Rm 173
1910 w Glue st
DR

4980 E KELLOGG
48 E JOHN
AP   5 - 6

2,5
2,5

2,5

Basic Business Finance

Text and Cases

BASIC

BUSINESS

FINANCE

Text and Cases

By PEARSON HUNT, D.C.S.

Professor of Business Administration

CHARLES M. WILLIAMS, D.C.S.

Edmund Cogswell Converse Professor of Banking and Finance

and GORDON DONALDSON, D.C.S.

Associate Professor of Business Administration

ALL OF THE GRADUATE SCHOOL OF BUSINESS

ADMINISTRATION, HARVARD UNIVERSITY

Revised Edition

1961

RICHARD D. IRWIN, INC.

HOMEWOOD, ILLINOIS

REVISED EDITION

First Printing, September, 1961
Second Printing, November, 1961
Third Printing, August, 1962

Library of Congress Catalogue Card No. 61–16917

PRINTED IN THE UNITED STATES OF AMERICA

Preface

Preface to the First Edition

A VOLUME such as this represents the work of many persons and complete acknowledgment of all those who have contributed to it is impossible. However, we would like to mention specifically the contribution of those whose part in the preparation of this book has been particularly significant.

First were those business leaders whose active co-operation made possible the preparation of case problems from actual situations. Unfortunately it is necessary that they must remain anonymous.

A number of past and present members of the Faculty of the Harvard Business School played important roles in the preparation of the case material. In particular, we would like to acknowledge the vital contributions of Professors Leonard C. R. Langer and Robert Vandell. Professors Leonard Marks, Jr., and James T. S. Porterfield also had primary responsibility in the preparation of particular cases. Finally there are the Research Associates and Assistants who handled the field work and drafts of a number of cases: Donald S. Howard, Paul R. Judy, Samuel Schwartz, and Dan S. Tucker.

Several prominent businessmen were especially helpful in reviewing and commenting on sections of the text dealing with their fields of especial competence. These included Charles L. Moore of The First National Bank of Boston; Frank A. Petito of Morgan Stanley & Co.; Charles E. Goodhue of Goodwin, Procter & Hoar; and Peter F. Coogan of Ropes, Gray, Best, Coolidge, and Rugg. Professor John Lintner of the Harvard Business School acted in a similar role on the chapter dealing with Dividend Policy.

To our efficient secretaries, Catherine M. Smith, Lois I. DeAndrade, and Carol M. Fields go our hearty thanks for their prodigious and ever-cheerful secretarial and editorial work. We are grateful also to Mrs. Elizabeth Dalton who prepared the index.

Preface to the Revised Edition

SINCE 1958, when the first edition of this book appeared, there have been significant developments in several aspects of financial analysis, and we have tried to give them their proper place in this revision. Also, we have had the benefit of many helpful suggestions from those who used the first edition. So far as possible, we have taken their advice. The result, we hope, is a better-integrated and up-to-date treatment of the subject, without the omissions and difficult spots of the first edition.

To the list of those to whom we are indebted for assistance in the writing of cases we are glad to add: M. Colyer Crum, John A. Griner III, Roger Stark, and particularly Roy C. Satchell, who has prepared more than half of the cases new in this edition. We accept full responsibility for the case material as well as for the text.

Miss Carolyn Stubbs, Associate in Research in our School, did much of the work necessary to bring up to date the various statistical tables. She also edited much of the text, and made many other valuable contributions. Catherine M. Smith and Carol M. Fields again handled a mountain of materials with efficiency and good nature.

Without such help, this book would never have appeared.

PEARSON HUNT
CHARLES M. WILLIAMS
GORDON DONALDSON

Graduate School of Business Administration
Harvard University, June, 1961

Table of Contents

PART I. INTRODUCTION

PART II. THE MANAGEMENT OF ASSETS AND THE NEED FOR FUNDS

List of Cases

PART I

Introduction

Chapter 1

Introduction

IN THIS introductory chapter of *Basic Business Finance: Text and Cases,* we shall begin by describing the finance function in business. Having explained what this book is about, we then describe the design of the book—the point of view from which we approach the subject, the users for whom the book has been prepared, the needs we seek to meet through inclusion of both textual and case problem materials, the objectives of the text and of the cases, and how each should be used. Then we shall briefly outline the substantive plan of the book, that is, the major subject areas covered and the order of their presentation.

After this introduction to the book as a whole, we shall turn to an over-all look at the need for funds in business. The importance of using funds effectively and widely used methods of measuring the effectiveness with which funds are being employed are then considered.

The Finance Function in Business

This book is concerned with the finance function of business and how it can be carried out effectively. Viewed narrowly, the finance function is simply the task of providing the funds needed by the enterprise on terms that are most favorable in the light of the objectives of the business. This concept has the merit of highlighting a central core of the finance function—keeping the business supplied with enough funds to accomplish its objectives. Certainly, seeing to it that the business has the funds to pay its current bills and to support programs embarked upon is a basic part of the finance function. Getting the needed funds in the most suitable way and on the best terms possible also is clearly a central part of the finance job.

But the finance function is broader than one of funds procurement

3

or supply. It is also concerned with the effective utilization of funds in the business. Money has a cost, and it is seldom available to the firm in unlimited amounts. Decisions in the firm that involve a need for funds should take into account the costs and problems involved in getting the funds and balance these with the added profits or other advantages that can be gained through the use of the added money. To illustrate, the production manager of a manufacturing firm is urging the construction of a new plant. The new plant, he argues, will result in lower production costs and a higher profit for the firm. Yet, to build the new plant will require a large outlay of cash and necessitate heavy borrowing. The financial aspects of the problem do not stop with a decision that the funds *can* be obtained or even with the decision that they can best be raised in a particular way—say, through an issue to the public of twenty-year first-mortgage bonds. Instead, the financial considerations extend toward questions of whether the added profits from the new plant adequately compensate for the costs and risks involved in the borrowing. Further, are there alternative methods of getting the same or some of the profits at much less financial burden? Would, for instance, modernization of the existing plant at half the total cost and three quarters of the cost savings achieved by a new plant be a better alternative? Or could the funds required for the new plant be used to better advantage in research devoted to new products that could be produced efficiently with the existing facilities? The financial function cannot be separated out and divorced from questions of the effective use of funds in the business.

Perhaps another example will make our broad concept of the financial function more readily understood. The board of directors of the company is considering what dividends to declare on the common stock of the company. Certainly, the board will wish to take into account the financial needs of the business and the opportunities for using the funds that have been made available from profits in the business. But the board will also be concerned with such matters as the objectives and desires of the stockholders, the likely impact of alternative dividend decisions on the short-run and long-term market price of the stock, and the consequent effect of its own dividend action on the ability of the company to sell more common stock at a favorable price in the future.

Further, few firms enjoy financial positions so strong that planning can go forward and decisions can be made on the assumption that any funds required by the plans and decisions will be obtained. Indeed, in a great many less affluent concerns the present or potential supply of funds and the financial aspects of important decisions may well be of dominant importance. The financial situation often is such that the current and future operations of the business must be shaped to fit the funds available, rather than the reverse.

Even the relatively specialized or central-core aspects of the broad financial function—those related to supplying the needed funds— are not to be regarded as narrow or separated from the operations of the business, as we shall see in detail later in this book. The need for funds in a business is affected by every activity of the business and by virtually everything that happens to the business. In order to understand and meet its needs for funds efficiently and astutely, the financial officer must understand the business and keep in touch with all phases of its operations. Probably no other functional area of business is so intimately interrelated with other areas of the business as is the finance function. The successful financial man in business must be not only a "money man"; he must be a businessman.

Organization to Carry Out the Finance Function in Business

The financial function, broadly considered, is much the same in its basic aspects in all businesses. That is to say, financial considerations exist in virtually all concerns, whatever their size or nature. The details of the function may differ widely, but the basic and important features of the job to be done are universal in nature. Many of the important aspects of the financial function are carried on by the top management of the company—the president, executive vice president, the board of directors, or top management committees. The board of directors, with the advice of the president, treasurer, or other senior officers, may well make the final decision on such issues as the decision to build a new plant in our previous illustration. Though final decisions in the financial area may be taken by the board or other officers with over-all responsibility in the firm, the financial officers have an important responsibility to contribute to good decision making on issues that cut across functional areas of the business. They should see to it that the financial implications of broad decisions are clearly brought out and are understood by those who must make the final decisions.

The ways that enterprises organize to carry out the finance function differ widely, however. In very small concerns the head of the firm often assumes direct and virtually sole responsibility for marketing, production, finance, and still other functions. In medium and

large concerns a separate financial department headed by an officer
with a title such as treasurer or vice president–finance may be assigned primary responsibility for funds supply aspects of the finance
function. In some concerns, responsibilities in the broad financial
area are divided between a treasurer and a controller who, in addition
to his usual duties as the chief accounting officer of the firm, may be
assigned responsibility for such aspects of the finance function as financial forecasting and the appraisal of the effectiveness with which
funds are used in various parts of the business. In many large concerns, both the treasurer and the controller report to a chief financial
officer who often has the title, vice president–finance. To minimize
problems of terminology, we shall refer to the officer with primary
responsibility for the financial function as the chief financial officer
or simply the financial officer, be his literal title president, general
manager, treasurer, or controller.

As is suggested by the nature of the finance function, the chief financial officer usually is one of the senior officers of the firm reporting
directly to the president or executive vice president and is an important member of the "top management team."

The Design of This Book

This book is written from the point of view of the chief financial
officer in an operating business, a man with responsibilities for getting
a job done well. His job involves a need to make or take part in specific decisions and hence is oriented toward responsible recommendations and action rather than abstract theorizing. This viewpoint of the
active businessman is in contrast with that of some finance textbooks
which seem to be written more from the viewpoint of a detached observer and reporter of the business scene, or with other books written
primarily from an investor's viewpoint. It is also in contrast with still
other books on finance which are written more or less implicitly from
a public or governmental policy point of view, such as that of a con-
gressman heading a committee which has an interest in the financing
of business.

The primary emphasis in the book is on financial decision making
and administration in a going concern. We do deviate somewhat
from our going-concern framework in the chapters dealing with business failure and the financing of new enterprises. Even here, however,
the emphasis is on the special problems which management may face
at either end of the life cycle of an individual business organization.

Our general adherence to the point of view of internal management does not preclude our occasionally looking at business as might an outside analyst—investor, trade creditor, etc.

Since we take a point of view encompassing that of the chief financial officer, we are much concerned with what we term "the funds point of view." While the chief financial officer, along with the president and other top officers, has a real interest in profits and the effective use of assets, typically he has the direct and primary responsibility for seeing to it that the firm does not run short of funds. The term *funds* is often used here and elsewhere synonymously with *cash* or *money*, but a more accurate and complete definition of *funds* would be *the means of payment*. Thus, the purchase of raw materials requires funds; but for a time, at least, credit supplied by the seller can take the place of cash as the medium by which ownership of the materials was accomplished. As the man responsible for seeing to it that the firm has the means of payment it desires, the chief financial officer appropriately is strongly oriented toward a funds point of view.

The book is designed to provide the principal materials for a course intended to meet the needs of students with diverse interests. It seeks to provide a solid basis for further development in the finance area on the part of those students who plan to take additional courses in finance, perhaps with the hope of making a career in the field. But it also is written with the needs in mind of those students who may go into business without any more academic work in finance. We hope to give these students a sufficient appreciation of key financial problems that they will develop at the least an awareness of these problems and their importance in business management. We also hope to give them enough feel for financial problems that they will be able to understand and work effectively with financial specialists in overlapping problem areas. Finally, we hope to give a solid enough base that those students who reach top management positions through, say, sales or production specialties, can return to the subject of finance and further build competence in the area on their own. For these needs, we regard a reasonably thorough treatment of a limited number of basic problem areas as more useful than a rapid sweep over a more comprehensive list of financial topics.

In this book, textual material and case problems are combined, on the premise that the basic course in finance should serve two major purposes. The text seeks primarily to inform—to provide the student with useful background information about the financing job in business. The case problems are designed to help the student develop some rudimentary skills in thinking through financial problems and in reaching sensible decisions for action.

To be more specific, one of the functions of the textual material is to supply a virtual kit of background facts in key areas of our subject. For example, before introducing cases dealing with problems in raising funds, we describe the major suppliers of funds to business and the economic and operational conditions which govern the arrangements under which they make funds available to business. Particularly important sources of funds, such as the commercial banks, are treated at some length.

We do not attempt to be exhaustive or encyclopedic in our description. At a number of points, we refer—usually in footnotes—to more extensive works on the particular subject under discussion; and we urge the student whose interest is captured by particular aspects of the subject to refer to these books, both for their more extended coverage and for an interpretation of the subject that often is different from ours.

In addition, part of the text material is devoted to introducing techniques of analysis or interpretation of material that can be useful in handling the case problems or in business. For example, a chapter is devoted to discussion of techniques of forecasting future needs for funds and problems in their use.

Still other parts of the text go well beyond the task of painting a factual background or describing financial techniques and attempt to develop basic ideas on some important issues. We hope thereby to stimulate rather than close out student thinking on these issues. In most instances where we have put forward our own ideas on debatable subjects, the student will have a chance to test the usefulness of these ideas in dealing with related issues raised in the cases.

We should make clear, however, that we do not attempt in the text to supply the answers to the case problems that follow. Rather, we hope through the text to bring the student along to a point where he can comprehend the problems posed in the cases and work out sensible answers to these problems. In other words, we hope through the text to equip the student with useful tools for attacking the issues raised in the cases.

Since few students will have had previous training through case problems, some discussion of the case problems is appropriate. The cases are essentially descriptions of actual business problems faced by real firms. The names, and sometimes other nonvital facts, have usually been disguised to conceal the true identity of the firms—indeed, the use of a disguise is usually a condition of permission by the firm for us to use the material. Usually, too, the actual facts of the business situation have been simplified somewhat by omission or alteration of peripheral aspects.

The case problems are intended to be much more than illustrations. Typically, they are problems calling for solution. Seldom is there a single "right" answer to the problem presented, but some actions clearly are better than others that might be suggested. The student should be prepared to defend his particular proposals for action and to give in some detail the reasons for his choice of alternatives.

The case problems do not follow a standard pattern but present considerable variety. Some are primarily analytical, in which a major part of the job is defining the real problem to be solved. Others state the problem and put the focus on working out solutions to the problem posed. In some instances, likely alternatives are rather fully described, and the student need only choose between these alternatives in the light of the circumstances. Still others pose a problem but leave to the student the task of proposing the likely alternatives and of choosing between them.

Perhaps it will be useful for us to indicate what we hope the student will do with the cases if he is to get maximum benefit from them. First, we strongly urge the student to try to put himself into the case situation—to identify himself with the businessman grappling with the problem. By accepting this intellectual role playing, the student tackles the problem from a definite point of view and, at the same time, in effect, is accepting intellectual responsibility for dealing with the problem. A second step is the marshaling of the facts of the situation especially pertinent to the problem. It is our aim to supply in the cases all the essential facts bearing on the problem available to the businessman in the real situation. If we fail to supply data that the student feels are vital and that might in fact have been available in the actual situation, the student is urged to make the assumptions as to the facts he considers most reasonable and to go on with his analysis on this basis. Usually, the student will find more facts in the case than will really be useful, so that he must distinguish between the pertinent and the irrelevant in the information furnished in the case.

After the pertinent facts have been marshaled, the students may have to diagnose the real problem to be solved and to develop alternatives if the problem and alternatives are not given in the case. In weighing alternative courses of action, it often is helpful to prepare a list of the pros and cons of each alternative. Then the importance of each advantage and disadvantage must be weighed. Sometimes, a single pro may outweigh in importance a dozen minor cons.

Finally, and most important, the student should arrive at a decision on the case problem that makes sense. And as we have said, he should be prepared to support his position in detail.

Effectiveness in dealing with the case problems will not be easily acquired. Indeed, progress on the part of the student toward real skill in problem solving and decision making is about all that we can realistically hope will result from use of this book. Many students will find the case problems difficult and demanding. On the other hand, they should find the case work interesting and their efforts on it rewarding.

The Substantive Plan of the Book

It may be helpful to review briefly the major subject areas to be covered and indicate the order in which they are taken up in the book. We first are concerned with helping the student understand the nature of the need for funds in business. The nature and amount of funds needed to operate a business are grounded on the nature of its operations. We seek to help the student to see how operational decisions affect the need for funds and how changes in operations, such as changes in the policy of the firm toward granting credit to customers, affect the finances of business. Attention is directed, in turn, to the investment in inventory, in receivables, in cash and near-cash investments, and in fixed assets. Methods by which the financial officer can play a useful part in controlling the need for funds are also examined.

We then discuss techniques of analyzing the past and current financing of the business as a means of understanding the past needs for funds and the way they have been met.

From a focus on understanding past needs, we then shift to the problems of forecasting future needs for funds. Techniques for organizing information on the future operations of the business into specific forecasts of funds needs are introduced and discussed.

Next, the problem of how the needed funds should best be obtained is taken up. Sources of short-term funds are explored, and the negotiation of suitable terms with these sources is considered. Raising intermediate- and then long-term funds is taken up next and at considerable length.

In considering long-term sources, we deal first with the basic security types and examine their role individually and collectively in
the allocation of risk, income, and control. At this stage the analysis
is kept in the simplest terms possible so that the essential features will
be more readily apparent. This is followed by a chapter concerned
with dividend policy and the retention of earnings as a source of
funds.

With a clear understanding of the basic sources of long-term
funds, it is then appropriate to turn attention to a number of the more
important variations in long-term capital contracts and observe how
these evolve to meet the recognized needs of suppliers and users of
capital. This section includes detailed consideration of lease contracts and a chapter devoted to the measurement of the cost of capital
in individual issues.

This section is followed by two chapters which describe the markets
for corporate securities. Here, we are concerned not only with filling
in a factual picture of the long-term capital market but also with the
normal procedures by which business taps this market for new
funds. These chapters are followed by one devoted to the role of government in regulating aspects of the long-term capital market. One
objective here is to give a brief description of the nature of present-
day regulation with special emphasis on the role of the Securities
and Exchange Commission. More importantly, however, the chapter
seeks to bring out the impact of such regulation on the financial practices and policies of individual business corporations.

The next-to-last section of the book takes up a number of special
aspects of business finance under the general heading of "Financing
Growth and Readjustment." Here, the financial problems peculiar
to the new small-scale business are presented in some detail. Other
chapters deal with the financial implications of mergers and the
closely related problem of valuation, the evolution and reconstruction
of corporate capital structures, and the problems surrounding the
business during a period of serious financial difficulty, including the
event of failure.

The final chapters of the book deal explicitly and in some detail
with one of the major areas of corporate decision making—the selection of long-term investment opportunities. This subject is touched
on at a number of points throughout the text but largely in descriptive
rather than analytical terms. Here, the current analytical concepts
are described and include time adjustment, the ranking of investment
opportunities, and the determination of a cutoff point. This section is

perhaps the most difficult part of the book conceptually and is appropriately left until the reader has a firm grasp on all major dimensions of the finance function in the business firm.

The Need for Funds: An Over-all Look

"You've got to have money to make money!" This business adage is a simple recognition that most enterprises need funds in order to operate profitably. The typical manufacturing firm, for example, needs to maintain some stocks of goods, to extend credit to its customers, to carry a bank account, and to have plant and productive equipment. While the amounts needed in the individual firm are influenced by many factors and developments, and fluctuate over a period of time, the typical going business has and must maintain a substantial continuing investment in inventory, credits to its customers (receivables), cash in banks, and plant and equipment.

Table 1–1 shows the assets and liabilities of all United States manufacturing corporations at the end of 1960. Together, these corporations owned assets valued at almost $256 billion. Inventories amounted to over $60 billion, or 23.6 per cent of their total assets. Notes and accounts receivable totaled nearly $40 billion, or 15.6 per cent of the total assets. Cash and U.S. government securities, which are a popular medium for investment of cash not needed immediately, together amounted to almost $28 billion, or 10.8 per cent of the total. The net investment in property, plant, and equipment was also huge—over $100 billion, or 39.3 per cent of the total. Together, these four major types of assets represented 89.3 per cent of the total assets of U.S. manufacturers.

In building an understanding of the financing of business, it is useful to think of the various assets as representing the investment of funds. Viewed in this light, the outstanding investment in inventory reported on the balance sheet represents funds absorbed or tied up in inventory on that date. If the inventories are built up, more funds are absorbed, or used, in maintaining this type of asset. If the inventories are reduced, funds are released for other uses. In many respects the analogy of a sponge is appropriate. An increase in inventory or other assets soaks up cash or funds; a squeezing-down of the inventory sponge frees cash for other uses.

Looking at the changes in the aggregate balance sheets for U.S. manufacturers from December 31, 1959, to December 31, 1960, as shown in Table 1–2, we see that the investment in every type of asset except U.S. government securities was expanded during 1960. The

TABLE 1–1

ESTIMATED BALANCE SHEET, ALL U.S. MANUFACTURING COMPANIES

(Dollar Figures in Millions)

	December 31, 1960	Percentage of Total
ASSETS		
Cash on hand and in bank....................	$ 15,437	6.0%
U.S. government securities....................	12,217	4.8
Accounts and notes receivable, net..............	39,916	15.6
Inventories..................................	60,360	23.6
Other current assets.........................	5,890	2.3
Total Current Assets.....................	$133,820	52.3%
Gross property, plant, and equipment...........	$193,843	75.8%
Less: Reserve for depreciation................	93,351	36.5
Net Fixed Assets.......................	$100,491	39.3%
Other noncurrent assets......................	$ 21,494	8.4%
Total Assets..........................	$255,804	100.0%
LIABILITIES AND STOCKHOLDERS' EQUITY		
Short-term loans from banks (original maturity of one year or less)........................	$ 7,882	3.1%
Trade accounts and notes payable..............	20,223	7.9
Federal income taxes accrued..................	9,435	3.7
Instalments due in one year or less on long-term debt....................................	2,135	0.8
Other current liabilities......................	13,607	5.3
Total Current Liabilities...................	$ 53,282	20.8%
Long-term debt due in more than one year........	$ 31,290	12.2%
Other noncurrent liabilities...................	3,609	1.4
Total Liabilities.........................	$ 88,181	34.5%
Reserves not reflected elsewhere................	$ 1,992	0.8%
Capital stock, capital surplus, and minority interest	68,529	26.8
Earned surplus and surplus reserves.............	97,102	37.9
Total Stockholders' Equity.................	$167,623	65.5%
Total Liabilities and Stockholders' Equity..	$255,804	100.0%

SOURCE: Federal Trade Commission and Securities and Exchange Commission, *Quarterly Financial Report for Manufacturing Corporations: Fourth Quarter, 1960* (Washington, D.C.: U.S. Government Printing Office, 1961), p. 34.

NOTE: In this and other tables in the book the figures have been rounded to the nearest whole number. Hence, totals do not always agree.

TABLE 1-2

ESTIMATED BALANCE SHEET, ALL U.S. MANUFACTURING COMPANIES

(In Millions)

	December 31, 1959	December 31, 1960	Net Change
ASSETS			
Cash on hand and in bank..............	$ 15,298	$ 15,437	+$ 139
U.S. government securities.............	14,411	12,217	− 2,194
Accounts and notes receivable, net.......	38,056	39,916	+ 1,860
Inventories.........................	57,922	60,360	+ 2,438
Other current assets..................	5,311	5,890	+ 579
Total Current Assets..............	$130,998	$133,820	+$ 2,822
Property, plant, and equipment.........	$180,134	$193,843	+$13,709
Less: Reserve for depreciation........	85,664	93,351	+ 7,687
Net Fixed Assets.................	$ 94,471	$100,491	+$ 6,020
Other noncurrent assets...............	$ 19,033	$ 21,494	+$ 2,461
Total Assets...................	$244,502	$255,804	+$11,302
LIABILITIES AND STOCKHOLDERS' EQUITY			
Short-term loans from banks (original maturity one year or less).........	$ 6,664	$ 7,882	+$ 1,218
Trade accounts and notes payable.......	20,019	20,223	+ 204
Federal income taxes accrued...........	10,792	9,435	− 1,357
Instalments due in one year or less on long-term debt.................	1,871	2,135	+ 264
Other current liabilities................	12,873	13,607	+ 734
Total Current Liabilities............	$ 52,219	$ 53,282	+$ 1,063
Long-term debt due in more than one year	$ 29,500	$ 31,290	+$ 1,790
Other noncurrent liabilities.............	2,329	3,609	+ 1,280
Total Liabilities...................	$ 84,048	$ 88,181	+$ 4,133
Reserves not reflected elsewhere.........	$ 2,937	$ 1,992	−$ 945
Capital stock, capital surplus, and minority interest...................	65,269	68,529	+ 3,260
Earned surplus and surplus reserves......	92,247	97,102	+ 4,855
Total Stockholders' Equity.........	$160,453	$167,623	+$ 7,170
Total Liabilities and Stockholders' Equity......................	$244,502	$255,804	+$11,302

SOURCE: Federal Trade Commission and Securities and Exchange Commission, *Quarterly Financial Report for Manufacturing Corporations: Fourth Quarter, 1960* (Washington, D.C.: U.S. Printing Office, 1961), p. 34.

increases in receivables, inventory, and net fixed assets represented particularly large uses of funds. Some funds were released for other uses by reduction of the investment in government bonds.

Under this same concept the items on the liability side of the balance sheet can appropriately be regarded as sources of funds. In Table 1–1, it can be seen that total debts of U.S. manufacturers on December 31, 1960, amounted to over $88 billion, or 34.5 per cent of total assets. Stockholders, by buying stock in the companies and leaving profits in the businesses, have been, in effect, the source of almost $168 billion, or 65.5 per cent of the total assets.

The funds required to increase the investment in one asset may be provided by the squeezing-down of the investment in another asset— for example, the added need for funds created by an inventory build-up might be met by drawing down the investment in cash. Alternatively, the needed funds might be secured by increasing a liability—for example, by added borrowing from banks. Or the use could be matched through the sale of more stock—or an increase in the stockholders' investment in the company.

Turning again to Table 1–2, we see that the large increase in assets of manufacturing companies during 1960 was financed through increased credit from all the major sources except federal income taxes accrued, through important increases in the ownership accounts, and by the drawing-down of the investment in U.S. government bonds.

Organized and careful analysis of sources and uses of funds over a period of time, as reflected in balance sheet changes, can be a useful aid to understanding the needs of a business and how they have been met. In Chapter 8, we shall explain in some detail the technique of such analysis—which is built around the construction of statements of sources and uses of funds. At this point, it will suffice if the student recognizes clearly that the various assets represent the use or investment of funds, that increases in these assets absorb or use funds, and that decreases in particular assets free or release funds.

Underlying Objectives of Resource Management

The basic reason for being of most business enterprises is to build maximum sustainable values for the owners. True, enlightened owners and managers recognize that the firm also has responsibilities to its customers, its employees, its community, and perhaps to the firm itself as a total organization. But the obligation of management to use the funds contributed to its care by the owners to the maximum advantage of the owners is a paramount one.

Generally, the end objective of building values for the owners can better be served if profit performance is viewed in relation to the scale of resources committed to the enterprise. To illustrate, suppose that an entrepreneur who has set up two businesses is reviewing their progress. In Business A, in which he has invested $500,000, annual profits are $50,000. Business B, which produces profits of $25,000, required an investment of only $100,000. Surely, on these facts, Business B is to be regarded as the more successful investment, since the profit return on the $100,000 investment is 25 per cent, while that on the $500,000 investment is only 10 per cent.

The validity and usefulness of return on investment as a basic business objective for the owners and as a prime measure of performance of their steward management is gaining increasing acceptance. The increasing acceptance rests on solid grounds. First, the return-on-investment objective inherently recognizes the value of capital—the fact that its owners could use their funds to advantage in other ventures—and that capital is seldom available for an enterprise in unlimited amount. Second, it puts a premium on economical use of capital in the firm. Third, use of this performance criterion and objective points to broad avenues for improvement of performance.

Return on investment can usefully be calculated in terms of the return both on total investment of the firm (total assets) and on that portion of the total resources of the firm which represents the owners' contribution. Let us illustrate.

Firm X has total assets of $400,000, sales of $1,000,000, and net profit after taxes of $40,000. Return on investment can usefully be calculated as follows: *Rate of Return on Asset Investment Equals Rate of Profit on Sales Multiplied by the Rate of Turnover of Assets.* In our example the rate of profit on sales is 4 per cent ($40,000 profit/$1,000,000 sales). The rate of turnover of assets is 2.5 ($1,-000,000 sales/$400,000 assets). So the return on asset investment in this case was 10 per cent (4 per cent times 2.5).

Now, let us assume that Firm X in the following year increased sales to $1,200,000 and net income after taxes to $48,000, but also increased assets to $600,000. The rate of profit on sales remained at 4 per cent ($48,000/$1,200,000), but investment turnover fell to 2.0 ($1,200,000/$600,000). Consequently, rate of return on asset investment fell to 8 per cent (4 per cent times 2.0), reflecting the less effective use of assets. Had Firm X's management been able to achieve the expanded sales and profit results on the old investment base of $400,000, it would have boosted the turnover rate to 3.0 and the return on asset investment to 12 per cent (4 per cent times 3.0).

It should be apparent that success in boosting return on asset investment can be achieved by progress along either of two broad avenues—by increasing the rate of profit on sales or by increasing investment turnover. Investment turnover, in turn, can be raised by increasing sales more than assets or by cutting assets more than sales are reduced. Put differently, increases in sales or profit returns on sales enhance return on investment only if the investment is held to a less than proportionate increase.

From an ownership viewpoint the rate of return on *owners' investment* is more significant in many respects than is the rate of return on *total asset investment.* In calculating return on owners' investment, the investment base is narrowed by deducting from total assets the total debts of the firm.

Returning to Firm X, let us make the unlikely assumption that Firm X had no debts during the year it earned 10 per cent on asset investment. Since all the assets were provided by the owners, the return on owners' investment also was 10 per cent. Now, let us assume that the same sales results were achieved in the following year, but that $200,000 of ownership funds were replaced with borrowed funds and that interest charges cut the $40,000 profit after taxes to $36,-000. The shift to greater use of debt and consequent increase in turnover of the owners' investment increased the return on owners' investment from 10 to 18 per cent (3.6 per cent times 5). This simple example points up the fact that so long as after-tax interest costs are less than the rate of return on *asset investment,* the rate of return on *owners' investment* can be increased by increasing the proportion of borrowed money to ownership funds. This is simply another way of saying that if assets can be made to earn more than the cost of borrowed money, financing through debt is profitable to the owners.

Balanced against the attractions of the opportunity for boosting return on owners' investment through increased use of debt are the added financial risks imposed by borrowing. If interest or agreed loan repayments cannot be met on schedule, creditors can force bankruptcy of the firm. And in liquidation or reorganization of the firm, creditors' claims must be met in full before the owners can recover any of their investment. The decision as to the optimum balance in financing through debt and ownership funds is one of the most important financial decisions in most firms, and one discussed at length later in this book. Suffice it here to recognize the impact of the debt/ownership relationship on the return on owners' investment.

Different Routes to a Satisfactory Return on Investment

Widely varied approaches can lead to a gratifyingly high return on invested capital. Let us examine the results of several successful firms with quite different approaches.

First, let us look at Minnesota Mining and Manufacturing Company, which in 1959 showed a return of 16.8 per cent on total year-end asset investment and 23.2 per cent on owners' investment. How were such striking results achieved? The answer lies primarily in a rate of profit on sales unusually high in manufacturing, 12.7 per cent. (The average profit on sales of 1,944 leading manufacturers in 1959 was 5.8 per cent.[1]) Coupled with an asset turnover of 1.32 and an ownership investment turnover of 1.82, the high profit rate produced an unusually high return on total investment and, despite only modest use of debt, on the owners' investment.

Red Owl Stores, a Northwestern food chain, in contrast, earned only 1.04 per cent on sales in its 1960 fiscal year. Turnover of asset investment was, however, 5.59; and turnover of ownership investment, reflecting substantial debt financing, was 12.42! Consequently, the company earned 5.6 per cent on total assets and 12.9 per cent on owners' investment.

The Dayton Power and Light Company, an Ohio electric and gas utility, earned 11.76 per cent on total sales in 1959. Turnover of assets, as in the case of most utilities, was low—only 0.35. Since, again like most electric utilities, much debt was used, turnover of owners' investment was much higher—0.79. Though return on total assets was just 4.1 per cent, return on owners' investment was 9.3 per cent.

The Need for Pressures toward Effective Use of Assets

As our endorsement of the usefulness of the return-on-investment concept indicates, we believe that vigorous, well-thought-out, and continuing management effort to keep the firm's assets working hard and productively is essential to the success of the business. The financial officer can and should play a leading role in these efforts.

This emphasis may appear misplaced or platitudinous without full recognition of the basic pressures that exist in most enterprises, and

---

[1] First National City Bank (New York City), *Monthly Letter*, April, 1960.

particularly in highly profitable ones, toward extravagant or indulgent use of resources. Some of these pressures stem from seemingly innate human qualities—the human animal is not by nature thrifty or wise in his use of resources. For example, all of us like to have the latest and best tools with which to work. And many, if not most, people tend to equate "bigger" with "better." Personal empire-building tendencies also seem almost innate. Further, the sheer convenience of abundant resources at hand is attractive—witness the number of financially pressed families who embrace the luxury and convenience of a second or even third family automobile. Participation in business—especially in a business owned by someone else—does not convert the human animal into a machine that grinds out economically rational decisions.

Even in enterprises whose management generally is imbued with concern for return on investment or similar goals stressing maximum productivity of resources, certain sources of pressure toward indulgent use of assets can be identified. One such is the common preoccupation of managment personnel with specialized responsibilities with the gains from increased sales or cost cutting which can be achieved with more capital. Production managers are likely to be keenly aware of possibilities of greater output or of cutting production costs with added laborsaving equipment (larger equipment investment). An expensive shutdown due to exhaustion of raw material stocks provides an obvious push toward the carrying of greater stocks. The sales manager can be expected to be vigorous in exposing the potential for bigger sales through more generous credit extension (larger receivables) or through more complete stocks of goods for sale (larger finished goods inventory). Such added use of resources *may* appear to boost over-all return on investment and be desirable. But too often, the partisans of such actions overlook or underemphasize important but less obvious operating costs involved in higher asset accumulation and the costs of the added capital investment required.

The carrying of added raw material stocks, for example, may well mean a need for greater storage facilities, higher property taxes, insurance, and other costs of protecting and caring for the stocks. Further, risks of loss through physical deterioration, obsolescence, or price declines may be significant and yet inadequately recognized. Similar operating costs and risks of loss are likely to be significant in the case of all other types of assets—with the exception perhaps of cash itself.

The *net* gains, after full allowance for the added operating costs and risks of loss of values involved in added investment, must be compared with the costs or economic burden of the added investment. The objective, of course, should be one of balance—of insuring that the savings or added revenues from more assets match or exceed the costs of the capital involved. The return-on-investment concept basically is a device to see that the added assets "pay their way" and to point up the price in lower return on investment of less productive investment.

But even adherence to return-on-investment doctrines does not insure adequate management recognition of the problems of raising the funds to finance the added investment. In large, prosperous firms the assumption that funds can readily be secured for any investment judged worthy may in fact be justified. But in a great many firms—particularly new, smaller, or less successful concerns—the problems in financing even obviously desirable investment may be formidable, often controlling. Here, management must balance the advantages of moves that call for more capital against the financial problems of getting the needed money. The interest of the financial officer here is immediate and direct. In such cases, imaginative effort may reveal ways in which many, if not all, of the gains of proposals for added investment can be garnered with smaller or no added investment. *Often, the easiest and best way to raise funds is to avoid the need for them.*

In Chapters 3, 4, 5, and 6, we focus in turn on a discussion of the nature of the investment in inventory, in receivables, in cash and temporary investments of cash, and in property, plant, and equipment. In the case of each asset, we shall indicate the relative importance of the investment in business generally and in various industries. Then, we shall consider the major factors or variables affecting the size of the investment in the individual firm. We shall briefly review the cash flows associated with the asset. Then, some techniques of analysis of changes in the account are introduced. Further, in each instance, distinctive problems in controlling and managing the investment are discussed. Through each of the chapters, we attempt to build student understanding of the nature of the need for funds associated with each asset, so that he will have an appreciation of the business decisions or events that underlie the dollar demands associated with each type of asset.

After our separate consideration of the major assets, we then shall turn to discussion and problems involving the total business and its financing.

Chapter 2

The Nature of the Corporation in the United States

ANY PERSON visiting even the smallest business district of a town in the United States will observe, if he turns his attention to the matter, that the business which is carried on is owned in a variety of ways. There will surely be shops, dealerships, and services that are owned and operated by one person. Some of these may even have a sign showing the name of an individual and the abbreviation *Prop.*, indicating "Proprietor." Other activities will be found to be owned by a group of persons acting as partners. This will certainly be the case for any law office or medical center, and it will often be the case for other activities where a few persons have decided to join together to form a business. It is not always possible to judge that a firm is a partnership purely from its name, but the use of personal names (Smith & Jones) or the words *and Company* often furnish a clue.

Mixed in with these organizations, which are to be recognized as persons or groups of persons engaged in business, the observer will see, by the use of the abbreviation *Inc.* (Incorporated) or *Corp.* (Corporation) in the name, that certain firms are designated as having corporate form. Agencies, plants, and offices of larger businesses will be among those which bear the corporate designation. In most communities, for example, our observer is likely to find the business office of the local unit of the American Telephone and Telegraph Company, the largest private corporation in the United States. And of course, on the shelves of all the stores the products of corporate business will greatly outnumber the goods that were made by other types of firms.

As he looks for the names which indicate that a business has corporate form, the observer will see the somewhat puzzling fact that

21

many of the smaller firms are also incorporated. If he should conclude that there must be a variety of reasons why people choose to incorporate their businesses, he would be on the right track.

The differences between the types of ownership are of more than passing importance to all of us. Their significance begins to become apparent whenever one wishes to establish a relation with a firm that requires a commitment of some sort. Who is authorized to speak for the business? Will the business survive those who now speak for it? Where and how much is the ultimate liability of the firm, in case damage is done to me? How can I invest some of my funds in this firm? What participation in control would I have? Any one of these questions has different answers, depending upon the type of business organization that is used. The reader should be able to answer them, among others, after study of this chapter.

Legal Patterns Fall into Two Groups

In order to indicate how some of the questions can be answered, it is necessary to identify the various bodies of rules within which a business must operate. We refer to these rules as *legal patterns,* of which several are available for choice by those who wish to set up a business organization. A complete treatise would describe even those, such as the *business trust* and the *joint stock company,* which are at present of small importance in the United States. The principal avenues of choice lead to the *corporation* on one side and to the *partnership* or to the *proprietorship* on the other, and our discussion will deal chiefly with them. The major concern of this material will therefore be to explain the characteristics of the corporation, on one hand, and the partnership-proprietorship, on the other, so that the reader can understand the factors that enter the decision-making process when the choice is being made for a firm. For the present the business trust can be regarded as very like a corporation, and the joint-stock company as a corporation except for the legal liability that attaches to its owners. A preliminary distinction can then be drawn between the partnership-proprietorship, which is simply a certain person or group of persons in business, and those businesses of corporate type, where there is a legal entity apart from the persons who own and operate the firm.

Present Importance of the Corporation
in the United States

Since the corporation has become the predominant form of doing business in the United States, we can well begin our examination of the subject by a review of some important statistics about the varying importance of the corporation in various sectors of the economic activity of the nation. While we shall confine ourselves to the factual situation in the United States, it will be of interest to note that in general the same conditions will be found in any industrialized country where private enterprise plays an important part. Table 2–1 shows

TABLE 2–1

COMPARISON OF RELATIVE IMPORTANCE OF INCORPORATED AND UNINCORPORATED
ENTERPRISES AS MEASURED BY PERCENTAGE OF TOTAL NET INCOME
BEFORE TAXES, BY INDUSTRY, FOR THE YEAR 1959

INDUSTRY	BEFORE-TAX CORPORATE INCOME	
	Millions of Dollars	Percentage of Industry
All industries............................	$47,021	50.2%
Communications and public utilities..........	5,378	98.7
Manufacturing...........................	25,173	93.7
Mining..................................	918	76.6
Finance, insurance, and real estate...........	5,713	68.0
Transportation...........................	932	54.2
Wholesale and retail trade..................	5,588	30.6
Contract construction......................	802	14.8
Services.................................	642	5.2
Agriculture, forestry, and fisheries...........	54	0.4

SOURCE: Office of Business Economics, Department of Commerce, *Survey of Current Business*, July, 1960 (National Income Number), Tables 45 and 56, pp. 27 and 30.

not only that one half of the business income is earned by corporations, but also that this form of business organization is dominant wherever large-scale units are needed for efficiency.

To explain more fully the reasons for the use of the corporate form, we now turn to an examination of its characteristics in some detail. They have been organized under the major headings: "Legal Entity," "State Sanction—Corporate Powers," "Financial Contracts," and "Tax Status." In each section, primary attention will be given to the corporation. The partnership-proprietorship and other patterns will be referred to only where there are major differences of concern to those selecting the legal pattern of a business.

Legal Entity

The reader should note that the American culture of today provides natural acceptance of the idea that one normally does business with an entity which is separate from the persons dealt with. One thinks of a business as separate from the personal interests of its owner. This division is a complex one, involving characteristics that are not always desirable, but it is important to recognize that it does exist. There is acceptance in our culture of the idea that a business unit is a separable entity, and the law has been specific in making the separation in the case of the corporation, so one can speak of the legal entity that exists in addition to the cultural entity that is generally accepted.

A useful definition of a *corporation* is: ". . . an association of persons which is in many respects treated as if it were itself a person. It has rights and duties of its own, which are not the rights and duties of the individual members thereof. . . . The rights and duties of the members descend to the successive members of the corporation."[1]

This statement is both the definition of a corporation and an explanation of the meaning of the term *legal entity*. The corporation has status before the law as a person. This means that courts will consider the corporation as a person which may enter into contracts, sue or be sued, and so on, quite independently of the individuals who own its securities. Thus, while the culture confers a sort of entity upon any business unit, the law confines this privilege to the corporation. The other forms of organization are recognized only as groups of individuals.

It should be noted that the conferring of personality upon the corporation does not mean that this kind of person has all the rights and privileges of a natural person. Obviously, there are many types of contract, such as marriage, that a corporation cannot enter into, and there are many types of conduct which corporations cannot undertake. There are, in fact, many laws limiting corporate privileges. The significant thing is that a corporation does have certain important elements of a separate personality in the eyes of the law.

Characteristics of the Corporation Associated with Legal Entity. Certain characteristics of a corporation may be associated with its legal entity. (1) There is the duty to have a corporate name, although as a privilege, other types of firms may select names. (2) There is the privilege of a term of existence which is completely independent of the lives of any natural persons. (3) There is a provision for a board of directors to represent the owners, who may be a great many persons. (4) There is the privilege that the corporation may hold title to property and enter into contracts of all sorts without binding the individuals who own the corporation to the obligations it has undertaken. Finally, and often of great importance, (5) the separate entity

---

[1] Cecil T. Carr, "Corporation," *Encyclopaedia Britannica* (11th ed.; New York: Encyclopaedia Britannica Co., 1910–11), Vol. VII, p. 190.

is subject to different rules of taxation. This last matter will be the subject of a separate section of this chapter.

The foregoing characteristics are available only in limited form, if at all, to the other forms of business organization, and none has all of them. None of them, except the business trust in a few states, has legal entity, but in practice the difference is less sharp than at first appears. In the case of a joint-stock company, it is usually found that certain officers stand in a representative capacity for all the stockholders, so that while they do not absorb any of the stockholders' liabilities, they represent them in lieu of a corporate personality. A partnership operates under the rule—exactly contrary to that for the corporation—that any partner may act for the partnership in matters related to the business of the partnership, except where the limitation on the partner is indicated clearly and publicly.[2] The grant of such power to a partner is a necessary convenience if business is to be done efficiently, but it has served as the disruptive force that has caused the dissolution of many firms.

The Corporate Name.   The duty to select a corporate name includes as a requirement that the name indicate the fact of incorporation.[3] In the United States, this is usually done by using the word *Incorporated* as the last word of the corporate title. This is usually abbreviated and read as *Inc.* The word *Corporation* (Corp.) is sometimes used. One also finds *Limited* (Ltd.), which is the standard British and Canadian practice but appears in the United States only to lend a sort of prestige to the name. Some states have laws which permit the use of *The _____ Company* to distinguish a corporation. Other distinguishing words are used in other countries. The French *Société Anonyme* is worth noting because it points out the separate entity characteristic of the corporation.

Most states now permit any form of business unit to adopt a firm name. Often, there is some designation in the title that indicates the type of legal pattern that is used. Business trusts usually have the word *Trust* in their names.[4] Limited partnerships must indicate that

---

[2] In such case the person is known as a *limited partner* and can take no part in the management of the partnership. He is simply a supplier of capital. A major difficulty faced by limited partners is that states other than that in which the partnership was formed may make the limited partner equally liable with the other partners for debts created in the outside state.

[3] Insurance *companies*, trust *companies*, and *banks* are usually corporations, though their names may not indicate the fact. These enterprises are incorporated under special laws regulating banking and insurance.

[4] The phrase *the trust problem* to designate the problem created by large-scale enterprise is an historical accident arising from the fact that the first "trusts" used the business trust form. Later, "trusts" used the corporate form much more frequently.

some of the partners do not have unlimited liability, but do not do so in their names. In most states the fact of limited partnership is disclosed in a Certificate of Limited Partnership, which is filed with the Secretary of State and is thus a matter of public record. The ordinary partnerships and other forms of business use the words *and Company* frequently.

Term of Life. Most corporations avail themselves fully of the privilege of indefinite existence by stating no termination date in their basic documents. Those which do usually find it easy to extend their life by amendment. One author has selected an apt simile by comparing the corporate society to a river. The water in the river, symbolizing the parties to the corporation, is ever changing. The general river, however, does not change; and one thinks of the river as the same entity, even though much water has flowed through it.

The characteristics of a corporation which have just been described can be summarized in the eloquent and frequently quoted words of John Marshall: "A corporation is an artificial being, invisible, intangible, and existing only in contemplation of law. Being the mere creature of law, it possesses only those properties which the charter of its creation confers upon it, either expressly or as incidental to its very existence. . . . Among the most important are immortality, and . . . individuality; properties by which a perpetual succession of many persons are considered the same and may act as a single individual."[5]

Important differences exist with respect to the period of life of the other types of organization. The corporation and the joint-stock company may enjoy perpetual lives. The business trust must limit itself according to the "rule against perpetuities," generally to twenty-one years after the life of some named person.[6]

The historic rule is that a partnership must dissolve upon the death, incapacity, or withdrawal of any partner, except a limited partner. The same is, of course, true of an individual proprietorship. A great many partnership agreements provide in detail the procedure to be followed upon the withdrawal of a partner. A few states permit partnerships to survive without the signing of a new contract. Thus, in many cases a new partnership is formed to take over the affairs of the old one without any disturbance of the business. It must, however,

---

[5] *Trustees of Dartmouth College* v. *Woodward,* 4 Wheat. (U.S.) 518, 636 (1819). In his first sentence the learned justice was paraphrasing Sir Edward Coke. Case of Sutton's Hospital, 10 Coke's Reports 1, 32*b* (1613).

[6] This gives rise to the device of listing several children, with the provision that the longest individual life shall be used to measure the life of the business.

be noted that no such arrangement can avoid the necessity of evaluating the interest of the withdrawing partner, or of paying this value to the partner, or his estate, or other representative. The payment may be made in notes of the new partnership, if this was provided for by the original partnership agreement, but any such notes must be payable in a reasonable time.[7]

Despite the devices that can be created by advance agreement, the process of dissolution of a partnership and creation of a new partnership is usually a period of strain even with goodwill from all parties. It may impose severe financial burdens upon the continuing business. Thus, the disadvantages of mortality lead many partnerships to shift to the corporate form. The same is true, of course, of the individual proprietor, if he desires to see his business continue after him.

The Board of Directors. In the proprietorship the ultimate powers of decision are in the hands of the owner. In the partnership, as stated above, any general partner may act for the partnership. In the case of the corporation, most of the powers of ownership are placed in the hands of a board of directors. There are certain questions of such importance that they must be referred to a stockholders' meet-

---

[7] The following quotations from a partnership agreement show the extent of complexity sometimes encountered in partnership agreements. Note that the partnership contract foresees problems of valuation as well as liquidation.

Profits and Losses. Salaries of partners shall be treated as expenses. Net profits or losses for each calendar year shall be entered as follows:

a) Net profits or losses up to and including 10% of the aggregate capital accounts shall be credited or charged to partners in proportion to their capital accounts;

b) One-half of any remaining net profits or losses up through the next 6% of the aggregate capital accounts shall be credited or charged proportionally to the several capital accounts, and the other half shall be credited or charged against the partners in equal shares; and

c) All net profits or losses for each year over 16% of the aggregate capital accounts shall be credited or charged in proportion to the several capital accounts.

New Partners. New partners may be elected not less than 60 days after proposal for membership, by the vote of at least two-thirds of the members owning at least two-thirds of the firm's capital.

Withdrawal or Death of a Partner. A partner may withdraw at any time by agreement with the Executive Committee or by giving one year's notice. Withdrawal may be required by a two-thirds vote of members owning two-thirds of capital. Such withdrawal or death shall not work a dissolution of the firm. In case of the withdrawal or death of a partner, the interest of such former partner shall be determined and paid as follows:

a) The amount credited in his drawing account shall be paid on 30 days' notice.

b) His credit balance in the capital account, as shown by the last previous balance sheet plus or minus subsequent charges and corrections for the profit or loss of the year, with interest at 6% per annum until payment, shall be paid by the firm in 10 equal annual installments, with such anticipation in the payment of installments as the firm may decide. Such unpaid balances shall be treated as a debt of the firm.

ing for a vote. These include decisions to merge with another firm, to change the privileges of a class of stockholders, and others of like importance. But in the normal course of affairs the board of directors makes decisions as if the directors were owners, as long as its members act honestly and in good faith. From this situation of representative government comes the possibility—and often the fact—of a separation of ownership from control.

Adolph Berle and Gardiner Means, in their pioneering study,[8] defined location of the control of a corporation as follows: ". . . we may say for practical purposes that control lies in the hands of the individual or group who have the actual power to select the board of directors (or its majority). . . ."[9] In the active sense of day-to-day management, this definition is entirely true, and it is therefore appropriate to study first the location of the voting power which can be used at corporate meetings. Every corporation will have at least one class of shareholders whose members have voting power. In the majority of corporations, all the voting power is found in the common stock, on the basis of one vote per share.

Any shareholder may be elected a director at the annual meeting of the shareholders; but since his holding need be only one or a few shares, his own position as owner may be nominal. In the smaller firms, especially those *closely held* corporations where the ownership of shares is concentrated in a few hands, the membership of the board will be able to know the desires of the stockholder group, and to act accordingly. In the larger, *publicly held* corporations the directors may be unable to sense the desires of a group of shareholders of diversified characteristics. Although there has been a movement to persuade shareholders in the publicly held corporations to attend meetings, the proportion of such owners who do in fact attend has been and will continue to be small. Most persons entitled to vote at such meetings execute a *proxy*, which names someone who is authorized to cast the vote of the absent shareholder. There are, as our readers doubtless know, occasional proxy fights where opposing interests solicit the vote of the shareholder; but the majority of corporations have peaceful annual meetings at which the existing management, having solicited proxies, has a controlling majority of the votes at the meeting. The terms *management controlled* and *minority controlled*

---

[8] Adolph A. Berle, Jr., and Gardiner C. Means, *The Modern Corporation and Private Property* (New York: Macmillan Co., 1933). Used by permission. The statistical section has become out of date, but the legal analysis is as cogent as ever.

[9] *Ibid.*, p. 69.

are used to describe corporations where the *proxy system* is relied on to provide the incumbent group with the votes needed to elect its nominees to the board of directors.

As far as the large publicly held companies are concerned, the present situation has been aptly described by Mason:

The one-hundred-and-thirty-odd largest manufacturing corporations account for half of manufacturing output in the United States. The five hundred largest business corporations in this country embrace nearly two thirds of all nonagricultural economic activity. These or similar figures are reiterated with such frequency that they tend to bounce off our heads rather than to penetrate. But by now we are all aware that we live not only in a corporate society but a society of large corporations. The management—that is, the control—of these corporations is in the hands of, at most, a few thousand men. Who selected these men, if not to rule over us, at least to exercise vast authority, and to whom are they responsible? The answer to the first question is quite clearly: they selected themselves. The answer to the second is, at best, nebulous. . . .[10]

There are a great many factors to be appraised before one can form a judgment about the desirability of such a situation. Suffice it to say here that corporations are governed by elected boards of directors, which are supposed in legal theory to represent the interests of the owning investors. In many corporations, especially the closely held ones, they do. In other corporations, it is not easy for the members of the board to be identified as representatives of any ownership interest. Most directors under such circumstances act in what they believe to be "the best interests of the corporation"; but the exact meaning of that term is not clear—nor can it be, for the corporation is nothing more than an artificial being, with no interests of its own. One much-quoted attempt to provide guidance is the following:

. . . Business firms are man-made instruments of society. They can be made to achieve their greatest social usefulness—and thus their future can be best assured—when management succeeds in finding a harmonious balance among the claims of the various interested groups: the stockholders, employees, customers, and the public at large. But management's responsibility, in the broadest sense, extends beyond the search for a balance among respective claims. Management, as a good citizen, and because it cannot properly function in an acrimonious and contentious atmosphere, has the positive duty to work for peaceful relations and understanding among men—for a restoration of faith of men in each other in all walks of life.

. . . .

Those two words, "fair" and "reasonable," mark the asserted claims not only of a corporation's stockholders but of all other groups as well. Very

---

[10] Edward S. Mason (ed.), *The Corporation in Modern Society* (Cambridge, Mass.: Harvard University Press, 1959), p. 5.

few groups ever believe that they make unfair or unreasonable claims. But often what one group thinks fair is regarded as entirely unreasonable by another. It takes professional judgment, experience, and knowledge of the consequences of specific decisions to resolve all the claims and to keep all the groups in cooperative support of the joint enterprise.

This reconciliation of interest is not always as difficult as it may seem. It is in part a matter of recognizing true long-term interest, as distinguished from interests that may seem real because they are more immediate.[11]

In view of the widespread ineffectiveness of shareholder control, the reader may be disposed to conclude that the common shareholder should be considered as just another source of funds along with the bondholder and preferred stockholder. We disagree with this interpretation for two reasons: (1) The common shareholder alone possesses the legal right to control the management and the business, whether he exercises it or not; and (2) the common shareholder continues to bear the fundamental risks of the business, whether or not he dictates its policies. This leads us to the position that questions of financial policy (which are the matters of principal importance throughout this book) *should* be determined from the point of view of the interests of the common shareholders *existing at the time the policy is being determined*. This interest, when determined, can then enter the balancing process that is implicit in the quotation from Abrams that we gave above.

Limited Liability. As distinguished from other forms of business organization, the corporate form offers *limited liability* to its owners. The following comment has been made on the typical provision of corporation law on stockholders' liabilities: "Stockholders are liable to creditors of their corporation for unpaid stock subscriptions. In addition, the law in some states lists other conditions under which stockholders incur liability. Receiving unlawful distributions in the form of either dividends or payments on dissolution, or voting approval of other proposals which unlawfully reduce the corporation's capital are among [such] conditions."[12]

 While the legal obligations of a proprietor or of any member of a partnership are described as *unlimited liability*, experience indicates that business creditors are reluctant to levy upon personal assets, if only because of the cost involved. When they do, they often find that most of the assets in the partner's family are in the name of the wife, or some other person not a partner. Such insulation from

---

[11] Frank W. Abrams, "Management's Responsibilities in a Complex World," *Harvard Business Review*, May, 1951, pp. 29–30.

[12] Commerce Clearing House, Inc., *Corporation Law Guide* (Chicago, 1959), Par. 511 [Par. 658].

liability is common and expected. It reflects the cultural acceptance of the business as separate from the personal interests of the owners. Nevertheless, where one considers the incorporation of a small firm, the grant of limited liability is often a factor of considerable weight in the decision.[13]

On the side of the publicly held corporation, where limited liability exists as a matter of law, it is now so universally a characteristic of securities that investors take it for granted. The need for this feature is therefore no longer an issue of the investment world. There is, however, one corollary of the grant of limited liability which corporate management needs to bear in mind. The capital contributed by the shareholders is to be kept separate from any earnings that may be received and held by the corporation. Dividends may not be paid out of such capital.

State Sanction—Corporate Powers

All of the material above, which is centered on the legal entity enjoyed by the corporation, has implicit in it the fact that the corporation exists by the grace of legislative power. Artificial persons are created only by legislative action, and the sovereign has always been the agency upon which depends the opportunity to create corporations.

General Incorporation Laws of the States. For some years past, beginning with New York in 1811, each of the states of the United States has had a "general corporation law," paralleled by a "general banking law" and the like, which permit persons to charter a corporation for any legal purpose, provided they meet certain requirements, which are the same for any applicant.[14] The terms of the laws vary greatly among the states, and some of the differences will be referred to where they are pertinent, but they have the common characteristic of the relative ease with which a corporation can be created. The necessary papers are drafted and filed, moderate fees are paid, et cetera, all within the terms of the statute and without real difficulty.

Incorporation is not difficult in any state, but few states match Delaware, where it is possible for a firm in Wilmington to advertise that out-of-state persons may employ it to handle all the necessary procedure of incorporation, with the result that: "Corporations are

---

[13] The limited liability feature of an incorporated business may be of little use if a banker or other creditor insists on having the debt contract personally endorsed by the principal stockholder(s).

[14] In the case of banks and other financial corporations, the minimum capital requirement may be substantial. Certain types of business, such as utilities, cannot be set up without a finding by a commission that they are "convenient and necessary."

organized, by-laws adopted and records mailed to counsel on the same day. . . . The first meeting is held in Wilmington. Personal attendance of the incorporators is not required. . . . Thus the organization is brought up to the point of holding the first meeting of directors for electing officers and commencing business. This meeting may be held when and where convenient to the directors and forms are furnished as a guide for its procedure."

Many older corporations still do business under charters granted in the time when each charter was a separate legislative act. Some of them have unusually broad provisions. The charter of Dartmouth College deserves special mention, since it raised the constitutional question of whether a state could amend a grant of powers which it had at one time made. It was decided, in a famous opinion of John Marshall,[15] that the grant could not be amended. While this decision is still law, one should not be confused by its effect. The result has been that every existing general corporation statute contains a provision which reserves to the state the right to amend a charter granted thereunder.

Federal Corporations Result from Special Enactment. No general corporation statute exists as a part of the federal law, though the Congress has the power to enact one and bills have been submitted for the purpose. There is a general banking law, known as the National Banking Act, under which are chartered banks with the privilege, and duty, of carrying in their title the words *National Bank* (or N.B.A.). Similar laws provide for federal savings and loan associations, national farm loan associations, and other credit agencies; but for the formation of a general business corporation, one looks to the various states.

The federal Congress has chartered numerous corporations by special enactment. These fulfill some governmental purpose, often of a financial nature. The Federal Reserve banks, the Federal Land banks, the Reconstruction Finance Corporation, and the Inland Waterways Corporation are examples of the use of federal statute to create a corporation. On the other hand, the Congress has sometimes provided for the formation of a governmental corporation under state law. This is true, for instance, of the Commodity Credit Corporation of Delaware.

The Definition of Corporate Powers. The saying "The corporation has limited powers" reflects the admitted fact that a corporation can have only the powers that the state permits it to assume. Nevertheless, the statement is misleading. In practice, those who

---

[15] *Trustees of Dartmouth College* v. *Woodward*, 4 Wheat. (U.S.) 518 (1819).

form corporations draft their own definition of powers and provide the powers they desire within the broad limitations of the general law.

At the time a corporation is formed, its powers will be defined by (1) the statutes of the state, which apply to all its corporations; (2) the *certificate of incorporation* (or *charter*, or *articles of association*), which is drafted by those desiring to form the corporation and applies only to the specific firm; and (3) the bylaws, further defining the corporation's powers, which are also drafted by the incorporators.

The Corporation Law. Corporations are subject to all law that affects business affairs, but the corporation statute of a state deals with the special characteristics of a corporation, and it is to the provisions of such a statute that one turns when the powers available to a corporation are to be described.

Anyone with imagination who studies carefully any piece of legislation will soon be able to think of situations where the application of the wording of the statute is uncertain. When lawyers speak of "untested" provisions of a statute, they refer to clauses whose meanings have not yet been the subject of a judicial decision. There is no other way to discover the meaning of a difficult clause than by waiting for a lawsuit to develop and observing the court's conclusion. Then it is said that the clause has been "interpreted."

For this reason, it must be realized that the corporation law of a state is far more than the text of the legislation. It includes this text and all the judicial decisions relative to it. From this fact flows a reluctance on the part of legislators to change long-standing and fully interpreted clauses of legislation. There is always uncertainty about the exact meaning of proposed provisions which may cause hesitancy in their use and costly litigation before their interpretation. Among the reasons for the popularity of Delaware in the past as a state of incorporation has been the fact that its corporation law has been the subject of much litigation, so that at present the meaning of the statute is well settled.

Although from time to time, judicial decisions tend to confuse rather than clarify the law, the longer the corporation continues to be the principal pattern used by business units, the more nearly perfected its law will be in every detail. Thus, as time has gone by, the greater has become the margin of preference for the corporation over the joint-stock company and the business trust.

Articles of Incorporation and Bylaws. Most general corporation laws make it clear that the state no longer values its privilege to limit the powers of corporations formed for general business purposes. Under such circumstances, it is not surprising that a cautious draftsman may state the proposed powers broadly enough to avoid any necessity of later amendment. The case of the Public Works Emergency Leasing Corporation (Delaware, 1934) has been chosen to show how broad the powers may be, despite the more limited immediate purpose of the incorporators (in this instance, the Secretary of the Interior and two other government officials).

The articles of incorporation of this organization specify that it is to have perpetual existence. The powers include those:

To undertake . . . any project eligible to be included in the comprehensive program of Public Works to be prepared pursuant to the provisions of the Recovery Act.

To collect fees, tolls, and other charges in the construction of [public works].

To cause maintenance and operation of edifices, structures, and buildings of every kind, nature, or description.

To furnish, equip, operate, manage and maintain projects and structures of every kind, nature, or description, and to do any and all things necessary, suitable, or convenient in connection therewith, including without limitation the supplying of heat, steam, water, gas and electricity and transportation, telephone, and any other facilities or utilities necessary, suitable, or convenient.

To carry on its functions in the State of Delaware or in any other State, Territory, or locality . . . without restriction or limitation as to amount.

To acquire personal property of every kind, nature or description and in any manner to acquire, hold, use, or dispose of any franchises, licenses, grants, concessions, patents, trade marks, trade names, copyrights, or inventions granted by or existing under the laws of any government or subdivision thereof.

To acquire, by purchase, exchange or otherwise, all or any part of or any interest in the properties, assets, business and goodwill of any one or more persons, firms, associations, or corporations engaged in any business for which a corporation may now or hereafter be organized under the laws of the State of Delaware; to pay for the same in any lawful manner; to hold, operate, reorganize, liquidate, sell, donate, or in any manner dispose of the whole or any part thereof; and, in connection therewith, to assume or guarantee performance of any liabilities, obligations, or contracts of such persons, firms, associations, or corporations, and to conduct in any lawful manner the whole or part of any business thus acquired.[16]

At this point the reader is reminded that this description refers to incorporation under general laws, not under banking, insurance, or other special laws. The draftsman cannot entirely "encompass the world in the English language," as certain activities are in the pur-

---

[16] Small wonder that a somewhat unsophisticated commentator found in this charter evidence of a conspiracy to socialize the nation!

view of other laws. Thus, the extremely broad charter of the Chesapeake Corporation, a railroad holding company, concedes the following restrictions:

Nothing herein contained is to be construed as authorizing the Corporation to carry on the business of discounting bills, notes or other evidences of debt, or receiving deposits of money, or foreign coins, or buying and selling bills of exchange, or of issuing bills, notes or other evidences of debt for circulation as money. . . .

Nothing herein contained shall be . . . construed to give the Corporation any rights, powers, or privileges not permitted by the laws of the State of Maryland. . . .

Despite the possibility that narrow definitions of powers may prove embarrassing at a later time, a substantial number of cases exist where the powers that are taken are narrowly stated. This is particularly true of small firms, where the intent of the incorporators is to take advantage of certain of the attributes of the corporation without freeing the future management in every particular. Quite frequently, one finds that the transfer of stock is limited to certain procedures that give the corporation's directors control over additions to the stockholder group.

Since the bylaws of the corporation are drafted to implement the articles of incorporation, it can be expected that they will not alter the conclusions suggested by the above paragraphs: that the general corporation law of most states does not, in fact, limit the freedom of incorporators to set up a corporation of their own design. While many corporations do operate with closely defined powers, many others do not, and the state is a passive agent. The legal pattern of the corporation need be no more restrictive than that of the noncorporate enterprise.

The state is also a passive agent in the taking of powers by firms that select patterns other than a corporation. A proprietorship is the most free of any special limitation upon its business. Partnerships are, in most states, the subject of a special partnership law; but in the making of the partnership contract, a basic document similar to corporate articles and bylaws, draftsmen are as free when it comes to the particular matter of defining the nature of the business to be undertaken.

Important Distinctions Remain. The basic differences already referred to in this chapter are (1) that the corporation is a legal entity, and thus that its parties may separate its affairs from their own more completely than is possible under other legal forms;

(2) that the corporation has the possibility of an unlimited term of existence; (3) that each member of a partnership, except a publicly announced limited partner, may act in the name of the partnership; (4) that a partnership must go through a dissolution upon the death of a partner, and a new partnership must succeed it; and (5) that the liabilities of a corporation do not attach to its owners or its managers.

An important basic difference not so far mentioned, and one that cannot be avoided completely by clever draftsmanship, is the limitation put upon a corporation's power to do business in any state. This limitation comes from the general recognition that a corporation is not a person in the sense used in the Constitution of the United States, which guarantees that each state shall confer upon a citizen of any state all those rights which it confers upon its own citizens. In contrast, an out-of-state corporation, "foreign" to a state in which it desires to do business, is always required to pay certain fees and to maintain a local office. In some states, it may be required to indicate which of its powers it proposes to use in the state; and in a few cases, it may be denied permission to do business at all. Such restrictions are possible under the general rule of a decision of the United States Supreme Court, quoted below, but the "comity" referred to in the quotation keeps the number of restrictions small.

. . . The corporation being the mere creation of local law can have no legal existence beyond the limits of the sovereignty where created. . . . The recognition of its existence even by other states . . . depend purely upon the comity of those states—a comity which is never extended where the existence of the corporation and the exercise of its powers are prejudicial to their interests or repugnant to their policy. Having no absolute right of recognition in other states, but depending . . . upon their assent, it follows . . . that such assent may be granted upon such terms and conditions as those states may think proper to impose. They may exclude the foreign corporation entirely; they may restrict its business. . . . The whole matter rests in their discretion.[17]

Although the comity of the states and reliance on laws of general application have kept the number of restrictions upon foreign corporations small, the added expense alone results in the practice that most corporations incorporate in the state of their principal place of business. On the other hand, several large corporations have chosen as the state of their incorporation some state where the franchise taxes are low or some desired corporate practice is known to be legal.

Table 2–2 shows the state of incorporation and the state in which

---

[17] *Paul* v. *Virginia*, 8 Wall. (75 U.S.) 168 (1869).

TABLE 2–2

STATE OF INCORPORATION AND LOCATION OF GENERAL OFFICE
OF TWENTY LARGEST UNITED STATES CORPORATIONS

Name of Company	Location of General Office	State of Incorporation
General Motors Corporation.......	Michigan	Delaware
Standard Oil Company (New Jersey).......................	New York	New Jersey
Ford Motor Company............	Michigan	Delaware
General Electric Company........	New York	New York
United States Steel Corporation....	New York	New Jersey
Socony Mobil Oil Company, Inc....	New York	New York
Gulf Oil Corporation.............	Pennsylvania	Pennsylvania
Texaco Inc......................	New York	Delaware
Chrysler Corporation.............	Michigan	Delaware
Swift & Company................	Illinois	Illinois
Western Electric Company, Inc....	New York	New York
Du Pont (E. I.) de Nemours & Company....................	Delaware	Delaware
Bethlehem Steel Corporation......	New York	Delaware
Standard Oil Company (Indiana)..	Illinois	Indiana
Westinghouse Electric Corporation.	Pennsylvania	Pennsylvania
Armour and Company............	Illinois	Illinois
General Dynamics Corporation....	New York, Washington	Delaware
Shell Oil Company...............	New York	Delaware
Boeing Airplane Company........	Washington	Delaware
National Dairy Products Corporation........................	New York	Delaware

SOURCE OF COMPANY NAMES: *The Fortune Directory of the 500 Largest U.S. Industrial Corporations*, Supplement to *Fortune*, July, 1960 (New York, 1960), p. 132. Copyright, 1960, by Time, Inc.
SOURCE OF OTHER DATA: *Moody's Industrial Manual, 1960*, except *Moody's Public Utility Manual, 1960*, for Western Electric Company, Inc.

the general office is located for the twenty largest United States industrial corporations (1960).

Financial Contracts

No single corporate characteristic does more to explain the corporation's overwhelming importance in the present-day American economy than its ability to create financial contracts of innumerable types. Any business may be referred to as a "bundle of contracts," for this phrase is used to point out that, as of any moment, the activities of any going concern, no matter what its form of organization, are defined in innumerable ways by the contracts into which it has entered. Such contracts, in fact, define the activities of a business from day to day far more then the basic documents referred to above. The bundle includes contracts of purchase and sale, contracts of employment, real estate lease contracts, and all the other types of business contracts that will be found to be in force in any going concern.

Contracts of the type just referred to do not distinguish a corporation. The distinction is found in the greater variety of financial contracts possible to a corporation because of its long span of existence and its ability to limit the liability of investors. When contrasted with the partnership or any business unit whose life is measured by that of some individual, the corporation offers much greater continuity, and thus the basis for long-term arrangements, such as bond or preferred stock issues. When contrasted with the joint-stock company, the corporation offers in its financial contracts less risk of loss, because of the feature of limited liability. Finally, the entity conferred upon the corporation permits it to make contracts of the nature of mortgages upon its property without the cumbersome detail that attends the use of instruments of this nature in connection with partnerships.

The term *corporate securities,* as used in finance, usually refers to stocks, bonds, and other evidences of contracts for funds.[18] Actually, existing security contracts, as used by corporations, vary in detail almost as widely as the range of the imagination, for there is as little restraint upon the draftsman of corporate securities as upon the draftsman of the articles of incorporation and bylaws that create the corporation. But examination of the innumerable corporate securities that have been issued shows three characteristics prevailing among them. Their terms are made *suitable* to the needs of particular buyers; they provide for the *division* of the contract among many investors; and they permit *transfer* of the benefits of the contract from one investor to another.

| *Suitability: Debt versus Ownership.*   Much of the art of financial management is applied to the drafting of corporate financial contracts that are suitable to the circumstances of the corporation and the investor. But although the variety of individual cases is almost infinite, the contracts fall into two main classes: those which create debt and those which recognize ownership. The distinguishing characteristic of debt is that a contract of this nature contains a promise to pay money under stated conditions. The law conveys to the holder of a debt the right to enforce his claim by court action, if necessary. A contract of participation in ownership, on the other hand, does not

---

[18] Originally, the term may have been restricted to contracts under the terms of which the promises were secured by the pledge of something of value—"the security"—but the use of the term is now far more genral.

contain a promise to pay but merely conveys an opportunity to participate in such distributions as shall be voted by the directors of the corporation. Thus, as a minimum, the holder of a debt of a corporation is more certain of receiving payments according to the terms of his debt contract than is the holder of a share in ownership.

Out of this distinction, with all the variety that can be applied in individual cases, arises the possibility of drafting corporate financial contracts that are suitable to a variety of investors. Those desirous of relative certainty of payment will be offered debt contracts, broadly referred to as *bonds* or *notes*. Others, anxious to participate as owners when profits expand, will be buyers of shares of ownership, usually referred to as *common stock* or *capital stock*.

A middle position, that of *preferred stock*, often appeals to investors desiring a larger return than that offered by debt contracts; but in law, this type of contract enjoys none of the certainty of a debt obligation. The dividend, though having priority over common stock, is only paid when voted by the directors.

For example, the life insurance companies of the United States, with investments in the securities of business and industry totaling approximately $49.9 billion at the close of 1959,[19] are heavy buyers of corporate bonds. Their investment policy, reflecting the nature of their obligations, calls for an emphasis on safety of return rather than on any prospect of great profit. Corporations obtain funds from this enormous investing industry by creating bonds and preferred stocks which confer a priority of claim on earnings (and perhaps also on assets). In return, the insurance companies agree to take a lower annual return on their investment than would be required to satisfy a prospective buyer of stock under most market conditions.

2 *Divisibility.* Any corporate financial contract may, and usually does, provide that its terms shall apply ratably to each of many fractional parts evidenced by documents that shall be issued to a total representing the entire contract. Such parts may then be sold to as many separate investors as desire to participate in the provisions of the financial contract.

For example, a corporate mortgage contract involving a loan of, say, $20 million, may be evidenced by 20,000 bonds, each of $1,000 denomination. Each bond contains on its face a summary of the contract of debt. It is considered as evidence of a 1/20,000 interest in the benefits of the contract.

---

[19] Institute of Life Insurance, *1960 Life Insurance Fact Book* (New York, 1960), p. 71.

The exact mechanism of accomplishing this result varies from case to case, but the essence always is that many investors may participate by buying as much of the total issue as may suit their plans. The result is that a corporation may obtain enormous quantities of funds from the small purchases of many security buyers, including those who are not professional investors. In no other way could one obtain the great aggregations of wealth that have been accumulated by the major corporate businesses of the United States. In fact, the great corporations rely on "OPM"—Other People's Money—to use the designation made famous by Justice Brandeis.

The American Telephone and Telegraph Company, the largest private corporation in the United States, can be used as an example. At the end of 1960, this corporation published a consolidated balance sheet showing assets totaling $22,558,283,000. It had obtained $2,090,611,000 of these assets by entering a variety of short-term contracts classed as "current liabilities."

The balance was made up in part of debt contracts totaling $7,232,239,000. This sum represented a considerable number of issues and types of bonds issued by the parent company and its subsidiaries. The total number of bondholders is unknown, but it is undoubtedly very large.

Substantially all of the remainder of the total assets of the company were represented by 223,518,483 shares of stock, owned by 1,911,484 shareholders. The average holding was about 117 shares.

Such an example serves to explain the essential feature of the financing of large corporations. The corporation, contrasting with the partnership-proprietorship, provides for the building of great sums out of small individual investments.

Transferability. The documents evidencing participation in corporate financial contracts can be made freely transferable, and in the typical case the contract so provides. Details vary from case to case, but the essence is that a holder of a security may transfer it at any time to some person who will take it. If the transaction is a sale, the price is negotiated between the investors. It must be recognized that the corporation is not a party to the transfer. It has received funds from the original investor, and subsequent transfers do not affect this sum. There is merely a transfer of parties on one side of the corporate contract. In fact, the corporation frequently receives no notification of the transfer. By contrast, a member of a partnership cannot sell his interest without gaining the unanimous approval of his fellow partners to the proposed new partner.

No corporate characteristic is more responsible than this feature of transferability for the enormous growth of corporate enterprises. *Suitability* provides a variety of investment media; *divisibility* provides the means for the accumulation of a great whole out of many small parts; *transferability* allows the investor to choose the time for his own purchase and sale.

Liquidity through sale is relied on by both small and large investors who would not be willing to commit funds to a single enterprise for as long as the business might need it. Thus is created a paradoxical condition in which businesses receive funds for long-term purposes such as the building of hydroelectric dams, while investors receive securities that may be converted into liquid funds by sale. We have already presented statistics showing the extent of such ownership by stockholders in the United States.

As a necessary result of the transfers that take place so frequently, there has developed the whole organization of security dealers and securities exchanges which are a vital part of the system of corporate finance. These institutions will be described more fully in later material.

Transferability, while it is a necessary condition for size, is not always a desired characteristic for small corporations. Frequently, the owners of a closely held corporation may reject the idea that any stockholder should be able to sell his interest to any one at any time. In such a case the solution is provided by the inclusion in the articles of incorporation of provisions restricting transfer. Here, as elsewhere, the ingenuity of the draftsman is the limit to the terms of the limitation. The only general rules are that the limitation must be provided in advance, or imposed with the consent of the security holder, and that the limitation must apply equally to all the holders of any class of security to which it is applied.

An example that is frequently encountered among closely held corporations requires the security holder first to offer his security to the directors of the corporation. A procedure for setting the price for the sale is specified. If the directors do not act favorably within a specified time, the security holder is free to sell in the open market. It is of doubtful legality to forbid the stockholder to sell his holding under all circumstances.

Tax Status

A review of the major considerations that need attention before making the choice of the legal form of doing business must include the topic of income taxation. There is little difference in the treatment of the various types of business units as far as property and similar taxation is concerned. There is some disadvantage to the corporation because it must pay fees to maintain its corporate status in each state wherein it does business, but such payments are minor considerations. On the other hand, there are significant differences between the proprietorship, or the partnership, and the corporation in tax treatment of income derived therefrom, and this can be of real importance in the choice of one or the other of these organizational forms.

For those who have not studied the federal income tax law, a brief introduction to some of its provisions is necessary. The reader will recognize that in our attempt to be brief, we shall necessarily describe a complex situation only in approximate terms. First, the law recognizes two types of income: *capital gains* and *ordinary income.* There are also, of course, *capital losses* and *ordinary losses.* Capital gains or losses result from transactions involving the sale of a capital asset, as opposed to a product offered for sale, where the selling price is above (or below) a value based on what was originally paid for the asset. The most important type of capital transaction for the present discussion is the gain or loss resulting from the sale of a corporate security by an investor, who may seek his gain in this way rather than by the receipt of dividends.

Ordinary income and losses result from the ordinary business activities of the taxpayer. This class includes, in the case of an investor, interest and dividends on securities.

The distinction between capital gains and ordinary income is important because capital gains are taxed at rates equal to one half the applicable rate for ordinary income, with a maximum of 25 per cent. When personal rates rise as high as 91 per cent, this is a matter of considerable importance.

The tax law treats a corporation, which is a legal entity, as a separate taxpayer and levies taxes on its ordinary income and capital gains without reference to the way in which this income is distributed or retained in the business. Unlike the progressive personal income tax, the corporate income tax since 1951 has been at a flat rate of 30 per cent on all taxable income plus a surtax of 22 per cent of income in excess of $25,000.

Any distribution to shareholders will then be considered part of their personal income, and will be subject to a personal income tax at a rate determined by the over-all income situation of the individual shareholder. The only relief from this double taxation of the distributed income of incorporated businesses is a modest one introduced in the 1954 Code. At the time this book was going to press (early 1961), even this provision was undergoing heavy criticism. Under this provision the first $50 of dividends received is not included as taxable personal income; and in addition, a credit of 4 per cent of dividends received in excess of $50 is provided as a deduction from the tax payable.

The idea of a separate tax on business income does not apply to the proprietorship or the partnership. As explained previously, business activity carried on under these forms is considered merely as an extension of the personal activities of the owner or owners; hence, business income is classed as personal income of the proprietor or partners. As personal income, it is subject to the personal income tax rates applying to the individual owners.

This basic difference in treatment has given rise to significant variations in the tax burden, depending not only on the legal form chosen for the business but also on the ways in which the income of the business is handled. Whether these variations favor the corporate form or the partnership-proprietorship depends on the particular circumstances of the business and its owners and, at least in part, on circumstances which the owners may not be able to foresee at the time the legal form is chosen. Some of the more generally significant implications of these differences will be outlined in the remainder of this section.

At first glance, it might be concluded that a 52 per cent levy on corporate income added to the personal tax on dividends to shareholders would make the corporate form distinctly unattractive from the tax point of view. This would be particularly true if all or a large part of the corporate earnings were regularly distributed in the form of dividends. On the other hand, if corporate earnings are retained in the business, they do not become personal income and therefore bear only the 52 per cent corporate tax, at least at that point of time. The opportunity of deferring, perhaps indefinitely, the receipt of the business earnings of a given period and the personal income tax associated therewith may be considered a major advantage by shareholders, particularly those whose personal income puts them in a tax bracket which is very high. There is a different opportunity, present only in a closely held company, to pay very high salaries to officers who are also shareholders. If such payments are allowed as "costs" by the income tax authorities, the 52 per cent tax is avoided, although, of course, the personal income tax remains.

One important possible advantage of this aspect of the corporate form is the opportunity of using earnings for business expansion without being first subject to the personal income tax—an advantage which would have particular appeal for the owner whose tax bracket is above 52 per cent. Further, the reinvestment of earnings makes possible their ultimate "withdrawal" as a capital gain rather than as dividend income, thus giving the advantage of the low capital gains tax. This results when there is an appreciation in the value of the stock as a result of reinvested earnings, with the shareholder receiving the benefit of the investment in a higher price for the stock when it is sold rather than in dividends during the time the stock is held.

There may also be some owners who have no desire to benefit from their investment during their lifetime. If the earnings can be reinvested without the depleting effect of the personal income tax and permanently retained in the business, the only tax which will bear on such earnings will be the tax on the value of the estate at time of death, a tax which would be paid in any case if the earnings were withdrawn and retained rather than spent.

It must be stressed, however, that the Internal Revenue Service has no intention of permitting the corporate form to be used simply as a device to avoid the personal income tax. The retention and reinvestment of earnings must have a valid justification in terms of normal and reasonable business practice. Although infrequently used, a special tax is provided by the Internal Revenue Code on the accumulated earnings of a corporation where it can be proved by the government that the purpose is to avoid the personal tax on dividends. The additional tax applies to unnecessarily accumulated earnings in excess of $100,000 and amounts to $27\frac{1}{2}$ per cent of the first $100,000 plus $38\frac{1}{2}$ per cent of accumulated earnings in excess of $100,000.

Even where it can be justified, the advantages of the corporate form arising out of the opportunity to defer the receipt of income may not be sufficient to outweigh the disadvantage of the added corporate income tax. There can be other disadvantages as well. The distribution received by the shareholder as dividends is personal income, regardless of its original source. The distribution received by the proprietor or partner retains the character as originally received by the business. Thus, a capital gain to the partnership is also a capital gain to the partners, whereas a capital gain to the corporation passed along as a dividend to its shareholders becomes personal income and is taxed as such. On the other hand, a potential advantage to the corporation lies in the handling of business losses. Because of the way the tax law stands, a net loss for a given year in a partnership could be used by the partners only as an offset against personal income in that year. A net loss to a corporation would have an advantage as a tax offset in certain past and future years.

From the foregoing, the reader can see that very few general statements can be made about the advantages of a corporate form of doing business from a tax point of view. The advantage will depend on the exact nature of the interests involved in the particular case, with emphasis probably being given to the degree of interest the owners may have in cash dividends in the near future, and to the uses the corporation may be expected to have for funds for expansion, debt retirement, and other purposes.

Probably in order to reduce the importance of the tax factor in the decisions of smaller businesses about the form of organization which they will use, the 1954 revision of the Internal Revenue Code provided that certain unincorporated businesses could be taxed as corporations and that certain small corporations could be taxed as partnerships. The reader is referred to Section 1361 for details. If a business once elects to be treated in one or another of these ways, it cannot change its choice at a later date without the consent of the Director of Internal Revenue.

The Effect of Size on Choice

The corporation has been said to dominate the business section of the American economy. This is true because large-scale enterprises almost exclusively use the corporate form in order to raise the great amount of funds they need. A few joint-stock companies exist, but they present no advantages to overcome the unlimited liability of their owners. There are some business trusts, but these have difficulty in gaining recognition because they have ill-defined terms of life and because they find that some states do not recognize them. They do provide a chance of greater centralization of control, but this is not often the determining factor. Thus, it is very seldom that a large-scale enterprise will adopt any form other than that of the corporation.

Much greater diversity exists among smaller firms. The advantage of security flotation loses much of its force. Instead, the factors of length of life, limitation of liability, centralization of management, fees, and income taxation assume greater importance. The result of such considerations on the selection of the form of organization varies with the details of a particular business, and the predispositions of its managers.

PART II

The Management of Assets and the Need for Funds

Chapter 3

Inventory Management and the Need
for Funds

Goods carried for ultimate sale in the normal course of operations make up the bulk of business inventories. Included also in inventory but usually of minor importance are stocks of supplies—goods not intended for sale but needed in operating the business, such as coal for the heating plant, lubricants for machines, and paper for the office. Manufacturing, wholesale, and retailing firms typically maintain a large investment in inventory, and its management is a highly important function. United States manufacturers on September 30, 1960, had $60.5 billion, or 23.8 per cent, of their total assets tied up in inventory. Wholesalers had 29.4 per cent of total assets in inventory, retailers 32.2 per cent.

Reflecting their sale of services rather than goods, the inventories of concerns in the electric utility, transportation, and service industries consist almost entirely of supplies and are of relatively minor consequence financially.

A Focus on Manufacturers' Inventories

In this chapter, we shall discuss aspects of inventory management of especial significance to the financial manager. We have chosen a focus on inventory management in manufacturing concerns for several reasons. One is the sheer size of manufacturers'[1] inventory investment and its importance to them. Further, the problems of managing manufacturers' inventories are relatively complex. If they can be understood, the basic concepts involved can be applied to inventory

---

[1] Manufacturers account for more than one half of all business inventories. Retailers account for about 25 per cent, wholesalers 15 per cent.

CHART 3-1

INVESTMENT IN INVENTORY OF CORPORATIONS IN SELECTED INDUSTRY GROUPS, AS A PERCENTAGE OF THEIR TOTAL ASSETS, TAX YEAR ENDED JULY, 1957–JUNE, 1958

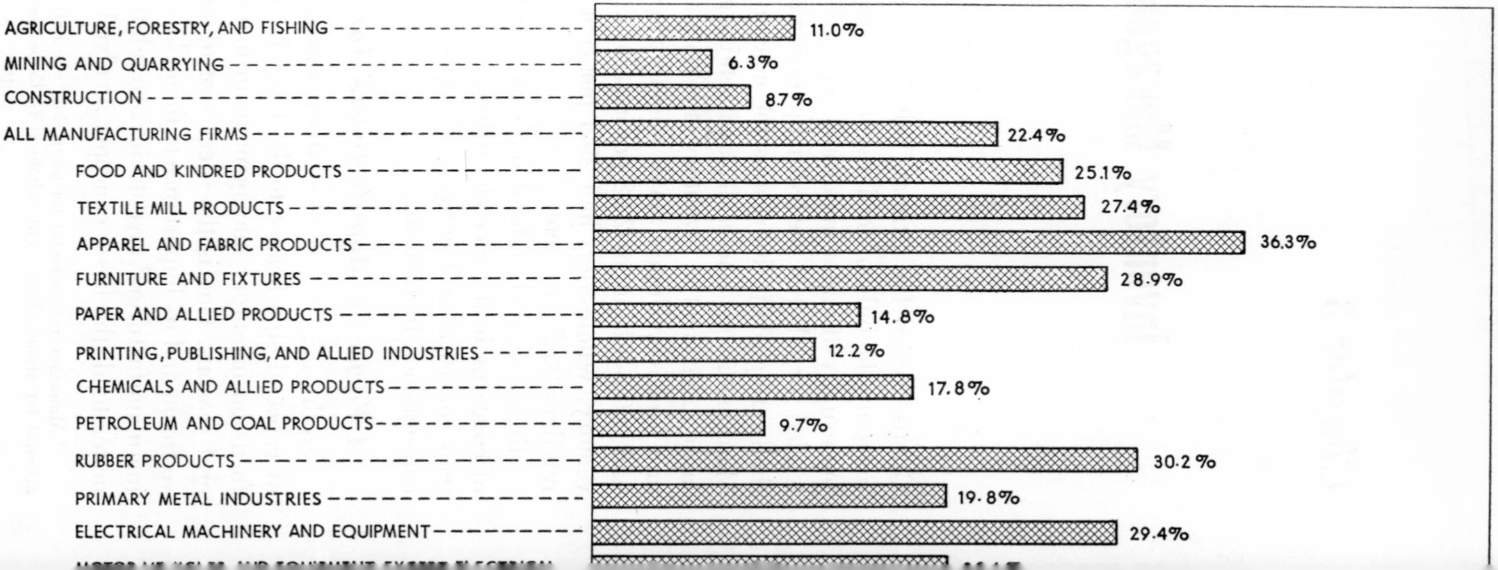

Industry Group	Percentage
AGRICULTURE, FORESTRY, AND FISHING	11.0%
MINING AND QUARRYING	6.3%
CONSTRUCTION	8.7%
ALL MANUFACTURING FIRMS	22.4%
FOOD AND KINDRED PRODUCTS	25.1%
TEXTILE MILL PRODUCTS	27.4%
APPAREL AND FABRIC PRODUCTS	36.3%
FURNITURE AND FIXTURES	28.9%
PAPER AND ALLIED PRODUCTS	14.8%
PRINTING, PUBLISHING, AND ALLIED INDUSTRIES	12.2%
CHEMICALS AND ALLIED PRODUCTS	17.8%
PETROLEUM AND COAL PRODUCTS	9.7%
RUBBER PRODUCTS	30.2%
PRIMARY METAL INDUSTRIES	19.8%
ELECTRICAL MACHINERY AND EQUIPMENT	29.4%

OTHER TRANSPORTATION EQUIPMENT — — — — — — — 36.8%

OTHER MACHINERY — — — — — — — — 31.7%

OTHER FABRICATED METAL PRODUCTS — — — — — — 28.4%

ALL PUBLIC UTILITIES — — — — — — — 2.5%

TRANSPORTATION COMPANIES — — — — — — 2.2%

COMMUNICATION COMPANIES — — — — — — 2.8%

ELECTRIC AND GAS COMPANIES — — — — — — 2.6%

WHOLESALE FIRMS — — — — — — — 30.4%

ALL RETAIL TRADE FIRMS — — — — — — — 32.2%

FOOD RETAILERS — — — — — — — 27.6%

GENERAL MERCHANDISE RETAILERS — — — — — 29.0%

APPAREL AND ACCESSORIES RETAILERS — — — — — 37.5%

FURNITURE AND HOUSEHOLD FURNISHINGS RETAILERS — — — 28.9%

BUILDING MATERIALS AND HARDWARE RETAILERS — — — 37.3%

0   5   10   15   20   25   30   35   40   45   50
PER CENT

Source of Data: Internal Revenue Service, U.S. Treasury Department, *Statistics of Income, 1957–58: Corporation Income Tax Returns* (Washington, D.C.; U.S. Government Printing Office, 1960), Table 3, pp. 31–38, and Table 5, pp. 41–66. The percentage investment in inventory for the corporations in each industry group was computed from aggregate balance sheets submitted by the individual corporations with their income tax returns. Some 508,000 corporations in the selected industry groups submitted balance sheets; these corporations accounted for virtually all the corporate sales reported in their industries.

problems of retailing and other types of business. Also, most manufacturers' operations are subject to rapid change, and the dynamic
quality of their inventory problems makes them a particularly interesting subject for study.

While the inventory investment is an important one for manufacturers generally, the relative importance of inventory varies widely
between industry groups—as Chart 3–1 brings out. Note, for example,
that inventory represented more than one third (36.3 per cent) of the
total assets of apparel and fabric manufacturers, but less than one
tenth (9.7 per cent) of the total assets of manufacturers of petroleum
and coal products.

The Varied Make-up of Manufacturers' Inventories

Although the inventory investment usually is shown on published
balance sheets as a single figure, the total "inventory" of the typical
manufacturing company is a composite of one minor (supplies) and
three major types of inventory:

1. Raw materials[2]
2. Work in process
3. Finished goods

Each of the major categories of inventory differs significantly
from the others, so that analysis of the inventory investment and its
management can be most meaningful if each category is thought of as
a separate and distinct "animal."

As can be seen from the breakdown of inventories on October 31,
1960, below, for manufacturers as a whole the three major categories
are of somewhat similar magnitude.[3] Work in process is particularly

PERCENTAGE OF TOTAL INVENTORY INVESTMENT

	All Manufacturers	Durable Goods Manufacturers	Nondurable Goods Manufacturers
Raw materials...............	31.9%	27.1%	38.6%
Work in process............	28.4	39.5	13.2
Finished goods.............	39.7	33.4	48.2
	100.0%	100.0%	100.0%

---

[2] For simplicity of presentation, we shall use the term *raw materials* in a broad
sense—that is, to include with basic materials all parts, subassemblies, and components
purchased from other firms but not yet put into the manufacturer's own production
processes.

[3] Department of Commerce, *Survey of Current Business*, January, 1961, p. S–5.

important for durable goods producers; for nondurable goods manufacturers (textiles, food, gasoline, and the like), it is of much less consequence than raw materials or finished goods.

The Investment in Raw Materials

The balance in the raw materials inventory account is a summation of the dollar values of all raw materials owned but not yet put into the production process. The total investment swells with new purchases and shrinks as materials are issued for entry into the production process.

Virtually all manufacturing concerns must carry some stocks of raw materials. But the size of the raw materials inventory normally is very much subject to management decision and control. Turnover is greatest if inventories are held to an absolute minimum relative to sales. But as we have seen, return on investment is determined also by sales volume and profit margins. The aim of inventory management then is not simply to squeeze down inventories but rather to maintain stocks at that level which best reconciles turnover and profit considerations and hence maximizes return on investment.

What are key considerations in the fixing of optimum levels of raw material stocks? For manufacturing industries broadly the following are especially important:

1. The volume of "safety stocks" needed to protect against material shortages that interrupt production.
2. Considerations of economy in purchase.
3. The outlook for changes in the prices of purchased materials.
4. The volume of production and sales anticipated.
5. The operating costs of carrying the stocks.
6. The costs and availability of capital.

The decision as to what level of inventory of key materials represents an appropriate degree of protection against "out of stocks" that halt production is a particularly important and tricky one. Especially critical are the speed and reliability with which suppliers can be counted on to fill orders. For example, if there are several suppliers who keep large stocks of an item available for immediate shipment, the user can safely carry a smaller inventory of this item than of others which suppliers must make to order and hence require a long "procurement lead time." In recent years, New England manufacturers of silverware have been able to get overnight delivery of silver bullion from New York suppliers who carry large stocks ready for immediate shipment. Consequently, many silverware manufacturers

have decided that two or three days' stock of silver is adequate to provide reasonable assurance that operations will not be impeded. Similarly, a New York doughnut maker, whose main plant was located
near flour mills, carried only a few days' supply of flour. The same
manufacturer, however, who used large quantities of dried egg yolks
imported from the Orient, carried several months' supply of egg
yolks.

Threats to continued materials availability by such events as an industry-wide strike also affect inventory levels. For example, in early
1959, when a strike of steelworkers was in prospect, users of steel
built up very large stocks—and were glad they had when a long strike
did develop.

Also, supplies of raw materials may be available only at certain
times of the year. The steel mills in Cleveland, Ohio, or Gary, Indiana,
which depend on iron ore from the Mesabi Range in Minnesota, find
it necessary to build up huge piles of iron ore in the summer and fall
in order to continue production through the winter, when ice on the
Great Lakes prevents economical water transportation of the ore.

Another factor in setting "safety stock" levels is the extent of
loss through higher costs or lost sales that would result from out-of-
stock shutdowns. Production halts can have near-catastrophic consequences in some firms, a relatively minor impact in others.

Considerations of purchase economy may affect stock levels. Purchasers of large lots frequently can command favorable prices from
suppliers and lower transport costs. For example, small paint manufacturers often buy minor ingredients in economical carload lots, even
though a carload may last them several months. This method of purchase is of particular importance to smaller concerns and to processors using small quantities of a wide variety of commodities or purchased parts.

Many companies modify inventory levels with the outlook for
price changes, building up stocks if price increases are anticipated
and trimming them when prices are expected to soften. During the
last half of 1950, when prices were rapidly rising because of the fight-
ing in Korea, manufacturers increased their raw materials inventory
by $3.5 billion, or 30 per cent. In most companies, price speculation
is not, however, a dominant factor in stock levels; in fact, under conditions of heavy demand, uncertain supply, and rising prices, it is
often hard to draw a clear line between "speculation" and sensible
protection of material supply. Of course, price speculation involves

risks of loss as well as gain, since price trends often shift rapidly and erratically.

In most enterprises the conditions of availability of supply, opportunities for economies of purchase, and attitudes toward future prices do not shift very rapidly.[4] Less constant is the rate of anticipated use of materials which is geared to production and sales volume. Most inventory level aims are expressed in terms of so many days or weeks of production requirements. The tonnage of iron ore adequate in mid-1959 for a month's production at near-capacity rates would be highly excessive for operation below 50 per cent in late 1960. The anticipated rate of usage probably is the most important single factor affecting materials inventories. The tendency of purchased materials inventories of all durable goods manufacturers to move with sales and new orders is illustrated in Chart 3–2.

---

[4] This is *not* to imply that changes in materials availability are of little significance. Note, for example, the following comments from a *Wall Street Journal* article of February 10, 1961, on shifting inventory policies:

"'Despite a substantial pickup in sales to distributors since the first of the year, we intend to adhere to the policy of getting along with smaller stocks of parts and raw materials,' says a spokesman for Admiral Corp., Chicago-based manufacturer of major appliances and television sets. 'We're simply able to live on smaller stocks and order at more frequent intervals.'

"'Expected order increases are making us a little more optimistic about putting something on the shelf,' says Paul Fischer, plant manager for Hyster Co., Portland, Ore., lift truck manufacturer. But he indicates the ease of getting steel is leading the company to put off adding to its stocks of this key raw material for the time being. 'Steel mills are operating more or less as warehouses,' he says. 'They're giving 10-day deliveries where it would normally take two or three months.'"

Indeed, some observers, commenting on widespread inventory reductions in late 1960 and early 1961, see evidence of a long-term trend toward greater inventory turnover. Thus, a writer in the November, 1960, *Monthly Review* of the Federal Reserve Bank of New York comments:

"Some of the factors underlying the weak demand for inventories thus far this year may prove to be long run in nature. Various structural forces, previously concealed by cyclical movements and strike effects, may be causing a secular downtrend in the inventory level required to support a given volume of sales. Although the evidence for such a trend is not conclusive, inventory-sales ratios during cyclical expansions have been progressively lower in each of the successive postwar business cycles. At the distributive level, where the differences among recent cycles are quite clear, inventory needs have probably been reduced relative to sales, not only by some recent shifts in the urgency of consumer buying, but also by the increasing importance of large-scale self-service stores and of chain stores with centralized order procedures and the opportunity to shift stocks quickly among branches. At both the distributive and manufacturing levels, the more flexible transportation opportunities offered by combinations of truck, rail, and air facilities have cut down the relative volume of goods 'in transit.' Some shifts in the composition of output may also have reduced stock needs; for instance, the rapidly growing chemical industry reportedly requires a small volume of goods in process relative to final output. Greater reliance on 'production to order,' increased use of high-speed computers for inventory control, and development of techniques for determining the most efficient location of plants and warehouses may all also play some part in a tendency to conserve inventories."

The cost of storage and other expense of caring for the materials, along with risks of loss through deterioration or obsolescence, also must be taken into account in determining optimum inventory levels.

Thus far, we have talked of size of inventory primarily in terms of physical volume. The financial burden of these inventories, of course, is measured in dollars; a general rise in prices heightens the dollar investment required to maintain a given volume of goods. True, a sus-

CHART 3–2

SALES, NEW ORDERS, AND AVERAGE PURCHASED MATERIALS INVENTORIES,
ALL DURABLE GOODS MANUFACTURERS, 1939–60

(In Billions of Dollars)

SOURCE: *Economic Report of the President* (Washington, D.C.: U.S. Government Printing Office, January, 1961), p. 167.

tained price rise often increases profits as low-cost materials eventually are sold in the form of higher priced finished goods. But the added "inventory profits" left after income taxes usually are inadequate to provide funds needed to replenish stocks with the then higher cost new materials. Conversely, a decline in prices may have the net effect of so reducing the dollar commitment to inventory that the cash account is swelled despite reduced lower profit inflows.

Clearly, the more obviously financial considerations—the costs of the funds tied up in raw material and the financial problems of raising those funds—are of keen significance in the determination of optimum material inventory levels. Since these apply equally to in-process and finished inventories, we shall defer comment on these aspects until later in this chapter.

The Cash Flows Associated with Raw Material Inventories

For purposes of financial planning the financial officer is particularly concerned with the cash flows connected with inventory. From a cash flow standpoint the crucial dates connected with the purchase of raw materials are the dates by which the invoices for the materials must be paid. Typically, the business concern will not have to pay cash at the time of purchase. Instead, an account payable, due perhaps in thirty days, is created at the time of purchase. The cash outflows resulting from purchases of raw materials can be planned for by setting up a schedule of future payments. In the illustration below, assume accounts payable were $1,500 on December 31, and that purchase terms called for payment in thirty days:

	January	February	March	April	May	June
Expected raw material purchases..........	$2,000	$4,000	$8,000	$7,000	$6,000	$2,000
Cash required to pay accounts payable—raw materials during month............	1,500	2,000	4,000	8,000	7,000	6,000

No cash inflows occur when raw materials are put into production. Instead, cash inflows come only when finished goods are sold for cash or, if sales are on credit, when the related accounts receivable are collected weeks or months later.

Investment in Work-in-Process Inventory

As the name suggests, this category of inventory comprises the goods in the process of being manufactured. From an accounting viewpoint a part of the investment in goods in process at any one time consists of the original cost of the raw materials. Added to the material costs transferred to the work-in-process account are the accumulated cost charges for wages and other direct costs of manufacture applied to these raw materials, together with an allocation of overhead costs such as heat, power, and plant supervision. Thus, the balance sheet value assigned to work-in-process inventory at any particular date is the summation of all costs assigned up to that date to the partially completed products.

What are the main determinants of the amounts of funds locked up in work-in-process inventory? To what extent is the size of the investment dictated by the nature of the operations? And to what degree can managerial policies shape the volume of the funds commitment?

The length of the complete productive process clearly has a major influence on the value of the inventory undergoing processing at any one time. An extreme illustration is furnished by a canner of peaches. Less than a day is normally required to pick, grade, process, can, label, and package peaches. Naturally, the canner's work in process at any date will be negligible in relation to annual sales. In contrast, consider the case of a manufacturer of large aircraft. Production and assembly of the complicated aircraft typically will extend over many months; at any one time, once production is well under way, the aircraft company will have accumulated a sizable investment in aircraft in all stages of completion, from raw stampings of aluminum to aircraft undergoing final tests before being ready for delivery.

While the length of the process is to a large degree dictated by the technology involved, the inventory investment nevertheless is subject to some managerial control. For example, the aircraft manufacturer working on a contract for two hundred planes may try to cut production costs by making all of a minor assembly in one production run, even though many of the items will not be needed for final assembly for many months. As we can see, a decision to produce components in long or short runs—at first thought purely a production problem—has definite financial implications. The calendar days required to produce an item may be cut down by adding second or third production shifts. By such moves, total output may be increased without a proportionate increase in work-in-process inventory levels. Conversely, any events that interrupt the production process—for example, the delay in receipt by a tank manufacturer of the subcontracted gun turrets for the tanks—act to lengthen the over-all process and to increase the funds tied up in work-in-process inventory.

The amount of costs incurred in the particular manufacturing process, often referred to as the "value added in manufacture," also affects the size of work in process. A very simple and inexpensive operation, even if extended over a long period—such as the aging of wines—requires little outlay beyond the cost of the materials involved.

The volume of production—assuming a constant length of process—is also a major determinant of work in process. If other factors are equal, as production increases, the amount invested in work in process increases. And as volume of production operations is curtailed, the investment in in-process inventory drops. As we noted earlier in connection with raw material inventory, production generally is geared to anticipated sales. Hence, the amount of funds tied up in work in process might also be expected to fluctuate directly with sales expectations and perhaps somewhat less directly with actual sales levels.

Chart 3-3 plots average monthly inventories of work in process, monthly sales, and new orders of durable goods manufacturers. As in the case of raw material inventories, the amount of funds tied up in work in process tends to vary with the level of sales and new orders.

CHART 3-3

SALES, NEW ORDERS, AND WORK-IN-PROCESS INVENTORIES
OF ALL DURABLE GOODS MANUFACTURERS, 1939-60
(In Billions of Dollars)

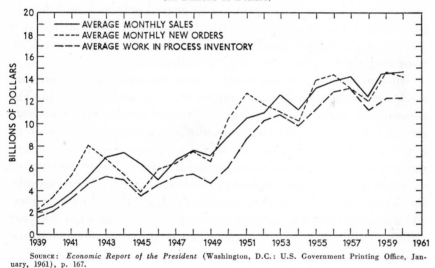

SOURCE: *Economic Report of the President* (Washington, D.C.: U.S. Government Printing Office, January, 1961), p. 167.

The price levels of raw materials used, wages, and other items that enter into production costs also influence the dollar investment in in-process inventories.

Cash Flows Associated with Work in Process

As indicated above, the accounting for work in process involves accumulation of accounting charges for raw materials used and for various expenses of manufacture and overhead, including depreciation charges. The flow of funds out of the company in connection with manufacturing, of course, will not coincide in timing or in amount with these accounting charges. No checks are written or payments made when raw materials are moved from the company's storerooms into production. Rather, the cash payments associated with raw materials occur when the accounts payable generated by the raw material purchases are paid. Further, payment of manufacturing costs—such as those for wages and salaries—seldom takes place at the time when these obligations are incurred. One item of expense—depreciation— calls for no cash payment at all. In planning the outflow of funds to support manufacturing, then, it is necessary to determine which of the anticipated expenses will require payment and to schedule these payments according to the time when they will be made.

The Investment in Finished Goods Inventories

Finished goods inventories build up with additions from the production line and are cut down with sales. Finished goods inventories can be minimized if production can be geared only to firm orders in hand. Many manufacturers—particularly those of specialized machines—avoid finished goods inventory, other than of spare parts, almost entirely by producing only to order.

Most manufacturers find it advantageous or necessary to maintain stocks of finished goods ready for shipment as orders come in. The pressures to carry sizable stocks of finished goods may stem from considerations of production convenience and economy and/or of marketing effectiveness. Where demand for the products is in small or uneven increments, production for stock permits longer production runs and more even and efficient production scheduling. For example, the demand for skis is concentrated in the late fall and early winter. Ski manufacturers can achieve steady production through the year only by building up heavy stocks of finished skis in advance of the selling season.

Some manufacturers must produce for stock because vital raw materials are available only on a seasonal basis, while customers' demand is spread throughout the year. The California canner of peaches, for example, must process the fruit when it ripens in July and build up a huge finished inventory if he is to meet orders spaced throughout the year.

Sales considerations may dictate an ability to fill orders without delay. In many lines, competition for sales forces maintenance of stocks near customers so that fast delivery can be promised.

A number of firms with far-flung distribution systems have reported success in the use of mathematical models and electronic computers to work out distribution patterns and inventory locations and levels that best reconcile considerations of customer service, manufacturing and distribution costs, and inventory turnover.

Under World War II conditions of restricted supply, intense demand, and heavy production against government order, many manufacturers operated with almost no finished inventories. Return to more competitive conditions saw manufacturers rebuild finished goods to a more normal relationship to sales—as is shown in Chart 3–4.

In some industries, such as seasonal apparel, manufacturers have attempted over the years to force retailers to carry a larger part of the inventory burden—a burden in terms of space and risk as well as investment—with limited success. Of course, if the manufacturer is in a

CHART 3–4

SALES, NEW ORDERS, AND AVERAGE FINISHED GOODS INVENTORIES,
ALL DURABLE GOODS MANUFACTURERS, 1939–60

(In Billions of Dollars)

SOURCE: *Economic Report of the President* (Washington, D.C.: U.S. Government Printing Office, January, 1961), p. 167.

very strong position vis-à-vis the retailers, he may be able to force inventories on the dealers. Thus, Henry Ford in 1923 was seriously short of funds to meet bank loans; at the same time, large stocks of unsold Fords were accumulating at the plant. Mr. Ford simply shipped large numbers of unordered cars to his dealers with drafts calling for cash payment attached to the shipping papers. The dealers were forced to provide cash and accept the inventory burden or yield their dealerships. However, few manufacturers today possess either the commanding position or the willingness to take the risks of such action.

Optimum finished goods stock levels, like those of raw materials, are usually set in terms of so many days' or months' anticipated sales. Thus, *over time,* finished goods inventories tend to move directly with sales volume.

But in the short run, finished stocks may well vary inversely with sales. If sales fall below expectations, and production is not cut back sharply, unsold goods pile up. Despite strenuous efforts to forecast sales accurately, a great many manufacturers (and retailers) are confronted with unexpected, and often inexplicable, declines in sales which pose poignant problems. Seldom can production be cut back or expanded rapidly without severe organizational strains and higher unit costs. If the sales drop proves short-lived, holding production steady and accepting temporarily swollen inventories may well maximize return on investment. But if sales stay off, inventories pile up, and even more drastic production cutbacks ultimately are needed to bring inventories into line with the reduced sales prospects. Many manufacturers have experienced severe cash stringency, sometimes leading to business failure, as a result of freezing too much of their resources in finished goods for which timely orders failed to develop.

Unexpected sales spurts also present inventory management problems. Unless production and inventory levels are boosted, service to customers may suffer, and sales opportunities may be lost. But if production is boosted and the sales surge proves temporary, excess inventory results. The critical role of sales forecasting in effective inventory management can hardly be overemphasized. Increasing effort is being devoted by the managements of many companies to improve their "feel" for their customers and their intentions, and to respond rapidly and perceptively to shifts in demand. But the problem of anticipating changes in sales remains a difficult one—especially where a wide range of products is involved.

Careful and fast accounting procedures and systems are important to the control of inventory, particularly in companies carrying a large number of different items at many points. In most firms, running tallies of items on hand are corrected by reconciliation with physical count only infrequently, so that fast and accurate record keeping is essential to efficient stock control. More than a few companies have lost control of inventory through deficiencies in accounting procedures.

The impact on cash of an inventory build-up or decline is usually a deferred one. The immediate cash flow impact of a sales decline and inventory build-up is minimal as cash flows in from collection of the receivables from sales at the old high level. But the decline in sales means fewer new receivables, and a sharp drop in inflows occurs when the smaller volume of receivables comes due and is collected.

Risks in Inventory Investment

The two decades since 1940 were ones of general prosperity and broad commodity price increases. Nevertheless, there have been enough sharp drops in the prices of important commodities to remind businessmen that heavy inventory positions, particularly in standard commodities with free markets, expose their firms to risks of loss through sustained price declines. For example, the market price of crude rubber[5] fell from \$0.46¼ a pound to \$0.28¾ between June and December, 1960. Generally, the vulnerability to price declines is greatest on standard raw materials and least on differentiated finished goods.

More significant in recent years have been the risks of inventory obsolescence. Changing customer tastes, as in high-style merchandise, may make old finished goods, work in process, and even raw materials unsalable and nearly worthless. Nor is vulnerability to obsolescence restricted to luxury consumer goods. Changing needs of industrial customers, new production techniques, or product improvements by competitors may force changes in product specifications and design that cut values of old model stocks and components or materials distinctive to the earlier models. As the rate of technical change and product development shows evidence of acceleration, avoidance of undue hazards of inventory obsolescence becomes more urgent.

In addition, the numerous firms whose resources are limited must be particularly wary of the risks to their liquidity—indeed, their solvency—in tying up too much of their limited capital in hard-to-move inventories.

Aids in the Analysis of the Investment in Inventory

The financial and other officers of the company are seldom alone in their interest in the company's inventory investment. Because of the importance of this asset group to the financial condition of the concern, important stockholders, the credit analysts of commercial banks or other lenders, and the credit men of important suppliers are also interested in discovering and understanding significant movements in inventory or its turnover. Unless the "outside" analysts re-

---

[5] The prices indicated are for No. 1 ribbed smoked sheets, New York basis.

ceive more information about inventories than is usually available from published financial statements, the degree of penetration of analysis and understanding they can hope to achieve is limited. This is particularly true if only annual statements are available and inventories are reported in a single, lump sum. Yet some calculations can be made which often prove useful, especially in raising questions which may indicate the desirability of further inquiry.

The same general methods of analysis used by outside analysts, which we shall discuss below, can be pushed further and used with greater precision by the financial officer of the firm, who has full access to available sources of data. For example, while the outside observer must often work with a single inventory figure, the financial officer of the firm would have available figures for each major type, and indeed for each major item, of inventory and thus should be able to arrive at more meaningful conclusions.

It is often helpful to determine whether changes in inventory investment are in line with changes in the volume of sales. As we have seen, the level of investment in inventory tends naturally and normally to vary directly with the volume of sales. Movements not in line with sales raise questions for further inquiry—for example, an increase in inventory levels substantially beyond that which might be expected from an increase in sales should stimulate the analyst to further investigation. Is this unexplained increase the result of accumulation of unsold merchandise, or inventory speculation in raw materials, or price level changes not reflected in selling prices, or some other factor?

Several methods are commonly used to determine the relationship between inventory and volume of sales. Let us consider the following facts to illustrate the more common methods. Total inventories reported by the XYZ Corporation on December 31, 1960, were $462,-000. Reference to earlier balance sheets shows that the inventory investment was $274,000 on December 31, 1959, and $270,000 in 1958. Reference to income statements reveals the following:

1960 Sales	$1,060,000
1959 Sales	880,000
1960 Cost of sales	860,000
1959 Cost of sales	702,000

Quick mental arithmetic indicates that inventories are up in 1960 and that they increased faster in 1960 than did sales. But the extent to which inventories relatively have outrun sales can be made more apparent through the use of ratios.

One ratio approach simply expresses year-end inventories as a percentage of the inventories that were sold during the preceding year. Since inventories are usually carried at cost on the balance sheet, the comparison is most often made with the cost of the inventories sold—that is, the cost of goods sold—rather than with sales which are measured by selling prices. In the case of the above example, it can readily be determined that 1960 inventories of $462,000 were 54 per cent of the $860,000 cost of goods sold in 1960 (462,000/860,000). In contrast, 1959 inventories of $274,-000 were only 39 per cent of the $702,000 cost of goods sold in 1959.

Another method of portraying the relationship between inventories on hand and those which were sold is through calculation of the times inventory "turned over" during the year. In 1960 goods valued at $860,000 were sold; so year-end inventories of $462,000 can be thought of as turning over 1.9 times (860,000/462,000). In contrast, similar computations in 1959 inventories and cost of sales showed a turnover figure of 2.6 times. Thus, turnover, based on year-end inventories, declined from 2.6 to 1.9 times.

Some analysts prefer to use the average of beginning and ending inventories in computing turnover ratios. It can be argued that use of average inventory figures gives a more accurate "turnover" figure, but it also plays down the influence of the recent inventory figure which is generally the item of particular interest to the analyst. Thus, turnover of *average* inventory in 1960 was 2.3 times [860,-000/(462,000 + 274,000/2)] and in 1959 was 2.6 times [702,-000/(274,000 + 270,000/2)]. It will be noted that the average turnover figures, being an average of beginning and ending inventories, changed less widely (from 2.6 to 2.3 times) than did the ending inventory turnover figure (from 2.6 to 1.9).

If a breakdown of inventory is available, percentage of cost of sales or turnover figures can be calculated for each category of inventory. Thus, changes out of line with sales movements can be pinpointed. For example, the build-up of inventory relative to sales shown in the XYZ Corporation might be found to be entirely in finished goods with materials and work in process down substantially.

Of course, if only annual sales and inventory data are available, important movements of sales and inventories within the year will not be discernible. In the case above, if sales in the last few months of 1960 had been unusually small, the large year-end inventory in 1960 would seem much heavier than it appeared to be in comparison with the rate of sales for the year as a whole.

In the case of firms that operate under essentially similar conditions, the comparison of inventory-sales ratios of one company with those of its competitors may prove useful in calling attention to distinctive policies of the subject firm.[6] On the other hand, as we have indicated earlier, it is extremely difficult to apply value judgments on the basis of quickly calculated ratios, and such ratios will usually suggest more questions than answers. As one writer has put it, ratios such as those of turnover provide many clues but few conclusions.

The Financial Officer's Role in Inventory Management

Seldom is the financial officer the corporate officer most directly concerned with inventory policies. Usually, purchasing and production officers are more directly concerned with raw material policies, production officers with work in process, and production and sales officers with finished goods inventories. But it should be clear that inventory policies have a very direct and important impact on the financial needs of the firm. The financial officer can do a good job of anticipating changes in the need for funds only if he thoroughly understands the implications of changing inventory policies and positions. Where finances are a limiting factor, he should be prepared to help directly in shaping inventory policies that are consistent with the realities of the firm's financial position.

But the financial officer's role should be much more than that of an informed observer—or monitor, if funds are short. Good inventory management is good financial management. Levels should be under frequent or constant review. When inventory levels are set, the financial officer can help in applying pressure against practices that slow turnover and debase return.[7]

---

[6] Among the sources of information on average inventory-sales and other ratios for different industries are the results of a continuing program of ratio analysis published periodically in *Dun's Review and Modern Industry*. For example, ratios in the retailing field were published in the October, 1960, issue, for wholesalers in various lines in November, 1960, and for manufacturers in thirty-six product lines in December, 1960.

[7] In one outstanding firm the financial officer was instrumental in the establishment of a highly productive program of periodic "turnover audits" in which questions like the following are investigated:

1. Are we exercising full vigilance against imbalances of raw material and in-process inventory that limit the utility of stocks to that of the item in shortest supply?

2. Are we employing the shortest procurement lead-time assumptions and leanest stock levels consistent with safety, recognizing that complete safety has a prohibitive cost?

To firms short of funds, imaginative exposure and full exploitation of opportunities to cut inventory investment can be highly rewarding in reduced capital requirements. The advice of one experienced businessman speaking to a group of small manufacturers, "When you need money, look to your inventories before you look for your banker," deserves more than a smile.

Even if funds are plentiful, the financial officer should be prepared to participate actively and helpfully in the formulation of inventory policies designed to speed turnover and maximize return on investment. Our discussion has indicated some of the key considerations in setting and trying to hold to optimum inventory levels—levels that represent the best reconciliation of profit and turnover objectives.

---

3. Do we keep the heat on uncompleted production items held in suspension to get them into salable condition?

4. Do we press hard enough to keep production schedules firm, so that unneeded materials and in-process inventories don't accumulate? Does purchasing get early notification of production schedule changes?

5. Do we move vigorously to dispose of goods that are obsolete, surplus, or for any other reason unusable for production?

6. Are we continually striving to shorten the production cycle? Are we careful to be sure that long production runns are worth the cost and risks of the extra inventory investment?

7. Is design engineering making maximum use of standard materials and components available from suppliers' shelves on short notice?

8. Are we quick enough to use special pricing to move extremely slow-selling finished items?

9. Are we doing all we can to flatten out seasonal sales patterns that bulk up inventories?

Chapter 4

Receivables Management and the Need for Funds

MOST business sales are made on credit. Credit sales do not result in immediate cash inflows but rather in creation of accounts or notes receivable from the customers. Reflecting the time lag between sales and inflows of cash as receivables are collected, receivables represent a major and continuing investment for those firms selling on credit. United States manufacturing corporations, which sell primarily on credit, had almost $42 billion, or 16.6 per cent of their total assets, tied up in receivables on September 30, 1960. Wholesaling firms, which also sell largely on credit, had on a recent date $12.2 billion in receivables, or 33.9 per cent of their total assets. In the case of retailers generally, cash sales are sizable. Some types of retailers, such as the food chains, sell exclusively for cash and thus avoid any investment in receivables. Nevertheless, data for all retailing corporations showed a total investment in receivables of $9.1 billion, or 24.6 per cent of total assets. While not so large in the aggregate as the investment in inventories, the investment in receivables clearly is an important one for American business.

That the significance of the receivables investment varies widely among industry groups is brought out by Chart 4–1, which draws on comprehensive data from balance sheets submitted with corporate income tax returns.

Form of Receivables

The bulk of credit sales are made on *open account*. That is, the seller keeps a simple book record of the obligations arising out of sales and does not ask his customers for formal acknowledgment of their debts or for signed promises to pay. In case of dispute the seller has the customer's order, copies of the sales invoice, and shipping papers as evidence of the validity of the debt.

At one time, decades ago, it was the common practice of many business firms to ask their customers to sign unsecured *notes,* or written promises to pay by a stated date the amount of credit extended on routine credit sales. This practice was especially common in product lines customarily sold on long credit terms. The holder of an ordinary note receivable does *not* enjoy any priority of claim to payment over open-account creditors in the event of a debtor's bankruptcy and subsequent liquidation of his assets for distribution to creditors. But the signed note does provide strong legal evidence of the validity of the debt; and written stipulation of a due date, together with the practice of note collection through banks, provides psychological pressure for prompt payment at maturity. Too, the mechanics of charging interest on notes are simple. Further, usually it is easier to use notes from customers than accounts receivable as security for bank loans. Despite these advantages the use of notes in routine domestic trade credit by manufacturers and wholesalers has given way to the currently predominant practice of sale on open account.

Although most retail credit sales are also made on an open-account basis, "big 'ticket items"—durable goods of considerable value, such as automobiles, television receivers, and refrigerators—commonly are offered for sale on terms which call for instalment payments extended over many months. Such sales are customarily made subject to the terms of conditional sales contracts which give the seller (or his assignee) the right to recover the merchandise if payments are not made as agreed upon in the contract. Usually, a significant cash payment, often 20 to 30 per cent of the retail price, is required. And unlike the case in routine open-account credits, significant interest and other credit charges are added to the cash sales price.

The retailer may retain the instalment sales obligation. More commonly, instalment contracts are sold to banks or specialized sales finance companies. Some retailers, such as Sears Roebuck, have formed subsidiaries to hold and collect instalment credits. Some manufacturers, who have found easy credit vital to the ability of final users to buy their products, have established sales finance subsidiaries to buy the instalment "paper" of customers of their dealers. Thus, major farm equipment makers, such as John Deere, now finance not only the sale of equipment to dealers for inventory but the dealers' sales to farmers as well. Indeed, some farm equipment manufacturers

CHART 4-1

INVESTMENT IN NOTES AND ACCOUNTS RECEIVABLE, LESS RESERVE, OF CORPORATIONS IN SELECTED INDUSTRY GROUPS, AS A PERCENTAGE OF THEIR TOTAL ASSETS, TAX YEAR ENDED JULY, 1957–JUNE, 1958

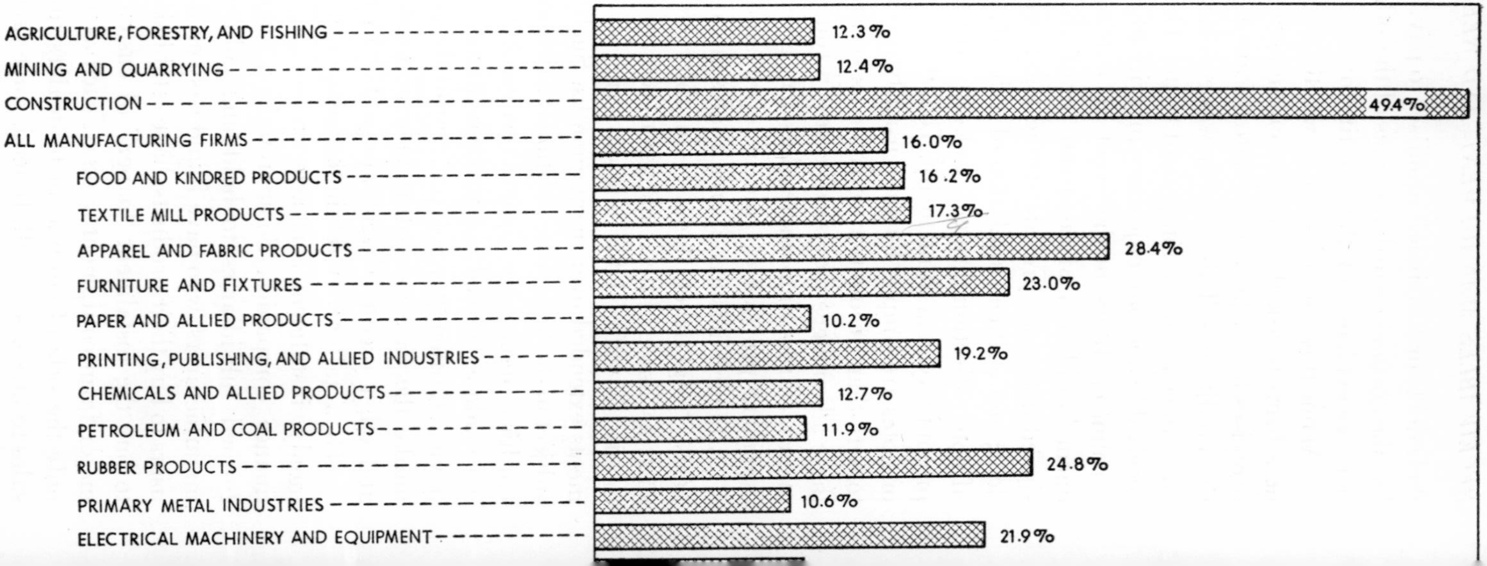

Industry Group	Percentage
AGRICULTURE, FORESTRY, AND FISHING	12.3%
MINING AND QUARRYING	12.4%
CONSTRUCTION	49.4%
ALL MANUFACTURING FIRMS	16.0%
FOOD AND KINDRED PRODUCTS	16.2%
TEXTILE MILL PRODUCTS	17.3%
APPAREL AND FABRIC PRODUCTS	28.4%
FURNITURE AND FIXTURES	23.0%
PAPER AND ALLIED PRODUCTS	10.2%
PRINTING, PUBLISHING, AND ALLIED INDUSTRIES	19.2%
CHEMICALS AND ALLIED PRODUCTS	12.7%
PETROLEUM AND COAL PRODUCTS	11.9%
RUBBER PRODUCTS	24.8%
PRIMARY METAL INDUSTRIES	10.6%
ELECTRICAL MACHINERY AND EQUIPMENT	21.9%

Category	Per Cent
OTHER TRANSPORTATION EQUIPMENT	31.9%
OTHER MACHINERY	19.5%
OTHER FABRICATED METAL PRODUCTS	18.5%
ALL PUBLIC UTILITIES	4.0%
TRANSPORTATION COMPANIES	5.6%
COMMUNICATION COMPANIES	3.2%
ELECTRIC AND GAS COMPANIES	2.9%
WHOLESALE FIRMS	33.2%
ALL RETAIL TRADE FIRMS	23.6%
FOOD RETAILERS	10.8%
GENERAL MERCHANDISE RETAILERS	23.9%
APPAREL AND ACCESSORIES RETAILERS	23.9%
FURNITURE AND HOUSEHOLD FURNISHINGS RETAILERS	45.6%
BUILDING MATERIALS AND HARDWARE RETAILERS	31.0%

PER CENT

0   5   10   15   20   25   30   35   40   45   50

SOURCE OF DATA: Internal Revenue Service, U.S. Treasury Department, *Statistics of Income, 1957–58: Corporation Income Tax Returns* (Washington, D.C.: U.S. Government Printing Office, 1960), Table 3, pp. 31–38, and Table 5, pp. 41–66.

also finance the resale by their dealers of other makes of used equipment acquired as trade-ins on new equipment.

In recent years an increasing number of manufacturers of industrial equipment also have found it necessary or desirable to offer instalment credit terms to their business customers. Most manufacturers of machine tools and of equipment for service industries, such as dry cleaning equipment, for example, offer credit terms extending over as much as three to four years. A number have formed finance companies to take over these credits or have arranged their resale to other finance companies. Usually, these credits are extended on conditional sales contracts. Since the instalment credit terms include substantial finance charges, companies whose finances are strong generally prefer to purchase equipment on the normal trade terms and open account.

In international trade, relatively few sales are made on open account. Instead, a number of distinctive credit instruments, chief among them the *letter of credit* and *banker's acceptance*, are used; and arrangements have been developed to meet the particular problems that surround international commercial transactions. These will be discussed in Chapter 11.

Objectives in the Management of the Investment in Receivables

In the typical firm the financial officer has operating responsibility for the management of the investment in receivables. Reporting directly to him in most firms is the head of the credit department, which carries out the work of granting credit and supervising the collection of receivables. In addition to his role in overseeing the administration of credit, the financial officer is in a particularly strategic position to contribute to top management decisions as to the best credit policies for the firm.

Unless the firm's own finances are closely limited, the basic objective of receivables management, like those of inventory management, should be that of maximizing return on investment. Policies which stress short credit terms, stringent credit standards, and highly aggressive policing of collections clearly will work to minimize bad debt losses and the tie-up of funds in receivables. But such policies may well restrict sales and profit margins, so that despite the low receivables investment, rate of return on total investment of the firm is lower than that attainable with higher levels of sales, profits, and receivables. Conversely, extremely lenient or sloppy credit extension may well inflate receivables and bad debts without compensating increases in sales and profits. Clearly, the objective of receivables management should be the achievement of that balance which in the particular circumstances of the firm results in the combination of turnover and profit rates that maximizes the over-all return on investment of the firm.

Again, we should recognize, however, that limited financial resources of the particular firm may force greater restraint in receivables than would be ideal from a return on investment viewpoint. If the availability of funds is restricted, their use in inventory, equipment, or other areas offering even higher return may dictate severe restraint on credit administration. Or if the financial position of the firm is so precarious that a major bad debt loss would be disastrous, extreme caution in credit administration, though costly in forgone profit and return opportunities, may nevertheless be wise.

Now, let us turn to a consideration of the major determinants of the size of the investment in receivables in the individual firm, with especial attention to those particularly subject to management influence and control.

Major Determinants of the Size of the Investment in Receivables

Of particular importance in shaping the size of the firm's investment in receivables are the following factors:

1. The terms of credit granted customers deemed creditworthy.
2. The policies and practices of the firm in determining which customers are to be granted credit.
3. The paying practices of credit customers.
4. The rigor of the seller's collection policies and practice.
5. The volume of credit sales.

Let us look briefly at each of these factors which underlie and determine the size of the investment in receivables.

In theory, each firm is free to specify whatever terms of sale best suit its objectives and circumstances. It may sell only for cash on delivery in order to avoid tying up its funds in receivables and risking bad debt losses, perhaps consciously conceding the added sales that might be achieved through selling on credit. Or it may use the extension of generous credit as an aggressive selling tool—one used-car retailer in Boston currently is advertising that he will sell cars to any customer "whose credit is good" on terms of "no down payment, 48 months to pay." Further, the seller is free to change his terms of sale.

In actual practice, competitive pressures tend to push the individual firm to offer credit terms at least as generous as those of most of its competitors. Over a long span of years, particular terms of sale have become traditional in many product lines. Buyers have come to expect these terms to such an extent that new suppliers joining an industry usually offer the "customary" terms of sale of the industry as the course of least resistance. Thus, manufacturers of wire goods usually sell on terms of "2/10, net 60." This notation means that a discount of 2 per cent is allowed if payment is made within 10 days of invoicing, and payment regardless of discount is expected within 60 days. Customary terms on many products call for payment within 30 days, although sometimes on an "E.O.M." basis, that is, within 30 days after the end of the month of sale. Terms on a few products are quite long; for example, uncut diamonds usually are sold on terms of six to nine months.[1]

Most firms make their "customary terms" available to all customers whom they have judged worthy of this credit. Changes in the customary terms of sale generally are made only infrequently; in many firms and industries the customary terms have remained constant over decades.

Of course, there are important exceptions to the generalizations of the above paragraphs. For example, some firms in industries where terms are relatively standardized between sellers offer terms generally more lenient than their competitors, or are willing to make negotiation of special terms of sale a common practice. In the highly competitive textile industry in 1957, many firms, while announcing no general departure from the terms customary in the industry, reportedly were granting especially generous terms to so many of their customers that their formal terms had become more nominal than real.

At any rate, it should be clear that the credit terms granted customers are an important determinant of the size of the investment in receivables—if other factors are constant, the longer the credit terms offered, the larger will be the investment in receivables.

It is interesting to note that the outstanding receivables of U.S.

---

[1] For a list of customary terms of sales for 162 types of products, see T. N. Beckman and Robert Bartels, *Credits and Collections in Theory and Practice* (6th ed.; New York: McGraw-Hill Book Co., Inc., 1955), pp. 591–96.

manufacturers on September 30, 1960, represented some 46 days' sales at the rate of sales reported for the preceding quarter.

The policies and practices of the individual firm in deciding which of its customers should be granted its customary terms of credit also affect the size of its investment in receivables. The firm's customary credit terms typically are extended only to those customers which are adjudged acceptable credit risks. Terms of cash on order or on delivery, or shorter than usual credit terms, may be used for sales to "poor risks" or to concerns for which available information is insufficient to establish their credit standing. Different firms apply different standards in appraising the creditworthiness of their customers. Speaking generally, the more liberal the standards used in extending credit, the larger will be the investment in receivables. Some firms modify their standards in granting credit with the sales outlook, taking greater risks of bad debts when demand is slack. Most firms, however, appear to change their standards infrequently and then only within relatively narrow limits. We shall have more to say at a later point in this chapter on how credit risks are evaluated and controlled.

The actual paying practices of customers also have an impact on total credit outstanding. For example, many firms offer customers a discount for early payment. Firms offering terms of 2/10, net 30 give their customers the option of taking discounts and paying within 10 days or forgoing the discount and waiting until 30 days to pay. The choice exercised by the customers clearly affects the amount of credit outstanding. Further, even where inflexible terms are quoted, customers may take liberties with them. Customers who buy primarily from sellers offering, say, 30-day terms, often ignore shorter terms of minor suppliers and pay all bills on the same basis. In other cases, important customers deliberately and habitually take extra time to settle their trade obligations. In such instances, rather than risk losing the valuable sales outlets, the sellers may allow their stated terms to be exceeded. Still other customers, who are financially hard pressed, may let their debts run as far overdue as their creditors will tolerate.

While many firms are careful to meet all their trade obligations when due, others appear all too willing to take advantage of tolerant suppliers. The closeness with which the supplier follows up on overdue accounts and the degree of pressure he brings for prompt payment have a material effect on the paying practices of many customers and hence on the level of outstanding receivables.

The most important variable affecting the level of the receivables investment is the volume of credit sales. If the other variables we have discussed remain constant, the level of receivables may be expected to vary directly with changes in sales volume. As sales increase, receivables expand, absorbing funds. As sales fall off, the related receivables decline, releasing funds. Unless long credits are granted, the time lag between changes in sales volume and proportionate changes in receivables is short.

Since the determinants of the investment in receivables other than sales volume typically do not change rapidly or drastically, *most of the important changes in the amount of outstanding receivables can be traced to changes in sales volume.* Conversely, important variations in the outstanding receivables of firms whose sales volume has been constant must be attributed to changes in credit terms, in the standards for granting credit, in the paying practices of customers, or in the rigor with which collections are policed.

The Work of the Credit Department

Since the financial officer usually is responsible for the effective functioning of the credit department, it is appropriate that we review the key functions and major problem areas in the effective administration of trade credit.

The work of the credit department consists of three main activities. First, the department must approve the granting of credit to particular customers. Second, it must police the collection of receivables to insure that efforts are made to collect the debts when due. Finally, in the case of accounts which appear to have "gone bad," that is, accounts of customers who apparently cannot or do not intend to pay, it must determine and carry out appropriate efforts to collect the accounts and avoid loss.

Sources of Credit Information

Although the usual standards for extension of trade credit are not severe, prospective customers seldom are automatically extended normal credit terms. Typically, before shipment of a sizable order to a new customer, the credit department conducts a quick investigation to determine whether the company is justified in extending its normal credit terms to the new customer. Usually, the investigation must be a rapid one lest the prospective sale be lost as a result of delays in clearing the credit. In checking on the creditworthiness of the prospective customer, the credit department can take advantage of a widespread network of credit information for data other than those provided by the customer. If the customer is a concern of any size, the department can probably obtain, at moderate cost, a credit report from one of the companies which make a business of collecting and supplying such information. The largest firm of this sort, Dun & Bradstreet, Inc., operates on a national basis and usually is able to supply information about the background and experience of the principal executives of the concern, a summary of its history and methods of operation, notation of any bankruptcies or compromises with creditors on the part of the firm or its executives or owners in the past, and also income and balance sheet data. Further, the credit agency periodically conducts "trade checks" on concerns on which they maintain files. The agency contacts the major suppliers of the firm to learn their collection experience with the firm. The experience of major suppliers is summarized in the credit report and includes present credit outstanding, amount past due, recent high credits, and whether the concern usually pays on time.

In addition to the large national credit information firms, a number of industry trade associations operate a credit information service. Further, local mercantile credit agencies, dealing mainly in information about the credit standing of individuals, operate in almost every city; these are widely used by retail establishments whose potential sales to individual customers hardly justify extensive credit investigations of their own.

Commercial banks serve an important function in the exchange of credit information. Usually, the banks stand ready to help customers' credit investigations. If the subject of the credit investigation is not a customer of the bank, upon request the bank will commonly contact other banks that are familiar with the subject's reputation and financial standing.

The company's own salesmen, who may well have visited the subject concern in getting the order, may be of help. However, sales personnel often are more concerned about the booking of the sale than the collection of the ensuing debt, and their information must be interpreted accordingly.

Where it appears necessary, the credit department can contact the prospective customer directly either to discuss questionable aspects of the credit or to round out the file of information. In determining how much time and effort to devote to accumulation of credit information and its analysis, credit managers must balance the costs of added information against the benefits from the degree of improvement in the credit decisions that can be expected as a result of the more refined analysis. Usually, a balance is indicated that is far short of the complete analysis that theoretically could be made.

Evaluation of Credit Risk

Once the available sources of information have been utilized and a mass of data accumulated, the data must be interpreted and the credit decision resolved. In digesting the facts and reaching a credit decision, many credit men more or less explicitly keep in mind, as basic criteria, the "Four C's of Credit—Capital, Capacity, Character, and Conditions." *Capital* obviously refers to the financial resources of the company as indicated primarily by the balance sheets. *Capacity* has reference to the experience of the principals and the demonstrated ability of the concern to operate successfully, the latter to a good degree indicated by the profit record of the company. *Character* refers to the reputation of the owners and management for honesty and fair dealing. Information reflecting unfavorably on the integrity of the principals is especially important because time and cost considerations limit the extent and thoroughness to which investigation can be pushed, and a clever rascal is likely to be able to present an outwardly attractive situation. The criterion *Conditions* suggests the possibility of placing special limitations or restrictions on the extension of credit to doubtful accounts.[2]

In most companies a minor fraction of the credit accounts cause a very high percentage of the credit department's headaches. Chronically slow in paying but quick to claim faulty merchandise, these problem accounts dilute turnover and enrich correspondence files. The cost of credit mistakes is not measured by bad debts alone but by the trouble and expense of collection efforts and litigation in the case of accounts that ultimately are collectible.

We do not mean to suggest that business bad debt losses in themselves are trivial; all active nonfinancial corporations reporting for income tax purposes showed aggregate bad debt expenses of $918.7 million in a recent year. In relation to total sales, the figure was modest—only 0.14 per cent—but the absolute amount, even after allowance for the likelihood that the reported expense exceeded losses actually realized, is not one to be dismissed lightly.

On the basis of information easily gathered, it seldom is difficult

---

[2] The term *conditions* is also used by some in a very different sense. These persons use the term to stress the importance of the business conditions or level of prosperity of the customer's industry as a factor affecting his creditworthiness.

for trained credit men to spot those accounts—both new and ones on the books—which are inherently high-risk accounts. The key problem in credit evaluation is to decide which of the admittedly higher risk accounts are to be given credit, how much, and under what conditions. At one time the ability to avoid credit losses was widely regarded as the complete measure of the success of a credit manager. Measured by such standards, the credit manager had every incentive to turn down the credit requests of questionable customers. This concept of credit evaluation clearly is a gross oversimplification; the credit manager who maintains a credit policy so strict that credit losses never occur is properly suspected of turning away profitable business.

In deciding what credit risks to accept, the credit department should balance the risks of loss and the burdens involved in possibly tying up funds in slow-paying accounts against the value to the firm of the prospective sales involved. Commonly, the value of added business is high enough to justify a high degree of risk taking in trade credit, particularly if unused capacity is available, and if the incremental production and sales can be accomplished at limited added out-of-pocket expense. Under such circumstances, it may take only a few months of sales to a marginal customer for the marginal revenues from added sales to offset completely the risk of full loss on the outstanding receivables balance. Consider the case where a customer buys $10,000 of goods a month and actually takes 60 days to pay, disregarding 30-day terms. If the seller's out-of-pocket costs for the added sales are 70 per cent, on annual sales of $120,000, it gains $36,000 in added profits in return for tying up and risking an average of $20,000 in outstanding credit. If the account were to stay active for only seven months, the added revenues from $70,000 sales, or $21,000, would more than match complete loss of a 60-day-old account.

Once an initial credit to a new customer is approved, it is customary for the credit department to approve continued shipments to the customer provided the shipment does not bring the outstanding balance due from the customer above a designated high limit established for that customer. Shipments on orders that would mean exceeding the high limit or *credit line* on the account are then subject to review by the credit executives. Credit lines usually receive periodic routine review, often on an annual basis, and are revised only if important changes develop.

Policing the Collection of Outstanding Credits

The credit department also has the work of supervising or policing the accounts to see that customers are billed promptly and that slow-paying customers are reminded in effective fashion of their delinquency before it becomes serious. Books have been written on the art of gentle but effective "needling" of slow-paying customers so that prompt payment may be obtained without giving offense and jeopardizing future business.

In getting prompt payment of receivables, credit men are aided by the moral pressures stemming from the general recognition that failure to pay promptly will receive widespread publicity in trade circles and reflect adversely on the credit standing of the firm. Furthermore, for continuing customers the credit department has a more drastic weapon at hand; it can cut off future shipments on credit unless overdue accounts are given attention. Once either supplier or customer has ceased active business, this pressure vanishes. Also, the threat of unfavorable publicity is a minor one to concerns in severe and well-publicized difficulty.

Collection of inactive and long-overdue—or "sour"—accounts involves difficult problems. In such circumstances, normal pressures on the debtor to make payment are not likely to be effective, and bad debt losses or excessive expense and effort in collection can be avoided only through skillful action. Initial efforts should be designed to discover the real reasons for the debtor's delinquency. If the debtor appears able to pay, vigorous collection procedures are in order. If the account is small, often it is best to turn the account over to a specialized collection agency, which, for a substantial percentage of the debt, assumes the task of collection. These agencies typically act with great vigor, and they are set up to handle such operations with a minimum of expense. Direct legal action by the seller in the case of small accounts often involves legal expense and managerial effort disproportionate to the amounts involved. This is especially true since persons seeking to avoid legal obligations frequently attempt to challenge quantities or qualities of the goods involved and to do anything else they can to make the collection effort so tiresome that it will be abandoned.

In the case of important customers who freely acknowledge the debt but are in such financial difficulties that payment in full is difficult, somewhat different tactics are in order. If the creditor insists on his full legal rights and brings suit to collect the debt, he may only force the company into bankruptcy. When bankruptcy results, the affairs of the company are put in the hands of the courts, usually federal, for reorganization or liquidation under the supervision of court-appointed officials. If liquidation of the company results, the assets left after payment of the legal and administrative expenses of bankruptcy are divided among the creditors. Typically, the net proceeds from asset liquidation permit only a modest partial payment to trade creditors. Further, unless the sales outlet can be replaced, the future sales that might have been made to the customer are lost with his demise.

Consequently, it is often desirable for the creditor to seek a compromise settlement with an embarrassed customer that will get some payment yet permit the customer to stay in business. Unfortunately, if the customer has many other debts, as is typical, a compromise settlement may not be feasible unless other creditors will join in the compromise, since any unpaid creditor can demand his legal rights and throw the debtor into the courts. As a practical matter, it is not easy to get scattered creditors to work together to postpone or compromise their demands for payment. To help in bringing about such concerted action on the part of creditors, standing creditors' committees in some industries and cities provide a continuing organization to bring the credit officers of the co-operating concerns together in particular cases as the need arises. Although compromise settlements are difficult to accomplish when many creditors are involved, the results of many such efforts have been relatively successful. In fact, experience dictates that the possibility of compromise settlement should be carefully investigated before resort is had to the more drastic use of full legal remedies, which often prove remedies in name only.

Aids to the Analysis of the Investment in Accounts Receivable

We have noted that the level of the investment in trade receivables can be expected to fluctuate in direct relationship with the volume of sales, provided sales terms and collection practices do not change. Naturally, credit officials, financial officers, and others associated with the finances of the concern are interested in detecting any tendency toward more lenient credit extension, as would be suggested by tendencies of collections to slow up and slow-paying accounts to increase. Consequently, these interested parties look carefully at the relationship of receivables to recent credit sales. The comparison of receivables to sales can take several forms. One comparison simply expresses outstanding receivables as a percentage of sales. Unless sales terms are unusually long, the existing receivables should be the product of recent sales. Consequently, persons within the firm, who have available recent monthly or quarterly sales data, compare recent monthly or quarterly sales to the reported receivables. As an illustration consider the following data:

Sales fourth quarter, 1960	$1,860,000	
Accounts receivable, Dec. 31, 1960		$967,200
Sales fourth quarter, 1959	1,200,000	
Accounts receivable, Dec. 31, 1959		492,000

Let us assume in this case that the analyst is the financial officer, who knows that sales during each quarter were at a relatively even rate. It can be quickly determined that the 1960 receivables are 52 per cent of the last quarter's sales ($967.200/1,860,000 = 52$ per cent). Looking back to 1959, it can be readily seen that receivables then were only 41 per cent of the preceding quarter's sales. Thus, the analyst can see that the large increase in receivables in 1960 is not simply the natural result of the growth in sales, and he is alerted to the need for further inquiry as to the reasons for the slowing of payments.

The relationship between sales and receivables is also expressed in terms of *days' sales outstanding*. In 1960, in the approximately 90 days of the last quarter, sales equaled $20,666 a calendar day. Thus, the receivables on hand at December 31, 1960, equaled 46.8 days' sales ($967.200/20,666 = 46.8$ days). Using the same method of calculation, the 1959 receivables represented 36.9 days' sales at the 1959 rate of $13,333 a day. A comparison of 46.8 days currently outstanding against 36.9 last year thus also reveals the apparent slow-up of receivables. The result in days' sales outstanding also permits comparison with stated terms of sale. If the above company is offering 30-day terms, it is apparent that these terms are being abused significantly.

Outside analysts often have only annual sales totals to compare with year-end receivables. If sales are steady through the year, the comparisons drawn from the data can be meaningful. But if sales fluctuate through the year, a comparison of year-end receivables with sales at the annual rate can be misleading. For example, if a firm sold on net 30-day terms and had monthly sales of $100,000 for January through November and $250,000 in December, it might well have receivables outstanding on December 31 of $250,000. Yet, in comparison with the annual sales of $1,350,000, or *average* monthly sales of $112,500, the $250,000 in receivables would appear unduly high.

Of course, if monthly sales are known to follow a consistent seasonal pattern year after year, the analyst can compare a year-end receivables/annual sales ratio with those of the same date in earlier years. The results should be comparable in relative if not absolute terms. Yet, as we have suggested earlier, receivables should be compared with *recent* sales data whenever such data can be obtained.

A useful management control device for review of the condition of receivables is the *aging schedule*. As the name suggests, this is a tabulation of receivables outstanding according to the length of time they have been outstanding. Each account, or a broad sample of accounts, is broken down according to the date of sale, and the results are summarized in a tabulation such as the following:

Outstanding less than 30 days	$677,040	70%
Outstanding 30 to 59 days	212,784	22
Outstanding 60 to 89 days	58,032	6
Outstanding 90 days or over	19,344	2
	$967,200	100%

The aging schedule reveals any tendency for very old accounts to accumulate and provides a valuable supplement to the various receivables to sales ratios. Since the outstanding receivables are appraised in terms of the associated dates of sale, the tabulation automatically recognizes recent bulges or slumps in sales. Many financial officers have such schedules prepared in routine at periodic intervals, and commercial banks and other lenders to firms with important investments in receivables frequently ask for aging schedules.

While it is possible for the recent receivables to contain accounts of very weak concerns, the fact that the large percentage of existing accounts are for recent sales and only a very small percentage are quite old nevertheless *suggests* that the quality of the accounts is good. Conversely, a schedule revealing a substantial percentage of accounts long overdue brings to light the need for vigorous action if significant bad debt losses are to be avoided. Without an aging schedule, the existence of many long overdue accounts could be obscured in average figures heavily influenced by the very prompt payment of most of the accounts.

Accounting for Accounts Receivable

The accounting for accounts receivable involves a large volume of record keeping, calling for rapid and accurate recording of sales and payments. The accounting theory, however, is simple. When a sale is made, the appropriate amount is added to an account kept for each customer and thus included in the total of accounts receivable. As payments are received, the fact of payment is noted on each account, and the total of accounts receivable is decreased at the same time cash is increased.

Most concerns recognize the fact that some of their sales on credit will not be paid and set up an account called Reserve for Bad Debts or Provision for Bad Debts. An amount equal to the portion of sales which it is estimated will prove uncollectible is charged to income as Bad Debt Expense, and an equal credit is made to the Reserve for Bad Debts. When it is determined that a particular account receivable will not be collected, it is taken off the books by reducing accounts receivable and the Reserve for Bad Debts by an equal amount. Many firms, in reporting their accounts receivable on the balance sheet, show "Accounts receivable, net"—in other words, after subtraction of the Reserve for Bad Debts.

Cash Receipts from Receivables

In planning when and in what amounts cash will be received as a result of credit sales, the critical dates are the dates when receipts of payment for credit sales can be expected. Thus, forecasts of credit sales must be converted into estimated collections of accounts receivable in order to determine cash receipts from such sales. Usually, an average figure based on past experience is employed as a measure of the time lag between sales and collection of the related receivables. Thus, if the average collection experience has been thirty days and there is no reason to anticipate a change in this figure, the receipts from future sales on credit can be scheduled a month behind the sales. Appropriate deductions should be made for bad debts if there is reason to believe they will prove significant.

Chapter 5

Management of Cash and Near-Cash Reserves and the Need for Funds

UNITED STATES manufacturing corporations on September 30, 1960, had an investment of almost $30 billion in *liquid assets*—cash and readily marketable U.S. government securities. This amount represented more than 10 per cent of the total assets of these corporations. In some industry groups the percentage of total assets tied up in cash and near cash was much higher—manufacturers of motor vehicles and equipment had 17.4 per cent of total assets in liquid form, drug manufacturers 16 per cent. For nonmanufacturing firms, as the data in Chart 5–1 show, the investment in liquid assets also is a major one. Obviously, the commitment to cash and "near-cash" securities of American business is a significant one; seemingly much less readily apparent is the susceptibility of these assets to effective management devoted to maximizing their productivity along the lines discussed in the chapters on inventory and receivables management. Indeed, many firms that long have sought to maximize turnover and return on inventory, receivables, and fixed assets appear to have devoted relatively scant attention to the very real potential contribution to higher over-all return through close attention to and skillful management of investment in cash and near-cash reserves. The taunt, "Physician, heal thyself," can properly be directed at financial officers who have stressed turnover considerations to other corporate officers without exploiting the opportunities for maximizing the productivity of liquid assets. Although top management can be expected to have a keen interest in the liquidity of the firm and in the shaping of policies governing the cash and near-cash accounts, the direct and

CHART 5-1

Investments in Cash and U.S. Obligations of Corporations in Selected Industry Groups, as a Percentage of Their Total Assets, Tax Year Ended July, 1957–June, 1958

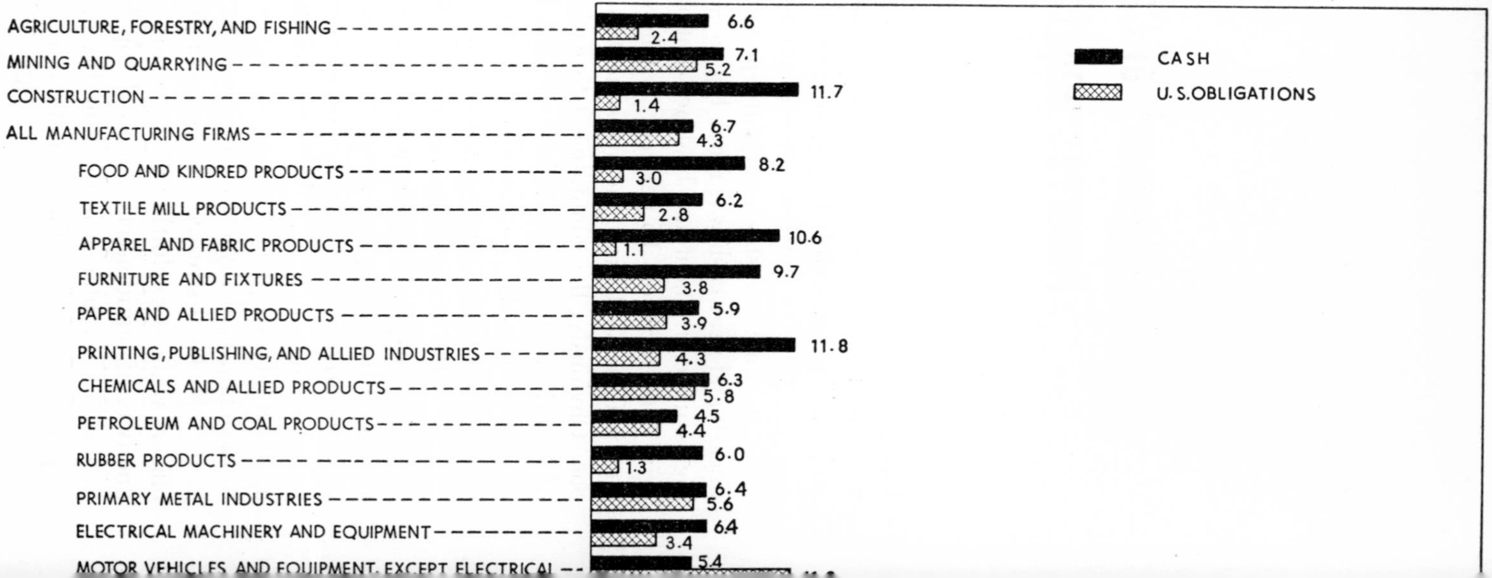

■ CASH
▨ U.S. OBLIGATIONS

AGRICULTURE, FORESTRY, AND FISHING ----- 6.6 / 2.4
MINING AND QUARRYING ----- 7.1 / 5.2
CONSTRUCTION ----- 11.7 / 1.4
ALL MANUFACTURING FIRMS ----- 6.7 / 4.3
FOOD AND KINDRED PRODUCTS ----- 8.2 / 3.0
TEXTILE MILL PRODUCTS ----- 6.2 / 2.8
APPAREL AND FABRIC PRODUCTS ----- 10.6 / 1.1
FURNITURE AND FIXTURES ----- 9.7 / 3.8
PAPER AND ALLIED PRODUCTS ----- 5.9 / 3.9
PRINTING, PUBLISHING, AND ALLIED INDUSTRIES ----- 11.8 / 4.3
CHEMICALS AND ALLIED PRODUCTS ----- 6.3 / 5.8
PETROLEUM AND COAL PRODUCTS ----- 4.5 / 4.4
RUBBER PRODUCTS ----- 6.0 / 1.3
PRIMARY METAL INDUSTRIES ----- 6.4 / 5.6
ELECTRICAL MACHINERY AND EQUIPMENT ----- 6.4 / 3.4
MOTOR VEHICLES AND EQUIPMENT, EXCEPT ELECTRICAL ----- 5.4

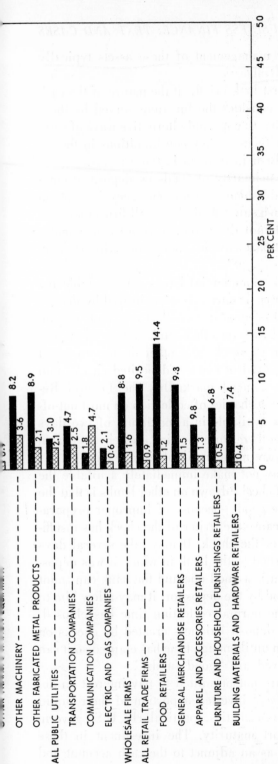

PER CENT

OTHER MACHINERY — — — — — — — — 8.2 / 3.6

OTHER FABRICATED METAL PRODUCTS — — — 8.9 / 2.1

ALL PUBLIC UTILITIES — — — — — — — 3.0 / 2.1

TRANSPORTATION COMPANIES — — — — — 4.7 / 2.5

COMMUNICATION COMPANIES — — — — — 1.8 / 4.7

ELECTRIC AND GAS COMPANIES — — — — — 2.1 / 0.6

WHOLESALE FIRMS — — — — — — — — 8.8 / 1.6

ALL RETAIL TRADE FIRMS — — — — — — 9.5 / 0.9

FOOD RETAILERS — — — — — — — — 14.4 / 1.2

GENERAL MERCHANDISE RETAILERS — — — — 9.3 / 1.5

APPAREL AND ACCESSORIES RETAILERS — — — 9.8 / 1.3

FURNITURE AND HOUSEHOLD FURNISHINGS RETAILERS — — 6.8 / 0.5

BUILDING MATERIALS AND HARDWARE RETAILERS — — — 7.4 / 0.4

Source of Data: Internal Revenue Service, U.S. Treasury Department, *Statistics of Income, 1957–58: Corporation Income Tax Returns* (Washington, D.C.: U.S. Government Printing Office, 1960), Table 3, pp. 31–38, and Table 5, pp. 41–66.

immediate responsibility for management of these assets typically rests with the chief financial officer.

In this chapter, we shall first look briefly at the nature of the cash and near-cash accounts; then consider the functions served by these investments, the costs of the investments, and alternative ways of serving these functions; and then focus on key considerations in the establishment of optimum levels of investment in these assets.

The *cash account* consists primarily of funds on deposit at commercial banks. In retail establishments, some currency is kept on hand for change making on cash sales. And almost all firms maintain a small *petty cash fund* for minor disbursements most conveniently made in cash. But for the most part, *cash* is synonymous with bank account balances.

Not all funds on deposit at commercial banks are available for disbursement. Part of the balance is normally immobilized by *float*—the time required for the bank of deposit to collect the funds due on checks deposited which are drawn on other banks. Over the years, through the air transportation of checks and other devices to speed their movement, the time required to convert deposited checks into "available funds" has been reduced markedly. The Federal Reserve banks, which handle the mechanics of collection on most out-of-town checks, now make funds available in a maximum of two days to banks turning checks over to them for collection. For checks drawn on banks near at hand, funds are made available in one day.

A second reason banks may not make immediately available the balances created by deposit of checks drawn on other banks is that the checks may turn out not to be good—because of improper preparation or, more importantly, because the writer of the check has insufficient funds on deposit to cover the check. It may take several days before a "bad check" is returned to the bank in which it was deposited. If the depositor's account is a good one and the bank can count on bad checks being made good by the depositor, it may allow him to draw on funds as soon as the normal collection time has elapsed. Otherwise, it may insist that deposit balances created by checks on other banks not be drawn upon until enough time has elapsed so it can be confident the funds involved are "good funds."

Since commercial banks are not permitted to pay interest on demand deposits, many firms have invested a portion of their liquid funds in readily marketable securities, particularly U.S. government bills and notes of short maturity. The investment in these securities may be thought of as an adjunct to the cash account and

termed *near-cash reserves*, since they can normally be speedily converted into cash without significant loss in market value. Until cash is
needed, some interest income is realized.

The Functions of the Investment in Liquid Assets

The investment in liquid assets may serve one or all of several
main functions. First, some cash is necessary for operational reasons.
Not only is currency needed for change making and petty cash funds,
but a bank account is necessary in the collection of checks received
and in order that the firm may have the great advantages of making
payments by check. Banks levy service charges on active accounts,
unless the deposit balance is large enough to compensate for the
bank's costs in servicing the account. Most companies seek to keep
deposit balances at a high enough level to avoid service charges. Further, as we have noted, a part of the operating cash is immobilized until checks are collected. Firms with widespread activities commonly
find it operationally desirable to maintain bank accounts in the cities
where their more important operations are conducted, even though
major balances are carried in one or a few banks.

If the daily cash receipts almost exactly matched the daily outflow, the total cash balances would not have to be very large to meet
the purely operational needs described above. Such even flows, however, seldom can be expected. Consequently, the cash account serves
the added function of absorbing the normal ebbs and flows in funds
through a business from day to day and week to week. For example,
most department stores buy from suppliers whose terms call for payment around the tenth of each month, while their major receipts
come in more evenly through the month. Unless they are to borrow for
midmonth needs, routine cash balances must be sufficient to cover the
heavy outflow around the tenth, even though the balances may be
large soon after the first of the month.

Liquid asset balances are also swelled by accumulation of funds in
anticipation of major outlays for such items as planned expansion of
inventories or receivables, dividend payments, income tax payments,
debt retirement, and purchase of major items of equipment. Commonly, prudence dictates that the funds for such purposes be raised
well in advance of the scheduled payment date to insure that they can
be met without strain. For example, if a major building program is to
be financed through the sale of securities, the company may well prefer to sell the securities and have the funds in hand before firm contracts for the construction are let, even though the payments for the

construction will not be required for many months or even years into the future.

Further, many managements like to keep "extra" cash on hand as an "opportunity fund" to permit rapid exploitation of attractive opportunities for investment that may present themselves—exploitation of a research finding pointing up a new product possibility, an unexpected chance to buy up another company, and the like.

An additional highly important function of the cash and near-cash accounts is that of providing a defensive or protective reserve against unexpected drains on liquidity. Interruptions to production and sales as a result of a strike, a transportation tie-up, or a fire in a major plant can rapidly deplete cash. A sudden decline in sales or an extremely bad year with heavy losses may create major cash drains at a time which is unpropitious for borrowing or for selling securities. Further, major adverse changes in the firm's competitive position may call for heavy expenditures at times when new capital is relatively unavailable. Moreover, the adverse developments setting up heavy cash needs may well be linked, so that the pressures on cash are multiple in nature. In uncertain times—and when is the future outlook entirely serene?—it is highly comforting to all those dependent on a business to know that it is "well heeled." To Benjamin Franklin is attributed the observation that in adversity a man can count on only three truly reliable friends: "a faithful dog, an old wife, and money in the bank."

Considerations of bank relationships also have an important influence on the size of deposit balances maintained. Deposits are vital to the banks; naturally, large and less active deposit accounts are especially valued by the bankers. And to the firm the favorable regard and active support of its major banks can be valuable in a variety of ways. First, the banks are in a position to supply a variety of tangible services, such as the provision of credit information, beyond the routine ones of servicing deposit accounts. Second, the bankers, by virtue of their experience and wide contacts, often can render important intangible services such as the discovery of attractive merger opportunities or advice as how best to raise needed capital.

Highly important to many firms is the fact that banks will be particularly interested in meeting the credit needs of those customers who have maintained desirable deposit accounts. In recent years, many banks have had more loan opportunities than money to loan. When credit must be rationed, the value of the deposit account becomes a major, often critical, factor in bankers' decisions as to which would-be borrowers are to be accommodated and on what terms.

Indeed, most banks insist that business borrowers maintain deposit accounts with them. Many require a *compensating balance* equal to a stated percentage of loan balances or credit lines. In recent years, for example, most banks have required finance companies, which typically borrow from many banks, to carry deposit balances equal to 20 per cent of their loan or to 15 per cent of their credit line when they are not borrowing. If the firm normally would carry a sizable account with its bank anyhow, the compensating balance requirement is more nominal than burdensome. If not, the balance requirement effectively increases the amount of credit needed and the cost of the usable funds.

Some business executives attach prestige values to a highly liquid position. Certainly, an illiquid position can adversely affect credit and other appraisals of the firm. But once an obviously strong position is reached, it is highly doubtful that further liquidity adds any material prestige value. One businessman in North Carolina some years ago took great pride in sending New York and other banking connections annual balance sheets which showed substantial cash and no current liabilities. The reaction was less one of respect than of amusement, of skepticism as to the validity of his accounting, and of sympathy for harried clerks who must have been frantically paying bills on New Year's Eve.

Finally, it should be recognized that the cash balance is to an extent a residual figure—the net result at any time of a multiplicity of inflows and outflows. If unforeseen or unexpectedly heavy inflows swell the account, redundant cash may be carried for a long time before decisions as to its use are made and implemented. Consequently, the level of a firm's cash at any particular time may be as much the result of happenstance as of conscious decision and plan.

Near-Cash Reserves

Once deposits are built up to levels adequate to meet the operating and other objectives in carrying bank deposit balances, the financial officer can well consider investing excess cash in income-producing securities. If these funds are invested in securities which have a ready market and are subject to little risk of loss of market value, the functions of a reserve of liquidity against planned or unexpected needs can be met and some income derived. Treasury bills and other short-term obligations of the U.S. government are particularly popular investment media for liquid corporate funds. The market for these securities is broad and active, and a wide choice of maturities is available, including tax anticipation note issues designed especially to appeal to financial officers desiring to "fund" income tax liabilities. Charts 5–2 and 5–3 show the fluctuations in aggregate corporate investment in cash and government securities in recent years.

Interest income on U.S. investments is fully taxable, and the available pretax return on short-term securities has been modest in recent

CHART 5–2

MANUFACTURING CORPORATIONS—CASH AND SALES, 1947–60
(In Billions of Dollars)

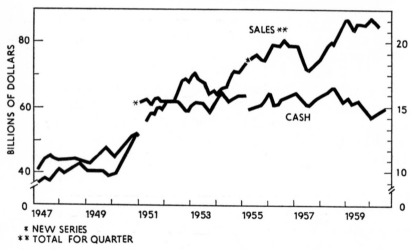

* NEW SERIES
** TOTAL FOR QUARTER

SOURCE: Federal Reserve Bank of Philadelphia, *Business Review*, March, 1961, p. 8.

years (the yield on new issues of thirteen-week bills fluctuated between 0.58 and 4.66 per cent during 1958 and through 1960). Some financial officers have invested near-cash reserves in tax-free municipal securities and in other securities offering higher net income than governments, but many have regarded liquidity and protection of principal as objectives paramount to income and hence have confined their investment to short governments.

Unless the amounts available for short-term investment are substantial, the income to be derived from conservative investment is so modest as to offer little advantage over leaving the funds on deposit. Consequently, smaller firms seldom find it worth while to bother with short-term investment; and the bulk of the $19.7 billion investment in U.S. government securities by nonfinancial corporations on December 31, 1960,[1] was held by medium-sized and large corporations. Despite the huge size of the aggregate business investment in cash and near-cash reserves, it is well to remember that a great many firms operate by choice, or more often by necessity, on very modest cash reserves and have no excess funds to invest in near-cash reserves.

CHART 5–3

CORPORATE CASH BALANCES AND GOVERNMENTS, 1947–60
(In Billions of Dollars)

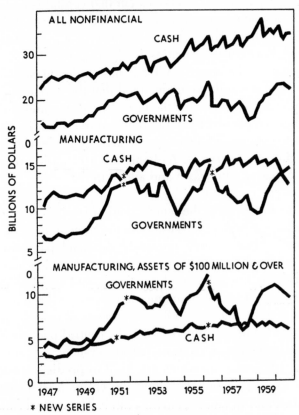

* NEW SERIES

SOURCE: Federal Reserve Bank of Philadelphia, *Business Review*, March, 1961, p. 8.

Investment of Cash in Near-Cash Reserves

Many of the reasons for carrying large liquid reserves can be illustrated by reference to the American Telephone and Telegraph Company (A.T.&T.), a holding company for the operating telephone companies in the Bell System which provide telephone service

[1] Securities and Exchange Commission, *Statistical Bulletin*, April, 1961, p. 15.

for most of the country. A.T.&T. carries the largest investment in cash and marketable securities of any U.S. nonfinancial corporation. The total cash and marketable securities (primarily short-term U.S. government securities) account of the System on December 31, 1960, amounted to $1,173 million, or 5.2 per cent of total assets. As regulated utilities, the telephone companies are restricted in the rates they can charge. Most regulatory commissions seek to restrict the telephone companies' earnings to a "fair return" on total capital employed in their businesses. To the extent that capital is tied up in cash and low-return temporary investments, the return on stockholders' investment is diluted. Hence, the cost of carrying a sizable investment in cash and low-return securities is significant.

In considering the reasons A.T.&T. has chosen to carry such large liquid reserves, it should be understood that the parent company acts as a sort of central banker for the operating companies. Certain cash balances must be carried by the parent and the subsidiary companies with banks to compensate them for the activity in clearing checks and drafts and for other services. As bank balances build up above these levels, the excess is withdrawn and added to the central pool of funds with the parent company.

One of the functions of the central pool of funds is to provide funds needed for large payments anywhere in the System, most of which can be scheduled. They include quarterly dividend payments, interest payments on bonds, payments of income and excise taxes, income taxes withheld by law from employees' pay, and social security taxes, which are collected by the companies and turned over to the U.S. government at regular intervals. Large payments to contractors for new facilities can also be scheduled. Thus, the central pool covers uneven but predictable outflows of cash for the system.

Certain needs come up which are hard to predict—such as funds needed for repair of damage along the entire East Coast suffered from Hurricane Donna in September, 1960. The central fund must be prepared to meet such unpredictable cash needs on call.

In addition, the Bell System in recent years has had to raise huge sums through almost continuous sale of new securities. The proceeds of such sales are held in the central fund until needed. System expansion to meet public needs for service should not be subject to interruption through any demoralization of the capital markets which might interrupt the sale of new securities. While A.T.&T. would doubtless find it difficult to "stay out of the market" for new funds for long periods, it is deemed desirable to keep on hand enough funds so that new offerings could be deferred for at least several months if such action seemed urgently desirable.

Finally, as a very large enterprise aware of its great public responsibilities, the Bell System wants to keep in a sound, reasonably liquid condition against the general uncertainties of the times, and in striking a balance between too much in liquid reserves and too little, doubtless would prefer to have been on the safe rather than the sorry side of a theoretically perfect balance.

The Costs of Carrying Cash and Near-Cash Reserves

In contrast to investment in inventory or receivables, the investment in cash involves little if any risks or operating costs. And as we have seen, near-cash reserves can be invested at little expense or risk so as to produce 1 or 2 per cent after-tax income. But the carrying of cash and near-cash reserves beyond irreducible operating needs cuts asset turnover and rate of return. Maximum productivity of these assets should be sought as vigorously as of inventory, receivables, or other commitments. Yet, various studies have indicated that in many companies the opportunities for effective cash management have been little exploited. Indeed, it appears clear that some firms use huge balances as an expensive substitute for careful management of liquid resources.

Approaches to Boosting Turnover of Cash and Near Cash

The success of some able managements in increasing the productivity of their liquid funds while still meeting the needs of their firms points up useful approaches to more effective management of liquid resources. First, it is useful for the financial manager to identify carefully and explicitly the functions to be served in his firm by the liquid accounts. Then, he can proceed to analysis of the minimum amounts necessary to meet adequately these purposes and of alternative ways in which they might be met more economically.

Many firms have found that the operating needs for cash can be cut sharply through various devices of "money mobilization." In most firms, cash equal to several days' sales is tied up in the process of receiving check payments from customers and converting them into usable bank balances. From the customer's viewpoint, receivables are paid when he puts a check in the mail. Yet, several days may elapse while the check is in the mail, after receipt and before deposit, while receipt and accounting routines are accomplished, and while the bank in which it is ultimately deposited converts the check into "good funds." With the aid of their banks a number of firms have developed comprehensive programs of money mobilization which have cut several days off this process. These programs typically employ procedures for customers' remittance to nearby "collecting banks," which speed collection of the checks and simply forward to the receiving firm the essential information for accounting for the receipts. Wire transfers of balances from collecting banks to the major "paying banks" also contribute to the minimizing of balances needed for operating purposes. In smaller firms, simple programs such as organized effort to cut the time used in office routines of processing incoming checks can be rewarding in freed funds.

As we have seen, a major and rather universal reason for carrying sizable operating balances stems from intramonth or intermonth fluctuations in inflow and outgo of cash. Of course, one way of being sure of not being embarrassed by unexpected overdrafts is to carry bank balances surely large enough to meet any conceivable operational net outflows. Yet, careful study of past patterns of receipts and payments and organized effort at forecasting probable future cash flows may well indicate that a very much lower operating cash balance will prove adequate to meet the anticipated periodic drains of cash and to cover reasonable margins of error in forecasting. Further, the analysis and forecasting effort may expose opportunities to reduce the fluctuations. For example, a change in selling terms from ones calling for payment in 10 days after the end of the month to a straight 20 days after invoicing may eliminate peaking of midmonth inflows and permit smaller operational balances without hurting sales.

Careful forecasting of future cash receipts and expenditures may also indicate that heavy outflows such as those on tax payment dates can be satisfactorily met through temporary pulldown of bank balances or other devices that make unnecessary the accumulation of extra funds for these purposes long in advance.

The extent to which it is desirable and wise to maintain liquid reserves against unpredictable opportunities for effective permanent investment and/or possible events draining cash is inherently difficult to determine. The very uncertainty of the need to draw on the reserves, the difficulty of measuring the undesirable consequences of lost opportunities or financial embarrassment stemming from insufficient reserves and of putting a value on the protection against financial risks afforded by large reserves, make judgments about the ideal size of such reserves—if any are to be carried—highly subjective. Yet, aspects of the problem can be usefully pinned down and the area of subjective judgment narrowed. The likely cash impact of the various sorts of events to be guarded against should be analyzed carefully—frequently, it may be determined that the probable flows of cash involved will be largely offsetting and net outflows less formidable than would be thought. Thus, a major decline in sales with accompanying losses that drain cash may well permit a reduction in inventories that, along with the shrinking of receivables, frees cash that more than matches the cash drain from operating losses. The likelihood that various unfavorable events will occur simultaneously should also be considered. Conceivably, each of the four infielders on a baseball team could be injured at the same time. But it is much more likely that one or two utility infielders will be enough to provide a reasonable "bench." Or analysis of the likely opportunities to buy other businesses may disclose the probability that sellers will prefer an exchange of common stock to a straight cash sale.

Further, alternative methods of meeting unpredictable cash needs should be thoroughly canvassed. If the firm maintains reserves of borrowing power, careful cultivation of potential creditors may provide satisfactory assurance that the needed funds can be raised expeditiously. If firm assurance that credit will be available when needed is desirable, revolving credit lines may be established; the common fee of one half of 1 per cent for unused funds under a firm revolving bank or insurance company credit arrangement may be a much more economical form of insurance against cash stringencies than large cash reserves—even those invested at modest return. Those firms with obvious reserves of borrowing power that long have carried unused liquid reserves would seem to be striking an unnecessarily conservative balance between risk and return.

Establishing Optimum Levels for Cash and Liquid Reserves

The determination of the optimum balance between turnover and the advantages of abundant liquidity represents an important management decision, and one that must be made and reviewed in the light of the distinctive circumstances and objectives of the individual firm. General rules of thumb—one that is slow to die out is that cash and near-cash reserves should be equal to one month's normal expenditures—should be recognized as shallow substitutes for the kind of vigorous, if difficult, analysis and thoughtful judgment that should be applied to the determination of optimum levels.

Our discussion should have indicated major considerations in the decision—the extent of unavoidable fluctuations in operational cash flows; the susceptibility of flows to forecasting; the effort and skill devoted to cash forecasting; the degree of vulnerability to unpredictable major cash drains; the transitional period available when unexpected drains develop; the extent to which alternative sources of emergency funds can be made available, particularly through cultivation of reserves of borrowing power; the opportunity for more profitable use of funds elsewhere in the business; the current and potential importance to the firm of strong bank relationships; and the degree of financial conservatism. We do not mean to suggest that the final decision as to optimum levels should be by rigid formula. The weighing of the reduction in risks afforded by large balances against the costs of the "insurance" provided must be a subjective matter, in which different managements faced with the same facts would reach different final judgments. We do urge the careful assembly of the facts and considerations on which final judgments are to be made.

Analyzing the Investment in Liquid Resources

In the absence of the kind of data we have discussed, which would make possible more meaningful judgments as to the adequacy of liquid resources, financial analysts outside the firm have developed several ratios as rough, but sometimes useful, measures of the liquidity of subject firms. Widely used as a rough measure of liquidity is the *acid test* or *net quick* ratio which compares the total of cash, near-cash reserves, and trade receivables with the total of current liabilities. Although the wide variation among firms limits the significance of any average figure, it might be noted that this ratio for all U.S. nonfinancial corporations was 1.24 on June 30, 1960. Also used rather widely are ratios which compare cash and near-cash reserves to sales and to total current liabilities. At midyear 1960 the cash and U.S. security holdings of U.S. manufacturing corporations equaled 27.5 days' sales, and the ratio of these accounts to their total current liabilities was 0.50.

Chapter 6

The Investment in Fixed Assets

IN PRECEDING chapters, we have discussed the necessary commitment of funds in cash, inventories, and trade credit, pointing out the continuing nature of the basic investment of funds in these categories, despite the movement of individual items through the process of production and sale. In this chapter, we turn to the investment of funds in assets where the permanent nature of the underlying need for funds is paralleled by the more enduring characteristics of the assets themselves.

The most important group of these assets is the *fixed assets,* also termed *capital assets.* To quote Kohler: "Included in the fixed-asset family are land, from which the flow of services is seemingly permanent, buildings, building equipment, fixtures, machinery, tools (large and small), furniture, office devices, patterns, drawings, dies. . . . The characteristic fixed asset has a limited life (land is the one important exception), and its cost, less salvage, is distributed over the periods it benefits by means of provisions for depreciation."[1]

Many businesses also have investments of consequence in *intangible assets,* which represent investments having no physical existence in themselves, but rather rights to enjoy some privilege. Examples are patents and investments in the securities of other companies. If the value of the intangible assets is expected to have a limited life, their cost usually is distributed by charges similar to depreciation, known as *amortization.*

Importance of the Investment in Fixed Assets

The technology of the industry in which a company operates largely determines the quantity of funds it must commit to fixed as-

---

[1] Eric L. Kohler, *A Dictionary for Accountants* (2d ed.; Englewood Cliffs, N.J.: Prentice-Hall, Inc., 1957), p. 209.

CHART 6-1

Investment in Net Capital Assets of Corporations in Selected Industry Groups as a Percentage of Their Total Assets, Tax Year Ended July, 1957–June, 1958*

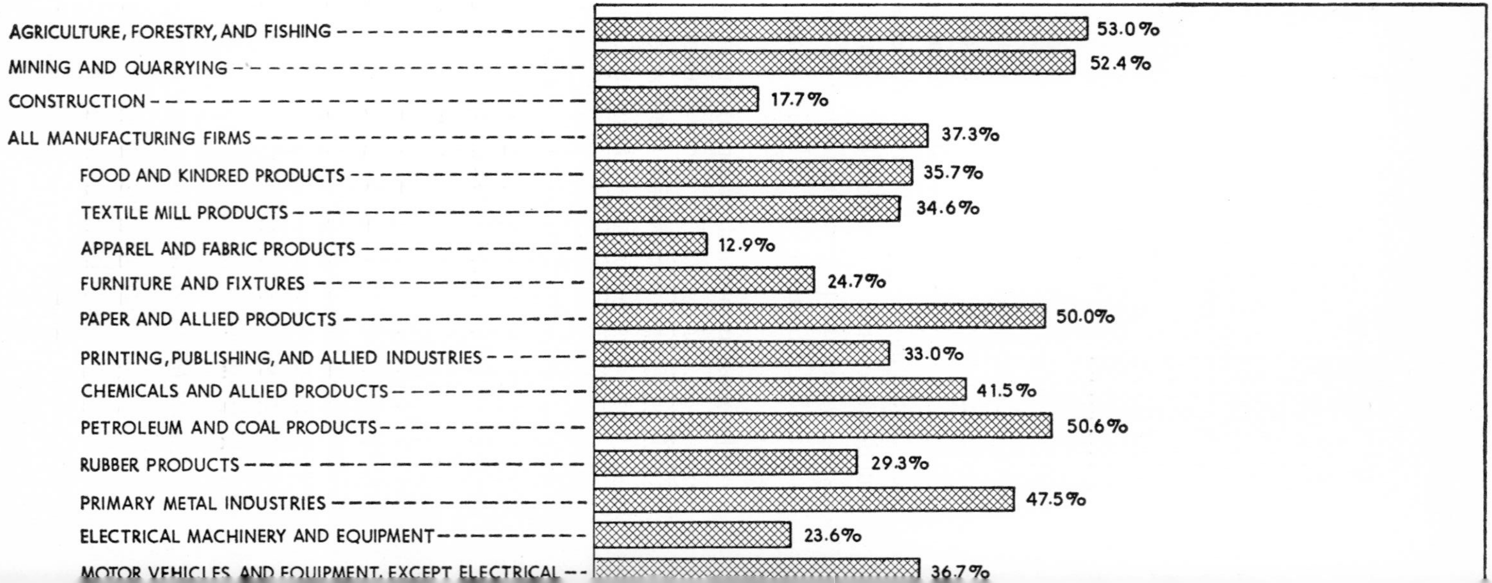

Industry Group	Percentage
AGRICULTURE, FORESTRY, AND FISHING	53.0%
MINING AND QUARRYING	52.4%
CONSTRUCTION	17.7%
ALL MANUFACTURING FIRMS	37.3%
FOOD AND KINDRED PRODUCTS	35.7%
TEXTILE MILL PRODUCTS	34.6%
APPAREL AND FABRIC PRODUCTS	12.9%
FURNITURE AND FIXTURES	24.7%
PAPER AND ALLIED PRODUCTS	50.0%
PRINTING, PUBLISHING, AND ALLIED INDUSTRIES	33.0%
CHEMICALS AND ALLIED PRODUCTS	41.5%
PETROLEUM AND COAL PRODUCTS	50.6%
RUBBER PRODUCTS	29.3%
PRIMARY METAL INDUSTRIES	47.5%
ELECTRICAL MACHINERY AND EQUIPMENT	23.6%
MOTOR VEHICLES AND EQUIPMENT, EXCEPT ELECTRICAL	36.7%

OTHER MACHINERY – – – – – – – – 27.2%
OTHER FABRICATED METAL PRODUCTS – – – – – 31.7%
ALL PUBLIC UTILITIES – – – – – – 80.0%
TRANSPORTATION COMPANIES – – – – – 71.8%
COMMUNICATION COMPANIES – – – – – 79.7%
ELECTRIC AND GAS COMPANIES – – – – 87.6%
WHOLESALE FIRMS – – – – – – 12.7%
ALL RETAIL TRADE FIRMS – – – – – 22.9%
FOOD RETAILERS – – – – – – 35.8%
GENERAL MERCHANDISE RETAILERS – – – – 23.6%
APPAREL AND ACCESSORIES RETAILERS – – – – 14.8%
FURNITURE AND HOUSEHOLD FURNISHINGS RETAILERS – – – 9.8%
BUILDING MATERIALS AND HARDWARE RETAILERS – – – 15.6%

PER CENT

0   10   20   30   40   50   60   70   80   90   100

* SOURCE OF DATA: Internal Revenue Service, U.S. Treasury Department, *Statistics of Income, 1957–58: Corporation Income Tax Returns* (Washington, D.C.: U.S. Government Printing Office, 1960), Table 3, pp. 31–38, and Table 5, pp. 41–66.

sets. While other factors influence the investment of individual firms in fixed assets, firms in the same industry generally tend to have a similar portion of their total assets in fixed assets. Thus, no electric utility company can avoid a heavy investment in generating and/or distributive facilities. Since these utilities have little need for inventories and only moderate receivables, it is not surprising to note from Chart 6–1 that fixed assets represent over four fifths of their total assets.

In the aggregate, United States manufacturers' investment in fixed assets was $100.5 billion, or 39.3 per cent, of their total resources on December 31, 1960. Chart 6–1, which is based on earlier but more detailed data, shows the relative importance of fixed assets to manufacturers in various industry groups. As might be expected, primary metal manufacturers, such as the steelmakers, have a relatively high commitment in plant facilities. In contrast, note the low investment in fixed assets of apparel manufacturers. The technology of the garment industry is very simple compared to that of steelmaking. Much of the needed machinery, such as sewing machines, is relatively simple and inexpensive, and is available on rental. Specialized buildings are not required, and the "loft space" available for rent in New York and other garment centers meets the needs of many manufacturers.

The reference to the garment industry has indicated another significant determinant of the required investment in fixed assets—the extent to which needed plant or equipment is available on reasonably satisfactory rental terms. Rental of office space is especially common, even among the largest and most affluent concerns. Of 129 new office buildings put into place in Manhattan (New York City) during the fifties, only 28 were owner-occupied. Many retailers, and some manufacturers whose space needs are not distinctive, are able to meet their major building needs through rental. For a long time, certain leading manufacturers of office and plant equipment, notably International Business Machines Corp. and United Shoe Machinery Corporation, have made their products available on rental terms. But in recent years an increasing variety of productive equipment—from refrigerator trucks to automatic machine tools—has become widely available on a rental basis, both from equipment manufacturers and from specialized leasing firms. Long-term leasing of industrial and commercial plant also has come to represent a financial alternative to ownership and debt financing. Since most long-term leases deserve to be evaluated as a form of long-term financing, we shall discuss such leasing in the long-term financing section of this book.

Another determinant of fixed asset investment of particular importance to firms with limited finances is the degree to which the need for facilities, particularly highly specialized and expensive equipment, can be avoided through subcontracting of work or outside purchase of parts and components requiring special equipment. For example, if a machinery builder can arrange to have the electroplating of certain parts performed by an outside specialist in this work, he may be able to avoid otherwise necessary ownership of expensive and little-used plating equipment. Or the small wheat farmer may find it wiser to have his wheat harvested by custom combiners than to own a little-used combine. One of the less widely recognized strengths of American industry lies in the extent to which finished product manufacturers can rely on specialized manufacturers for particular parts or components. By virtue of their large volume as suppliers of their specialty items to many end-item manufacturers, these specialty manufacturers can make economic use of highly specialized and expensive equipment that would be burdensome if production of these items were widely diffused.

In some fields, used equipment or old plant, available at prices that are far below those of new facilities, may be satisfactory. This is particularly likely to be true in areas where the rate of technological change in production methods has been moderate or slow. Their use can materially reduce the required investment in fixed assets, and firms with limited financial resources should carefully investigate the possibilities of buying used facilities before committing themselves to heavier investment in new fixed assets.

Distinctive Aspects of the Investment in Fixed Assets

In earlier chapters, we have stressed the central importance in asset management of concern for over-all return on investment, and there should be no need to belabor the point that these same considerations apply with equal force in fixed asset management. Indeed, certain distinctive aspects of investment in fixed assets make it especially important that new fixed assets be acquired only after searching consideration of the impact on investment return. First, proposed additions to fixed assets are commonly in sizable increments which can be considered deliberately and consciously as discrete proposals. Given reasonable foresight, it is usually possible to plan new acquisitions sufficiently far ahead that analysis of their desirability can be appropriately organized and deliberate.

Second, the purchase of plant and equipment (or their long-term lease) represents a financial commitment that will be binding over a period of years. If boosts in inventory, receivables, or liquid reserves prove unwise, or if funds stringencies make it necessary, management often can act to cut back these investments and free the funds involved in a matter of weeks or months. But the typical fixed asset investment can be recovered only through operations over a period of years. Further, uncertainty of return, as well as time, is very much involved. For example, demand for the products to be made with a new machine may not develop as expected, so that operations do not return the investment in the form of added profits and coverage of depreciation. Or new methods of production may make the machine expected to have an economic life of ten years obsolete in three.

Third, the loss in forced sale of excess or obsolete equipment and facilities typically is great. For example, the automobile manufacturer faced with unsold stocks of an unsuccessful model can usually find economy-minded buyers for the unsold cars coming forward to buy the cars at reductions of 10 or 20 per cent. Buyers for specialized productive equipment and facilities designed especially for manufacture of this model are likely to be found only at prices which are a small fraction of their book value—if at all.

In brief, investments in plant and equipment are inherently illiquid, that is, retrievable only over years and then only under conditions of uncertainty. Consequently, it is important that purchases of new plant or important items of equipment be made only after particularly careful consideration of the prospects of recovery of the investment from operations, with appropriate return, and of the financial effects of tying up substantial amounts of funds for long periods.

Major Funds Flows Related to Fixed Assets

From the cash flow viewpoint the costs of fixed assets take on importance as the funds are actually expended by the firm. A major construction project may well require substantial payments during the period of construction, perhaps as long as several years before any productive activity can be commenced. One of the authors has visited a new rubber plantation on the Amazon River where large expenditures for land clearance, dwellings for workers, and nursery plants were not expected to become productive for at least ten years.

Although this type of project is exceptionally long, the lead time for an ordinary factory building is often two years.

On the other hand, fixed assets may be acquired under a time payment contract where (usually after some initial expenditure for a *down payment*) the actual funds are expended during the use of assets. Again, if the use of fixed assets may be acquired by lease, there is no transfer of ownership, and the actual flows of funds take place during the period of use as the rent is paid. The first step in looking at a fixed asset project from a funds flow point of view is, therefore, to ask, "When must payments be made?"

Another flow of funds must also be considered. It is the net effect of inflows and outflows which occurs because the fixed assets have been acquired and put into operation, and can be referred to as *funds provided by operations.* In collecting information to permit the determination of this quantity, the analyst must be careful to choose only those flows of funds whose magnitudes change because the particular capital investment project has been undertaken. Such a search is sometimes easy, as when the project does not displace or compete with some existing operation. Sometimes, the determination is difficult. To illustrate the major cash flows in fixed asset investment, we shall now look at a simple project, a new motel to be added to an existing chain of motels.

Our motel will cost $200,000, and we estimate that its useful life is ten years. To determine the funds provided by operation of this motel, we estimate that cash rentals will bring in $40,000 a year, while in the same period we shall incur and pay for the following expenses:

Heat, light, janitorial, and other services	$10,500
Repairs and maintenance	500
Income and real estate taxes, cost of borrowed money, and all other items	5,000
	$16,000

For the time being, we prefer not to explore the question of how income taxes are determined; the topic gets considerable attention later on. The table above shows that for the year in question, the net inflow of funds from operations is $24,000. How should this quantity be considered by management? Does it constitute funds that can be used for any corporate purpose? Must a portion of it be regarded as tied to the particular investment in some way?

Any business operation that produces a net gain in funds does so throughout a period of time, and not in a single sum at the end of the period. Thus, in our example the gain of $24,000 will be simply the cumulative result of the operations of the period. Absent special action to that end, the funds will not be segregated as they are received, and there will be no special box or bank account where they can be found at the end of the year. All we can say with assurance is that management will have at its disposal $24,000 more in funds than if the motel had not been in operation. Surely, the funds will be in liquid form immediately after receipt; and they may well be kept in such form, but not certainly. It all depends on how management decides to use the funds, and the possibilities cover all types of transactions.

Having looked at one year of operations, let us try to foresee what problems management will face at the end of the ten-year life of the motel. If one of the vital concerns of management is that of *preserving* the earning power of the investment in this motel, much more must be done than simply to try to regain the original investment of $200,000. Let us suppose that in looking forward to the tenth year of the life of this project, management estimates that the earning power of the motel can be extended for a new period of time by the expenditure of $100,000 for extensive alterations. It is then management's task to see to it that the needed funds are available in liquid form, either from accumulated funds provided by operations over the first ten years, or from available credit, or otherwise. This same task, in different magnitude, would confront management if it found that rising prices made an investment of $275,000 necessary and desirable. It cannot be overemphasized that recovery of the cost of the original investment does not assure the availability or adequacy of funds to provide for its continuation or replacement.

The Impact of Depreciation Accounting on Cash Outflows for Income Taxes

As we shall emphasize, charges to income for depreciation do not in themselves affect the total inflow of cash from operations. However, the allowance of depreciation expense as a deduction from income subject to taxation does have an important effect on the outflows of cash necessary to satisfy tax requirements. For this reason, it is desirable that we devote attention to the accounting for depreciation for tax purposes. As an accountant views the $200,000 investment in the motel at the beginning of the ten-year period, he finds he must record an outflow of funds of that amount. Among the principal concerns of accounting is the determination of income, year by year (or more generally period by period), and for this purpose the expenditure of $200,000 is obviously not an expense to be charged wholly to the first year of the ten. The accountant, therefore, *capitalizes* the expenditure by "booking" $200,000 as fixed assets. There then ensues the procedure referred to by Kohler: "The characteristic fixed asset has a limited life . . . and its cost, less salvage, is distributed over the periods it benefits by means of provisions for depreciation."

A widely used method (known as the *straight-line method*) of providing for the depreciation of the $200,000 motel in ten years would be to take one tenth of its cost as an expense each year, deducting $20,000 from the gross income (along with the other costs), and reducing the capitalized value of the fixed asset accordingly. If this were done, the income statement of our sample year of operations would become:

Rental income	$40,000
Expenditure of funds	16,000
Funds provided by operations	$24,000
Depreciation	20,000
Net Profit	$ 4,000

While this income statement is decidedly more useful to those who are studying the profitability of the firm, especially from year to year, it must be emphasized that the charging of depreciation, itself, does nothing that alters by as much as one cent the amount of funds provided by operations. All that has happened (apart from the income tax effect discussed below) is that the $24,000 has been divided into two accounts, one called Depreciation and the other Net Profit.

Business income taxes in the United States are levied on net profits, so that all allowable expenses are deductible from gross revenues before the "net income subject to tax" is determined. Treasury regulations govern the admissibility of items as deductible expenses. Depreciation is one of the acceptable charges.

The consequence of any allowable expense is a reduction of the tax liability. Taking the annual depreciation of the motel as $20,000 and the income tax rate as 52 per cent, there will be a reduction in net profits of $20,000 and therefore a decline in the tax liability of (0.52) $($20,000$) = $10,400. In other words, the depreciation expense permits retaining $10,400 more net funds after taxes than would otherwise be possible. This is referred to as the *tax shield*, which is always the full amount of the deductible item multiplied by the applicable tax rate. How much this shield can be depends, of course, on the amount of depreciation permitted by the tax authorities to be used for tax purposes.

The tax authorities are particularly interested in seeing that the estimates of useful life used in setting depreciation rates are not unreasonably short. Treasury estimates of reasonable life for several hundred items of plant and equipment are given in its *Bulletin F*. Beyond these indications the Treasury reserves the right to look at any pertinent evidence in the particular case in evaluating estimates of life proposed by taxpayers. Treasury interest in the matter, however, extends only to the depreciation claimed in tax returns as a business expense deductible before determination of taxable income. Some thoroughly reputable companies go so far as to keep two sets of property records and charge depreciation for their own accounting purposes differently from the charge for purposes of accounting for income tax. Such firms believe that the tax treatment of depreciation does not result in the most useful figures for internal use or for reporting to the public.

So far, we have spoken only of straight-line methods of allocating depreciation to annual periods. Under liberalized tax laws enacted in 1954 regarding depreciation, two other major methods of allocating depreciation to annual periods were authorized. In effect, these newly authorized methods permit larger amounts of the total depreciation to be charged in the early years of useful life of newly acquired assets. Since the total charged as depreciation under any method cannot exceed the cost of the item to its owner, the new methods do not alter the total depreciation that can be charged off as a business expense, nor is the total life of the asset reduced. Thus, given constant tax rates, the ultimate total of tax liabilities is not reduced by shifts in the timing of depreciation deductions.[2] By advancing the time when much of the depreciation can be taken as an expense, however, they do permit the postponement of part of the tax liability and give the firm the use for a time of the funds that otherwise would have been paid in taxes at an earlier date.

The two alternate methods are the *declining balance* and the *sum-of-the-years'-digits* methods. Under the declining balance method a uniform rate, which may be as much as twice the straight-line rate, is

---

[2] Under certain circumstances, if a depreciable asset is sold for more than the depreciated balance for tax purposes, the gain can be treated for tax purposes as a capital gain taxable at 25 per cent or less. If the firm has reduced its income taxable at 52 per cent by depreciation charges taken on this equipment, it realizes *tax savings* of 27 per cent or more on the exchange of any added depreciation tax deduction for capital gain taxation. But this and other less important exceptions do not destroy the general validity of the textual observation.

applied to the undepreciated asset balance. In the case of an investment for a ten-year period the annual rate would be twice the straight-
line rate of 10 per cent, that is, 20 per cent; but the charge for each
year would be determined from the application of the 20 per cent
rate to the declining book value of the asset. At any time during the
life of the asset a shift may be made to the straight-line method for the
undepreciated balance. As an example, we give the computation of
the depreciation charges for the $200,000 motel as a part of Ta-
ble 6–1.

The years'-digits method is better explained than defined. The
amount that can be taken as depreciation in each year is established
by use of a fraction. In this fraction the numerator is the number of
years of useful life remaining, and so changes each year. The denominator in all years is the number representing the sum of the digits
of years of full life of the property. For the motel, the denominator would therefore be $1 + 2 + 3 + 4 + 5 + 6 + 7 + 8 + 9 +
10 = 55$, and in the first year the depreciation would be $^{10}\!/_{55}$. For the
ten years the amounts would be as shown in Table 6–1. *of original
investment*

Remembering that it is almost always advantageous for a firm to
have funds at its disposal early rather than late, one can see that the
newer methods are preferable, and we find it surprising that many
firms cling to the straight-line technique.

Business Investment and Depreciation

For American business as a whole the cash outflows associated with
the acquisition of new fixed assets and the cash inflows from operations measured by depreciation charges are huge. Compared below
are the expenditures of American corporations for new plant and
equipment from 1954 through 1960 and the depreciation charges of
corporations in these same years.[3] In each case the amounts are expressed in billions of dollars.

	1954	1955	1956	1957	1958	1959	1960
Expenditures for new plant and equip-ment..............	22.4	24.2	29.9	32.7	26.4	27.7	31.0
Depreciation charges..	13.5	15.7	17.3	19.1	20.2	21.5	23.0

As can readily be seen, the total cash inflows associated with depreciation in recent years fell well short of equaling the outlays for

---

[3] *Economic Report of the President* (Washington, D.C.: U.S. Government Printing
Office, January, 1961).

TABLE 6-1

COMPARISON OF THE RESULTS OF THREE METHODS OF ALLOCATING DEPRECIATION OF A $200,000 MOTEL OVER TEN YEARS*

	STRAIGHT LINE, 10% RATE		DECLINING BALANCE, 20% RATE		YEARS'-DIGITS		
	Allowable Depreciation	Undepreciated Cost, Year End	Allowable Depreciation	Undepreciated Cost, Year End	Rate	Allowable Depreciation	Undepreciated Cost, Year End
At purchase.	.....	$200,000	.....	$200,000	.....	.....	$200,000
First year.	$20,000	180,000	$40,000	160,000	10/55	$36,364	163,636
Second year.	20,000	160,000	32,000	128,000	9/55	32,727	130,909
Third year.	20,000	140,000	25,600	102,400	8/55	29,091	101,818
Fourth year.	20,000	120,000	20,480	81,920	7/55	25,455	76,363
Fifth year.	20,000	100,000	16,384	65,536	6/55	21,818	54,545
Sixth year.	20,000	80,000	13,107	52,429	5/55	18,182	36,363
Seventh year.	20,000	60,000	13,107†	39,322†	4/55	14,545	21,818
Eighth year.	20,000	40,000	13,107	26,215	3/55	10,909	10,909
Ninth year.	20,000	20,000	13,107	13,107	2/55	7,273	3,636
Tenth year.	20,000	0	13,107	0	1/55	3,636	0

* For simplicity, the table is based on the somewhat unrealistic assumptions that the estimated useful life of the motel is ten years and that there will be no salvage value at the end of the period.

† These calculations assume a shift from declining balance to straight-line depreciation at the beginning of the seventh year. It should be noted that if there were a salvage value, the timing of the shift would be more difficult to determine. Whereas the straight-line and years'-digits methods base depreciation on cost less salvage, depreciation in the declining balance method is based on cost. If a shift is made to the straight-line method, however, depreciation must be based on the unrecovered cost at that time, reduced by salvage.

NOTE: A simplified comparison of the three methods applied to a $100 asset with a ten-year useful life is given in Paragraph 14,148 of *Prentice-Hall Federal Taxes, 1961* (Englewood Cliffs, N.J.: Prentice-Hall, Inc., 1961).

new plant and equipment during these years, but the gap has narrowed. The difference, in part, is the reflection of a net increase in physical facilities of American business during these years. But it also reflects the fact that depreciation is generally calculated merely to return the cost of depreciable assets over their useful life. In the recent period of rising prices, even simple replacements have usually cost more than the original cost of the asset replaced.

A growing number of accountants, professors, and company executives, notably those of the U.S. Steel Corporation, have argued strenuously that depreciation charges should take into account changes in the costs of replacing the depreciable assets rather than simply aiming to distribute the historical costs of the assets over their useful life. In general, the organizations that speak for the accounting profession and the tax authorities have insisted that for purposes of income determination and for balance sheet purposes, depreciation should be based on cost.

Summary of Funds Flows Related to the Ownership of Fixed Assets

Now, let us recapitulate our main points regarding the cash flows related to acquisition and ownership of fixed assets. In planning the cash outflows related to the acquisition of fixed assets, care should be taken to schedule the outflows in payment for the assets as they actually will be made, since their timing may differ materially from the time at which ownership of the assets is reflected in the accounting records of the firm. Further, cash inflows from operations are *not* reduced by the acknowledgment of depreciation as an expense appropriate for purposes of income determination. The amount of depreciation which can be taken as a deduction from taxable income does, however, have a significant effect on the timing of cash outflows required to satisfy income tax liabilities. So the firm's pattern of allowable depreciation deductions does affect its depreciation tax shield and hence the timing of its cash outflows for taxes.

Further, the tax-free recovery through operations of the original cost of fixed assets will not, in a period of rising costs, supply a sufficient inflow of funds, even if segregated and accumulated for the specific purpose, to pay for replacement of the assets with higher cost physical equivalents. To maintain a constant level of physical facilities over a long period of rising costs, added funds are required to match the excess of replacement over original fixed asset costs.

Since American business has been adding to its stock of fixed assets, acquisition in the postwar years of fixed assets has represented a major use of funds and one well in excess of the operational cash inflows measured by depreciation. This has been true despite the impact of liberalized tax laws governing the timing of tax-deductible depreciation charges.

The Total Business Outlay for Fixed Assets in Recent Years

The aggregate outlays of business for new fixed assets are great enough to have a major impact on the total demand for funds by business and hence on the conditions of the capital market faced by the individual firm needing external financing. Further, the volume of business spending on fixed assets both influences and is influenced by the over-all level of the economy. Consequently, a brief review of aggregate business spending on fixed assets in recent years may be useful.

As can be seen from Chart 6–2, during the period from 1930 through 1941, the expenditures of American business on new plant and equipment were very low—just about equaling the use or depreciation of equipment and plant. During the war years, business expenditures on plant and equipment fell behind the heavy use of physical facilities. For a period of sixteen years the *net* investment of American business in fixed assets actually declined.

Since 1945, as is apparent from Chart 6–2, expenditures for plant and equipment have surged sharply upward. Total corporate outlays for new plant and equipment during the 15 years from 1946 through 1960 amounted to more than $343 billion. Although dollar depreciation also increased, the outlay for new plant and equipment outran depreciation and retirements in each of the 11 years by a significant margin, so that the net investment in plant and equipment for business as a whole has increased substantially.

Several reasons appear to account for the increased outlays on plant. The low rate of capital expenditures during 1930 to 1945, together with rapid technical development and heavy wartime usage, meant that much of the nation's facilities in 1946 were worn or obsolete. A second basic cause has been the rise in population under conditions of general prosperity, in which the effective demand of the population for goods and services has been great and rising. The development of new products—television, diesel locomotives, synthetic fibers, air conditioning, to mention a few—and radical changes in others, such as the extension of dial telephoning, called for new or expanded facilities. Changes in productive processes and methods, such as in oil refining, have been important. Further, the rise in labor wage rates and the periodic shortages of labor have accelerated a

CHART 6-2

Business Expenditures for New Plant and Equipment, Selected Years, 1929–60

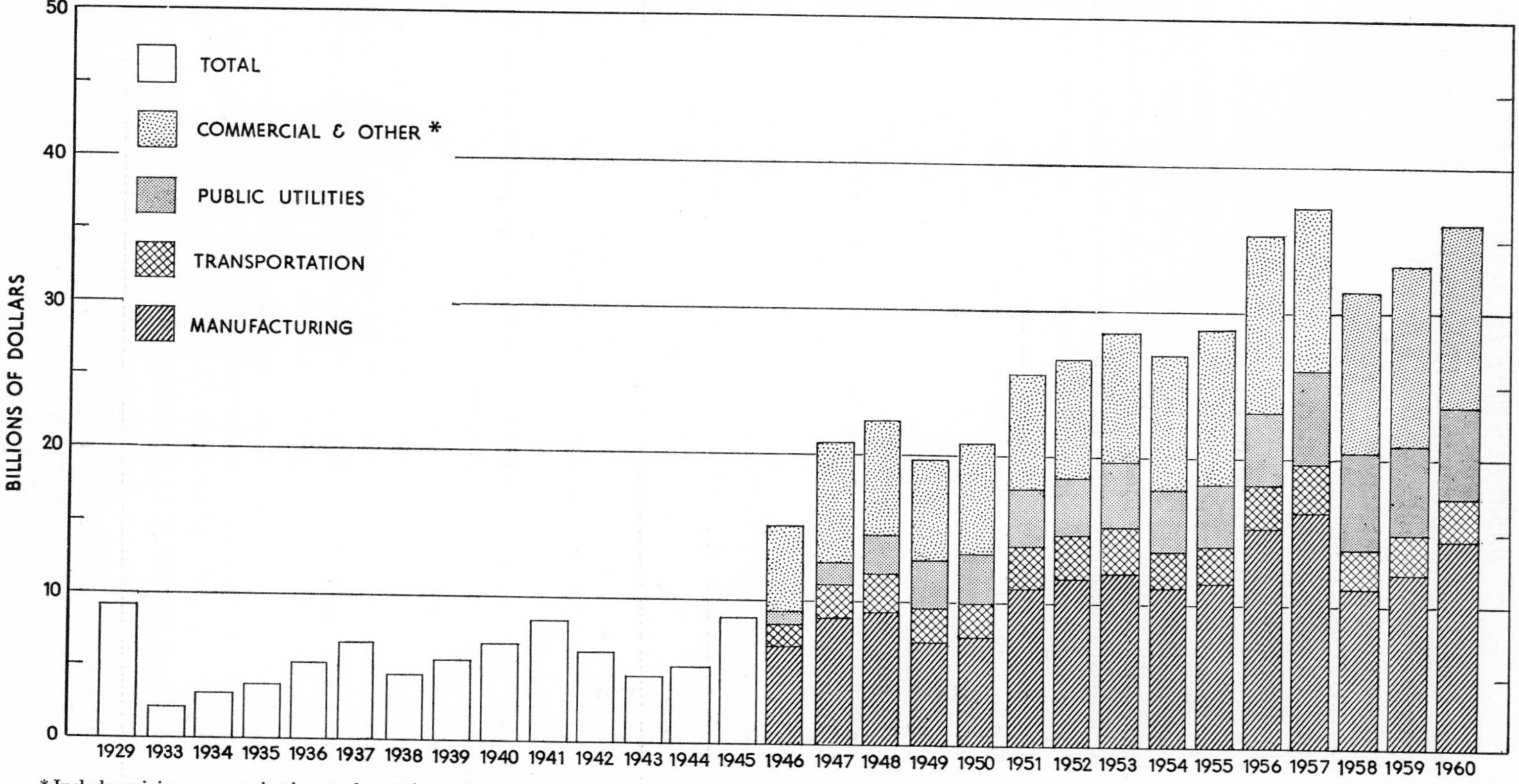

* Includes mining, communication, trade, service, and financial.
Source: For 1929–44 data, Moody's Industrial Manual, 1956, p. a7. For 1945–56 data, Economic Report of the President (Washington, D.C.: U.S. Government Printing Office, January, 1958), Table F-30. For 1957–60 data, Economic Report of the President (January, 1961), Table C-30.

BILLIONS OF DOLLARS

Legend:
TOTAL
COMMERCIAL & OTHER *
PUBLIC UTILITIES
TRANSPORTATION
MANUFACTURING

long-term trend toward greater use of laborsaving machinery. Adding
to the costs of new facilities has been a trend toward provision of improved working facilities—for example, air conditioning in plants,
offices, and stores. Important also in adding to the dollar cost of new
construction and equipment outlays has been the general rise in price
levels since 1945.

Finally, it would be most inappropriate for authors of a book on
finance to overlook the facilitating role of finance in making possible
the huge outlays on plant and equipment. The fact that the necessary
cash or credit needed to finance the outlays has been forthcoming on
terms judged reasonable must be included among the major reasons
for the postwar upsurge in business spending for plant and equipment.

The investment in new fixed assets can be broken down into acquisitions for three different but proximate objectives:

1. To expand capacity for producing existing or new products.
2. To gain savings by replacement of existing facilities with others that
   cut costs or produce other benefits such as higher quality output.
3. To replace worn-out or otherwise unserviceable assets.

Major emphasis in the fixed asset expenditure programs of manufacturing companies as a whole has shifted in recent years from expansion of capacity to modernization and replacement. Some 54 per
cent of total outlays on new fixed assets in 1956 was for increased capacity; in 1959, only 39 per cent was for expansion, 61 per cent for
modernization and replacement.[4] Since recession years heighten
pressures for cost cutting, the level of outlay for modernizing and
replacing tends to be much less volatile than does that for increased
capacity, which is directly affected by changing anticipations as to
future product demand.

Of business's total spending for fixed assets in 1959 and 1960,
about 70 per cent was for machinery and other equipment, and only
30 per cent for buildings. Only in the commercial sector (chain
stores, hotels, and office buildings) was building predominant. In
manufacturing, 80 per cent of the total was for machinery and other
equipment.[5]

Aids in the Analysis of the Investment in Fixed Assets

As we emphasized early in this chapter, commitments of funds to
fixed assets typically are for long periods into the future and usually

---

[4] McGraw-Hill Publishing Company, Inc., *Business Plans for New Plants and Equipment, 1960/1963* (13th Annual Survey; New York, 1960).

[5] *Ibid.*

are difficult and costly to reverse. Often, they are in large increments. Consequently, it is important that the firm carefully establish and apply a valid pattern of analysis of the impact of proposed investments on the rate of return on the investment involved. The importance and inherent complexity of such analysis and selection among opportunities for fixed asset investment appear to us to justify the extended treatment of this subject which we undertake in Chapter 30.

The impact of fixed asset outlays on the firm's financial needs and position also typically is major. Unduly heavy commitment of available resources to relatively illiquid fixed assets—even ones of promising long-term earning power—can precipitate major liquidity problems and, indeed, in extreme situations, make it impossible for the firm to meet maturing obligations. In Chapter 8, we shall consider some leading ratios used to measure liquidity and the impact of the firm's fixed asset investment on its liquidity, and Chapter 9 discusses the forecasting of cash needs.

At this point, it may well suffice to note that ratios similar to those applied to the investment in inventory and receivables can also usefully be applied to fixed assets. Thus, net fixed assets can be expressed as a percentage of total assets. Also, the turnover of net fixed assets in sales (sales/net fixed assets) is useful as a quick, if rough, index of the efficiency of use of fixed assets. Those firms which, by the nature of the technology of their industry, can hope to achieve only low turnover of fixed assets, notably utilities, can achieve a satisfactory return for their shareholders only if a high rate of profit can be achieved on sales (or revenues) and/or relatively heavy use can be made of low-cost debt money. Firms, on the other hand, that can achieve a high turnover of fixed assets, such as retail food chains, may well be able to achieve a high return on assets with only a moderate rate of profit on sales.

Chapter 7

Spontaneous Sources of Credit

THE FINANCIALLY prudent bachelor who is about to acquire a wife, whom to avoid argument we shall regard as an unqualified asset, will give careful thought as to how he can finance the needs that maintenance of this "investment" involves. He will quickly dismiss the rosy rationalization that two can live as cheaply as one and calculate how much the new investment will add to his recurring need for funds. Suppose that he calculates this as $200 a month. Now, if his bride brings with her an assured income from a trust fund of $100 a month, which she wants to contribute to meet family needs, the careful planner is entitled to consider the net need for funds in his matrimonial "investment" as reduced by the source that comes with the need. So he must meet an added need of only $100 a month.

In preceding chapters, we have discussed at length how continued investment in particular assets is a necessary feature of most business operations. Before we turn to further consideration of analysis of past and, then, of future needs for funds, and ways to meet these needs, we should recognize that successful business operations give rise not only to needs for funds but, happily, to certain significant sources of credit. In the normal course of profitable operations, three major sources of continuing credit tend to develop without especial effort or negotiation. Together, these sources, like the bride's independent income, constitute a substantial offset to the need for funds in the business. Since they grow out of normal patterns of profitable operation without especial effort or conscious decision on the part of owners or managers, they can be thought of as "spontaneous" or self-generating sources, which reduce the amounts of funds that the managers must raise from other sources. It is for this reason that we consider these particular sources in advance of our discussion of sources in general.

NORMAL TRADE CREDIT

The first and most important of these spontaneous sources is the trade credit normally provided by suppliers of the company. As we have seen, most raw materials, supplies, and other items purchased on a recurring basis are available on purchase terms which permit a delay in payment. The credit standards imposed by sellers which buying firms must meet in order to get credit on their purchases seldom are severe. Concerns whose purchases bear a reasonable relationship to their capital and scale of operations, and which can show some liquidity, seldom have difficulty in qualifying for the credit terms normally offered by suppliers.

For American business in general, trade credit represents a quite significant source of funds. For all manufacturing companies, total trade payables amounted to $19.4 billion, or 7.6 per cent of all assets, on September 30, 1960. In the case of manufacturers of apparel and related products, trade payables represented 23.3 per cent of all assets—this source almost matching their investment in inventory.[1] In some companies which buy on very generous credit terms and have a short and inexpensive manufacturing operation, and which sell on short terms, the trade credit virtually finances their entire operations, making it possible for them to do a very large volume of business with a minimum of ownership funds and negotiated credits. For example, we learned recently of a manufacturer who insisted that he could finance his working capital needs for the manufacture of parachutes under a government contract on an investment of his own funds of only $17 for each $1,000 of annual sales. Making this possible was the combination of generous credit from suppliers, a simple and fast production operation, and fast collection from the government.

Trade credit is a particularly important source of funds for smaller companies. Many financially weak small firms that find it difficult to negotiate loans from banks or other institutional lenders are able to qualify for trade credit. The importance of trade credit to smaller firms is evidenced by available data on manufacturing concerns. On September 30, 1960, manufacturing firms with assets under $1 million enjoyed trade credit amounting to 19.2 per cent of their total assets. In contrast, manufacturers with assets over $1 bil-

---

[1] Federal Trade Commission and Securities and Exchange Commission, *Quarterly Financial Report for Manufacturing Corporations: Third Quarter, 1960* (Washington, D.C.: U.S. Government Printing Office, 1960).

lion relied on trade credit to the extent of only 6.1 per cent of their total assets.[2]

Normal credit terms offered by many suppliers leave purchasers the option of earning a discount by paying within a certain period or of having longer credit without the discount. Very common, for example, are terms of "$2/10$, net 30"—that is, the buyer can deduct a 2 per cent discount from payments made within 10 days, or he can take 30 days to pay without discount. Using the full 30 days is quite permissible under such terms, but the buyer pays a high price for the extra 20 days of credit. By taking the extra 20 days on a $1,000 purchase under such terms, the purchaser gets the use of $980 for an extra 20 days at the cost of the discount forgone of $20. In effect, the purchaser is paying 2.04 per cent ($^{20}\!/_{980}$) for the use of the $980 for 20 days, or one eighteenth of a year. In terms of annual interest, the cost of continued loss of the discount is almost 37 per cent (2.04 per cent times 18).

Some suppliers let their terms be regarded as somewhat nominal, taking no action to speed collection until payments become well overdue. If the supplier's terms were nominally $2/10$, net 30, but he actually permitted payment in 60 days, the buyer then gets credit for 50 extra days, or $^{50}\!/_{365}$ths of a year, bringing the cost of discounts forgone in terms of annual rates down to 14.8 per cent. Failure to take discounts is still expensive, even when nominal terms are stretched considerably.

Firms which are short of funds find it tempting to "lean on their suppliers" by delaying payment of trade debt well beyond due dates. Where loss of discounts is not involved, the extra credit taken at the expense of suppliers appears to be "cost-free" credit. Further, suppliers are likely to be the most indulgent of the firm's creditors, particularly if they are well financed and are earning a good profit on the sales to the firm. Some managers have become masterful tacticians in stretching their trade credit to a point just short of the breaking point. Tactics used in making full use—or perhaps we should say "abuse"—of trade credit include "selective payment" of trade debts, which is a euphemism for testing and taking full advantage of the limits of indulgence of each major creditor, concentration of purchases with the most lenient suppliers, and periodic cleanup of overdue accounts on a rotating basis as a means of reducing pressures

---

[2] *Ibid.*

from suppliers. Many firms have been able to stay in business only through continuous heavy use of trade credit over many years.

As a general rule, taking of cash discounts wherever available, and prompt payment of trade debt when due, represent sound long-run business and financial practice. Not taking discounts is expensive. Too, as we indicated, the network of exchange of credit information is sufficiently well organized and extensive in this country that the payment record of firms becomes a matter of widespread knowledge. A record of promptly meeting all its obligations adds much to the general reputation of the firm. Further, the way the firm handles its obligations to trade creditors will have an impact on its ability to get credit from banks and other lenders. Also, in a sellers' market, where demand pushes hard on supply, "slow-pay" customers may find themselves at a real disadvantage in competing for scarce supplies. In the long run, the tangible and intangible benefits flowing from a record of prompt payment of trade obligations are impressive.

Analyzing Changes in Trade Payables

It should be apparent from the foregoing discussion that the three major determinants of the size of the accounts or notes payable are the terms offered by suppliers, the payment practices of the firm, and the volume of purchases. In most concerns the terms offered by suppliers and the firm's policy as to payment of trade debt do not change frequently. Consequently, the major element back of most changes in the level of trade payables is variation in the volume of recent purchases.

Outside analysts are often anxious, however, to detect any evidences of shifts in policy or practice toward "slow pay." Yet, increases in accounts payable in themselves do not suggest "slow pay"—instead, as indicated above, they are more likely the result simply of a larger volume of purchases. Consequently, analysts typically seek to determine whether changes in the amount of payables outstanding are in line with changes in the volume of purchases. The methods by which payables are compared to purchases are similar to those by which receivables are compared to sales, as are the problems of interpreting the results of the comparison. One method of comparison is to express payables as a simple percentage of recent or annual purchases. A second is to convert outstanding payables into a figure of "days' purchases outstanding." As was the case in computing "days' sales outstanding," a single day's purchases are computed and divided into the outstanding payables. A third method of comparing purchases and payables is to compute the "turnover" of payables by dividing the payables, either year end or average of beginning and ending payables, into total purchases for the period.

Each of the purchases/payables ratios should, when compared with similar ratios for earlier periods and with terms of purchase common for the type of goods purchased, bring to light tendencies toward slowing up or speeding up in payment. Of course, as was true of receivable/sales comparisons, it is most desirable to use *recent* purchase figures wherever they are available, since fluctuations in the level of purchases within an annual period will distort a comparison of annual purchases with the payables at the end of the year which relate to relatively recent purchases only.[3]

Analysts particularly interested in the condition of a firm's accounts payable sometime require an aging schedule of the payables. This schedule simply breaks down the payables according to the time they have been outstanding. An aging schedule serves to bring to light the existence and extent of overdue accounts.

In forecasting cash outflows of a concern, the dates when payments for purchases are due, rather than the dates of purchase themselves, are of key concern. Consequently, in planning cash outflows arising out of purchases, it is necessary to prepare a schedule of purchases and then, using time lags appropriate to the customary terms of purchase, to construct a schedule of required payments of trade payables.

ACCRUED EXPENSES

The typical concern is supplied with many services on a continuing basis with the suppliers of such services not expecting payment immediately upon rendering the service. For example, it is common practice in many businesses to pay the labor force weekly, clerical and supervisory personnel biweekly, and executive personnel monthly. In the accounting sense, an expense is created when the services are rendered. But since payment is not made at once, a liability is created, usually termed an *accrued expense*. In effect, the company is getting some credit from the wage earner and other suppliers of services. A related source of funds of some significance to important

---

[3] In many cases, no data on purchases may be available to the outside analyst. In such cases, an analyst with some knowledge of the industry may be able to estimate the annual purchases from cost of sales and annual inventory figures. Assuming a constant rate of purchases, a highly approximate but possibly useful appraisal of the condition of the payables can be made.

employers stems from established patterns of payment to the federal government of old-age benefit and income taxes which employers must withhold from employees' pay. Employers have until the fifteenth of the month following the month in which these taxes are withheld to deposit them in an authorized bank. Effectively, the employer has the use of these funds for an average of one month. In the aggregate, the credit represented by accrued expenses is of some significance. On September 30, 1960, all United States manufacturers reported "other current liabilities," which were chiefly accrued expenses, of $12.4 billion, or 4.9 per cent of their total assets.[4]

Normally, there is little opportunity to postpone the outlays connected with accrued expenses. Thus, the volume of accruals tends to vary with the level of operations. However, if wages and salaries are a major item, the size of accrued expenses shown on the balance sheet will be affected by the date on which employees are paid in comparison with the date on which the balance sheet is computed. Just after payday, the amount will be small.

ACCRUED INCOME TAXES

Under our tax laws, corporations operating at a profit are required to share such profits with the federal government and in many cases with state governments. Thus, every time profits are computed, a liability to the government for its share of the profits should be recognized. In accounting for federal income taxation, the claim of the government to a portion of accruing profits is usually recognized each time profits are calculated by adding an appropriate amount to a liability account variously termed Accrued Income Taxes, Reserve for Income Taxes, or Provision for Income Taxes. Although the government lays claim to a percentage of the profits as they are made, it does not require payment of the taxes due until well after the time the profits are earned and the liability for taxes is created. As long as a company is making profits and thus incurring an income tax liability, then, it will have a liability to the government for taxes. As new tax obligations are recognized, these add to the liability, while periodic payments to the government to extinguish old tax debts reduce the total tax liability. Thus, we have the somewhat strange circumstance in which the government continues as a major creditor of profitable corporations and the liability to the government represents, in effect, a continuing "source" of funds.

---

[4] Federal Trade Commission and Securities and Exchange Commission, *op. cit.*

Until 1951 the time lag between receipt of income and required payment of taxes approximated one year. The Revenue Acts of 1950 and 1954 provided for progressive cuts in the time lag in payments so as to move corporations closer to a "pay as you go" basis. Since 1959, corporations with an annual tax liability of less than $100,000 have been required to pay the taxes due on the income of a particular year in equal instalments on March 15 and June 15 of the following year. Estimated tax liability in excess of $100,000 must be paid as follows: 25 per cent of the estimated tax due in excess of $100,000 must be paid by September of the year earned, 25 per cent of the estimated tax by December 15. The remaining unpaid taxes on the year's earnings must be paid in equal amounts by March 15 and June 15 of the following year. Thus, a corporation with steady earnings and total income tax liability of $1 million a year typically accrues taxes and makes payments as follows:

Date	Taxes Paid in Quarter	Taxes Accrued in Quarter	Balance of Accrued Taxes
June 15, 1960...............			$500,000
September 15, 1960..........	$225,000	$250,000	525,000
December 15, 1960...........	225,000	250,000	550,000
March 15, 1961.............	275,000	250,000	525,000
June 15, 1961...............	275,000	250,000	500,000
September 15, 1961..........	225,000	250,000	525,000
December 15, 1961...........	225,000	250,000	550,000

Unless the tax laws are changed, the payment pattern in following years will be the same. As can be seen, the lag between receipt of income and payment on taxes due on that income will be at least six months. Thus, the corporation with continuing profits can anticipate a large, uneven but continuing liability for accrued U.S. income taxes. This is, in effect, a spontaneous source of funds for profitable corporations. The liability for accrued federal income taxes of all U.S. manufacturing corporations amounted to $9.4 billion, or 3.7 per cent of their total assets, on September 30, 1960.[5]

So far, we have assumed that the corporation continues to make profits and to accrue a liability for new taxes during the year. What happens if a profitable concern ceases to be profitable and just breaks even? Clearly, it must pay off its liability for back taxes on schedule. But it is not adding to the Accrued Income Taxes account, since it is making no profits. The "spontaneous" source that it enjoyed while

---

[5] *Ibid.*

profitable disappears. So it not only loses the inflow of funds from net profits after taxes but must pay off its liability for back taxes. The squeeze on funds from a shift from profitable to break-even operations is thus a "double-barreled" one, as many concerns have learned to their sorrow.

If losses are realized, partially compensating relief may be obtained through application for refunds of taxes paid in earlier profitable years. Operating losses may be carried back three years, or forward for five years. If carried back, the losses reduce the taxable income of the previous year and the taxes due on that income. Provision is made for rapid processing of claims for the difference between the taxes actually paid and the taxes due on the income of the earlier year remaining after deduction of the loss carried back. Of course, the tax refund will in no case exceed 52 per cent of the losses suffered.

In planning cash outflows of corporations related to income taxation, the significant dates are the dates when tax payment must be made. The federal government is not an indulgent creditor, and it is wise to make the required payments strictly on schedule.

In the case of concerns organized as individual proprietorships or as partnerships, the business enterprise in the eyes of the law and of tax regulations normally has no entity apart from that of the proprietor or the partner-owners. Consequently, such businesses incur no income tax liability on their income. Instead, the individual owners are expected to report their share of the business earnings in their personal tax returns and to pay taxes on this income at the rates of personal income taxation applying to their income. Therefore, the income statements and balance sheets of individual proprietorships and partnerships make no provision for income tax obligations.

Under a relatively recent change in U.S. tax law, businesses operated as individual proprietorships or partnerships may, if a variety of conditions are met, elect to be taxed as if they were corporations.[6] The number desiring and qualifying for such distinctive treatment has not been large.

---

[6] See Internal Revenue Code, 1954, Sec. 1361.

PART III

Analysis of Past Financing and Future Funds Needs

Chapter 8

Interpreting Financial Statements

THE five-year-old who has not yet added reading to his growing skills must call on someone else to convert the symbols on the printed page, so meaningless to him, into his favorite story. To the neophyte, the figures in balance sheets and income statements may be almost as much of a jumble as is the printed page to the nonreader. But to the analyst, skilled in drawing out their meaning, the financial statements can tell a rich story of what has happened in a business in terms of its financial operation and condition.

In the business world, effort is devoted to financial analysis not only by internal management but by "outsiders" such as trade creditors, bank lenders, bond investors, and shareholders. The objectives of the analyst shape the focus of his analysis. The security analyst considering a purchase of common stock, after a quick check to make sure that finances are not strained, tends to center his efforts in gaining clues as to the future profitability of the subject company. The trade creditor is much more concerned with the short-term ability of the company to meet its maturing debts and with aspects of the financial situation bearing directly on this.

The amount of time and effort devoted to analysis of a particular situation also varies with the objectives of the analyst. Bankers considering a large loan to a customer for the first time will devote a great deal more time and care to their analysis than will the trade creditor in his annual review of the data on a small, satisfactory customer.

The nature of the analysis and the degree of conclusiveness of the results depend much on the amount and quality of the data available. Trade creditors in routine seldom are furnished more than summary financial statements, supplemented modestly by credit agency reports. The individual investor usually has little more than the financial information published in the annual report or in a prospectus.

127

EXHIBIT 8–1

cenco *Instruments*

CONSOLIDATED BALANCE

ASSETS	1960	1959
Current assets:		
Cash	$ 773,206	$ 1,270,806
Government securities, at cost which approximates market	—	407,477
Accounts receivable, less allowance (1960, $56,500; 1959, $35,000) for doubtful accounts	3,699,515	1,958,945
Inventories, at the lower of cost (average or first-in, first-out) or market:		
Finished and resale merchandise	4,029,140	3,300,921
Work in process and parts	946,858	775,866
Raw materials and supplies	563,920	315,643
Goods in transit	237,712	175,320
	5,777,630	4,567,750
Total current assets	10,250,351	8,204,978
Property and equipment, at cost:		
Land	71,977	71,977
Buildings	417,901	417,901
Machinery, equipment, and office furniture and fixtures	1,267,223	1,157,120
	1,757,101	1,646,998
Less allowance for depreciation	985,028	903,382
Total property and equipment, net . . .	772,073	743,616
Other assets:		
Prepaid expenses and deferred charges	104,287	114,274
Investment in and receivables from foreign subsidiaries, not consolidated	250,559	56,383
Excess of cost of investment in subsidiaries over net tangible assets acquired	616,406	128,604
Other assets	19,260	1
Total other assets	990,512	299,262
	$12,012,936	$ 9,247,856

See accompanying notes to financial statements.

CORPORATION *and subsidiaries*

SHEET *April 30, 1960 with comparative figures for 1959*

LIABILITIES	1960	1959
Current liabilities:		
Notes payable to bank . . . . $	500,000	—
Accounts payable	872,916	488,002
Accrued expenses	650,016	449,533
United States and Canadian taxes on income	999,456	500,616
Total current liabilities	3,022,388	1,438,151

Long-term debt:

	1960	1959
Fifteen-year 5⅛% notes of Central Scientific Co., payable in annual installments of $100,000, 1961 to 1963; $125,000, 1964 to 1968; $175,000, 1969 to 1972; and $425,000, 1973.	2,050,000	2,150,000

Stockholders' equity:

	1960	1959
Capital stock of $1 par value. Authorized 2,500,000 shares; outstanding: 1,033,504 shares in 1960; 1,013,479 shares in 1959	1,033,504	1,013,479
Capital in excess of par value (note 4)	1,967,428	1,565,482
Retained earnings (note 2)	3,939,616	3,080,744
Total stockholders' equity	6,940,548	5,659,705

	1960	1959
	$12,012,936	$ 9,247,856

In contrast, the commercial banker considering a large loan is usually in a position to get from the company a great deal of additional information, such as breakdowns of inventory and aging schedules of receivables and payables, sales and production plans, product-line profitability estimates, and the like.

If a thorough analysis is desired and the full data needed are not available, or if the suspicion exists that the firm involved is trying to hide or confuse its real situation, the financial analyst must be a virtual detective in order to ferret out the full facts and piece together the story they tell.

In Exhibits 8–1, 8–2, and 8–3, we reproduce the financial statements and president's report to stockholders of Cenco Instruments Corporation as presented in its 1960 annual report to stockholders. Cenco manufactures scientific instruments for sale to industry and to educational institutions as aids in the teaching of science subjects. The financial data presented in its annual report are typical of those made available in routine to stockholders, trade creditors, and the public.

Those interested in Cenco's progress during the year can make some significant observations from a quick scanning of the financial data. Readily apparent, for example, is the sizable increase in sales and in net profits. But the person who is equipped with basic techniques of financial analysis can use these to shape up a much more meaningful picture of Cenco's financing. With these tools, he can make clearer the changes in Cenco's financial needs during the year and how they were met. He can also get a much clearer picture of Cenco's financial position at year end and how it changed during the year. In short, he can shape the data into a story of what happened.

Let us use the Cenco data as an illustration of the application of techniques of analysis and see what kind of a story we can put together. In so doing, we should be alert to the limitations of our data and to the danger of drawing unwarranted conclusions from our analysis. We must recognize that management, with its knowledge of the business and its access to full financial details, can make a much more complete analysis and draw value judgments from it with much keener insight and confidence than can we, working only from summary financial information.

SOURCE AND USE OF FUNDS ANALYSIS

What were Cenco's needs for funds during the year? How did management move to meet these needs? To shape answers to these

EXHIBIT 8–2

cenco *Instruments* CORPORATION *and subsidiaries*

CONSOLIDATED STATEMENT OF EARNINGS AND RETAINED EARNINGS

Year ended April 30, 1960 with comparative figures for 1959

	1960	1959
Net sales	$21,107,533	$15,032,904
Cost of sales	13,545,966	9,691,891
Gross profit	7,561,567	5,341,013
Operating expenses	4,958,728	3,753,720
Operating profit	2,602,839	1,587,293
Other charges, net	70,138	53,145
Earnings before taxes on income	2,532,701	1,534,148
United States and Canadian taxes on income	1,364,000	805,000
Net earnings for the year	1,168,701	729,148
Retained earnings at beginning of year	3,080,744	2,654,887
	4,249,445	3,384,035
Dividends paid—30c a share	309,829	303,291
Retained earnings at end of year	$ 3,939,616	3,080,744

Depreciation expense included in the above statement amounted to $192,061 for 1960 and $159,908 for 1959.

See accompanying notes to financial statements.

basic queries about its financial management, we can usefully apply source and use of funds analysis, also termed *funds flow analysis*.

By *funds*, we mean money or other means of payment. For example, an increase in inventory absorbs or uses funds. If the increase in

EXHIBIT 8-2—*Continued*

Notes to Financial Statements

April 30, 1960

(1) The consolidated financial statements include the accounts of all subsidiaries operating in the United States and Canada.

(2) The loan agreement relating to the 5½% fifteen-year notes provides, among other things, for certain restrictions upon the payment of dividends. At April 30, 1960 consolidated retained earnings amounting to approximately $2,135,000 were free from these restrictions.

(3) Under the terms of a restricted stock option plan approved by the stockholders in 1951 options on 2,025 shares were exercised during the year at a price of $12.825 a share. Options to purchase 10,000 shares at a price of $21.375 a share were granted during the year in connection with the acquisition of a subsidiary company.

At April 30, 1960 there remained 56,975 shares under option at option prices of $12.825 and $21.375 a share, of which 20,000 shares are exercisable during the year ending April 30, 1961. At April 30, 1960, 15,000 shares were reserved for the grant of further options under the plan.

(4) The increase of $401,946 in capital in excess of par value represents the excess of market value at date of issuance over par value of shares issued during the year, of which $23,946 was in connection with stock options and $378,000 was in connection with the acquisition of a subsidiary.

(5) The company's subsidiaries are obligated under long-term property leases expiring in 1968, 1976, and 1980 for which the aggregate annual rentals are approximately $93,000.

ACCOUNTANTS' REPORT

PEAT, MARWICK, MITCHELL & CO.

CERTIFIED PUBLIC ACCOUNTANTS

10 SOUTH LA SALLE STREET

CHICAGO 3, ILL.

The Board of Directors
   Cenco Instruments Corporation:

   We have examined the consolidated balance sheet of Cenco Instruments Corporation and subsidiaries as of April 30, 1960 and the related consolidated statement of earnings and retained earnings for the year then ended. Our examination was made in accordance with generally accepted auditing standards, and accordingly included such tests of the accounting records and such other auditing procedures as we considered necessary in the circumstances.

   In our opinion, the accompanying consolidated balance sheet and consolidated statement of earnings and retained earnings present fairly the financial position of Cenco Instruments Corporation and subsidiaries at April 30, 1960 and the results of their operations for the year then ended, in conformity with generally accepted accounting principles applied on a basis consistent with that of the preceding year.

Peat, Marwick, Mitchell & Co.

Chicago, Illinois
June 9, 1960

inventory was financed by an increase in accounts payable, a need for funds was met not with money outflow but with credit. The increase in a liability, accounts payable, served as a source of funds. Source and use of funds analysis is built around a statement of

EXHIBIT 8–3

President's Report to Stockholders:

April 30, 1960 nears the completion of the first five-year reconstruction plan of your company, and the fifth year of consecutive increases in sales and earnings. We finished the year with better than a 40% increase in our volume and a 60% increase in our after tax earnings.

April 30, 1960 showed a record volume for the year of $21,107,533 compared with $15,032,094 the previous year. Earnings advanced from last year's $1,534,148 to $2,532,701 before taxes, or $1,168,701 after taxes, compared with last year's $729,148. The per share earnings this year mounted to $1.13 from last year's 72c. The percentage of net profits on our volume increased to 5.5 as against last year's 4.8 and 2.8 five years ago. Our educational business showed the largest increase over last year, but the industrial division, too, showed a substantial gain.

Much of our growth was attributable to the new proprietary items we brought to market this year. As illustrated in another portion of this Annual Report, Cenco begins the 1961 fiscal year with 35 additional new products developed by our own and our research affiliates.

On the manufacturing side we are on constant vigil to improve efficiency in production and the utilization of the most advanced methods of operation.

To take advantage of increased leverage to our shareholders during this period of growth, your management intends to augment its finances in the near future by the issuance of $5,000,000 in convertible debentures.

An acquisition division has been established and is examining a number of situations that fit into our over-all picture. We are particularly on the alert for the more sophisticated scientific companies available. Naturally, acquisitions will only be made where an attractive deal can be consummated for their inclusion in the Cenco family.

June 2nd will mark the formal opening of our new Breda, Holland plant. After only two months of manufacturing operation, Cenco Instrumenten Maatschappij N.V. is already in the black, and is definitely an active participant in the European Common Market.

Our country has come to realize that it has as much to fear from technological warfare as from missiles, hydrogen and atomic bombs. To help with the war of technology, your company has dedicated itself to the development and the production of the finest educational and scientific research instruments and equipment that the world has to offer. Cenco's technical men are on the alert everywhere for any and every new development that can help us in this monumental effort.

We wish to take this opportunity to again express our gratitude to our management and to our loyal working force, whose efforts and support are speedily molding our dreams into a reality.

John J. Gorrecht
Chairman of the Board

Alfred A. Stielin
President

funds flow in the business for a period. The first step in preparing this statement is the calculation of the net changes in the various asset, liability, and net worth accounts from one balance sheet date to another. The net changes in the accounts are then sorted out according to whether they represent a source or a use of funds. Listed in the *use* column are:

Increases in assets (for example, an increase in inventory)
Decreases in liabilities (e.g., payment of a bank loan)
Decreases in net worth (e.g., payment of dividends)

Conversely, the following changes provide funds and hence are *sources:*

Decreases in assets (such as reduction of inventory)
Increases in liabilities (such as increases in accounts payable)
Increases in net worth (such as from sale of common stock)

Using this approach, let us list the changes in the various Cenco accounts in its 1960 fiscal year:

USES OF FUNDS

In Thousands

Increases in assets:

Increase in accounts receivable, net..............		$1,741
Increase in inventories:		
Finished and resale merchandise................	$728	
Work in process and parts....................	171	
Raw materials and supplies...................	248	
Goods in transit............................	63	
		1,210
Increase in machinery, etc......................		110
Increase in investment in and receivables from foreign subsidiaries, not consolidated........		194
Increase in excess of cost of investment in subsidiaries over net tangible assets acquired....		488
Increase in other assets.........................		19

Decreases in liabilities:

Decrease in long-term debt......................		100
Total Uses...............................		$3,862

SOURCES OF FUNDS

Decreases in assets:

Decrease in cash...............................	$ 498
Decrease in government securities................	407
Decrease in prepaid expenses and deferred charges....................................	10

Increases in liabilities:

Increase in notes payable to bank................	500
Increase in accounts payable.....................	385
Increase in accrued expenses....................	200
Increase in accrued U.S. and Canadian income taxes.....................................	499
Increase in allowance for-depreciation............	82

Increases in net worth:

Increase in capital stock.........................	20
Increase in capital in excess of par value.........	402
Increase in retained earnings....................	859
Total Sources..............................	$3,862

The above classification of net balance sheet changes can be made more meaningful if we take advantage of information furnished by the income statement. We noted above that an increase in retained earnings provided $859,000. The income statement shows that the $859,000 is a net figure; net earnings after taxes were the source of $1,169,000, while $310,000 was used to pay dividends to the common stockholders. Surely, these flows are material, and the fund-flow statement is made more useful if we show the net earnings as a source and the dividend payments as a use of funds in place of the figure for the net increase in retained earnings.

Our treatment of the use of funds for "machinery, equipment, and office furniture and fixtures" has also been unnecessarily cursory. We have shown as a source only the net increase of $82,-000 in the Allowance for Depreciation account. Yet, from the income data, we note that depreciation charges were $192,000; and as was explained in Chapter 6, this amount can be regarded as a cash inflow from operations. Consequently, we can replace the $82,000 net increase figure in the source column with the $192,000 figure.

But this throws the source and use statement out of balance and raises the question why the allowance for depreciation balance increased only $82,000 when $192,000 was added or credited to that account during the year. Clearly, there must have been charges of $110,000 ($192,000 minus $82,000) to this account.[1] Such charges occur when items of equipment are sold or scrapped; at that time the amount of depreciation accumulated against the equipment disposed of is removed from the depreciation reserve. And of course, the original cost of the equipment is removed from the machinery account. Thus, the $110,000 was not the full amount of funds expended on new equipment, but a net figure after credit of an additional $110,000 for equipment disposed of.

Thus, we can add $110,000 to the $110,000 and show $220,000 as funds used to buy equipment.

Perhaps this will be clearer, at least for students familiar with accounting, if expressed in "T-accounts."

Allowance for Depreciation

Balancing figure presumed to represent cost of equipment disposed of	110	Balance, end of 1959	903
		Depreciation in 1960	192
			1,095
			110
	110	Balance, end of 1960	985

[1] Note that conceptually this $110,000 is different from the $110,000 increase in machinery, etc., shown as a use of funds in the tabulation above.

Machinery, Equipment, and Office Furniture and Fixtures

Beginning balance	1,157	Equipment presumably disposed	
Balancing figure for cost of new		of	110
equipment acquisitions	220		
	1,377		
	110		
Ending balance	1,267		110

Our statement of sources and uses now appears as follows:

USES OF FUNDS

In Thousands

Increases in assets:

Increase in accounts receivable, net		$1,741
Increase in inventories:		
Finished and resale merchandise	$728	
Work in process and parts	171	
Raw materials and supplies	248	
Goods in transit	63	1,210
~~Increase in machinery~~		~~110~~
Acquisition of machinery, etc.		220
Increase in investment in and receivables from		
foreign subsidiaries, not consolidated		194
Increase in excess of cost of investment in subsidiaries		
over net tangible assets acquired		488
Increase in other assets		19

Decreases in liabilities:

Decrease in long-term debt		100

Decreases in net worth:

Dividends paid		310
Total Uses		$4,282

SOURCES OF FUNDS

Decreases in assets:

Decrease in cash		$ 498
Decrease in government securities		407
Decrease in prepaid expenses and deferred charges		10

Increases in liabilities:

Increase in notes payable to bank		500
Increase in accounts payable		385
Increase in accrued expenses		200
Increase in accrued U.S. and Canadian income		
taxes		499
~~Increase in allowance for depreciation~~		~~82~~
Depreciation charged without outlay		192

Increases in net worth:

Increase in capital stock		20
Increase in capital in excess of par value		402
~~Increase in retained earnings~~		~~859~~
Net earnings from operations		1,169
Total Sources		$4,282

Now, we can draw on our funds flow analysis to summarize Cenco's financing in the year. Would the paragraphs below fairly tell the story?

During 1960, Cenco experienced a major need for funds to match sharp increases in receivables and in all types of inventories, apparently related to the big increase in sales. Acquisition of a domestic subsidiary was financed through exchange of a small number of newly issued common shares, but a modest investment in a foreign subsidiary contributed to the need for other funds. No new plant facilities were acquired; and the moderate outlays for machinery, equipment, and office furniture and fixtures were almost matched by operational inflows related to depreciation.

A variety of sources was drawn on to finance the expansion of receivables and inventories. The substantial net income, largely retained, met almost one third of that need. The combined increases in the spontaneous liabilities, particularly the large tax accrual related to the higher earnings, were an almost equally important source. Management also utilized the funds invested in U.S. securities and drew down cash by more than one third. Despite these moves, external funds were needed, and $500,000 was raised through short-term bank borrowing. That management anticipated further and continuing need for external funds in the future was evidenced by the president's announcement of plans to sell a large issue of convertible debentures.

But our opportunities for possibly useful analysis of Cenco's financial data have by no means been exhausted by our review of funds flow management. We have done little to probe profits beyond noting their increase and the funds they have provided. Remaining unanswered are such relevant queries as: Was the profits increase due solely to higher volume of sales, or were margins increased? Did management succeed in getting a higher gross margin over cost of goods sold? Did operating expenses increase in line with sales? How was profit return relative to total assets? To owners' investment? Nor have we explored the big increases in receivables and inventory to see whether they were in line with sales increases. Beyond noting the pulldown of liquid assets, we have not looked into the financial condition of the company as revealed by the latest balance sheet. Nor have we devoted attention to the developing capital structure of the firm and the extent to which it is relying on the use of debt relative to ownership funds. Exploitation of the opportunities for further analysis can be aided by purposeful ratio analysis.

But before we turn to a discussion of ratios and their application to the Cenco data, some further general comments on funds flow analysis are appropriate.

Professional accountants making up source and use of funds statements for clients where full facts are available often undertake further refinement of the statement to remove from the tabulation any transactions which were merely "paper transactions" not actually involving any flows of funds. Thus, if Cenco were found to have increased the asset values for balance sheet purposes simply by writing up the values of existing plant by $1 million with a corresponding increase to capital surplus, deductions of $1 million would be made from both the source and the use side so as to keep the flow of funds statement "pure." Seldom does the outside analyst have enough information on transactions of this sort to attempt such refinements in the source and use of funds statements he constructs.

The reader should appreciate the fact that the source and use of funds statement, as we have constructed it, and as it is generally prepared, does not attempt to picture all flows of funds through a business during the period. Note that from the operating statement, we picked up only *net* profits and the noncash expense depreciation. Left off the source side were the remainder of the sales dollars received, and the cash expenses paid during the year do not show up on the use side. Many other transactions within the year are not shown. For example, Cenco might have borrowed from banks for short periods and repaid the loans several times during the year; these intraperiod flows would not show up in our statement, which deals primarily with *net* changes during the year.

While it is more thorough to bring all known flows during the period into the source and use statement, in practice such statements seldom show more than does our revised one for Cenco. The source and use statement is often put together in somewhat different form, though with essentially the same information.

THE USE OF RATIOS IN FINANCIAL ANALYSIS

Ratios, discriminately calculated and wisely interpreted, can be useful tools of financial analysis. Ratios are simply a means of highlighting in arithmetical terms the relationships between figures drawn from financial statements. A great number of ratios can be computed from the basic financial statements—for example, the relationship of Cenco's accrued expenses to its net investment in fixed assets can be readily calculated as 84.2 per cent (650/772). But does this relationship have any significance? None is apparent, so that the 84.2 per cent figure is meaningless and its calculation distracting.

Ratios will be meaningful and useful, then, only to the extent that significant relationships exist between the figures selected for comparison through ratios. And as we earlier pointed out, the viewpoint and particular interests of the analyst will make some relationships of especial interest to him. The more commonly used ratios fall into one of three generic groupings according to their use. These main groups or families of ratios are:

1. Measures of profitability
2. Measures of asset use
3. Measures of financial condition

Let us identify and discuss these ratios in the practical context of their use in the analysis of the Cenco data.

Ratios in the Measurement and Analysis of Profitability

Sales and Profit Comparisons. The absolute figures for profit take on more meaning when compared to sales. Widely used as a measure of profitability is the percentage ratio of net income after taxes to net sales—or to total income if income from sources other than sales is material. In Cenco, the 1960 net profit after taxes on sales was 5.54 per cent, calculated as follows:

$$\frac{\text{Net Income after Taxes}}{\text{Net Sales}} = \frac{1,169}{21,108} = 5.54\%.$$

The corresponding ratio for 1959 was 4.85 per cent. Thus, it is apparent that Cenco's increased profits in 1960 were not solely the result of higher sales but were attributable also to success in taking down into net profit a higher percentage of total revenues from sales.

Since the burden of income taxation can vary from year to year, operational results often are measured in terms of net income before taxes compared to sales. In Cenco, net profit before taxes was 12 per cent of sales, up from 10.2 per cent in 1959.

Sales and Expense Ratios. Management and those outside analysts particularly interested in profit performance and the control of expenses compute many expense/sales ratios. Outside analysts, who commonly have no breakdowns of expenses beyond the summary ones presented in published income statements, make frequent use of "100 per cent statements"—that is, convert each of the expense and profit items in the income statement into percentages of net sales. The Cenco income statement, in percentages, appears on page 140.

The percentage statement makes it apparent that Cenco's higher net profit percentage in 1960 is due in part to an increased gross profit or *gross margin* percentage, but more importantly to control

	1960	*1959*
Net sales.................................	100.00%	100.00%
Cost of sales.............................	64.18	64.47
Gross profit...........................	35.82%	35.53%
Operating expenses.......................	23.49	24.97
Operating profit.......................	12.33%	10.56%
Other charges, net.......................	0.33	0.36
Earnings before taxes on income...........	12.00%	10.20%
Income taxes.............................	6.46	5.35
Net Income after Taxes..................	5.54%	4.85%

of operating expenses so that they did not increase so fast as sales. These favorable factors more than offset an increased tax burden. With its more complete information about various expense items, management can make a similar but much more detailed expense/profit analysis.

Profits Compared to Assets

Readers should already be familiar with rate-of-profit-return ratios, two of which are particularly important as gauges of profitability which take into account the resources employed in generating the profits. The first of these compares after-tax profits with total assets. Thus, Cenco's 1960 profit-on-assets ratio is found to be 9.73 per cent:

$$\frac{\text{Net Profit after Taxes}}{\text{Total Assets, Year End}} = \frac{1,169}{12,013} = 9.73\%.$$

We can come to the same rate-of-return figure through use of return-on-sales and asset turnover figures, as described in Chapter 1.

$$5.54\% \times \frac{21,107}{12,013} \text{ or } 1.757 = 9.73\%.$$

The 9.73 per cent return in 1960 compares with a return of 7.88 per cent in 1959.

An equally or more important measure of profitability is the rate of return on owners' investment. Reflecting its use of debt, Cenco's profits equaled 16.84 per cent of the year-end stockholders' investment (1,169/6,941) compared with 12.88 per cent in 1959.

A refinement of the rate-of-return ratios uses average rather than year-end asset or owners' investment figures. In a growing firm the use of average figures results in higher rates of return than those on year-end figures.

Ratios as Measures of Asset Use

In Chapter 3, we emphasized the significance of the relationship between inventories and sales, and described key ratios used to depict this relationship. We suggest that the reader review this material. Now, let us apply the ratios discussed there to Cenco. First, we can note that despite the large dollar increase, total year-end inventories as a percentage of sales fell off from 30.39 per cent of sales in 1959 to 27.37 per cent in 1960. Similar checks on each type of inventories show that each, except the minor goods in transit, increased at a rate less than that of sales.

The same relationship can be expressed in terms of turnover (sales/inventory). Since inventories are usually carried at cost, a more precise measure of physical turnover can be obtained by dividing inventories into cost of sales rather than sales. As might be expected, turnover increased from 2.12 times to 2.34 times.

In Chapter 4, we introduced some ratios useful in appraising the investment in receivables. The first of these simply expressed receivables as a percentage of sales. Cenco's receivables were 13.03 per cent of sales in 1959, 17.53 per cent in 1960. Thus, unlike inventories, receivables went up faster than sales.

The growth in receivables relative to sales is brought out, perhaps more sharply, by calculation of "days' sales outstanding," or collection period. It will be recalled that this ratio is calculated in two steps, the first being determination of an average day's sales:

$$\frac{\text{Annual Sales, 1960}}{365} = \frac{\$21,108,000}{365} = \underline{\$57,830.}$$

In the second step the average day's sales are divided into year-end receivables:

$$\frac{\text{Year-End Receivables, 1960}}{\text{Average Day's Sales}} = \frac{\$3,700,000}{\$57,830} = \underline{64 \text{ days.}}$$

The 64-day figure at the end of 1960 compares with a 47.6-day figure at the end of 1959.

The net investment in plant can also be compared with sales: Cenco's net plant investment in 1960 was only 3.66 per cent; in 1959, it was 4.95 per cent. In terms of turnover (sales/net plant), the very high rates of 27.34 times and 20.22 times call attention to the high volume of sales achieved by Cenco on its very limited fixed asset investment. Partial explanations are suggested in the note that subsidiaries lease property and in the fact that the finished goods inventory is labeled "finished goods and *resale merchandise*"—apparently, some of Cenco's sales are of products made for it by other firms. Yet, the question raised by the ratios as to how Cenco can achieve such high sales relative to plant investment remains one that the analyst anxious to understand fully Cenco's operation will want to investigate further.

Ratios as Measures of Financial Condition

Liquidity Ratios. Several ratios are used as measures of liquidity—that is, they are concerned with short-term obligations and the assets that are more readily convertible into the means of payment. Outside analysts who lack detailed data about the anticipated cash flows of the business use the liquidity ratios as rough indices of the likely ability of the subject firm to meet its near-term obligations, or of possible need to raise additional funds through borrowing or stock issues.

Perhaps the most widely used of any ratio is the *current ratio,* which is simply the current assets divided by the current liabilities. Using Cenco's figures, we find the following:

$$\frac{\text{Current Assets, Year End, 1960}}{\text{Current Liabilities, Year End, 1960}} = \frac{10,250}{3,022} = \underline{\underline{3.39}}.$$

The 1960 ratio of 3.39 compares with that of 5.71 a year earlier. The strength of Cenco's current ratio, despite the decline during 1960, reflects the predominance of receivables and inventory in its asset structure and its substantial net worth and long-term debt.

Despite its wide use—which suggests that analysts think it revealing—the current ratio is at best a very crude measure of the financial health of a firm and its ability to meet its debts. An example of the limited conclusiveness of the current ratio as a measure of debt-paying ability arises out of the fact that inventory is included in current assets. Actually, the inventory may be of limited salability, particularly in the short run. Consider the situation of a manufacturer of ice skates at the end of March with the following summary balance sheet and the strong current ratio of 3 to 1:

Cash	$ 10,000	Current liabilities	$100,000
Receivables	10,000		
Inventory	280,000		
	$300,000		

This firm could still be in financial difficulty if the $100,000 of current liabilities were all due within a month, while inventory could be sold without severe loss only over a period of many months.

Recognized for what it is—a very rough and not necessarily conclusive indicator of liquidity—the current ratio can be useful in the absence of better information or as a small part of a more complete and discerning analysis. In the case of Cenco the decline in the current ratio from 1959 to 1960 does call attention to a significant decline in liquidity during the year.

The current ratio is also used by creditors as a measure of the extent that current asset values could shrink in liquidation of the firm and still be adequate for repayment of current creditors—fixed assets and long-term debts left aside. Thus, the current assets of a firm with a 4.0 current ratio could shrink to one fourth and still match the current debts.

Another widely used ratio is one called the *acid test* or the *net quick* ratio. This ratio is like the current ratio except that inventory and prepaid expenses are excluded. Using the 1960 Cenco figures, we see the following results:

$$\frac{\text{Cash, Marketable Securities, and Receivables}}{\text{Current Liabilities}} = \frac{773 + 3700}{3022} = \underline{1.48}.$$

The 1960 figure, 1.48, represents a sharp drop from that of 1959, 2.53. But it indicates that Cenco's cash and receivables, without reference to inventory, still exceed current liabilities by a large margin.

A third ratio used to assess liquidity compares cash and marketable securities to current liabilities. Reflecting the lower liquidity from the pulldown of cash, the liquidation of the investment in governments, and the increase in current liabilities, Cenco's ratio fell from 1.17 in 1959 to 0.256 in 1960. While one should not conclude that cash is unduly small, the decline in the ratio does call attention to the sharp decline in liquidity during the year.

A fourth ratio used to assess liquidity is one which compares the level of cash and near-cash accounts to average daily cash payments:

$$\frac{\text{Cash} + \text{Marketable Securities}}{\text{Average Daily Cash Payments}}.$$

Since no figures for daily outflows are available in the case of Cenco, this ratio cannot be calculated by outsiders. Here again, speaking broadly, the ratio is open to "ifs, ands, and buts." A firm with strong, little-used lines of credit with banks or other creditors can well afford to operate with a lower cash balance relative to the size of its outflows than can a firm without such "credit backstops" in reserve for use if cash stringencies develop.

In Chapter 7, we indicated the usefulness of comparing trade payables with recent purchases. Two ratios were recommended: (1) payables as a percentage of purchases during a recent period and

(2) payables expressed in terms of average day's purchases outstanding:

$$\frac{\text{Payables Outstanding}}{\text{Average Day's Purchases}}.$$

In the Cenco illustration the annual report does not give data on purchases. Management, of course, would have the necessary data for the calculations.

The Source of Funds for the Business: Comparisons of Borrowed Funds with Ownership Funds

Of much interest to many analysts is the relative use of debt and of ownership funds in the concern. A useful and simple way of depicting the extent of debt financing is to calculate the percentage of total assets provided by all creditors. As shown by the calculations below, in Cenco, debt as a percentage of total assets increased somewhat in 1960:

$$\frac{\text{Total Debts, 1960}}{\text{Total Assets, 1960}} = \frac{5,072}{12,013} = 42.22\%.$$

$$\frac{\text{Total Debts, 1959}}{\text{Total Assets, 1959}} = \frac{3,588}{9,248} = 38.8\%.$$

It is interesting to note Cenco's plans to issue $5 million of convertible debentures. If none of the $5 million were used to pay off existing debts, total debt would increase to 59.2 per cent of the expanded total assets.

Another widely used ratio for relating debt and ownership financing is the *net worth to debt* ratio. Since *net worth* means the same thing as *ownership funds*, this ratio is computed by dividing ownership funds by total debts. Using the Cenco illustration, the results for 1960 would be:

$$\frac{\text{Total Net Worth, 1960}}{\text{Total Debt, 1960}} = \frac{6,941}{5,072} = 1.37, \text{ compared with } 1.58 \text{ for 1959.}$$

In the public utility and railroad industries, debt is often shown as a percentage of *total capitalization.* This ratio is the same as the total debt/total assets ratio except that current liabilities are deducted from both denominator and numerator. Thus, the ratio becomes:

$$\frac{\text{Total Debt less Current Liabilities}}{\text{Total Assets less Current Liabilities}}.$$

Speaking generally from a creditor's viewpoint, the lower the percentage of debt financing to total assets, the better. The creditor can regard the ownership funds as representing a buffer protecting him from loss. If, for example, debt is only 20 per cent of total assets, the assets could shrink in liquidation to one fifth of the balance sheet values and still be sufficient to cover debt claims, since creditors are entitled to be paid out in full before the owners are entitled to anything. In contrast, if total debts amount to 90 per cent of total assets, a shrinkage of more than 10 per cent would leave the creditors "under water."

Of course, the amount of debt that the business can reasonably carry depends on many factors, to be discussed at length in a later chapter. A public utility with stable earnings and favorable prospects may safely finance a much larger percentage of its assets with debt than can, say, a manufacturer with a past record of erratic profitability who produces a single specialty product of uncertain long-term demand.

As we observed earlier, the conclusion that a particular ratio depicts a good or bad condition may rest with the analyst's viewpoint. One suspects that the holders of Cenco's outstanding long-term debt might well prefer a slower expansion financed predominantly by retained earnings or equity issues to faster expansion with convertible debentures which, if the company's fortunes wane, would remain unconverted as debt. Yet, to the common stockholders the convertible debentures may well represent the most feasible means of financing desirable rapid expansion.

Increasing the Usefulness of Ratio Analysis

In our analysis of Cenco, we have looked only at the balance sheets at the end of Cenco's 1959 and 1960 fiscal years and at operating results for two years. We could add depth to our analysis by extending it backward over a much longer span of years. The calculation of ratios for a span of years may bring to light important trends unapparent in analysis focused on short periods. Further, marked changes in the ratios from those characteristic of the past may signal important changes in industry conditions or in management policies deserving further investigation. Thus, data on the use of debt relative to equity financing over, say, a ten-year period would make clearer whether the rise in the debt percentages shown in 1960, and promised for 1961, was in line with a long-standing management policy of gradually expanding reliance on debt or a sharp departure from past debt policies. Similarly, the profit ratios for 1960 would take on more meaning against the background of profit ratios over a longer period. If profit ratios have bounced up and down from year to year in the past, the 1960 improvement would be much less encouraging than if it were found to be in line with a long and steady trend toward wider margins and greater sales.

It can also be helpful to compare the funds flow data and the ratios of the subject firm with those of competitors in the same industry. Many trade associations and other industry groups collect and publish data for firms in the industry, often classified by size or specialized activities within the industry. If the firms within industry groups operate along similar lines and under reasonably comparable conditions, comparison of the subject firm's ratios with industry ratios can add much to the analysis. It should be emphasized that deviations from typical industry ratios should not be judged as being undesirable per se. For example, the firm under study may show a much higher investment in receivables relative to sales than its competitors. At first thought, it might appear that the subject firm was guilty of dangerously lax credit policies. But in fact, the high ratio may be simply the reflection of a conscious management policy of competing for sales through especially liberal credit policies; and this policy might be paying off handsomely to the firm in the form of higher sales and profits, and even return on assets, than it otherwise would have achieved. In other words, deviations from "normal" may mean simply that the firm operates differently, not less effectively. Further, the ratios are drawn from the accounting data of the firm, and differences in accounting policies and practices between firms naturally limit complete comparability between their respective ratios.

In recent years the moves of many firms toward diversification into multiple-product lines that cut across traditional industry groupings has made more difficult comparison of these firms with industry indices. Indeed, a number of firms are sufficiently unique to defy close comparison with any other. However, it may still be possible for management of these concerns to make useful ratio comparisons among certain of their divisions or subsidiaries, and of these units with ratios drawn from other firms in the industries in which these units operate.

Since this discussion is already an extended one, we shall concede in our analysis of Cenco the advantages of depth of analysis that might have been gained through comparison with Cenco ratios of earlier years or with industry ratios. Let us see what we can add from our admittedly limited ratio analysis to the interpretative comments on Cenco's statements that were based only on the funds flow analysis. The reader is asked to compare the following with what he would regard as the major points from the analysis worthy of inclusion in a summary commentary. There is abundant room for differences in view as to the more significant points for comment and emphasis.

Cenco's 1960 sales increased 40.4 per cent over 1959; profits were up 60.3 per cent. The disproportionate profit increase reflected a small increase in gross margin and a larger cut in the percentage of the sales dollar consumed by operating expenses, which more than matched an increase in Cenco's effective tax rate. Though heavy inventories are carried (turnover of cost of sales was 2.34), the inventory increases were less, proportionately, than that of sales. Year-end receivables were up much more than sales, the collection period rising from 47.6 to 64 days. This might well warrant inquiry. The high (20.22 times) turnover of plant in terms of sales of 1959 was boosted further to 27.34 times. Profit return on total assets at year end increased to 9.73 per cent from 7.88 per cent, while return on shareholders' investment jumped from 12.88 per cent in 1959 to 16.84 per cent.

Reflecting the various financing moves, liquidity ratios all showed sharp declines, but the acid-test ratio at year-end 1960 still was 1.48. Liquid assets were 25.6 per cent of current liabilities, down from 117 per cent. Management increased its use of debt, as shown by an increase in the percentage of debt to total assets from 38.8 to 42.22 per cent. If none of the proceeds of the forthcoming $5 million convertible debenture issue is used to repay existing debts, the debt percentage will rise to some 59 per cent of total assets.

Actually, the above summary of the results of the ratio analysis could well be blended into the earlier comments drawn from the funds flow analysis for a more compact single statement of the results of our financial analysis.

At several points in our discussion of ratio analysis, we have counseled caution in the interpretation of ratios. Hasty or overconfident judgments as to the facts behind the ratios can prove dangerously wrong. For example, the increased collection period in Cenco *might* reflect credit or collection difficulties. But other possible interpretations may, upon inquiry, prove the real explanation. For example, public school administrative agencies are notoriously slow in processing and paying bills. A shift in the mix of total sales toward more sales to schools could well explain the change. Or it might simply be due to very heavy sales in the weeks before the fiscal year end. Ratios are mechanical tools of analysis; they never should be used standing alone as arbitrary standards of excellence. As aids to judgment, they can be helpful; as mechanical substitutes for thinking and judgment, they can be worse than useless.

Chapter 9

Forecasting Future Needs for Funds

VIRTUALLY ALL financial managers do some sort of forecasting of the future needs for cash of their business. Yet, in many firms the forecasting is so limited in scope, haphazard, based on rules of thumb of dubious reliability, or on such a short-term basis that many of the potential gains from careful, organized planning of cash needs are lost. As a practical matter, the major issue connected with cash planning in most concerns is not whether any cash planning will be attempted but rather how far the managers should go in putting their cash forecasting into organized, systematic, and careful form.

Effective forecasting of cash needs, like any kind of forward planning, calls for mental effort, co-operation of the nonfinancial executives, and time and energy. The advantages to be gained must justify the effort involved. Actually, in the typical firm the potential benefits from fully effective forecasting of cash needs can be great. The benefits include the following:

1. Pretesting of the financial feasibility of various programs before moves are made that are difficult to retract.
2. Facilitation of the raising of additional funds that may be required.
3. Increased confidence in the firm's management on the part of lenders or other sources of funds.
4. Provision of a control device or check points useful in exposing deviations from plans.
5. Improvements in utilization of funds, particularly of cash balances.

Systematic cash forecasting pushed well into the future provides the necessary data for review by top management as to the advisability of projected plans and programs in the light of their probable impact on the company's finances. In most concerns the supply of available funds is by no means unlimited, and the plans of the company must be shaped to fit the financial capabilities of the firm. Once the needs implicit in proposed programs are set forth, those programs involving undue outlays can be cut back or reshaped before embarrassing commitments are made. For example, a medium-sized manufacturing concern had expanded profitably over the years without particular cash stringencies to signal the need for careful cash planning. Rather casually, management undertook the construction of a new plant and office building, the expansion of civilian sales, and a large government manufacturing contract, all of which, it developed, called for heavy cash outlays at about the same time. Some of the needs for cash, such as the heavy cash outlays involved in moving to the new location, and the extent and timing of the other needs were not calculated or appreciated by top management. Consequently, a serious shortage of cash developed, which had to be met through hasty and improvised borrowing arrangements on highly disadvantageous terms. Very serious embarrassment was narrowly averted. To use a nautical analogy, careful cash planning would have pointed up the financial rocks and shoals ahead before the course of the business was firmly set. Further, in many cases where no major new programs calling for large cash outlays are planned, many diverse and individually small needs can combine to "sneak up" insidiously and confront management with unexpected cash stringency.

When the cash forecasts indicate that programs desirable on balance will result in the need to raise additional funds, the advance warning gives the company time to "turn around" in planning and executing programs to raise funds. Many methods of raising funds—sale of common stock, for example—normally require several months in consummation. Unanticipated cash stringencies leading to hasty "crash program" efforts to find funds often result in the company's assuming loan repayment or other commitments it subsequently finds difficult to meet.

Furthermore, advance discussion and planning of financial needs with lenders or other sources of money tend to inspire confidence that management is "on top of its problems." For example, two young men promoting a new enterprise appeared at a commercial bank to discuss prospective loan needs of their business several months in the future. With them, they brought a full outline of their plans, with schedules showing financial needs under various alternative plans of action. The banker, who was more accustomed to seeing loan applicants only after financial needs had become immediate and urgent, was impressed and offered a substantial credit.

The banker was even more impressed (and the young businessmen were almost equally surprised in view of the many variables involved) when their cash forecast for the program selected proved accurate almost to the dollar.

Cash forecasts can be valuable as a control device as well as an aid to planning. Once plans are agreed upon and programs are under way, the forecasted levels of cash can serve as check points against which actual results can be compared. Significant deviations from expected levels serve as signals that the program is not moving along as it should and hence requires top management attention and action. Alternatively, deviations may indicate that the plans were unrealistic and should be revised in the light of unforeseen or uncontrollable developments.

While cash forecasting is especially important for firms whose financial resources are limited, it can also be useful in affluent concerns by pointing up opportunities to use liquid funds more profitably. For example, in one very large, wealthy, and liquid company, only a modicum of financial planning was done prior to a postwar management reorganization. The new financial management undertook a wide range of planning activities, including cash forecasting. The cash forecasts revealed that existing cash balances were unnecessarily high. Subsequent investment of unneeded cash in income-producing securities reportedly contributed income sufficient to more than cover the costs of a wide range of valuable planning activity.

Techniques of Forecasting the Need for Funds

Two different methods of forecasting future cash needs are widely used. These are the cash flow forecast method and the projected balance sheet method. In this chapter, we shall explain the essential nature of each approach and outline for each method the basic procedures in building a forecast of cash needs. Each method will be illustrated by reference to a simple situation, but we do not wish to imply that a single format can be applied mechanically to any business situation. While the essentials of forecasting are broadly applicable, the details of the approach should be adapted to fit the distinctive needs and circumstances of the subject business. The related case problems are relied upon to help the student get a working understanding of how to apply the basic techniques to the requirements of specific business situations. It is suggested that the student use this chapter to get a basic idea of how to go about forecasting cash needs in advance of the case work on forecasting, and then as reference material in handling the cases. Finally, we suggest that the student review the chapter carefully after he has worked with the forecasting cases. Much of the generalized discussion here will have more meaning after the student has struggled with the specifics of the case problems.

The Cash Flow Forecast

The most basic and comprehensive method of predicting the amount and the time of future cash needs is through preparation of a cash flow forecast or, as it is often called, a *cash budget*. Essentially, the cash flow forecast is a tabulation of the plans of the firm in terms of their impact on the receipts and expenditures of cash in future periods. The basic theory of the cash flow forecast is simple—it seeks merely to predict when and in what quantity receipts of cash will come into the firm and when and in what quantity payments of cash will be made. It is not much of an oversimplification to think of the cash forecast as a timed prediction of additions to and deductions from the company's bank accounts.

In the cash forecast, all anticipated receipts of cash are included, regardless of whether or not they represent income in the accounting sense. Thus, included along with collection of cash from sales and receivables arising out of sales are cash receipts from such sources as sale of securities or sale of fixed assets. Similarly, the tabulation of payments should include, along with routine payments of accounts payable, wages, salaries, rents, etc., any planned payments of taxes, dividends, loan repayments, or outlays for equipment or buildings. It should *not* include expense items which do not represent outlays of cash, such as the allowance for depreciation and the allowance for bad debts.

Usually, the financial planner is interested in revealing not only the total outflow and inflow over an extended period, such as a year, but also the timing of the cash flows within this period. In most cash forecasts, receipts and payments are broken down by months. If uneven inflow and outgo are anticipated within the monthly intervals, it may be necessary to break the forecast down into weekly or even daily periods if maximum needs are to be brought to light.

Some concerns vary the time period breakdown of the cash forecast according to how far into the future the forecast is projected. One concern, for example, has a program of cash flow forecasting that extends five years ahead. Estimates for the next month are broken down by days, for the following eleven months by months, for the next twelve months by quarters, and for the ensuing three years only by annual periods. This pattern is based on two arguments, the first being that highly detailed information as to timing is needed only for short periods ahead. The second is that the accuracy of the estimating decreases markedly as the forecasts are pushed out into the future and consequently that the distant forecasts are too uncertain to justify more than general planning for the needs suggested by them.

We have described the cash flow forecast as a tabulation of the plans of the business in terms of the effect of these plans on the cash account. As such, the results of the cash flow forecast will prove only as accurate and as reliable as the underlying planning on which the forecast is based. And as we have seen in earlier chapters, virtually all of the significant activities of the firm affect its flow of funds. Thus, for complete effectiveness in his work the forecaster of cash flows needs comprehensive and accurate data on what the operations of the firm will likely be.

The task of assembling the background data for the cash flow forecast is made much easier if the firm operates under profit budgeting. Under profit budgeting, profit objectives are set for the firm, and operations are planned to produce the desired results. Revenues and expenses are forecasted in detail; and if necessary, the plans are altered so as to produce the desired end results. Some firms employing profit budgeting use the budgets exclusively as planning devices and make no effort to use the estimates as a continuing control device to force actual operations to conform to the plans. Many others go further and do attempt to control operations in such a way that the targeted profit goals actually are realized. Where the budget is used as a control as well as a planning device, provision is typically made for revision of the original targets, if unforeseen or uncontrollable factors make them inappropriate.

Where operations of the firm are closely geared to careful plans, and planning assumptions are revised to reflect changes in the outlook, it is possible for the cash forecaster to maintain cash forecasts that are much more likely to prove accurate and reliable than is possible in other firms that utilize budgets for planning alone or that attempt no formal planning, simply "playing it by ear."

Where profit budgets exist, they supply much of the background information needed for preparation of a cash flow forecast. The task of forecasting cash flows becomes one of simply translating these plans, which are stated primarily in terms of accounting income and expense, into cash flow terms, as described later in this chapter. Actually, although the use of profit budgeting is growing, most firms still do not have a carefully organized profit budget program. Yet, cash flow planning, though on a less solid footing, may still be highly useful to them. Under such circumstances, what information must the financial officer assemble, and how can he organize it into a cash flow forecast?

Probably the most critical estimate in cash flow forecasting is the forecast of sales. Usually, sales represent the primary source of cash receipts. Further, the operations of the business requiring cash outlays are typically geared to the anticipated volume of sales. Particularly closely tied to sales are the purchases of materials and outlays directly related to manufacturing. In compiling sales forecast data, the financial officer must usually rely heavily on the active co-operation of the sales department. Ideally, the sales department will provide a sales forecast in terms of both physical units and dollar value, and this will be checked and approved by top management.

Let us assume, for purposes of illustration, that the financial officer of the Able Company is preparing a six-month cash forecast beginning in January, to be broken down into monthly periods. Putting ourselves in his place, we shall assume that the best estimate of sales we can get calls for sales of $200,000 per month in the first three months, $250,000 per month for April and May, and $300,-000 in June. Ten per cent of the sales are expected to be for cash, the remainder on credit terms. On the basis of the experience of the firm, we estimate that the receivables arising out of sales will be collected approximately one month after sale. It is further estimated that the outstanding receivables on December 31 will amount to $185,000 and that these will all be collected in January. No bad debts are expected. The sales forecast now can be converted into a schedule of cash receipts from sales, expressed in thousands of dollars, as follows:

	Jan.	Feb.	March	April	May	June	Total
Total sales............	$200	$200	$200	$250	$250	$300	$1,400
Credit sales............	180	180	180	225	225	270	1,260
Receipts from collection of accounts receivable.	185	180	180	180	225	225	1,175
Cash sales.............	20	20	20	25	25	30	140
Cash receipts—sales....	$205	$200	$200	$205	$250	$255	$1,315

Note that the collection of the receivables from sales is scheduled to lag one month behind the credit sales. Thus, the $225,000 credit sales of April are shown as cash receipts of May.

Now, let us take into account any anticipated receipts from sources other than sales, such as the proceeds of sale of fixed assets or of new security issues. The only cash receipts apart from those arising from routine sales, already tabulated, which are anticipated are from the planned sale for cash of used equipment no longer required, amounting to $40,000 in April and $30,000 in June. With this information, we are ready to put together a summary schedule of forecasted cash receipts, expressed in thousands of dollars:

	Jan.	Feb.	March	April	May	June	Total
Cash receipts—sales....	$205	$200	$200	$205	$250	$255	$1,315
Proceeds from sale of used equipment..	....	....	....	40	....	30	70
Total Cash Receipts........	$205	$200	$200	$245	$250	$285	$1,385

Now, let us turn to the forecast of cash payments. As we have said, many of the operations of the company are geared to the sales forecast. It serves as the basis for the development of manufacturing schedules that will provide the products needed for sale and inventory. The production schedules indicate the timing and amount of labor, material, and additional equipment needed. On the basis of the material needs established by the production schedules, procurement officials can be expected to prepare schedules of planned purchases of materials and of equipment. A major step in building the forecast of payments is the conversion of the purchase schedules, employing appropriate assumptions as to the terms of sale that will be offered by suppliers, into a schedule of anticipated payments of the accounts payable arising out of these purchases. Any purchases for cash usually are best listed in a separate schedule.

Let us assume that the purchase schedule drawn up in the Able Company calls for purchase of materials costing $70,000 in each of the first three months and $90,000 a month thereafter. All are to be purchased on 30-day payment terms, and the accounts payable will be paid promptly when due. The company is also planning to buy two major items of equipment costing $200,000 each, one for delivery in January and the second in June. Sixty-day terms are expected on these items. In addition, routine replacement of minor equipment items of $5,000 per month is expected, also purchased on

60-day terms. Miscellaneous cash purchases of $1,000 per month are also planned. The outstanding payables together with miscellaneous accrued expenses on December 31 are estimated at $110,-000, all due in January.

With these data, we can schedule the planned purchases and, from this schedule, prepare a schedule of planned payment for purchases, expressed in thousands of dollars:

	Jan.	Feb.	March	April	May	June	Total
PLANNED PURCHASES							
Cash purchases..........	$ 1	$ 1	$ 1	$ 1	$ 1	$ 1	$ 6
Production materials.....	70	70	70	90	90	90	480
Replacement equipment..	5	5	5	5	5	5	30
Special equipment........	200	....	....	....	....	200	400
PAYMENT FOR PURCHASES							
Trade payables outstanding on December 31...............	110	....	....	....	....	....	110
Cash purchases..........	1	1	1	1	1	1	6
Production materials.....	....	70	70	70	90	90	390
Replacement equipment..	....	....	5	5	5	5	20
Special equipment.......	....	....	200	....	....	....	200
Total..............	$111	$71	$276	$76	$96	$ 96	$726

The wage costs established by the production program next are tabulated and brought into a summary schedule of payments when they are expected to be paid. Usually, wages are paid weekly so that the payments closely coincide with the incurring of wage expense. In our illustration, wage payments of $50,000 were scheduled for each of the six months. Other manufacturing costs, such as light and power, were estimated to require payments of $10,000 each month.

General and administrative expenses, such as rents, salaries, travel expense, and property taxes, should next be tabulated and included in the summary schedule of payments in the month of payment. The total of these is estimated to call for payments of $25,-000 each month.

Income tax payments, scheduled repayment of existing loans, dividends, and other nonroutine items of significance are usually listed separately in the summary payments schedule. The only such payments anticipated in the Able Company are income tax payments of $20,000 in March and again in June, and a dividend payment of $40,000 in January.

Having satisfied ourselves that no prospective payments have been overlooked, we can now bring the anticipated payments together in a summary schedule of payments, expressed in thousands of dollars:

SUMMARY CASH PAYMENT SCHEDULE

	Jan.	Feb.	March	April	May	June	Total
Payments for purchases .	$111	$ 71	$276	$ 76	$ 96	$ 96	$ 726
Wages paid............	50	50	50	50	50	50	300
Other manufacturing payments.......	10	10	10	10	10	10	60
Payments of general and administrative expenses........	25	25	25	25	25	25	150
Payments of income taxes...........	....	....	20	....	....	20	40
Dividend payments.....	40	....	....	....	....	....	40
Total Payments....	$236	$156	$381	$161	$181	$201	$1,316

Now, let us bring the summaries of payments and receipts together and calculate the *net* cash inflows or outgoes for each month by subtracting the total payments from the total of anticipated receipts. An additional calculation of cumulative inflow, or outgo, should next be made. When matched with cash on hand at the beginning of the period, it is then possible to calculate the additional cash needed (or excess cash above minimum needs) in order to maintain the minimum cash balance desired. In our illustration, assume that cash on hand on December 31 amounted to $65,000. Further, let us assume that after consideration of all the aspects bearing on the subject (such as those discussed in Chapter 5), management decided that it wished to maintain a cash balance of no less than $50,000:

SUMMARY SCHEDULE OF CASH FLOWS
(In Thousands)

	Jan.	Feb.	March	April	May	June	Total
Total Receipts.............	$205	$200	$ 200	$245	$250	$285	$1,385
Total Payments............	236	156	381	161	181	201	1,316
Net inflow or outgo ( )......	$(31)	$ 44	$(181)	$ 84	$ 69	$ 84	$ 69
Cumulative inflow or outgo ( )...............	(31)	13	(168)	(84)	(15)	69	69
Beginning cash.............	65						
Minimum cash.............	50						
Cash above minimum needs or cash shortage ( ) end of month.................	(16)	28	(153)	(69)	0	84	84

It can be seen that a substantial shortage of cash can be expected in March, but that operations of the business should generate enough net cash inflow in April and May so that the need for extra funds should last little more than two months. A brief analysis of the data reveals that the shortage is primarily attributable to the payment in March for the $200,000 equipment item scheduled for January purchase and for March payment. Confronted with our evidence of the forthcoming shortage of cash, management can plan to finance the needs by borrowing or other methods. Alternatively, it can reconsider the plans, perhaps postponing the $200,000 equipment purchase until March or April, in order to reduce the need for funds during this six-month period.

We should emphasize again that those expenses which do not by their nature require cash outlay are not included in the cash forecast. Thus, we did not include the important expense item for manufacturers, depreciation, among the payments listed in our illustration. On the other hand, appropriately, we did include the payments for equipment purchased (except for the second purchase, for which payment was not due until July) and of dividends, even though they are not treated as expenses.

Our cash forecast illustration was based on a single set of plans for the business. Where alternative plans of operation are under consideration, it will often prove helpful to run cash forecasts based on each alternative plan. This permits the financial officer to determine the cash impact of each plan and to help top management decide on the best alternative in the light of this information.

The Essential Nature of the Projected Balance Sheet Method

The projected or *pro forma* balance sheet method of forecasting funds requirements is built around a forecast of the size of key balance sheet items at a selected date or dates in the future. Four major steps are involved in building a balance sheet forecast. The first involves forecast of the net investment required in each of the assets in order to carry out operations at the level planned on the date involved—say, a date six months ahead. Second, the liabilities that can be counted on without especial negotiation are listed. Third, the net worth on that date is estimated. The total of projected assets is then compared with the total sources of funds—debts and net worth. If the total of assets required exceeds the total for expected liabilities and net worth, the difference represents the additional sources that must be negotiated if operations and the build-up of assets to desired levels are to proceed as planned. On the other hand, should the sources exceed the assets required, the excess presumably indicates the additional cash above the desired minimum level that will be on hand.

Put another way, in using the balance sheet approach, the forecaster is reasoning essentially as follows: To carry out our plans, certain predictable investment in assets is required. On the other hand, we can count on certain routine sources of credit. The owners' investment in the business as of the future date can also be predicted. If our indicated sources fall short of meeting the desired investment in the various assets, the amount by which the sources must be expanded or asset investment held down is made apparent. If the expected sources more than cover the needed asset investment, a measure is provided of the cash cushion above minimum working balance needs or of cash available for uses beyond those envisioned in the original planning estimates.

Major Steps in Preparing the Projected Balance Sheet

With this general explanation of the approach in mind, let us now look more closely at each of the key steps in preparation of a projected balance sheet forecast. Let us assume that the subject firm has prepared fairly definite estimates of sales through to the date of the projected balance sheet, and that in the light of the sales expectations, manufacturing and procurement schedules have been drawn up in some detail. Let us also assume that profits for the period have been budgeted.

A first item to be estimated is the anticipated investment in accounts receivable on the forecast date. As we have seen, a major determinant of the size of the receivables investment is the volume of sales. From past records of sales and receivables, the forecaster can determine what the relationship of receivables has been to sales in the past. The ratio suggested by past experience then should be adjusted in the light of any anticipated changes in credit terms, in the leniency with which credit will be granted, or in any other factor that might affect the receivables balance. The adjusted ratio then can be applied to the forecasted sales immediately preceding the forecast date.

Inventory needs can also be projected on the basis of "normal" inventory/sales relationships in the past. Alternatively, if purchase, production, and sales plans have been worked out in detail, the value of inventory that will be left on hand at the forecast date can be directly determined, using the approach: Beginning inventory plus purchases plus value added in manufacture less cost of goods sold equals value of inventory left on hand. All inventory values should be in terms of cost rather than selling prices.

The investment in fixed assets should next be forecasted. Planned purchases of new plant or equipment are added to the existing net investment in fixed assets, and planned depreciation subtracted in order to arrive at the estimated net investment in fixed assets on the forecast date.

Taking into account the considerations discussed in Chapter 5, the minimum cash balance that the firm would wish to carry is next determined.

Turning to the liability side of the balance sheet, the level of accounts payable on the forecast date must next be calculated. Based on the schedule of planned purchases, the assumed purchase terms, and the policy of the firm in meeting the due dates of trade payables, the purchases for which payment will not yet have been made on the forecast date can be tabulated and entered on the projected balance sheet as the anticipated accounts payable.

Accrued wages and other accrued expenses can also be calculated by reference to the production schedule, allowing for the usual lag between the incurring of the wage and other expense items and the required payment of the accrued expenses.

The amount of accrued income tax can be estimated directly if the probable profits and income tax rates are known. To the currently outstanding balance of accrued income taxes, the taxes accrued on income to be earned before the forecast date are added. Scheduled payments of taxes are then deducted to arrive at the amount of accrued taxes which will be outstanding on the forecast date.

Next, existing net worth must be adjusted for planned sales of stock, stock retirements, or any other such changes in prospect. Further, the addition to surplus from retained earnings (net profits after taxes less planned dividend payments) must be reckoned. The profits forecast is usually based on a projected income statement.

Let us suppose that when all the anticipated assets and all liability and net worth items are added up, the totals show $1.2 million for assets and $1.05 million for combined liabilities and net worth. Somehow, an additional $150,000 must be secured from owners or creditors if the $1.2 million level of assets is to be reached. Thus, the balancing figure, when planned assets exceed anticipated liabilities and net worth, represents the additional funds needed to permit the planned asset investment—or else the dollar extent by which the investment in assets must be reduced in order to bring it into line with available sources of funds.

On the other hand, if the sources exceed the assets needed, the excess presumably will accrue as cash above the required minimum amount.

It must be emphasized that the projected balance sheet method of forecasting depicts funds requirements as of the particular balance sheet date only. It does not show varying needs in the interim period. In the case of companies whose needs fluctuate sharply from month to month, or seasonally, a forecast of needs based upon construction of a balance sheet as of a single distant date can be highly misleading. Maximum needs during a future period will be brought out only if the dates for projection of balance sheets are carefully selected so as to represent the balance sheet situation at times of maximum strain—that is, dates on which the combinations of heavy asset commitments and below normal liabilities and net worth are most severe.

Some forecasters, using the projected balance sheet approach, attempt to meet the problem of interim fluctuations by setting the minimum level of cash desired at a high enough level to take care of short-lived peak needs within the forecast periods. As indicated earlier, this can be a costly method of meeting peak and temporary needs.

Our outline of procedures useful in fashioning a projected balance was based on the assumption that detailed plans for the business existed and were available to the forecaster—information of a sort that would have permitted preparation of a full-fledged cash flow forecast showing interim needs as well as those on the balance sheet date. But one of the attractions of the projected balance sheet approach is that it can be used to make rough—yet often highly useful—forecasts in situations where detailed forward plans of the sort necessary for cash flow forecasting do not exist.

Consider, for example, the following problem. A program of sales expansion is being considered by the Baker Company. The owners of the company have said they will be willing to advance any added funds needed to finance the expansion but have asked whether they can look forward to the return of these additional advances within a year. Consequently, the question is raised: "If we double sales in the next year, what will be our need for additional funds at the end of one year?"

Let us see if we can answer the query by means of a projected balance sheet a year ahead.[1] The current balance sheet is as follows:

Cash	$ 50,000	Trade payables	$120,000
Receivables	120,000	Accrued expenses	60,000
Inventory	240,000	Accrued income taxes	30,000
Net fixed assets	400,000	Net worth	600,000
Total Assets	$810,000	Total Liabilities	$810,000

In the past year, sales amounted to $1.2 million and profits were $120,000 before taxes. Income taxes were at the rate of 50 per cent. Production and sales were at a relatively even rate, and the sales at the doubled rate are also expected to be achieved evenly through the coming year. In the past, receivables and inventory have borne approximately the same relationship to sales as currently. Profits of 12 per cent before taxes, 6 per cent after taxes, are expected on the new volume of $2.4 million. No dividends are planned. The Baker Company's productive facilities are adequate for the expanded volume, and new equipment to be purchased will about equal the depreciation to be charged during the year. Since detailed plans do not yet exist, other than for sales, we shall have to draw liberally on the relationships between the various assets and sales in the past as guidelines for estimating the needed investment in these assets at the doubled volume of sales.

Turning first to the estimate of receivables, we note that the current $120,000 figure represents approximately 10 per cent of annual sales at the $1.2 million volume. In the absence of indications that this relationship will not continue at the higher sales volume, we can estimate the receivables on $2.4 million sales at $240,000.

A similar approach to the inventory figure suggests a doubling of the current inventory to $480,000. Since the new acquisitions of fixed assets are expected to equal the depreciation to be charged, we can carry $400,000 forward as our net investment in fixed assets.

Now, let us assume that after considering all aspects of the problem, it is decided somewhat arbitrarily that $75,000 will provide an adequate minimum level of cash for the expanded operations.

Accounts payable in the past have fluctuated with the volume of purchases, which in turn have varied with sales. Similarly, accrued expenses have tended to vary with the level of production, which also has moved with sales. Consequently, we can forecast with some confidence a doubling of these items with a doubling of sales.

---

[1] This simplified example disregards the special treatment applicable to the first $100,000 of estimated tax liability as explained on page 122.

The accrued income tax item currently is one half of the last year's income taxes. Since the income tax rate of 50 per cent is assumed to remain constant, our taxes on profits of $288,000 (12 per cent of $2.4 million sales) should amount to $144,000. If the schedule of required payments is assumed to remain the same, then we can expect one half of the $144,000 taxes, or $72,000, to remain outstanding as accrued taxes a year hence.

Net worth should increase by the amount of the profits after taxes, or $144,000, to a projected total of $744,000. Putting these estimates together, we get the following projected balance sheet:

Cash	$ 75,000	Trade payables	$ 240,000
Receivables	240,000	Accrued liabilities	120,000
Inventory	480,000	Accrued income taxes	72,000
Net fixed assets	400,000	Net worth	744,000
	$1,195,000		$1,176,000

Desired asset position	$1,195,000
Anticipated liabilities and net worth	1,176,000
Additional Sources Needed	$ 19,000

Thus, we see that on the assumptions built into the above forecasted balance sheet, additional funds of $19,000 will be required a year hence to support operations at the $2.4 million sales level. Although, as is true of any forecast, the estimate is only as reliable as the assumptions on which it was based, it does give an approximate answer to the owners' question which prompted this forecast. We can assure the owners that if operations proceed as we expect them to, they will need to keep only $19,000 in added investment in the firm for more than a year.

Upon reflection, it should be apparent that the balance sheet does not picture the maximum amount the owners will have to advance during the coming year if sales are to be built up to the $2.4 million annual volume at once. Receivables and inventory presumably will be doubled almost at once in line with the immediate doubling of sales. While trade payables and accrued expenses also can be expected to increase rapidly, the accrued income tax liability and, more importantly, the net worth account will only gradually be built up through retained earnings to the year hence totals. Thus, the need for additional funds should peak at a high figure soon after the higher sales volume is reached. Our projected balance sheet as of a year ahead, though it supplies an answer to the specific question posed, definitely does *not* show the maximum amount the owners will have to advance the company in the interim months. A further balance sheet projection as of the anticipated date of maximum need or a monthly cash flow forecast will be necessary in order to establish this figure.

So far, we have spoken of the projected balance sheet method primarily as an alternative to the cash flow forecast approach. Actually, when a cash flow forecast has been made, it is a relatively simple matter to round out the forecast data by preparation of projected balance sheets also. If consistent assumptions are used in the two approaches, the cash flow forecast and projected balance sheets should yield identical estimates of cash as of corresponding dates.

Some Basic Problems in Effective Cash Forecasting

An important practical limitation to effective cash forecasting by either method, but especially to cash flow forecasting, is suggested by our earlier discussion. We refer to the fact that virtually all of the firm's operations affect its need for cash; and hence, in order to forecast cash needs closely, comprehensive and detailed planning data are required. Most ot these data cover operational areas outside the direct responsibility of the financial officer. It is seldom hard for the financial officer to get his management associates to agree in theory that careful planning is important and desirable. But it often is more difficult, when day-to-day problems are clamoring for their attention, to get other department personnel to devote time and effort to the less obviously urgent task of planning well into the future. Unless the top management appreciates the value of good forecasting and insists that planning is given appropriate attention throughout the organization, getting the necessary data on which to base his cash forecasts is likely to be a continuing problem for the financial officer.

Even if top management appreciates the need for careful planning and organizes to do a good job of it, the realistic forecaster knows that no matter how well he does his work, he cannot expect to prove exactly right in his forecasts. Most businesses operate in an atmosphere of change, and predictions of an inherently uncertain future necessarily are subject to error. Of course, the degree of predictability of the future varies among firms. Some are highly vulnerable to sharp fluctuations in sales or to disruptions of their plans owing to such events as strikes or the breakdown of key equipment. For example, firms whose sales are directly dependent on the vagaries of the weather have difficult cash forecasting assignments. Manufacturers of fertilizer being sold in areas where its use

by farmers is sharply influenced by the season's rainfall face forecasting problems inherently more formidable than those of firms
whose sales are made against firm orders placed long in advance of
production.

Yet, even in those firms where the future is hard to predict, the
choice is not one of planning or not planning. Rather, it is one of the
degree to which the difficult job of planning is thought through and
organized. And there is much that the firm whose future operations
are inherently difficult to plan can do to make its forecasting as helpful as possible and to reduce management's problems of "staying
on top" of the finances of the firm.

First, in the highly variable situation, it is particularly important
that management recognize the likely margins of error inherent in
its forecasts. So, at the least, management can avoid the hazards involved in attaching false connotations of accuracy in forecast data
based on inherently tenuous assumptions.

Second, in situations where different assumptions as to key variables reasonably can be made, it may be helpful to prepare several
different forecasts, each employing a different basic assumption as
to the key variable. This, in effect, permits the financial officer to
determine, "If this happens, then this will be the effect on cash
. . . , etc." For example, a forecaster for the fertilizer concern referred to earlier might well run different forecasts using sales estimates based on normal, on heavy, and on sparse rainfall, and thus be
forewarned as to the cash implications of each development. Along
the same lines, some firms find it helpful to put together forecasts
under combinations of assumptions that would picture likely minimum and maximum, as well as most probable, needs for the future
period.

Third, frequent revision of the forecasts as the future unfolds
helps to keep them attuned to changing conditions and to provide as
much advance notice as possible of developing changes in the need for
funds. In the very dynamic firm the forecasts must be adjusted
almost continuously if they are to be helpful in detailed financial
planning.

Fourth, the organization of the firm and the way its finances are
handled can be adjusted to fit the degree of variability of its future
needs. For example, the firm subject to sudden, hard-to-predict cash
outflows might well plan to carry a much larger cash balance than
would be appropriate in a firm whose future needs were subject to
more accurate prediction.

Further, experience with forecasting in the firm should lead to development of improved methods, both of preparation of forecasts and of their interpretation, which will reduce to a minimum the inherent margins of error. Learning by trial and error has its place in forecasting.

When forecasts of cash needs are prepared for use by top managers or outsiders such as bank lending officers, the forecaster should include with the forecast data a careful statement of the key assumptions upon which his forecasts were based. This gives the reviewer a better basis for understanding the figures and an opportunity to form his own judgments as to the validity of the key assumptions. Further, subsequent revisions of the forecasts based on differing assumptions can be more readily understood and appraised.

Long-Range Financial Forecasting

Companies which require long-range planning for fixed asset expansion commonly prepare rough cash forecasts extending far into the future. Electric power companies, for example, commonly plan their capital expansion programs five, ten, and even fifteen years ahead of actual construction. The tabulations of required outlays for such expansion are known as *capital budgets*. The theory back of this special form of forecasting is much the same as for the ordinarily shorter and more comprehensive cash forecasts. However, in forecasting needs for long periods in the future, most forecasters focus their attention on a few key items and rely on ratios and other approximate methods in "guesstimating" secondary items. Thus, an electric utility might well concentrate on estimating sales volumes and physical facility needs, relying on ratios of normal receivables to sales as the basis for computing the needs relating to receivables at the forecasted sales levels. We shall devote more attention to this subject in later chapters.

PART IV

Short- and Intermediate-Term Sources of Funds

Chapter 10

The Effective Use of Bank Credit

"BUT WHERE will we get the dough?" The job of answering this question so often raised in management councils usually falls to the financial officer. In framing answers to this basic query, it is necessary for management first to decide whether the need for funds can best be met through use of short-term, intermediate, or long-term sources. Let us first define our terms. While there are no clear-cut theoretical dividing lines between short-term, intermediate, and long-term sources, a distinction can be drawn that is useful though arbitrary. For our purposes, credits that do not by their terms specifically make funds available for more than one year will be regarded as short term. Thus, loans which call for payment in one year or less, even though they may be repeatedly renewed, are classed as short term. In contrast, sale of preferred and common stock and of bonds represents long-term financing. In a middle-ground classification as *intermediate-term financing*, we put loans which must be repaid in over one but no more than fifteen years.

In this and the two following chapters, we shall focus on sources of short-term funds. In Chapter 13, we shall center on sources of intermediate funds or *term loans;* and in later chapters, we shall discuss how long-term funds are obtained.

In Chapter 7, we discussed the spontaneous sources of short-term funds of great importance to American business. Speaking of business broadly, the credit available as normal trade credit from suppliers, as accrued expenses, and as accrued income taxes, in total amount far exceeds the amount of short-term credit secured from lenders on a negotiated basis. However, a great many concerns rely heavily on short-term borrowings from commercial banks and a variety of other sources. To distinguish these latter sources from the spontaneous sources, we refer to them as *negotiated sources.*

169

The more important sources of short-term credit secured under special or *negotiated arrangements* include the following:

1. Loans from commercial banks.
2. Sale of commercial paper.
3. Loans from finance companies.
4. The use of factoring.
5. Loans from private lenders.
6. Advances from customers.
7. Special credits from suppliers.
8. The use of banker's acceptances.
9. The use of United States government sponsored or supported programs designed to supply financial aid to business.

THE IMPORTANCE OF UNDERSTANDING
THE SOURCES OF CREDIT

Immediately following the attack on Pearl Harbor on December 7, 1941, Rear Admiral Yokoyama, the Japanese naval attaché in Washington, together with two naval officer associates, was interned at Hot Springs, Virginia. For several months there, they had full access to the American press and could add to their knowledge of America and the American Navy. When their diplomatic exchange ship arrived in Japan in August, 1942, they were met at dockside by an officer of the Naval General Staff and taken directly to headquarters. They were allowed to see no one and to read no Japanese newspapers. The idea was that they should use their fresh knowledge of America and the U.S. Navy to play the role of the United States leaders in an extended war game. In this game, Admiral Yokoyama was to conduct the war against Japan as he thought the American commanders should and would. Thus, through this and other measures the Japanese sought to know and understand their adversary and to forge their own plans in the light of this understanding.

Fortunately, the negotiations of businessmen are unlike the wars of nations, and the gains of one need not be at the expense of the other. Business relationships *can* be profitable and satisfactory from the viewpoint of *each* party—indeed, if they are to endure, the arrangements must be good ones from the standpoint of each concern involved. But effective business planning and negotiation, just as certainly as military planning, must be grounded in a basic understanding of the circumstances and thinking in the organizations with which a relationship is to be developed. The more that can be learned about how their managers operate, their aims, their procedures, the logics of their operations, and the human prejudices and irrationalities of their managers as well, the more likely it is that arrangements can be made that will meet their needs and situation and yet will be a "good deal" for the initiating firm.

This philosophy certainly is pertinent in the case of the businessman hoping to make good use of potential sources of credit. This chapter and the two that follow are intended to help the reader to gain a basic understanding of banks and other lenders to business, and their lending attitudes and practices.

IMPORTANCE OF BANK CREDIT TO BUSINESS

American business firms depend on their commercial banks for a wide range of important services. Carried on with such smooth routine that it is taken virtually for granted is the service of the banks in handling the mechanics of payment by check. A very high percentage of the nation's business transactions are settled by check, and the number of business checks handled annually by the banks runs into the billions. Business firms in 1960 carried some $64 billion on deposit in more than six million bank accounts. But in this chapter, we are interested primarily in the nation's banks as sources of credit for business and the manner in which these sources can be tapped effectively by business concerns.

The commercial banks are a highly important source of business credit. While banking statistics do not isolate the amount of total bank credit going to business, it is likely that as much as half of the $118.4 billion of commercial bank loans outstanding at the end of 1960 were for business purposes. To the $41.9 billion of commercial loans shown in Chart 10–1, we could appropriately add considerable portions of the amounts in several other loan categories that directly or indirectly were for business purposes. The great growth of bank lending in recent decades is also brought out in Chart 10–1.

Federal Reserve System studies of member bank loans as of October 5, 1955, and October 16, 1957, provide a wealth of information on the lending of member banks, which together accounted for some 86 per cent of all commercial bank loans. On the 1957 date, business firms had outstanding 1,286,600 loans from member banks. Table 10–1 presents a classification of these loans according to the business of the borrower. Since many firms borrow for short periods, the total number of loans or the amount of bank credit outstand-

CHART 10–1

LOANS OF U.S. COMMERCIAL BANKS AS OF DECEMBER 31
(In Billions of Dollars)

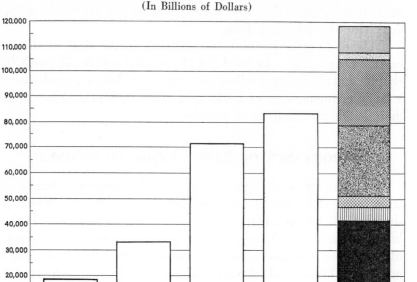

SOURCE: *Federal Reserve Bulletins.*

ing on a single date substantially understates total business use of bank credit.

The *availability* of bank credit is of much importance to a great many companies that may not borrow at all for extended periods. To these companies the banks serve as a "backstop" or reserve source of cash. As we have seen, it is often difficult for the businessman to forecast with precision or full confidence the amount of funds his business will need during a substantial period in the future. Many unpredictable events can create the need for cash. If the business has a good credit standing with its bank and knows it can borrow if unexpected needs develop, it can undertake larger scale and more risky operations than would be feasible in the absence of the reserve of borrowing power at the banks. For many businesses, it is entirely uneconomical and in some cases impossible for the business itself to

TABLE 10-1

Business Loans of Member Banks of the Federal Reserve System, 1957 and 1955, by Business of Borrower

(Estimates of Outstanding Loans)

Business of Borrower	Amount of Loans				Number of Loans*	
	In Millions of Dollars		Percentage Distribution		In Thousands	Percentage Distribution
	1957	1955	1957	1955	1955	1955
All businesses	40,618	30,820	100.0	100.0	1,317	100.0
Manufacturing and mining, total	16,144	11,283	39.7	36.6	225	17.1
Food, liquor, and tobacco	2,392	1,838	5.9	6.0	36	2.7
Textiles, apparel, and leather	1,683	1,689	4.1	5.5	31	2.3
Metals and metal products	5,527	3,235	13.6	10.5	59	4.5
Petroleum, coal, chemicals, and rubber	3,750	2,646	9.2	8.6	28	2.2
Other	2,792	1,875	6.9	6.1	72	5.4
Trade, total	8,386	6,539	20.7	21.2	517	39.2
Retail	4,589	3,476	11.3	11.3	411	31.2
Wholesale	2,982	2,312	7.4	7.5	96	7.3
Commodity dealers	815	751	2.0	2.4	9	0.7
Other, total	16,087	12,988	39.6	42.2	575	43.7
Sales finance companies	3,095	2,872	7.6	9.3	13	1.0
Transportation, communication, and other public utilities	4,169	2,906	10.3	9.4	44	3.4
Construction	1,980	1,691	4.9	5.5	105	7.9
Real estate	2,976	2,405	7.3	7.8	76	5.7
Services	2,262	1,783	5.6	5.8	239	18.2
Other nonfinancial	1,605	1,340	3.9	4.4	98	7.5

* Comparable data on number of loans were not included in 1957 survey.

Source: *Federal Reserve Bulletin*, April, 1956; April 1958.

hold idle cash in reserve for such possible needs. The value to American business of unutilized but potential bank credit, though inestimable, is unquestionably great.

In the interests of undistorted perspective, we should recognize that bank credit is a much smaller source of funds for business than the spontaneous sources, notably trade credit. But for business generally, the banks represent the dominant source of negotiated short-term credit. For most smaller firms and a large percentage of medium-sized firms, bank loans represent the paramount source of negotiated credit—long, intermediate, and short term. For very strong and larger firms that can sell bonds in the capital markets, bank credit represents one of several important sources of credit open to them.

There is abundant evidence of the relatively great importance of bank credit to small business. As Table 10–2 makes clear, almost

TABLE 10–2

BUSINESS LOANS OF MEMBER BANKS, 1957, BY SIZE OF BORROWER

SIZE OF BORROWER (TOTAL ASSETS, IN THOUSANDS OF DOLLARS)	AMOUNT OF LOANS		NUMBER OF LOANS		AVERAGE SIZE OF LOAN (IN THOUSANDS)
	Millions of Dollars	Percentage Distribution	Thousands	Percentage Distribution	
All borrowers............	40,618	100.0	1,280.6	100.0	31.7
Less than 50.............	1,456	3.6	504.7	39.4	2.9
50–250.................	5,256	12.9	494.3	38.6	10.6
250–1,000...............	6,302	15.5	157.6	12.3	40.0
1,000–5,000.............	6,775	16.7	48.2	3.8	140.5
5,000–25,000............	5,912	14.6	13.3	1.0	445.7
25,000–100,000..........	4,893	12.0	5.4	0.4	901.6
100,000 or more.........	8,815	21.7	6.5	0.5	1,363.5
Not ascertained.........	1,207	3.0	50.7	4.0	23.8

SOURCE: *Federal Reserve Bulletin*, April, 1958, p. 396.

1,000,000 of the 1,280,600 business loans of member banks in 1957 were to firms with total assets of less than $250,000. For most of the smaller businesses the banks were the only source of negotiated credit open to them. A Department of Commerce study in the midfifties showed that bank loans constituted nearly 80 per cent of all negotiated credit for a broad sample of established small and medium-sized firms. For newly established firms in the sample, bank loans accounted for nearly 70 per cent of all loans.[1]

Several factors contribute to the especial importance of bank credit to smaller business. First, banks generally are actively interested in making small as well as large business loans. The borrowers

[1] McHugh Loughlin and Jack N. Ciaccio, "Financing Small Business in the Postwar Period," *Survey of Current Business*, November, 1955.

usually are well known to their banks, and the extent of the credit investigation is not so great as to make the costs of extending small business loans prohibitive. Second, there are commercial banks in almost every town in the country, and local firms are likely to find their local bank interested in helping enterprises which contribute to the community's economy. Further, small businesses generally are less strongly capitalized and their internal sources of funds less adequate than in the case of large firms; many, if not most, are chronically short of funds. Apart from the relatively small number of "glamour firms" with outstanding prospects, smaller firms, and many of intermediate size, find the capital markets ill-suited and unreceptive to their needs. The inability to tap other institutional sources makes it especially important that the managers of small and intermediate-sized firms make effective use of the credit facilities of their commercial banks.

That bank credit is not restricted to established firms with demonstrated earning power is indicated by the fact that 107,000, or 8.4 per cent, of the loans reported in the Federal Reserve study of October, 1957, were to businesses less than two years old. The bank loans outstanding to these new firms totaled almost $2 billion.

THE STRUCTURE OF U.S. COMMERCIAL BANKING

U.S. commercial banks are distinguished from the two other major deposit institutions—mutual savings banks and savings and loan institutions—by their ability to accept demand deposits subject to check as well as time and savings deposits. The savings accounts of mutual savings banks and the share accounts of savings and loan associations are invested predominantly in residential mortgage loans and in U.S. bonds. The savings institutions play an important role in the financing of home construction, but their lending to business outside the construction industry is very limited.

Although commercial banks typically accept both demand deposits subject to check and interest-bearing time deposits, the demand deposits of commercial banks as a whole are more than twice their time deposits. The deposit accounts of business firms are carried predominantly at commercial banks. While the commercial banks make home mortgage loans, they specialize in loans to business and to individuals. Unless reference to the contrary is made, hereafter when we speak of "banks," we refer to commercial banks.

The federal government and each of the states have enacted specialized legislation governing the operations of commercial banks. Further, banks are subject to continuing supervision of their activities by one or more public agencies. The regulations applicable to a particular bank are governed in part by its decision to incorporate as a *national* or as a *state bank.*

At the end of 1958, about one third of the nation's 13,486 commercial banks were incorporated as national banks and as such were subject to federal banking legislation. The 4,549 national banks, however, held over half of the total bank assets. The remaining banks have chosen to incorporate under the laws of the states in which they are located.

Primary responsibility for supervision of national banks rests with the U.S. Comptroller of the Currency. The Comptroller has a sizable staff which reviews periodic reports from the banks and conducts field examinations of the banks' affairs. A team of examiners visits each national bank at least once a year to examine the condition of the bank and to check compliance with pertinent laws and regulations. The examiners give particular attention to the bank's investment in loans and securities. Responsibility for supervision of state banks typically rests with a state banking department whose examiners perform a function similar to that of the national bank examiners.

By law, all national banks must be members of the Federal Reserve System. State banks may apply for membership in the Federal Reserve System. To date, most of the state banks have not sought membership, but enough of the larger state banks have become members so that member banks hold almost 85 per cent of all commercial bank assets. State banks joining the System become subject to Federal Reserve regulations and to supervision and examination by the System.

In addition, all national banks and 96 per cent of the state commercial banks have a portion of their deposits guaranteed by an agency of the U.S. government, the Federal Deposit Insurance Corporation.[2] Since the FDIC assures depositors of the safety of their deposits (up to $10,000 in each account), it naturally is interested in seeing that the bankers manage depositors' money with due regard for avoidance of losses or illiquid investments that would impair their ability to meet their deposit liabilities. The FDIC, too, has a staff of examiners.

---

[2] At the end of 1959, 317 state commercial banks were not insured by the FDIC. These banks held less than 1 per cent of total commercial bank deposits, however.

A few of the detailed restrictions on bank lending are of general interest to business borrowers. For example, national banks are subject to a "legal limit" on the amount they can lend to a single borrower. Unsecured loans to one borrower may not exceed 10 per cent of the bank's combined capital stock and surplus. Most state banking laws also have provisions aimed at forcing diversification in loan portfolios, but the precise legal limit may well be different from that of a national bank in similar circumstances. Although the regulations governing specific banks may differ in detail, the similarities are more striking than the differences, and the typical business borrower is unlikely to be materially affected in his use of bank credit by the differences.

The most important point for the businessman to appreciate with respect to bank regulation and supervision is that the bankers operate under certain definite and vigorously enforced restrictions on their lending activity.

In terms of numbers, most of the nation's commercial banks operate as unit banks from a single office. Over the years, there has been vigorous and continuing debate in the United States as to whether it is wise public policy to permit individual banks to establish branches. The various states have come to different conclusions. At the end of 1960, 14 states, including Illinois, Texas, and Wisconsin, refused to permit their banks to establish branches. On the other hand, 15 states, including California and Connecticut, permitted state-wide branch banking. The largest bank in the country, the Bank of America National Trust and Savings Association, operated more than six hundred branches in California cities and towns and nine branches overseas. The remaining 19 states permitted some branch banking but restricted it to certain areas within the state.

Branch banking is more completely established in other countries than in the United States. Eight banks dominate the commercial banking business in Canada, as do five in England. A few large banks with many branches also characterize the commercial banking systems of Italy, Belgium, France, West Germany, and Japan.

Commercial Banking as a Business

So much has been written and said about the obligations of banks to their depositors, to their borrowing customers, to their communities, and to the general public that it is easy to overlook the basic fact that our commercial banks are also private businesses, owned by the stockholders, operating to make a profit for the stockholders.

They are not charitable institutions or organizations operating exclusively, or even in large measure, for the public welfare as such.

It is true that most banks are operated in the interests of *long-run profitability* rather than for "the fast buck." Few bank shareholders invest in bank shares for quick speculative profit. Most managements identify the long-run interests of their banks with the prosperity of their customers and the long-term economic health of their communities. Further, few broad-minded bankers challenge the social need for substantially more supervision and regulation of bank affairs in the depositors' and the public interest than is appropriate for most other businesses. Nevertheless, *banking is a business,* with profit-making the mainspring and basic objective of banking operations.

Banks have been aptly described as "dealers in debts." The basic features of the commercial banking business are relatively simple. When a commercial bank is started, the stockholders, by purchasing common stock, commit capital as a continuing investment in the business. Then the bank receives deposits, subject either to withdrawal without advance notice in the case of checking accounts or *demand deposits,* or subject to withdrawal upon advance notice as *time* or *savings deposits.* In practice, the requirement of advance notice before withdrawal of savings deposits typically is waived, and such

TABLE 10–3

SUMMARY BALANCE SHEET,
ALL U.S. COMMERCIAL BANKS
December 28, 1960

	Total in Millions	Percentage of Total
ASSETS		
Cash on hand or on deposit with other banks..........................	$ 47,200	18.7%
Loans, net of reserves for bad debts......	118,160	46.7
Investments in securities:		
U.S. government securities............	61,320	24.2
Other securities.....................	20,830	8.2
Other assets..........................	5,550	2.2
	$253,060	100.0%
LIABILITIES		
Demand deposits......................	$150,350	59.4%
Time and savings deposits.............	73,030	28.9
Other liabilities......................	8,570	3.4
Capital...............................	21,110	8.3
	$253,060	100.0%

SOURCE: *Federal Reserve Bulletin,* January, 1961.

deposits are also readily withdrawable. Interest typically is paid on savings deposits but cannot be paid on demand deposits.

Deposits are debts of the bank; if it is to stay in business, the bank must be prepared to meet deposit withdrawals *at all times*. Banks typically get most of their funds from depositors. As can be seen from Table 10–3, depositors provided 88.3 per cent of all commercial bank assets at the end of 1960; the owners, 8.3 per cent. Banks typically earn profits by investing a substantial amount of the deposited funds in interest-bearing loans to individuals and business firms or in income-producing securities. Obviously, the banks, in investing the deposit funds, should so invest them that ability to meet potential withdrawals is not jeopardized. Just how much "liquidity" of assets is enough in the particular circumstances of their banks is one of the difficult decisions facing bank managers.

Table 10–4 shows how important the income from loans and investment in securities is to commercial banks generally. Interest from loans accounted for 61.7 per cent of the total operating income of commercial banks in 1959. Interest on investments produced 23.6

TABLE 10–4

SELECTED INCOME DATA, 1959,
ALL U.S. INSURED COMMERCIAL BANKS

	In Millions	Percentage of Current Operating Income
Income from loans......................	$5,969	61.7%
Interest on investments.................	2,278	23.6
Service charges on deposit accounts.......	532	5.5
Other current earnings..................	890	9.2
Total Current Operating Income......	$9,669	100.0%
Current operating expenses..............	6,264	
	$3,405	
Losses on security sales, charge-offs of loans, and transfers to reserves less recoveries, profits on securities sold, and transfers from reserves..........	1,033	
Net profits before income taxes..........	$2,372	
Income taxes.........................	884	
Net profits after taxes..................	$1,488	
Cash dividends........................	776	
Net Income Added to Capital........	$ 712	

SOURCE: Federal Deposit Insurance Corporation, *Annual Report* (Washington, D.C.: U.S. Government Printing Office, 1959).

per cent of total revenues, while service charges on deposits returned 5.5 per cent and other income the remaining 9.2 per cent.

The net income after taxes of commercial banks in 1959, which was $1,488 million, represented only 0.63 per cent of average total assets held by the banks in that year. Yet, this was enough to represent a net return of 7.94 per cent on the average investment of stockholders during 1959. It is apparent that banks depend for profitable operations on effective employment of the funds entrusted to their care by depositors as well as stockholders.

The rates charged on loans are influenced by a variety of factors. The rates charged by the large metropolitan banks, sometimes termed "money market banks," are more sensitive to changes in the supply and demand for credit than are the rates charged borrowers by smaller banks. Chart 10–2 shows the rates charged by large New

CHART 10–2

CURRENT RATE (PER CENT) ON NEW PRIME COMMERCIAL LOANS*

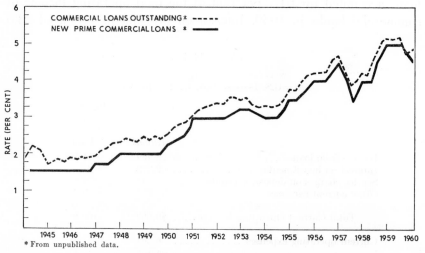

* From unpublished data.

York banks on "prime" commercial loans—those on short-term loans to firms of the highest credit standing—and the average rates on commercial loans received by New York banks over a period of years.

BANK LENDING STANDARDS AND PROCEDURES

Basic Economics of Bank Lending

As emphasized earlier, commercial banks are in business to make money for their stockholders. Income from interest on loans is a major source of bank income. But it is *net* income from lending that counts—income after allowance for losses and for other costs of the lending operation. Naturally, in their effort to maximize their net profits, banks compare loan opportunities with other investment opportunities open to them. In recent years, there has been an abundant supply of U.S. government bonds available to banks with cash to invest. It is appropriate for bankers to regard the government bonds as entirely free of risk of nonrepayment. In recent years, banks have been able to earn 3 per cent or more on certain government bonds held to maturity. In appraising the risks and return from loans to private businesses, the bankers can appropriately ask that the amount of interest they can receive above the "risk-free" 3 per cent at least compensate for the risk of default by the prospective borrower.[3] Theoretically, banks might appropriately consider making loans of any degree of risk, however great, by simply charging an interest rate high enough to compensate for the estimated risk of nonrepayment and return a profit on the business. In some cases, such a charge might run to 20, 30, or even 50 per cent. Actually, for many years in this country, both custom among bankers and legal requirements have restricted the maximum interest rates banks charge. Six or 7 per cent has been the normal ceiling on the interest rates banks have charged business borrowers.[4] Loan applications involving high risk are referred to other lending agencies which are in a position to charge rates more nearly commensurate with the high-risk appraisal.

Bank Credit Contrasted with Trade Credit

The gain to the bank from risk taking on a typical loan is in striking contrast to the gain to the typical manufacturer from risk taking in extending trade credit to a customer. Consider the following illustration. A manufacturer sells on 30-day credit terms to a particular customer. The customer's credit position has deteriorated, and the manufacturer must decide whether or not to grant him 30-day payment terms. Assume that the manufacturer is not selling his full capacity and that the sales involved will be lost if he does not offer the 30-day credit terms. If the manufacturer sells $10,000 a month to this customer and collects the account receivable in 30 days, he will have

---

[3] As a means of cementing close relationships with borrowers and of boosting deposit funds, many banks require borrowers to keep deposit balances with the bank. The amount of the "compensating balance" required is usually 10 to 20 per cent of the amount of the loan. The fact that a part of the funds loaned must be kept on deposit may be regarded as indirectly boosting the rate of interest on the net funds actually made available to the borrower.

[4] Exceptions to this generalization do exist. For example, in the case of some loans repayable in instalments over a two- or three-year period, a 5 or 6 per cent rate is applied to the full amount of the loan. Thus, the effective interest rate on the loan balances actually outstanding is much larger than the nominal rate.

just $10,000 at risk at any one time, assuming sales at an even rate. In a year, he would turn over the $10,000 receivable twelve times, achieving sales of $120,000 while risking no more than $10,000 at any one time. If profit before taxes on the sales is 10 per cent, a not uncommon figure, he will realize $12,000 profit on the $120,000 yearly sales (in addition to any contributions to the manufacturer's fixed costs) in return for his continuing risk of $10,000. On the other hand, if a banker loaned the shaky customer $10,000 at 6 per cent interest for a year, he would get $600, less any cost associated with making the loan. If he could get 3 per cent for his money in "risk-free" government bonds, the banker's return for risking $10,000 would be something less than $300 a year, in contrast to the $12,000 or more return of the manufacturer. Obviously, in his own economic interest the banker must take a very different view of the risk he is willing to undertake in the situation than should the manufacturer in his extension of trade credit.

Contrast between Owner's and Creditor's Return for Risk Taking

It is important also to appreciate the very significant difference in the gain from risk taking of a banker whose lending agreement provides only for a fixed and limited interest return for his risk taking[5] and the gain from risk taking of shareholding investors who, as owners, participate fully in the profits of the business. Consider, for example, the position of a banker asked to make a loan to a newly established business which appears highly risky but may be very profitable. If the business proves highly profitable, the bank will get its money back with only the fixed amount of interest as its reward for its courage and capital. The owners, on the other hand, in return for their capital ventured, will get all the profits after taxes of the venture, whether they are 10 per cent, 20 per cent, or even 100 per cent per year. Viewed in this light, it is obvious that the limited and fixed return available to the bank does not justify its taking risks in providing capital that a partner or common stockholder participating fully in prospective profits might well regard as reasonable.[6]

---

[5] Some European banks have invested money in business enterprises on a common stock or ownership basis, but U.S. commercial banks do not.

[6] An experienced Canadian banker, Mr. A. B. Jamieson, writing in *Chartered Banking in Canada*, published in August, 1953, by the Ryerson Press, Toronto, makes this same point in these terms:

"In many cases where a banker is approached for a loan, the financial position of the prospective borrower is such that what he really needs is more risk capital. When the

Traditional Theories of Sound Commercial Bank Lending

As we have seen, commercial bankers must limit their risk taking to situations that promise an acceptable return after allowances for the risk of losses. The bankers also must have regard for investing the banks' funds in such a manner that the demands of depositors can be met at all times. What kind of loans do bankers regard as appropriate in view of these basic considerations? Or put most simply: "What sort of loans are the bankers looking for?" Although few bankers would give exactly the same answer, over the years one type of loan has been generally regarded as particularly suitable for commercial banks. This "ideal" loan for commercial banks is a short-term, self-liquidating loan for productive or commercial purposes.[7] The words *short term* are usually interpreted to mean a period of a few months, normally less than six, and certainly not more than twelve months. *Self-liquidating* indicates that the loan is for a purpose that will provide the means for repayment in the normal course of opera-

banker points this out, perhaps the applicant's response is 'If I get someone to put money in my business, he will expect a proportionate share of the profits; if I get money from the bank, all it will cost is the interest on the loan.' With such an answer the banker can tell the applicant he is showing exactly why the loan should not be made. The bank does not share in the profits of the business; therefore, it should not put up money which might be lost if the business proves unsuccessful."

[7] Adam Smith, writing in 1776, set forth the arguments in favor of short-term, self-liquidating loans in the following terms:

"What a bank can with propriety advance to a merchant or undertaker of any kind, is not either the whole capital with which he trades, or even any considerable part of the capital; but that part of it only, which he would otherwise be obliged to keep by him unemployed, and in ready money for answering occasional demands. . . .

"When a bank discounts to a merchant a real bill of exchange drawn by a real creditor upon a real debtor, and which, as soon as it becomes due, is really paid by that debtor; it only advances to him a part of the value which he would otherwise be obliged to keep by him unemployed and in ready money for answering occasional demands. The payment of the bill, when it becomes due, replaces to the bank the value of what it had advanced, together with the interest. The coffers of the bank, so far as its dealings are confined to such customers, resemble a water pond, from which, though a stream is continually running out, yet another is continually running in, fully equal to that which runs out; so that, without any further care or attention, the pond keeps always equally or very near equally full. Little or no expense can ever be necessary for replenishing the coffers of such a bank. . . .

. . . . .

". . . A bank cannot, consistently with its own interest, advance to a trader, the whole or even the greater part of the circulating capital with which he trades; because, though that capital is continually returning to him in the shape of money, and going from him in the same shape, yet the whole of the returns is too distant from the whole of the out-goings, and the sum of his repayments could not equal the sum of its advances within such moderate periods of time as suit the conveniency of a bank. Still less could a bank afford to advance him any considerable part of his fixed capital; of the capital which the undertaker of an iron forge, for example, employs in erecting his forge and smelting-house, his work-houses and warehouses, the dwelling-houses of his workmen, etc.; of the

tions of the business. For example, consider the case of a fertilizer manufacturer whose sales are heavily concentrated in spring and early summer, and who wants to mix and bag the fertilizer at an even rate throughout the year. Consequently, the manufacturer's investment in inventory increases sharply during the winter months. A bank loan in early winter to provide the funds for the seasonal investment in inventory would meet what is presumably a temporary need. As the peak inventory is reduced through sales in the spring months, accounts receivable are built up. When the accounts receivable are collected, the Cash account of the fertilizer company will build up and permit repayment of the loan. Consequently, if operations, sales, and collections proceed as expected, the loan to finance the temporary expansion of inventory can be regarded as self-liquidating.

The short-term, self-liquidating type of loan has several basic attractions to commercial banks. Since the normal operations of the borrowing company will provide the means of repayment in a relatively short period, risk of repayment should be subject to fairly careful analysis and in most cases be judged tolerable. Too, since such loans are essentially temporary, the bank avoids getting "frozen into" a particular loan situation. That is, it avoids investing capital to supply a normal and continuous need of the business. In cases where it does provide for a permanent need, if the bank wants its money, it can insist on repayment only by seriously upsetting the operations of the borrowing company. Further, the use of short maturities affords the bank officers an opportunity to review the situation if renewal is needed, and perhaps to insist on changes in the terms of the credit or in the operation of the business. Also, emphasis on short-term lending

---

capital which the undertaker of a mine employs in sinking his shafts, in erecting engines for drawing out the water, in making roads and waggon-ways, etc.; of the capital which the person who undertakes to improve land employs in clearing, draining, enclosing, manuring and ploughing waste and uncultivated fields, in building farmhouses, with all their necessary appendages of stables, granaries, etc. The returns of the fixed capital are in almost all cases much slower than those of the circulating capital; and such expenses, even when laid out with the greatest prudence and judgment, very seldom return to the undertaker till after a period of many years, a period by far too distant to suit the convenience of a bank. . . . [The] money which is borrowed, and which it is meant should not be repaid till after a period of several years, ought not to be borrowed of a bank, but ought to be borrowed upon bond or mortgage, of such private people as propose to live upon the interest of their money, without taking the trouble themselves to employ the capital; and who are upon that account willing to lend that capital to such people of good credit as are likely to keep it for several years."

Adam Smith, *An Inquiry into the Nature and Causes of the Wealth of Nations* (Modern Library; New York; Random House, Inc., 1937), pp. 288–92. The attention of the authors was directed to this quotation by a similar reference by H. V. Prochnow in his book, *Term Loans and Theories of Bank Liquidity* (New York: Prentice-Hall, Inc., 1949).

provides the bank with a degree of asset liquidity which it would not have if its assets were invested in longer-term credits. Finally, for many years—or more precisely, from 1914 to 1934—it was possible for the banks to use only such short-term, self-liquidating notes as security for loans from the Federal Reserve banks. The possibility of such borrowing or *rediscount* by the banks gave additional liquidity to the short-term credit extensions.

If this be the ideal, in actual practice few American banks have restricted their lending to it. A basic reason for the gap between theory and practice is that the demand from business for this type of credit seldom has been great enough to absorb fully the bank funds available for lending. Many loans were made on nominally short terms when there was little prospect that the business actually would be able to repay the loan at the stated maturity date. Both lending bank and borrower expected that renewal would be granted.[8] In such situations the banks usually attempted to have the borrower make an annual "cleanup" or repayment of the loans and thus demonstrate that the firm was not fully dependent on the bank for permanent capital. Often, the annual cleanup was more nominal than real. The author recalls one case where for many years a borrower provided his bank with an annual cleanup by shifting his borrowing to a bank across the street for a few months of each year. Each bank was able to show on its loan ledgers an annual cleanup of the loan. There have been many such cases.

Further, almost all commercial banks make a certain number of loans against real estate or other security on a continuing basis in the conviction that the liquidity needs of the bank permit and the security against loss justifies continuing investment of a part of the banks' assets in such loans.

In the period after 1934, commercial banks found it particularly difficult to invest the bulk of their funds in short-term, self-liquidating loans. At the same time, a continuing decline in interest rates reduced the attractiveness of investment in government bonds or high-grade

---

[8] A study by the Federal Reserve Bank of Cleveland of loans in the Fourth Federal Reserve District (Ohio and parts of Pennsylvania, Kentucky, and West Virginia) provided impressive evidence of the extent of continuous bank borrowing through renewal of short-term loans. While only one third of the dollar amount of the notes outstanding of business borrowers were over one year old, nearly two thirds of the business loans were outstanding to business firms who were continuously in debt to the same bank for more than a year. Further, only 6 per cent of the amount of notes were five years old or more, but 25 per cent of the outstanding loan volume was to firms continuously in debt to the same bank for five years or longer! Details of this study are described in the *Monthly Business Review* of the Federal Reserve Bank of Cleveland, September, 1956.

corporate bonds. Consequently, certain other types of loans came to be regarded more favorably, both in theory and in practice. Thus, many banks undertook *term loans* to businesses of particularly strong credit positions and profit prospects. These term loans called for serial repayment and extended over periods of ten years or more, although more commonly they were limited to five years.

Revolving loans were also made against the security of accounts receivable, inventory, or machinery, even though there was every reason to believe that the borrowers would continue to need most of or all the credit for a period of years. Of course, the commercial banks are willing to invest only a portion of their assets in such relatively non-liquid loans. Bank supervisory agencies have come to regard a reasonable proportion of such loans as both acceptable and desirable. Consequently, while self-liquidating, short-term loans are still regarded by most bankers as ideal for bank purposes, other types of loans in amounts not inconsistent with liquidity needs are considered appropriate outlets for bank funds.

Differences between Banks and Bankers

So far, we have spoken of the lending policies and practices of commercial banks as a group and perhaps implied a uniformity of approach to lending. Actually, many factors condition the loan practice of particular banks and bankers. Consequently, while there can be general agreement along the lines suggested above, there are important differences in the lending practices between banks and even between loaning officers in a single bank. What are some of these factors that make loan officers react differently toward similar loan opportunities? They include: (1) The basic policies of banks toward risk taking differ. Some managements prefer to remain conservative, perhaps in a conscious concession of gross income to peace of mind. (2) Banks have different concepts of appropriate loyalty to borrowing customers. The erstwhile First National Bank of New York for many decades was famous for the care with which it entered into lending relationships with its customers. Once it decided to meet the needs of a customer, it was equally famous for standing by its customer in good times *and* bad. Other New York banks loaned more freely in good times but felt more at arm's length with their borrowers. (3) Differences in the nature of the deposit liabilities of banks create different liquidity needs. Lending policies of banks with a large number of inactive, stable deposits can differ from those of banks with a few very large but volatile deposits which may be quickly withdrawn. (4) Banks tend to specialize in particular types of loans, developing especial experience and confidence in their ability to gauge risks in their specialties. For example, one New York bank has developed a particularly large business in shipping loans. Too, a wool dealer would be more likely to find credit in a Boston bank, while an oil producer would usually find a Dallas bank more interested in lending against security of oil production runs. (5) The amount of assets a particular bank already has invested in loans obviously affects its willingness to undertake new loans. As general credit conditions tightened during the fifties, many banks with substantial loan credit outstanding reviewed requests from new borrowers very severely, preferring to save some lending power to meet the possible additional credit needs of old customers. (6) As indicated earlier, legal regulations to which they are subject, such as the limitation of amounts that can be loaned to a single borrower to a fixed percentage of permanent capital, can make for differences between banks. (7) Perhaps most important are the twin facts that loans are made by men, not machines, and that the appraisal of the risks of most loans is in the last analysis a matter of personal judgment. No bank lending officer has a crystal ball that reveals the future to him. Within a single bank, individuals with different personality, experience, and status frequently form very different judgments on particular loan requests. A lending officer who has just had important loans for which he was responsible "go sour" and is wondering what to do about them is likely to look differently on a new loan request before him than would another more confident colleague. Banking is still an art.

General Procedures in Making New Loans

As we have said, there are many differences among banks and bankers in procedures and practices of lending. However, most banks follow a relatively similar procedure in considering an initial loan request from a prospective borrower. A first formal step consists of an application by the prospective borrower for a loan of a stated amount. Let us assume that the president of a small manufacturing concern visits his bank and, after a discussion with a bank lending officer, fills out a loan application form. Immediately, the bank undertakes to accumulate information about the background, experience, business and personal reputation of the company and its management, its record with suppliers for prompt payment of its trade debts, the reasons the company needs the loan, sources of funds for repayment, its record as to profitability in past operations, and recent balance sheets detailing its assets and liabilities.

With the aid of specialized credit techniques, lending officers of the bank review the accumulated information and reach a decision as to whether and on what terms the proposed loan represents a good investment. In most banks the lending officers have authority to make loans within certain limitations of bank policy and according to their own experience and status. In the case of large or complicated loans, the loan officer typically arrives at a recommendation on the loan; but final decision on the application is made by a committee of officers and, in some cases, by the board of directors of the bank. In other words, while particular loan officers have much influence in the final decision on important loans, the ultimate decision often rests with a group of senior officers.

In many instances, prospective borrowers do not need a bank loan immediately but would like to determine, perhaps many months in advance, what the viewpoint of the bank will be toward a subsequent request for a loan. In such cases, most banks are willing to consider a request for a *line of credit* at the bank. The prospective borrower usually discusses with a loaning officer in detail his anticipated needs for credit in advance of the need, and the request is considered in much the same fashion as if he were asking for an immediate loan. If the borrower's situation is a strong one and the loan looks clearly attractive, the bank may decide to extend a line of credit to the customer. This represents an assurance by the bank that, barring major changes in the borrower's situation, the bank will be willing to lend up to a stated amount to the borrower. Once a line of credit has been opened, when the company wants the money the bank lending officers review the situation of the company primarily to determine that no major changes have in fact occurred. If not, the loan will be granted. The line of credit, while it is not a contract and does not absolutely guarantee the borrower that the loan will be forthcoming, does serve to let him know how he stands with the bank. In many cases, it permits the prospective borrower to embark on operations that will probably require bank credit with reasonable assurance that such credit will be forthcoming. Lines of credit are usually extended for periods of one year or less.

Banks are sometimes willing to make a firm commitment to lend particularly strong customers a stated amount whenever the borrower wants to borrow, or "to take down" the amount involved. Typically, the borrower is asked to pay a small amount (often one fourth of 1 per cent, but up to one half of 1 per cent) in return for the definite commitment of the bank to make the loan when requested.

Form of Loan

In a number of other countries, bank credit is extended in the form of authorized overdrafts. That is, the borrowing customer is permitted to overdraw his deposit balance at the bank up to an agreed-upon amount. Often, there is no written evidence of the debt except the checks drawn on the account and the account itself, which serve as evidence of the debt. Interest is calculated periodically on the average amount of the overdraft. This arrangement is perhaps the simplest and in some respects the most logical of lending arrangements. In this country the deposit and the loan accounts of a borrowing customer are kept separately by the banks.[9] When a company borrows money, its authorized officers sign on its behalf a written agreement to repay, known as a *note*. The note, typically in the form shown in Exhibit 10–1, serves as evidence of the debt and states the terms of the credit extension. Except in the case of very large borrowings, it is customary to make the note for a term of at least 30 days, even though the borrower may actually need the funds involved for only a few of the 30 days. From the borrower's point of view, such a note arrangement is obviously less flexible than the authorized overdraft approach.

The interest charged by the bank usually is deducted at the time the loan is made. Thus, on a $10,000, three-month note at 4 per cent per annum, interest of $100 would be deducted, $9,900 being deposited to the credit of the borrower. This is known as *discounting* the note. Under an optional form commonly used on notes of more than one year, the full amount of the loan is advanced, with payment of the interest called for upon repayment of the principal amount of the loan.

If the repayment of the loan is to be secured by the borrower's pledge of valuable assets as specific security for the loan, in addition to the preparation of the note as evidence of the debt, preparation of documents conveying a security interest in the asset pledged will also be involved. The effective use of security in lending arrangements and the review of the more common methods of secured lending will be the subject of a separate chapter.

---

[9] Some U.S. banks have adopted personal loan plans that have many features of authorized overdraft lending.

EXHIBIT 10-1

TYPICAL PROMISSORY NOTE

No. 3696

Boston, Mass.,   July 16,   19 57 $ 1000.00

Thirty days   after date   I   promise to pay to the order of
ROCKLAND-ATLAS NATIONAL BANK OF BOSTON
at said bank

One Thousand - Dollars
for value received.

If any party liable hereon as maker, endorser, guarantor or otherwise shall die, make assignment for the benefit of creditors, or if a receiver of any such party's property shall be appointed, or if a petition in bankruptcy or other similar proceeding under any law for relief of debtors shall be filed by or against any such party, this obligation at the option of the holder hereof shall forthwith become due and payable. Each such party hereby waives demand, notice and protest and any defence by reason of any extension of time for payment or other indulgence granted to any party liable hereon, and agrees to pay all costs and expenses of collection, including reasonable attorney fees. The obligations of all makers shall be joint and several.

Any moneys or other property at any time in the possession of the holder belonging to any of the parties liable hereon as maker, endorser, guarantor or otherwise, and any deposits, balance of deposits, or other sums at any time credited by or due from the holder to any such parties, may at all times be held and treated as collateral security for the payment of this note and any other liability of the maker herein referred to whether due or not due, and the holder may at any time apply such deposits or other sums or property against the amount due or to become due hereon or set off such amount against any claim of any of said parties against the holder.

Alexander Hammond

NEGOTIATING A BANK LOAN

The businessman who can be confident that he will never need bank credit is in a position to treat his bank relationship lightly. But the businessman who may need bank credit at some time in the future *can do much* to improve his chances of getting the necessary credit on favorable terms when it is needed.

The earlier discussion of the differences in lending practices among banks and bankers should suggest the wisdom (and the difficulty) of judicious selection of the bank with which to do business. Since it takes time to build the mutual understanding and confidence basic to a good banking relationship, unnecessary change should be avoided. Since, apart from lending, services are rather similar from bank to bank, the likely reaction to future requests for credit should be a major factor in selection of a bank.

Paving the Way for Credit Applications

The work of building a favorable climate for loan requests should begin long before the credit is needed. Company officers should devote substantial effort to building up a background of information and goodwill with the bank. They should seek to know well the lending officers with whom they may deal, and to be known well and favorably by the lending officers, before they go into the bank with outstretched palms. Specifically, the banker should be told that credit might be asked in the future, so that he will accumulate a file of basic data on the company. At least annually, preferably quarterly, the bank should be furnished balance sheets and income data along with a verbal fill-in on the current operations and future outlook of the business. Information provided the banker should be more than "sales talk." Unfavorable information, as well as good news, should be discussed candidly. A loan officer familiar with a business over a period of years and confident that he has a complete picture of the company will be much more competent in working out a satisfactory loan arrangement, and certainly more comfortable in doing so, than in a situation completely new to him. Such knowledge promotes future confidence.

A further factor has become particularly important in recent years when loan demands have increased faster than the deposits of many banks, particularly the large city banks which loan heavily to national corporations. We refer to the renewed interest of bankers in deposit balances. Concerns that have kept, and will maintain, sizable deposit balances with a bank will find their requests for loans receive more favorable attention than those of equally creditworthy firms which have favored the bank with smaller deposits.

Supporting the Loan Application

Before applying for credit, the prospective borrower should attempt to analyze his own situation from the perspective and point of view of the bank lending officer. He should anticipate the banker's questions and have careful but convincing answers ready. While the detailed questions will vary with the situation, a number of the following will almost surely be raised:

1. Why has he left his former bank connection?
2. Why does the business need funds?
3. How much is needed?
4. How and when will the loan be repaid?
5. What are the possibilities that the plans of the company will miscarry?
6. If the plans miscarry, what will be the situation of the company, and how will it meet its commitment to the bank?
7. What is the background, character, and experience of the principal executives and/or owners of the business? This question will be particularly pointed and detailed in the case of the small company, where the success of the company is especially dependent upon only a few persons.
8. What is the record of profitability in the company?
9. What is the current financial position of the company?

In general, the better the evidence of careful planning, the more convincing will be the loan application. The banker must be confident that the managers of the borrowing company are and will stay "on top of their business."

Recent financial statements, preferably audited by a certified public accountant, should be submitted with loan requests. Highly desirable as supporting data are carefully prepared cash flow forecasts and projected balance sheets extending beyond the term of the loan requested. These projections should be invaluable in indicating the nature, timing, and amount of the need for funds and the cash inflows that will provide the means of repaying the loan—in other words, properly drawn, they provide ready answers to key questions in the banker's analysis. In those cases where the forecasts are based on tenuous assumptions, alternate forecasts on other assumptions may well be put before the banker so that he can fully understand the more important variables that will affect the borrower's funds requirements.

In emphatically stressing the value of cash flow projections, both in planning loan requests and in supporting loan applications, we recognize that only a modest, though growing, number of bankers customarily require them. Until the use of projections becomes more universally routine, as we believe will in time be the case, the financial officer who recognizes their value has the opportunity to add especial strength to his firm's credit request by voluntary submission of forecast data to his bankers.

Few bankers will be willing to finance operations or projects that do not promise to succeed. But there are few "sure things" in business, and risks of failure are present in some degree in almost all projects. Consequently, the answers to questions 5 and 6, above, are of particularly keen interest to the bank lender whose return for risk taking typically is small. In a very real sense the investment of the owners in the business serves as a protection or buffer against loss by the creditors should the venture fail. Naturally, the bank lender will be keenly interested in the size of this buffer in relation to the debts of the business and its adequacy to absorb the shrinkage in asset values from operations so unfavorable that failure of the firm results. Again, we can refer to classic and highly pertinent observations of the eighteenth-century writer, Adam Smith:

Traders and other undertakers may, no doubt, with great propriety, carry on a very considerable part of their projects with borrowed money. In justice to their creditors, however, their own capital ought, in this case, to be sufficient to ensure, if I may say so, the capital of those creditors; or to render it extremely improbable that those creditors should incur any loss, even though the success of the project should fall very much short of the expectation of the projectors.[10]

Just how much ownership capital the lender will deem enough to provide the desired protection is a matter of judgment in the light of the circumstances of the particular case. The greater the chances are of failure and of major shrinkage in the asset values should liquidation of the enterprise prove necessary, the greater, generally, will be the ownership capital the lender will require in relation to his and other debts of the enterprise. In virtually all instances the bank lender will give important attention to the size of the ownership investment relative to the borrowings on the enterprise.

In interviews with bankers representing more than 670 banks, members of a Federal Reserve System research group sought to determine the more important reasons for banker rejection of credit re-

---

[10] Smith, *op. cit.*, pp. 291–92.

quests of small business firms. Each bank was asked to rate the relative frequency with which each of a list of reasons for rejection had occurred. Responses were in terms of "frequent, occasional, rare, or never." In Table 10–5 the percentage of all banks responding

TABLE 10–5

RELATIVE FREQUENCY OF VARIOUS REASONS FOR REJECTIONS
OF SMALL BUSINESS LOAN APPLICATIONS

Reasons for Loan Rejections Involving Small Business	Percentage of All Banks Citing Each Reason as "Relatively Important"
Reasons involving creditworthiness of borrower:	
1. Not enough owner's equity in business	93
2. Poor earnings record	85
3. Questionable management ability	84
4. Collateral of insufficient quality	73
5. Slow and past due in trade or loan payments	69
6. Inadequacy of borrower accounting system	51
7. New firm with no established earnings record	48
8. Poor moral risk	41
9. Other reasons	6
Reasons involving bank's over-all policies:	
1. Requested maturity too long	71
2. Applicant has no established deposit relationship with bank	49
3. Applicant will not establish deposit relationship with bank	36
4. Type of loan not handled by bank	33
5. Line of business not handled by bank	21
6. Loan portfolio for type of loan already full	19
7. Other reasons	4
Reasons involving federal or state banking laws or regulations:	
1. Loan too large for bank's legal loan limit	23
2. Other reasons	9

SOURCE: Federal Reserve System, *Financing Small Business*, report to the Committees on Banking and Currency and the Select Committees on Small Business, U.S. Congress (Washington, D.C.: U.S. Government Printing Office, 1958), Part II, Vol. III, p. 415.

either "frequently" or "occasionally" to each of the reasons is presented.

Keeping a Good Bank Relationship

Bank relationships should be built to last. Well maintained, a good bank relationship grows stronger over the years and can become a priceless asset to a business. A cornerstone of a good banking relationship is continual diligence in meeting all commitments to the bank precisely and scrupulously. The spirit and letter of all agreements should be honored by the borrower. When it is unduly difficult or impossible to meet the commitments, every effort should be made to advise the bank *in advance* of developing trouble. In such fashion the banker is assured of the interest of the company in respecting its agreements and doubtless, for this knowledge, will be more receptive to requests for adjustments in the agreement when clearly necessary.

Secondly, the borrower should keep the bank informed of major developments in his business, even though there is no expectation that these developments necessarily will affect the borrowing arrangement adversely. The bank lending officers like to feel that they are accurately informed as to the affairs of their borrowing customers and prefer to hear of major developments affecting the company promptly and from company officers. In the absence of confidence that they are in complete and continual contact with their borrowing customers, the bank officers must depend on the unreliable and often distorting services of the "grapevine."

Third, as suggested above, candor is extremely important in a continuing relationship. It is not very difficult for a glib person to sell a "bill of goods" to a banker once and perhaps twice, but the passage of time will help even an unsophisticated banker recognize a "phony" for what he is. A continuing relationship can be built only on continuing, mutual confidence.

Fourth, to restate a point made earlier, a good banking relationship, like a good marriage, is worth cultivating. "Cultivation" includes, wherever possible, the maintenance of deposit balances of a size attractive to the bank.

Much of the above comment and advice will seem commonplace and obvious to many readers. It is offered in the full knowledge, however, that a great many businessmen very much neglect their bank relationships and would profit greatly by following the guidelines to good banking relationships we have outlined.

Chapter 11

Nonbank Sources of Short-Term Credit

HAVING discussed in Chapter 7 the spontaneous sources of short-term credit normally available to business in routine, and in Chapter 10 the use of bank credit as a short-term source, we can now turn to a review of other sources of short-term funds for business. While the aggregate credit to business from the "other sources" is much less than that provided by the spontaneous sources or the banks, the importance of these sources to the particular firms who can advantageously tap them is often great.

The Commercial Paper Market as a Source of Short-Term Funds

To several hundred concerns of strong credit standing the commercial paper market is an important source of short-term funds. *Commercial paper* refers to short-term promissory notes, generally unsecured, which are sold through commercial paper dealers or directly to investors. The investors in commercial paper include banks and other financial institutions; but in recent years, nonfinancial concerns with excess funds to invest on a short-term basis have been the major buyers of commercial paper.

Notes sold in the commercial paper market typically are written in denominations or multiples of $5,000 and with maturities of from one to nine months. Ninety-day maturities are particularly common. Some firms sell commercial paper on a continuing basis; others borrow through its sale only to meet seasonal and other temporary needs.

The setup and pattern of operation of the commercial paper market is such that it is at the disposal only of borrowers with high credit standing. Prospective users of commercial paper must be relatively large, with a net worth of at least $500,000 and commonly $5 million or more. Credit records and pay-out prospects must be excellent. Also, commercial paper borrowers are expected to have open and unused bank borrowing lines which could be drawn on, if necessary, to replace the commercial paper borrowing. Finally, the firm name should be one recognized immediately by investors as an excellent credit risk.

According to an unpublished analysis, 327 firms in a wide variety of industries sold commercial paper in 1960. A summary of the industry distribution of these firms follows:

Finance companies	118
Manufacturers:	
Textiles	26
Food and related products	32
Metal products	22
Leather products	8
Lumber, wood, paper, and rope	7
Cigars and cigarettes	7
Other manufacturers	27
Wholesalers	37
Retailers	32
Miscellaneous	11
	327

Borrowing through commercial paper is an old practice dating back more than a century. Chart 11–1 traces the fluctuation in total volume of commercial paper outstanding in recent decades. The decline in the use of commercial paper during the 1930's will be noted, as well as the post-World War II increase, attributable largely to finance companies. Some four fifths of the total dollar volume of commercial paper since 1945 has been issued by finance companies who use it to supplement other borrowing. The finance companies are the main source of the commercial paper shown in Chart 11–1 as placed directly with investors.

A principal attraction of borrowing through commercial paper lies in the relatively low rates of interest at which this borrowing can be accomplished. If the borrowing firm can meet the exacting standards for use of commercial paper, it can ordinarily obtain short-term funds thereby at effective interest rates significantly below the interest rates charged by commercial banks. Chart 11–2 pictures this rate differential in recent years.

The notes sold in the commercial paper market do not provide for interest as such. Instead, an effective interest rate is established by sale of the notes at a discount from face value. Thus, a six-month note for $100,000 sold by a "prime name" in March, 1961, at the

CHART 11–1

COMMERCIAL PAPER OUTSTANDING AT YEAR END, 1918–60

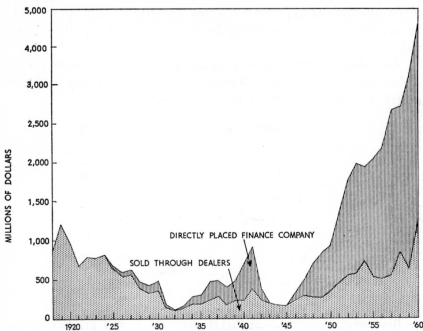

SOURCE: Data for 1918–47 are from Federal Reserve Bank of Chicago, *Business Conditions* (Chicago, August, 1955). Data for 1948–60 are from *Federal Reserve Bulletin*.

then prevailing market rate of 3 per cent per annum would net the borrower $98,375, which is the amount left after deduction of interest discount of $1,500 and the dealer's commission of 0.25 per cent per year for the six-month bill, $125.

Finance Companies

The label *finance company* is used loosely in business circles. In the absence of a more crisply definitive term, we use the term *finance companies* to refer to the several thousand firms that are in the business of lending money, yet cannot be classified as banks, insurance companies, or other forms of traditional financial institutions. This rather broad definition includes many companies which specialize in one or more of several widely different types of lending. However, a few of the largest finance companies, such as the Commercial Credit Company and C.I.T. Financial Corporation (C.I.T.), directly, or through subsidiaries, offer a wide range of lending services. Finance companies, regardless of their special lines of business, raise their funds in much the same general fashion. Almost all are corporations

CHART 11–2

SELECTED SHORT-TERM MONEY RATES

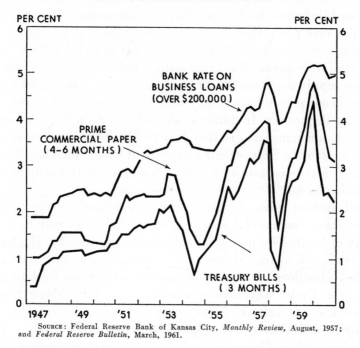

SOURCE: Federal Reserve Bank of Kansas City, *Monthly Review*, August, 1957; and *Federal Reserve Bulletin*, March, 1961.

with a significant ownership equity, often in the form of both common and preferred stock. On the basis of the equity investment and profitable records, finance companies have been able to borrow relatively large amounts through short-term bank loans and through sale of commercial paper and a variety of long-term debt instruments. For example, the consolidated balance sheet of C.I.T. on December 31, 1960, showed ownership funds of approximately $327 million compared with total debts of $1,939 million. By borrowing at lower rates than they charge on their loans, the finance companies hope to cover their expenses and enhance the return on their stockholders' investment.

Most of the finance companies specialize in direct lending to individuals and are called *personal finance* or *consumer finance companies*. Household Finance Corporation is the largest company of this type. On December 31, 1960, these firms had outstanding instalment loans of $4,212 million.[1] Another group of firms are known as *sales finance companies*. These firms specialize in the purchase from re-

[1] *Federal Reserve Bulletin*, February, 1961.

tailers of the instalment receivables arising out of retail sales of auto-mobiles, household appliances, industrial equipment, farm equipment, mobile homes, boats, and other durable goods sold on the instalment payment plan. The total instalment credit held by sales finance companies at the end of 1960 was estimated at $11.1 billion.[2] Given the fact of widespread instalment selling, the sales finance companies in effect supply the funds that firms selling on instalment credit would have to acquire elsewhere if they were to carry the investment in receivables themselves. In addition, these firms do a large volume of wholesale financing; that is, they loan to distributors and retailers of the above items to finance their inventory of unsold merchandise. The inventory serves as security for these loans, which typically are on a continuing basis.

Still another group of firms, variously termed *business finance companies* or *commercial finance companies,* lend directly to a wide variety of businesses, mainly of small and medium size. The bulk of their lending is against the security of assigned accounts receivable, but they also do a significant amount of lending on inventory and equipment. Under special circumstances, these firms also extend unsecured loans to valued clients, but the volume of their unsecured lending is small. Rates charged, translated into annual interest terms, range from 12 to 24 per cent, with 16 per cent a common figure. Most of their business customers are ones that could not qualify for equivalent bank credit; the borrowing relationship typically is a continuing one over a period of years, ending when the position of the borrower has sufficiently improved so that it can shift to lower cost sources.

Industry sources estimate the "total volume of commercial financing" in 1960 at $10 billion, up from $2 billion in 1950.[3] In view of the turnover of receivables and other assets against which the total advances were made, the credit extended at any one time was only a fraction of the $10 billion annual total. Nevertheless, the volume of such credit is significant and has grown steadily through boom and recession years alike.

A limited number of finance companies specialize in providing a distinctive financing service known as *factoring.* Factoring is essentially the purchase of accounts receivable. It has become sufficiently important to warrant separate discussion later in this chapter.

---

[2] *Ibid.*

[3] William J. Drake, "Report on Commercial Financing and Factoring in 1960," *Proceedings of Sixteenth Annual Convention of the Commercial Finance Industry* (New York: National Commercial Finance Conference, Inc., 1960).

As we have suggested, the lines between the various types of finance companies often are blurred. A breakdown of the receivables acquired during 1960 and those outstanding on December 31, 1960, in the course of the finance company operations of Commercial Credit Company and its subsidiaries indicates the varied kinds of financing supplied by this leading diversified firm:

RECEIVABLES ACQUIRED DURING 1960
(In Millions)

Motor retail	$ 660.9
Farm equipment, mobile homes, and other retail	306.5
Loan receivables	239.5
Motor wholesale	1,343.6
Factoring, open accounts, leases, other wholesale notes, and mortgages	1,737.4
Total	$4,287.9

RECEIVABLES OUTSTANDING ON DECEMBER 31, 1960
(In Millions)

Automobile, retail	$ 701.5
Automobile, wholesale	200.9
Farm equipment, wholesale and retail	250.7
Mobile home, appliance, and other, retail and wholesale	213.5
Factored receivables	163.3
Business loans secured by accounts receivables	106.3
Fleet leasing	47.0
Industrial equipment	58.9
Personal or direct loan	158.9
Sundry	6.0
Total	$1,907.0

The diversified lending operations of companies like Commercial Credit Company suggest a characteristic important to many business borrowers. Generally, the better finance companies have won a reputation as venturesome and imaginative lenders. Their willingness to consider lending to companies in difficult situations, and their skill and resourcefulness in setting up lending arrangements that meet the pressing needs of borrowers yet hold the lender's risks to tolerable proportions, have made them an invaluable source of credit for many companies and won them an important role in the economy.

The Use of Factoring

As an alternative method of converting accounts receivable into cash, many firms can look to factoring, a service offered by factoring concerns and a very limited number of commercial banks.[4]

---

[4] Among the larger firms active in factoring are three subsidiaries of C.I.T. Financial Corporation: Commercial Factors Corp.; William Iselin & Co., Inc.; and Meinhard & Co.,

For many decades, factoring has been very important in the textile industry, and this industry was still the source of 80 per cent of total factoring business in 1960.[5] In recent decades, its use has spread to many other industries. Factoring perhaps can best be understood if major distinctive aspects of a factoring arrangement are compared with those of a loan secured by assignment of accounts receivable. As we shall see in Chapter 12, under the typical accounts receivable loan arrangement the borrower still holds title to his accounts receivable,[6] and the lender expects him to absorb losses if particular accounts are not paid. The firms owing the accounts normally are *not* notified that their account is pledged and continue to send their payments to the borrower. In contrast, the typical factoring arrangement has the following characteristics:

1. The factor *purchases* accounts acceptable to him without recourse. That is, if the accounts are not paid, the loss is the factor's. The client no longer carries factored accounts receivable on his balance sheet, in effect having converted them into cash.[7]

2. Firms owing the accounts receivable to client firms are notified that the account has been sold to the factor and asked to remit directly to the factor.

3. As implied above, the factor seldom agrees to buy all of the accounts receivable of a client firm; instead, he retains the right to screen the accounts and select those acceptable to him. The client firm can continue to sell to customers whose accounts are unacceptable to the factor, but it must carry them itself and assume all risks on them.

4. Under the typical factoring arrangement the client maintains a running account with the factor. As receivables are sold to the factor, the proceeds are put at the client's disposal in this account. Often, clients are given the privilege of overdrawing their account with the factor, or, in effect, of borrowing on an unsecured basis, in addition to drawing against the proceeds of the factored accounts. Also, interest is normally credited by the factor on funds left with him.

Inc. Textile Banking Co., Inc., a subsidiary of Commercial Credit Company; Walter E. Heller & Co.; United Factors, Inc.; James Talcott, Inc.; and John P. Maguire & Co. are also among the largest firms doing factoring.

The First National Bank of Boston, the Trust Company of Georgia, and the Bank of America National Trust and Savings Association are among the few commercial banks which have developed a factoring service on an important scale.

[5] Drake, *op. cit.*

[6] The borrower pledging accounts receivable shows the pledged receivables on his balance sheet. Good accounting practice requires note, however, of the fact that they are pledged as security.

[7] Where the factor advances less than 100 per cent of the receivables, the borrower carries his equity in the receivable among his assets. Thus, if $500,000 of accounts are factored but only 90 per cent is advanced, the client would show accounts receivable of $50,000 on his balance sheet.

Usually, the factor's charges are computed and assigned to the client's account once a month. The computation of the factor's net charges, involving a variety of charges and credits, is a somewhat complex one. This complexity, together with the fact that the factor provides certain distinctive services, such as credit investigation, collection, and the absorption of bad debt losses, makes difficult a clear-cut comparison of the costs of factoring with the costs of alternative methods of raising funds. However, factoring is widely regarded as a relatively high-cost method of financing. Outside the textile industry, factoring has been used most widely by firms with annual sales in the $500,000 to $10 million range.

Definitive data on the total volume of funds furnished business by factoring firms are not available, but industry sources estimate the annual volume of receivables factored during 1960 at $6 billion.[8] This figure for annual purchases of receivables suggests that the funds made available at any one time by the factors—that is, the average investment in receivables by all clients of factors that was eliminated by factoring—amounted to something less than $1 billion.

Private Lenders

In past decades a number of private individuals who had accumulated considerable wealth, particularly in the smaller cities and towns of the nation, made a practice of lending money. While most of their loans took the form of long-term notes, they did some short-term lending to businesses, particularly smaller local concerns. While no statistical information is available on the loans of individuals to businesses, there is strong reason to believe that the amount of such lending currently is small.

In the larger cities, there are still individuals who make business loans, usually to firms that cannot find enough credit elsewhere. Rates charged are very high, often amounting to annual rates of 24 per cent or more on the funds supplied. The little information that is available about such lenders suggests that they are truly a "source of last resort" and that they should be dealt with most cautiously— preferably not at all.

Customer Advances and Prepayments

Some companies are able to get substantial aid from customers in the form of advances against orders for future production and delivery, or by special arrangements under which partial payments are

---

[8] Drake, *op. cit.*

received prior to completion of an order or contract. Such financial aid from suppliers is most important to producers of large, specialized equipment, where the time and expense involved in production are great. For example, R. Hoe & Co., which makes high-speed printing presses, reported customer advances of $3 million on September 30, 1959, when total assets of the company were $14.6 million.

Most contract builders depend heavily on customer advances and/or contractual agreements under which they are authorized to bill customers as certain costs are incurred in connection with the partially completed contract. For example, Foster Wheeler Corporation designs, manufactures, and installs power plant, chemical plant, and oil refinery equipment. At the end of 1959, Foster Wheeler showed on its balance sheet advance payments from customers of $10.9 million against total assets of $77.1 million. In addition, costs and accrued profits on contracts in process were shown at $11.3 million, which represented total costs and profits covering $122.3 million of uncompleted contracts *less* $111 million already billed customers on the uncompleted contracts. Had Foster Wheeler not been able to collect from its customers in advance of completion, its total financial needs would have been more than twice what they were.

Special Credit from Suppliers

In our earlier discussion of trade credit from suppliers as a spontaneous source, we did not discuss the possibilities of obtaining through negotiation special additional credit from suppliers. Under certain circumstances, sellers are willing to grant somewhat longer terms than those made available in routine to all their credit customers. In a number of instances, buying firms have been able to negotiate with the seller special terms for the financing of an especially large or otherwise unique purchase order. Illustrative of such possibilities was the reported willingness of the Hammond Organ Company to offer to new distributors of Hammond's products term credits as large as twice the distributor's equity investment. According to the vice president of finance of Hammond: "We will offer loans up to 200%, to be retired in three years, at an attractive interest rate. This capital financing program will help us put into business those who have expressed interest in owning a studio but who have not had the necessary capital."[9]

Not infrequently, hard-pressed firms are able to arrange with im-

---

[9] *Wall Street Journal*, October 31, 1960.

portant suppliers to put outstanding overdue open-account payables on a note basis with maturities deferred for a period of months or years. In such cases, it is usually expected that new purchases will be on open account and regular terms, and will be paid promptly when due; it is the prospect of further business and an improved relationship that encourages suppliers to accept deferred payment arrangements on old payables. Needless to say, suppliers enter into such deals with reluctance.

Another form of special credit is the use of special credit terms designed to encourage distributor or retailer inventory stocking well ahead of their normal selling season. In such cases the supplier offers "seasonal datings," that is, special credit terms which require payment only after the retail selling season is well advanced. Special credit terms also are often made available in the case of promotional stocks.

A number of firms have formed finance company affiliates to help dealers finance inventories of their products as well as to take over retail instalment sales contracts. Some firms are willing to support bank borrowing by customers with credit guaranties or agreements to buy back unsold inventories of their products. Suppliers also may provide financial aid to their customers to permit them to acquire specialized equipment necessary to handle their products. A number of dairy products producers help customers acquire refrigeration equipment. Grain companies may finance customers' purchases of bulk feed storage facilities. Oil companies may help finance the construction of filling stations.

Speaking generally, suppliers are most likely to consider granting special credit terms when all or most of the following circumstances exist: The customer is one who can be expected to buy important quantities of goods in the future if the special terms are granted; the customer can get equally satisfactory products from other suppliers; the supplier itself is well financed; the supplier expects to operate at a rate short of full capacity, and marginal production costs are low; and there is evidence that the need for special credit will not last indefinitely. If the supplier is making a large profit margin on marginal increments of sales, the chances of his agreeing to a special credit deal are enhanced greatly.

Reliance on suppliers for unusual credit arrangements can have weighty disadvantages, including the loss of bargaining power on price, delivery, and other terms. However, firms hard pressed for funds should not overlook the possibility of negotiating special credit terms for new purchases, extended payment terms on existing payables, or other forms of assistance from major suppliers.

Credit Instruments Used Predominantly in Foreign Trade: The Banker's Acceptance

Certain credit instruments, of which the *banker's acceptance* is the most important, are used primarily in connection with the financing of imports from and exports to foreign countries. The financing of foreign trade involves many distinctive instruments and practices, detailed description of which is best left to specialized books on the subject. We shall briefly discuss here the banker's acceptance and its use, both because of its importance in foreign trade and as an example of the specialized instruments of credit that have been developed to meet special needs.

The banker's acceptance begins as a *draft* or demand for payment, drawn on a bank, asking the bank to pay a stated amount to a stated firm or its assignees at a definite date. When the bank on which it is drawn agrees to make the payment by writing "Accepted" on the draft (along with the signature of an authorized official of the bank), it becomes a banker's acceptance—or an obligation of the accepting bank. Of course, the bank will only accept drafts in behalf of customers who have made the necessary previous arrangements with the bank and convinced it that they in turn will repay the bank upon maturity of the acceptance. The accepting bank charges a commission of at least 1½ per cent for the use of its name and credit.

An illustration may help to explain how the banker's acceptance is used as a source of credit by business firms. Let us assume that a New York manufacturer of topcoats desires to import a $20,000 shipment of Harris tweed from a manufacturer in Scotland. The Scottish manufacturer is anxious to make the sale and will be willing to defray the costs of extending the credit the American importer wants on the deal—say, ninety days from shipment.

The New York garmentmaker—who, we shall assume, has a good credit standing with his New York bank—arranges to have his bank open a *letter of credit* in favor of the Scottish tweed manufacturer. This document states that the New York bank will honor—or accept —drafts drawn on the New York firm, provided they are drawn in accordance with detailed terms stated in the letter of credit. When shipment is made, the Scottish firm prepares a ninety-day draft on the New York firm in accordance with the letter of credit and presents it to its local bank. That bank will advance the funds—actually, the pound equivalent of $20,000 less interest and fees—to the Scottish company and forward the draft along with shipping papers, the ocean bill of lading, etc., to its New York correspondent bank, which presents it to the New York manufacturer's bank for acceptance. If all papers are found to be in order, the New York manufacturer's bank accepts the draft, and it becomes a *banker's acceptance.*

Since there is an open market in bankers' acceptances based on their very strong credit standing as a result of the bank's acceptance, the Scottish bank could readily arrange its sale and thus recoup the dollar equivalent of the funds it had advanced. The American manufacturer gets the credit he wants, the risks to all parties except the accepting bank are minimal, and the sales transaction is completed. The credit transaction is completed when in ninety days the acceptance is presented to the New York bank and paid by it; and the bank, in turn, looks for repayment to the New York manufacturer.

Of course, the accepting bank depends heavily on the credit of its customer—the New York importing manufacturer. It may release the goods to him upon arrival only under a security arrangement, or it may satisfy itself that it can safely accept the draft without requiring security when the goods are released to the manufacturer.

Since the Scottish firm, or its bank, usually is in a poor position to assess the creditworthiness of the American customer, the use of the letter of credit and the insertion of the American bank's credit into the picture through its acceptance is an important, and often vital, part of the trade arrangement.

Although bankers' acceptances are used predominantly to finance the movement of goods in international trade, they are also used to a modest extent for domestic transactions where goods are used as security. In one field, the domestic storage and sale of raw cotton by cotton dealers, bankers' acceptances are a major method of financing. At the end of 1960, bankers' acceptances outstanding were estimated at $2,027 million, of which $308 million represented domestic transactions. Bankers' acceptances, like commercial paper, are bought and sold on a discount basis. Discount rates during December, 1960, averaged 2.88 per cent, a rate approximating that of prime commercial paper, and only modestly above the rate of U.S. government ninety-day bills.[10] The low rate reflects the high credit standing of bankers' acceptances as obligations of the banks.[11]

---

[10] *Federal Reserve Bulletin,* February, 1961.

[11] For a more complete description of the use of acceptances and the market for them, see Federal Reserve Bank of Cleveland, *Monthly Business Review,* January, 1961.

U.S. Governmental Sources of Short-Term Funds

In recent decades the United States Congress has enacted a number of laws providing for federal government financial assistance to business enterprise. Most of these programs have been directed at meeting financial needs which have been intermediate or long term rather than short term as we have defined it. In view of the great variety in the provisions for governmental financial assistance, however, a classification of the purposes of federal financial assistance to private concerns may be helpful. The legislation providing for governmental financial assistance seems to fall into four rough categories.

1. Broad-scale government loans to business under depression conditions, in which the normal sources of financial assistance to business are inadequate for business needs, or where the economic welfare of the country suggests the wisdom of lending standards more lenient than those normally considered appropriate by lenders for profit.
2. Legislation under which governmental agencies seek to fill gaps in the financial structure of the country believed to exist under normal economic conditions.
3. Aids to suppliers to the government of military items.
4. Special aids to particularly deserving groups such as military personnel returning to civilian life and the victims of floods, tornadoes, or other disasters.

Broad-Scale Government Financing to Business under Depression Circumstances

During the depression of the 1930's, several governmental agencies were established to loan public funds to business firms in need of aid because of depressed conditions. The Reconstruction Finance Corporation was the most important agency set up for this purpose, and it granted loans on a massive scale to a wide variety of businesses, both large and small. Most of the RFC loans called for periodic repayment over a period of years. During World War II, this agency also provided much aid to industries vital to the war effort. Finally, in 1953, the RFC was put in the position of winding up its affairs. By that date, it had loaned more than $12 billion. A very large percentage of the RFC loans were ultimately repaid. In the event of general depression the federal government probably would again establish credit facilities of the RFC type.

Government Efforts to Fill Gaps in the Availability of Credit

Even under prosperous conditions, Congress has concluded that private financing agencies have not met fully the needs of all segments of socially desirable business. Most important of the gaps have been in the availability of intermediate loan capital for smaller businesses, in the loan capital available to farmers, and in credit on export sales. Various agencies have been set up to assist small businesses to meet their capital needs. The most recent of these, the Small Business Administration, in 1953 was given the authority both to make direct loans and to guarantee portions of loans to small business by banks and other private lenders. The Small Business Administration has described the business loan program in these words:

Section 207 (a) of the Act gives the Small Business Administration authority *to make loans to small business enterprises when credit is not otherwise available on reasonable terms.*[12] The loans are intended to fill a gap in the financing provided small firms by private financial institutions and are designed to stimulate and preserve the initiative, independence and enterprise of small businesses. To the greatest extent possible, the Small Business Administration is striving to provide this credit in cooperation with private lending institutions. Its success in this is evidenced by the fact that about two-thirds of all loans approved are in participation with banks and other financial institutions.

In order to expand financial assistance to small business concerns and to promote a balanced national economy, the Bank–Small Business Administration participation loan plan offers the greatest possible benefit to the participating institution consistent with the intent of the Small Business Act. For example, the plan enables a bank to broaden its lending activities, while maintaining desired liquidity of assets. The bank is assured a fair return on money loaned and is able to give better service to its depositors.

In the administration of its lending program under Section 207 (a) of the Small Business Act, the Small Business Administration is governed by the policies established by the Agency's Loan Policy Board and the requirement of the Act that *"loans be of such sound value or so secured as reasonably to assure repayment."*[12] The Agency applies the most liberal interpretation of these policies and requirements possible, consistent with sound credit principles, but at the same time is fully aware of its responsibility to protect Government funds. Therefore, each loan application is thoroughly analyzed and a loan is never approved or declined without full consideration of all factors concerned. The Agency's lending program is under continual study, and the area in which credit can be provided safely is being constantly reviewed.

Under the policies described above, the SBA has developed an active business loan program. By June 30, 1960, the SBA had considered 42,994 loan applications and had approved 20,232 of these, totaling $955.2 million. The average size of the loans made was $57,053. Despite the relatively low maximum interest rate of 5½ per cent, a number of loan requests have been canceled after approval;

---

[12] Italics supplied.

through June, 1960, a total of $744.2 million had been disbursed on 16,471 loans. Of this amount, 28 per cent was disbursed by participating banks or other financial institutions.

Thirty-two per cent of the number and 45 per cent of the amount of loans approved were to manufacturers. Retailers and service firms accounted for a large percentage of the remaining loans approved.

It is interesting to note the reasons given for loan rejections by this "source of last resort," as summarized in Exhibit 11–1.

EXHIBIT 11–1

U.S. SMALL BUSINESS ADMINISTRATION
REASONS FOR DECLINING BUSINESS LOAN APPLICATIONS
January 1 through June 30, 1960

Reasons	Number	Per Cent of Total
Total Reasons*......................	4,264	100.0
Lack of reasonable assurance of ability to repay loan (and other obligations) from earnings............................	1,564	36.7
Collateral, considered along with other credit factors, not deemed sufficient to protect the interest of the government...	931	21.8
Disproportion of [loan requested and of] debts to [tangible] net worth before and after loan...........................	923	21.6
Need for loan funds not demonstrated.....	327	7.7
Inadequate working capital after the loan..	284	6.7
The result of granting the financial assistance requested would be to replenish funds distributed to the owners.........	68	1.6
Other—including size, policy reason.......	167	3.9

* Total number of reasons is in excess of the number of applications declined (1,936) because in most instances, two or more reasons for declination were given.

SOURCE: Small Business Administration, *Fourteenth Semiannual Report for the Six Months Ending June 30, 1960* (Washington, D.C.: U.S. Government Printing Office, 1960).

Under Section 207 (*b*), as amended, of the Small Business Act of 1953, the SBA is also authorized to make loans to assist in the rehabilitation of homes and businesses which have been damaged by floods, storms, or other natural disasters. In addition, the SBA is empowered to give loan assistance to businesses suffering economic loss as a result of drought conditions where there is any reasonable chance of rehabilitation. In the words of the SBA: "Loans can be made only to the extent of actual losses (apart from those of drought) not covered by insurance, and, as in the case of regular business loans, cannot be approved if the financing is otherwise available on reasonable terms."

Since the disaster loans are intended as a rehabilitation measure, much more liberal credit standards are applied to them than would be prudent for the agency's business loans. Interest rates, too, are lower (3 per cent). Through June, 1960, 9,241 disaster loan applications, totaling $93.3 million, had been approved.

The SBA also has important administrative responsibilities under the Small Business Investment Act, which we shall discuss in a later chapter.

Mention should also be made of the development credit corporations that have been established in a number of states and localities. The purpose of these organizations is to support employment and economic activity in their areas by extending financial or other support to firms that cannot secure the needed funds from conventional lenders. Most of the development corporations operate with local government encouragement and in some cases public funds, but most are privately financed. Although they make short-term loans, their loans are mainly of intermediate term and call for instalment repayment. Typically, security is required. The first development corporations were established in New England; in seven years through 1960 a rather typical one of these, the Massachusetts Business Development Corporation, had made or participated in 139 loans totaling $16 million. As the Massachusetts Business Development Corporation experience suggests, the volume of lending of these corporations has been modest.

Governmental financial aid to farmers has taken a variety of forms. Suffice it for our purpose here to recognize that sizable governmental programs exist to help the farmers finance both long-term and short-term needs.

Section 13 (*b*) of the Federal Reserve Act, enacted in 1934, authorized the twelve Federal Reserve banks under certain circumstances to make direct loans to business. Through December, 1957, a total of 3,786 applications had been approved, amounting to $841.3 million. Most of the approved loans were not actually used, however; and currently, this program is inactive.

One student of the subject commented that government programs of loans to private business, such as those of the RFC, the Federal Reserve banks under Section 13 (*b*), and the SBA, shared the following characteristics:[13]

1. Avoidance of competition with private lenders and the related emphasis on participation arrangements with private lenders. . . .
2. Emphasis on secured loans.

[13] Carl T. Arlt, "Government Loan Programs for Small Business," chap. xii in *Financing Small Business* (Washington, D.C.: Board of Governors, Federal Reserve System, 1958).

3. Elaborate procedure of loan processing involving counseling on business management matters.
4. Large proportion of loan applications denied.
5. Relative inflexibility of interest rates over time and absence of differentials for varying size, risk, and maturity of loans.
6. Intermediate-term financing for working capital purposes.
7. Large proportion of loan approvals for manufacturing enterprises.
8. Subsidy aspects of programs.

Especially important among the government-sponsored organizations active in the support of export sales by U.S. firms has been the Export-Import Bank, a government-owned corporation. The "EX-IM Bank" makes loans to foreign governments and private concerns which permit them to purchase machinery and other products from U.S. firms. In addition, the EX-IM Bank participates with American exporters and U.S. commercial banks in extending short- and intermediate-term credit to foreign buyers on specific export transactions, such as the sale of textile machinery to a Colombian textile manufacturer. The scale of EX-IM Bank lending has been substantial. New credits in its fiscal year ended June 30, 1960, totaled $499.6 million; and outstanding loans at year end, $3,231.8 million.[14]

Financial Aids to Military Suppliers

During World War II, it was vitally important that production of war goods not be hampered by the financial limitations of otherwise desirable suppliers. Accordingly, a variety of forms of financial aid to military suppliers was developed. Most forms were continued in use after the war, although used more selectively, or were revived during the Korean conflict. As long as defense outlays continue at a high level, the financial aids to military suppliers will continue to be of great importance.

The more important financial devices to help private business assist in the defense effort include the following:

1. Government Construction and Equipping of Plants with Government Money. For many important items the government provides the basic facilities and equipment, and private concerns operate the facilities, providing—sometimes with government aid—the necessary working capital and management for operations.

2. Authorization of Rapid Amortization of New Facilities and Equipment Important Immediately or Potentially for Defense Pur-

---

[14] Export-Import Bank, *Annual Report, 1960* (Washington, D.C.: U.S. Government Printing Office, 1960).

poses Which Are Acquired, Owned, and Operated by Private Concerns. In time of emergency a method of depreciation was available under our federal tax laws to those firms who obtained, for certain new assets, a *certificate of necessity* from a military procurement agency. The certificate stated that the assets in question were necessary for defense purposes and that otherwise they would not be constructed. In such cases *accelerated amortization* was allowed on all or part of the cost of the assets and the investment could be depreciated in five years. This was avowedly an incentive plan designed to induce capital investment where desired by the government, and it was effective because of the large size of the tax shields provided in the first five years of a project. The certificates could no longer be granted after December 31, 1959.

3. Government Guaranties of Commercial Bank Loans to Military Contractors. The program of government loan guaranties, known as the "V–Loan" program, is designed to help private firms get commercial bank credit to aid them in financing working capital needs arising out of performance under specific defense contracts. Under this program the contractor negotiates a loan with his commercial bank. The bank typically agrees to advance a percentage (often 80 per cent, but sometimes higher) of the contractor's inventory and receivables connected with the military supply contract. As a means of encouraging the bank to make the loan through reducing the risks of loss to the bank, the buying service—Army, Navy, or Air Force— guarantees repayment to the bank of a percentage, often 80 or 90 per cent, of the bank's advances to the contractor. The banks must pay a percentage of the interest charged on the loan to the government for its guaranty, the amount of the payment varying with the percentage of the total loan guaranteed.

From revival of the V–Loan program in 1950 through August, 1960, 1,573 V–Loans were authorized, totaling $3.3 billion. On August 31, 1960, V–Loans amounting to $281 million were outstanding.[15] In recent years, use of the program has declined greatly.

4. Progress Payments. Military contracts may authorize payments to the contractor before any deliveries of finished products are made. Progress payments are made as work proceeds under a contract on the basis of costs incurred or upon accomplishment of stages of completion of the project. They have become traditional for production contracts involving a "long lead time," or preparatory pe-

---

[15] *Federal Reserve Bulletin*, September, 1960.

riod of six months or more between the beginning of work under a contract and deliveries of finished products. Progress payments are widely used in the procurement of aircraft, ships, guided missiles, and a variety of other expensive items that involve lengthy design and production schedules. It was estimated in August, 1957, that $25 billion of outstanding contracts were of a sort qualifying for such payments, and that the United States had advanced some $4 billion on partly completed contracts.[16] After September 1, 1957, progress payments on new contracts based on costs were limited to 70 per cent of the contractor's total cost outlays or 85 per cent of his direct labor and materials costs. Slightly higher percentage payments were permitted small business firms.

5. *Advance Payments.* Under certain circumstances, the terms of military contracts may authorize advance payments to prime contractors prior to and in anticipation of performance under the contracts. As distinguished from progress payments, advance payments do not require previous work on the contract. It is Defense Department policy to authorize advance payments only if no other method of financing will meet the contractor's needs. Special procedures, including the use of special bank accounts, designed to protect the government's interests, are involved in advance payments. Advance payments are used, for example, where the work under the contract is of such a secret nature that other financing methods, such as V–Loans, would be inappropriate. Although somewhat cumbersome in use, advance payments have the attraction to the contractor of minimizing the use of his own funds in contract work.

We should make clear that the government is sparing in its extension of the various financing aids to contractors, and many military suppliers cannot qualify for any of them. For example, a food manufacturer supplying a standard ration item under competitive bid types of contracts would likely receive no financial assistance from the government in fulfilling the contract.

Where financing aid is to be extended suppliers, current Defense Department policy favors the use of loan guaranties, in preference to either progress payments or advance payments. Progress payments are preferred to advance payment.

Programs of Aid to Especially Deserving Groups

An example of programs of this sort is the provision by legislation for governmental guaranties of certain loans by banks or other pri-

---

[16] *Wall Street Journal,* August 14, 1957, p. 8.

vate agencies to ex-servicemen. Greatest use of these loan guaranties by veterans has been for the purchase of homes. However, guaranties of up to 50 per cent and a dollar amount of $2,000 can be obtained for business ventures that have good promise of success. Through 1959, 233,760 loans, totaling $651 million, involving credit for business ventures of veterans, had been made under this continuing but decelerating program. It is interesting to note that defaults were reported on 42,632, or 18 per cent, of these loans through 1959; claims for Veterans Administration reimbursement were filed on 15,885, or about 7 per cent of the loans.[17]

The disaster loan program of the SBA, discussed earlier, is another example of this sort of government financial aid.

---

[17] Administrator of Veterans Affairs, *Annual Report, 1959* (Washington, D.C.: U.S. Government Printing Office, 1960).

Chapter 12

The Effective Use of Security in Business Borrowing

A VITAL feature of much business borrowing is the granting to lenders of a security interest in particular assets of the borrower. A large percentage of the commercial bank credit, and virtually all of the credit granted business by commercial finance companies and governmental agencies, is predicated on the pledge of security.

A comprehensive study of business loans by member banks of the Federal Reserve System in 1957 revealed that 856,000 of the 1,281,-000 business loans outstanding at these banks, or 66.8 per cent, were supported by collateral.[1] Table 12–1 is adapted from a table in that study. Comparison with earlier studies in 1946 and 1955 indicates that the use of security in commercial bank lending to business increased modestly during the post-World War II period.

The use of security is particularly important in the bank borrowing of small and medium-sized firms. This conclusion is supported by the Federal Reserve study, which disclosed that secured loans, while representing 66.8 per cent of the total *number* of business loans, accounted for $20,426 million, or 50.3 per cent, of the total *amount* of bank credit to business.[2] The lower dollar amount percentage reflects the fact that most large loans are made on an unsecured basis. As might be expected in view of the general tendency for the financial strength of business firms to increase with asset size, the study showed that the use of security varied inversely with the size of the borrowing firm. Thus, 76.5 per cent of the bank credit extended firms with total assets of between $50,000 and $250,000 was on a secured

---

[1] *Federal Reserve Bulletin*, April, 1958.

[2] *Ibid.*

TABLE 12-1

RELATION OF SECURED LOANS TO TOTAL BUSINESS LOANS OF MEMBER BANKS, 1957, WITHIN SIZE-OF-BORROWER GROUPS

SIZE OF BORROWER (TOTAL ASSETS, IN THOUSANDS OF DOLLARS)	AMOUNT			NUMBER		
	Total Loans (in Millions of Dollars)	Secured Loans		Total Loans (in Thousands)	Secured Loans	
		Millions of Dollars	Percentage of Total for Size Group		Thousands	Percentage of Total for Size Group
All borrowers*.........	40,618	20,426	50.3	1,281	856	66.8
Less than 50..........	1,456	1,141	78.4	505	344	68.2
50–250...............	5,256	4,023	76.5	494	325	65.7
250–1,000............	6,302	4,543	72.1	158	104	65.9
1,000–5,000..........	6,775	4,056	59.9	48	29	60.7
5,000–25,000.........	5,912	2,661	45.0	13	6	48.5
25,000–100,000.......	4,893	1,381	28.2	5	2	31.7
100,000 or more......	8,815	1,546	17.5	6	2	34.7

* Includes a small amount of loans to borrowers whose size was not ascertained.
SOURCE: Adapted from *Federal Reserve Bulletin*, April, 1958, p. 403.

basis, while only 17.5 per cent of the credit extended firms with assets above $100 million was secured.[3]

As we have seen, commercial finance companies are important lenders to business. A very high percentage of their loans to business is extended against security. Since the finance companies generally have been willing to loan to companies inherently more risky than commercial banks have cared to accommodate, they have been especially vigorous and imaginative in developing ways of taking security as a means of curbing their risks in lending.

The lending to business by governmental and semigovernmental agencies has been predominantly on a secured basis. A major proportion of the Reconstruction Finance Corporation loans were made against specific security. The loans currently made by the Small Business Administration, and loans supported by governmental guaranties to aid in the financing of war and defense production, such as those under the "V–Loan" program, typically are predicated on the grant of a security interest to the lender.

Why Borrowers Offer Security to Lenders

The paramount reason most borrowers offer lenders a security interest in their assets is simply to enhance their borrowing power. Many American concerns, particularly very large ones, enjoy such excellent profit prospects and strong financial positions that they do not need to offer security—they can get sufficient credit on suitable terms on an unsecured basis. But a great many more enterprises are able to boost their attractiveness to lenders materially by skillful concession of security interests in their assets.

To many firms with uncertain prospects or limited ownership funds, little or no credit, other than that from the spontaneous sources described in Chapter 7, is available on an unsecured basis. Only by offering security attractive to lenders are they able to get loans at all. In other words, to these firms, use of security in borrowing is not really a matter of choice but the *sine qua non* of any debt financing. For still other concerns in less weak circumstances, some credit may be available on an unsecured basis, but much larger amounts may be borrowed if security is offered.

In the case of other borrowers, offering security may be desirable primarily as a means of obtaining more favorable credit terms— lower interest rates, longer maturity schedules, or less restrictive

---

[3] *Ibid.*

covenants—than could be obtained through unsecured borrowing. For example, many railroads use locomotives or other rolling stock as security under equipment trust certificates, a borrowing device referred to later in this chapter. The repayment record of equipment trust certificates over past decades has been so excellent that it is usually possible for even the strongest railroads to borrow through equipment trust certificates at lower net interest rates than could be obtained through unsecured borrowing for comparable periods.

Why Security Is Valuable to the Lender

Why do lenders so frequently prefer a "secured position" to the status of an unsecured creditor? As suggested earlier, lenders take collateral primarily as a means of reducing the risk of loss through nonrepayment of their loans. The risks of loss may be reduced by a secured position in several ways:

1. Under many security arrangements, close contact with the borrower is required in order to maintain an effective secured position. As a by-product of the security arrangement, the lender often gains a more intimate, complete, and up-to-date acquaintance with the borrower's affairs than he would have obtained as an unsecured creditor.

2. Under many security arrangements the lender obtains a close and continuing control over assets vital to the borrower's business. This control helps to prevent the sale or diversion of assets that the lender is looking to as an ultimate source of repayment of his loan. Some lenders would be willing to accept an unsecured status *provided* no other creditor could obtain a prior claim. By taking key assets as security, the lender assures himself that these assets cannot be pledged to another lender who would thereby gain priority over unsecured lenders. If the lender has full confidence in the borrower, he may seek to gain this same objective through an agreement that the borrower will not pledge assets to other lenders. Such compacts, known as *negative pledge* agreements, are used with some frequency.

3. Finally, and most basically, if the borrower encounters serious financial difficulties and cannot meet his obligations, the secured lender expects to enjoy a prior claim to the security and to the net proceeds from its disposition. Under certain circumstances, if the borrower cannot meet his commitments to the secured lender, the lender can seize and sell his security to satisfy his debt without ever becoming a party to developing bankruptcy proceedings. Alternatively, if all of the distressed borrower's assets are placed under the supervi-

sion of a bankruptcy court for distribution to creditors or for reorganization of the business, the secured lender expects to be able to establish his prior claim over unsecured creditors to the proceeds of his security.

Taking over security does not necessarily mean the full satisfaction of the debt obligation. In the event that sale of the security does not net enough money to pay off the debt in full, the secured lender usually can obtain a *deficiency judgment* for the unsatisfied portion of the debt. However, for this portion of his debt, the lender ranks as an unsecured or general creditor of the firm and shares pro rata with other unsecured creditors in any proceeds available for them.

As we shall see in a later chapter, most sizable firms that enter bankruptcy do not undergo complete liquidation of their assets. Very often, the total value of the firm as a reorganized, going concern is judged to be greater than the probable net proceeds from liquidation and dispersal of its assets. Consequently, the firm is reorganized and continues in business. The treatment accorded secured creditors in reorganization is influenced strongly by the value of the secured assets under the alternatives of liquidation or reorganization. Secured creditors with claims of assets vital to the operation of reorganized firms frequently have been paid out in full while unsecured creditors suffered heavily. Consequently, the priority ranking of creditors strongly influences their vulnerability to loss in reorganization, as well as in bankruptcy leading to complete liquidation. At worst, secured creditors of bankrupt concerns generally fare substantially less badly than unsecured creditors.

It should be emphasized that the legal rights to a security interest in particular assets can be no more valuable than the assets themselves. If the assets prove of limited value in sale or use, the priority that attaches to the proceeds of this security likewise will be of limited value.

What Assets Make Good Security

Not many decades ago, only *real property*—land and buildings —and marketable securities found widespread use as security for loans. In recent decades the situation has changed markedly. Today, every major type of business asset is used as security for loans in significant volume. Accounts receivable, inventory, equipment, and even claims not yet appearing as assets on the balance sheets of borrowers (such as anticipated rental receipts for property rented under long-term leases) now serve as collateral on an important scale.

Back of the broadening security base for business borrowing have been several developments. Important among these have been major developments in the legislation covering the use of business assets such as inventory and receivables as security. Further, lenders have much improved their skills and techniques in taking and administering a secured position. Vitally important, too, has been the increasing conviction on the part of lenders broadly that such assets as accounts receivable, properly handled, can constitute good security against loss to the lenders.

Of course, this does not mean that in a specific situation a potential lender will conclude that all or any of the firm's assets represent good collateral. Rather, it means that lenders are increasingly willing to take a searching look at almost any asset for its possible value as security. If lenders are to regard a particular asset as attractive security, it must meet three basic tests:

1. The lender must be able, under applicable laws (usually state legislation) to obtain a legal security interest in the asset that is clearly valid and sustainable against challenge in the courts.
2. The mechanics of the security device and of supervision of the security interest must be such that they can continue in force without undue expense and trouble to either borrower or lender.
3. The asset must be one that can reasonably be expected to continue to have value over the projected life of the loan. This value must be recognizable and realizable; that is, the lender must be able to forecast with some confidence that even under adverse conditions, he will be able to convert the asset into enough cash to cover his advance.

Establishing a Legally Valid Security Interest

The legislation governing the means of taking security and the rights and obligations of secured lenders primarily is state legislation, although certain provisions of federal bankruptcy law are pertinent. Although progress has been made toward relatively uniform legislation in some areas relating to secured borrowing (in the use of warehouse receipts, for example), important differences between the provisions of the various state laws remain in many other areas.[4]

---

[4] There is reason to hope for and expect great progress in the future toward relative uniformity in legislation relating to many aspects of commercial transactions, including the granting of security, as an outgrowth of almost herculean efforts which have gone into the development of model legislation called the "Uniform Commercial Code." Many important legal and business organizations have endorsed this proposed legislation, which is put forward in the hope that it will be adopted virtually intact by many, if not all, of the fifty states. The Uniform Commercial Code became the law of Pennsylvania in 1954; and by 1961, Massachusetts, Kentucky, Connecticut, New Hampshire, and Rhode Island also had adopted the Code. It is to be hoped that many more of the states in which the

Many of the differences in state law represent different approaches to the solution of basic problems. One such problem is how best to balance the desires of borrowers and of secured lenders for simple methods of effecting a legally valid pledge and, in many instances, for a minimum of publicity regarding the fact that security is being given, with fair treatment of unsecured lenders and other interested "third parties." In fairness, trade creditors or other lenders are entitled to an opportunity to learn that assets of the borrower that they might otherwise regard as supporting their loans are, in fact, pledged to other lenders. And the interests of persons who might otherwise purchase in good faith assets already pledged, which the borrower had no right to sell, also deserve consideration.

The difference in the way various states have reconciled the conflicting interests of the various interested parties can be illustrated by laws regarding *notification* of the fact that accounts receivable are being assigned as security. In a number of states in early 1961, no public notice is required for accomplishment of a legal assignment; all that is necessary is for the borrower to sign an agreement assigning his receivables to the lender. In some states the agreement can be written to include receivables arising out of future sales as well as those receivables already on the books; but in other states, confirmatory assignments are required after the account comes into existence. A growing number of states require that a statement that receivables are being pledged be recorded and available as a matter of public record at a designated public office, usually the office of the Secretary of State at the state capital. The idea here is that credit agencies such as Dun & Bradstreet, Inc., will check such sources and make the fact of pledging widely known to interested parties through

---

Code is under active consideration will adopt it soon. While this might be the least important of many desirable consequences, its widespread adoption would permit a substantial simplification and shortening of this chapter. A group of Pennsylvania bankers are reported in the *Banking Law Journal*, January, 1961, p. 12, as replying to critics of Article 9 of the Code, that dealing with use of security, as follows:

"Six years' experience has convinced us that Article 9 is one of the very best features of the Code and that the new simplified procedure which it makes possible in connection with the taking of personal property as security for loans has saved Pennsylvania banks and their customers hundreds of thousands of dollars in the six years of the Code's operation.

"Instead of being uncertain whether to use a chattel mortgage or a conditional sale contract or a trust receipt or any other device which is meticulously described in a separate act and in connection with which there must be observance of certain technical requirements—each form of security having a different set of requirements—the Code makes it possible to take a 'Security Agreement' in any form, and to perfect the lien by filing in a public office a 'Financing Statement.'

"We in Pennsylvania have had no difficulties in operating under Article 9."

their credit reports. Or interested parties can themselves check with the designated office to determine whether pledging arrangements exist. One state, North Dakota, insists that the company pledging its receivables mark its accounts receivable records in such a way that persons visually inspecting these records can see that particular accounts have been pledged. In several states the use of receivables as security has been restricted because of the cumbersome and somewhat strange legal requirement that concerns owing the receivables be notified of their pledge or because of the existence of uncertainties regarding the precise legal requirements for a valid pledge.

The practice of pledging *real property,* such as land and buildings, is centuries old; but business practice and the law related to the use of *personal property*—inventories, equipment, receivables, and the like—as security on a significant scale is of relatively recent origin. Some legislatures, and many courts in interpreting the legislation, seem to look on the pledge of such property with distaste and have demonstrated extreme concern that secured lenders do not get undue advantage. The newness of much legislation dealing with security, the fact that such legislation has not been thoroughly tested and clearly interpreted through judicial decisions, and the general hazard of interpretations unfavorable to secured lenders stemming from deep-seated prejudice against secured lending, along with the diversity in state legislation regarding security, all dictate that this discussion of the legal requirements for a valid security interest be couched in general terms. We want to provide the reader with a helpful but *general* background understanding of the major legal devices by which lenders can acquire a security interest; yet, at the same time, we emphatically advise both borrower and lender in actual transactions involving pledging of security to obtain the advice of lawyers familiar with applicable law in their jurisdictions in order to make sure that their contemplated lending arrangements are legally sound both in principle and in detail.

One generalization has broad validity in all legal jurisdictions: *Lenders must exercise great care in taking a security interest and in maintaining it.* If the borrower gets into financial difficulties and bankruptcy ensues, typically unsecured creditors also will be in the picture. It will be to the unsecured creditors' advantage to have as much as possible of the proceeds of the bankrupt's assets put in the pool for division among unsecured creditors. Consequently, counsel for unsecured creditors can be expected to exploit any opportunity to challenge the claims of secured creditors to a priority security interest in the more valuable assets. If counsel for unsecured creditors can find significant flaws in the prior claims, they may well succeed in having the court deny the validity of the security interest, so that the "secured lender" finds himself unwittingly and unwillingly a general creditor. In effect, lenders against security must walk a legal tightrope in order to insure that their claim to a security interest can stand up under challenge in the event the claim needs to be asserted.

BORROWING AGAINST RECEIVABLES

Discounting Notes Receivable

In an earlier chapter, we noted that it was once common practice for manufacturing and wholesale firms to sell to retailers on credit terms of several months. The credit instrument in such sales was the unsecured promissory note of the customer. Commonly, the seller *discounted* or borrowed against these notes at his bank. The bank held such notes in its possession and presented them, through correspondent banks, for collection at maturity. Since the discounting bank required endorsement of the notes by the seller, they were known as *two-name paper*; and if either buyer or seller had a good credit standing, the notes represented good support for the bank's advance. No priority of claim over unsecured creditors of either firm was involved, however.

In recent decades the volume of business borrowing through discounting of notes receivable has shrunk. The decline in such financing has resulted not from bankers' unwillingness to discount notes of responsible concerns but from changing business practice in terms of sale. As we saw earlier, most businesses now sell on short terms and on open account. Consequently, even though those firms still selling on notes from creditworthy customers have little trouble converting such notes into cash, the over-all volume of such transactions in domestic trade now is small.

While the use of notes receivable in routine trade credit has declined, there has been a sharp increase in the sale of machinery and equipment and consumer durable goods on terms which call for monthly instalment payments over a period of several years. Typically, the manufacturer or retailer granting such credit retains legal title to or a security interest in the equipment, and the debt is evidenced by notes or sales contracts which are assignable to lenders. The discounting of notes secured by equipment will be discussed later in this chapter under "Borrowing against Equipment."

Borrowing against Accounts Receivable as Collateral

Since most business concerns sell on credit and on open account, the typical firm has a big investment in accounts receivable. The attitude of banks and other commercial lenders toward accounts receivable as security has changed substantially in the last twenty-five years. In earlier periods, many lenders, particularly commercial banks, hesitated to enter into loan agreements with accounts receivable as security. Generally, they took accounts receivable as security only as a means toward the "working-out" of loans which had "gone sour." As a consequence of the association of accounts receivable pledging with financial difficulties, the use by a business of its accounts receivable as security for loans was widely regarded as evidence of serious financial weakness on the part of that firm.

Despite this early stigma and the problems involved in lending against accounts receivable, this form of lending has become important in recent decades. Basic to the growth is the solid fact that accounts receivable represent the closest asset to cash timewise and the asset of soundest value of many would-be borrowers. For example, many small, financially weak shoe manufacturers sell on short terms to large retail chain stores or department stores whose credit is excellent. Too, much progress has been made in the development of procedures for efficient and low-cost handling of the extensive paper work necessarily involved in lending against accounts receivable. Aware of fraud hazards in this sort of lending, lenders have had considerable success also in developing policing techniques which reduce the opportunities and temptations for fraud. These include periodic inspection of the borrower's receivables records and selective verification, often through a public accounting firm, of the receivables through confirmation by the customers of the amounts they owe the borrowers.

Other important measures of curbing the risk in loaning against accounts receivable have come into widespread use. Perhaps most important among these are the following:

1. Lenders reserve the right to select the accounts that will be acceptable to them as security. Effort is made to screen out and exclude from the security base overdue accounts and current accounts from concerns financially weak or with a poor reputation for payment.
2. Accounts typically are accepted *with recourse*. That is, the borrower agrees to replace those accounts that are not paid reasonably promptly with acceptable accounts not overdue, or to reduce the loan accordingly.

3. Perhaps most important is the usual practice of loaning only a percentage of the full face amount of the accounts pledged. For example, if the lender advances only 75 per cent of the face value of the accounts pledged, the 25 per cent margin is available to cover prompt payment discounts, goods returned by the customer for credit, and demands for allowances for faulty merchandise or damaged goods, and accounts that prove uncollectible. If these are expected to be high, a wider margin of safety is sought through establishment of a lower percentage of loan to accounts pledged.

4. Typically, a maximum limit also is established on the total amount that will be loaned, regardless of the total value of the security. This ceiling recognizes that the general credit of the borrower is also back of the loan and that this added protection is diluted when the receivables loan becomes very large relative to the total resources of the borrower.

Now, let us get some idea of the mechanics of receivables borrowing by reviewing typical terms of loan agreements drawn up to cover bank loans against receivables. Points covered in the loan agreement commonly include the following:

1. The term of life of the lending arrangements. Although provision often is made that the loan secured by receivables is payable on demand of the lender, there is usually an understanding that the loan will continue for a considerable or indefinite period. Many receivables loans continue for years, terminating only when the company no longer needs to borrow or has prospered to a point where it can get satisfactory credit on an unsecured basis.

2. Agreement that the bank may screen the accounts to determine which represent acceptable security, and an outline of the procedures by which accepted accounts that become overdue are replaced or the loan base is reduced.

3. The percentage that the bank will loan against the face amount of receivables.

4. The maximum dollar amount of the loan against receivables.

5. The evidence that the borrower must submit in support of the validity of the accounts. In some cases, only a simple listing of the customers and the amounts owing from each is required. In other cases the borrower may be required to submit such evidence as original invoices, or signed receipts from shipping companies, for the goods giving rise to the account receivable.

6. Authorization to the lender to inspect the borrower's books upon demand or to undertake other methods of checking up on the validity of the receivables given as collateral.

7. The frequency with which the borrower can bring in new accounts to add to the security base and thus permit greater borrowing, as well as as the interval within which he must bring in the money collected from pledged accounts to pay down the loan. In some cases, collections and new accounts added are brought in daily, and a new calculation is made of security base and loan balance. Since most firms make new

credit sales and collections each day, both the gross value of the accounts given as security and the loan amount totals are shifting ones. Specific receivables pledged change, and the total pledged and borrowed rises and falls; but normally, some accounts remain outstanding, and so does the loan against the receivables.

A typical loan agreement pledging accounts receivable as security is shown in Exhibit 12–1.

Who Makes Accounts Receivable Loans?

Commercial banks, commercial credit companies, and factoring concerns are the principal financial concerns that lend against accounts receivable on a major scale. In commercial banking circles, it is now widely recognized that accounts receivable can represent satisfactory security, and most large banks now stand ready to make such loans as part of a well-rounded lending service to business. Since such lending often implies relatively steady lending, requires more paper work and generally more trouble to service than most loans, and necessitates some specialized knowledge and procedures, many smaller banks have shown little interest in making such loans.

As indicated earlier, commercial credit companies pioneered in accounts receivable lending, and such lending still accounts for a substantial portion of their total lending volume. While factoring concerns, as explained earlier, finance receivables primarily on a purchase basis, they also do a certain amount of lending against pledge of receivables.

Costs of Borrowing against Accounts Receivable

Since companies borrowing against receivables tend to be of less than average financial strength, and since the continuing borrowing arrangement involves relatively high expense and trouble to the lender, the costs of such borrowing tend to be higher than on unsecured loans to stronger companies. When the interest rate charged by banks to prime credits on an unsecured basis is around 4 per cent, the interest rate on accounts receivable loans will likely be 6½ to 7 per cent; and additional charges for servicing the account, amounting to an annual cost of 1 or 2 per cent, are common. Total charges by nonbank lenders commonly amount to an annual rate of 12 to 18 per cent of the credit supplied, and often are higher.

BORROWING AGAINST INVENTORY

As we have seen, most business firms have a substantial portion of their resources invested in inventory. And many in need of credit

EXHIBIT 12-1

TYPICAL LOAN AGREEMENT WITH THE ASSIGNMENT OF ACCOUNTS RECEIVABLE AS SECURITY

Commercial Service Department Agreement

AGREEMENT made this 15th day of March 1957, by and between ROCKLAND-ATLAS NATIONAL BANK OF BOSTON, a national banking association having its principal place of business in Boston, Massachusetts, hereinafter called the Bank, and The Hammond Company of Boston, Mass. hereinafter called the Borrower.

1. This agreement refers to proposed loans by the Bank to the Borrower on the security of assignments of accounts receivable tendered to and acceptable to the Bank at a percentage of the face value of such accounts as from time to time established. The percentage initially established for loans to be made in pursuance hereof is 6 %, which percentage may be changed from time to time at the election of the Bank. The term "net face value" for the purposes of this agreement shall mean the face amount of the assigned account, less all discounts and credits to which the account-debtor may be entitled. In consideration of such loans, and the services to be rendered by the Bank in connection herewith, the Borrower shall pay monthly to the Bank such rate of interest and such service charge, computed on the daily net loan balance, as may from time to time be established. The intent of this agreement is to provide a basic arrangement for loans secured as aforesaid and, under ordinary circumstances, the Bank will continue to make loans to the Borrower in pursuance hereof until ten (10) days after written notice to the Borrower of the Bank's intention to discontinue making such loans; provided, however, that the Bank may discontinue making such loans at any time without notice to the Borrower when, in its uncontrolled discretion, it shall deem it inexpedient to do so and provided further it is understood that the Bank will not make loans hereunder except to the extent the security offered therefor in each instance is, in its uncontrolled judgment, satisfactory and sufficient. All loans hereunder shall be evidenced by Borrower's demand promissory notes payable to the order of the Bank. It is understood and agreed, as a condition of granting loans from time to time hereunder, that the Borrower will not borrow on the security of accounts receivable from, or sell or discount receivables to, any factor, discount company or other financial institution without first notifying the Bank of its intention to do so, and, unless in each case the Bank shall in writing permit such borrowing, selling or discounting, the Borrower shall not be entitled to the privilege of further loans in pursuance of this agreement.

2. The Borrower from time to time shall assign the aforementioned accounts receivable on forms to be supplied by the Bank. Such assignments shall assign, transfer and set over to the Bank the accounts receivable and contracts therein listed including all moneys due and to become due thereunder and including the right of stoppage in transit and every other right, title and interest of the Borrower in and to the property or merchandise sold, shipped and delivered in pursuance thereof, whether returned, refused, re-routed, re-consigned or re-shipped. Such assignments shall secure the loans made in connection therewith and any other direct or indirect liability or liabilities of the Borrower to the Bank then due or to become due or that may thereafter be contracted. The Borrower shall deliver promptly to the Bank at its request invoices, original bills of lading and such other documents as may be necessary or convenient in connection with such assignments. The Borrower shall promptly make such entries on Borrower's books of record and account as the Bank from time to time shall require to indicate that such accounts are assigned to the Bank. The Bank shall have the right at all reasonable times to audit and inspect the Borrower's books of record and account. The Borrower shall furnish the Bank with balance sheets of the Borrower's financial condition certified by an approved public accountant at such times as the Bank may from time to time request.

3. The Borrower agrees and warrants that all accounts receivable assigned or to be assigned hereunder shall represent bona fide sales made by it to the respective debtors whose names appear in the accounts so assigned or to be assigned to the Bank; that delivery of all of the merchandise so sold shall have been made on or before the time of such assignments; that at the time of such assignments such accounts shall be free of credits, set-offs and counterclaims (not disclosed in said assignments); that the Borrower at the time of any such assignment shall have full title and right to assign the accounts therein assigned and will defend the Bank's title to the same and will indemnify and save harmless the Bank from the claims and demands of all persons adverse to the interest of the Bank in and to any account assigned to it, or to moneys or other property, or the value thereof, received by the Bank in pursuance of assignments hereunder and moreover the Borrower will exonerate and reimburse the Bank for all expenses, including attorneys' fees, incurred by it with respect to all such claims and demands.

4. The Bank may at any time apply any deposits, balance of deposits, or other sums at any time credited to, or due from it to, the Borrower against the amount due or to become due on any loan made by the Bank to the Borrower in pursuance hereof. The Bank shall have the right from time to time to demand additional security if in its judgment the value of the existing security shall at any

any promissory note given hereunder, the Bank will release such portion of the accounts assigned to it or of collections thereon received by it (and not applied against the Borrower's notes) as, in its uncontrolled judgment, is excess security, but the Bank in any event may select the security so to be released by it.

5. The Borrower shall deliver or transmit to the Bank, on the day of the receipt thereof and in the form received, all cash, checks, drafts, notes, acceptances and other instruments of payment received by the Borrower in payment of or as security for any account assigned to the Bank; and all such cash, checks, drafts, notes, acceptances and other instruments of payment may, at the option of the Bank, be applied by the Bank against any indebtedness or obligation of the Borrower to it whether or not then due and payable; provided, however, that notwithstanding any such application, the obligation of the Borrower to the Bank shall not thereby be reduced or discharged if, for any reason, the Bank does not receive the avails of any such instrument of payment or if, for any reason, it is required at any time to pay over any part of such cash or avails, or the equivalent thereof, to or for the account of any other person. Any merchandise or other property returned by or acquired from any debtor with respect to any assigned account will be received and held by the Borrower in trust for, and as the property of, the Bank, and upon the request of the Bank, such merchandise or other property will be delivered to the Bank, and thereupon the Bank may sell or otherwise dispose of the same for its own account and apply the net proceeds from any such sale or other disposition to any indebtedness or obligation of the Borrower to it after deducting reasonable expenses of such sale or other disposition and of any transportation, storage or other charges incurred by it.

6. The Bank shall have the right at any time and from time to time directly to enforce, collection of the assigned accounts, either in its own name or in the name of the Borrower, and authority is hereby irrevocably given to the Bank so to do. Moreover, in the event of a default by the Borrower in the performance of its obligations hereunder or in the making of any payment due to the Bank or upon the filing of a petition by or against the Borrower under any of the provisions of the Federal Bankruptcy Act, as from time to time amended, or upon the making by the Borrower of an assignment for the benefit of creditors or upon the appointment of a receiver or liquidator for the Borrower or for any of its property, the Bank may sell, at its election, at public or private sale all or any of the assigned accounts and any other property acquired by it in pursuance of this agreement or of assignments given hereunder without advertisement or notice to the Borrower or to any other person or persons. The Bank, its officers, attorneys and agents may bid and purchase at any such sale, if public. The Bank may reimburse itself from the proceeds of collections and sales of the assigned accounts for expenses, including attorneys' fees, incurred by it with respect thereto, or with respect to the recovery, preservation or storage of property acquired by it hereunder and may apply the remaining proceeds therefrom against the obligations of the Borrower to it, whether or not then due and payable.

7. The Bank, in its sole discretion and without notice to the Borrower, may settle with or compromise with or grant time or other indulgences to any of the debtors named in the aforementioned assignments and may make, take or release security from or to such debtors. The Borrower hereby waives presentment, demand and protest of any note, draft or other instrument for the payment of money received by the Bank in any dealings hereunder.

8. The Borrower hereby agrees to execute such other instruments of title or assurance as may be necessary or convenient to render fully effectual the security intended to be afforded hereby. For a like purpose the Borrower hereby authorizes the Bank to send in its own name or in the Borrower's name such notices with respect to the assigned accounts as may be necessary or convenient. The Bank, likewise, may endorse in the Borrower's name checks, drafts, notes, acceptances or other instruments of payment received in pursuance of said assignments and/or this agreement.

9. No waiver of any provision of this agreement on any occasion shall operate as a waiver on any future occasion; nor shall any delay in enforcing any provision hereof operate as a waiver thereof.

10. This agreement shall enure to the benefit of and be binding on the parties, their heirs, executors, administrators, successors and assigns. The terms and provisions of this agreement and assignments given in connection therewith shall be governed in all respects by the laws of the Commonwealth of Massachusetts.

IN WITNESS WHEREOF, the parties have executed this agreement as a sealed instrument on the date first hereinabove written.

ROCKLAND-ATLAS NATIONAL BANK OF BOSTON

By Thomas Oaks, Vice President

The Hammond Company

By John Lake, Treasurer

C S 2

have inventory with characteristics that make it good collateral for borrowing. Of the 799,100 secured bank loans covered in a 1955 Federal Reserve study summarized in Table 12–2, some 47,400 loans

TABLE 12–2

SECURITY PLEDGED ON BUSINESS LOANS AT MEMBER BANKS
OF FEDERAL RESERVE SYSTEM, OCTOBER 5, 1955,
BY TYPE OF SECURITY

(Estimates of Outstanding Loans)

MAJOR TYPE OF SECURITY	AMOUNT OF LOANS (IN MILLIONS)	NUMBER OF LOANS (IN THOUSANDS)	PERCENTAGE DISTRIBUTION	
			Amount	Number
Unsecured..................	$15,105	386.1	49.0	32.6
Secured.....................	15,700	799.1	51.0	67.4
Total, All Loans..........	$30,805	1,185.2	100.0	100.0
SECURED				
Endorsed, comaker, or guaranteed................	$ 2,755	185.9	17.5	23.3
Receivables and other claims...	2,813	52.9	17.9	6.6
Inventories..................	1,448	47.4	9.2	5.9
Equipment...................	2,194	218.5	14.0	27.3
Plant and other real estate.....	3,592	164.4	22.9	20.6
U.S. government securities.....	182	8.5	1.2	1.1
Other bonds.................	165	2.6	1.0	0.3
Stocks......................	1,002	39.1	6.4	4.9
Life insurance and savings accounts..................	447	53.8	2.8	6.7
Other security..............	1,102	26.1	7.1	3.3
			100.0	100.0

SOURCE: "Security Pledged on Business Loans at Member Banks," *Federal Reserve Bulletin*, September, 1959.

representing 9.2 per cent of the total amount and 5.9 per cent of the number were secured by inventory.

What Inventory Makes Good Collateral?

An outstanding characteristic of the investment in inventory of a great many firms is its heterogeneity. The typical manufacturer, for example, has on hand raw materials, work in process, finished goods, and supplies; and each of these categories consists of a variety of items of different sizes, shapes, and grades. In considering the possibilities of bolstering a credit application by giving the lenders a security interest in particular inventory, it can be helpful to appraise the inventory in terms of the qualities that lenders look for in deciding whether a particular commodity will be good security.

The physical characteristics of the goods are of basic importance. Clearly, lenders prefer products that are not vulnerable to physical deterioration during the terms of the credit. Wheat of low moisture content, properly stored, resists deterioration for long periods, for example, in contrast to fresh peaches, which may go soft, even under refrigeration, in a matter of hours. While conditions of storage can affect perishability risks, it is possible to generalize that lenders are little interested in taking as security those commodities subject to substantial risks of physical deterioration.

Relatively homogeneous products generally are preferred to commodities whose grade or quality is diverse or hard to measure. For example, lumber of a single type, grade, size, and shape would be easier to appraise and keep tallied than lumber of diverse kinds, grades, and shapes.

Although bulk is not necessarily undesirable, commodities of high value relative to bulk generally are preferred.

It is perhaps more important that the commodity be one that reasonably can be expected to continue to have resale value. No lender wants to take over inventory and have to dispose of it. But he wants to be confident that if he must, he can find a ready buyer at a good price. What factors help build such confidence? First is a record of price stability in the past. Some products, such as wool, have records of rapid and wide price fluctuations in contrast to the relative price stability of such items as sheet steel.

Second, the existence of a broad, local market for the commodity heightens the possibility that buyers can be found at a relatively small reduction in price. Such a broad market is more likely to exist if the commodity is a relatively standard one. High-style items with a narrow local market, such as women's high-style dresses in a small Midwestern town, could be compared with uncut yard goods of a popular grade and color suitable for men's suits, located in New York City, center of the garment industry. Usually, raw materials have a broader market than semiprocessed or finished goods where the process of manufacture has created distinctive features.

Third, the existence of frequent selling transactions in an organized market with published price quotations helps the lender to follow trends in value of the product with minimum effort.

Fourth, as is true of any asset considered as security, the commodity must be such that the borrower can give the lender a clear-cut security interest without undue inconvenience or disruption of his business operation and associated expense. For many would-be borrowers against inventory, this is a major problem area. Consider the highly diverse circumstances under which inventories are held— pulpwood at the paper mill awaiting processing, cattle in the farmer's feed lot for fattening, refrigerators on the floor of the appliance retailer, oil reserves still underground, the food processor's stocks of frozen foods located in cold-storage warehouses in a number of cities. These few items suggest the need for a variety of legal procedures and for imagination on the part of lenders if they are to obtain a valid security interest and keep track effectively of their collateral. And indeed, much progress has been made in the development of legal and operational procedures that can offer adequate protection to the lender while minimizing the inconvenience and expense to the borrower.

Several different legal methods of giving lenders a security interest in inventory are in widespread use. The basic features of the more important types of arrangements will be described briefly.

1. Borrowing against Inventory Covered by Warehouse Receipts. Under this well-established method, physical custody of the

EXHIBIT 12–2

EXAMPLE OF A WAREHOUSE RECEIPT
Front Side of Receipt

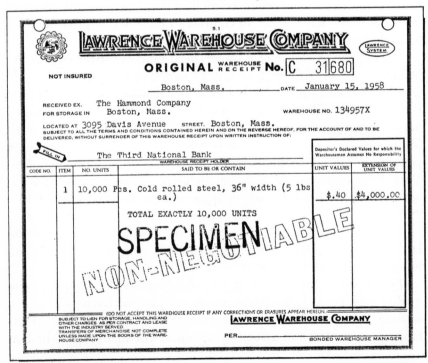

EXHIBIT 12-2—*Continued*

Provisions Stated on the Reverse Side of the Receipt

The face hereof is a copy of original Non-Negotiable Warehouse Receipt bearing the same number and date hereof. This copy is for purposes of certification and record only and is not a Warehouse Receipt. Any references on this copy to the face of such original Non-Negotiable Warehouse Receipt or the face of this copy includes only that portion of the original Warehouse Receipt or this copy above the words "Lawrence Warehouse Company Office Copy" set forth on the face hereof.

* * * * *

I (We) the undersigned, certify and guarantee that the face hereof is a true copy of the face of the Lawrence Warehouse Company original Non-Negotiable Warehouse Receipt bearing the same number and date hereof and this copy has been compared by us with the original.

I (we), the undersigned, hereby certify and guarantee that I (we) are the legal owners of the commodities set forth on the face hereof and that the quantity and quality stated thereon are correct and that I (we) have delivered the same as of the date hereof to the Lawrence Warehouse Company for warehousing purposes in accordance with the terms of our storage agreement with them. I (we) hereby authorize the Lawrence Warehouse Company to issue a Non-Negotiable Warehouse Receipt bearing the same number and date hereof covering the above mentioned commodities in the name of

The Third National Bank at _____

Depositor _____ The Hammond Company _____

By _____ John Doe _____

* * * * *

I, the undersigned, certify and guarantee that the face hereof is a true copy of the face of the Lawrence Warehouse Company original Non-Negotiable Warehouse Receipt bearing the same number and date hereof and this copy has been compared by me with the original.

I hereby certify that I received on _____ **January 15** _____ 19.**58** into my custody as

Bonded Warehouse Manager of the Lawrence Warehouse Company at its _____ **Boston,** _____

_____ **Mass. Warehouse No. 134957X** _____ Warehouse No. _____
the commodities set forth on the face hereof and have issued an original Non-Negotiable Warehouse Receipt covering the above mentioned commodities. Such original Non-Negotiable Warehouse Receipt was issued and signed by me and such commodities will be released by me from the above mentioned warehouse only in accordance with Lawrence Warehouse Company written instructions which I have heretofore received or may hereafter receive. I realize that to issue or sign such original Warehouse Receipt and the copies thereof or to release such commodities otherwise than in accordance with such written instructions violates the terms of my employment by the Lawrence Warehouse Company and constitutes a fraud upon that Company and the holders of its Warehouse Receipts.

Lawrence Warehouse Company Bonded Warehouse Manager _____

* * * * *

INSTRUCTIONS TO LAWRENCE WAREHOUSE COMPANY BONDED
WAREHOUSE MANAGER

IMPORTANT: The Lawrence Warehouse Company Bonded Whse. Mgr. making out and signing the original Non-Negotiable Warehouse Receipt bearing the same number and date hereof must forward this signed copy of such Warehouse Receipt **ON THE DATE HEREOF** to the Lawrence Warehouse Company office, the address of which is included in its written instructions addressed to such Bonded Warehouse Manager.

goods pledged is placed in the hands of a warehousing company which, at the direction of the borrower, issues a *warehouse receipt* made out in favor of the lender. An example of such a receipt is given in Exhibit 12–2. As custodian of the goods, the warehousing firm releases them only upon the instructions of the lender. Properly handled, the warehousing arrangement gives the lender firm control over the collateral. Much of the moral risk inherent in other kinds of inventory financing, where physical control of the goods is left with the borrower, is avoided. The legislation of the various states relating to the pledge of commodities under warehouse receipts is relatively uniform and well tested, so that the legal uncertainties that relate to many aspects of secured lending are relatively small in the case of lending against warehouse receipts.

Warehousing arrangements are of two major types—*public* and *field*. In the case of public warehouses the goods are brought to the warehouses for storage—for example, wheat moved into the public grain warehouses that dot the sky lines of farm belt towns and cities. Lenders have long looked with favor on the public warehouse receipt security arrangement, and it has worked well from the borrower's viewpoint in the case of commodities that can be left undisturbed in the warehouse for long periods of time—such as whiskey being aged or wheat stored after harvest awaiting processing into flour.

Yet, many firms have their own storage facilities convenient to their manufacturing facilities or markets and want to avoid the trouble and expense of moving inventory to and from the warehouse-man's facilities. Further, they wish to add to and draw from ware-housed stocks frequently or continuously. To meet such needs, several warehousing firms[5] offer a *field warehousing* service. Under a field warehouse arrangement the warehousing firm leases storage facil-ities of the borrower and posts signs to signify that goods stored therein are in its exclusive custody, to be used as security. Commodi-ties are put in the custody of the warehousing firm,[6] which issues warehouse receipts covering these segregated goods in the name of the lender. We should make clear that the warehousing firm performs only a warehousing function, making it possible for banks or other lending organizations to advance loans against the security of the goods covered by the warehouse receipt. Under the typical field ware-house receipt loan the lender advances a percentage of the value of the commodities covered by the warehouse receipt. When the borrow-ing firm wants to withdraw goods for processing or sale, it arranges with the lender to pay down that portion of the loan advanced against

---

[5] Among the leading field warehousing firms are Lawrence Warehouse Company and American Express Co.

[6] Care must be taken that the borrower in fact has no control over the goods. To be legally valid, the warehousing arrangement must put "continuous, exclusive, and notori-ous possession" in the hands of the warehousing firm.

the particular goods involved, and the lender authorizes the warehouseman to release the goods to the borrower by surrendering the warehouse receipts.

The field warehousing arrangement is a highly ingenious method of facilitating the extension of credit and has come into widespread use in recent decades. One of the first industries to make heavy use of field warehousing was the California food-canning industry. The typical canner's manufacturing operation was highly seasonal, but sales were spread through the year. Customarily, the canner had a large investment in finished goods at the end of the canning season. The field warehousing arrangement permitted the canners to get substantial bank credit against the collateral of the canned goods and yet fill shipment orders through the year with minimum inconvenience and expense.

Over the years, field warehousing has been used for a wide variety of commodities, including such items as coal in hopper cars on a railroad siding (locked switches into the main railroad line were in the control of the field warehouseman), logs in a mill pond, and watch movements stored in a large file cabinet.

2. Borrowing against Inventory Covered by Trust Receipts. Most of the states have adopted similar legislation covering lending against inventory under trust receipts. Lending arrangements under trust receipts typically involve three parties: for example, the manufacturer of automobiles, the automobile dealer, and the commercial bank lending to the dealer. If a shipment of cars to the dealer is to serve as security, the manufacturer transfers title to the cars and receives payment for them from the lending bank. The lending bank, in turn, delivers custody of the cars to the borrowing dealer under a *trust receipt agreement*, which specifies what the borrower may do with the cars. In the case of finished goods held for resale, such as the automobiles on the premises of the dealer, the agreement will provide that the goods may be sold but that the borrower will use the proceeds from sale promptly to pay off the loan. If the trust receipt agreement covers raw materials awaiting manufacture, the borrower typically agrees to hold the material in trust until he puts it into process, whereupon he covenants to pay off the loan secured by that material. An example of a trust receipt is given in Exhibit 12–3.

The goods in trust must be specifically identified in the trust receipt, and the lender must devote reasonable care to policing the agreement to insure that the borrower carries out his responsibilities under the trust agreement. The fact that the borrower can put the

EXHIBIT 12-3

EXAMPLE OF A TRUST RECEIPT

| Credit or Agreement No. 19357 | Draft or Note Dated Jan. 20, 1958. | Face Amount Draft or Note $6000.00 | Due Nov. 20, 1958 |

ROCKLAND-ATLAS NATIONAL BANK OF BOSTON

TRUST RECEIPT

S. S. _____ Boston, Massachusetts __January__ ___, 19___

The undersigned (hereinafter called the "Trustee") hereby acknowledges receipt from Rockland-Atlas National Bank of Boston (hereinafter called the "Entruster") of the goods, documents or instruments specified below and agrees and acknowledges that a security interest in said goods, documents and/or instruments, and in any goods represented by said documents, remains in or hereby passes to the Entruster.

Commercial Invoice —Northeastern Supply Company – Inv. No. 39560 dated Jan. 16, 1958,
Consular Invoice   as attached, covering 100 electric motor units
Certificate of Origin
Insurance Certificate
Weight Note
Warehouse Receipts
Delivery Orders
Bills of Lading

In consideration of such receipt and other valuable consideration, the Trustee agrees to hold said goods, documents and/or instruments in trust for the Entruster and subject to its security interest, to be used promptly by the Trustee without expense to the Entruster for the following purpose(s) checked below but for no other purpose and without liberty to pledge the same or, unless hereafter expressly provided, to sell the same:—

☐ 1. To transfer to carrier.
☐ 2. To transfer to warehouse.
☐ 3. To deliver said goods to _____ who have/has agreed to purchase the same.
☐ 4. To sell said goods, subject to the following limitations (if any). _____

☒ 5. To manufacture or process said goods and to sell the same, whether or not manufactured or processed.
☐ 6. To make Customs entry and obtain inspection by the appropriate U. S. authorities.
☐ 7.

A. If the purpose numbered 1 be checked above—Proper and sufficient negotiable bills of lading.

B. If the purpose numbered 2 be checked above—proper and sufficient warehouse receipts to the order of or in the name of the Entruster.

C. If either of the purposes numbered 3, 4 or 5 be checked above, or if any liberty of sale is stated under 7 above—The proceeds of the sale of such goods, documents and/or instruments in whatever form received, to be applied by the Entruster under the terms of the Credit, Agreement, Draft, or Note referred to above and/or to the payment of any obligations for which said goods, documents and/or instruments are security or were security before this transaction and of any obligations arising as part of this transaction and of any renewals of any such obligations. If such proceeds be notes, bills receivable, acceptances or in any form other than cash, they shall not be so applied by the Entruster until paid; the Entruster, however, shall have the option at any time to sell or discount such items and so apply, conditionally upon final payment of such items, the net proceeds thereof. The Entruster shall have full power to compromise and collect such proceeds in its own name or that of the Trustee.

D. If the purpose numbered 6 be checked above—(1) Payment in good funds in Boston for the Invoice value thereof, together with all bank and other charges, if any, as soon as the merchandise has been admitted into this country, by the appropriate U. S. authorities. (2) If the merchandise is not admitted by the appropriate U. S. authorities, the Trustee will deliver to the Entruster immediately the notice of detention and/or rejection issued by the appropriate U. S. authorities, together with a letter officially signed, (a) agreeing to hold the merchandise intact for the account of the Entruster in the same condition as arrived and inspected by the appropriate U. S. authorities and further agreeing not to alter its condition in any manner whatsoever unless so permitted in writing by the Entruster and (b) further agreeing to deliver to the Entruster upon demand the merchandise so detained and/or rejected. (3) If the merchandise is admitted in part only, by the appropriate U. S. authorities, Clause (1) will apply to that portion so admitted and Clause (2) will apply to that portion so detained or rejected.

E. If a purpose numbered 7 is stated and checked above the Trustee shall:

The Trustee agrees to pay all expenses and charges in connection with said goods, documents, instruments and any proceeds thereof, and will at all times while the same are in its hands hold said goods, documents, instruments and proceeds separate and distinct from any property of the Trustee and capable of identification and will definitely show such separation in all its records and entries. The Entruster shall have the same security interest in any additions or improvements to goods as it had in the goods themselves.

The Trustee will at all times keep such goods fully insured at the Trustee's expense in favor of, and to the satisfaction of the Entruster against loss by fire, theft and any other risk to which said goods may be subject, and will forthwith pay over to the Entruster any funds recovered under any insurance on said goods. The Trustee will at any time on the demand of the Entruster deliver to it the insurance policies in such form as to enable the Entruster to collect any loss directly.

The Entruster may at any time cancel this arrangement and take possession of, and upon demand of the Entruster the Trustee agrees to deliver to the Entruster, said goods, whether or not manufactured or processed, and any documents representing the same, or said instruments (until delivery of said goods and documents or said instruments to the purchaser(s) pursuant to a sale hereby authorized and the receipt by the Trustee of the proceeds of such sale) and the proceeds of any sale, wherever the said goods, documents, instruments, or proceeds may then be found. As to articles manufactured by style or model, the Trustee's interest therein may be forfeited, at the election of the Entruster, in the event of any default on the part of the Trustee, against cancellation to the extent and as provided by law of the Trustee's then remaining indebtedness with respect to such articles.

The Trustee agrees to deliver to the Entruster on demand accurate records and copies of all accounts with respect to said goods, documents, instruments or proceeds thereof and to execute any assignments or other documents in connection therewith which the Entruster may require, and the Trustee further agrees that there will be no offsets or credits against any claims or accounts constituting proceeds of said goods, documents or instruments and guarantees payment of said claims and accounts in full.

The Trustee agrees that the Entruster is not responsible for the correctness, validity or genuineness of any documents referred to herein or for the existence, character, quantity, quality, condition, value or delivery of any goods purported to be represented thereby. No waiver of any rights or powers of the Entruster or consent by it shall be valid unless in writing signed by the Entruster. The rights and powers herein given the Entruster are in addition to those otherwise created.

............The Hammond Company............, Trustee

............By John Lake, Treasurer............

material into process or sell it, as the trust agreement specifies, *before* he makes settlement with the lender can be a major convenience to the borrower, but it also involves risk to the lender. Accordingly, the moral standing and reputation for integrity of the borrower are particularly important to the lender considering a trust receipt financing arrangement—more so than in the case of warehouse receipt financing.

The trust receipt device has been heavily used by distributors and retailers of new automobiles, and major equipment and appliance items, who borrow to finance their working inventories of these items. Since the trust receipts must specifically identify the security, new trust receipts must be prepared as the borrower adds and disposes of particular items of inventory. The problem of specific identification and the burden of paper work in trust receipt financing makes the trust receipt an awkward or unsuitable device for securing highly diverse, fast-moving, or hard-to-identify inventory such as work in process. Under the recording statutes of most states the trust receipt is a less awkward instrument than the alternative devices, the *chattel mortgage* or the *conditional sale,* but perhaps less flexible than another alternative device, the so-called *factor's lien.* Each of these devices is discussed later. The trust receipt device is feasible only for a series of transactions between the same buyer and seller. Thus, it can be highly useful in financing the purchase by a dealer of new cars from the manufacturer, but not for financing his purchase of used cars from a great number of sellers.

3. *Borrowing against Inventory Pledged under a Factor's Lien.* Within recent years, about half of the states, including New York, California, Illinois, Ohio, and other commercially important states, have made statutory provision for the granting of a security interest in inventory by means of a *factor's lien agreement.* The factor's lien arrangement is distinctive in that it permits blanket assignment to a lender of the entire stocks of the borrower, whether in a raw, in-process, or finished state. The lien can extend over long periods, during which time the actual stocks held by the borrower under the factor's lien may turn over several times and the dollar value may rise and fall substantially. Often, arrangements for loans against inventory under such a blanket assignment are combined with loans against the receivables created when the inventories are sold, so that the lender takes both inventory en masse and receivables as security.

Typical factor's lien agreements are multipage documents. However, the essence of the agreement—a general and continuing assignment of inventories and receivables created therefrom—is apparent in the initial paragraphs of a typical agreement (see Exhibit 12–4).

As in the case of the trust receipt arrangement, the factor's lien leaves practical control over the inventory with the borrower and calls also for a strong sense of moral responsibility, as well as accounting care, on the part of the borrower. Too, much of the inventory pledged, particularly if work in process is a large percentage of the total, may have a low value upon forced sale. Consequently, lenders under the factor's lien arrangement usually are willing to loan only a modest percentage of the book value of inventory pledged. In one case known to the authors, where a factor was lending to a manufacturer of Venetian window blinds, the factor determined that he could safely advance only 20 per cent of the cost of the inventory. Since the factor's lien arrangement is adaptable to heterogeneous, fast-moving inventory, it has found considerable usage by banks, business finance companies, and factoring concerns in the growing number of states which have made legal provision for its use. However, some lenders hesitate to use it because of its departure from historical security concepts.

4. *Inventory Pledges under Chattel Mortgage, an Instrument Which Conveys to the Lender a Security Interest in Specifically Identified Goods.* The chattel mortgage is an old, well-established, and widespread legal device. Farmers holding cattle in feed lots for fattening over a period of months have made particularly heavy use of the chattel mortgage in posting such livestock as security for bank loans. As we shall see, however, the chattel mortgage instrument is more widely used for items of machinery and equipment than for inventory. The choice of the best device to use in creating a security interest must be made in the light of all the circumstances, including particularly the state laws governing security transactions.

BORROWING AGAINST FIXED ASSETS

Borrowing against Equipment

The continuing long-term trend toward mechanization in manufacturing, farming, service, and even retailing (use of vending machines, etc.) has been accompanied by increasing investment in equipment by firms in these fields and by growing use of equipment as security for loans.

Much of the credit to businesses secured by equipment is extended initially by manufacturers or sales concerns supplying new ma-

EXHIBIT 12–4

EXTRACTS FROM A TYPICAL FACTOR'S LIEN AGREEMENT

1. The Bank shall have a lien upon such merchandise of the Borrower as is from time to time after the execution of this Agreement designated in one or more separate written statements dated and signed by the Borrower and delivered to the Bank, and upon the accounts receivable or other proceeds resulting from the sale or other disposition of such merchandise (hereinafter called the "accounts") to secure the Bank for all loans and advances made to or for the account of the Borrower at any time during the period of   years from   , together with interest thereon and also to secure the commissions, obligations, indebtedness and expenses properly chargeable against or due from the Borrower and to secure the amounts due or owing upon any notes or other obligations given to or received by the Bank for or on account of any such loans or advances, interest, commissions, obligations, indebtedness, charges and expenses.

2. The Borrower covenants that at the time the Borrower designates any merchandise as being subject to this Agreement for the purpose of transferring to the Bank a lien upon such merchandise, the Borrower will be the lawful owner of the merchandise so designated and will have good right to designate, consign, pledge, sell, assign and transfer the same; that said merchandise will be free from all liens and encumbrances; and that the Borrower will warrant and defend the same against the lawful claims and demands of all persons.

The Borrower hereby covenants with the Bank as follows:

3.1 The Borrower will forthwith designate to the Bank all merchandise owned by the Borrower on the date hereof and located at any premises owned or rented by the Borrower, and will promptly after its acquisition designate to the Bank all additional merchandise (as so defined) including merchandise returned by customers, received by the Borrower at any such premises.

3.2 The Borrower will not remove any of the merchandise, lien upon which is transferred to the Bank, from the premises or place of business of the Borrower designated in the statement creating the lien, without the written consent of the Bank, *provided, however,* that the Borrower may sell any such merchandise in the ordinary course of its business.

chines. Many vendors of important items of new equipment accept from purchasers who make a significant down payment (often 20 to 33 per cent) notes calling for payment of the remainder of the purchase price plus interest and other charges over a period of months, in some cases as many as sixty. Generally, the seller requires a down payment and monthly payments sufficiently large so that the outstanding debt over the life of the credit remains less than the estimated net resale value of the equipment if repossession becomes necessary. The seller takes a security interest in the equipment, the most common security device being a *conditional sale contract,*[7] under which the seller retains legal title until the buyer has met all terms of the sale agreement. Under the terms of the conditional sales contract, the seller has the right to repossess the equipment if the contract terms of payment are not met. Alternatively, chattel mortgages are taken on the equipment, but their use is less frequent, partly because the word *mortgage* has undesirable connotations to some borrowers.

Many vendors who offer instalment payment terms to purchasers of their equipment cannot, or prefer not to, maintain a large investment in such instalment receivables. Most finance companies, and in recent years a number of commercial banks, have been willing to extend credit based upon such instalment notes secured by an assignment of the vendor's security interest (the conditional sales contract or chattel mortgage) in the equipment. Usually, financing of the instalment notes receivable is with recourse to the vendor, so that the financing agency has the obligation of the buyer of the equipment, the assigned security interest in the equipment, and the right of recourse to the vendor to support the obligation. In addition, a portion of the payment to the seller is often withheld by the financing agency as a "dealer's reserve" until the note is paid. A typical conditional sales contract and its related dealer assignment are shown in Exhibits 12–5 and 12–6.

In recent years a number of manufacturers and a few large retailers of equipment and consumer durables have set up wholly-owned subsidiaries to take over the parent firm's investment in extended receivables. Typically, these "captive finance companies" borrow heavily from banks and bond issues; frequently, their debts are supported by parent company guaranties.

Concerns purchasing new equipment may find it cheaper or other-

---

[7] As in the case of most other security devices, considerable variety exists in the legislation of the states relating to conditional sales contracts.

EXHIBIT 12-5

TYPICAL CONDITIONAL SALES CONTRACT

CONDITIONAL SALES CONTRACT
ROCKLAND-ATLAS NATIONAL BANK
OF BOSTON

AGREEMENT MADE AT Boston, Mass.
(City and State)

January 10 19 58, between The Hammond Company, 3095 Davis Avenue.
(Purchaser's Name and Address)

Boston, Mass. hereinafter called "Purchaser", and

Marshall Equipment Corporation, 20 Columbus Place, Boston, Mass. hereinafter called "Seller".
(Seller's Name and Address)

Purchaser (which term hereinafter shall include all who sign as purchaser, jointly and severally) agrees to buy and Seller agrees to sell the property described below and all accessories and equipment connected therewith hereinafter called "Property", upon the following terms, for the TOTAL TIME PRICE set forth below. Purchaser accepts and acknowledges receipt of said Property in its present condition, after examination.

DESCRIPTION OF PROPERTY

1 Brockton Forklift Truck, 5-ton, Model L, Serial No. 4935D6, Motor No. 69340 - M - 1

TERMS OF SALE

1. TOTAL CASH SELLING PRICE—Delivered (Including extra equipment —3M adapter———— $ 500.00 $ 5,100.00

2. DOWN PAYMENT: (a) Cash.......... $ 1500.00

(b) Allowance on Trade-In 1949 Brockton 105A4 601-N......... $ 600.00 $ 2,100.00
(Year) (Make) (Serial No.) (Motor No.)

3. DEFERRED BALANCE (Item 1 minus Item 2)......... $ 3,000.00

4. FINANCE CHARGES......... $ 540.00
THE FINANCE CHARGES PROVIDED HEREIN ARE NOT REGULATED BY LAW.
THEY ARE A MATTER FOR AGREEMENT BETWEEN THE PARTIES.

5. NET TIME BALANCE in 35 monthly installments of $ 99.00 $ 3,540.00
(Sum of Items 3 and 4) in 1 ...... $ 75.00

Purchaser agrees to pay to Seller or his assignee the NET TIME BALANCE as set forth above, in consecutive monthly installments commencing one month from date, with interest at 6% per annum on each installment after the due date thereof and, after the expiration of five days following default, reasonable costs of collection. Title to the Property shall remain in Seller until TOTAL TIME PRICE is paid in full. Title to any and all additions and attachments, whensoever added, shall become part of the Property and subject to the terms hereof. No warranty with respect to the Property, either expressed or implied, is made by Seller, and Purchaser accepts Property under manufacturer's warranty only, if any. It is contemplated that this contract may be assigned to Rockland-Atlas National Bank of Boston to facilitate the financing of the purchase herein made and, in consideration thereof, Purchaser agrees, with respect to the exercise by said bank, as assignee, of any rights hereunder, not to assert any defense or claim of setoff, counterclaim or recoupment which Purchaser has or may acquire against the Seller. In the event that any installment payment provided for herein remains unpaid for five days after its due date or upon the failure of the Purchaser to perform any other obligation hereunder within five days after performance is due, then all unpaid installments herein provided for shall, at the option of the Seller or his assignee, forthwith become due and payable. On or upon any default by the Purchaser hereunder, the Seller or his assignee may repossess the Property and may do so without liability for trespass and without responsibility for any articles left in the Property and thereupon (after such redemption period as provided for by law) the Seller or his assignee may sell the Property at public or private sale without notice or publication (except as may be required by law) and at any such public sale the Seller or its assignee may bid and be a purchaser thereat. In the event of the repossession and sale of the property for default in payment of any part of the TOTAL TIME PRICE, all sums paid on account of such price and any sum remaining from the proceeds of a sale of such repossessed Property, after deducting the reasonable expenses of such repossession and sale, shall be applied in reduction of such price, and that if the net proceeds of such sale exceed the balance due on such price, the sum remaining shall be paid to the Purchaser. However, if the net proceeds of such sale are less than the balance then due, Purchaser agrees to pay upon demand to the Seller or his assignee, as liquidated damages for any aforementioned default, the amount of such deficiency, together with reasonable expenses of collection, including reasonable attorneys' fees. Purchaser further agrees that he will not remove the Property from the State in which he now resides without the written consent of the Seller or his assignee, and authority is hereby given to the Seller and his assignee to examine and inspect the Property at any reasonable time. Purchaser further agrees that he will not sell, mortgage, encumber or dispose of the Property or his interest therein and will keep the same free from taxes, encumbrances, liens or other charges, and in good condition at all times. Purchaser gives Seller and his assignee full power and authority to prove any losses covered by insurance, to adjust and collect claims and to receive and endorse (in Purchaser's name) checks or drafts in payment of such claims, however the same may be payable, and to apply the net amount so collected (after deduction of costs of adjustment and collection) against the NET TIME BALANCE then remaining unpaid, whether or not then due and payable, and, in case of a sale of the Property upon Purchaser's default, to cancel all insurance and receive the premium refunds. Purchaser, on any installment due date, may prepay the entire then unpaid NET TIME BALANCE, and upon such prepayment shall be entitled to an allowance less an acquisition cost of $10.00. The allowance shall be equal to that proportion of the finance charge as the sum of the subsequent periodical balances (which would have been due as of each installment date thereafter except for such prepayment) bears to the sum of all the periodical balances as of each installment date, according to the schedule of installment payments hereinabove set forth, computed without regard to such prepayment.

NOTICE TO PURCHASER. DO NOT SIGN THIS CONTRACT IN BLANK.

EXECUTED IN TRIPLICATE AS AN INSTRUMENT UNDER SEAL.

Signature of Seller..(Seal)   Signature of Purchaser..(Seal)
(In ink)   (In ink)

By...Henry Marshall, President..   By...John Lake, Treasurer..
(Owner, Officer, Firm Member and Title)   (Owner, Officer, Firm Member and Title)

Purchaser hereby acknowledges receipt of a copy of this contract..
(Purchaser's Signature)

ORIGINAL FOR BANK

Form TS-5-R·52

EXHIBIT 12-6

DEALER'S ASSIGNMENT OF INTEREST IN A CONDITIONAL SALES CONTRACT

DEALER'S ASSIGNMENT

For valuable consideration, the receipt whereof is hereby acknowledged, the undersigned does hereby sell, assign and transfer to the Rockland-Atlas National Bank of Boston, his, its, or their right, title and interest in and to the conditional sale contract on the reverse side hereof and the property referred to therein, with power to take legal proceedings in the name of the undersigned or itself in respect thereto, and the undersigned warrants that said contract is genuine and enforceable according to its terms, that all statements made therein are true, that the parties thereto had full legal capacity to enter into said contract, that the said property is free from all claims, liens or encumbrances (except said contract) and said property has been delivered and accepted in pursuance of said contract.

Also, for the aforementioned consideration, the undersigned guarantees to said assignee the prompt and due performance of the said contract by the Purchaser therein named and of all obligations arising therefrom. No defense to liability hereunder shall result from any surrender, release, or waiver by said assignee of any interest in said property, or by any action taken, or election of remedies made, by said assignee with respect to said contract. The undersigned hereby waives notice of defaults of the Purchaser and agrees that said assignee may at any time and from time to time grant extensions of time or other forbearance, indulgence or favor to the Purchaser or his assigns and the undersigned hereby waives generally all suretyship defenses and defenses in the nature thereof.

Executed as an instrument under seal at ..... Boston, Mass. ....by the Seller named in said contract on the
........Eleventh.................day of ....January..........1958.

By.....Henry Marshall, President.....................................(Seal)
(Owner, Officer or Firm Member, with title)

wise preferable to borrow directly from banks or finance companies in order to pay the vendor the full purchase price in cash. Such a direct lender often takes a chattel mortgage on the equipment to secure his advance, normally an amount significantly less than the purchase price. Repayment of the notes is scheduled on an instalment basis, again at a rate calculated to keep the loan balance below resale value upon repossession. A standard chattel mortgage agreement covering an item of industrial equipment, and under which promissory notes would be written, is shown in Exhibit 12–7.

Instalment financing is used for a great variety of equipment—from barber chairs to giant diesel earth movers—and by a wide variety of businesses. Large corporations of strong credit standing are less likely to use the device, but many strong railroads are outstanding exceptions to this generalization. For a long time, major railroads have been buying locomotives and other rolling stock through use of *equipment trust certificates,* which can in many ways be regarded as a specialized form of instalment equipment financing. Insurance companies have been major buyers of equipment trust certificates.

Speaking broadly, credit against equipment is restricted mainly to new or highly serviceable used machinery. The rapid obsolescence of many types of equipment reduces the resale value of much used, though serviceable, equipment to near scrap values. Consequently, a would-be borrower will find it much easier to get substantial credit on new than on old equipment, even though the used equipment is physically sound and is carried on the owner's books at substantial value.

Costs of credit against equipment vary widely. Equipment trust certificates of strong railroads have long carried low interest rates, while financially weak concerns buying equipment subject to rapid depreciation in value may well pay fees amounting to an annual interest rate on the balance owed of from 12 to 24 per cent.

More than 27 per cent of the secured commercial bank loans covered in the 1955 Federal Reserve analysis were secured by equipment. Since the equipment loans were typically for small amounts, they were about 14 per cent of the total dollar amount of secured loans.

Borrowing against Plant or Other Real Estate

Businessmen are inclined to regard their investment in brick and mortar—in plant and built-in or fixed equipment—as excellent po-

EXHIBIT 12–7

Typical Chattel Mortgage Agreement

Chattel Mortgage

KNOW ALL MEN BY THESE PRESENTS, that....The Hammond Company..

of.............Boston................................ Massachusetts, hereinafter called the "Mortgagor", for a valuable consideration paid by Rockland-Atlas National Bank of Boston, a national banking association, hereinafter called the "Bank", the receipt whereof is hereby acknowledged, and to secure the payment of --two thousand five hundred---------dollars, payable with interest as provided in a promissory note of even date, and to secure any other direct or indirect liabilities or obligations of the Mortgagor to the Bank, due or to become due, or that may hereafter be contracted, does hereby grant, sell, transfer, deliver and mortgage unto the Bank the following goods and chattels, and all accessories, attachments and equipment connected therewith or hereafter added or attached thereto, viz:

.........................Brockton Mobile Conveyor, 6 ton per hour.........................

.........................capacity, with auxiliary power unit and payload gear box;.........................

.........................Mfrs. Serial No. M3694.........................

together with all property of like kind now owned or hereafter acquired by Mortgagor and any and all additions, accessions and substitutions thereto or therefor, all hereinafter called or referred to as the "Property".

TO HAVE AND TO HOLD all and singular the Property unto the Bank, its successors and assigns to its and their own use and behoof forever.

The Mortgagor hereby covenants with the Bank that the Mortgagor is the lawful owner of the Property, that the same is free from all encumbrances, that the Mortgagor will defend the same against all claims and demands whatsoever of any and all persons at any time claiming the same or any interest therein, that the Property will not be removed from the Commonwealth of Massachusetts without the written consent of the Bank, that the Mortgagor will not assign, sell or offer to sell, or transfer the Property, or any interest therein, that the Mortgagor will keep the Property at all times insured against fire (including comprehensive coverage so-called) and such other insurance and in such amounts as shall at all times be satisfactory to the Bank and by policies delivered to and payable to the Bank as mortgagee and in such form and in such companies as the Bank shall approve, and that the Mortgagor will not permit or suffer any strip or waste or improper use of the Property nor permit an attachment of the Property or any part thereof.

tential security under mortgage arrangements.[8] Particularly is this impression likely to be strong if the plant facilities are handsome, costly, and built to last for a long time. Yet, our earlier observation

---

[8] The mortgage device of granting to lenders a security interest in real estate is a very old one. Since ownership of residential property is so commonly financed by borrowing, with the home used as security under a mortgage (or a similar form used in several states called a deed of trust), mortgage law has become detailed and complicated in all of the states. Generally, commercial or industrial real estate is mortgaged under the basic mortgage laws applying to residential property.

EXHIBIT 12-7—*Continued*

Provided, nevertheless, that if the Mortgagor shall pay the aforementioned note and all interest thereon at the times and in the manner stipulated therein and shall perform and observe all of the covenants herein and in said note expressed to be performed or observed by the Mortgagor and shall then be under no other liability or obligation of any kind or description to the Bank, then this mortgage and also the said note shall be void.

But upon any default of the Mortgagor in the payment when due of the principal or interest on said note, or in the performance or observance of any of the covenants, terms, conditions, liabilities or obligations contained or referred to herein or in the said note, the Mortgagor hereby authorizes and empowers the Bank to sell the Property subject to this mortgage, either as a whole or from time to time in parts, together with all improvements and additions thereto, at private sale or at public auction, and either for cash or on credit, first giving notice in writing of the time and place of any such sale by mailing at least five (5) days before such sale such notice by registered mail addressed to the Mortgagor at the Mortgagor's last address known to the Bank or by leaving at least five (5) days before such sale such notice with the Mortgagor or with a person in possession of the Property claiming the same or first publishing notice of such time and place once in each of three successive weeks in one of the principal newspapers, if any, published in any city or town (otherwise in one of the principal newspapers published in any county) where this mortgage is properly recorded or where the Property is situated and the Bank or any person or persons in its behalf may purchase at such sale or sales, if at public auction, and the power of sale hereunder shall not be exhausted however many times exercised. The proceeds of such sale or sales shall be applied to the payment or reimbursement of all costs and expenses of such sale or sales, including all reasonable attorneys' fees, and including all costs, charges and expenses incurred or sustained by the Bank in relation to the Property or in discharging the claims or liens of third persons affecting the same, and the balance to the payment pro tanto of the said note or other liabilities or obligations secured hereby, and paying over the surplus, if any, to the Mortgagor.

Upon any default hereunder and the sale of the Property or any part thereof subject to this mortgage, the Bank shall have the right to cancel any insurance on the Property and to require payment to it of any unearned premiums thereon.

And it is agreed that until default in the performance or observance of any of the covenants, terms, conditions, liabilities or obligations contained or referred to herein or in said note, the Mortgagor may retain possession of the Property and may make use of the same in his personal affairs or in ordinary course of business, as the case may be, but may not subject the same to unusual or excessive exposure, hazards, or wear, but after any such default, the Bank may take immediate possession of the Property and for that purpose may, so far as the Mortgagor can give authority therefor, enter on the premises in which the Property or any part thereof is located, and may remove the same therefrom.

If there be more than one person executing this instrument, the term "Mortgagor" as used herein shall be deemed to apply to each of them and the covenants and agreements herein shall be joint and several. It is further agreed that this instrument shall bind and inure to the benefit of the heirs, executors, administrators, successors and assigns of any designated by the term "Mortgagor".

In Witness Whereof the Mortgagor has executed this instrument as an instrument under seal this   25th   day of   August   1957 .

Witness

..............J. O. Dain..............................   ....The Hammond Company..........

....John Lake, Treasurer..........

that few lenders are willing to make a loan against security if they really expect to have to take over and liquidate the security in order to settle the loan is particularly valid in the case of loans against plant as security.

Industrial plants have, in the view of many lenders, particular weaknesses as loan collateral. A first weakness is that firms wanting to borrow against fixed assets often want the money to finance added investment in fixed assets. Since recovery of this investment by the borrower through depreciation or added profits normally takes many years, his investment is relatively illiquid. Further, action to seize and sell, or *foreclose,* a company's productive establishment is indeed a drastic step, often fatal to the company, and hence one taken by lenders with real reluctance. Third, the process of foreclosure is, in many states, a time-consuming one, with the debtor retaining rights to reclaim his property over a considerable time. Fourth, and most basic, is the high degree of uncertainty regarding resale value upon foreclosure. If the difficulties of the borrower that lead to default and foreclosure are the result of generally depressed conditions in his industry, as frequently is the case, the number of firms interested in buying the foreclosed plant may be limited indeed. Prosperous and expanding companies which might be buyers often prefer to build a new plant designed and located to meet their particular requirements. In such circumstances, the added expense of building to their own needs may result in lower operating costs and in long-run economy, so that they are not interested in the older, foreclosed plant at any price.

Furthermore, relatively few plants are truly general purpose facilities. Most contain much built-in equipment or special features for a particular productive activity that limit the potential market for the property. Highly specialized plants such as foundries have attraction and value only to other foundry companies, and they may well share the slack business or other unfavorable developments that led to the trouble of the borrower.

This is not to say that industrial facilities have no value as collateral. There is widespread mortgaging of plants as security—almost 21 per cent by number and 23 per cent by volume of secured loans in 1955 were secured by plant and other real estate. But much of their use as security is not due to the attractiveness of plants as collateral. Lenders often take the security as a means of added control over a borrower for a loan they are making essentially on an unsecured basis. That is, many loans that are nominally against plant security are in fact regarded by the lender as primarily unsecured, with some possibility of added security in the plant because of its value to the borrower. If the property is essential to the borrower, or to a reorganized company in the event of bankruptcy, the lender may get better treatment at the hands of the court owing to his claim against the vital, if nonresalable, plant.

BORROWING AGAINST SECURITIES AND LIFE INSURANCE

For various reasons, concerns owning government bonds or other securities may prefer to raise needed funds by borrowing against the securities rather than by selling them. The mechanics of pledging securities are relatively simple and easily accomplished. Although the borrower retains ownership of the securities, he assigns an interest in them to the lender, who holds physical possession as security for the loan. The note or other debt instrument specifies the terms upon which the lender can dispose of the securities and apply the proceeds toward the debt. A typical ninety-day note against securities as collateral is shown in Exhibit 12–8.

If the securities are marketable government bonds or corporate securities traded actively on national security exchanges, the borrower seldom will have difficulty finding lenders willing to loan a high percentage of the market value of the securities. If the securities are those of little-known subsidiaries or other companies whose securities have limited markets, prospective lenders can be expected to consider carefully the factors that will probably affect the future value and marketability of the securities, and to loan only a portion of their appraisal of the value of the securities. In 1955, 6.3 per cent of the total number of secured member bank business loans and 8.6 per cent of the total amount were against pledged securities.

Many firms carry life insurance policies on key personnel of types that in time accumulate considerable cash surrender value. The rights to matured or cash surrender value can be assigned to bank or other lenders as security for loans. Much of the lending against securities or cash surrender values of life insurance policies is by commercial banks, ordinarily at near prime interest rates.

USE OF COMAKER, ENDORSEMENT, OR GUARANTY OF LOANS

Over 23 per cent of the secured member bank loans to business in 1955 were secured in the sense that other concerns or individuals accepted direct or contingent obligations for the loans. As will be noted by reviewing Exhibit 10–1 (page 190), a plain note can be signed by several parties, each party becoming a *comaker* of the note, and all parties jointly and severally assuming the obligations of the promise to pay. As another technique of security, a lender may ask for an *endorsement* of a borrower's note by a third party. The third party, by signing a note on the reverse side, grants to the lender full recourse to his resources (unless otherwise stated) in case the borrower fails to honor the debt. In a third and more flexible arrangement, a third party signs a guaranty agreement covering all debts of the borrower to the lender and thereby obviates the necessity for each note or other

EXHIBIT 12-8

A TYPICAL PROMISSORY NOTE WITH SECURITIES AS COLLATERAL

C119-A

NON-PURPOSE "STOCK" COLLATERAL TIME LOAN

BOSTON, MASSACHUSETTS _____ January 5, _____ 19 58 _____ $5,000.00

Ninety days _____ after date, for value received, I/we promise to pay to the order of

at said Bank Five thousand – Dollars

THE FIRST NATIONAL BANK OF BOSTON

having deposited with said Bank, as collateral security for payment of this and any and all other liabilities, direct or indirect, absolute or contingent, due or to become due, now existing or hereafter arising, of mine/ours or either of us to said Bank, its successors or assigns, the following property, viz.:

Fifty (50) shares American Telephone and Telegraph Company – common stock

I/We agree to either deliver to the holder additional security or make payments on account, to the holder's satisfaction, should the value of the security at any time held decline, or should the holder or any officer or anyone acting in behalf of the holder deem such security to be insufficient by reason of the decline in the market value of any part thereof.

This note and any or all of the liabilities above mentioned shall, at the option of the holder, become immediately due and payable without notice or demand upon the occurrence of any of the following events: (a) failure of the undersigned with or without demand or notice, to deliver additional security or make payments on account to the holder's satisfaction as above agreed; (b) default in the payment or performance of any liability or obligation of any of the undersigned, or of any maker, endorser or guarantor of any liability or obligation of any of the undersigned, to the holder; (c) failure to pay when due any premium on any life insurance policy held as collateral herefor; (d) death, dissolution, termination of existence, insolvency, business failure, appointment of a receiver of any part of the property, of assignment for the benefit of creditors by, or the filing of a petition in bankruptcy, or the commencement of any proceedings under any bankruptcy or insolvency laws or any laws relating to the relief of debtors, readjustment of indebtedness, reorganization, composition or extension, by or against, any maker, endorser, or guarantor hereof.

The undersigned do hereby fully authorize and empower the holder, on the non-performance of any promise made herein, or the non-payment of any of the liabilities above mentioned, or the occurrence of any of the events specified in the next preceding paragraph, or at any time or times thereafter, to sell, assign and deliver all of the security herefor or any part thereof, or any substitutes therefor, or any additions thereto, at any Broker's Board, or at public or private sale, at the option of the holder, or any officer or anyone acting in behalf of the holder, without advertisement or any notice to the undersigned or any other person, and the holder, its officers or assigns may bid and become purchasers at any such sale, if public, or at any Broker's Board. Right is expressly granted to the holder at its option to transfer at any time to itself or to its nominee any securities pledged hereunder and to receive the income thereon and hold the same as security herefor, or apply it on the principal or interest due hereon or due on any liability secured hereby.

Any deposits or other sums at any time credited by or due from the holder to any maker, endorser or guarantor hereof and any securities or other property of any maker, endorser or guarantor hereof in the possession of the holder may at all times be held and treated as collateral security for the payment of this note and any and all other liabilities, direct or indirect, absolute or contingent, due or to become due, now existing or hereafter arising, of said respective maker, endorser or guarantor to the holder. The holder may apply or set off such deposits or other sums against said liabilities at any time in the case of makers, but only with respect to matured liabilities in the case of endorsers or guarantors.

The holder may at its option, whether this note is due or not due, demand, sue for, collect, or make any compromise or settlement it deems desirable with reference to collateral held hereunder. The holder shall have no duty as to the collection or protection of collateral held hereunder or any income thereon, nor as to the preservation of any rights pertaining thereto beyond the safe custody thereof. No delay or omission on the part of the holder in exercising any right hereunder shall operate as a waiver of such right or of any other right under this note. A waiver on any one occasion shall not be construed as a bar to or waiver of any such right and/or remedy on any future occasion.

Every maker, endorser and guarantor of this note, or the obligation represented hereby, waives presentment, demand, notice, protest, and all other demands and notices in connection with the delivery, acceptance, performance, default or enforcement of this note, assents to any extension or postponement of the time of payment or any other indulgence, to any substitution, exchange or release of collateral, and/or to the addition or release of any other party or person primarily or secondarily liable. Nothing in this paragraph shall be construed to prevent any maker, endorser or guarantor from paying this note on its stated maturity.

The undersigned will pay all expenses of every kind of the enforcement of this note, or of any of the rights hereunder, and hereby agree to pay to the holder on demand the amount of any and all such expenses incurred by it. After deducting all legal or other expenses and costs of collection of this note and all legal or other expenses and costs of collection, storage, custody, sale and delivery of collateral held hereunder, the residue of any proceeds of collection or sale shall be applied to the payment of principal or interest on this note or on any or all of the other liabilities aforesaid, due or to become due, in such order of preference as the holder shall determine, proper allowance for interest on liabilities not then due being made, and any overplus shall be returned to the undersigned.

As herein used the word "holder" shall mean the payee or other endorser of this note, who is in possession of it, or the bearer hereof, if this note is at the time payable to the bearer.

Under the provisions of Regulation U issued by the Board of Governors of the Federal Reserve System pursuant to the authority of the Securities Exchange Act, I/we certify that this loan is not made for the purpose of purchasing or carrying any stock registered on a National Securities Exchange.

Address	3095 Davis Avenue	_Signed by_	The Hammond Company
	Boston, Massachusetts		Alexander Hammond
			President

debt instrument being individually endorsed. Guaranty agreements are particularly common in the case of closely held corporations whose owners have substantial personal resources and are willing to put these resources behind the firm's borrowing. An example of a guaranty agreement of this nature is shown in Exhibit 12–9. Also, it is common for parent companies to guarantee loans to their subsidiaries.

Obviously, the value to lenders of any of these arrangements varies with the financial resources of the comaker, endorser, or guarantor. It is interesting to note that lenders, by obtaining endorsement or guaranty of corporate debts by share owners, in effect break through the limited liability feature of the incorporated business.

We should make it clear that the comaker, endorsement, or guaranteed loans are not secured loans in the sense that the lender gets any priority over the other general creditors of either the comaker or endorser of the note. The use of the comaker simply gives the lender a general claim on two persons or firms, rather than one.

SUBORDINATION OF CERTAIN DEBT CLAIMS TO OTHER OBLIGATIONS

In recent years the practice of subordination by a creditor or group of creditors of certain of their rights as creditors to another creditor or class of creditor has become sufficiently important to deserve attention here. Subordination is accomplished through contract between the interested parties and as such can take whatever form the interested parties can agree upon.

One of the most common uses of subordination is by stockholders of closely held corporations who are also creditors of their corporations. Tax considerations have been especially important in recent years in stimulating stockholders to make part of their investment in their company in the form of loans to the company. In negotiating bank credit, agreement by the stockholder-creditors to subordinate their own loans to those of the bank may materially improve the chances of getting bank loans. In such cases the subordination is usually stated both in terms of maturity (for example, agreement that no debt to stockholders will be repaid so long as the bank loan is unpaid) and in terms of bankruptcy leading to reorganization or liquidation. The subordination agreement often is drawn to provide that in the event of bankruptcy the favored creditor—in this case, the bank—is entitled to stand in the place of the subordinated creditors

EXHIBIT 12–9

A TYPICAL ENDORSEMENT AGREEMENT

GUARANTY

For valuable consideration, the receipt of which is hereby acknowledged, the undersigned guarantee(s) due fulfillment to The First National Bank of Boston, (herein called the "Bank") of all obligations of___The Hammond Company___
to the Bank, whether direct or indirect, absolute or contingent, due or to become due, now existing or hereafter arising, which are incurred prior to the receipt by the Bank of written notice of the revocation of this guaranty by the undersigned or written notice of the death or incapacity of the undersigned, which notice of revocation, death or incapacity shall not affect rights acquired by the Bank prior to its receipt. If in reliance upon this guaranty the Bank grants loans or extensions or takes other action, after the death or incapacity of the undersigned, or the revocation of this guaranty by the undersigned, but prior to the receipt by the Bank of said written notice thereof, the Bank's rights shall be the same as they would have been had said death, incapacity or revocation not occurred, and the undersigned agrees to indemnify the Bank and save it harmless from and against all loss, cost, liability and expense which the Bank may incur or suffer by reason of any action so taken by it. The maximum liability of the undersigned hereunder shall be
_ Fifty Thousand ($50,000) _Dollars
(Insert the number of dollars, or the word "unlimited")
and liability up to this maximum shall continue, regardless of the payment, reduction, creation or any change in the amount of obligations, until each and all of the above mentioned obligations have been paid and satisfied in full.

The undersigned waives presentment, protest, notice of acceptance of this guaranty, notice of any loans made, extensions granted, or other action taken in reliance hereon and all demands and notices of every kind in connection with this guaranty or the obligations hereby guaranteed; assents to any renewal, extension or postponement of the time of payment or any other indulgence, to any substitution, exchange or release of collateral, and/or to the addition or release of any other person primarily or secondarily liable; and agrees to the provisions of the notes and/or other papers evidencing the obligations hereby guaranteed.

This guaranty shall inure to the benefit of the Bank and its successors and assigns and shall be binding upon the undersigned and the executor(s), administrator(s) and/or other legal representative(s) of the undersigned. If this guaranty is signed by more than one person it shall be the joint and several obligation of said persons.

This instrument is intended to take effect as a sealed instrument.

Witness my/our hand(s) this   20th   day of November   1956

Alexander Hammond

EXHIBIT 12–10

ILLUSTRATION OF A SUBORDINATION AGREEMENT

SUBORDINATION AGREEMENT

Whereas the...... Hammond Company.., a

Massachusetts ....corporation having its usual place of business in...... Boston, Mass.

....

(hereinafter called the "Borrower"), is indebted to the undersigned...... Alexander Hammond

in the sum of....... — — — $100,000.00 — — — — — — — — — — — ~~scope appear~~ —evidenced by the note(s) of the Borrower

Dated	Payable	Amount
June 10, 1957	June 10, 1959	$100,000.00

Whereas the Borrower and the undersigned have requested that The First National Bank of Boston grant to the Borrower ~~a loan or advance~~ an additional loan or advance ~~in extension of time for the payment of the Borrower's indebtedness to the Bank~~ but the Bank has indicated that it is unwilling to grant such request unless the undersigned shall subordinate all of the present and future indebtedness of the Borrower to the undersigned to the present and future indebtedness of the Borrower to the Bank;

Now, Therefore, in consideration of the premises and as an inducement to the Bank to grant to the Borrower, a loan or advance, or an additional loan, or an extension of time, as the case may be, and in consideration of the granting thereof, the undersigned hereby agrees with the Bank to subordinate and hereby subordinates all present and future indebtedness of the Borrower to him to any and all indebtedness now owing or hereafter owing by the Borrower to the Bank, and for the consideration aforesaid, the undersigned agrees with the bank that—

1. He will not at any time accept or receive from the Borrower any payment of principal or interest on account of, or any collateral for, any indebtedness of the Borrower to him and will not otherwise take or permit any other action prejudicial to or inconsistent with the Bank's priority position over the undersigned created by this agreement, until all the indebtedness of the Borrower to the Bank has been paid in full.

2. In the event of any petition in bankruptcy being brought by or against the Borrower, and in the event of any other proceedings for the liquidation of the Borrower, either by its voluntary action or otherwise, he will assign and pay over to the Bank, to the extent necessary to satisfy the indebtedness of the Borrower to the Bank in full with interest to the date of the receipt of such payments, any and all dividends and payments with respect to the indebtedness hereby subordinated to which he would be entitled in any such proceedings.

3. In the event of any proceedings affecting the Borrower under any bankruptcy or insolvency laws or any laws relating to the relief of debtors, readjustment, composition or extension of indebtedness, or reorganization of corporations or other debtors, any payment to which he would be entitled under any plan of reorganization approved by the Court shall be paid to the Bank to be applied on the Borrower's indebtedness to it, and any securities or other property issued or issuable to him under any such proceedings shall be assigned and delivered to the Bank to be held by it subject to the same terms of subordination to the claim of the Bank as are created by this instrument with respect to the present indebted-

or convenient to preserve for the Bank the benefits of this subordination agreement and will execute all agreements which the Bank may request for that purpose, and he hereby assigns, transfers and sets over to the Bank his claim against the Borrower whether evidenced by notes, book entries or otherwise, and without imposing upon the Bank any duty with respect to preservation, protection or enforcement of such claim, or any note or notes evidencing the same, constitutes and appoints the Bank and each of its executive officers his true and lawful attorney for the following purposes:

(a) To collect any dividends or payments which would otherwise be payable to him on any liquidation of the Borrower or in any proceedings affecting the Borrower under any bankruptcy or insolvency laws or any laws relating to the relief of debtors, readjustment, composition or extension of indebtedness, or reorganization of corporations or other debtors.

(b) To prove his claim in any such proceedings.

(c) To accept or reject, to the extent to which he would be entitled to accept or reject, any plan of reorganization in any such proceedings.

(d) To accept any new securities or other property to which he would otherwise be entitled under any such plan of reorganization or proceedings.

(e) And in general to do any act in connection with any of such proceedings which he might otherwise do, it being understood that the Bank shall account to him for any dividends or payments received by it in excess of the amount necessary to satisfy its claim in full with interest.

5. He will and does hereby deposit with the Bank, to be held by it until all future indebtedness of the Borrower to the Bank has been paid in full, the note(s) evidencing the Borrower's indebtedness to him.

6. No action which the Bank, or Borrower with the consent of the Bank, may take, or refrain from taking with respect to any indebtedness of the Borrower to the Bank, or any note or notes representing the same, or any collateral therefor, or any agreement or agreements (including guaranties) in connection therewith, shall affect this agreement or the obligations of the undersigned hereunder. If all indebtedness of the Borrower to the Bank is at any time or times hereafter paid in full and thereafter the Borrower again becomes indebted to the Bank, the provisions of this agreement shall apply to said new indebtedness unless before the same is incurred the undersigned notifies the Bank in writing to the contrary. If, in reliance upon this agreement, the Bank grants loans or extensions or takes other action, after the death or incapacity of the undersigned or the termination of this agreement by the undersigned, but prior to the receipt by the Bank of written notice of said death, incapacity or termination, the Bank's rights shall be the same as they would have been had said death, incapacity or termination not occurred, and the undersigned shall indemnify the Bank and save it harmless from and against any loss, cost, liability or expense which it may incur or suffer by reason of any action so taken by it.

7. This agreement is intended to take effect as a sealed instrument and to be binding on the executor(s), administrator(s) and/or other legal representatives of the undersigned. If it is signed by more than one person it shall be the joint and several obligation of said persons.

In Witness Whereof, the undersigned has hereunto set his hand this..........31st..........day of

January..................., 1958......

....
Alexander Hammond

when assets are distributed and thus be entitled to payment in full before the subordinated creditors are entitled to anything. An example of a subordination agreement between an important stockholder and creditor of a borrowing company and its bank is shown in Exhibit 12–10.

Often, it is said that such subordination agreements, from the viewpoint of the favored creditor, make the subordinated debt money the equivalent of equity funds as a protective cushion in the event of bankruptcy. Actually, from the viewpoint of the favored creditor, debt subordinated to his debts may be better than equity because the favored creditor acquires, for his exclusive benefit, the subordinated creditor's rights as a *creditor* of the company.[9]

Consider the following simplified examples:

BALANCE SHEETS, IN SUMMARY, BEFORE BANKRUPTCY

Company A		*Company B*	
Total Assets............	$500,000	Total Assets............	$500,000
Bank loan..............	$100,000	Bank loan..............	$100,000
Due trade and other		Due trade and other	
creditors.............	200,000	creditors.............	200,000
Loan from stockholders, sub-		Common stock and surplus.	200,000
ordinated to bank.......	100,000		
Common stock and surplus.	100,000		
Total Liabilities.........	$500,000	Total Liabilities.........	$500,000

Note that the only difference between the two balance sheets is that $100,000 of the owner's investment in Company A is in the form of debt which has been subordinated to the loan to the company from the bank. Now, assume that each company found it impossible to meet maturing obligations and was forced into bankruptcy leading to liquidation. Assume that in each company, enough cash was available to pay the expenses of bankruptcy and to pay certain preferred creditors in full, leaving thereafter $220,000 in cash for all other creditors.

In Company A, a 55 per cent distribution to creditors ($220,000 divided by 400,000) is sufficient to pay the bank in full, since it is entitled to $55,000 on its debt directly and, under the subordination agreement, is entitled to enough (in this case, $45,000) of the subordinating creditor's share to permit repayment of the $100,000 due the bank in full.

In Company B, however, a similar net amount for distribution to

---

[9] A disadvantage is that the holder of the subordinated debt may have greater power than the holder of an equity of the same amount to initiate bankruptcy proceedings at a time when the favored creditor would prefer to avoid such proceedings.

all creditors, $220,000, would permit a 73.3 per cent pay-out to each creditor ($220,000/$300,000). In this instance the bank is able to collect only $73,333 on its $100,000 credit. Trade and other creditors fare better than in Company A, getting paid $146,666 in comparison with $110,000 in Company A. The owners get nothing in either case.

In the discussion and examples above, we have considered only one of the important types of subordination agreements. Other circumstances in which subordinations are used include subordination by an entire class of creditors, such as trade creditors, as a means of encouraging new credit to keep a valued customer in business. Further, in nondistress circumstances, many concerns, particularly finance companies, have succeeded in selling to the public subordinated debentures which by their terms subordinate certain rights of the holders of these securities to those of other creditors.

Some Cautions Regarding the Giving of Security

Earlier in this chapter, advantages that borrowers might obtain from effective use of their assets as security for loans—greater credit, lower interest rates than on unsecured borrowing, etc.—were discussed. It is appropriate at this point to consider the serious disadvantages that can result from injudicious giving of security.

First, the increased availability of credit by giving security may encourage excessively heavy use of debt. Any borrowing involves risk to the borrower—financial risk added to the normal risks of doing business. The increased risks of debt should be appreciated and accepted only after careful and full consideration.

Secondly, for many firms, there is great advantage (not to say comfort) in retaining reserves of borrowing power for use in financial extremity or to finance particularly desirable investment opportunities that may develop. Obviously, security, once committed, no longer is available as the basis for further credit; and the firm which ties up all of its attractive security is in the same exposed position as the general who has committed all his reserves to battle. When secured borrowing is undertaken, the borrower should appreciate that if he concedes more security than really is required and further credit subsequently is needed, it may be hard indeed to get the old lender to release security or to dilute his own cushion by lending more against the same security.

Third, most firms depend heavily on continued trade credit from suppliers, extended on an unsecured basis. As the firm commits more and more of its best assets as security for loans, the trade creditors increasingly depend on the shrinking and poorer assets left unpledged. While it is difficult to determine in advance the exact extent to which pledging of assets can be carried without jeopardizing the continued availability of trade credit, excessive pledging of assets *can* result in impairment or loss of credit from alert suppliers and other unsecured creditors.

Chapter 13

Negotiating Intermediate Credit: The Term Loan

IN CHAPTER 10, we classified the sources of funds according to the length of time for which the business could count on having the funds. Classified as intermediate credit are loans of from one to fifteen years. Credits on terms of less than one year are short term, while we regard those of over fifteen years as long term.

Although the focus in earlier chapters was on short-term credit, the discerning student will note that some of the borrowing arrangements discussed earlier actually represent intermediate credit. For example, equipment purchased under conditional sales contracts on terms that provide for a down payment and for monthly repayment of the remainder over as many as sixty months is bought in part on short-term and in part on intermediate credit. It is possible also to argue that many loans based on the pledge of receivables or inventory are in substance intermediate credit even though nominally payable on the demand of the lender, because of the presumption on the part of both borrower and lender in most of these arrangements that the loans will be continuing over a period of years.

The focus in this chapter is on one form of intermediate credit—the *term loan*—which has assumed great importance to American business in the last twenty-five years. After identifying key characteristics of present-day term loans, we briefly review the history and growth of term lending. Then we describe current term-lending practice with an emphasis on the measures taken by lenders to control the risks inherent in this type of lending. Assuming the borrower's viewpoint, we next focus on the advantages and disadvantages of term credit, and how borrowers best can negotiate suitable term credit and maintain term borrowing relationships.

Key Characteristics of the Term Loan

The term loan has taken on several key and distinguishing characteristics. First, as suggested by our earlier classification, term loans are for a period of at least one year and can be for as much as fifteen years' maturity. Second, periodic or serial repayment typically is required. Although many term loans call for equal repayments during each year of the life of the loan, the schedule of repayments customarily is designed to fit the circumstances of the borrower as well as the needs of the lender. Third, the relationship between the borrower and the term lender is a direct one. Although intermediaries may bring borrower and lender together, the terms of the loan usually are worked out directly over the conference table by representatives of the lender and the borrower. Although two or more lenders may combine in providing the money under a single term loan agreement, the number of lenders is usually small. Fourth, the direct relationship between borrower and lender permits a "tailor-made" loan agreement. The typical term loan agreement has many provisions. As long as a borrower carries out the commitments agreed to in the loan agreement, the lender can require payment only in accordance with the maturity schedule specified. However, failure to comply with any important provision of the agreement accelerates the maturity of the loan so that the lender legally may demand payment of the full amount.

The History and Growth of Bank Term Lending

Two major types of financial institutions, commercial banks and life insurance companies, are now of dominant importance as sources of term loans for business. The history of term lending by both banks and insurance companies is a short one; neither type of institution did a significant amount of term lending before 1935. Both became term lenders on an important scale as recovery from the Great Depression developed during the latter half of the thirties.

For the commercial banks, deliberate entry into term lending represented a particularly important break with traditional ideas of appropriate bank lending. As we have seen, commercial banks get their funds for lending primarily from demand deposits. And we have noted the general and long-standing acceptance of the theory that demand deposits should be loaned out primarily or virtually exclusively on short terms. It is true that in practice, banks made many loans on terms nominally short that really represented intermediate credit in the sense that both borrower and lender anticipated that the loans would be renewed rather than repaid at maturity of the note. Nevertheless, the deliberate and definite commitment of loan funds for a period of years represented a noteworthy departure from traditional theory and practice. A variety of factors affecting the supply and demand for bank credit contributed to the initial term lending around 1935 and its subsequent continued growth. Among the factors increasing the willingness of bankers to make term loans, probably the most important was the fact that from the mid-thirties to the mid-fifties the demand from business for short-term credit of the traditional sort was insufficient to absorb the funds the banks had available to lend. Economic recovery from the Great Depression, the success of certain depression-born governmental agencies with longer term loans repayable in instalments geared to estimates of the borrower's ability to pay, the inauguration of deposit insurance and waning fears of massive deposit contraction, and increasing acceptance by bankers and bank supervisory agencies of the concept that the liquidity needs of the banks would not be compromised by a moderate amount of term lending all provided encouragement to its growth.

At least equally important was the fact that a great many creditworthy businesses needed and wanted intermediate credit rather than, or in addition to, temporary short-term credit. As particular banks aggressively expanded their term lending, competing banks experienced pressure from their customers for similar accommodation, and many reluctant bankers were forced into term lending to keep their institutions competitive.[1]

By 1946, term loans had grown to represent one fifth of the total number and one third of the amount of member bank loans to business. During the great expansion of bank credit to business in the following decade, the proportion of total bank credit in term loans expanded further. The member bank survey on October 16, 1957, revealed that $15.4 billion of the $40.6 billion of total loans to business by these banks, or 38.0 per cent, represented term credit. The increasing inability of many banks since 1955 to satisfy fully the avid business demand for bank credit has fostered growing reluctance on the part of many bankers further to increase their term loan portfolios. When bankers must ration credit among their creditworthy

---

[1] For an excellent survey of term lending through 1940, see N. H. Jacoby and R. J. Saulnier, *Term Lending to Business* (New York: National Bureau of Economic Research, Inc., 1942).

customers, they can use a given amount of funds for lending to satisfy the needs of a larger number of short-term than of long-term borrowers. Furthermore, bankers point out that if an undue proportion of loanable funds is tied up in term credits to strong, big firms, which could have borrowed through public issues of bonds, other borrowers, who possess no other sources of credit than their banks, are deprived of access to short-term funds. Nevertheless, it is difficult for the bankers to turn down term credit requests of highly valued customers, and data on the lending of large New York banks show that term loans grew from 51 per cent of their business loans in 1957 to 57 per cent on January 25, 1961.[2]

More than half of the $15.4 billion of term credit outstanding at member banks in 1957 was to borrowers with assets of more than $5 million. However, term credit was outstanding to more than 479,100 firms; most of the smaller term loans were secured by fixed assets or equipment, along the lines described in Chapter 12. The industry distribution of bank term loan borrowers is shown in Table 13–1.

TABLE 13–1

OUTSTANDING TERM LOANS TO BUSINESS OF MEMBER BANKS
OF FEDERAL RESERVE SYSTEM
As of October 16, 1957

Business of Borrower	Amount (in Millions)	Term Loans as Percentage of Total Bank Loans to Industry Group
All businesses	$15,421	38.0
Manufacturing and mining:		
Food, liquor, and tobacco	485	20.3
Textiles, apparel, and leather	314	18.6
Metals and metal products	1,905	34.5
Petroleum, coal, chemicals, and rubber	2,763	73.7
Other manufacturing and mining	1,067	38.2
Retail trade	1,387	30.2
Wholesale trade	600	20.1
Commodity dealers	88	10.8
Sales finance companies	266	8.6
Public utilities	2,839	68.1
Construction	596	30.1
Real estate	1,307	43.9
Services	1,194	52.8
Other nonfinancial	611	38.1

SOURCE: *Federal Reserve Bulletin*, April, 1959.

[2] Federal Reserve Bank of New York, *Monthly Review*, February, 1961.

Life Insurance Company Term Lending to Business

The entry of life insurance companies into term lending on a sizable scale during the late thirties represented a much less radical shift from their traditional lending activities than was the case for commercial banks. The maturities of obligations to the policyholders supplying funds to the life insurance companies are both long term and subject to reasonably precise actuarial prediction, so that they have relatively little need for liquidity in their investment portfolios. Before 1935, life insurance companies had invested heavily in medium- and long-term bonds, particularly of railroads and public utility companies. These were purchased in the open market or from investment bankers marketing public issues.

Under the pressure of competition for desirable investments during the thirties, more and more insurance companies began to enter into direct negotiation with public utility and industrial concerns leading to direct purchase of entire new debt issues. Since many business borrowers wanted intermediate credit, many of these direct placements—or *private placements,* as they came to be called—took on the essential characteristics of term loans.[3] To some extent the insurance companies competed directly with commercial banks as term lenders to the larger and better grade borrowers. For the most part, however, bank interest centered in terms loans of less than five years, and to a lesser extent in five- to ten-year maturities, and the insurance companies concentrated on term loans of five to fifteen years. In a number of cases, banks and insurance companies have worked together in making particular term loans, the banks taking the portion of the total loan with earlier payment schedules and the insurance companies the longer term portions.

As their experience with directly negotiated term loans proved favorable, insurance companies have tended to make term loan money more freely available to medium-sized companies and to companies of less than the highest credit standing. In recent years a number of insurance companies have made term loans of $100,000 to $500,-000, although the expense of investigating and servicing smaller loans discourages keen interest in loans of such size. A few large life insurance companies have set up special units to make term loans to smaller businesses, but the volume of such lending is small.

---

[3] In insurance company terminology the label *direct placements* is used much more widely than *term loans.* The terms of most insurance company direct placement loans are such that they can appropriately be considered as term loans.

At the end of 1960, life insurance companies had an investment of almost $47 billion in business debt securities. This total includes bonds purchased in the open market or from investment bankers upon first issue as well as direct purchases. Of the direct purchases a considerable portion represented term loans as we have defined them, but the amount cannot be estimated from published industry data. Probably the amount exceeds the total of term loan credit from banks. In any case the insurance companies represent a highly important and continuing source of intermediate credit for business.

CURRENT TERM LENDING PRACTICE

The commitment of loan funds directly to a borrower for a period of years has basic implications keenly important to the lender. Recognizing and understanding these implications helps much toward understanding key features of term-lending practice.

A basic fact that the lender must face in considering a loan for a period of years is the near certainty of major change in the situation and affairs of the borrower before the loan is repaid. Five, ten, or fifteen years is long enough in our dynamic and competitive economic environment for material developments to occur in the management of any borrowing enterprise, in its products, its markets, its competitive position, its industry, and in the general level of the economy in which it operates. Of course, lenders have always had to cope with change. But the extent, speed, and intensity of change in our present-day economy particularly complicates the job of working out lending arrangements that will stand up for years under rapidly shifting circumstances.

A related and rather obvious point is that risk increases with uncertainty, and that uncertainty increases as the length of the loan commitment is extended. If term lending is to be extended beyond those few companies with particularly outstanding prospects and those seemingly invulnerable to unfavorable developments, while the risks in lending are to be held to proportions consistent with the interest income, lenders must exercise imagination, skill, and vigor in working out provisions that will minimize the risks inherent in the unpredictable but certainly changing future.

Insurance company investment officers have long been buyers of long-term bonds and hence are experienced in gauging long-term risks. However, a continuing market exists for many such bond issues. The market price quotations to some extent provide a continuing check on the owner's appraisal of the creditworthiness of the issuer. And except for the largest bondholders, the existence of the market offers an opportunity for the investor to sell his holdings if deterioration in the credit is foreseen. In the case of bank term loans and debt issues bought privately by insurance companies, there is no organized market for the debt obligations, and the lender must live with his mistakes as well as his successes.

In the case of short-term or continuing credits subject to periodic review and renewal, bank lenders are less firmly committed to their borrowing customers. As conditions affecting the loan change, the bankers have the opportunity to reconsider or realign the credit and its terms at renewal dates.

Measures by Lenders to Restrict Risk

During almost three decades of active term lending, lenders have developed a variety of measures to restrict the risks inherent in term credit. As in the case of all "bargaining for funds," the final provisions of a credit reflect the bargaining strength of the parties as well as the objectives of each party. When credit was easy and the supply of funds for loan investment exceeded the demand, as was true of most years between 1935 and 1955, competitive pressures commonly forced concessions on the part of the lender that in periods of active loan demand and less avid competition among lenders, as in early 1960, were successfully resisted. But regardless of what competing lenders might do, the intelligent lender must at all times keep his risk taking in line with his prospective rewards for risk taking.

Distinctive Aspects of the Credit Analysis

Since most term loans are for sizable amounts, as well as for considerable periods of time, the credit analysis of a typical term loan application is more comprehensive and thorough than for short-term credits. The industry in which the company operates and its vulnerability to downturn in business conditions is the subject of close scrutiny. Industries with a history of vulnerability to cyclical changes in demand are obviously less attractive than those which have stood up well under depression conditions.

Particular emphasis in the analysis is placed on the long-term profit prospects of the borrower's industry and of the company within the industry. Loan repayment over a period of years is highly dependent on profitable operations. The protection afforded by even a very strong asset position can be swept away by only a few years of heavy losses. Looked upon with favor are companies with a diversified line of products which have built-in protections against especially rigorous competition. Such protections include particularly strong quality features in their products, research effective in developing profitable new products, strong consumer brand loyalty, and fixed asset requirements great enough to discourage entry into the field by new competitors. Established, stable product lines are preferred over high-style or novelty items. It is not surprising that companies in the chemical, oil, and public utility industries, all requiring heavy capital investment and regarded as having favorable long-term profit prospects, have been particularly important term loan borrowers.

Term lenders place much stress on appraisal of the competitive effectiveness of the applicant's management. Certainly, an alert, able, and aggressive management is essential if even those companies most successful in the past are to make the adaptations necessary to keep ahead of competition in a dynamic economy. But as intangibles, the character and skill of management are not easy to measure and project into the future. For example, the past success of a particular company may be due largely to a top management team that is nearing retirement, so that another generation of management, as yet not fully tested, may hold the key to the future. However, if the lending institution has had a long relationship with the would-be term borrower, its officers have had considerable opportunity to get a useful, if inconclusive, size-up of the caliber of those who will guide the borrower's affairs in the future. Put most simply, the question to be answered is: "Are these the kind of men able to 'light on their feet' if major problems knock them off balance?" or "Will these people do all right, come what may?"

The emphasis on profit prospects and the relative de-emphasis of balance sheet analysis does not mean that such items as the working capital position or the relationship of debt to ownership funds are ignored. It is more an implicit recognition that even though working capital is adequate for the apparent near-term needs of the company. and the debt/equity position is reasonable, the long-term maintenance of a healthy balance sheet must hinge on profitability, which not only provides funds for debt service but forms the basis for equity or other financing as needed.

As the length of term credit is extended, the analysis becomes closer to that of a reasonably conservative and astute common stock investor and less like that of the typical short-term creditor.

Repayment Provisions

One of the main protections against risk built into term loans is the typical provision for instalment repayment beginning soon after the credit is extended. From the outset of the loan the borrower is forced to think of repayment and to plan for it as an integral part of his financing. Most lenders prefer to set repayment schedules that leave no large "balloon payment" until the final maturity date. Indeed, many see a need by the borrower for deferral of large amounts to the final maturity as a confession of weakness in the loan application. While conditions at final maturity *may* be sufficiently favorable to permit refunding or extension of the unpaid amount, there is no assurance that this will be the case.

Provision for instalment repayment from cash provided by retained earnings compensates to some degree for the risks inherent in term loan commitments, inasmuch as the size of the loan is reduced as time goes on. At the same time as repayment is made from cash from retained profits, the ownership equity (in the form of earned surplus) increases, so that the debt/ownership relationship is improved both by reduction of the debt and by the retention, in a balance sheet sense, of the earnings in the business. Some have labeled term loans repaid out of profits as programs of *forced reinvestment of earnings*.

In setting repayment schedules, effort is made to forecast cash flows from earnings and other sources and, after allowing for anticipated cash needs of the business, to shape the timing and amount of the repayments to the anticipated "cash throwoff," or cash-generating capacity of the business. Particular reliance is placed on profits as a source of funds for loan repayment. Depreciation as a source of cash is not ignored in the analysis of anticipated cash flows. However, most lenders prefer to consider the cash generated from depreciation and not committed to the purchase of new fixed assets only in appraising the margin of safety left the borrower should profits fall off. Regarded in the same light is the extra cash that might well be made available as a consequence of a decline in sales and the associated release of funds due to lower inventories and receivables. Furthermore, few lenders like to count on the full anticipated profits to cover loan repayments, preferring to have a comfortable cushion against unforeseen difficulties in a substantial excess of anticipated profits over loan repayment requirements.[4]

Of course, the ironical observation that "them what has gits" applies to loan repayment scheduling. In the case of companies with excellent prospects for large, continuing profits, which could afford fast repayment, the lender is less anxious to get his money back quickly and more prepared to accept the risks of a long loan with smaller repayments. Conversely, lenders are more anxious to keep short the term of loans to companies with more uncertain profit potentials, and shorter term means higher instalment payments. Speaking generally, effort is made to compensate for higher risk by shorter repayment schedules.

Not uncommon is a provision requiring repayment of a percentage of profits in addition to the fixed minimum instalment. This contingent requirement is common where the credit analysis suggests the likelihood of very large but fluctuating profits. From the lender's viewpoint, it provides an opportunity for getting paid "while the getting's good" without embarrassing the borrower if profits prove only moderate.

Since profit forecasts are at best estimates, "tailoring repayment to cash throwoff" remains an art rather than a science. The repayment schedule frequently is a major bargaining issue during the term loan negotiation, the borrower seeking the most lenient terms the lender is willing to supply.

Typically, provision for prepayment at the option of the borrower is also made in the term loan agreement. Commonly, prepayments are applied to reduce the principal in inverse order—that is, applied against the most distant instalment rather than the one next due, so that they are not a substitute for regular repayments. Usually, lenders insist on provisions calling for prepayment fees, but this is often a matter for bargaining.[5]

---

[4] One eminent banker explained his approach to scheduling term loan repayment in the following terms: "My own homely method, over a number of years of term lending, has been to arrive at the term of the loan backwards, which is, perhaps, the way I do a lot of things. Having been satisfied with the desirability of the amount of the loan requested, and then having satisfied myself from a cash flow sheet or forecast as to the actual annual cash throw-off or debt paying ability and having reduced that figure, perhaps arbitrarily, to provide some elbow room for the borrower in the event of unforeseen conditions, I then divide the amount of the loan by the figure thus obtained and the resultant figure is the number of years that the loan should run." Hugh H. McGee, "Term Lending by Commercial Banks," *15th New England Bank Management Conference* (Boston: New England Council, 1945), October 11, 1945.

[5] In actual practice, many commercial banks waive the penalty payments on early repayments by customers with large deposit balances. Insurance companies have become

Curbing Risk through Restrictive Covenants

It has long been the practice of firms borrowing through the sale of bonds to make their securities more attractive to prospective buyers by including certain guaranties or "protective provisions" in the basic contract between the issuer and the bondholders. For example, it is common for the corporation to give assurance that additional long-term debt will be issued only under certain specified circumstances—or, in some cases, not at all. Typically, a corporate trustee is appointed who is charged with the responsibility of seeing to it that the issuing firm carries out the obligations spelled out in the bond contract.

In the case of bond issues sold to investment bankers for resale to the public, the investment bankers, in a sense, represent the prospective buying public in bargaining with the company to get provisions that make the terms of the bond contract attractive from the viewpoint of the potential bond investors. Once the bonds are issued, it becomes difficult and cumbersome, as a practical matter, to modify the bond indenture covenants. So there is a strong tendency for bond issuers to seek the flexibility afforded by the minimum of restrictive covenants that the investment banker believes investors will accept.

The direct relationship between borrower and lender implicit in the term loan affords greater opportunities for the lender to restrict the risks he sees in the commitment by means of restrictive agreements specifically drawn to suit the needs of the two parties. Furthermore, most term loans are made in the expectation that should events make particular provisions unduly burdensome, the lender, as a continuing lender anxious for more business, will agree to reasonable modifications. Where only two, or a few, parties to the term loan must be satisfied, the mechanics of change of the loan provisions are much more easily accomplished than in the case of bond issues, where several hundred or thousand holders must be persuaded to acquiesce to changes desired by the issuing firm.

Most term lenders have become skilled and resourceful in working out provisions that are acceptable to the borrower yet provide important protection against risk of serious deterioration of the credit. Since lender and borrower are free "to agree to anything they can agree to," much variety is found in the restrictive provisions from

---

increasingly insistent on significant prepayment premiums and on flat prohibitions of refunding of the loan to take advantage of lower interest rates.

one term loan to another. However, the provisions used with particular frequency fall into the following categories:

1. Restrictions on major changes in the borrower's business.
2. Restrictions on additional borrowing.
3. Provisions relating to maintenance of working capital.
4. Restrictions on diversion of assets.
5. Provisions relating to security.
6. Other provisions.

A first set of provisions represents assurance against certain types of changes that could alter substantially the nature of the borrower's business and hence of the term loan. These include prohibitions during the life of the loan of the following:

1. Sale of the assets of the company other than in the normal course of business—for example, sale of an obsolete machine would be permitted; sale of a plant would not. Sale and lease-back deals often are prohibited.
2. Merger of the company with other companies.
3. Major changes in the management of the company.

The prohibition of such actions is intended to make them subject to the consent of the lender. For example, if the borrower were able to present a strong case for selling a major plant, the lender might well waive his rights under the provision, perhaps insisting that a portion of the proceeds be applied toward prepayment of the term loan. In effect, if the other terms of the credit are to continue, the lender has a veto power over such actions, but one that a reasonable lender anxious for more lending business in the future presumably would use with discretion.

What happens if the borrower breaks the agreement without permission of the lender? The basic and typical penalty for uncorrected breach of any major provision of the term loan contract is the automatic acceleration of the maturity of the loan—that is, the lender may insist upon payment of the full amount outstanding and take legal action to assert his rights. If the borrower cannot find the funds to repay, the lender is in the "driver's seat" legally and may well demand drastic action by the borrower even if he does not choose to precipitate bankruptcy proceedings. So the provisions can have real force.

Provisions restricting or prohibiting additional borrowing are very common and may take one or more of several forms. If security is not taken, a *negative pledge clause* frequently is used—that is, no assets may be pledged as security to other lenders. Presumably, the borrower would be able to get large additional loans on an unsecured basis only if the firm was in a strong financial condition. In any case the negative pledge agreement protects against the possibility that another lender could get a prior claim to assets otherwise behind the term loan and other unsecured credits.

In addition, other long-term debt may be prohibited entirely or alternatively, permitted only if the company's statements meet certain ratio requirements such that the financial position of the company is so strong that the additional risk of the further debt clearly is tolerable.

Many companies seeking term loans borrow also from banks or other short-term lenders for seasonal or other temporary working capital needs, and the continuation of such borrowing may be entirely sound from the viewpoint of both the borrower and the term lender. Hence, provisions regarding short-term borrowing frequently seek only to prevent excessive short-term borrowing—by fixing a maximum limit on such borrowing—and to bar long-term borrowing in the guise of short-term notes continuously renewed—by a requirement that the company be out of debt to the banks (for other than the term loan) for a significant period each year.

Another group of provisions seeks to guard against continuing deterioration of the current position of the borrower. The long-term profits looked to for loan repayment may be jeopardized if the borrowing firm does not maintain sufficient working capital and current credit standing to permit normal conduct of its business. Furthermore, in the event serious trouble should develop and the lender is forced to look for repayment from liquidation of the borrower's assets, the lender would like to have the prospect of substantial pay-out from current assets—typically, the most liquid and often the highest yielding assets in bankruptcy—and heavy current borrowing would dilute the term lender's prospects of repayment from liquidation of current assets.

One of the most important of the requirements aimed at preservation of a strong working capital position is a limitation on acquisition of fixed assets. Undue diversion of cash into plant, equipment, or long-term investments may hamper normal operations and jeopardize repayment of the loan. Consequently, term lenders frequently demand restriction of fixed asset acquisition to an amount no greater than the funds supplied from depreciation charges or to a fixed dollar maximum. Such limitations are often the subject of vigorous bargaining and, over the full life of the term loan, are among the provisions most frequently modified by mutual agreement.

Many lenders rely on a requirement that the current ratio of the borrower be maintained above a minimum figure, such as 2 to 1, counting on this requirement for protection against excessive current borrowing or undue diversion of liquid resources into fixed assets. A minimum "net quick" ratio requirement is also included frequently.

Another provision used in lieu of—or, more commonly, in combination with—the minimum current ratio or net quick ratio requirement insists on maintenance of net working capital above a stated minimum dollar amount or above a minimum figure which is a multiple of the amount of term loan outstanding.

The student may well ask if such requirements, assuming the ratio or minimum amounts required are reasonable, are not redundant, inasmuch as the borrower will want to maintain a healthy current position as a matter of prudent financial management anyhow. Thus, are they not like admonition to a swimmer that he must not drown— a bit unnecessary? In many instances, it is true that the borrower will not let his current position deteriorate deliberately; yet, such deterioration may occur as a result of losses or other factors that he has been unable to control. In such cases, this family of ratios has particular value to the lender in that by accelerating the maturity of the loan, it puts the lender in a position to insist on measures he thinks will help the situation *before the financial position of the company has become desperate.* In effect, violation of these provisions, deliberate or involuntary, signals the need for concern with the situation and, at the same time, puts the lender in a position to insist on remedial action while there may still be finances and time sufficient for the working-out of solutions to the problems that created the tight current position.

A fourth family of restrictive covenants is drawn upon to guard against undesirable diversion of assets to owners or managers. One of the most common and direct of these is explicit limitation of the salaries or other benefits paid top management. Such a limitation is particularly common in the case of small, closely held companies where major stockholders are also employees and could, in the absence of restrictions, "milk the company" through excessively large salary withdrawals.

More important in the case of larger companies is the frequent inclusion of restrictions on dividend payments, particularly to common stockholders. The restriction on dividends takes various forms and degrees of severity, depending largely on the strength and bargaining power of the borrower. For even stronger borrowers, lenders frequently insist that future dividends be paid only out of future earnings so that the surplus "cushion" at the time the loan is granted is not reduced. In other instances, dividends may be prohibited entirely until repayment has been completed or, alternatively, has reached a certain level. The dividend restriction provision is often a matter of extended bargaining.

Other provisions relate to security. As we have indicated, lenders that do not insist on taking particular assets as security for a term loan frequently insist on a negative pledge clause. Some lenders regard the no-pledge clause as effectively providing many of the benefits of a secured position over a period of years. Other lenders, perhaps more realistically, put much more emphasis on security as a protection against risk and, as a matter of policy, take a mortgage on fixed assets whenever the borrower will agree to it.

Certain other common requirements can be grouped in a catchall classification, "other provisions." These include periodic certification by a senior officer of the borrowing firm that the borrower has complied with all of the provisions of the loan agreement, as well as assurance that the borrower will provide audited financial statements annually, along with unaudited statements on a monthly or quarterly basis and such other information as the lender reasonably may request from time to time.

While most term loans provide for a fixed interest rate, provision for a flexible interest rate has been made in many cases. In such cases, the rate is usually tied to the prime bank rate for short-term loans or the rediscount rate of a Federal Reserve bank with provision for a constant differential between the base rate and the term loan interest rate. Such a flexible rate provision affords the lender some protection against loss of income during a subsequent major rise in interest rates but, of course, conversely protects the borrower against declining rates.

In recent years, most banks have insisted on formal provision for compensating balances in their term loan agreements. Commonly, the deposit balance requirement is fixed as a percentage of the loan, with 20 per cent a frequent figure. To the extent that the required balance exceeds the deposit balance the borrower would carry anyhow, the requirement increases the effective interest on the funds the borrower can use in his business.

Incentive Financing

In recent years a number of companies have been able to negotiate term loans from insurance companies that otherwise might well not have been available to them by agreeing to provide "financial incentives" to the lenders. The term *incentive financing* is used to refer to directly negotiated intermediate or long-term loans to business firms by institutional investors, which provide for actual or contingent compensation (usually of an equity nature) in addition to fixed interest payments. Mirroring the flexibility made possible by direct negotiation, as well as the ingenuity of the parties involved, the devices used to allow the lender to share to some extent in the future success of the borrower have taken varied forms, ranging from an outright grant of common stock to a stipulated participation in net profits. Particularly popular is the granting of an option to purchase a specified number of common shares, the option being in the form of detachable warrants permitting the purchase of the shares at stated prices over a designated period.

While the use of incentives in term lending is not new, it first appeared in significant volume in 1956, and its subsequent growth has been closely correlated with the intensity of business demand for long-term funds. While incentive financing may not necessarily be the creature of tight money, tight-money conditions certainly stimulated the use of incentives. An additional stimulant of importance was the buoyant or "bull" market for equities existing concurrently with tight money. The bull market is a factor which naturally tends to increase the attractiveness of either actual or potential equity participations.

The volume of incentive financing has been moderate but significant, and the interest of many insurance companies in incentive lending has introduced a real element of flexibility into insurance company term lending. The use of incentives has been most common in companies that fall into the following categories:

1. New companies without established earnings records but with good prospects.
2. Companies in high-risk industries.
3. Companies in new industries.
4. Small companies with inherent risk qualities stemming from such factors as lack of diversification.

5. Sound companies requesting full loans, viz., loans in amounts larger than those suggested by an application of the traditional credit standards, such as debt/equity ratios.[6]

Term Loans from the Borrower's Viewpoint

Inherent Disadvantages or Problems. The big advantage of term loan credit to most borrowers is the contractual assurance of credit for a set period of years. Armed with a credit made available under terms explicitly set forth in writing, the borrower can enter into plans and projects for the use of the funds consistent with the terms of the credit. Usually, these involve long-term investment of the borrowed funds in equipment, plant, or other assets that will "pay out" only over a period of years. Yet, it follows clearly from the foregoing discussion of restrictive covenants typical of term loans that the assurance of credit is a *conditional* one, dependent upon the borrower's meeting fully the terms of the loan agreement throughout the life of the credit. The "accelerated maturity" feature of the loan agreement can be a severe penalty for acts of default by the borrower. Even if the lender does not avail himself of his rights to insist upon accelerated payment of the loan, the lender may well be able to insist upon new terms and restrictions that are very onerous from the borrower's point of view.[7] In effect, the defaulting borrower must "bargain while flat on his back"—an unenviable position, to put it mildly.

Consequently, the astute term borrower must appraise the proposed terms with care and foresight. If he plans carefully and bargains skillfully, the restrictions arrived at may be entirely reasonable and represent a quite tolerable risk to assume. But even though they are judged acceptable, it must be recognized that the restrictions inherently do reduce the flexibility of management, at least to some degree.

Essentially, the major disadvantages of term borrowing, however, are those of any borrowing. Lenders expect debts to be repaid; the

---

[6] For a more detailed discussion of incentive financing, see Charles M. Williams, and Howard A. Williams, "Incentive Financing—A New Opportunity," *Harvard Business Review*, March–April, 1960.

[7] Some astute bankers who have read this chapter disagree with this emphasis. They argue that as a practical matter the strong legal position of the bank in the event of default is misleading and that in most cases, exercise of their legal rights is less feasible than efforts to work out the difficulties over a long period. In such efforts, they insist, the co-operation of the borrower's management is almost essential. While recognizing the merits of the point, it seems to the authors only to temper somewhat the points in the text and not to invalidate them.

penalty for nonrepayment can be severe. Further, loan funds are not like water from an ever-flowing spring—the more a borrower draws on his ability to borrow, the lower is the level of additional borrowing power for future expected or unexpected needs. Debt money is "unfriendly money"; it repels other money, unless it is used so profitably as to attract additional equity investment.

The typical term loan involves only one or a few lenders. The term loan borrower is dealing with an informed, sophisticated lender, who can be expected to be vigorous in protecting his sizable investment. Compared with the creditors in the form of small investors who buy a widely distributed issue of bonds, the term lender is a fast-moving, informed creditor who has such a big stake in the credit that he can be expected to follow it carefully and to defend his rights effectively.

While the term lender can usually be presumed to be an intelligent and reasonable creditor who will react sensibly to requests for modification of the loan agreement, it is important that the borrower recognize an inherent or potential conflict of interest between himself and the lender. Many possible modifications that seem clearly desirable from the borrower's point of view will not be attractive to the lender. Consider, for example, the situation of a borrower who sees opportunities for expansion into a new field that promises big profits but contains substantial risks. The borrower might well, in view of the profit outlook, be willing to assume the risks to him of more debt and hence want the term lender to waive restrictions on further debt. But the term lender, who gains little from extra profits from expansion, may well, intelligently and reasonably, refuse to increase his risks by permitting the expansion of debt.

Other disadvantages of term borrowing are less basic but in some cases may be of significance. Except in rare instances, the interest rates required by term lenders are higher than on short-term loans, although for all but the weakest borrowers the cost differential is usually less than 1 per cent—and it may be as little as one fourth of 1 per cent. More significant to those would-be borrowers to whom a public issue of debt securities is an available alternative method of borrowing is the fact that direct lenders normally will insist on an interest rate somewhat higher—one half of 1 per cent or so —than the rate at which the borrower could sell bonds publicly. Further, insurance companies have been vigorous in their insistence on protection against early refunding of direct loans, and their requirements on these and other protective terms usually are somewhat more stringent than those necessary in order to sell a debt issue publicly. Too, in the case of term loans from banks, and to a much lesser extent from insurance companies, even the least stringent repayment schedules the borrower can negotiate from these sources may well call for faster repayment than would be necessary if bonds were sold publicly.

Concerns that have never come under the "full disclosure" requirements of the Securities and Exchange Commission and that have borrowed before only on a short-term basis may find irksome the relatively full investigation of a term lender. Certainly, the borrower should expect to have few secrets and should anticipate having any "skeletons in the corporate closet" exposed to the view of the lender. However, term lenders are accustomed to respecting the confidences of borrowers and can usually be counted upon to treat confidential data in proper fashion. And surely, the disclosure of facts to a single lending institution is much less distasteful to a reticent firm than would be the public disclosures involved in public offerings of bonds or other securities subject to the informational requirements of the SEC.

Advantages of Term Credit. The major attraction of term credit to many business concerns has already been stated implicitly or directly several times, and needs only brief restatement and emphasis here. It is simply that the intermediate maturities of term loan credit fit the need for funds of many would-be borrowers. Granting that the credit is available for the full term only if the provisions of the loan are met, at least the repayment and other requirements of the lender are definite and known, and are fixed so long as the borrower can keep his obligations under the agreement. Being definitive, they can be planned for.

Some borrowers who have been successful in financing medium-term needs with renewed, short-term borrowings are apt to over-emphasize the restrictions of the term loan and to overlook the fact that the lender, as he considers each renewal of the short-term notes, has certain minimum standards for continued credit very much in mind, even though they may not be discussed as such with the borrower and renewal seems routine. In other words, the requirements spelled out in the term loan are *not necessarily* more stringent than those the lender in fact requires upon renewal of a short-term credit. And lender attitudes are not always constant or, indeed, fully rational; at least, in the term loans the lender is committed to a definite, constant set of standards and requirements.

The direct negotiation implicit in the term loan has a number of advantages to the borrower. Term loans typically can be negotiated faster and at less expense than public issues of debt securities. The major inescapable "issue costs" of term loans are those of legal counsel. In the case of term loans placed with insurance companies, borrowers frequently employ the services of an investment banking firm as an adviser in planning the financing and as an agent in searching for the most suitable lender and in negotiating terms. The usual charge for such services— 1 to 1½ per cent of the principal amount—while significant, is less than the charge the investment bankers typically make as underwriters of public issues of debt securities. In term borrowing, disclosure of information is only to the lender(s), not to the general public; and the time and trouble of preparing the registration statement and prospectus necessary in larger public offerings also are avoided. Altogether, the mechanics involved in arranging a term loan are less than those of a typical public issue.

Many borrowers want to make firm arrangements for funds that they will not need in hand for some months or even years. For example, a company planning a new plant may well want to complete the borrowing necessary to finance the expansion before firm contracts are let, even though actual payments to the contractor will be necessary only as work on the plant progresses. Under such circumstances, funds raised from a public issue of securities before construction contracts are signed are likely to remain relatively unproductive for an extended period. Term lenders, however, will commonly permit the borrower to *take down* or draw against the loan in increments corresponding with his planned needs. This added flexibility can mean significant interest savings for the borrower.

To many firms who could qualify for term loans the alternative of a public issue of debt securities is not available. The cost of term credit to these firms is likely to be much lower than the cost of funds raised through sale of common or preferred stock. Many owners of smaller companies are extremely reluctant to concede the degree of control over the corporation that may well be involved in a major issue of common stock. The interference by the term lender with the control exercised by the borrower's management is restricted to that explicit in the loan agreement provisions so long as these are met. While it is not prudent, of course, for the borrower to count on the willingness of the lender to agree to any modification of the term loan the borrower might like, the fact that reasonable and appropriate changes can probably be made is a major advantage of the term loan.

One further advantage of term borrowing from banks or insurance companies has been particularly apparent during recent periods of tight money. That is the fact that most term lenders look upon their borrowers—or at least the ones with whom their experience is favorable—as valued clients whose reasonable needs for money deserve precedence over those of new customers. Consequently, the borrower who has repaid on schedule has available what amounts to an "inside track" to funds needed in the future. One large insurance company, for example, has reported that 60.7 per cent of the dollar volume of its direct placement loans to business in a recent year was to old customers.

NEGOTIATING EFFECTIVE TERM LOAN ARRANGEMENTS

For most term borrowers, it is highly important that the term loan arrangements be negotiated effectively. What aids to successful term borrowing can be suggested? Our more important suggestions can be grouped under the following headings:

1. Top management's role in negotiating term credit.
2. The need for understanding term loan theory and practice.
3. The search for a suitable lender.
4. Appraisal of provisions and selective bargaining.
5. Maintaining the term loan relationship.

Top Management's Role in Negotiating Term Credit

While many financial matters are appropriately delegated to financial specialists, especially in larger firms, term borrowing is not one of them. The working-out of a credit arrangement that can stand up over a period of years calls for careful planning of a variety of aspects of the firm's operations. The more clearly the future needs of the business for facilities, for working capital, for dividends, etc., can be formulated, the more effectively can the plans for financing through term credit be brought into harmony with the over-all plans and objectives of the firm.

Top management's responsibilities toward term lending are not limited, however, to formulation of the plans which are to serve as the basis for term borrowing that will fit in with those plans. For the desires of the would-be borrower must be reconciled with the needs and demands of the lender. Almost inevitably, the give-and-take of bargaining over specific provisions raises questions that can only be resolved by top management. For example, only top management and the board of directors should assume final responsibility for the reconciliation of dividend objectives with lender proposals for restricting dividend pay-out.

In brief, term borrowing is intertwined with many matters of significance to top management. Top management understanding and participation in the planning and decision making that is a part of effective term loan negotiation are essential to term borrowing that serves, rather than stifles, management's objectives.

The Need for Understanding Term Loan Theory and Practice

Most business leaders are involved in the planning and negotiation of term loans only infrequently, or the process is entirely new to them. Important term lenders are at it continuously. As outlined earlier in this chapter, an important body of theory and practice has developed in term lending. Clearly, a basic understanding of *term loan theory and practice* by would-be borrowers is a prerequisite if they are to be fully effective in tapping term loan credit. Much of this chapter has been devoted to providing such basic background; other more detailed sources of information are also available.[8] The borrower, from study of such material and of his own situation, can help to establish the limits of bargaining within which he must operate and to see ways he can meet the needs of the lender at minimum sacrifice of his own key interests.

As we have noted, many firms who seek to tap insurance company term loan credit—and to a much smaller extent, bank term loan credit—enlist the advice and counsel of investment bankers in approaching lenders and in working out suitable terms. Legal counsel who are experienced in this area may also be of great assistance. But such advice should supplement rather than substitute for top management understanding of term lending.

The Search for a Suitable Lender

The search for the most suitable lender should begin long before the actual approach for funds is made, since the lead time necessary for "feeling out the market" and for properly building the

---

[8] For example, see H. V. Prochnow, *Term Loans and Theories of Bank Liquidity* (New York: Prentice-Hall, Inc., 1949); and Jacoby and Saulnier, *op. cit.*

groundwork for a request for term credit is long. If the advisory services of an investment banking firm are to be used, it should be brought into the picture while the financing is still in the early planning stage. If investment bankers are employed, they are prepared to "carry the ball" in the search for the most suitable lender. The following comments on this subject are more pertinent to those cases where investment bankers are not used.

Other things being equal, for all but firms known nationally, the canvass of possible lenders should begin close to home—since local sources are more likely to have built up a knowledge of and confidence in the firm. The size of local lenders is not necessarily a barrier to their use. If the local banks or insurance companies are not large enough to meet the full need alone, the possibility exists of their enlisting the participation of other lenders in meeting the needs of the borrower.

Yet, seldom are "other things equal." Most lenders have developed somewhat distinctive attitudes and policies toward term lending and have decided preferences for particular kinds of loans and loan terms. It is seldom really difficult for a discerning borrower to ascertain the reputation of particular term lenders. One of the best sources of such information is other term borrowers, who can report on their experience with particular lenders. To paraphrase an advertising slogan, to find out about term lenders, "Ask the Man Who Owes One."

Careful advance investigation and preselection of the best lender to approach are particularly important because of a strong prejudice among lenders against "shopping around" for a borrowing proposal. Many lenders flatly refuse to consider a loan application—and to undergo considerable trouble and expense in the process—if the borrower is engaged in serious discussion of the loan with even one other lender. In other words, custom dictates that the borrower select the lender with whom he wants to do business in advance of serious discussion and exhaust the possibilities of a satisfactory agreement with that firm before turning to other lenders.

As indicated earlier, in periods of tight money, lenders are more likely to accommodate old customers than new applicants to whom they owe no loyalty and with whom they have had no experience. The nature of the credit analysis described earlier further suggests the wisdom of building a good relation with the most likely term lender well in advance of "putting on the touch." And finally, since the association of term borrower and lender may well become an intimate and extended one, it is well that compatibility be pretested as far as is feasible.

Appraisal of Provisions and Selective Bargaining

The shrewd borrower enters the bargaining conference in which the amount of the loan, the repayment terms, and the various restrictive covenants are to be worked out only after he has considered carefully the provisions the lender may propose and their probable impact on his company and its future operations. Once he has forearmed himself with knowledge of term lending practice, the major limiting factor on the borrowing management's skill in appraising the terms is the extent and degree of accuracy of the future planning of the company. If plans for the future are vague and uncertain, skillful bargaining is difficult, if not impossible.

Particularly important to the borrower are the terms of repayment. Some firms are content with the haphazard approach of seeking credit as large and a repayment schedule as lenient as the lender's indulgence will grant. Yet, the borrower has as much or more to lose from too much borrowing as the lender; and usually, he is in a better position keenly to appraise his own repayment capacity. Speaking generally, the borrower should estimate as carefully as he can, through cash flow forecasting, his future "cash throwoff" from operations and borrow no more than can be repaid easily—allowing a comfortable margin between his forecasted means of repayment and the contractual repayments. The more uncertain or unreliable the forecast, the greater should be the planned margin of safety. If reasonable margins between the repayment demanded by the lender and the capacity to repay cannot be projected, serious doubt is thrown on the wisdom of borrowing, and curtailment or abandonment of the borrowing plans is suggested.

An important issue in assaying ability to repay is the extent to which cash from depreciation should be relied upon for loan repayment. To the extent that the borrower can be sure of having no need for the funds so generated to acquire new assets or for other purposes, it is reasonable to regard these funds as available for loan repayment. Most concerns, however, have continuing needs for equipment replacement or for additional facilities; and in these circumstances, it is prudent to regard the funds generated from depreciation as available only in emergencies. And of course, the funds from depreciation are not automatically available when needed—the urgent need for funds must be foreseen and normal equipment purchases halted well in advance of the repayment date if important amounts of depreciation funds are to be accumulated and free for application against the debt.

A related issue concerns the wisdom of counting on, even as an emergency source, the funds that might be expected to accumulate as a result of a decline in sales leading to a reduction of receivables and inventory. There are "catches" here: The reduction-of-inventory assumption is valid only if production is cut back to more than match the decline in sales and if the inventory on hand proves salable. Further, if the funds from current asset pulldown are used for loan repayment, additional funds will be needed to support a recovery in sales, if and when it occurs. Finally, a severe drop in sales may well be accompanied, if fixed costs are high, by heavy losses which eat into the funds created by working capital liquidation. So, current asset liquidation, though possibly a major source of cash, should be regarded at best as a qualified, or "iffy," source of funds for loan repayment.

Turning now to the appraisal of the restrictive covenants and the need for selective bargaining, the key problem here is to separate those restrictions that may well prove burdensome from those with which compliance is painless—which require policies that the borrower would in ordinary business prudence follow anyway. Separating the onerous from the innocuous again requires forecasts over the life of the loan. A requirement that no dividends be paid during the life of the loan might not appear very objectionable if the company were owned by a few stockholders who had little need or desire for dividends. But should the company want to sell common stock to the public, dividend payments may be essential to the sale of the stock at a good price, and the provision barring dividends would become highly restrictive.

Of course, few borrowers can expect to have the bargaining go all their way. The secret of successful bargaining is to discover and concede those points which are important to the other party but represent relatively minor concessions to you, and vice versa.

The interest rate is a good illustration of a feature which is very important to the lender, yet of lesser significance to many borrowers. The range for bargaining on the interest rate proposed by the lender is usually small—one half of 1 per cent or less. Since the lending institution lives largely on its interest income, the fraction of 1 per cent is important to it. Yet, the cost to the borrower is reduced by the inclusion of interest as a business expense before calculation of income tax—hence the *net cost* is more than halved for most companies. More importantly, the borrower typically expects to make 10 per cent or more on the borrowed funds, so that availability of the credit and freedom from onerous restrictions commonly are much more vital than the difference in cost that would result from concentrating his bargaining power on the interest rate.

Maintaining the Term Loan Relationship

Even with the best possible advance planning at the time the term loan is negotiated, it may become highly desirable for the borrower to secure the lender's agreement to modification of the loan terms at some time during the life of the loan—or to further credit at some later date. In his own interest the borrower should act to keep the lender's good regard throughout the loan.

It is hard to overemphasize the importance of providing the lender with good and candid information about the company, not only at the outset of negotiations but throughout the loan as well. Since the lender has an important financial stake in the enterprise, his interest in timely notice of major developments affecting it—favorably and unfavorably—should be taken for granted and freely met.

In the case of term loans from banks, a strong relationship is promoted by efforts to keep substantial deposit balances with the lending banks. It is important also to a good relationship that the borrower fully understand the loan agreement and the logic back of the provisions so that he can conscientiously live up to the spirit as well as the legal letter of the loan agreement. Grudging or nominal compliance works against mutual good will.

If modifications of the agreement are needed, the borrower should give the lender as much notice as possible of the impending need for change and carefully work out appropriate modifications to propose. Similarly, as the borrower has unfavorable developments to report, he should have plans worked out to cope with these developments. While the lender wants to know of impending problems, he does not want them thrust in his lap for solution. Instead, he is entitled to evidence that the borrower is making constructive plans to overcome his own problems.

Yet, in the final analysis, there is no adequate substitute for effective performance—the meeting of commitments—as the foundation for a sound and viable borrower-lender relationship.

PART V

The Long-Term Capital Structure

Chapter 14

The Basic Security Types

EARLIER in this book, it was pointed out that corporate securities fall into two main classes: contracts of debt and participations in ownership. Three main types were named: *bonds* or *notes* in the first class, and *preferred stock* and *common stock* in the second. The reader may already be aware that there are in common use a great many different kinds of bonds as well as a variety of preferred and common stock forms. To the beginner in finance, it would be a very difficult assignment to get this confusing array of securities clearly fixed in mind.

Fortunately, this is not at all necessary or desirable, at least at this stage of our study. As will be brought out in this chapter, the first step is to gain a clear understanding of the fundamental characteristics of the three basic security forms—the bond, the preferred stock, and the common stock. It is these characteristics which are of primary importance in decisions relating to long-term finance. Later, when the basic analysis has been well established, we shall introduce the subject of the bargaining process between issuer and investor and the many special kinds of bonds and stocks which have been produced in an effort to meet special needs and circumstances.

The Bond: The Basic Promises

The responsibility of a company to those who have supplied funds through the purchase of its bonds is essentially the very simple obligation of anyone who has borrowed money, namely, to repay the sum at the promised time and to compensate the lender for the use of his money by the payment of an interest charge while the debt is outstanding. A formal statement of this obligation is found on the face of the *bond certificate* held by each individual or institution participating in the loan. The precise details of the legal contract between the issuing company and the bondholders is to be found in a document known as the *bond indenture*. A copy of this document is held and enforced by a *trustee under the indenture*, who represents the bondholders as a group.

The following is a condensed version of the wording of a typical bond certificate:

> The A.B.C. Corporation . . . for value received, hereby promises to pay to bearer on the first day of August, 1975, the principal sum of—ONE THOUSAND DOLLARS—and to pay interest on said principal sum at the rate of three and three-quarters per cent (3¾%) per annum semiannually on the first day of February and the first day of August in each year until payment of said principal sum. . . . This is one of a duly authorized issue of bonds of the Company . . . of the aggregate principal sum of $5,000,-000. . . .

To cite a recent bond issue, we may take the case of the Allied Chemical Corporation. In April of 1953, Allied Chemical raised the sum of $200 million through the sale of bonds. In exchange for the use of these funds for a period of twenty-five years, the company contracted to pay interest to the bondholders on April 1 and October 1 of each year to 1978 (3½ per cent annually) and to repay the principal amount on April 1, 1978. The semiannual amount of interest at the time of issue was, therefore, $3.5 million.

There are no qualifications to this time series of payments. The certificate does *not* say "if earned" or "if the financial condition of the company permits"—but simply, "hereby promises to pay." To fail to do so at any point constitutes a breach of a legal contract, which act (under almost all bond contracts) entitles the bondholders to declare the entire sum due and payable and to take court action to recover the loan. This process is known as *acceleration of maturity*.[1] We referred to it before in discussing term loans. It is clear that if the business is to continue without a financial crisis, there is no alternative to a literal adherence to its promises. Herein lies the hazard of debt financing to the issuer and the advantage of bond ownership to the investor. A bond will not be well regarded unless both sides see a considerable margin of safety to assure the performance of the promises in the bond contract even if events turn out badly.

To a company such as Allied Chemical, with sales of $545 million in the year in which the bonds were sold, the addition of $7 million to annual costs of operation may seem unimportant. It must be remembered, however, that this is a charge against the remaining

---

[1] Debtors are not permitted to default willfully in order to pay off burdensome debt.

income after making payment of the year's costs of operation. In the year 1953 the *net earnings* of Allied Chemical *before interest and federal corporate income taxes* were $89 million. This relationship between net income available for the payment of fixed charges ($89 million) and the fixed charges on the debt ($7 million) is a significant ratio in financial analysis. Analysts often refer to this ratio as *times interest earned*; in this case, 12.7 times.[2] Another way of expressing this relationship is to divide $7 million by $89 million, thus to measure the fraction of income needed to carry the interest. In this case, it is 7.9 per cent.

Sinking Funds

The reader is reminded that the debtor must meet each promise to pay at the time it becomes due. Therefore, in viewing this margin of net income over fixed charges on debt, it must be borne in mind that corporate gross revenues fluctuate from year to year and that net earnings fluctuate even more to the extent that the costs of operation are inflexible. Thus, it is possible that a margin of earnings such as that shown by Allied Chemical could shrink rapidly, although perhaps only temporarily. The range of possible fluctuation varies, of course, from one industry and one company to another.

In modern practice, corporate debt contracts usually provide for partial repayment of the debt at intervals, usually yearly. Such requirements are generally referred to as *sinking funds*. In the case of the Allied Chemical issue, the bond indenture required that in addition to interest payments the corporation must make the following sinking fund payments to the trustee, who will call bonds by lot, pay them, and thus cancel the corporate liability to that extent:

1959–63	$ 7 million annually
1964–68	9 million annually
1969–73	11 million annually
1974–77	13 million annually

Such payments do not always provide for complete retirement of the debt by maturity; and often, there is a substantial final payment on the maturity date, commonly known as a *balloon payment*. However, to the extent that is required by the sinking fund provision, a portion of the debt is repaid prior to the official maturity date, and these

---

[2] Note that we recommend that the earnings used in this ratio be taken before both interest and taxes. Where there is more than one bond issue, it is better practice to relate total charges to total income available for such charges, rather than taking each issue separately.

funds must be provided by the debtor out of earnings or other sources.[3]

It is to be noted that these repayments of the principal are just as mandatory as the payments of interest, and any failure to pay on the dates specified will accelerate the maturity of the whole issue. The following is a typical indenture provision on this point:

Default

SECTION 1.   The following events shall be events of default under this indenture and the term "event of default" or "events of default" shall mean, whenever the same is used herein, one or more of the following events, to wit:

. . . .

(*b*) Default shall be made in the due and punctual payment of any installment of interest on any of the bonds hereby secured when and as the same shall become due and payable . . . and such default shall continue for a period of thirty (30) days; or

(*c*) Default shall be made in any installment of any sinking fund provided for in any series of bonds hereby secured, and such default shall continue for a period of sixty (60) days; . . .

SECTION 2.   In case any one or more of the events of default shall happen, then . . . the Trustee may, and upon the request in writing of the holders of at least twenty-five per cent (25%) in principal amount of the bonds hereby secured at the time outstanding, shall, by notice in writing delivered to the Company, declare the principal of all bonds . . . together with all accrued and unpaid interest thereon, if not already due, to be due and payable immediately. . . .[4]

It is obvious that management must consider the sinking fund, as well as the annual interest payments, when deciding whether or not to issue bonds. Times interest earned is, therefore, often an unreliable measure. A more inclusive measure will be suggested below.

The Flow of Funds Related to the Bond

Stripped to its purely financing implications, a bond is an instrument which commits the corporation to certain outflows of funds at

---

[3] The bond indenture may provide, as an alternative to a cash payment, the equivalent in par value of bonds repurchased by the issuing company. If these are available on the market at less than par, the cash drain involved will be somewhat less than the indicated sinking fund obligation. In other cases the company must expend a set amount of money, leaving the number of bonds acquired to be determined by the market price.

In some issues a corporation has the option to use funds to retire some of the debt or to buy new assets of specified types. It is argued that the new investment serves to protect the debt by adding value and earning power.

[4] Kimberly-Clark Corporation indenture as cited in *Bond Indentures* (Michigan Business Cases, Financial Management Series, No. 20) (Ann Arbor: Bureau of Business Research, School of Business Administration, University of Michigan, 1935), p. 18.

specified times. The combined amounts of interest, sinking fund, and final maturity payments are referred to as the *burden, service,* or, less elegantly, *cash drain* of the bonded debt. In addition to the obligation to meet the burden annually, there is also the obligation to repay at maturity that portion of the original issue which has not been redeemed by the application of the sinking fund. This would not present a problem in the Allied Chemical case, since only 6.5 per cent of the original issue of $200 million would remain outstanding in the year of maturity. There are, however, many bond issues which either have no sinking fund provision or provide for only a partial retirement by this means. As a result, the sum outstanding and due for repayment at the maturity date is of an entirely different order of magnitude from that required for annual servicing of the debt. For example, United States Plywood Corporation $25 million issue of 5¼ per cent debentures, dated April 1, 1960, and due in 1985, carries a maximum semiannual sinking fund payment of $455,000. If no bonds were redeemed except as required by the sinking fund provision, $7 million would be due and payable on April 1, 1985. This is, clearly, a major fraction of the original borrowing.

The fulfillment of this obligation might well appear to present an impossible strain on the earnings and cash position of the company in the year 1985. It is obvious that since the maturity date is known at the time of issue, a management which intended to eliminate the debt would be guilty of negligence if it left plans for repayment of this sum until the final year. Actually, management may have no intention of terminating its borrowings at that point but rather may expect to find the solution in a new issue of bonds, the proceeds of which will be used to repay the holders of the old bonds. This process, known as *refunding,* will be discussed in more detail in Chapter 27. It can, however, be noted that one of the major immediate causes of business failures is the inability to pay maturing obligations. Usually, the basic causes of failure are different, but a large maturity is often the event that forces the failure.

The Tax Implications of Debt Service

In observing the role played by debt and other basic security types in the long-term financing of individual companies, it is necessary to develop one or more simple measures of significance so that objective comparisons can be made among companies and over time. Before we turn to a description of these measures, however, it will be helpful to identify one of the important elements of such comparisons, namely, the effect of associated payments on the company's corporate income tax position.

With regard to debt, it is particularly important to have a clear understanding of the differences between interest and sinking fund payments in this respect. The reader will be aware that in the United States, income taxes are levied on *net income*, that is, on the sum remaining from gross income after the deduction of all costs. Among the expenditures accepted as "costs" for tax purposes, and thus deductible in computing the income upon which the tax is based, is interest on debt.

In order to bring out the significance of this, we present a revised and simplified version of the Allied Chemical income statement for 1959, adjusted to a 52 per cent federal corporate income tax rate and assuming no prepayment of the debt (which, in fact, there was):

		(*In Thousands*)
Net sales.		$720,000
Cost of goods sold and operating expenses.	$499,000	
Depreciation and depletion.	55,000	
Selling, general, and administrative expenses.	69,000	623,000
Gross income from operations.		$ 97,000
Other income.		5,000
Earnings before interest and income tax.		$102,000
Bond interest.		7,000
		$ 95,000
Federal income tax (@ 52%).		49,400
Net Income after Taxes.		$ 45,600

Now, let us suppose that instead of financing by bonds, the company had raised the $200 million by the sale of stock. The relevant portion of the income statement would then have appeared as follows:

Earnings before interest and income tax.	$102,000
Federal income tax (@ 52%).	53,040
Net Income after Taxes.	$ 48,960

A comparison of these two sets of figures shows that the use of debt has reduced taxes by $3.64 million, or 52 per cent of $7 million. Thus, it can be said that the *after-tax cost* of the debt is $3.36 million, because this is the net increase in costs caused by the debt.

Since we are constantly relating interest and other payments associated with corporate securities to the company's taxable income, it is frequently desirable to identify the exact amount of the tax which would be payable on an equivalent amount of taxable corporate income. This we will call the *tax related*. In the example above, the tax related to the bond interest of $7 million is $3.64 million.

It must be emphasized that the privilege of deducting debt costs for purposes of income tax computation does not extend to sinking fund payments. Although such payments involve a cash drain similar to the payment of interest, the sinking fund payment is in fact a repayment of part of the liability, which is the principal of the bonds, and cannot be counted as a cost any more than the original proceeds of the loan received by the company would be counted as income. A *sinking fund* should therefore be regarded as a contractual commitment defining how earnings, or a part of earnings, shall be used. That is to say, they must be retained in the business to permit the payment of a portion of the debt. We referred to this as forced reinvestment when discussing term loans. Interest, on the other hand, is an expenditure necessary to have the use of the funds, just as wages are an expenditure necessary to obtain the services of employees.

It may be added that this line of reasoning does not apply to dividends on stock. In contrast to the treatment of bond interest as a cost, dividends are considered as a distribution of the net income of the business to the owners and, as such, are not deducted when computing the corporate income tax. This applies to dividends on preferred stock as well as to dividends on common stock.

The Burden of Debt: Measures of Significance

In the analysis of the capital structures of individual companies, there are two commonly used methods for measuring the importance of debt. One is the simple and obvious statement of total debt as a *percentage of total capitalization* (often referred to as the *debt ratio*). In the case of Allied Chemical the year-end balance sheet related to the income data of 1953, previously cited, shows capital stock and surplus of $344 million. Adding this to the long-term debt of $200 million gives total capitalization of $544 million. The debt is 36 per cent of this. The other method is that which was described on page 289, namely, *times interest earned*, which relates total bond interest to the earnings from which bond interest must be deducted in arriving at net profit for the period. Both of these measures have the advantage of simplicity and clarity, and both can be derived directly from conventional financial statements.

Throughout this book, however, we have emphasized that numerical values are of little use unless they are meaningfully related to the objectives of the analysis. In this respect the two measures cited above, although widely used by borrowers and lenders alike, have some serious limitations. These will be discussed more fully in Chapter 16. At this point, it is sufficient to state that our primary concern regarding the burden of debt is with the capacity of the borrower to make the cash payments required by the debt contract. It makes sense, therefore, to derive a measure of significance in terms of cash flows: *times burden covered*. The reader has already been told the elements of the cash flow which represent the *burden* of a debt. These are:

1. The interest.
2. The sinking fund.
3. The final payment at maturity.
4. The tax related to the above items.

As we have pointed out, the amount of burden cannot be judged to be large or small except as it is related to the cash inflows available to meet it. The elements on this side of the comparison may be approximated by taking the figure for *earnings before interest and taxes (E.B.I.T.)* from the annual income statement and adding back noncash charges, the principal item of which is depreciation.

A table for the analysis of the burden of debt may be prepared in the following form. We have filled in the initial information, except the tax related, from the Allied Chemical example, using boldface type. The data are for the year 1959, the first year in which the sinking fund requirement applied. The reader should note carefully that some figures appear in the Amount before Tax column, and some in the Amount after Tax column. Great care must be taken to assign the initial information to its proper class, for any combination of before-tax with after-tax figures is as meaningless as the traditional example of adding horses and apples. The next step is to complete the table. The formula for converting from before-tax to after-tax amounts, or vice versa, is $\text{Before} = \dfrac{\text{After}}{(1-r)}$ where r is the applicable tax rate.

After completing the table, the reader should observe the meaning of the figures in each line. Starting with the before-tax amount of interest, as explained above, the tax related represents the tax shield provided by the use of debt, and the after-tax amount is the net payment. In the case of the sinking fund, the before-tax amount is what the company has to earn in order to have the required sinking fund after taxes, and the tax related is what the name implies. In the case

	Amount before Tax (in Thousands)	Amount of Tax Related (52%) (in Thousands)	Amount after Tax (in Thousands)
(A) Interest...................	$ 7,000	$ 3,640	$ 3,360
Sinking fund................	14,580	7,580	7,000
(B) Total cash burden...........	$ 21,580	$ 11,220	$ 10,360
(C) Income, 1959, before interest and taxes..*E.B.I.T*..	$102,000	$ 53,040	$ 48,960
Depreciation charged, 1959....	114,580	59,580	55,000
(D) Approximate Net Cash Inflow from Operations......	$216,580	$112,620	$103,960

of the income, the before-tax figure is the E.B.I.T. The tax related is
computed from it, and the after-tax figure shows what the net income
would have been if there had been no tax shield from the use of debt.
We have already entered this tax shield in the line for interest; to use
it again would be double-counting. The line for depreciation shows in
the before-tax column the amount that the company would have had to
earn if depreciation were not tax-deductible. The tax related is the
figure that reduces this amount to the actual charge.

We now have two sets of figures that are consistently measured,
both before and after tax, and we can use either column to calculate
the following ratios, which are frequently encountered in financial
analysis.

Group 1: Times Interest Earned $= \dfrac{C}{A} = \dfrac{102,000}{7,000}$ or $\dfrac{48,960}{3,360} = 14.6$

% Income Required for Interest $= \dfrac{A}{C}$ $= 6.9\%$

Group 2: Times Burden Covered by Funds Inflows $= \dfrac{D}{B}$ $= 10.0$

% Funds Flows Required to Carry Debt $= \dfrac{B}{D}$ $= 10.0\%$

In the tabulation above, Group 1 represents the income point
of view. The ratio of times interest earned is the one that has
been most frequently used by analysts in the measurement of the
safety of bond issues. It is presented by every standard financial
manual; and it is embedded in the laws of those states which regulate the investment practices of certain types of investors, such as
trustees, insurance companies, and savings banks. Despite this use, it
is now becoming clear that the more important point of view is that of

funds flows, where the appropriate ratios are those of Group 2. In these ratios, we confront all the burden of a debt in a year with all the funds available to meet it.[5]

We shall have more to say later on about these ratios and the others we shall encounter in this chapter. The reader should be sure that he understands what they are, how they are computed, and what lies behind them. May we emphasize that no method which gives unequal ratios from before-tax and after-tax figures is properly designed. It is also to be remembered that before-tax and after-tax figures cannot be combined. A very common error, for example, is to add interest and sinking fund without taking account of the tax-related items. Thus, it would be meaningless to speak of the burden of the Allied Chemical debt as being the sum of the interest charges of $7 million and sinking fund payments of $7 million, since one is in before-tax dollars and the other is in after-tax dollars.

There are reasons which lead us to recommend that the reader make it a practice, where possible, to use the before-tax basis: (1) In comparisons of different companies, there can be significant differences in the tax levy which are not apparent in the information available. (2) For the same company over a period of time, there will surely have been significant changes in the basis and rate of tax from one year to another, which will affect the results and again may not be apparent in the data used. (3) Finally, if the company should sustain a loss in any year, the full interest payment must still be met. (Of course, to the extent that the bond interest increases the deficit for the year, a tax credit may be taken later against earnings of other years.) For these reasons, our comparisons will be made primarily in terms of burden before taxes, earnings before interest and taxes (which we abbreviate to E.B.I.T.), and depreciation charged.

Summary: The Bond

Let us now summarize briefly what has been said about a bond. The typical bond contract requires the repayment of the principal amount on a specified maturity date and regular interest payments

---

[5] In our first edition, we proposed that analysts having the funds point of view should use: Times Burden Earned $= \dfrac{C}{B}$. Many analysts do so, arguing, as we did, that depreciation should not be considered as an item available for debt coverage. It is true, of course, that burden is only one of several types of commitment of funds, capital expenditures and dividends being among other important ones. But since depreciation bears no necessary relationship to capital expenditures, we now prefer the direct comparison of funds flowing in with funds flowing out in the form of debt service.

while the bond is outstanding. The consequences of default at any time are that the debt matures at once. The bond contract may also require payments into a sinking fund in partial or total anticipation of the repayment of the principal amount. The total annual payments required by the bond contract are referred to as the burden, service, or cash drain of the debt and may be measured in terms of their effect on corporate income only after allowance for the corporate income tax. Times interest earned is a frequently used test of the safety of a debt, but it pictures only one element of the burden. Times burden covered is a more inclusive test.

The Common Stock

In contrast to the bondholders, the common shareholder has no promise from the company to which he may turn for an assurance of income or the return of his investment. The absence of any specific financial commitment on the part of the corporation to the shareholder is reflected in the wording of the stock certificate, an example of which appears below:

This is to certify that _____ is the owner of _____ fully paid and nonassessable shares of the par value of $20 each of the common stock of the A.B.C. Company, Inc. . . . A statement of the designations, preferences, privileges and voting powers, and the restrictions and qualifications thereof, of the Preferred Stock . . . and of the Common Stock . . . is printed on the reverse side hereof, and this certificate . . . shall be subject to all the provisions of the Certificate of Incorporation . . . to all of which the holder by acceptance hereof assents.

Dated _____ Signed _____

The basic purpose of the certificate is simply to indicate that the person named is a shareholder of the company and to indicate the extent of his participation as measured by the number of shares owned. No payment in the form of dividends is promised or implied. No repayment of the original principal is anticipated, since the money supplied by the common shareholder is considered to be an investment for the life of the business. The principal assurance given the holders of the common stock is the basic right of ownership—the right to decide matters of corporate policy either directly, by vote at regular or special meetings of the shareholders, or by delegating their powers of control to a board of directors of their own choosing.[6]

Thus, the corporation has no specific financial commitments to its

---

[6] It should be noted that stock records show the name and address of the "holder of record," while most bonds are payable to the bearer. A company may not be able to communicate directly with its bondholders!

shareholders of a nature that would make the expenditure of cash at any point of time mandatory. Of course, profits which are not paid out in cash dividends remain in the business; and if wisely used, they will add to the value of the common shareholders' residual claim on the assets and earning power of the business. The realizable value to the shareholder of reinvested earnings depends on the extent to which they are reflected in a higher market price for the stock.

It is this absence of specific financial obligations which makes common stock so attractive and necessary as a basis of long-term finance in the business corporation, characterized as it is by fluctuating earnings in greater or lesser degree. Dividend payments can be adjusted year by year to the financial circumstances of the moment. This is not to imply that the management is free from pressures of a nonlegal sort for payment of dividends. It is apparent that a board of directors elected by the common shareholders will probably be sensitive to the wishes of those shareholders. Even when the directors are representative of the shareholders in name only, significant pressures are likely to exist. The most important of these relates to future financing. Companies which face a long-range program of growth, or even just the possibility of such growth, must keep in mind the fact that at some time in the future they may have to supplement existing equity capital with a new issue of stock. In order that the new stock be readily marketable, the outstanding stock must have an attractive record of stability and strength. A pattern of stability and growth in dividend payments is often the foundation for stability and growth in the market price of the stock. Obviously, then, the necessity for a sale of stock at a favorable price in the future can be a very practical and powerful incentive to pay dividends in the present.

However, the essential feature of stock remains, namely, that management can, if necessary, disregard these urgings and reduce or suspend dividend payments without breaking a legal contract or interfering in any way with the continuity of the business. This gives management a flexibility which it does not possess with fixed charge debt obligations.

In view of the absence of assured income in the case of common stock, it may seem surprising that many investors prefer to invest in stocks rather than in bonds. The reason is, of course, that the residual claim of the shareholders has its advantages as well as its disadvantages. The holder of a bond of Allied Chemical, cited earlier, will never under any financial circumstances receive for each bond more than $35 per annum interest income nor more than $1,000 at maturity. There is a limit to his gains which goes along with protection against loss. The shareholder, on the other hand, has no limit placed on possible participation in earnings. If the business prospers, it is quite likely that he will receive dividends which pay him a rate of return substantially above that which is paid to the bondholder; and if he liquidates his investment, he may also realize a capital gain over and above his original investment. Counterbalancing the uncertainty associated with a return which is dependent on earnings and the policy decisions of the directors is the prospect of greater rewards than can be obtained when the return is guaranteed.

The advantages of owning common stock seem all the greater in periods of general inflation, when the fixed income of bondholders becomes less and less attractive from the point of view of purchasing power. Many companies enjoy not only increasing profits in such periods but also increasing monetary values of their fixed assets, so that their common stocks are considered especially attractive investments.

The Flow of Funds Related to Common Stock and Its Measurement

In the case of bonds, we identified certain outflows of funds as committed because the corporation had entered into the bond contract. Although no such enforceable commitments are made to the common stockholder, two kinds of funds flows must be identified with this type of security. The first of these is an actual outflow of funds to the shareholder, in the form of such cash dividends as may be paid. This flow is of the same nature as the burden of a bond, and it is on an after-tax basis because the law does not regard it as a cost. The amount of the dividend is, therefore, an important measure. It is usually computed and expressed as the *dividend per share.*

The special nature of the common stock interest brings another flow into consideration. Since the common shareholder has the residual equity, he is entitled to consider as his all the earnings after prior charges, whether or not they are to be distributed as dividends. Funds earned but not paid out are known as *retained earnings,* or *reinvested earnings,* and they serve to add to the value of the stockholder's interest. A measure of equal importance to *dividend per share* is, therefore, *earnings per share.*

These two measures can be illustrated by referring to the Allied Chemical financial statements at page 292. The per share figures are arrived at as follows:

	(In Thousands)
Earnings before Interest and Income Tax (E.B.I.T.)............	$102,000
Deduct: Bond interest....................................	7,000
	$ 95,000
Deduct: Federal income taxes @ 52%......................	49,400
Net Earnings on Total Common Stock (19,906,318 shares)......	$ 45,600
Dividends on common stock...............................	$ 31,352
Net Earnings per Common Share (E.P.S.)....................	$ 2.29*
Dividend per Share.......................................	$ 1.57½

* For purposes of our example, we have used a 52 per cent tax rate rather than the actual taxes shown on Allied Chemical statements. Actual E.P.S. for 1959 was $2.51.

Note that the figures of $2.29 and $1.57½ per share are on an after-tax basis and that they may also be considered on a before-tax basis. Thus, in this case, it takes $95 million of before-tax earnings to produce the $45.6 million of earnings after taxes to which the common shareholders have claim. On a similar basis, it takes $65.26 million of before-tax earnings to enable the company to pay $1.57½ per share of dividends.[7]

A measure of the same nature as the ratio of earnings coverage for bonds or preferred stock is computed for common stock in the form of the *pay-out ratio*, which is the amount paid in dividends divided by the earnings:

$$\frac{\text{Dividend per Share}}{\text{Earnings per Share}} = \frac{1.575}{2.29} = 69\%.$$

It is a common practice of investors to relate earnings per share and dividends per share to the market price of the stock. Thus, *dividend yield* is the dividend expressed as a percentage of the market price at whatever point of time is significant in the analysis. The average market price for Allied Chemical common stock during 1959 was $58. Thus, the yield based on this price would be:

$$\frac{\text{Dividend per Share}}{\text{Average Price}} = \frac{1.575}{58} = 2.71\%.$$

The relationship between earnings per share and market price is most commonly expressed in terms of the *price/earnings ratio*, which in the Allied Chemical example would be:

---

[7] In making calculations or projections of earnings data where the exact tax is not known, our practice is to assume that the full federal corporate income tax applies, which at the moment is 52 per cent of taxable income.

$$\frac{\text{Market Price}}{\text{Earnings per Share}} = \frac{58}{2.29} = \frac{25}{1}.$$

Thus, the stock is said to be selling at twenty-five times earnings. This also can be expressed as an *earnings yield* similar to the dividend yield, as follows:

$$\frac{\text{Earnings per Share}}{\text{Market Price}} = \frac{2.29}{58} = \underline{3.94\%}.$$

Summary: Common Stock

In summary of this section on common stock, we can say that the holder of this stock has no enforceable promises relating to monetary payments. He shares in the residual values of the company, and benefits or loses without limitation as the company prospers or declines. The value of the stock depends not on promises to pay but upon the ability of the company to grow in value, and thus reinvested earnings will influence the price of the stock. Dividends depend upon management decisions, but there are several reasons why management will consider dividends when earnings exist. Useful measures of the position of a common stock include earnings per share, dividends per share, and ratios of earnings or dividends to price.

The Preferred Stock

The preferred stock represents a type of corporate financing which is somewhat paradoxical as between its nominal characteristics and its practical application. On the surface, it appears to provide the corporation with a security which couples the limited obligation of the bond with the flexibility of the common stock—a combination which would be unusually attractive to the issuer. Unfortunately, general experience does not bear out such expectations.

From the purely legal point of view the preferred stock is a type of ownership certificate and thus takes a classification similar to that of the common stock. Accounting practice recognizes this by placing preferred stock along with common stock in the net worth section of the balance sheet, and tax laws interpret preferred dividends as a distribution of net profits to the owners rather than a cost of the business, as in the case of bond interest. The preferred stock certificate is much the same as that for the common stock, stating that the named individual is the owner of a number of shares of preferred stock with such "designations, preferences, privileges, and voting powers, and the restrictions and qualifications thereof," as are shown on the face and reverse side of the certificate. Unlike the bond, the preferred stock does not contain any promise of repayment of the original investment; and as far as the shareholders are concerned, this must be considered as a permanent investment for the life of the company. Many preferred issues give the corporation the right to call in the stock and pay off the shareholders at a predetermined price, but there is no obligation to do so.[8] Further, there is no legal obligation to pay a fixed rate of return on the investment.

The special character of the preferred stock lies in its relationship to the common stock. When a preferred stock is used as a part of the corporate capital structure, the rights and responsibilities of the owners as the residual claimants to the asset values and earning power of the business no longer apply equally to all shareholders. Two types of owners emerge, representing a voluntary subdivision of the over-all ownership privileges. Specifically, the common shareholders agree that the preferred shareholder shall have "preference" or first claim in the event that the directors are able and willing to pay a dividend. In the case of what is termed a *nonparticipating* or *straight* preferred stock, which is the most frequent type, the extent of this priority is a fixed percentage of the par value of the stock or a fixed number of dollars per share in the case of stock without nominal or par value. For example, on October 16, 1956, the Commonwealth Edison Company released a prospectus for a new cumulative preferred stock. According to the prospectus, the preferred shareholders would be entitled to an annual dividend of 4.64 per cent of the par value of $100, payable quarterly, before the common shareholders would be allowed to receive a cash dividend. The *cumulative* feature, which is found in most preferred issues, means that before any common dividends can be paid, not only must the current preferred dividend have been paid but also the preferred dividends of previous years which have remained unpaid. The formal statement of this cumulative preference, taken from the Commonwealth Edison prospectus, is as follows:

No dividend may be paid or other distribution made on the Common Stock or on stock of any other class junior to the Preferred Stock, other than a dividend or distribution solely of shares of the Common Stock or of such other junior stock, and no Common Stock or such other junior stock may be purchased or otherwise acquired by the Company for a consideration, unless (1) all dividends on the Preferred Stock for all past quarterly dividend periods, and . . . for the current quarterly dividend period, shall

---

[8] Some preferred issues are subject to sinking funds.

have been paid or shall have been declared and funds set aside for such payments, and (2) all funds then and theretofore required to be paid into or set aside for any sinking fund or funds created for one or more series of the Preferred Stock shall have been so paid or set aside.

It must be emphasized that the prior claim of the preferred stock does not guarantee a fixed and regular rate of return similar to that on a bond—it merely establishes an order of priority in which the board of directors will pay dividends *if* it decides to do so. At the same time, it establishes a definite upper limit to the preferred shareholders' claim on earnings. Whatever the profitability of the Commonwealth Edison Company, the preferred shareholders of this issue will never receive more than the $4.64 per share per annum dividend.

In most cases the prior position of preferred stock extends to the disposition of assets in event of liquidation of the business. Again, the priority is only with reference to the common stock and does not affect the senior position of creditors in any way. It has meaning and value only if asset values remain after creditors have been fully satisfied—a condition which is by no means certain in the event of liquidation following bankruptcy. In the preferred issue cited above, the shareholders are entitled to receive $100 per share plus accrued dividends in the event of involuntary liquidation before the common shareholders participate in the remaining assets.

So far, we have considered the preferred stock in terms of the formal rights and responsibilities inherent in this type of security. The impression created is that of a limited commitment on dividends coupled with considerable freedom in the timing of such payments. In reality, experience with preferred stocks indicates that the flexibility in dividend payments is more apparent than real. The management of a business which is experiencing normal profitability and growth desires to pay a regular dividend on both common and preferred stock because of a sense of responsibility to the corporate owners and/or because of the necessity of having to solicit further equity capital in the future. The pressure for a regular common dividend in many cases assures the holder of a preferred stock in the same company that his regular dividend will not be interrupted even in years when profits are insufficient to give common shareholders a comparable return, for it is very damaging to the reputation of a common stock (and therefore its price) if preferred dividend arrearages stand before it. The fact that most preferred issues are substantially smaller in total amount than the related common issue means that the cash drain of a preferred dividend is often less significant than the preservation of the status of the common stock.

The result is that management comes to view the preferred issue much as it would a bond, establishing the policy that the full preferred dividend must be paid as a matter of course. The option of passing the dividend still exists, but it is seen as a step to be taken only in case of unusual financial difficulty.[9] Under such a circumstance, the obvious question presents itself: Why, then, use preferred stock as a means of raising permanent capital—why not use bonds instead? The primary advantage of the preferred stock becomes identical with that of a bond, namely, the opportunity to raise funds at a fixed return which is less than that realized when the funds are invested. On the other hand, the dividend rate on preferred stock is typically substantially above the interest rate on a comparable bond and is not allowable as a cost for tax purposes. Of course, the bond is more likely to have a sinking fund, so that the *burden* of bond and preferred may not be greatly different. Any differential in cost may be considered as a premium paid for the option of postponing the fixed payments. However, if management is reluctant to exercise this option, the cost differential may appear excessive.

The Flow of Funds Related to Preferred Stock

It is our opinion that for planning purposes, management should regard preferred dividends (and sinking funds, if any) as a fixed charge. This concept of preferred stock should therefore be reflected in quantitative analysis except when the viewpoint is that of senior creditors. The recommended management approach is seen in the following calculations. In the Commonwealth Edison Company example the total annual dividend payment on 400,000 shares of preferred stock would be $1,856,000. Like common dividends, preferred dividends are (except for certain older utility issues)[10] treated for tax purposes as a distribution of profits and not as a cost. Consequently, the sum of $1,856,000, which is a payment after taxes, may also be considered in terms of the before-tax income necessary to cover this payment. Assuming a 52 per cent federal corporate income tax, the figure would work out approximately as follows:

---

[9] The experience of the thirties is evidence of the fact that such periods do occur; and it must be recognized that in such conditions of severe economic recession, large numbers of preferred issues will stand in arrears.

[10] Internal Revenue Code, 1954, Sec. 247.

Preferred dividends........................$1,856,000
Tax related at 52% rate..................... 2,011,000
Required Before-Tax Income................$3,867,000

As a measure of the degree of assurance which the investor may place in the continuity of this dividend, we may use the same criterion suggested for bonds, namely, coverage. In discussing the ratios of times interest earned and times burden covered in connection with bonds, it was suggested that whatever particular issue happens to be under consideration, the calculation should include in the denominator the interest and sinking fund charges on *all* fixed debt.

Likewise, in considering preferred stock, our calculations should include the total burden of all securities which are equal or senior to the issue in question, because all must be paid if this class is to be. Thus, the ratio of times burden covered for preferred stock should have earnings before interest and taxes and depreciation in the numerator and in the denominator the total of the following, where they apply:

1. Total bond interest.
2. Total sinking funds on bonds plus tax related.
3. Total preferred dividends plus tax related.
4. Total sinking funds on preferred stock (if any) plus tax related.

The pertinent information in the Commonwealth Edison case, using the year 1955 as a base, was as follows (in thousands):

	Before-Tax Amount	Tax Related (52%)	After-Tax Amount
Earnings before interest and taxes....	$104,075	$54,119	$49,956
Depreciation......................	72,900	37,900	35,000
Approximate net cash inflow from operations...................	$176,975	$92,019	$84,956
Total interest on debt..............	$ 17,803	$ 9,258	$ 8,545
Sinking funds on debt..............	8,333	4,333	4,000
Total preferred dividends*..........	3,867	2,011	1,856
Total Burden..................	$ 30,003	$15,602	$14,401

* There was no sinking fund on preferred stock.

Times Burden Covered, including Preferred Stock: $\dfrac{176,975}{30,003} = 5.9$

It is often useful, especially where management regards a common dividend as a part of an established financial policy, to extend the calculation of burden to include the amounts related to the dividend on the common stock. For example, the table just above can be extended as follows (in thousands):

	Before-Tax Amount	Tax Re- lated (52%)	After-Tax Amount
Total burden (preferred).............	$30,003	$15,602	$14,401
Common dividends.................	68,720	35,734	**32,986**
Total Burden (Including Common).	$98,723	$51,336	$47,387

Times Burden Covered, including All Dividends: $\dfrac{176,975}{98,723} = \underline{\underline{1.8}}$

On page 300, we illustrated a form for calculating the effect of an existing or proposed capital structure on the position of the common shareholder as measured by earnings per share. This can be modified to take account of preferred stock, as seen in the following example based on Commonwealth Edison income data for 1955:

(In Thousands)

Earnings before Interest and Taxes..........................$104,075	
Deduct: Bond interest.................................... 17,803	
$ 86,272	
Deduct: Federal income taxes @ 52%..................... 44,861	
Net earnings after interest and taxes........................$ 41,411	
Deduct: Preferred dividends............................. 1,856	
Net Earnings on Common Stock...........................$ 39,555	

Net Earnings per Common Share (E.P.S.)(17,764,921 shares
    outstanding)....................................... $2.23

Summary: The Preferred Stock

To summarize what has been said about preferred stock, it is a security that offers no contractual guaranty of dividends, although it does define the amounts that may be received, and usually provides for the accumulation of dividends that are not paid. In fact, most preferred stocks are issued with the intent of management to pay the dividends on time; and for analytical purposes, they should be treated as a kind of debt, although they are not legally so considered. Preferred dividends cannot be considered as costs, and the income tax related to the dividend is part of the burden of the issue. If there is a sinking fund, it is part of the burden, too.

General Summary

As mentioned at the beginning of this chapter, we have confined our attention to the basic security types—bonds, straight preferred stock, and common stock. This has enabled us to examine the fundamental characteristics of these securities free of the distractions which would result if the discussion were extended to include the many modified forms of bonds and stocks. Later, in Chapters 19 and 20, it will be seen that these modified security forms evolve in the bargaining process between issuer and investor as variations in, or modifications of, the normal distribution of risk, income, and/or control found in the basic types. We defer a full discussion of this bargaining process and of the many bond and stock types it produces until after we have described the markets in which the issuers and investors are brought together.

We have in this chapter illustrated certain quantitative measures which we have found most useful in appraising the financial significance and effects of these basic security types. In particular, we have emphasized the ratios of times interest earned and times burden covered for senior securities and the measures of earnings per share, price/earnings ratio, and dividend and earnings yields for common stock. Throughout, a careful distinction has been drawn between before-tax and after-tax comparisons. Whether or not the reader accepts our preference for before-tax comparisons, it is essential that the calculations be consistently on one basis or the other and that the analyst be ready to use either.

Chapter 15

The Use of Securities to Allocate Risk, Income, and Control

IN THE last two chapters, we have described important characteristics of the basic security types taken separately. We shall now begin to consider how these securities relate to one another when they are used in combination in the financing of a single corporation. It is in the power of management to decide from time to time what type or types of security shall be used. It might be desirable to use debt, preferred stock, new common stock, or retained earnings—most often, in fact, some combination of these. It is therefore one of the tasks of financial management to decide on the "mix" of securities most suitable to the policies of the company.

As we begin to explore the determinants of the management decision about the most desirable capital structure, we shall find that the types of securities available permit the allocation of certain attributes of a business to security holders in varying proportions. Chief among these attributes are *risk, income* (or cost, depending on the point of view), and *control.* In this chapter, we shall see how these elements have been subdivided in a specific corporation, from which we can draw facts for illustration. We have chosen a company that makes use of bonds and preferred stock as well as common stock but otherwise presents an uncomplicated capital structure. It is the Continental Baking Company, and our data are taken from its financial statements for the year ended December 26, 1959.

At the time of our example, we see a company with total assets of $117 million and annual earnings before bond interest and federal income taxes of $20 million. The assets, of course, are funds which have been invested in the properties of the business. From our knowl-

308

edge of the make-up of a balance sheet, we know that the liabilities
and net worth side shows the sources from which the investment of
$117 million has come (see Table 15–1).

TABLE 15–1

CONTINENTAL BAKING COMPANY
CONSOLIDATED BALANCE SHEET
As of December 26, 1959
(In Thousands)

ASSETS

Current Assets:

Cash		$ 14,783
Accounts receivable		14,663
Inventories		20,785
Prepaid expenses		741
		$ 50,972
Deferred charges and other assets		2,305
Plant and equipment (net)		60,986
Good will less amortization		3,084
Total Assets		$117,347

LIABILITIES AND NET WORTH

Current liabilities		$ 22,967
Long-term debt		15,248
Cumulative preferred stock		12,800
Common stock		28,220
Earned surplus		38,112
Total Liabilities and Net Worth		$117,347

It is apparent from the balance sheet that with the exception of
the current liabilities, which by definition are due within a period of
less than one year, these sources are all on a long-term basis. In
Table 15–2, we have made a more detailed statement of the sources of
long-term funds, including several calculations that will be referred
to later in this chapter. The $94 million total shown is referred to col-
lectively as the *capitalization* or the *invested capital* of the company.
When we speak of the capitalization of a company, we are therefore
talking about the funds provided by the long-term creditors and the
owners—the latter through stock subscription and reinvested earnings.

The first on this list of long-term sources is long-term debt. It includes a twenty-year, 3 per cent debenture issue marketed in 1945,
due in 1965, which has been reduced by annual sinking fund payments to its present level of $10,123,000. The balance of the long-
term debt consists of two notes payable, the larger amount negotiated
in 1958, paying 4 per cent and due in 1962, and the smaller amount
negotiated in 1959, paying 3 per cent and due in 1964. The total debt

TABLE 15–2

DETAILS OF CAPITALIZATION OF CONTINENTAL BAKING COMPANY
As of December 26, 1959
(Dollar Figures in Thousands)

	Amount	Capitalization Ratios
Long-term debt:		
3% debenture bonds, due in 1965...........	$10,123	
3% note payable, due in 1964..............	625	
4% note payable, due in 1962..............	4,500	
	$15,248	16%
Preferred stock...........................	12,800	14
Total Debt and Preferred..................	$28,048	30%
Common stock equity:		
Common stock (par $5.00 a share), stated at..	$28,220	
Earned surplus...........................	38,112	
	$66,332	70 = S
Total Capitalization......................	$94,380	100%
Earned before Interest and Taxes...........	$20,188	21.4%

BURDEN

	Before Tax	After Tax (52%)
Interest, long-term debt....................	$ 502	$ 241
Preferred dividend.........................	1,467	704
	$ 1,969	$ 945
Sinking funds, due in 1960*................	569	273
	$ 2,538	$1,218

Times interest and preferred dividend earned = 10.2   = T

* Assumed to be paid at the end of 1960.

makes up 16 per cent of the capitalization, a relationship often referred to as the *debt ratio*. The diverse terms of these issues reflect the results of bargains made between the Continental Baking Company, which was the *issuer*, and various investors. They also reflect different market conditions at the times the debt was issued.

The funds provided by direct shareholder investment came in part from a preferred stock issue as well as from the sale of common stock. The preferred shareholders of Continental Baking made their funds available to the management on the promise of a limited dividend of $5.50 a share. This issue makes up 14 per cent of the total capitalization, and the *debt and preferred ratio* is 30 per cent.

The rest of the equity capital came through the sale of common stock. Although issued with a $5.00 par value, this stock had been sold over the years since incorporation at various prices, and the sum shown for common stock is the total of all amounts paid in by new stockholders to date. The shareholders, both preferred and common, invested without promised maturity and hence for an unlimited period so far as they were concerned. These issues make up an investment base which can be as permanent as the business itself.

The remaining item is the total of *retained earnings*. The figure of $38,112,000 is the sum total of those profits which have been realized over the years since incorporation (net of any losses) and have been reinvested in the business rather than distributed in the form of dividends. These earnings stand to the credit of the common shareholders, and the common shareholders' equity therefore includes them. Unlike the investment in stock, the earned surplus is an amount which the board of directors is legally entitled to distribute to the shareholders at any time. In practice, however, such action is unlikely to take place since most, if not all, of the funds provided by profits have long since become a permanent part of the asset structure upon which the present earning capacity is based. The reader is reminded that surplus represents a surplus of values, not of liquid assets, as some ill-informed people believe. Seventy per cent of the capitalization is represented by the common stock equities in this corporation. This is sometimes referred to as the *equity ratio*.

With the details of the capitalization of the Continental Baking Company before us, we now turn to the ways in which certain of the characteristics of the company have been allocated to the three types of securities that have been used.

The Distribution of Risk

Under a private enterprise system the prospects for individual gain are inevitably associated with the possibility of loss, and this hazard rests on those who have supplied the capital. The hazard shows itself in the uncertainty both of the income to be received and also of the recovery of the original principal invested. It is to the latter aspect that we turn under the heading of "risk."

If a firm fails to realize a profit and continues to spend more money than it takes in, the time will come when it is unable to meet its current obligations. When there is no longer enough to go around and some legal claims against the business remain unsatisfied, the company is said to be *insolvent* or *bankrupt*. If this occurs, certain legal procedures are instituted to assure a fair and orderly distribution of the remaining assets (in liquidation) or revision of claims (in reorganization), following a pattern of priorities established by the terms previously negotiated for the outstanding obligations of the company.

All debts are to be settled in full before any equity claim can be paid. Among the debts, there are certain claims which have top priority over all others. These are established by law and include tax liabilities and the legal expenses that arise because of the bankruptcy. All other debts have equal priority unless some specific collateral has been provided. Let us assume that the values of the assets of the bankrupt amount to 90 per cent of the debts after paying the special types mentioned above. Then all debts should receive 90 per cent of their amount, regardless of their form. The open account payable to a supplier ranks equally with the formal bond.

As we saw in Chapter 12, persons negotiating debt contracts can improve their position against the prospect of bankruptcy by arranging to have a secured position. In the field of long-term debt, a real estate mortgage is a common type of such a pledge, though many other forms exist, as will appear in a later chapter. We have already discussed the limits to the significance of collateral—the claim has priority only as to the value of the specific assets; and if the asset has ceased to produce a return on investment, that value may be seriously in question. Nevertheless, properly selected collateral can add substantially to the relative position of a debt claim in a bankruptcy.

The existence of such priorities as those just mentioned further strengthens the position of a creditor as contrasted with any holder of any equity security and further contributes to a creditor's willingness to lend funds and to take a fixed rate of return in the form of interest instead of requiring a proportionate share in the profits. The relatively low cost of raising money by the use of debt comes from the more certain position of the investor derived from his debtor position, supplemented in some instances by collateral.

It may be emphasized at this point that the position of creditor is a negotiated one, the result of a bargain between the firm obtaining funds and the person supplying them. The division of risk, therefore, is voluntary on both sides and must be consistent with the established policies of management. The management of a firm has a large amount of choice as to whether or not to permit debt and to give priorities, instead of raising funds by the issuance of equity securities.

The preferred stock contract is like a debt contract in that it confers a priority on its owner, but this is only superior to the common equity. All debts must be fully settled before any claim arising from a preferred stock can be met. In the previous chapter, we suggested that management should, for planning purposes, view preferred stock as if its claims were debt claims. While this is true of management, the preferred holder should always be aware that he does not have the protection against the ultimate risk of bankruptcy that any holder of a debt has. The intermediate position of preferred stock as to risk is reflected in its middle position with reference to cost.

Although financial failure occurs in only a minority of instances, and hence may seem unimportant, a priority position also influences the market value given to the securities of going concerns. Since the future is never wholly certain, the bonds of strong firms enjoy better markets than those of weak ones, and the bonds of any firm can be expected to exhibit more stable prices than the equity issues of the same firm, both in periods of poor economic results and in days of prosperity.

It is therefore within the power of a firm to increase the stability of the market price of some of the securities it issues, but only within the limits of amounts of claims that are reasonable in terms of the total capitalization, and only by creating a greater risk for the *junior* issues of the company.

Little needs to be added about the position of common stock with reference to the allocation of risk, because the matter is implicit in the preceding paragraphs. Management can weaken the position of common stock with reference to claim on assets for advantages which will appear below, but it cannot strengthen it, since the common stockholder is last in line and there is no one to whom he may turn for greater assurance of income or principal.

While the market price of a security is the result of many forces, it reflects in its stability or instability the degree of confidence that investors have in the security. In illustration of the effect of the uneven distribution of risk on the market prices of bonds, preferred stock, and common stock, we have chosen the 1957 record of three issues of the Erie Railroad and plotted them in Chart 15–1. The first is one of the bond issues under the consolidated mortgage. Not only is it a debt instrument, containing firm promises to pay interest and principal, but it is secured by the existence of a mortgage of property whose value is directly tied to these bonds, whatever happens to the Erie Railroad corporation.

Erie's preferred stock comes below a number of issues of bonds, so

CHART 15-1

ERIE RAILROAD COMPANY

Relative Changes in Market Price of Three Securities, Weekly, 1957

Prices of Week Ended January 4, 1957 = 100*

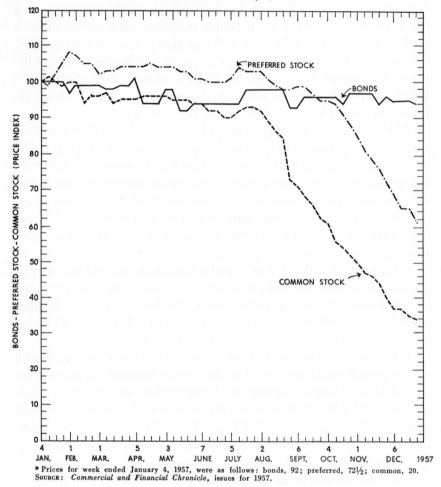

* Prices for week ended January 4, 1957, were as follows: bonds, 92; preferred, 72½; common, 20.

SOURCE: *Commercial and Financial Chronicle*, issues for 1957.

far as priority of claim for dividends is concerned. It would receive nothing in liquidation until every debt of any nature had been settled in full. Thus, it is not surprising to find that its price was more responsive to the developing pessimism in 1957.

Erie's common stock, which bore not only the risks of the railroad business but also those created by the promises made to bond and preferred issues (those *senior* to it), was considered much more risky, as Chart 15-1 shows.

For the same basic reasons, if the outlook in 1957 had been for growing railroad prosperity, one could expect the common stock to rise as steeply as it fell. The preferred and bond issues would respond in their more sedate ways.

From the point of view of management in a going business, what happens in the event of failure is secondary to the question of what needs to be done to avoid failure. The practical concern of management at the time of signing a debt contract, as far as risk is concerned, is the extent to which the increase in the total of fixed cash payments resulting from the new interest and sinking fund commitments makes the task of avoiding failure (cash insolvency) more difficult. A rational appraisal of the risk element would relate expectations on the magnitude and timing of cash inflows to cash outflows, particularly to mandatory cash outflows, in an effort to anticipate the chances of being "out of cash" at some time in the future and to determine how these chances are affected by the additional fixed cash commitments. In this regard, the principal amount of the debt is meaningful only when it is translated into the terms of repayment. Since there are wide variations in these terms as between different debt contracts, it is necessary to examine the sinking fund requirements in detail for each debt issue of the company.

To illustrate this point, we return to the Continental Baking Company case. Table 15–2 translates the $15,248,000 of long-term debt shown on the December 26, 1959, balance sheet into the equivalent schedule of cash outflows which Continental Baking must provide for the repayment of these debts, as defined by the contracts. Note that these sinking fund payments are after-tax dollars.

Since the terms of repayment illustrated in Table 15–2 are negotiated and are open to a considerable range of variation, it can be seen that the degree of risk presented by a debt of any given principal amount can be altered somewhat by management if it chooses to give priority to this in its negotiations with the creditor before the signing of the contract. Thus, for example, extending the life of the loan by ten years could substantially reduce the annual cash drain required to retire the debt by the maturity date. Naturally, the opportunity to modify the risk in this manner will depend heavily on the bargaining position of the borrower and the risk standards of the lender.

The Allocation of Income

The Continental Baking Company reported for 1959 the amount of $20,188,000 as earnings before interest and taxes. This can be related to the year-end capitalization of $94,380,000 to show a return

on invested capital of 21.4 per cent. Despite the fact that the corporation earned this return, it paid only 3 per cent on the funds raised by
some of its long-term debt, and 4 per cent on the rest. The $5.50 per
share preferred stock dividend, on a before-tax basis, required 11.5
per cent on the funds provided by this issue. Clearly, the holders of
the senior securities of this company were satisfied with relatively low
returns on their investment. They preferred to receive fixed incomes
and to enjoy stable market values rather than to participate in all the
risks of the business.

The safety granted to these holders of senior securities was obtained by increasing the risk of the investment of the common equity
shareholders, who promised fixed returns and granted priorities in
liquidation to the holders of the bonds and preferred stock. By this
acceptance of greater risk, the common equity created for itself the
expectation of greater return on the investment of the common stock.
This process has long been known as *trading on the equity*, a term
which indicates that a bargain has been made between the classes of
securities, as is indeed the case. It is also referred to as *leverage*, although we prefer to join those who reserve the word for another meaning, which will appear in a few paragraphs.

Trading on the Equity

A diagram will serve to indicate the nature of the bargain as far as
the allocation of income is concerned. Chart 15–2 has been drawn
with the horizontal axis representing the $94,380,000 invested capital
of the Continental Baking Company. The line has been subdivided
into the amounts provided by the various classes of securities, as tabulated in Table 15–2 (page 310). The vertical axis represents rates of
cost or return, so that the area of the rectangle *ABCD* is the product of
the rate of return on capital and of the capital itself, or the $20,188,-
000 earnings before interest and taxes.

On the base representing the capital contributed by each of the senior securities, rectangular areas are shown which represent the
amounts of cost required to support these securities. These claims
must be met before the common equity can receive anything, thus
adding some risk to the equity position. On the other hand, the amount
of the senior claims is fixed, and any earnings above these fixed
amounts benefit the common shareholders. We have shown this in our
diagram by transferring the irregular area above the fixed charges to
an equal area based on the amount of the common equity. It will be
seen that the effective return on the amount of common equity capital

CHART 15-2

EFFECTS OF TRADING ON THE EQUITY IN THE CONTINENTAL BAKING COMPANY, 1959

(Dollar Figures in Thousands)

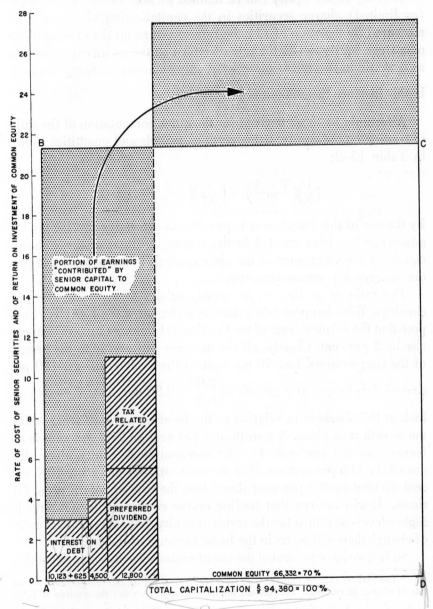

has risen from 21.4 per cent to 27.5 per cent. These rates are, as will be recalled, on a before-tax basis.

Trading on the equity can be defined as follows: the use of fixed (or limited) charge securities in the capitalization of a company, measured by the ratio of (1) the rate of return on the existing common stock equity to (2) the rate of return on the entire capitalization as it would have been if there were only common stock outstanding. In this instance the amount is $\dfrac{27.5}{21.4} = 1.3$.

A formula has been derived for the quick computation of the ratio of trading on the equity, using certain symbols and quantities shown in Table 15–2:

$$\left(\frac{1}{S}\right)\left(\frac{T-1}{T}\right) = \left(\frac{1}{0.7}\right)\left(\frac{9.2}{10.2}\right) = 1.3.$$

By the use of this formula, it is possible to determine precisely what advantage has been created in the income position of the common equity by the acceptance of the risks implicit in the promises to pay the charges for senior securities.

The ratio of trading on the equity relates to a certain level of earnings. What happens when there is a change in the E.B.I.T.? Suppose that the earnings rate of the Continental Baking Company should rise by 2 per cent. Clearly, all the increase will accrue to the benefit of the shareholders, i.e., 70 per cent of the capital will get 100 per cent of the change, or a growth of $\dfrac{2.0}{0.7} = 2.86$ per cent. We can now look at this increase in relation to the level of earnings from which the growth took place. A growth of 2 per cent on 21.4 per cent is an increase of 9.3 per cent. For the common stock equity alone, the growth is 2.86 per cent on 27.5 per cent, or 10.4 per cent; 10.4 per cent divided by 9.3 per cent shows that the rate of return grew 1.1 times.[1] It will be seen that trading on the equity results not only in higher levels of return for the residual equity, but also in higher rates of change than will occur in the basic earnings of the company.

So far, we have presented the use of senior securities in a favorable

---

[1] The authors suggest that the term *leverage* be reserved for this effect of debt on the rate of change in earnings. The formula for its measurement, using the symbols of Table 15–2, is $\left(\dfrac{T}{T-1}\right)$. For further discussion, see Pearson Hunt, "A Proposal for Precise Definitions of 'Trading on the Equity' and 'Leverage,'" *Journal of Finance*, September, 1961, pp. 377–86.

light, when seen from the point of view of the holders of the common stock. If this be so, why do corporations not adopt the policy of borrowing all that anyone can lend? There are two reasons for some reluctance, although the second is only a reflection of the first.

Effects on the Cost of Capital

First is the fact that as the proportion of debt in a capitalization rises, the investor's appraisal of the quality of the debt falls. Higher cost of borrowed money is the result. Furthermore, as just shown, both the volatility and the riskiness of the common stock are increased, so that the investor's appraisal of the stock is also changed. From these changes comes the second reason, namely, that the appraisal of the quality of a company's securities will take the risk into account. A more highly "leveraged" capitalization will be made up of more costly elements. Any change in the debt ratio will, in theory, be reflected in the cost of each of the elements of the capitalization.[2]

Although this theoretical formulation is very important, it is equally important for us to say that the quality ratings of securities are not sensitive to small changes in capitalization ratios, particularly when burdens seem to be covered amply. Most persons with experience in the field will agree that in many corporations, there is considerable room for maneuver before major changes in quality ratings will occur.[3]

Just how far a company may go in accepting risk in order to improve the position of its common stock depends to a great extent on the predictability of the flows of funds through the nonfinancial parts of the firm. In the next chapter, we shall explore this and other factors leading to debt/equity policies. Suffice it to say here that corporations with stable and predictable sales tend to use debt instruments more heavily than corporations in other industries. An exception is the railroad industry, where heavy debt structures exist because of the high regard for their stability in the past. At present, broadly speaking, railroads are borrowers because they cannot sell stock, and their earnings are low. The following debt/equity ratios, by industry ag-

---

[2] For further discussion, see "The Theory of the Capital Structure of the Firm," by Eli Schwartz, in *Journal of Finance*, March, 1959, pp. 18–39.

[3] Per contra, see "The Cost of Capital, Corporation Finance and the Theory of Investment," by Franco Modigliani and M. H. Miller, in *American Economic Review*, June, 1958, pp. 261–97, where it is argued that the total market value of all the securities in the capitalization of a company will not change despite the nature of the securities making it up.

gregates for the end of the third quarter of 1960,[4] may be of some interest:

All manufacturing corporations, except newspapers.................24.6%
Manufacturers of motor vehicles and equipment....................12.7
Manufacturers of lumber and wood products, except furniture.......34.5
Manufacturers of textile-mill products...........................25.4
Manufacturers of apparel and other finished products.............43.7
Manufacturers in petroleum refining and related industries...........18.0

The Location of Control

In Chapter 2, we said that the control of a corporation can be considered as being in the hands of those who have the voting power to elect the board of directors of the corporation. Such power is obviously centralized when a person or group holds a majority of the voting stock. On the other hand, many corporations, even among those of small size, have issued some voting shares to holders who are not part of the management group, so that a threat to control may develop if new issues of voting shares are created or, perhaps, if a preferred stock dividend is passed.

In many cases, therefore, the location and distribution of voting power is an important part of the planning of security issues. There must always be a voting stock outstanding.[5] Sometimes, however, the common stock is "classified," with one class having all the rights of such stock and the other class having all of them except voting power. Many investors are not interested in participating in management, even to the minute degree of making use of a proxy; so there is a market for nonvoting common shares. Some years ago, however, in 1926, the New York Stock Exchange adopted a rule against accepting any future nonvoting common stocks; and although other exchanges have not followed suit, nonvoting common has tended to become a device that is adopted with hesitation.

There are rare instances where voting power is not proportionate to the number of shares held. Most co-operative corporations allow

---

[4] Based on data in Federal Trade Commission and Securities and Exchange Commission, *Quarterly Financial Report for Manufacturing Corporations: Third Quarter, 1960* (Washington, D.C.: U.S. Government Printing Office, 1960), pp. 12–27.

[5] The Great Northern Railway Company, for example, has never issued a common stock. Its preferred stock has the voting power. There is also the unique case in Virginia where a corporation acquired all its voting stock from a bank which had taken it over as collateral from the owner, who had defaulted on a loan. Although sympathizing with the management for its efforts to "bail out" the former owner, the probate court ordered the transaction rescinded. It is beyond the powers of a company to extinguish all its voting stock.

but one vote to each stockholder, for example. A "reform" of corporate voting power, which has strong proponents and opponents, is the scheme of *cumulative voting*, where all the nominees for office are voted for at once, and a shareholder is allowed the number of votes resulting from his number of shares multiplied by the number of persons to be elected to the board. The reader will see that this system allows minorities to elect members to the board roughly in proportion to their relative shareholding. The argument rages as to whether such minority representation assists or hinders the proper working of a board of directors. The right to vote cumulatively is assured by a number of states, namely:[6]

Alaska	Illinois	Montana	South Carolina
Arizona	Kansas	Nebraska	South Dakota
Arkansas	Kentucky	North Carolina	Washington
California	Michigan	North Dakota	West Virginia
Hawaii	Mississippi	Ohio	Wyoming
Idaho	Missouri	Pennsylvania	

All national banks also have cumulative voting.

In recent years, preferred stocks have not received general voting power, although there are still outstanding many older issues with full voting privileges. Instead, it has become customary to confer voting power on the preferred in the event that its dividends or sinking funds fall into arrears for longer than a specified period. Provisions range from the transfer of all voting power from the common to the preferred, a most rare case, to the power to elect a minority of the board of directors to represent the interests of the preferred stock. Such a power in the case of nonpayment of the preferred dividend is very different from the acceleration of maturity which occurs upon the default of a bond, and has led one of the authors to say that a preferred stockholder has a pillow while a bondholder has a club with which to threaten management.

Before one can take into account the question of the location of voting power, one must have a thorough understanding of the way in which the holders of voting power can be expected to use it. Many corporations have well-established managements whose direct supporters have very few votes. Yet, their nominees are regularly elected to

---

[6] C. M. Williams, *Cumulative Voting for Directors* (Boston: Division of Research, Harvard Business School, 1951), p. 8; and Commerce Clearing House, Inc., *Corporation Law Guide* (Chicago).

the board of directors through the operation of the proxy system, as described in Chapter 2. A successful proxy fight could unseat the existing management; but if the nonmanagement shareholders are widely scattered, and if there are no large blocks held by persons ready to take leadership, the proxy system can be relied on to provide the necessary support for management.

There is risk in minority control, however, and many managements holding majorities find it almost impossible to consent to any plan which endangers the "absolute" control which they have. (It is not in fact "absolute," for minority interests must always be considered fairly when policies are made.) In our view, small and growing corporations have too often chosen to borrow rather than to sell voting shares because of excessive fear of the risks to management of a public holding of voting control. But the actual appraisal of the risks is too complicated for a general statement. The matter must be studied on a case-by-case basis.

Bondholders, like other creditors, do not have a vote; and as long as the corporation lives up to the terms of the debt contract, they can take no action. The actual situation, however, is less permissive than it seems to be at first glance, for both bond indentures and preferred stock contracts usually contain clauses known as *protective provisions* specifying what the corporation will do (*affirmative covenants*) or will not do (*negative covenants*) during the time the particular security is outstanding. To cite a few examples: Corporations may promise not to pay dividends, even on preferred stock, unless earned; they may promise to set aside certain funds for the replacement of assets; and so on. The existence of such clauses leads us to suggest supplementing the definition of *control*, given in Chapter 2, so that it reads: ". . . We may say for practical purposes that control lies in the hands of the individual or group who has the actual power to select the board of directors (or its majority). In most corporations a measure of control is exercised by the promises that have been made in contracts in force at any moment."

We now return to the instance of the Continental Baking Company to cite examples of major ways in which the control of its policies has been determined by the terms of senior security issues.[7]

> (1) Debenture 3s, due 1965.
>> *a*) Except for refunding . . . company will not create . . . any additional funded debt unless immediately thereafter consolidated

---

[7] *Moody's Industrial Manual, 1960,* pp. 756–57.

net tangible assets shall be at least twice consolidated funded debt, and consolidated net earnings shall (1) equal for 12 consecutive months of 18 months next preceding, or (2) average for three fiscal years next preceding, at least 3 times annual interest charges on consolidated funded debt. . . .

  b) Company will not declare any dividends (except stock dividends) or make any distribution on or purchase or redeem . . . any capital stock if immediately thereafter the amounts so applied after December 30, 1944, would equal or exceed the sum of (1) consolidated net income from December 30, 1944 . . . (2) $2,000,000, and (3) net proceeds from sale after December 30, 1944, of capital stock. . . .

(2) $5.50 Cumulative Preferred Stock.

  a) Voting Rights—Has no voting power unless six quarterly dividends . . . are in default when preferred . . . is entitled to elect one additional director; and if accrued dividends have not been paid in full, at next succeeding annual meeting . . . preferred is entitled to elect one more additional director. . . .

  b) Affirmative vote or consent of 66⅔% of preferred necessary to amend provisions to affect rights of preferred adversely, or to restrict voting rights as above.

There are many types of protective covenants found in security issues. It is one of the places where the limit of possibility is set only by the ingenuity of the draftsman. The actual terms of issues are reached by bargaining between the issuing corporation and some agency representing the investors' interests. We deal further with this subject in the chapters on the bargain for funds. Suffice it to say here by way of summary that questions of control enter into the selection of corporate securities not only with reference to the powers granted to vote at annual meetings, but also in terms of the detailed contractual provisions that may be agreed upon for specific issues.

Summary Grid

The contrasting characteristics of bonds, preferred stock, and common stock with respect to the distribution of income, risk, and control may be summarized in the form of an analytical "grid." Students are urged to use such a grid in getting an over-all appraisal of the balance of security types in the capital structure of a corporation. After a time, the scheme of classification will become habitual and need no longer be done on paper unless the structure is very complex. The grid in Table 15–3 is illustrated with reference to the Continental Baking Company's capitalization as of 1959 (see Table 15–2, page 310).

TABLE 15–3

Basic Security Types	Income	Risk	Control
Bonds	Fixed payment of 3 per cent annually on outstanding debentures through 1965; 4 per cent and 3 per cent annually on outstanding notes due in 1962 and 1964, respectively. Sixteen per cent of capitalization.	Contractual obligation to pay interest and repay principal on specified dates. Total outstanding debt as of December 26, 1959, $15,248,000. Sinking funds, 1960, $273,000.	No voice in management other than through terms of bond indentures (see page 322).
Preferred stock	Prior claim to earnings of $5.50 per share on 128,000 shares before payments of dividends on common. Dividends cumulative. Fourteen per cent of capitalization.	Board has power to suspend dividends without penalty other than (1) suspension of common dividends, (2) election of one or two directors by preferred shareholders. No sinking fund.	No voice in management except when six quarterly dividends passed, when preferred may elect one or at most two directors to a thirteen-man board.
Common stock	Entitled to all earnings remaining after all prior claims deducted. In 1959, this amounted to $4.66 per share, of which $2.20 was paid out in dividends. Ratio of trading on the equity 1.3 (based on 1959 charges and earnings).	Basic risks of the business rest on the common shareholder, who has no legal claim except to the ownership of whatever remains after all other claimants have been satisfied. Debt/equity proportions at the end of 1959 are 16 per cent debt, 14 per cent preferred, and 70 per cent common equity.	Common shareholders elect the board of directors on basis of one vote per share.

Chapter 16

The Analysis of Alternative Security Issues

In the two preceding chapters, we have focused attention on the basic contracts by means of which a corporation acquires the use of external funds on a long-term basis. The reader is now familiar not only with the nature of these contracts—the common stock, the preferred stock, and the bond—but also with the effect each has on the incidence of the fundamental elements of investment—risk, income, and control. Up to this point, we have considered these securities in a general context as an important part of the institutional framework within which every business corporation operates.

We are now ready to move from the general to the particular and to view these securities through the eyes of the individual corporation facing a need for external funds at a point in time. Considered in this way, these basic security types are seen as alternatives in the solution of a specific financial problem; and we now turn to the analytical methods by which their potential effects may be compared as a preliminary stage in the decision-making process. As we proceed through the analysis, it will become clear to the reader, if it is not clear already, that a decision on the "right" balance of security types can be made only within the context of the individual corporation at a specific stage in its history, in full knowledge of its special circumstances and of the attitudes and objectives of its owners and management.

Before the reader becomes involved in the details of analysis, it may be helpful to provide him with a little perspective on business practice in this regard. The extent to which the choice of security types occupies the time and attention of the financial officer and the board of directors varies greatly from one company to another and within a single company from period to period over its life span. Obviously, the problem is presented when the company is first organ-

325

ized, though the choice may be simplified by the fact that one or more of the security types may not be available at that time. Subsequently, the frequency with which this type of decision has to be made depends on the rate of growth of the business, the capital requirements of growth, and the extent to which the needed funds can be generated internally. In some companies, even large and successful ones, the treasurer may never face a decision of this type during his period of office. In many businesses, new securities may be floated no more than three or four times over a twenty-year period. Obviously, in such companies the growth rate and capital requirements are such that they are substantially or entirely covered by retained earnings. In contrast, there are some companies which are issuing new securities every year.

Even where this problem is presented infrequently, however, it is of critical importance, with long-term financial implications. Usually, the need for additional external funds can be anticipated well in advance, so that there is time for a careful weighing of all relevant considerations. Further, it should be pointed out that although by far the largest proportion of funds for new business investment comes from internal sources, the choice between internal and external sources is an ever-present aspect of long-term financial planning. Every management has some control over the corporate rate of growth and the rate of earnings retention and therefore over the extent to which the need for external funds presents itself. Many managements consciously work to avoid the need for selling new securities; but in so doing, they are making a deliberate choice between equity capital generated internally and capital provided by the sale of stock or bonds. This choice is rational only if it includes a careful analysis of the effects of new external sources of funds.

Establishing a Point of View

For the individual company whose circumstances or policies require it to turn periodically to the external capital market for new long-term funds, there is a necessity for achieving a proper balance of the basic security types in its capital structure. What is a "proper balance," however, cannot be determined before we define a point of view from which the use of securities will be assessed. In studying what has occurred in actual cases, one can recognize several distinctly different viewpoints—such as those of the creditors, the management, "the company," the existing shareholders, and the prospective shareholders. It is clear that the relative advantages and disadvantages of securities in the corporate capital structure will appear very differently to individuals with varying relationships to the corporation. What is considered "best" by the bondholders may be viewed as less than best from some other point of view. Thus, for example, the sale of a new block of common stock would be welcomed by bondholders, since they would have prior claim to the earning power and residual values of the funds so acquired. The existing common shareholders, on the other hand, could be strongly opposed, particularly if the stock was sold below market price, because the new shares would dilute their participation in future net earnings. Specific illustrations of such effects will be found in the pages which follow. For management to reach a meaningful decision in a given situation, a point of view must be adopted and adhered to consistently.

In this regard, we adopt the viewpoint of the holder of common stock. It is his interests which are most clearly and intimately connected with the long-term prospects and objectives of the business. It is he who accepts (knowingly or not) the basic risks of ownership and whose resources are committed for the protection of others, including senior security holders. In contrast to this, the interests of the bondholder and preferred shareholder are negotiated and limited by contract. It is the common stockholders, acting as a group, who have the power to elect the board of directors, thus making the board—legally, at least—responsible to them. It seems reasonable to expect that the basic objectives of management will normally be identical with the objectives of the common shareholder and that management in its decisions should reflect this identity of interest.

Of course, this is not to say that in practice management should always take this point of view, nor that it should be interpreted so narrowly as to exclude from consideration the valid interests of others toward whom the company has important responsibilities—creditors, employees, customers, the general public. It is, however, an appropriate starting point for the consideration of problems such as the one posed in this chapter. It should be emphasized that if a new stock issue is in prospect, we narrow the point of view still further by identifying the company's interests with those of the *existing* common shareholders as opposed to the *new* common shareholders where a possible conflict of interest may develop (as, for example, in the pricing of the new issue).

With this point of view, the problem of balance in the capital structure can be brought into focus, though the solution is by no means obvious. Bonds normally offer the best alternative for maximizing earnings per share and do not affect the existing distribution of control. On the other hand, they involve more risk because of the fixed annual burden on cash, a burden which may well be substantially larger than that of other securities because of a sinking fund requirement. The preferred stock will normally appear less attractive than the bond in terms of the income consideration but, on the other hand, may be less risky as a result of a smaller annual burden on cash and more flexible terms of payment. There may also be a possible disadvantage in the voting feature written into many preferred stock issues. Common stock will appear least attractive to existing common shareholders because of the effect on earnings per share and the dilution of control that always takes place if new common shares are issued. On the other hand, since the new stock would be equal in status to the old, it does not add anything to the risks already present except, perhaps, to the question of the continuity of the common dividend.

It will be apparent that the choice of securities is a problem which cannot be solved in general terms or by any simple formula. There are pros and cons for each alternative, and the final choice must be left to individual judgment in each particular case. At the same time, however, if the analysis of these considerations is carried out in a thorough and objective manner, the resulting capital structure should, within limits, fit into a general pattern suited to the character of the industry in which the business operates.

A Problem for Analysis

The process of analysis of alternative security issues will be most meaningful if illustrated with reference to an actual company. In order to take full advantage of the knowledge built up in the two preceding chapters, we shall continue with the case of the Continental Baking Company. To do so, however, requires a modest departure from fact. Previous references to this company related to its capital structure as of the end of 1959. In order to preserve the time sequence, it will be assumed that the company developed a need for external funds in the early months of 1960 and was considering alternative sources. (In fact, the company financed its 1960 operations entirely through internal sources.) It is further assumed that the funds required amounted to $15 million and that the company was confining its consideration to the basic security types already outstanding—bonds, preferred stock, and common stock.

The market for the securities of Continental Baking during the early months of 1960 continued to be relatively stable. This stability gave some support for the assumption that current market values could be used as an adequate guide for the immediate future when the new securities would be offered. The common stock price appeared to be holding in the vicinity of $43 a share. The $5.50 preferred stock was selling around 102⅛ to yield 5.4 per cent to the new investor. Yields in the bond market had been showing an upward trend, but the trend had reversed in recent months. Continental Baking 3's of 1965, rated "A" by Moody's, were currently selling around 95 to yield 4.1 per cent to maturity.

While much of the challenge and excitement of new security issues lies in the uncertainty surrounding the price at which the securities will actually be sold, we shall for the moment by-pass the step of market analysis and assume that the following conclusions have been reached: The common stock can be sold at $40 a share, the $5.50 preferred stock can be sold at $100, and a new issue of twenty-year bonds bearing an interest rate of 4.25 per cent can be sold at par. Underwriting and legal and other costs incidental to the flotation of these issues will be ignored for the sake of simplicity. We now proceed to consider the implications of these three alternative methods of raising $15 million for the Continental Baking Company and its common stockholders, particularly with reference to the effects on the allocation of risk, income, and control.

Comparison of Alternatives: The Effect on Income

It will be apparent to the reader that in order to consider the income effect of a $15 million issue of one of these three security types, it is necessary to make some estimate of what the basic earning capacity of Continental Baking will be in the foreseeable future when the new securities will have become a part of the company's capital structure. Since few businesses are able to make meaningful detailed forecasts of earnings and cash flows beyond the period of a year, it seems appropriate to start with earnings expectations for the year 1960. Management's expectations, as revealed in the company's annual report for 1959, touched on the uncertainties of the general economic situation and on the upward trends of wage costs, but gave no indication of a radical departure from the earnings level of 1959.

This, then, becomes our starting point. Table 15–2 of Chapter 15 (page 310) showed that earnings before interest and taxes (E.B.I.T.) in 1959 were 21.4 per cent of total capitalization. Let us assume that in 1960 the company will earn 21 per cent, approximately the same rate of return, on the total permanent funds invested, including the $15 million of new funds. (This is, of course, somewhat optimistic, since it will take time for the new funds to find their way into profitable employment and they may not earn at the average level for company investment as a whole.) If this is the case, the effect on the earnings per common share resulting from the three alternatives will be as shown in Table 16–1.

TABLE 16–1

(Dollar Figures in Thousands)

	1959 Capital Structure and Earnings	1960 Earnings, Assuming $15 Million Expansion Financed through:		
		Bonds	Preferred Stock	Common Stock
Earnings before interest and taxes (21% of invested capital)....	$20,188	$22,970	$22,970	$22,970
Interest on debt.................	502	1,139	502	502
	$19,686	$21,831	$22,468	$22,468
U.S. federal income tax (at 52%)...	10,237	11,352	11,683	11,683
Net profit after taxes..............	$ 9,449	$10,479	$10,785	$10,785
Deduct preferred dividends.......	704	704	1,529	704
Net Earnings on Common Stock	$ 8,745	$ 9,775	$ 9,256	$10,081
Number of common shares......... outstanding (in thousands)...	1,875	1,875	1,875	2,250*
Earnings per share...............	$4.66	$5.21	$4.93	$4.48
Chart 16–1 reference point........		(3)		(4)

* Assuming new stock sold at $40 a share: 375,000 new shares.

It can be seen that on the basis of the anticipated effect on earnings per share—the criterion which we believe is of greatest immediate concern to the existing common stockholders—the most favorable result is produced by an issue of bonds, an E.P.S. of $5.21. This represents an improvement of 55 cents a share over the 1959 E.P.S. The improvement follows from the fact that the new investment is expected to earn 21 per cent before taxes, as compared with the effective cost of the debt, which is expected to be 4¼ per cent (before taxes). The preferred stock ranks second in terms of a favorable income effect, with an expected E.P.S. of $4.93. The increase in preferred dividends more than makes up for the lower interest payments under this alternative, so that the net result is less favorable to the common stockholder. The result is again more favorable than the 1959 E.P.S., since the 21 per cent return on the new investment exceeds the cost of the new preferred stock. Note here, however, that the comparison is not with the 5½ per cent dividend rate, but with the rate of before-tax earnings (11.46 per cent), which must be realized in order to pay the preferred dividends out of after-tax earnings without depleting what is left for the common shareholder.

The least attractive from the income point of view is the common stock alternative, where the anticipated E.P.S. is $4.48—18 cents a share below the 1959 level. Such dilution of earning power is unavoidable—unless the new stock is sold at such a favorable price that the increase in the earnings more than offsets the increase in the number of shares among which the new total of earnings after taxes and preferred dividends must be apportioned. Thinking in these terms, the "break-even" price for Continental Baking common stock at this time would be approximately $52, whereas the calculations were based on the assumption that the common stock would be sold at $40. Since the current market is only $43, improvement in E.P.S. as a result of the new investment financed through common stock is clearly out of the question at this time.

Thus, bonds, preferred stock, and common stock come out in a 1, 2, 3 ranking as far as the income effect is concerned. The question arises: Would this be true if corporate earnings in 1960 or any subsequent year prove to be different from the 1959 level? It is inherent in the nature of a dynamic economy that they will be. The critical question is therefore not whether the E.P.S. will differ from that shown in Table 16–1, but rather whether it will change so much and in such a manner that the ranking will change. We can, of course, test for this by substituting another earnings assumption in place of the 21 per cent return in Table 16–1. If this is done, the most sensible approach would be to estimate an upper and a lower limit for anticipated earnings and work out an E.P.S. calculation for each alternative at these two extremes. If the results show the same ranking at the extremes, then from an income point of view, one of these long-term sources will be clearly preferable to the other two.

It is possible, however, that the ranking may differ so that, for example, common stock would have the more favorable income effect at the lower level of earnings and bonds the more favorable effect at the upper level. In such a case, we need more information. This is best provided by the analytical device of a range-of-earnings chart, which will be the subject of the next section.

The Range-of-Earnings Chart as a Tool of Analysis

In considering the potential effects on earnings per share of alternative security types under varying assumptions with respect to future earnings, it is desirable to be able to observe these effects over the entire range of expected earnings and not merely at one or more points, the selection of which is bound to be somewhat arbitrary (as in Table 16–1). Given the assumptions of the case in question, there is a simple mathematical relationship between E.B.I.T. and E.P.S. for each one of the alternative security types. This can be represented graphically in what we call a range-of-earnings chart. Chart 16–1 pre-

CHART 16–1

RANGE-OF-EARNINGS CHART SHOWING COMPARISON OF BOND AND COMMON STOCK ALTERNATIVES AT DIFFERENT LEVELS OF E.B.I.T. IN TERMS OF EARNINGS PER SHARE

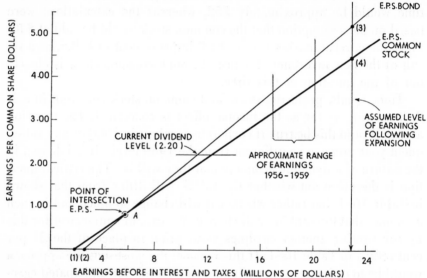

Graph based on following data: points (1), (2)—Table 16–2 (p. 333); points (3), (4)—Table 16–1 (p. 330).

sents a graph of the relationship for Continental Baking bond and common stock alternatives in accordance with the assumptions outlined in the preceding section. For the sake of simplicity, the preferred stock alternative has not been included, but it would be drawn in exactly the same manner.

The two lines show what the E.P.S. on the common stock would be for any level of E.B.I.T. from zero up to $24 million (*a*) if bonds were used to finance the new investment and (*b*) if common stock was used. It will be observed that in each case, it is a simple straight-line relationship. For this reason the line can be drawn merely by determining any two points on the line. We have already provided one point on each line; they come from Table 16–1, where the E.P.S. was calculated at the E.B.I.T. level of $22.97 million. These are shown as points (3) and (4) on Chart 16–1.

The second set of points may be established by answering the question: What level of E.B.I.T. would result in exactly zero E.P.S. under each alternative? The obvious answer is: that level of E.B.I.T. which exactly equals the total dollar amount of bond interest plus preferred dividends and their tax related. This gives two points along the base line of the chart, which will be joined to the related points derived from Table 16–1. The levels of E.B.I.T. which will produce zero E.P.S. in the Continental Baking example are shown in Table 16–2 and are plotted as points (1) and (2) on Chart 16–1.

TABLE 16–2

(Dollar Figures in Thousands)

	1960 EARNINGS, ASSUMING $15 MILLION EXPANSION FINANCED THROUGH:		
	Bonds	Preferred Stock	Common Stock
Preferred dividends and tax related (52%)..................... Bond interest...................	$1,467 1,139	$3,185 502	$1,467 502
E.B.I.T. necessary to cover interest and preferred dividends......	$2,606	$3,687	$1,969
Chart 16–1 reference point.........	(2)		(1)

The most striking feature of all such charts is the difference in slope of the two lines, resulting in an intersection point at some level of E.B.I.T. At this point the E.P.S. is the same for both alternatives ($0.82 in the Continental Baking case, Chart 16–1). For levels of earnings below this point the common stock has the more favorable income effect; for levels of earnings above this point the bond alternative has the more favorable income effect. The difference in slope is due to the fact that under each alternative the number of outstanding shares of common stock is different. For the common stock alternative, this obviously reflects the dilution effect of the new shares, which not only reduces the E.P.S. at any income line but, as was brought out in the preceding chapter (page 318), also changes the rate at which the growth of the whole company benefits the common shareholder.

Looking at the bond alternative in Chart 16–1, we can see that unless E.B.I.T. is above $5,793,000 (point A), the positive leverage of debt on earnings per share will not be realized.[1] This point becomes significant in relation to the range of earnings expected in the future. If it is expected that the lower limit of this range may fall below the intersection point, then the use of bonds may not give the desired leverage and therefore may not have the income advantage which we have assumed to be associated with this type of financing. If, on the other hand, the intersection point appears well below even the lower limit of future earnings, then the income advantage of bond financing seems assured. This appears to be the case for Continental Baking if the earnings of 1956–59 can be taken as a guide for the foreseeable future. The lower limit of this range is well above the intersection point. Thus, the impressions of Table 16–1 are confirmed.

The Comparison with Respect to Risk

In view of the comparatively low interest rates on the modest amounts of long-term debt carried by many business corporations and the fact that interest is treated as a cost for tax purposes, it is frequently found that bonds are the most beneficial alternative among long-term security types as far as the income effect is concerned. However, this is only one of several considerations even in a company which stresses profit maximization. A dimension of comparable importance is the effect these securities have on the risks of the business. This, we will find, not only requires ranking the alternatives in this respect—a relatively simple matter—but also requires some method of measuring incremental risk and of deciding how much risk is "too much." This latter problem turns out to be very difficult indeed.

As we have already explained in the two preceding chapters, the risk associated with debt derives from the contractual periodic pay-

---

[1] This "break-even" point on earnings per share between the bond and the common stock alternatives can be calculated algebraically, as follows:

Let
x = Break-even level of E.B.I.T.
I_1 = Dollar amount of interest without new bonds
I_2 = Dollar amount of interest with new bonds
PD = Dollar amount of dividends on preferred stock now outstanding
S_1 = Number of common shares if new stock is sold
S_2 = Number of common shares if new stock is not sold
TR = Tax rate

Then:

$$\frac{(x - I_1)(1 - TR) - PD}{S_1} = \frac{(x - I_2)(1 - TR) - PD}{S_2}$$

In our example:

$$\frac{(x - 502)(0.48) - 704}{2,250} = \frac{(x - 1,139)(0.48) - 704}{1,875}$$

$$x = \$5,791,000$$

ments which are due the bondholder regardless of the company's earnings or financial circumstances. Since bond interest is to be found on the income statement as a deduction from current earnings, it is not surprising to find that one of the most common measures of risk is a calculation of the excess or *margin of safety* of earnings available for bond interest over the amount of the interest payments. Of course, now that our focus has shifted from measuring the "cost" of debt to the size of mandatory payments, we must recognize that the periodic repayment of principal through a sinking fund provision poses just as much of a threat to corporate solvency as does interest. Failure to meet either payment would constitute a default of the contract. Thus, when measuring risk, our attention shifts to the total burden of debt represented by interest *and* sinking fund payments.

One way of measuring the adequacy of earnings for this purpose follows the form of analysis used in the section on income. Table 16–3

TABLE 16–3
(Dollar Figures in Thousands)

	1959 CAPITAL STRUCTURE AND EARNINGS	1960 EARNINGS, ASSUMING $15 MILLION EXPANSION FINANCED THROUGH:		
		Bonds	Preferred Stock	Common Stock
Net earnings on common stock (Table 16–1)...............	$8,745	$9,775	$9,256	$10,081
Sinking fund requirements on bonds....	273	1,023	273	273
Uncommitted Earnings on Common Stock......................	$8,472	$8,752	$8,983	$ 9,808
Uncommitted Earnings per Share......	$4.52	$4.67	$4.79	$4.36
Chart 16–2 reference point...........		(3)		(4)

continues the Continental Baking example where Table 16–1 left off, namely, at the point where net earnings on common stock had been derived. In order to take account of the drain on currently generated funds caused by the sinking funds on outstanding debt, we now proceed to deduct this amount and derive what we call uncommitted earnings on common stock and uncommitted earnings per share (U.E.P.S.). In this connection, it has been assumed that the new bonds are to be fully retired by maturity (in twenty years) through equal annual payments. The substantial annual burden which this imposes is seen in the fact that the bond alternative on a U.E.P.S. basis is only a slight improvement over the 1959 level and is actually inferior to the preferred stock alternative in this respect. It is still better than the common stock, however, having a margin of uncommitted earnings of 31 cents per share.

The significance of the comparison of the burden of these securities is seen even more clearly in a range-of-earnings chart. Chart 16–2

CHART 16–2

RANGE-OF-EARNINGS CHART SHOWING COMPARISON OF BOND AND COMMON STOCK ALTERNATIVES AT DIFFERENT LEVELS OF E.B.I.T. IN TERMS OF UNCOMMITTED EARNINGS PER SHARE

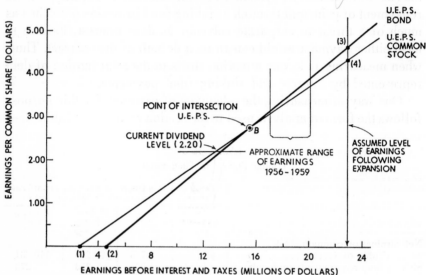

Graph based on following data: points (1), (2)—n. 2, p. 336; points (3), (4)—Table 16–3 (p. 335).

is similar to Chart 16–1 except that the lines now represent U.E.P.S. rather than E.P.S. Points (1) and (2) at the base of the chart indicate, for Continental Baking under the bond and common stock alternatives, the level of E.B.I.T. which just equals the total of bond interest and sinking fund payments plus preferred dividends on a before-tax basis.[2] Points (3) and (4) are taken from Table 16–3.

The most noticeable feature is the break-even point, the level of E.B.I.T. below which the common stock alternative would generate

	(In Thousands)	
	Bonds	*Common Stock*
E.B.I.T. necessary to cover interest and preferred dividends (Table 16–2)	$2,606	$1,969
Sinking funds (Table 16–3)	1,023	273
Tax related to sinking funds	1,108	296
	$4,737	$2,538

[2] Points (1) and (2) on Chart 16–2 are obtained as follows: Points (1) and (2) from Table 16–2, plus the sinking funds from Table 16–3, plus the tax related to the sinking funds.

more uncommitted earnings per share than the bond alternative. This level is $15.7 million compared with $5.8 million on an earnings per share basis. This has moved the point of intersection much closer to the 1956–59 range of earnings, revealing a significantly higher probability that the firm might face a year in which earnings were so low as to leave the company with less funds for dividends and other purposes under the bond alternative than under the common stock alternative. If E.B.I.T. falls below $15.7 million, where uncommitted earnings are $2.82 per share, the common dividend of $2.20 per share would be seriously threatened. It can be seen from Chart 16–2 that under such circumstances, it takes a higher level of E.B.I.T. to cover the dividend payment out of current uncommitted earnings under the bond alternative than under the common stock alternative ($13.3 million as compared with $12.8 million).

Thus, when we consider the factor of risk in terms of the burden of debt servicing on corporate funds flow, we have a means of measuring the impact of varying the amounts and proportions of debt in the capital structure. However, the basic problem of risk is still to be solved. It is apparent from Chart 16–2 that as debt increases, the level of E.B.I.T. required to cover the burden of the debt and the common dividends moves closer to the current range of earnings, and the chances increase that E.B.I.T. will be deficient in a recession period. How does a business decide on the point at which further use of debt to increase E.P.S. must be resisted because the risk has become "excessive"? At what point does the increasing risk overbalance the increasing earnings?

In practice, business resolves this problem in a variety of ways. There are many people in management positions who believe that any debt is too much debt. Few, however, are able to impose financial policies which exclude long-term debt entirely from the capital structure. Of the majority of businesses which do borrow at one time or another, many follow the practice of letting the creditor decide. Established financial institutions—commercial banks, insurance companies, investment bankers—have evolved what are generally considered to be conservative standards of debt capacity for a given industry. The simplest solution to debt policy is to stay within the requirements or recommendations of a trusted financial institution. A variation of this approach is to borrow as much as possible at the prime rate or within the requirements of an "A" rating, thus assuring some margin of unused borrowing capacity for unanticipated needs.

A second approach to debt capacity is to follow what appear to be the conventions of the industry by observing the debt policies of comparable companies. Here again, the borrower is passing the responsibility for a judgment on appropriate risk levels to someone else—in this case, his competitors. The argument in favor of such an approach is that the practices of the industry reflect a pooling of extensive experience and widely accepted decision rules are time-tested rules. There is the additional consideration that investors apply this test of comparability, and any company which is seriously out of line with comparable companies may be penalized in the capital market. However, in most industries the variations in corporate debt and other financial policies are broad enough to leave a considerable range within which individual choice can be exercised without being obviously out of line.

Thus, most borrowers have some type of operating debt capacity rule which they think of as being tailored to their individual circumstances. These rules commonly take one of two forms. The most common is the *percentage-of-capitalization* rule, which states that no new debt will be incurred if it raises long-term debt as a percentage of total capitalization above x per cent. The other, more frequently used by lenders than by borrowers, is the *earnings-coverage* standard, which sets a minimum required ratio between net earnings available for annual debt servicing and the total amount of the debt servicing. This latter standard relates directly to Chart 16–2, being the ratio of (a) the distance from the origin to the current (or an average) E.B.I.T. to (b) the distance from the origin to point (2). As the debt proportion increases, point (2) moves to the right, and the ratio decreases.

Where such standards as "30 per cent of capitalization" or "3 to 1 earnings coverage" come from is usually rather obscure. Evidence suggests that these so-called "individual" company standards merely reflect some widely accepted financial conventions or what may be described less reverently as financial folklore. The 30 per cent of capitalization rule is widely quoted in a variety of industrial and competitive situations. Oftentimes, the rules relate to individual circumstances only in the sense that they have been honored for many years by the company in question and have stood the test of time—*so far.*

For many businessmen, this is sufficient. For the company attempting to measure its own risks and establish its own margins of safety, however, the generalized rules of thumb offer little in the way of guidance as to how to approach the problem. It is not within the scope of this text to attempt a detailed description of how this admittedly very difficult problem may be approached. The measurement of the risk of cash insolvency or the lesser hazard of cash inadequacy is one of the most difficult elements of finance. A brief outline of the nature of what is required is all that will be attempted here.[3]

The Analysis of Risk in the Individual Company

Every business with variable and uncertain cash inflows must be concerned about the extent to which it is committed to fixed and certain cash outflows. Every addition made to these fixed outflows increases in some degree the possibility that outflows will exceed inflows at some point in time. If this deficiency is large enough and lasts long enough, there is the threat of exhaustion of cash reserves and consequent insolvency. Thus, an appraisal of the ultimate risk of debt is an appraisal of the probability of cash insolvency and must of necessity bring into consideration the entire structure of cash inflows and outflows. For the average established business with competent management and a sound competitive position, the primary concern about debt is with what might happen to cash flows in a business recession. The obvious answer is to observe what has happened in past recessions. However, net cash flows are acted on by a number of factors, and their behavior in any particular recession is the result of a particular combination of events—the magnitude and timing of the decline in orders, the collection experience on accounts receivable, the level of inventories, and the like—which is unlikely to be repeated.

Consequently, what is needed is an examination of the range of behavior of each major determinant of cash inflow and outflow—such as collection experience on accounts receivable and expenditures for direct labor—so that the picture of the behavior of recession net cash flows will include not only those combinations of events which have occurred but also those combinations which could occur within these expectations. Such an analysis, sometimes called *simulation,* can quickly become complex. There is a question as to how far it could or would be carried in practice. The theoretical ultimate would be to produce a series of estimates of recession net cash flows—some positive and, at the adverse limit, probably some negative—with estimates of the probability of occurrence of each. Thus, it might be estimated that the combined probability of events which would produce a cash deficiency was, say, one in thirty-five.

---

[3] A more detailed treatment of this subject is contained in *Corporate Debt Capacity* by Gordon Donaldson (Boston: Division of Research, Harvard Business School, 1961).

Ideally, this is the information management would like to have. Given estimates of the chances of various recession cash positions at, above, and below the "break-even" level, it is a simple matter to "plug in" the adjustment for any given increase in debt servicing and determine the revised probability of running out of cash. The management would then have to decide whether the advantages of debt were worth the increased risk as measured by the cash flow analysis. At this point, it should be emphasized that the decision on debt capacity has two distinct elements. One is the magnitude of the risk, as described above. The other is the willingness to bear risk, which is subjective and can be decided only by those who are to bear the risk or their appointed representatives. This latter element cannot be generalized; and for this reason, generalized debt capacity rules must always be viewed with suspicion.

Having briefly described the nature of a fully refined analysis of risk in the individual business, we must add that there are serious practical restraints on carrying it to its theoretical limit. These restraints relate to the availability of the data, analytical competence to handle the data, the cost of the analysis in terms of time and money, and, not the least of these, the attitude and motivation of management in substituting an elaborate analysis for rules of thumb which have kept the company out of trouble in the past. Fortunately, there are various compromises in refinement of the cash flow analysis, which produce useful results with a moderate investment of time and relatively simple analytical tools. These are in use by some businesses today as an important supplement to the more conventional debt capacity criteria.

One such tool is the range-of-earnings chart, previously described, which the authors consider to be the most meaningful way of introducing the risk analysis in terms of the summary data found in conventional financial statements. It does not provide precise answers, but it does serve to bring out the general characteristics of risk in the particular case. In the Continental Baking case, for example, the bond alternative does not appear to be a serious threat to the company's cash position. Considering the fact that this is a relatively stable industry and that even at the lower limit of the expected range of earnings, uncommitted earnings are still higher under the bond alternative than under the common stock alternative, a solvent and sound financial position appears to have a high probability of being achieved. When this evidence is added to that of the income analysis, the bond alternative appears substantially superior to the others as far as the existing common shareholders are concerned. Not all cases are so easy to classify as this one, however, and we have not yet covered the full range of considerations in making a choice of this kind.

The Comparison with Respect to Control

Turning to the consideration of control, we can state the implications of the three alternatives briefly. Neither a new bond issue nor a preferred stock issue would alter the control of the business as exercised through shareholders' meetings and the board of directors. As suggested by the outstanding preferred issue, a new issue of this class of stock might join in the election of a minority of directors in the event of a lapse in dividend payments. The exercise of the existing provision will not involve a major upset in control but merely representation on the board (two directors to be added to a thirteen-man board). The issue of common stock, however, does involve the problem of control directly, since each new share adds one new vote. To the extent that the stock is sold to new shareholders, there is a dilution of the control of the existing shareholders, the magnitude of which will be measured by the amount of new stock in comparison with the amount of stock presently outstanding.

A convenient measure of dilution may be made as follows: Divide the old number of shares by the total of old and new to be outstanding under the proposed plan. In the case of Continental Baking, this would be:

$$\frac{1,875,000}{2,250,000} = 83\%.$$

The figure of 83 per cent is the proportion of voting power that would remain for the old holders after the dilution. It is a factor that can be used by any holder to determine his future position. Thus, if a group held 51 per cent of the voting stock before the dilution, it would have $(0.51)(0.83) = 42$ per cent afterwards. As previously discussed, this may or may not be a major consideration in the choice of the security type, depending on circumstances. It is more frequently an important matter in the case of corporations with majority control, where any prospect of dilution of voting power may not be countenanced.

The Question of Marketability

While the considerations of income, risk, and control are basic to the problem of achieving a balanced capital structure, they are by no means the only considerations. In our initial presentation of the Continental Baking expansion, we very conveniently assumed away one of the major determinants in the choice of securities, namely, the ability of the company to market successfully $15 million of bonds, preferred stock, or common stock at this time. It must be remembered that the wishes of the prospective security holder are just as important as the wishes of the issuer in bringing the two together successfully. So far, we have considered only the interests of the latter.

In spite of the size, maturity, and reputation of the company concerned, we have no basis for assuming that Continental Baking could market with equal ease $15 million of a 4¼ per cent bond, a 5½ per cent preferred stock, or a common stock priced at $40. The securities market is at best highly complex and constantly changing. The services of men experienced in the ways of the market and in constant touch with it are required to approach a statement of the possibilities at a given point of time; and even then the statement will be tentative. The acceptable type, amount, and terms of the security to be offered will vary from time to time. This is not to suggest that Continental Baking could not have marketed all three types of securities in 1960 on the terms indicated but simply to indicate that the market could not be taken for granted. The securities markets will be discussed in some detail in Chapters 22 and 23. At this point, it is sufficient to recognize that in a given situation the factors which are considered of primary importance to the company and the common shareholders may be overshadowed by the consideration of what is acceptable to the prospective security holder.

Timing the New Security Issue

Related to the question, "Can the issue be sold?" is the question, "Is this the best time to sell it?" In prosperous times the large and successful business can usually sell an issue, provided it is willing to meet the investors' terms. In our Continental Baking example, we assumed these terms to be a 4¼ per cent interest rate on the bonds, a 5½ per cent dividend rate on the preferred stock, and a price of $40 for the common stock. However, we know that the securities market is dynamic, and a month or a year later the investors' terms on any or all of these securities might have changed significantly.

How this affects our decision depends entirely on our expectations as to the future trends in the securities market. If a consideration of risk, income, and control in this case pointed to the choice of stock, for example, as the desirable medium for financing current needs, management might still pause in its decision if it felt that by waiting for, say, a year, the stock could be sold substantially above 40. Since we started by assuming that the company could sell any of the three security types, such an expectation could lead to a decision to finance through debt on a temporary basis until a more advantageous price for the common could be obtained. Far-thinking management recognizes that financing in the long run will be a combination of debt and equity sources, and its ideal is so to time its approaches to the market as to minimize the cost of senior securities and minimize the dilution resulting from new common stock issues.

There are, of course, certain obvious limitations to the achievement of this ideal. The most basic is the dynamic nature of the market and our very limited capacity to anticipate trends. Obviously, there are considerable risks in waiting a year for this hoped-for rise in the market price of common. The company's expectation could be entirely wrong, and it might ultimately be forced to sell the common below 40. This brings up a second limitation, namely, that the issuing company cannot postpone equity financing indefinitely, since it must maintain a certain balance of debt and equity at all times. The opportunities for taking advantage of market trends have certain time limits placed upon them by these circumstances.

The question of timing is equally relevant with respect to the preferred stock and bond alternatives. In late 1959, yields on corporate bonds, which had shown a steady rise since 1958, reached a peak and began to decline; and this decline continued in the early months of 1960, when we assumed this decision was to be made. At such a time, there would be a strong temptation to wait a few months in the hope that the decline would continue. Since a long-term debt contract "freezes in" the interest rate for several years, the savings resulting from waiting could be substantial. Here again, short-term debt financing might be considered as a stopgap. In such a situation, as in the parallel case of a prolonged upward trend in the market price of common stock, where there is no termination point for the market trend in sight, management finds itself in a dilemma. An indefinite postponement of going to the market seems in order. On the other hand, experience teaches that there is always a termination point to such trends, and a recognition of this and the associated risks usually leads management to limit its consideration of timing to those advantages which can be realized by postponements not in excess of a year or two.[4]

It must be emphasized that in any case where the choice of security

---

[4] Some investment bankers would argue that even this limited period is too long, in view of the risks of an unpredictable market.

indicated by the basic considerations of risk, income, and control is influenced by the factor of timing, the full implications must be recognized. Assuming the investment must go ahead anyway, a delay in the use of debt or equity in the hope of a lower interest rate or a higher market price means that some alternative source must be substituted in the interim. The risks and costs of this interim method of financing cannot be ignored.

The Need for Flexibility

Although the matter of flexibility is involved in some of the considerations already discussed, it requires special emphasis. By flexibility, we mean the capacity of the business and its management to adjust to expected and unexpected changes in circumstances. Another way of expressing it would be to say that management desires a capital structure which gives it maximum freedom to maneuver at all times. Thus, this must be a consideration each time management changes its capital structure by a new issue of securities.

In part, this is just another way of stating the timing consideration. Many managements like to keep a "reserve" of borrowing power so that if at any time it seems more expedient to use debt than equity sources, they will be free to do so. This is an argument for not borrowing up to the limits suggested by considerations of risk and investors' standards. The idea of "unused capacity" is apparent in other aspects of financial management, as in the matter of excess "reserves" of liquid assets, for example, and in a flexible dividend policy which permits the company to reinvest more or less as it seems desirable. Flexibility achieved in this manner has a price, the price being the income forgone by the reduced leverage or the inactive assets.

Flexibility taken in a broader sense, however, means more than the capacity to use all sources of capital at all times. It relates also to the specific terms of the security issue and the ways in which these terms may restrict management's freedom of action in policy decisions. This is of particular importance in regard to senior securities. In the later chapters on the bargain for funds, the various features which may be attached to securities and the implications of these for the freedom of management in making future financial decisions are taken up in some detail. At this point, it is important to note that the specific terms of each alternative issue must be known before the consideration of effects on management flexibility can be properly assessed.

Chapter 17

Dividend Policy and the Retention of Earnings

IN THE preceding chapters dealing with sources of funds, primary emphasis has been placed on negotiated sources—those which are established through a contract with parties external to the user of the funds. This was apparent in the chapters dealing with short-term sources as well as those dealing with long-term sources. It has been recognized, however, either explicitly or implicitly, that in a going and profitable concern the primary continuing source of funds is the net cash inflow from operations—the cash remaining after all current expenditures have been provided for, including the customary disbursement to the owners in the form of cash dividends. Indeed, many companies operate for years entirely on retained earnings and quite independently of negotiated external sources. The balance sheet of every mature and successful company attests to the importance of this source by the fact that the main equity component of the capital structure is not stock issued and outstanding but rather earned surplus.

In our discussions so far, we have found it convenient to take internally generated funds as given and have focused on situations where the need for funds exceeded this source, thus creating the situation where external funds must be solicited. As a part of an orderly review of long-term financial policy, it is now appropriate to turn our attention to this source and consider the ways in which management influences the role played by retained earnings in the corporate capital structure. As this subject is commonly discussed, the decision to retain a portion of the corporation's earnings for investment purposes is made by the indirect process of deciding what portion is to be paid out to the shareholders in the form of dividends. This is at most,

345

however, a difference of emphasis and may merely be a question of semantics. In some companies the needs of the shareholders may be the dominant consideration and in others the needs of the company. In any case, both should be considered. However, following the convention, we take up the discussion in terms of dividend policy.

The Nature and Form of the Dividend

A *dividend payment* is a distribution to the shareholders of something belonging to the corporation, and specifically belonging to the stockholders themselves as owners of the corporation. If a company has more than one class of shareholders, a dividend might be declared to one class and not to another, or different amounts of dividend might be paid to each class. However, all shareholders of one class of stock must be treated alike, according to the number of shares they hold. Cash payments are the most frequently used method of distribution.

The material in this chapter concentrates upon the determination of policy for the payment of cash dividends. Before doing so, however, we shall give brief consideration to the other forms a dividend payment may take. Whatever the type of payment may be, it has the effect of reducing some of the value of the business. In the accounting sense, this means that the transaction has the effect of reducing the net worth of the business, specifically the surplus. The fact that all forms of dividend payment have this effect in common has led legislators to define the legality of dividends in terms of this surplus. It must be recognized that surplus is not itself a tangible thing which can be distributed. The debit to Surplus merely records the fact that a portion of the stockholders' equity in the business has been withdrawn, usually in the form of cash. The credit to Cash records the withdrawal of the tangible asset itself. We are already well aware of the fact that this withdrawal is not a cost of the business in either the economic, the accounting, or the income tax sense.

If cash is not distributed, the most common asset which is used is stock of another corporation held by the company. Beginning in 1948, Standard Oil of Indiana began to distribute shares in Standard Oil of New Jersey along with its cash dividend. The stock being distributed had been acquired in 1932 as a part of a sale of certain foreign properties. At the outset the distribution was on the basis of one share of New Jersey stock for each 100 shares of Indiana stock held. The company has continued to make a distribution of this stock along with its cash dividend in each year since 1948. Some companies which have decided to divest themselves of a portion of their activity incorporate it separately and then distribute the resulting shares to their shareholders. This is referred to as a *spin-off*. An example of a dividend of this type is seen in the case of Textron, Inc. In the year 1953, this company suspended its cash dividend and instead distributed one share of Indian Head Mills, Inc., for every ten shares of Textron, Inc., held by its shareholders. The cash dividend was resumed in the following year.

On occasion, other types of assets have been distributed as a dividend, such as the company's own products. It will be apparent, however, that the necessity of making the distribution on a per share basis puts practical limitations on the use of assets other than cash.

The definition of a dividend which has been adopted here, namely, that the payment must be one which reduces the value of the business, excludes the *stock dividend*, which has been frequently used in recent years. Such a distribution is not correctly termed a dividend. In this case the company distributes unissued shares of its own stock to the existing shareholders in proportion to the number of outstanding shares they hold. Normally, the stock which is distributed is the same class as that held by the recipients. If so, then the proportion of ownership held by each shareholder in the business remains exactly as before, except that he has more pieces of paper as evidence of this. If the stock distributed is of a class other than the one held by the recipients, then the relative position of these two classes will be affected. In either case, however, the total assets of the business remain unchanged —nothing of value leaves the business.

Such distributions of the company's own stock have come to be known as dividends because in many instances the transaction is recorded by reducing Earned Surplus by the par value of the new shares issued, the other side of the entry being an increase in Capital Stock outstanding. Since it is the authors' opinion that the stock dividend is a type of voluntary recapitalization similar to the stock split, it will be discussed in detail in Chapter 27, and no further reference to it will be made here. We turn now to the problems of practice and policy relating to cash dividends.

Dividend Payments a Matter for the Board of Directors

The power to declare dividends rests in all cases in the discretion of the directors of the corporation. It cannot be made into an obligation of the corporation by contract or otherwise. As we have seen previously, this is one of the basic distinctions between debt instruments and equity instruments. Even the strongest preferred stock will not receive dividends unless the directors take action to vote them. A decision not to pay a dividend may have unpleasant consequences, such as a change in the membership of the board of directors, or some other change provided for in the contract creating a preferred stock; but as long as the directors have used their judgment in good faith, there is no way to force a dividend by direct legal action.

On the other hand, business practice often tends to make certain dividend payments relatively secure. As a result, investors are justified in expecting the regular payment of dividends on the better grade of preferred stocks and even on some common stocks. But since this condition is the result of a management decision and not of legal obligation, it is more useful for us to leave elaborations of the reasons why such regular dividends can be expected from certain companies until after a study of the determinants of policy.

Although, as we have just said, the law does not force dividend payments, there are well-established legal rules defining precisely under what circumstances dividends must not be paid. The provisions of the corporation laws of the various states differ in detail on this matter, but the general rule is clear that dividends may be paid only out of realized earnings, and only if the paid-in capital of the business is not "impaired."[1] The historical origin of all these legal provisions is the desire to protect creditors; that is to say, that they are to be free to assume, first, that the owners of a corporation will not reduce by dividends the amount of its original paid-in capital, and, secondly, that the owners will not distribute "paper profits"—that is, those arising from transactions like upward revaluations of property not yet sold by the company.[2]

There is a financial rule of thumb which expresses the foregoing in deceptively precise and rather dangerous terms: "Dividends may be paid out of surplus." If this were to be rephrased as follows: "The measure of the maximum dividend a corporation can pay is the amount of the earned surplus," the rule would be more safely stated. One must always avoid giving any basis for the dangerous inference that a balance sheet surplus is the *source of payment* for anything.

---

[1] Special provisions exist for corporations with wasting assets, such as mining corporations, and for the exceptional cases when ordinary corporations wish to pay liquidating dividends.

[2] Accountants never tire of pointing out that the quantities of paid-in capital, and the amounts of earnings, both realized and unrealized, are extremely difficult to determine, so that the actual decision of the precise quantities involved may be very difficult.

In the precise legal language of the Uniform Business Corporation Act[3] the rule is expressed as follows. We add also the paragraph which states the penalties on corporate management for failure to observe the law. Note that these provisions merely establish the amount that *may* be distributed.

Section 24. *Dividends: Method of Estimating Fund for Payment of.*

I. Every corporation formed shall carry upon its books as a liability the amount of its capital stock as defined in Section I, subdivision X.

II. Amounts of surplus arising from an unrealized appreciation or revaluation of fixed assets shall be shown on the books of the corporation as a separate item apart from surplus profits or paid-in surplus.

III. In computing the aggregate of the assets of the corporation, the board of directors shall determine and make proper allowance for depreciation and depletion sustained, and losses of every character. Deferred assets and prepaid expenses shall be written off at least annually in proportion to their use as may be determined by the board of directors.

IV. No corporation shall pay dividends

(*a*) in cash or property, except from the surplus of the aggregate of its assets over the aggregate of its liabilities, including in the latter the amount of its capital stock, after deducting from such aggregate of its assets the amount by which such aggregate was increased by unrealized appreciation in value or revaluation of fixed assets;

(*b*) in shares of the corporation, except from the surplus of the aggregate of its assets over the aggregate of its liabilities, including in the latter the amount of its capital stock.

Section 25. *Liability of Directors and Shareholders for Dividends Unlawfully Paid or Corporate Assets Otherwise Unlawfully Returned.*

If any dividend be paid in violation of Section 24, or if any other unlawful distribution, payment or return of assets be made to shareholders,

I. The directors who knowingly, or without making reasonable inquiry, voted in favor thereof shall be jointly and severally liable to the corporation in an amount equal to the amount of the dividend so paid and the distribution, payment or return of assets so made;

II. Every shareholder who received any such dividend or any such distribution, payment or return of assets shall in the following instances be individually liable to the corporation in an amount equal to the amount so received by him:

(*a*) when no director is liable to the corporation as provided in subdivision I of this Section, or

(*b*) to the extent that the corporation is unable to obtain satisfaction after judgments recovered against directors upon the liability imposed by subdivision I of this Section.[4]

---

[3] Uniform Business Corporation Act as drafted by the National Conference of Commissioners on Uniform State Laws, 1928.

[4] *Ibid.*, pp. 49–52.

Payment of Dividends Greater than Earnings

Since the law in the United States permits the payment of dividends as long as there is an amount of earned surplus large enough to absorb the payment, it is possible for companies to pay more than the amount of current earnings in a period of low activity, if earned surplus was retained in previous profitable years. It is interesting to note that in certain other countries, companies are not permitted to draw upon past earnings in this way. Such is the case in England, where dividends may only be paid up to the amount of the earnings of the current year. In other countries, such as Italy, in addition, corporations are required to transfer a certain percentage of each year's earnings to a paid-in reserve account before dividends can be considered.

In the United States, if by operation during economic depression or for other reasons, companies find themselves without any surplus on their balance sheet to support the payment of a dividend, yet desire to make payments, adjustment of the corporation's capital structure can be made to transfer values from the stated or paid-in capital account to distributable surplus. This must be done after due notice to stockholders, followed by a vote taken at a meeting of stockholders entitled to vote. The publicity given to the move is considered to give adequate protection to creditors, in place of the absolute rule otherwise in force.

Limitation by Contract of a Company's Freedom to Pay Dividends

Since most companies would not consider the payment of dividends under conditions which would impair their capital, it is much more important to discuss the self-imposed restrictions on freedom to pay dividends which managements accept by contract in the bargain for funds. Many times, companies find it desirable to limit the ability of the directors to make dividend payments. As we have already seen, such promises are often made in loan agreements, and the same situation exists in many preferred stock contracts with reference to dividends on common stock. It is the existence of such provisions in the contracts of senior securities or in the charter or bylaws of a corporation that often leads to considerable restriction in the possibility of declaring dividends upon common shares. Anyone studying the position of a stock of a company must therefore include in his study reference to the *protective provisions* in senior securities.

The type of contractual limitation which restricts the freedom of a company to declare dividends is usually expressed in terms of the necessity to maintain a certain financial position, or a certain level of earnings. This type of provision has already been referred to in previous material, but it is useful to quote an example of a term-loan restriction here: "Company may not pay cash dividends on common or acquire stock in excess of consolidated net income after December 28, 1957, plus $2,500,000 and provided consolidated net working capital is not less than $10,000,000. At December 26, 1959, $4,073,247 of retained earnings were not so restricted."[5]

In the preferred stock contract the most frequently encountered provision defining when dividends may not be paid is that which requires the accumulation of unpaid preferred dividends. A typical provision of this type might read as follows:

The holders of the $6.00 preference stock shall be entitled to receive, if and as declared by the board of directors, dividends from the surplus of the company or from its net profits at the rate of $6.00 per annum, per share, and no more, payable quarterly on the first days of January, April, July, and October in each year. Such dividends shall be paid or declared and set apart for payment before any dividends shall be paid upon, or declared and set apart for, the common stock of the company, and shall be cumulative from and after January 1, 19—, so that if in any quarterly dividend period thereafter dividends at the rate of $6.00 per annum per share shall not have been paid upon, or declared and set apart for, the $6.00 preference stock, the deficiency shall be fully paid or declared and set apart for payment before any dividends shall be paid upon, or declared and set apart for, common stock of the company.

Taxation and Dividend Policy

Before we leave the topic of the legal rules imposed by statute and contract which limit freedom in the area of dividend policy, we should make brief reference to the laws of taxation, for there one can find examples of provisions which give strong incentive either to pay dividends or not to pay them, depending upon the law and the particular circumstances of a company. For example, frequent reference is made in financial journals to the paradoxical situation of the stockholder who does not want to receive dividends because he must pay a higher rate of personal income tax upon the dividends that he might receive than on capital gains that he may realize by selling the stock later on. Publicly owned corporations with scattered shareholders

---

[5] Term loan of General Baking Company, as stated in *Moody's Industrial Manual*, *1960*, p. 1136.

seldom have to worry about stockholders of this kind, but closely held companies do sometimes give consideration to this factor in determining the amount of cash dividends to be distributed. In view of this fact, there exist Sections 531–37 of the United States Revenue Code (1954), to which we have referred previously. It will be recalled that this provision of the Code may be used to penalize those corporations which unnecessarily retain earnings for the purpose of benefiting the personal income tax position of their shareholders. There exists a considerable body of specialized knowledge about how this provision must be regarded, but it will not be discussed here because of the narrow range of companies to which in fact it might be applied.

Laws of general applicability also exist which apply the power of taxation in such a manner as to give incentives to pay or not to pay dividends. From 1936 to 1939 the United States had in force a Surtax on Undistributed Profits, which in 1936 and 1937 caused many companies to increase their dividend payments (because of the extra tax which was levied on profits retained). In later years the rates of surtax were reduced, and the effect was much smaller, although in the same direction. On the other hand, beginning in 1947, Great Britain imposed a special tax on *distributed* profits. This has, of course, had exactly the opposite effect to the American law.

Procedure in Voting and Distributing a Dividend

In the United States, it has become customary to consider the question of dividends quarterly. In fact, when a company has been paying dividends regularly, a certain meeting of the board comes to be recognized as the *dividend meeting*, at which the matter of dividends comes up on the agenda. There are only a few companies in America which pay dividends at other intervals, such as monthly or annually. In other countries, this is not always the case. Particularly in those countries where the law requires that a corporation shall not pay more than it has earned in a particular year, it is not uncommon for companies to make payments on an annual basis after the determination of the earnings has been made by the company's accountant. Concerns in these countries which are rather sure of their earnings estimates may make advance payments, but they leave the bulk of the dividend to be paid at the end of the year. The relative infrequency of such payments and their unequal amounts makes the ownership of stocks a little less attractive to the average investor than is the case in the United States.

At the dividend meeting the board of directors considers not only the amount of the dividend but also the form it will take. In describing the procedure here, we shall concern ourselves only with cash dividends. The vote which the board takes will specify the amount, the date of payment, and the *record date.* Just after the dividend meeting a formal notice is often given to the financial journals in words like these:

"The board of directors has this day declared a quarterly dividend of 25 cents per share on the capital stock of this corporation, payable September 15, 1961, to shareholders of record August 30, 1961. Checks will be mailed." (Published August 16, 1961.)

The record date is established because it is necessary for dividend checks to be prepared for all the shareholders, and time is needed to make up these checks from an address list which will not change. Hence, a record date is established which is commonly a week or two weeks before the payable date. In the days before the development of fast-moving clerical machinery, the *transfer books* were *closed* for the period between the record date and the payable date, and no transfer of securities could take place, although, of course, sales and purchases did take place with the new owner waiting for formal transfer until the transfer books were reopened. At present, the closing is not necessary.

In the case of securities which are traded on registered exchanges, an *ex-dividend date* is established by the rules of the exchange. It is calculated from the record date with a time advance from that date to allow for the usual mechanics of delivery and transfer of securities that have been sold. On and after this ex-dividend date a stock is sold to the buyer without any right on his part to claim the dividend that has been declared. It goes to the former owner. Therefore, the market price of the stock should drop by the amount of the dividend involved between the closing price of the previous day and the opening price of the ex-dividend day. In fact, however, other market forces tend to obscure this change.

Beginning on the record date the dividend-paying agency or officer of the corporation prepares checks for the correct amount of the dividend to be sent to each shareholder. Oftentimes, the corporation takes advantage of this mailing to include *dividend stuffers:* letters to shareholders which contain information about the company and its affairs—quite frequently the most recent interim financial reports. The checks are placed in the mails either on the payable date or according to a schedule which will cause the checks to arrive at the address of record on the day the checks are payable.[6]

The Elements of a Dividend Policy

Before considering what we mean by the term *dividend policy*, we should take note of the fact that there are many companies which do not pay any dividends. This may be the result of an inability to realize the earnings which are the legal and financial prerequisite to such payments. It may also result from a deliberate policy of retention of all earnings for the purpose of financing growth. Such companies may come to be known as *growth companies*, and their shareholders should be those who prefer the idea of realizing their reward through capital gains rather than annual income.

The concept of a dividend policy implies that businesses through their boards of directors evolve a recognizable pattern of cash dividend payments which has a bearing on future action. Undoubtedly, some businesses do not have a dividend policy in this sense but rather act as if each dividend decision was completely independent of every other such decision. However, the results of a study of dividend policies in large industrial corporations in the United States strongly suggest that in the majority of cases, current dividend decisions are intimately related to previous dividend decisions.[7] In this study, cited below, Professor Lintner has concluded that management typically takes the existing dividend rate as its starting point and views the dividend decision as a question of whether or not to change this rate in the current period. He further concludes that while there is a feeling of responsibility to share increased earnings with the stockholders, there is a general resistance on the part of management to any change which may only be temporary and consequently a certain inertia which favors the continuance of the existing rate unless there are strong and persistent reasons to change. At this point, we simply report these findings without passing any comment as to whether or not such action appears to be a rational and sensible policy. It is clear that this action produces a strong tendency to regularity of dividend payments.

The term *regular dividend* has been used to mean a variety of

---

[6] Every corporation with any sizable list of shareholders always finds that a few checks are not cashed from each dividend payment, and these are accumulated in a special liability fund for later claim by the stockholders when they discover their right.

[7] See John Lintner, "Distribution of Incomes of Corporations among Dividends, Retained Earnings and Taxes," *American Economic Review*, Papers and Proceedings (May, 1956), pp. 97–113.

things. It may mean simply that a company has paid *something* in each year over a certain period. More significantly, it may mean regularity in dollar amount, for example, American Telephone and Telegraph's $9.00 per year paid without interruption from 1922 to 1959, at which time the stock was split and the dividend increased. The term may also refer to a regular *pay-out* as a percentage of earnings or a regular pattern of change in dollar amounts. Obviously, from the shareholders' point of view, there is a great deal of difference among these different forms of regularity.

It should be noted here that in the usage of the securities market the term *regular dividend* is employed in certain situations to draw a distinction between that portion of a cash dividend which is expected to continue from year to year and an additional payment, known as an *extra* dividend. An example of the use of such terms is seen in the following excerpt from the 1956 annual report of Standard Brands, Inc.:

> Dividends totalling $7,331,731 equivalent to $2.25 per share, were declared and paid on the common stock during 1956. This total, which compares with $2.15 per share paid during 1955, comprised quarterly dividends of $0.50 each, plus an extra dividend of $0.25 in December.
>
> A regular quarterly dividend of $0.50 per share was declared on the common stock, payable on March 15, 1957.

The significance of this distinction is that there is not the same commitment to continue the extra dividend as there is on the regular dividend. If and when the time comes when the added earnings upon which the extra dividend has been based prove to be permanent, the extra dividend is likely to become a part of the regular dividend, and the distinction would then be dropped.

When dividend payments in the past have shown a certain regularity, this becomes a basis for confidence in forecasting what future dividends will be. Unfortunately, regularity as applied to dividend payments is rarely if ever an absolute term, and what we really mean is that the business in question is more regular than some other businesses. Thus, a degree of uncertainty remains; and the vital question as to what may be expected in the future has—for the shareholder, at least—no sure answer.

In this situation, it is natural that shareholders of a public corporation search for clues as to the basis upon which management approaches the dividend question. Speaking generally, management is remarkably noncommittal on its future plans for dividend payments. The typical annual report dismisses the topic of dividends with a brief statement such as: "Quarterly dividends on the common stock totaled $1.20 per share." Most managements shy away from any statement which remotely resembles a promise for the future, and this is consistent with a literal interpretation of the traditional concept of a common shareholder as a guarantor of payments to others rather than the recipient of a guaranteed or promised payment. On the other hand, there are some companies which make comparatively forthright statements of intent as, for example, that which is found in the 1955 annual report of the Standard Oil Company (Indiana): "On June 30 we announced that our present intention for the next several years is to continue to supplement regular cash dividends by a special dividend in an amount sufficient to bring our total dividend declaration in any year to about 50 per cent of that year's earnings." This policy has been adhered to in the years since 1955.

Some companies come very close to a statement of dividend policy by the somewhat oblique method of commenting on past performance. Thus, for example, the annual report of General Electric for 1959 commented that dividends for the year were "62% of net earnings for the year, compared with 71% in 1958, and this compares with an average rate of 66% for the past 61 years." Other annual reports make similar, if somewhat less encouraging, comments on policy. Thus, the B. F. Goodrich Company's annual report for 1955 stated: "Dividends in 1955 reflect the company's practice in recent years of financing requirements for continued expansion and growth from earnings retained in the business." The report of American Motors for 1954 stated: "American Motors paid an initial dividend of 12½¢ in the June quarter. . . . No payments have been made since, our directors believing that it is advisable to conserve working capital until such time as future earnings warrant resumption of payments." At the time, the shareholders had no way of estimating how long it would be before dividends were resumed. In fact, they had to wait until 1959.

The Determinants of Dividend Policy

In the comprehensive study of dividend policy to which we referred earlier (see page 354), the typical established business was observed to take as its starting point the dividend rate of the preceding period and to be reluctant to depart from this rate (up or down) unless there were clear and compelling reasons to do so. This followed from a strong desire to avoid an erratic pattern of payments symptomatic of hasty decisions based on incomplete knowledge of the future. We now quote from Professor Lintner's article:

> . . . The principal device used to achieve this consistent pattern was a practice or policy of changing dividends in any given year by only part of the amounts which were indicated by changes in current financial figures. Further partial adjustments in dividend rates were then made in subsequent years if still warranted. This policy of progressive, continuing "partial adaptation" tends to stabilize dividend distributions and provides a consistency in the pattern of dividend action which helps to minimize adverse stockholder reactions. At the same time it enables management to live more comfortably with its unavoidable uncertainties regarding future developments. . . .[8]

At the same time, this study indicated a general agreement on the part of management that dividends should be related to current earnings. This was evidenced by widespread acceptance of some specific ratio of dividends to earnings as being reasonable for the company concerned. This pay-out ratio varied widely from company to company, but remained fixed for a given company over time. On the face of it, the idea of a fixed pay-out ratio runs contrary to the observed deep-rooted reluctance to change. In practice the reconciliation is brought about by the use of the pay-out ratio as a target, toward which the established dividend rate will be partially adjusted period by period.

The reader will observe that in this brief summary of a portion of the report on current business practice in the area of dividend decisions, we have only begun to touch on the basic determinants of dividend policy. Given the current business practice which is generally appropriate (or, at least, which is generally accepted by business as appropriate), there remain the unanswered questions as to how and why a company selects a particular target pay-out ratio and determines its rate of adjustment toward this target. Since we have been talking only about going concerns with an established record of dividend payments, there is also the question of how a company which is planning its first dividend payment will make this decision.

The fact is that we cannot arrive at a specific answer to any policy decision on a general basis since in the last analysis the decision must take into account the special circumstances of the individual case. On the other hand, careful observation and intelligent interpretation of general practice is of real assistance in narrowing down the

---

[8] *Ibid.*, p. 100.

area of study and in confirming the analysis in the individual case. Our next step, therefore, is to consider in general terms those determinants of dividend policy which are observed to be of major importance in the typical business situation. We shall then leave it to the reader to assess their applicability in the individual case and to fill in whatever additional considerations he may find to have a bearing on the decision.

1. Relation of Dividends to Earnings. As previously indicated, the starting point of dividend policy is the earnings of the business. We have seen that a business is legally entitled to pay dividends up to an amount equal to the net accumulated earnings of the business to date. Practically speaking, the upper limit on dividends tends to be set by the earnings of the current period, since the retained earnings of previous years generally become a part of the permanent investment of the business upon which current earnings are based. On the other hand, we have noted the observed inertia in dividend payments and the widespread reluctance to reduce, as well as to increase, dividends. In fact, it appears that the reluctance to reduce dividends is greater than the hesitancy in increasing them. It is also apparent, however, that a company cannot continue to pay dividends in excess of earnings over extended periods of time without impairing the future earning capacity of the business and therefore future dividends.

As a consequence, a rational dividend policy must take account of the amount and behavior of year-to-year earnings. Since dividend policy is by definition forward-looking, it must be based not only on earnings already realized, which provide the funds for the current dividend distribution, but also on anticipated earnings. The reader will be well aware of the fact that the pattern of change in earnings varies widely among industries and individual companies. Earnings may be so variable as to be largely unpredictable, or they may show a definite trend which may be up, down, or generally stable. They may be influenced by heavy leverage of senior securities, or there may be no leverage at all. Change from year to year may be abrupt or very gradual. The specific characteristics applying to a particular case are of obvious importance to a plan for the distribution of these earnings.

2. The Alternative of Reinvestment. In any dynamic business, there will be many alternative uses for the funds which are available to it. This applies to the funds provided from operations equally as much as to any other source. Consequently, dividend payments will be competing with other possible uses for the current earnings dollar. The basic choice that must be made by the board of directors is whether the earnings will be distributed to the shareholders or whether they will be reinvested in the business for strengthening of the existing earning capacity and for growth. Table 17–1 clearly indicates that with the possible exception of periods of general depression, the large majority of businesses consistently reinvest a substan-

TABLE 17–1

CORPORATE INCOME AND DIVIDEND PAYMENTS IN THE UNITED STATES, ALL INDUSTRIES, 1935–59

(In Billions of Dollars)

Year	Corporate Income before Tax	Corporate Income after Tax	Net Corporate Dividend Payments	Retained Earnings
1935........	3.1	2.2	2.9	− 0.7
1936........	5.7	4.3	4.5	− 0.2
1937........	6.2	4.7	4.7	0.0
1938........	3.3	2.3	3.2	− 0.9
1939........	6.4	5.0	3.8	1.2
1940........	9.3	6.5	4.0	2.4
1941........	17.0	9.4	4.5	4.9
1942........	20.9	9.5	4.3	5.2
1943........	24.6	10.5	4.5	6.0
1944........	23.3	10.4	4.7	5.7
1945........	19.0	8.3	4.7	3.6
1946........	22.6	13.4	5.8	7.7
1947........	29.5	18.2	6.5	11.7
1948........	33.0	20.5	7.2	13.3
1949........	26.4	16.0	7.5	8.5
1950........	40.6	22.8	9.2	13.6
1951........	42.2	19.7	9.0	10.7
1952........	36.7	17.2	9.0	8.3
1953........	38.3	18.1	9.2	8.9
1954........	34.1	16.8	9.8	7.0
1955........	44.9	23.0	11.2	11.8
1956........	44.7	23.5	12.1	11.3
1957........	43.2	22.3	12.6	9.7
1958........	37.7	19.1	12.4	6.7
1959........	47.0	23.8	13.4	10.5

SOURCES: Office of Business Economics, Department of Commerce, *U.S. Income and Output: A Supplement to the Survey of Current Business* (Washington, D.C., 1958), Table 1–8, pp. 126–27, for figures through 1955; *Survey of Current Business*, July, 1960, Table 2, p. 8, for figures for 1956–59.

tial fraction of current earnings. In view of the natural desire of the owners for an immediate income from their investment, there must be compelling reasons which would lead business to follow a regular practice of turning approximately 50 per cent of the earnings back into the business.

The obvious question presents itself as to which is the governing consideration—dividends or the needs of the business for new capital. In previous chapters, we have identified the problem of selecting new investment opportunities and of choosing the "right" combination of sources from which the necessary funds will be obtained. Later chapters will deal with this subject at greater length. The reader is now aware that common equity capital is generally a relatively high-cost source of funds; and from the point of view of maximizing profits, debt and preferred stock are preferable. On the other hand, businesses must have a balance of these sources; and if this balance is to be maintained, new financing means new equity capital sooner or later. Given this need, the alternatives are new common stock issues or retained earnings.

In Chapter 21 we shall develop an approximation of the cost of retained earnings and of new common stock issues. Some of the conclusions of that chapter are of significance here. One is that from a profit standpoint, new investments should not be made unless they are expected to earn a return which is at least equal to the cost of the funds which will be used to finance them. As a potential source of such funds, retained earnings are found to have a cost which is measured in terms of alternative investment opportunities of comparable risk outside the business, and this cost is incorporated into the general standard for a cutoff point on new investment. Obviously, if there are no investment opportunities which meet this standard, the source would not be used, and the earnings would be distributed as dividends.

On the other hand, we observe that where there are such opportunities, which must be financed in part by equity capital, there is strong pressure for the use of retained earnings rather than new common stock issues. In defining the cost of retained earnings, our reasoning leads us to the general conclusion that, although normally high relative to debt, it is significantly less than that for new stock issues. It is therefore quite conceivable that under circumstances of abundant opportunities for profitable expansion, all of the current earnings could be usefully retained in the business. In this situation the distribution of earnings to shareholders would appear to be contrary to their best (economic) interests, and any dividend policy which favored the maintenance of some dividend payment would be under considerable pressure.

There are also certain practical reasons why retained earnings appeal to management as a source of funds. As compared to other external sources, retained earnings have the advantage of being immediately available to the business as they are realized, and the decision is merely one of whether or not to continue to use them. There is no problem of negotiation with sources of supply and no uncertainty, at least as regards earnings realized to date. There is also the fact that the cost of retained earnings, in terms of alternative investment uses forgone, is less tangible than that for bonds or stocks, does not involve immediate and obvious cash drains, and therefore may tend to be given less weight by a management preoccupied with day-to-day financial problems.

The line of reasoning based on our discussion of corporate investment decisions would appear to lead us to the conclusion that, given the current level of earnings, dividend policy would be a sort of by-product of the capital budget. The dividends paid would fluctuate from year to year, depending on investment opportunities within the company as compared with those without, and would be that portion of current earnings which could not be profitably reinvested.

The reader will note that this does not appear to square with observed business practice, previously cited, which shows a strong preference for stability and regularity in dividend payments. However, the observed practice regarding dividends is not necessarily inconsistent with the idea of adjusting the proportion of retained earnings in accordance with investment opportunities. Viewed over a period of years, the policy of partial adjustment toward a fixed target pay-out ratio means that in a period of developing prosperity, rising earnings will always have a lead over rising dividends. As a consequence, there is increased earnings retention at a time when investment opportunities are becoming more numerous and more profitable. In a period of recession the same reluctance to change means that dividend payments tend to take an increasing proportion of current earnings and may even exceed them. Since this is a period when investment opportunities are few or nonexistent, the resultant decline in retained earnings is unlikely to be in serious conflict with management's investment objectives.

3. The Effect of Dividends on the Investment Worth of the Company's Stocks. A matter of primary interest to management, especially shareholder-oriented management, is the relationship of dividends and dividend policy to the investment worth of the common stock. This would appear to be directly related to the preceding discussion of reinvestment versus distribution because—in theory, at least—the investment worth of a stock at any given time would be the present value of the stream of earnings which is expected to flow from the investment. Since a dividend is by definition a distribution of something of value, it would seem that by reducing the earning assets of the business, the payment of a dividend would thereby reduce the investment worth of the stock below what it would have been if the funds had been retained.

Unfortunately, observation of the securities market fails to show an easy and uncomplicated relationship of this nature; in fact, the precise effect on market value of reinvestment and dividend policies is not at all clear. The analytical task of measuring the impact on market prices of any given consideration such as dividend payments is one of unusual complexity in view of the wide variety of possible considerations and the highly subjective process of translating these into quantitative terms. When we add to this the fact that the market is made up of many different kinds of investors with substantially different objectives and that emotion as well as reason has its influence, there is little reason to wonder that clear-cut answers are hard to come by.

However, there are some things which can be said by way of useful generalization to set the limits on this relationship between dividends and market prices. Let us first be clear that our primary interest is in the effects of dividend policy rather than the effects of any particular dividend payment. We have already noted that there is an observed pattern of market price in response to the periodic dividend payment which involves a build-up to the date when the list of dividend recipients is drawn up and a drop on the ex-dividend date by the amount of the dividend. Our interest here is in such policy questions as the probable effects on market price of regular versus fluctuating dividends, high versus low dividend pay-out, and changes in dividend pay-out.

These questions are of obvious importance to the common shareholders, whose opportunities for gain (or loss) include changes in market price of the securities as well as dividend income. They are also vital to management, even though it may not be closely identified with the common shareholder, for the equally obvious reason that these questions bear directly on the salability of new issues of common stock and on the number of shares which must be sold to raise a given amount of money.

One thing is clear, and that is that the market does not uniformly accept the line of reasoning we suggested at the outset, which implied that the more paid out in dividends, the less the value of what remained in the business. On the contrary, observation suggests that an increase in the dividend payment normally acts to raise market price rather than lower it, and there are several reasons why this should be expected. First, let us note that while there are some shareholders whose income tax bracket might lead them to prefer no dividends at all, the great majority of shareholders attach some importance to income as well as capital gains, and that a substantial number of individual and institutional shareholders consider dividends as all-important. The latter shareholders would, as a result, tend to discount to some extent the capital gains potential of reinvested earnings.

To these shareholders, reinvested earnings would be of interest primarily as a basis for the preservation of and increase in the current dividend rate. Expectations as to future dividends are normally based on the dividend record of the immediate past. If a company has had a record of regularity in dividend payments and the dividend rate has been recently increased, investors may very naturally expect that this increased rate will continue and thus be prepared to pay a higher market price for the stock. In view of the fact that such increases are usually small relative to the existing earning assets of the business, the market may well ignore the effect on earning capacity which might follow from reduced earnings retention. It is possible, of course, that extreme changes in dividend pay-out over short periods of time might raise questions as to future earnings and dividend-paying capacity. However, changes are frequently small enough, the remaining margin of earnings over dividends large enough, and the level of earnings sufficiently uncertain in any event that this aspect may be discounted completely.

It is not our intention here to leave the reader with the impression that dividends are all-important in market price determination but rather to bring out that they may be more important than has often been suggested in writings on the subject. We must continue to remind ourselves of the wide variations in shareholder objectives and among company shareholder groups, and remember that this has a major bearing on how they will respond to various dividend policies. There are, for example, the so-called "growth companies," which over long periods have paid out little or nothing in dividends and yet have experienced a steady rise in the market price of their stock and a flattering price/earnings ratio.

If, however, we conclude that there is the possibility, if not the probability, of raising the level of the market price by raising the dividend rate, this is of real significance in management decisions.

For example, it has a bearing on the question of new financing. Here, management may find itself in something of a dilemma. By raising the dividend rate, it may be possible to make a new issue more attractive, raise the issue price, and lower the number of shares required to be sold, thus reducing the dilution of equity and control. On the other hand, increased dividend payments mean less funds available from internal sources. The issue may turn on the extent of the response in market price which is expected to follow from the change in the dividend. In addition to the difficulty of forecasting the precise effect of the increase in dividend on market price, there is an ethical question as to whether it is appropriate for management to attempt to "manipulate" the market in this manner, particularly if it knows that the increase in dividend cannot or will not be maintained.

So far, we have been focusing on market price responses to changes in dividend pay-out. There is also the question of the relative desirability of stable dividend payments versus payments which follow closely the swings of business earnings. From the dividend study cited earlier, it would appear that the majority of established businesses have followed a dividend policy with the built-in assumption that shareholders prefer stability. If this is so, then we might conclude that the market price of a stock with a stable dividend payment should be higher than that of a similar stock with payments which fluctuate about an average of equal amount. In contrast to this, one investment authority maintains that a stable dividend policy is often attained at the cost of a comparatively low dividend pay-out, thus working to the long-term disadvantage of the shareholder.[9]

While it might be assumed that a company's dividend policy would be determined by its stockholders, it is sometimes claimed that the reverse is true, namely, that the company's dividend policy determines the stockholder group. Thus, a company with low pay-out and heavy reinvestment attracts stockholders interested in capital gains rather than current income subject to a personal income tax. A company with a stable dividend policy is said to attract those who look to it as a source of regular income. Likewise, a company with a high pay-out attracts those who emphasize immediate income. While there is undoubtedly some truth in this, the idea carries the questionable implication that any policy which suits the management is all right, since those shareholders who do not like it will sell out to those who do. Such an approach would have a certain appeal for manage-

---

[9] B. Graham and D. L. Dodd, *Security Analysis* (3d ed.; New York: McGraw-Hill Book Co., Inc., 1951), p. 596.

ment, particularly in those companies where a diverse stockholder group makes it difficult to develop a policy which suits everyone.

4. The Relation of Dividend Policy to Cash Flows and Liquidity. Whatever the considerations which dominate its thinking in the setting of dividend policy, management must take account of the obvious fact that dividends involve an outflow of cash and therefore that dividend payments must be fitted into the company's cash budget. Even when dividend policy is carefully tied to a capital budget which makes adequate provision for needed funds through retained earnings and other sources, the precise matching of cash inflows and outflows remains a problem.

The reader should now be well aware of the fact that a given number of dollars of earnings in a period does not automatically produce an equivalent sum in cash at the end of the period. In a dynamic business, profit as an element of the selling price is almost immediately subject to reinvestment in the working capital stream. Thus, the payment of a dividend at the end of the period often constitutes a diversion of funds from active use.

Because of seasonal, cyclical, or random variations in cash inflows and outflows, the cash position of the business must be subject to constant reappraisal. At any point in time, there may be many needs competing with dividends for the cash which is expected to be available over the forecast period. Some of these are mandatory, others optional and in varying degrees of urgency. Increases in working capital, replacement of productive equipment, payments to a sinking fund, retirement of debt—these are typical of alternatives which may have high priority. Shareholders may view dividends as a distribution of what is rightfully theirs, but the corporate officer responsible for the management of funds sees them as a reduction in usable cash, and it is an unusual company that could not usefully employ the cash in other ways.

In a business with a strained cash position, for any one of a number of possible reasons, dividends are likely to have low priority because of their noncontractual nature. Here, we can hardly justify the use of the term *dividend policy*, since dividends are likely to have been the result of a series of *ad hoc* decisions, each of which was dominated by the circumstances at the time. On the other hand, a business which is able to preserve a margin of liquidity at all times, through one or a combination of bank balances and highly liquid short-term investments and reserve borrowing capacity, is in a better position to put into practice a dividend policy which has a degree of consistency over time. The company is then able to draw on its reserves of cash, or its equivalent, to meet a temporarily unbalanced budget instead of using the alternative of cutting out planned expenditures of low priority.

5. *Other Considerations.* In any dividend policy decision, there may be a variety of considerations in addition to those already mentioned.[10] To suggest that those we have emphasized are more fundamental than some others is not to imply that they will be dominant at all times and in all situations. When one becomes familiar with the details of a particular business situation, other considerations will undoubtedly emerge; and in the last analysis, they may dominate the decision, at least for a time. Such factors as the dividend policy of other similar businesses in the same industry, restrictions on dividend policy imposed by debt contracts, the extent to which management identifies itself with the common shareholders, the nature of the capital structure, the existence of influential shareholders with special investment objectives, and other considerations must be weighed in the balance.

In view of the variety of considerations which may bear on the dividend question, it is unlikely that any one dividend policy will be completely satisfactory in all respects. Whatever course of action is chosen is likely to be a compromise of conflicting objectives. Thus, management is found in the familiar position of having to assess the relative importance of the relevant factors and choose that course of action which is of maximum advantage in the light of the circumstances of the business and the objectives of its shareholders. The task is sometimes complicated by the fact that this is one of those critical decisions which tends to bring into the open latent conflicts of interest between management per se and the shareholders, or between one shareholder group and another.

Dividends on Preferred Stock

The preferred stock, like the common stock, represents a share in ownership. Consequently, there can be no guaranty of dividends or of return of the original investment. As explained previously, the chief enforceable right possessed by the preferred shareholder is to receive dividends upon some predetermined basis before any distribution to the common shareholder. The decision as to whether to declare any dividends at all still rests with the board of directors. Thus,

---

[10] The reader may wish to read the list of considerations given by Professor Lintner on page 104 of the article cited earlier in this chapter.

unlike the payment of bond interest, which is mandatory, the payment of preferred dividends calls for a policy decision. It is useful to consider the reasons why the decision on preferred stock may differ from the decision on common stock of the same company at the same point of time.

The investor who buys preferred stock in preference to common of the same company expects greater assurance of regular income from such stock. This expectation is not based on any formal promise but rather on inferences drawn from the stock form and from the way in which management uses this form in its capital structure. The fact that the dividend is expressed as a fixed percentage or dollar amount, coupled with the cumulative provision that all unpaid dividends of prior years must be paid in full before any common dividend can be declared, implies an intention on the part of management to pay a regular fixed return if it is financially able so to do. Some managements accept this as a kind of moral obligation and will defer payment only under extreme conditions where payment would constitute an unnecessary hazard to the solvency of the business. This greater sense of responsibility in the case of preferred dividends is often reflected in management's efforts to keep an appropriate balance in the capital structure between a total of bonds and preferred stock, on the one hand, and common stock, on the other, so that the fixed charge of bond interest and the quasi-fixed charge of preferred dividends may be covered without strain.

A second reason for a variation in policy between preferred and common stock becomes apparent from a consideration of balance in the capital structure. It is, of course, obvious that if a dividend is to be paid at all, it must be paid equally to all shareholders of a given class of stock. If, as is often the case, the preferred issue is small relative to the common issue, the cash drain of a preferred dividend may be easily handled, whereas the cash drain of the common may not. This may still be true even if the company is not earning a return on total investment equivalent to the dividend rate on the preferred.

If the nature of the company or the state of the market is such that preferred stock is more salable than common, or if it is considered by management as better suited to its circumstances and objectives, then there will be pressure to keep the capital market receptive by maintaining regular dividend payments on preferred. If these conditions do not apply, or if the business is not in need of additional outside capital in the foreseeable future, the reaction of present or potential investors to dividend policy may be of little concern.

When the board of directors identifies itself with the interests of the common shareholder, as is usually the case, there will be a strong desire to maintain regular preferred dividends in order to permit the payment of common dividends. If successive preferred dividends are passed, it becomes increasingly unlikely that common dividends will be paid because of the accumulated arrears. This situation will be reflected in a depressed market price for both the common and the preferred stock. There have been many instances where preferred arrearages were so large that it was impossible to clear them up and the only hope for the common shareholder was to secure the consent of the preferred group to a recapitalization which wiped out the claim.

To these considerations which may lead to a somewhat different attitude on the part of management toward the preferred dividends may be added the matter of control. Preferred issues frequently provide that in the event that dividends are passed for a certain period of time, the preferred shareholders will come to have a voice in management. In its extreme form, this provision may give full voting

TABLE 17–2

PREFERRED STOCKS IN ARREARS

Preferred Stocks Listed on New York Stock Exchange

Date (Beginning of Each Year)	Total Number of Issues	Number of Domestic Issues In Arrears
1941	401	116
1942	398	98
1943	404	92
1944	392	69
1945	395	62
1946	388	48
1947	401	37
1948	415	30
1949	433	32
1950	440	33
1951	433	29
1952	441	26
1953	455	19
1954	461	20
1955	456	18
1956	432	17
1957	425	17
1958	424	18
1959	421	12
1960	415	9
1961	402	10

SOURCE: Department of Research and Statistics, New York Stock Exchange.

rights at shareholders' meetings on a "one vote per-share" basis, or participation may be restricted to the right to elect one or more directors. To a board of directors which is jealous of its power, this possibility may be taken very seriously.

For one or more of these various reasons, management will usually have a desire to keep preferred dividends current. On the other hand, there are times, particularly during depression periods, when it is unable to do so. A measure of the frequency of this occurrence is seen in Table 17–2, which shows how many of the domestic preferred stocks listed on the New York Stock Exchange were in arrears during the years 1941 to 1961. The high percentage in arrears in 1941 (over 25 per cent) reflects the aftereffects of the depression of the thirties.

PART VI

The Details of Specific Long-Term Financial Contracts

Chapter 18

Obtaining the Use of Assets without Ownership

In the past four chapters, we have presented the basic forms in which long-term capital can be obtained, and have developed a scheme of analysis to aid the financial manager in making his judgment of the pattern of obligations that best suits the ownership and other interests involved in a particular company. It is now time to turn to the more complex arrangements that exist as variations on the basic categories that we have been using so far. Each variation has its own advantages and disadvantages and thus may be most suitable for particular needs or conditions.

A complete catalogue of kinds of securities would be almost endless and never quite up to date, for the possibilities of special arrangements are limited only by the imagination of the draftsman. In the chapters in this part of the book, we shall therefore be dealing only with the principal variations, with the intent to show how these features come into being to meet special needs of issuer or of investor. Three chapters will be devoted to this material. The fourth and last chapter in this part of the book will deal with the computation of the costs of the principal types of issues, to enable the reader to analyze this aspect of the problem more explicitly.

Off-the-Balance-Sheet Financing

We shall first consider long-term rental arrangements, usually termed *leases*. From the points of view of finance and accounting, the unique feature of a leasing contract is that although the *lessee* is entitled to the use of the asset, legal title is retained by the *lessor*. In conventional accounting terms, leased property is not to be considered

373

or shown as an asset of the business, and the periodic obligations to pay rent are not liabilities until they become due. Thus arises the term *off-the-balance-sheet financing.*

There are many types of rental arrangements which are of short duration, or cancelable, or otherwise not important as alternatives to long-term ownership. A financial lease, with which we are now concerned, has two distinguishing characteristics. The first is the fixed nature of the obligation. Whenever a lease is noncancelable and runs over a long period of time, it produces a burden on the lessee similar to that of a debt. Secondly, under a financial lease a lessee promises payments which, in total, exceed the purchase price of the assets that are leased.

Usually also, though not necessarily, a financial lease is a "net" lease. That is, the tenant agrees to pay property taxes, maintain the property, etc., as if he were the owner.

Thus, a financial lease can be described as "a practicable alternative to ownership of the asset by the company, with the decision between owning and leasing turning on financial rather than operating considerations."[1]

Thus, once more, we see that the scope of finance is broader than the confines of a balance sheet. Management must provide the firm with the use of properties needed for its activities, either by ownership or by rental. We are familiar with the idea that assets are acquired by the creation of securities which appear as liabilities. The promises made under leases are just as binding as those under security contracts, although no asset or liability appears. In fact, we regard payments under long-term lease arrangements to be part of the burden of financing, and in the same category as the servicing of a bond issue.

The similarity which we see between leases and debt is based on the point of view of a going concern. The ultimate consequences of default under a lease are different from those if bonded debt exists. The lessor may repossess his property, but he may claim damages only for one year's future rent if a liquidation results from the failure, or three years' rent if the company undergoes reorganization. The holder of a bond, of course, is a creditor for the entire principal of his claim; but even if the bond is secured by a mortgage, the property cannot be taken away without a court order, which is seldom forthcoming unless a complete liquidation has been decided upon.

[1] D. R. Gant, "Illusion in Lease Financing," *Harvard Business Review*, March–April, 1959, p. 122.

Examples of Leasing Arrangements

The parties to contractual relationships that are found in a financial lease can be diagrammed as in Chart 18–1. In studying this chart, the reader should remember that the functions of selling, title holding, and investing may be performed by one company, two companies, or three.

The extent of the use of the lease form is indicated by the findings of Vancil and Anthony,[2] who heard from 386 nonfinancial corporations responding to a questionnaire. Of these, 53 per cent had arranged financial leases, with high figures of 93 per cent for integrated oil companies and 88 per cent for merchandising companies. The low figure was 48 per cent for the general class of industrials. Rental of real estate is, of course, a device long known and used in the business world, and the popularity of leases in oil operations and merchandising reflects this fact. The varieties of leasing arrange-

CHART 18–1

RELATIONSHIPS IN A TYPICAL FINANCIAL LEASE

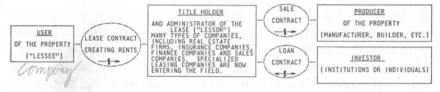

ments, however, are almost endless, with new variations being heard of frequently, as the use of this extremely flexible form of financing is extended. It is in the extension of its use that one sees the change. Today, one can find leasing arrangements offered for such items as office equipment, large and small computers, all kinds of production tooling, engines for aircraft, the aircraft themselves, entire corporations, general purpose buildings, and buildings built to the tenant's specifications.

Two examples may be helpful here. The first is the financing arranged by American Airlines, Inc., to provide the engines for its jet fleet. Each of the manufacturers of the jet engines established a subsidiary, which leased the engines to American Airlines on terms that amortized the purchase price and provided interest at about $4\frac{1}{8}$ per cent per year. The transactions "saved" the air line a capital investment estimated at $67 million at a time when public placement of

---

[2] R. F. Vancil and R. N. Anthony, "The Financial Community Looks at Leasing," *Harvard Business Review*, November–December, 1959, pp. 113–30, at p. 122.

stock would have been possible only at depressed prices, and when the company, because of existing loans, would probably have had to use subordinated debt if it had attempted to borrow in the investment market.[3] Other air lines have followed this initiative.

The second example is a more prosaic one. A variety store chain projected a branch to cost $225,000, a sum made up of land, $25,-000; building, $150,000; and certain equipment, $50,000. A group of investors in the area of the proposed store offered to build and equip it to the tenant's specifications, and to lease it for 25 years, with annual rentals as follows: first 10 years, $22,035; next 15 years, $11,583. The payments were computed to permit the lessor to amortize the $225,000 cost over the 25 years, while earning 6 per cent on the investment. The lease would be a "net lease," as defined above. Leases of this kind are very frequent, and we shall use this example to provide concreteness to our discussion.

Advantages and Disadvantages of Leasing

In the following paragraphs, we shall measure advantages and disadvantages as seen by the lessee—the user of the property. From the point of view of physical operations, it is usually unimportant whether the property is owned or rented. We shall therefore concentrate upon the advantages and disadvantages of financing by lease, in contrast to ways of financing ownership. More precisely, since a lease is to be regarded as a debt instrument, the contrast should be to some form of borrowing. The following topics need to be covered: the avoidance of investment, the effect of leases on borrowing power, the question of residual values, the role of taxation, and the cost of the arrangement.

Avoidance of Investment

A frequently cited advantage is that the company avoids the need to commit sizable quantities of funds at the time of acquiring the use of the property. Funds would be required by an outright purchase, or even mortgage financing. In the latter case a margin of value would ordinarily be required to be paid at the time of acquisition, with the amount of the mortgage providing the balance.

In evaluating this undoubted advantage of a lease, two points must be made. First, granted that the lease represents a way of putting funds (represented by the value of the property) at the disposal of the company, the lease will have its cost. The question must be asked:

---

[3] Data summarized from an unpublished thesis of Richard F. Vancil.

Will the company gain more from devoting its available funds to other uses? In many instances, analysis will show that ownership of a certain asset is more desirable than the alternative of leasing that asset and using company funds for another purpose, because the alternative does not promise a sufficiently high rate of return. Let us make this test for the variety chain chosen as an example. Here, properties that would cost $225,000 can be obtained without any initial investment. What alternatives are there that would permit earning more than the 6 per cent before-tax cost of the funds "released" by the lease?

A simple example, made without the refinements that would enter if we dealt separately with fixed and variable costs, is the following: The variety store chain of our example reports profits before taxes at the rate of 17.7 per cent on all assets. If all real estate were taken off the balance sheet, the rate of profit would be 20.8 per cent. It does not take any refinement to justify the conclusion that leasing at a 6 per cent cost will permit the company to use funds more profitably. In general, just as is always true when one considers any form of trading on the equity, there is advantage whenever the company can earn more on its assets than the fixed costs it incurs to obtain the use of those assets.

Further analysis reveals, however, the second qualification to the advantage of avoiding investment. The belief that the lease has "released" $225,000 for other business purposes is quite superficial. Such an idea contains the implicit assumptions that the funds in question exist in the business already, and that we can ignore the way in which they were obtained. The lease should be regarded as a case of a loan of 100 per cent of the needed funds—$225,000. Surely, the acceptance of the proposed lease will consume a portion of the company's total capacity to arrange debt financing. In purely logical terms the debt capacity that is consumed must be equal to that of borrowing to raise the same amount of funds.

In any actual case the comparison should be made with a debt contract that might actually be arranged. For our purposes at this time, we shall assume an issue of debenture bonds at 6 per cent, and the same schedule of payments as is called for by the proposed lease. This type of financing would create a balance sheet asset of $225,000, balanced by a debt of the same amount.

Further on in this chapter, we shall describe an analysis to determine whether it is better to borrow on these terms or to lease the property. Here, it is sufficient to point out that a lease uses up credit. One might expect that it would use up as much of the company's borrowing capacity as a loan of equivalent terms. Altogether too many leases have been signed without recognition of this matter.

Effect on Borrowing Capacity

Two factors exist, however, which sometimes permit a company to raise more funds by leases than by debt. One of these factors is that the title to leased property remains in the control of the lessor. It cannot be touched by the creditors of the lessee. If, instead, the property in question had been bought and financed by a mortgage and there were a default, the investor would have to await foreclosure, which is at best a slow and expensive process. In fact, if the property can be expected always to have a value to others, a lease may be the only way a financially embarrassed corporation can obtain the use of new equipment. For example, the financially weak Northeast Airlines, Inc., recently obtained the use of new jet-powered equipment through a leasing arrangement, and many a weak manufacturer has leased new tools when its general credit was exhausted. In order to obtain such a result, however, the criterion that the property is sure to be valuable to others must be met without any possibility of doubt. The more the leased property becomes special purpose, the more the general credit of the company limits its power either to lease or to borrow.

Another great advantage of the leasing arrangement is that it is available to finance amounts too small to be of interest to major institutional lenders or the public market. It is an important device in the expansion period of a small business.

A second factor that may sometimes permit a company to raise more funds by lease than by debt is that the burdens the lease creates are not evidenced by liabilities on the balance sheet. The result may be that certain grantors of credit will not take the leasehold obligations fully into account, and thus will be more liberal than if an equivalent debt were to appear. There is evidence that this situation does exist, despite the efforts of accountants, the Securities and Exchange Commission, and others to provide full disclosure.[4] As time

---

[4] The Committee on Accounting Procedure of the American Institute of Accountants has commented, in *Accounting Research Bulletin No. 43* (New York: 1953) (p. 126), as follows: "The committee believes that material amounts of fixed rental and other liabilities maturing in future years under long-term leases and possible related contingencies are material facts affecting judgments based on the financial statements of a corporation, and that those who rely upon financial statements are entitled to know of the existence of such leases and the extent of the obligations thereunder, irrespective of whether the leases are considered to be advantageous or otherwise. Acordingly, where the rentals or

goes on, however, this condition will dwindle in importance. What is perhaps more important to say is that no financial manager who contemplates a lease obligation should allow himself to be deceived. Contractual rental obligations are charges as fixed as the elements of the burden of bonds.

The Question of Residual Values

Strangely enough, leased property is often harder to leave than owned property. This paradox arises because one can sell the owned property at any time, while the leased property is under contract over the term of the lease; thus, the lessee may find that he has no choice but to continue in possession. Occasionally, therefore, a firm will choose ownership in order to preserve its flexibility as to the length of time it may choose to use the property.

An argument for ownership that is more frequently heard is based on the fact that leased property reverts to the lessor (together with all permanent improvements installed by the lessee) at the expiration of the lease. Certain types of property may enjoy a high sale value at the time the lease expires, and it may be desirable to hold title for the purpose of gaining from this residual value. The argument is especially attractive for well-situated real estate, since it is well known that substantial profits are often made in this way. While conceding the attractiveness of this line of thinking, we urge the reader to note carefully the fact that money which *may* be received in the distant future has far less value in the present than its future amount makes it seem to have. It is often far better to conserve funds for immediate purposes, as the earnings thus obtained will be more than the expected long-run windfall. Such would be the case, evidently, for the variety chain in our example, since it can earn 17 per cent or more on current funds.

---

other obligations under long-term leases are material in the circumstances, the committee is of the opinion that:

    a) disclosure should be made in financial statements or in notes thereto of:

      (1) the amounts of annual rentals to be paid under such leases with some indication of the periods for which they are payable and

      (2) any other important obligation assumed or guarantee made in connection therewith:

    b) the above information should be given not only in the year in which the transaction originates but also as long thereafter as the amounts involved are material; and

    c) in addition, in the year in which the transaction originates, there should be disclosure of the principal details of any important sale-and-lease transaction."

While this statement can be regarded as an authoritative guide to good accounting, it is by no means binding on all accountants in their audit certification of accounts. Compliance with the spirit of the statement still leaves much to be desired.

Tax Advantage in Leasing

Frequently, situations exist where everyone seems to gain except the tax collector. There are certain types of property, notably well-maintained urban real estate, whose market value tends to be more stable than the declining book value permitted by the optional methods of depreciation. In such cases the owner may gain by depreciating the property as fast as the law allows. After a few years the property is sold, and a capital gain is realized. Then another similar property is bought, and the process is repeated. Thus, a business which can shift its investments from one property to another may prefer ownership to leasing.

More generally, with reference to taxation, the lessee can charge all his annual payments as tax-deductible expenses over the life of the lease. He may find advantage in a shorter term of lease than the period usually allowed for the depreciation of the particular asset (although the new optional methods often will do as well). He can depreciate the cost of land, in the sense that he is paying for the land as he pays for the use of the property. Also, moneys spent for improvements on the leased property may usually be charged off during the remaining life of the lease. Each of these operations may give the lessee a tax shield (tax shield is discussed in Chapter 6) that is larger in earlier years than would be possible under ownership. In fact, the availability of larger tax shields from such sources is often the major reason for leasing instead of borrowing.

The Cost of the Arrangement

The actual schedule of payments called for by a financial lease is often quite complex. It is not always easy, therefore, to find the rate of interest which is implicit in the fact that the total to be paid under a financial lease is greater than the cash purchase price of the property. We shall deal with this problem more fully in Chapter 21. It is fair to say that the interest cost of the funds provided by a lease is seldom less than 0.5 to 1 per cent higher than could be arranged on a loan of equivalent amount. The discrepancy varies in relation to several factors, including the general credit standing of the lessee and the ease with which the leased property could be transferred to other uses following a default.

Ownership versus Leasing: An Example

In any actual case the analyst must compare the burdens of the proposed lease with those of an alternative borrowing, suitable to the actual condition of the company. In the example we are using, that of the proposed store property for the variety chain, we have assumed a debenture debt for the whole $225,000, with the same repayment terms and interest rate as the lease. This gives us the opportunity to compare ownership with leasing in an instance where the differences are confined to the tax treatment which is afforded leased property as contrasted with owned property. On one hand, we have a lease for 25 years. All of the annual rent is an expense. In the first year, for example, the payment of $22,035 results in a tax shield of $11,458, so that the net cash outflow is $10,577. Summing up all the 25 years, the total payments to the lessor will be $394,095. The net payments, however, will be $189,166 after taxes of 52 per cent.

In the case of the debt, the building has a depreciable life of 40 years. The equipment may be depreciated over 25 years, and the land not at all. Using the double declining balance method of depreciation, the first year's account will show interest and depreciation expense of $25,000, resulting in a tax shield of $13,000 and a net cash outflow of $9,035. The burden is less than that of the lease in the first year, because of the high charges for depreciation. Over 25 years, however, only $110,324 of the $150,000 building cost can be depreciated, and the land remains at $25,000. While the total payments will be the same as in the case of the lease, the net payments will be $222,774 after taxes. The difference, $33,604, is the tax shield not used in the 25 years under the debt arrangement.[5]

In Chart 18–2, the lines show the accumulation of the annual after-tax payments to the totals already mentioned. Despite the early advantage in favor of the bonds, the superiority of the lease in this instance appears to be obvious. It is well to remember that the superiority arises entirely from the fact that the lease permits "expensing" all the cost of the project in twenty-five years. When the depreciable lives of the assets are the same as the lease period, and land is not important, there is little to choose between borrowing and leasing. In such a case the higher cost of the lease may be the factor that tips the scales against it.

Even in our example, the bonds may still be the choice, if it be felt that the residual values in the property will exceed $33,604, as they well may. Before jumping to this conclusion, however, one must recall that the values are being regarded at the time the arrangement is starting. Is the *possibility* of some profit from ownership as valuable as the *certainty* of the funds released by the lease during the twenty-

---

[5] Directly computed, the figure is $33,632. The difference is due to rounding.

CHART 18-2

ACCUMULATED AFTER-TAX CASH OUTFLOWS IN ALTERNATIVE METHODS
OF FINANCING AN INVESTMENT OF $225,000

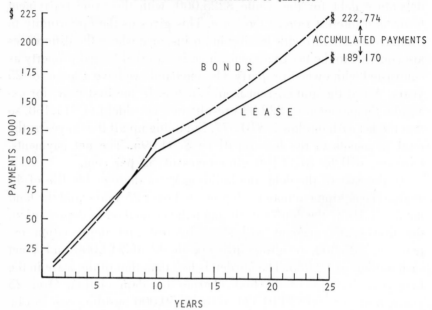

five years? The answer should be against ownership in many such cases.

Lease Obligations, Burden Coverage, and Debt Ratios

In Chapter 14, at page 291, we defined the burden of a debt and suggested certain ratios that are useful to relate the burden to the earnings or cash inflows of the borrower, and to measure the degree of trading on the equity. For analyzing a company with large lease obligations, we recommend including these lease payments as part of the financial burden and relating the burden thus found to earnings before interest, lease payments, and taxes (E.B.I.L.T.) instead of earnings before interest and taxes (E.B.I.T.). The necessary amounts can be determined from most published statements, and will, of course, be available to the management of a specific company.

Suppose, for example, we are to analyze the debt position of a company that reports an invested capital of $65,000, made up as follows:

Long-term debt.................................$15,000
Capital stock and surplus...................... 50,000
                                                        $65,000

The income statement shows:

(What is Trading on equity) (handwritten margin note)

E.B.I.T...	$14,000
Interest expense...............................	750
Taxable Income...........................	$13,250

We also learn from footnotes to the company's statements that there are long-term lease payments of $3,000 a year and that assets with a cost of $50,000 were provided under the lease. The figures above can be adjusted as follows:

Long-term debt and leasehold value..............	$ 65,000
Capital stock and surplus......................	50,000
	$115,000
E.B.I.L.T......................................	$ 17,000
Burden of debt and leases.....................	3,750
Taxable Income..........................	$ 13,250

We then find:

Burden coverage:

$$\text{Unadjusted} \ldots \ldots \ldots \ldots \quad \frac{14,000}{750} = 18.7$$

$$\text{Adjusted} \ldots \ldots \ldots \ldots \quad \frac{17,000}{3,750} = 4.5$$

Equity ratio:

$$\text{Unadjusted} \ldots \ldots \ldots \ldots \quad \frac{50,000}{65,000} = 77\%$$

$$\text{Adjusted} \ldots \ldots \ldots \ldots \quad \frac{50,000}{115,000} = 43\%$$

Ratio of trading on the equity:

$$\text{Unadjusted} \ldots \ldots \ldots \ldots \left(\frac{1}{0.77}\right)\left(\frac{17.7}{18.7}\right) = 1.2$$

$$\text{Adjusted} \ldots \ldots \ldots \ldots \left(\frac{1}{0.43}\right)\left(\frac{3.5}{4.5}\right) = 1.8$$

(handwritten margin notes: *equity 90* *Burden covrg ratio 107*)

Since a financial lease is to be regarded from many points of view as a debt, analysts often consider it desirable to place an imputed liability on the balance sheet. The liability will be offset, of course, by a new asset account of the same size. In this way, debt ratios and computations of the ratio of trading on the equity can be made to take lease obligations into account. As an example, we may refer again to the variety chain. Even if the lease is selected, one could for analytical purposes show an asset of $225,000 and a debt of the same sum.

If one is inside a firm, the alternate purchase price of leased property is usually available for such a purpose as that just mentioned. Analysts "on the outside looking in" may be forced to capitalize annual lease payments at some rate in order to get a figure to use. Controversy rages over the rate to be used, but the present authors feel that the yield on debenture bonds in the industry is a rate that will serve for most cases.

Sale and Lease-Back

Beginning in the mid-1930's a good many leases have been created by the sale and lease-back device. Once the lease created by this transaction is in force, the advantages and disadvantages treated above come into play in the ways described. The new element is that at the beginning the ultimate lessee and user of the property was the owner. Let us refer to this owner as A. Company A arranges to sell the property to B and to lease it back.

Two advantages may result to Company A from such a transaction. In the first place, liquid funds are obtained at once for whatever purpose they may serve. In return, the obligation to pay rent is undertaken. Many retail organizations, for example, have entered sale and lease-back arrangements to release funds committed to assets with low turnover. Secondly, new opportunities for tax advantage are created. If the sale price is less than book value, a loss is created that can be offset against other gains; if the sale price creates a profit, it is taxable at the capital gains rate. Yet, in either case the company continues to use the property.

Summary

We can summarize the place of the financial lease in the area of bargaining for funds by saying that its obligations are to be regarded as a form of debt, treated in financial analysis in the same way as the burden of a bond issue. Leases are used for both small and large transactions, and their variety is great. The tax treatment accorded to lease payments may make them less burdensome than an equivalent borrowing, although this is not always the case. Leases often assist in financing small or financially weak companies. They are often used by large companies to finance specific projects where the property is available on favorable terms, or when for some reason the time is not deemed propitious for the issue of new securities.

Perhaps this is the place to point out that the special advantages of leases in the tax field have led to very careful scrutiny of the real situation that lies behind the formal lease. Expert legal counsel is required for the complex task of drafting lease arrangements that will stand up against possible legal attacks either from creditors of the lessee (who would like to have the value of the property declared an asset of the lessee) or from the tax authorities (who would prefer to have the lease payments taken as instalments for an ultimate purchase). It is no game for the superficial or the unwary.

Chapter 19

The Bargain for Funds: I. Modifications of the Distribution of Risk

IN THE chapter on basic security types the fundamental characteristics of bonds, preferred stock, and common stock were described. In the succeeding chapters, it was shown how these security types, when combined in the corporate financial structure, can affect the distribution of risk, income, and control among corporate investors, so that these elements can be arranged to suit the needs of various types of investors. We believe that an understanding of the essential differences among the three types of securities was aided by confining attention to these securities in their simplest form.

We are now ready to extend our consideration of long-term finance to take account of the influence which variations in the circumstances and objectives of both issuers and investors have on the terms of the investment contract. Over a period of many years the basic security types have been subject to a considerable variety of modifications in an effort to have them meet more precisely the special needs of particular investors and business corporations.

It is not the purpose of this volume to provide a complete catalogue and description of all security types in present-day use. Such information is already available in a number of competent reference works. Rather, the purpose is to show, by reference to the more commonly used variations, how these features come into being in the bargaining process between issuer and investor. A secondary objective is to provide a simple framework for the classification of these variations of the basic types so that they can be appraised by the same analytical method as was used in Chapters 14 and 15 in considering the basic security types themselves.

The Bargaining Process

The specific terms under which a group of investors makes funds available to a business corporation are the result of a bargaining process between the investors and the management of the corporation. As in any bargain the final product is a workable compromise which embodies the essential objectives of both parties. For example, it is obvious that the investor will want to have the highest possible return on his investment and at the same time have the maximum assurance that the income will be received and the principal protected. The issuing company, on the other hand, will wish to minimize the costs associated with the financing and preserve the maximum flexibility in the payments to the investor. The terms of the actual security issue must somehow reconcile these conflicting objectives.

The use of the phrase *bargaining process* in describing the procedure by which the particular terms of a given security issue are developed and made final should not be taken as implying necessarily a formal negotiation around a conference table. As indicated in the chapters on the securities market, securities are commonly either sold directly to a single investor or offered publicly, in which case an investment banker is normally used as a middleman. If the securities are placed privately as, for example, with an insurance company, the terms of the issue will be worked out by direct negotiation with the insurance company's investment officers. The bargaining will include not only the basic considerations such as interest rate, maturity date, and sinking fund provisions but also any special features which accommodate the security to the particular circumstances and objectives of the issuer and/or investor. In such proceedings, it is necessary for the officers of the issuing company to know the limits of their bargaining position and to be flexible as suits their own advantage—to give a little here in order to gain a little there—for example, to consider offering greater security or a shortened maturity date if it means a lower interest rate, or offering a higher rate in order to preserve the right to call the issue. Thus, any special feature which offers a major advantage to one party is likely to have its price in concessions elsewhere in the terms of the issue.

The bargaining process in the case of a public offering is less obvious. The investors who ultimately buy the security are likely to vary considerably as to their circumstances and investment objectives. Consequently, even if they could be brought together for consultation, general agreement on specific terms would be highly unlikely. In fact, they will be offered a security with the terms already set on a "take it or leave it" basis. Under such conditions, it is hard to see the terms as negotiated between issuer and investor.

However, investors as a group do have an important though indirect influence on the character of new security offerings by the manner in which they have registered approval or disapproval of previous issues. As in the case of any product offered for sale, success depends on an accurate forecast of what the buyers want. "Consumer" tastes vary and change in the security market as in other markets, and considerable skill is required in planning the terms of a new issue, particularly since no one wishes to carry an inventory of unsold securities for an extended period of time. Since the typical corporation goes to the securities market infrequently, its officers are not sufficiently in touch with the market; and thus, when planning the terms of a new issue, the company usually turns to an investment banker or broker for advice. The investment banker is in a position to suggest the minimum terms which will bring a quick and complete sale, considering the condition of the market at the time. If the investment banker underwrites the issue, the investment banker in effect becomes the purchaser of the issue, and the issuing company negotiates the terms directly with him.

It should not be inferred from the concept of security planning as a negotiated procedure that each and every term of the issue is carefully weighed and debated before it is included. We start with the three basic and considerably standardized security forms of bonds, preferred stock, and common stock, the primary features of which have been well established in company law, corporate charters, and investors' standards. The precedent of accepted corporate practice in a given industry has a great deal to do with the form which new issues take. There are also the regulations of government agencies such as the Securities and Exchange Commission, which have an influence on the terms that shall be included or excluded, as well as the regulations of the organized exchanges. The general economic and business conditions at the time of issue have a bearing. All these things tend to narrow the range of security features which may be negotiated before the precise form of the security is finally decided.

It is important to recognize that when company officials make some concession in price, income, or other terms to a group of security holders in order to have a successful offering, what they concede is a portion of what would otherwise belong to other security holders. Likewise, the tangible gain to the company resulting from a security sale on unusually favorable terms is a gain to the other security holders. A sale of bonds at a relatively higher interest rate means lower net earnings per share of common stock. A preferred stock which has the cumulative feature means a greater hazard to common dividends than would be the case if it was noncumulative. A further common issue offered to new stockholders and priced at an unusual discount from market price in order to assure ready sale means added dilution of the investment of existing common shareholders. Thus, the ultimate bargain is not between the new security holders and management as such but rather between one class of security holders and another. In this connection, we remind the reader that we have consistently emphasized the desirability of viewing management as the representative of the common shareholder.

A Classification of Stock and Bond Features

In spite of the confusing array of special types of stocks and bonds in use today, it is possible to fit most, if not all, of these variations into the relatively simple analytical framework of Chapters 14 and 15. This comes about because most of these special security types or features turn out to be merely modifications of the normal distribution of risk, income, and/or control found in the basic security forms. Accordingly, we shall follow this basis of classification in our discussion of the more important special forms. As with most classifications, this approach is not without its limitations. For example, an income bond represents a modification of risk as well as income and could fit with equal justification under either category. This is not a serious problem, however, provided the classification is recognized as secondary to the objective of a clear understanding of the security in question.

A. Modifications of the Distribution of Risk: Bonds

1. The Pledge of Assets. As in the case of short-term debt, a loan in the form of a bond issue may be secured or unsecured. An unsecured bond is known as a *debenture.* The terms of such a bond are no less binding than those of a secured bond, and they rank ahead of all classes of stock in the fulfillment of these terms. However, the secured bond has the added protection of a prior claim over other creditors to certain specified assets in the event of default and liquidation. Thus, the effect of a pledge is to give a certain priority to one group of creditors over the claims of other creditors. The obvious intent of a pledge of or a lien against specific assets is to decrease the risk to the bondholder, and this may mean that the issue may be salable at a somewhat lower interest rate as a result. On the other hand, the primary protection for any bond lies in the earning capacity of the issuing company, so that the debenture of one company may involve less risk to the investor than the secured bond of another.

Almost any corporate asset may be pledged, but the laws are intricate, and so the forms of contract differ according to the type of property. The most common form of secured bond is that secured by a mortgage on all or some of the fixed assets of the business—land and buildings. This type of issue is known as a *mortgage bond* and is frequently found in industries which combine relatively stable earnings with a high proportion of the total investment in fixed assets, such as public utilities and railroads. The mortgage will contain a detailed description of the property pledged, so that it can be accurately identified in event of default. An abbreviated statement of such security is seen in the following example of Inland Steel Company's first 4½'s, Series L, issued in February, 1959, and due in February, 1989: "Secured equally and ratably with other series by first mortgage on (1) Indiana Harbor and Chicago Heights plants, (2) certain iron ore properties in Iron and Marquette Counties, Mich., and St. Louis and Crow Wing Counties, Minn., (3) coal properties of company, subject to certain exceptions, and (4) approximately 800 acres of vacant land in Porter County, Ind."[1]

It is a recognized fact that in the event of liquidation, business assets generally undergo shrinkage in value. This is particularly true of specialized fixed assets, where the cash realized in sale is likely to be considerably below the book value. In view of this, it is a general rule that the value of fixed assets pledged as security for a bond issue will be substantially larger than the amount of the debt. The usual upper limit for mortgage loans is two thirds of the cost of the pledged assets; and in some cases, it may be as low as one half. Obviously, this is one of the ways in which the creditor seeks to limit the risks involved in investment.

There are occasions when a bond issue is secured by a *second mortgage* on assets which have already been pledged on a previous issue. As the term implies, the holders of such securities take a secondary position to the holders of the first-mortgage bonds in the event of foreclosure and sale of the particular assets. On the other hand, they rank before other creditors as regards these assets. It will be ap-

---

[1] *Moody's Industrial Manual, 1960,* p. 1059.

parent that a second mortgage has an appeal to the potential bondholder only when the value of the pledged assets is substantially in excess of that necessary to provide protection under a first mortgage.

Some security provisions include property "hereafter acquired" as well as property in existence at the time of the mortgage. This is known as an *after-acquired property clause* and is found in many such mortgages as a feature to increase further the confidence of the investor by adding new assets to the pledge. More significantly, the effect of the clause would be to exclude additional first-mortgage debt, which would otherwise increase the fixed charges against earnings and thereby the risk to existing bondholders. The mortgage may also include a statement of certain exceptions to this clause in the case of property which bears a prior lien at the time of acquisition.

A second type of property which may become security for long-term debt is movable physical assets such as equipment, commonly referred to as *chattels*. The mortgages which cover such assets are broadly classified as *chattel mortgages*. This form is widely used in the transportation industry, and the best-known chattel mortgage is that on railroad rolling stock, the securities of which are called *equipment trust certificates*. It should be noted that the title to these assets is normally vested in a third party, a trustee, who leases the equipment to the user, the railroad, in exchange for a rental which is accumulated by the trustee on behalf of the certificate holders. This is a device further to insulate the property from the claims of other creditors. An example of a straight chattel mortgage is Trans World Airlines, Inc., equipment mortgage sinking fund $3\frac{3}{4}$'s issued in 1954, due in 1969, and secured by a general mortgage on aircraft and engines owned as of December 31, 1957, with the exception of certain specific aircraft and engines pledged under a bank loan or purchased under a conditional sale contract.[2]

A third type of property frequently pledged by certain types of businesses is investments in stocks and bonds or other instruments such as notes receivable. A bond secured by a pledge of such securities is known as a *collateral trust bond*. This type of collateral may be more or less effective as protection against the risk of default, depending on the character of the pledged securities and the strength and stability of the market for them. Such bonds would not normally be used by industrial companies, since few of them carry a sufficient

---

[2] *Moody's Transportation Manual, 1960,* p. 1387.

investment in marketable securities to support a bond issue. On the other hand, they are a natural form of bond issue for investment companies.

The features mentioned so far have been designed to reduce the risk to the investor. On occasion a feature is introduced which acts to increase the risk to the investor. Such is the case of the *subordinated debenture*. As we indicated previously in Chapter 12, a subordinated debt is one which would in the ordinary course of events be equal to or have priority over other debt but which for some reason has been placed in a secondary position to such debt. An example of the subordinated debenture is W. R. Grace and Company convertible subordinate debenture 3½'s, due in 1975, which were sold in 1955 for additions to plant, facilities, and working capital, and were "subordinated to all senior debt, including bank borrowings, current loans, etc."[3] Such subordination is necessary for new debt when existing debt contracts prohibit additional debt having equivalent or senior claim on assets and earnings. In order to make such bonds acceptable to the prospective holders, a higher interest rate may be necessary.

2. *Limitations on Additional Debt and Other Negative Pledges.* There are several ways in which creditors may seek to limit their risks by limiting the amount of additional debt and by other *negative pledges*. As we have indicated, the pledging of assets is in itself a limitation on additional debt by making these assets unavailable as prime security for another bond issue. To the extent that the limitation is successful, it acts to hold down the over-all proportion of debt in the capital structure, thereby improving the earnings coverage of the outstanding bonds beyond what it would be otherwise and reducing the risks assumed by the existing bondholders. From the company's viewpoint the acceptance of such limitations may be a means of gaining advantages in other ways—a lower interest rate and/or a better selling price for the bonds.

Most bonds secured by a mortgage of fixed assets are of the *closed end* type. This means that no additional bonds can be issued under the same mortgage, thus preventing the dilution of asset values per dollar of bond. In contrast, some mortgages are of the *limited open-end* type, which permit additional issues of bonds under the same mortgage provided certain conditions are met. An example of this is Michigan Consolidated Gas Company first-mortgage 3½'s, series

---

[3] *Moody's Industrial Manual, 1960,* p. 2929.

due in 1969. These bonds have an open indenture with the following provision regarding further issues:

Additional bonds may be issued (unlimited except as provided by law) equal to (1) 60% of lower of cost or fair value of net property additions after December 31, 1943, not theretofore bonded . . . (2) bonds issued hereunder and prior lien bonds retired but not theretofore bonded; (3) cash deposited with trustee for such purpose, but only if net earnings available for interest and depreciation for 12 out of 15 months next preceding are at least 2½ times annual interest on bonds to be outstanding and on all prior lien bonds outstanding; except that, in general, no earnings test is required to issue bonds (*a*) for refunding bonds issued by company or prior lien bonds, or (*b*) to reimburse company for monies expended or repay loans incurred for such refunding.[4]

Thus, it is apparent that even an open-end mortgage bond issue contains provisions designed to preserve a certain minimum protection of asset values and earning power for the bondholder. At the same time, the clause gives the issuer a degree of flexibility in the further use of debt. The specific terms of this provision are of obvious importance to both parties and would be a subject for negotiation in discussions preliminary to the sale of the issue.

Another example of a negative pledge is one commonly associated with debentures. It is often the case that a debenture is the only bond issue of a particular company. In order to protect against the hazard of a subsequent bond issue secured by a lien on assets, which would then take precedence over the debenture as to these assets, the terms of the debenture normally prohibit a future pledge of assets or outline the conditions under which such a pledge would be acceptable. For example, the Allied Chemical debenture 3½'s, due in 1978, are covered by the following provisions, known as the *equal and ratable security* clause:

Company and any subsidiary will not mortgage property unless debentures are equally and ratably secured therewith, except for (1) purchase money or existing mortgages up to 66⅔% of lower of cost or fair value of property, as provided and (2) other permitted liens. If on any consolidation or sale of substantially all properties, any property would become subject to a mortgage, debentures will be secured by direct prior lien thereon except for any existing lien.[5]

3. Method and Timing of Repayment. It is a characteristic of uncertainty or risk that, all other things being equal, the longer the pe-

---

[4] *Moody's Public Utility Manual, 1960*, p. 1609.

[5] *Moody's Industrial Manual, 1960*, p. 2814.

riod of time a debt will remain outstanding, the greater the risk to the bondholder. The longer he has to wait for the repayment of principal, the more difficult it becomes to forecast ability to pay with accuracy, and the less meaningful is the record of the immediate past upon which confidence is usually based. It follows from this that the risk to the bondholder may be modified by varying the timing and method of repayment of the debt. It also follows as a consequence that a significant lengthening of the maturity date of an issue will probably require a somewhat higher yield to the bondholder or some other concession in order to induce him to accept the increased risk.

The basic bond is repayable in a lump sum at a single known future date, which may be 15 or 20 years from date of issue. A very common modification of the lump-sum repayment of a bond issue is found in the *sinking fund bond.* Previous chapters have made the reader aware that some bonds require the issuing company to set aside a sum of money each year for the repurchase and retirement of some of the outstanding bonds instead of leaving repayment to the uncertain financial capacity in the year of maturity. Sinking funds may be set up in various ways. The terms of United States Plywood Corporation debenture 5¼'s, issued in April, 1960, and due in April, 1985, include the following sinking fund provisions:

> Cash (or debentures) to redeem at par following amounts of debentures each A & O: $335,000, 1963–66; $375,000, 1967–70; $420,000, 1971–76; $455,000, 1977–84; plus optional payments equal to minimum requirements. Payments are estimated sufficient to retire 72% of issue by maturity.
> Callable at 100 for sinking fund.[6]

A company such as United States Plywood, which has the option of buying in bonds for the sinking fund on the open market or calling them by lot, naturally will take the alternative which offers the lowest price. In any case the effect is to reduce the debt outstanding, provide some support for the market for the remaining securities when the issue is selling below call price, and increase the certainty of total repayment. The decrease in risk to the bondholder resulting from a sinking fund is a significant bargaining point when setting up the terms of a bond issue and one which should give the issuer a more favorable bargaining position in other respects. The disadvantage of such a feature to the common stockholders stems from the fact that the retention of earnings to meet the sinking fund requirement means, in effect, a gradual substitution of high-cost equity capital for low-

---

[6] *Ibid.,* p. 2746.

cost debt. Alternatively, the earnings could have been applied to new investments within the company or withdrawn and invested elsewhere. However, the practical significance for the stockholder may be small if the company is maintaining a continuous debt position through new bond issues which overlap the old.

Another type of bond which has a somewhat similar effect is the *serial bond*, where specific groups of bonds, all of which are covered by the same indenture, are repayable at predetermined dates. The significant difference between this bond and the sinking fund bond is that the bondholder knows in advance the exact life of his particular bond and can take this into account in the price he pays for it. The serial feature is not nearly so common as the sinking fund provision, but it continues to fill a need in certain situations and is frequently used in municipal finance. An example of a public utility issue is Indiana and Michigan Electric Company's 3.25 per cent serial notes, due in 1957–67 (issued on January 1, 1952). These notes were floated "for construction" and were sold to yield 2.75 per cent for the nearest maturity to 3.2 per cent for the farthest maturity. The various series were due as follows: $250,000, 1956–60; $500,000, 1961–62; $750,000, 1963–67.[7]

In contrast to the serial and sinking fund bonds, which work to reduce the risk to the bondholder, the *callable bond* provides a means by which the risks of debt financing to the management and the common shareholders can be reduced. The call feature gives the company the option of repaying all or some portion of the debt prior to maturity, as in the following example of Texas Company debenture 3⅝'s, issued in May, 1958, and due in May, 1983:

Callable—As a whole or in part at any time on 30 days' notice to May 1 incl. as follows:

1961........104½		1964........104
1967........103½		1970........103
1972........102½		1974........102
1976........101½		1978........101
1980........100½		1981........100¼
1983........100		

Optional redemption is also permitted up to $5,000,000 of debentures during each 12 months' period ending May 1, beginning with period ending May 1, 1969, at 100 and interest.[8]

The call feature gives the company the very real advantage of

---

[7] *Moody's Public Utility Manual, 1960*, p. 1248.

[8] *Moody's Industrial Manual, 1960*, p. 2894.

greater flexibility in its capital structure so that it can time repayment to suit its needs and objectives as they develop. It also enables the company to take advantage of lower market interest rates, should they occur prior to maturity, by calling in the old bonds and replacing them with new bonds at the lower rate. In this respect the company's gain is the bondholder's loss; therefore, the call feature may be a hotly debated issue. The small call premium may be quite inadequate to compensate the bondholder for having to reinvest his funds for the balance of the period at a lower rate of return. It is apparent that the call feature is one which may affect the distribution of income as well as risk.

The call provision is a good example of an indenture clause which is subject to change over time as the condition of the money market and the bargaining position of the borrower and lender change. In the period of declining interest rates which prevailed for many years, an unrestricted call provision was considered highly desirable by the borrower and was almost invariably included in the indenture as long as a strong demand for bonds by investors persisted. However, whenever their bargaining position permits, lenders are inclined to demand that limitations be placed on calls so as to slow down their turnover of investments and to preserve higher yields for a longer period of time.

4. *The Dividend Restriction.* Many bond issues carry a provision which to some degree limits the extent to which companies may distribute funds to shareholders in the form of cash dividends. The obvious objective is to preserve a cushion of equity investment and prevent any excessive depletion of the liquid position of the company. The precise form of such restrictions varies, but the following example of Sperry Rand Corporation sinking fund debenture 5½'s, issued in September, 1957, and due in September, 1982, is typical: "Company may not pay cash dividends on or acquire any stock unless consolidated net income after Mar. 31, 1957 plus $35,000,000 and net cash proceeds after that date from stock sold, exceed such payments after Mar. 31, 1957 plus such investments and advancements in excess of $20,000,000."[9]

Generally, the effect of such a clause is to freeze surplus at the time of issue. It should be noted that the situation in which the issuing company would find such a clause seriously restrictive is likely to be unusual. For this reason, and also because this feature has become so

---

[9] *Ibid.,* p. 1761.

common since the thirties, it is not often a major bargaining consideration.

Modifications of the Distribution of Risk: Stock

Preferred Stock. The major redistribution of risk as far as ownership certificates are concerned is that which takes place when a preferred stock is created. The basic characteristics of the preferred stock are already familiar to the reader. In addition to the usual priority as to earnings and assets, other features may be added to this stock which affect the risk position of the holders. Those features which are similar to provisions already referred to in connection with bonds will be described here briefly.

One of the potential hazards associated with preferred stock is the creation of additional securities at a later date which have an equal or senior position in the capital structure. Protection against this hazard in preferreds is a relatively new idea, but many issues currently outstanding contain restrictive provisions in this regard. These vary in the degree of limitation placed on management. They may apply only to new stock issues, or they may apply to new debt as well. The following example of the Kendall Company $4.50 cumulative preferred A illustrates the latter type:

> Consent of two-thirds of preferred necessary to (1) issue or assume any funded debt . . . if thereafter consolidated funded debt plus involuntary liquidating value of outstanding preferred of subsidiaries and of preferred and of any stock having priority or on a parity with preferred exceeds 75% of excess of consolidated tangible assets over consolidated current liabilities, (2) create or issue any stock having priority over preferred (3) alter or amend provisions of preferred.
>
> Consent of a majority of preferred necessary to create or issue additional preferred or any stock on a parity therewith. . . .[10]

Another feature of preferred stock which has been designed to decrease the risk of the shareholder is the *sinking fund*. This feature has become common in recent years. As mentioned previously in connection with bonds, the sinking fund presents a possible disadvantage from the common shareholder point of view. Nevertheless, investors —especially the casualty insurance companies—have demanded it. The reason lies in part in the unhappy experience of "default" on many oversized preferred issues in the thirties. It is also recognized that the market price of the stock benefits from some compulsory buying on the part of the issuing company.

---

[10] *Ibid.*, p. 763.

The payment may be required as a flat sum annually or may be tied to earnings on a percentage basis, thus automatically relieving the company of payments in years of losses. It should be noted that if the provision is in the form of a flat sum, failure to pay will not precipitate bankruptcy but may affect the relative voting position of the preferred and common shareholders. This is distinctly different from the effect of default of the sinking fund provision on a bond. The following is the sinking fund provision of the St. Regis Paper Company 4.4 per cent cumulative first preferred, series A, par $100:

Sinking Fund—Annually, and cumulative to extent of net income (after deduction of dividends on preferred and prior or equal stock, and sinking fund for any funded debt not to exceed the lesser of 3% of such debt or $1,200,000) for succeeding years, sufficient to retire by purchase or redemption at $100 per share and dividends, for (a) first 2 years, 2½%, (b) next 20 years, 4%, and (c) succeeding 3 years, 5%, of greatest number of shares of preferred at any time outstanding.[11]

As in the case of bonds, the risk to management and the common shareholder which preferred stock presents in the form of a rigid prior claim to earnings may be reduced by making the preferred *callable* or *redeemable*. This is essential in the issue where a sinking fund is required and is desirable in any case to give the company needed flexibility. The possible effect of this provision on market price of the preferred is the opposite of that of the sinking fund. The general effect of purchases for the sinking fund is to support the market price. The effect of a call feature, where the possibility of call appears a reality, is to hold down the market price to the call price when the general condition of the market might push it higher. An investor is seldom willing to pay more than the call price, even if the yield were attractive at the higher price, if the company might pick his number for redemption.

Common Stock. To the extent that the risks borne by senior security holders are lessened by the specific terms attached to their securities, the risks associated with the junior securities are likely to be increased, since the modification does not normally remove the risk but merely shifts it. Because the common stock stands last in line, there is no opportunity for the shifting of the basic risks by qualifications in the terms of the issue.

There is, however, one respect in which the risk may be reduced, and that is with regard to the dilution of equity values through additional issues of the same class of stock. The feature aimed at safe-

---

[11] *Ibid.*, pp. 851–52.

guarding the interests of existing stockholders is the *pre-emptive right*. This is the right to buy any additional issues of common stock on a prorata basis, before it is offered to new stockholders, on terms which are at least as favorable as those offered to the new shareholders. If dilution is involved in the offering price, the old shareholder can protect his position by buying a block of the new stock in proportion to his present holdings. This right may be required by state law, or it may be left to the bargaining process between the company and the shareholders. For common stock which does not have the pre-emptive right, new issues of common may or may not be first offered to existing shareholders before being offered to the public at large, depending on the decision of management. If the new common is priced substantially under the market, then it may result in lowered market value and earnings per share on the outstanding stock. We shall give further attention to various aspects of rights offerings of common stock in the chapters which follow.

Although most companies have only one class of common stock, which bears the main burden of financial risk, some companies have created two classes of common stock where the burden of risk may be divided unequally. Such stock, referred to as *classified common*, may differ only in respect to voting privileges and may be equal in all other respects. On the other hand, one class may be set up with a prior claim to dividends, in which case it becomes in essence a type of preferred stock, even though not so named. Such a provision obviously effects an uneven distribution of risk among the common shareholders. An example of this is Crown Cork International Corporation $1.00 cumulative participating Class A stock: "Has preference as to cumulative dividends of $1 per share and participates in any further distribution equally, share for share, with class B stock after latter has received noncumulative dividends of $1 per share in any year."[12]

Another interesting example of classified common stock is the A and B common issues of the Citizens Utilities Company. Both A and B stock carry one vote per share. However, dividends on Class A stock are payable only in stock, whereas dividends on B stock are payable in cash. Class A stock is convertible into B at the holder's option share for share, except at the time of cash dividend payments.[13] The two classes were issued as a part of a stock reclassification plan.

---

[12] *Ibid.*, p. 2219.

[13] *Moody's Public Utility Manual, 1960*, p. 481.

Chapter 20

The Bargain for Funds: II. Modifications of the Distribution of Income and Control

HAVING considered a number of the more common variations in the basic security types, which have emerged as a result of efforts to modify the distribution of risk, we now turn to variations where the primary focus is on the modifications of terms relating to income and control. Here also it is apparent that there is virtually no limit to what can be done, given the willingness of both parties to the contract. In spite of the large number of security types that has developed over the years, we have every reason to believe that this evolutionary process will continue in the future as needs and objectives change.

B. *Modifications of the Distribution of Income: Bonds*

In the bargain between the corporate borrower and the bondholder, there is no issue more vital to both than the interest rate which will be necessary to market the issue completely and quickly. In a private placement, this can be settled by direct negotiation, whereas in a public offering the issuer must estimate in advance of the offering what will be the minimum yield acceptable to the bondholder. In either case, however, once the coupon rate is accepted by both parties, the specific terms of payment follow a standard pattern—typically, a regular semiannual payment of fixed amount to maturity.

Two significant modifications of the normal income position of the bondholder are to be found in the convertible bond and the income bond. The *convertible bond* gives the bondholder the option of retaining his normal contractual claim or of exchanging his security for another security, usually common stock, on a ratio fixed at the time of issue of the bonds. The terms may be illustrated by Continental Baking Company convertible subordinated debenture 3⅝'s, issued on March 1, 1955, and due in 1980. The provision for conversion into common stock was stated as follows: "The basic conversion price shall be $34.50 per share of Common Stock to and including February 28, 1958, $37 thereafter to and including February 28, 1961, and $39 thereafter to and including February 28, 1965." Cash was to be paid in lieu of fractional shares, and there was to be no adjustment for interest or dividends. The conversion privilege was protected against dilution. As a result, when a stock dividend was paid on the common stock in September, 1955, the conversion prices were changed to $32.50 to February, 1958; $34.85 to February, 1961; and $36.73 to February, 1965.[1]

It will be apparent that this privilege has no realizable value to the bondholder unless and until the earnings and/or dividend performance of the common justifies a market price in excess of the conversion prices quoted. At that time the bondholder is able to acquire common stock at a bargain price and either take an immediate capital gain by selling the common or hold it for income and further appreciation. Thus, the bondholder has the option of retaining his contractual but limited claim on earnings or of taking advantage of the more favorable income position of the stockholder if and when this becomes a reality. It would appear that if there is any real prospect of conversion under favorable terms, the holder of the convertible bond has "the best of all possible worlds"—the protection of a bond plus the speculative opportunities of a stock. In this respect the bondholder's gain is the common shareholder's loss. When conversion takes place, high-cost equity capital is substituted for low-cost debt, and the common shareholder's equity is diluted by the addition of stock "sold" at a (conversion) price below market.

There are two principal reasons why companies are willing to consider a convertible bond. One is that circumstances may make it difficult to market a particular bond (for example, a subordinated debenture) at a reasonable coupon rate and the speculative feature is added to put the issue across. Thus, the conversion feature is often a sign of weakness, and convertible bonds often are found to have relatively low ratings. The other and perhaps more justifiable reason is found in the case of a company which prefers to finance by stock rather than bonds but finds the current bond market more favorable than the stock market. Being unwilling to sell stock at the price dictated by the existing market and at the same time able to sell a bond

---

[1] *Moody's Industrial Manual, 1956*, p. 1090.

which is convertible into stock at a higher price, the company sells the convertible bond in the expectation that it will be fully converted in the near future. If conversion takes place, the company has, in a sense, sold common at the higher price in an indirect manner.

To illustrate, the Continental Baking convertible debenture was issued on March 1, 1955, convertible immediately at $34.50 per common share. The range of Continental Baking common in the year preceding this date was 20¾–33, with the high prices being recorded in March. At the time the decision to float this issue was made, it was highly uncertain whether a common issue could be sold at or near $34.50. On the other hand, it was quite within the realm of possibility that even within the year the market price of the common could rise above this figure and thus make conversion attractive to the bondholders.

In practice, it is possible for the bondholder to realize his capital gain without actual conversion. The reason for this is that once the market price of common rises above the conversion price, the market price of the bond tends to rise along with it. The bond is no longer valued as a bond but rather on the basis of its conversion value. As a consequence, the bondholder can take his capital gain simply by selling the bond. This market result tends to prevent the issuing company from realizing its objective of replacing debt with common equity capital. In order to assure that this objective will be realized, convertible bonds are usually made callable.

For example, the Continental Baking convertible debentures were callable at 105 to February 28, 1958, and thereafter at 104¾ to February 28, 1961. If the hoped-for rise in the price of the common stock occurred (above $32.50 after September, 1955) and the price of the debentures began its corresponding rise but no conversion actually took place, the company would be in a position to precipitate conversion at any time that the debentures rose above 105 by issuing a call for redemption. The bondholders would then convert to avoid being paid off at the lower call price.

At the beginning of 1958, about $3.8 million of the $13 million issue of Continental Baking debentures already had been converted. The common stock price began a steady rise from 27¾ early in 1958, and the debentures were called for redemption on October 1, 1958, at 104¾. At the time of the call the common stock price was 41½. Almost $9.2 million debentures were converted during 1958, and only $36,000 were redeemed.[2]

---

[2] Continental Baking Company, *Annual Report, 1958.*

It will be recognized that the critical decision in establishing the terms of a convertible issue is setting the conversion ratio or conversion price. Normally, this price is above the current market price of common, although there have been issues where the convertible bond had an immediate value in conversion (for example, the American Telephone and Telegraph 4¼ per cent convertible debentures offered to shareholders of record as of January 24, 1958, convertible at $142 per common share, market price of stock on January 24, $172⅞). It is in the interests of the existing common shareholders to set the price as high as possible; but on the other hand, it must not be so high as to make conversion very remote and therefore valueless in the mind of the prospective bondholder. The setting of the conversion price on the Continental Baking issue is an example of an attempt to achieve both objectives.

It will be remembered that the terms of the Continental Baking issue included *protection against dilution*. This term means that the basis of conversion will be adjusted in the event of a subsequent stock split or stock dividend so as to preserve the original advantage. Thus, if the common stock is split 2 for 1, the conversion price offered to the bondholder will be cut in half.

Occasionally, the opportunity for capital gains is offered a senior security holder in a manner that does not require him to give up his preferred position. This is accomplished by attaching to the senior security *stock purchase warrants*, which entitle the holder to acquire common stock at a fixed price, intended to be favorable. If and when the warrants are exercised, the senior security remains outstanding— in contrast to the convertible security. Once again, to the extent that the senior security holder gains, the common stockholder loses.

An example of warrants is seen in Mack Trucks, Inc., subordinated debenture 5½'s, issued in September, 1956, and due in 1968: "*Warrants*, detachable and transferable by delivery. Holders have right to purchase one and one-third $5 par common shares at following prices per share to each September 1 inclusive: 1959, $40; 1961, $43; 1963, $45; 1965, $47.50; thereafter at $50 to September 1, 1966, when privilege expires."[3] The market price range for Mack Trucks common stock during 1956 (until the 4-for-3 stock split in December) was 42⅜–26¼.

The *income bond* is one which has not, until recently, been used in the financing of healthy corporations. Briefly stated, an income bond is one in which the interest payment is made contingent on earnings.

---

[3] *Moody's Industrial Manual, 1957*, p. 2312.

The payments may be cumulative or noncumulative. It differs from a preferred stock in the respect that the payment is mandatory if earned, whereas the preferred dividend is still at the discretion of the board of directors. This dependence on earnings constitutes such a radical departure from the normal debtor-creditor relationship that—in the past, at least—income bonds have been accepted by investors only when there appeared to be no alternative under conditions of severe financial difficulty or bankruptcy. In such instances the income bond emerges as a means of reorganizing under a workable capital structure, while at the same time preserving some of the priority of the bondholders who have accepted it in exchange for the regular bond form which they held but which was in default.

Recently, however, there has been a growing interest in income bonds by solvent and profitable businesses. The primary reason is that under current conditions of heavy corporate income taxation, the security offers the elements of flexibility found in a preferred stock, combined with the tax advantage of interest payments deductible as a cost. The result has been that the income bond has taken on a new respectability. In the subsequent chapter dealing with refunding and reorganization, we cite a recent example of a proposed exchange of income bonds for preferred stock. This is another example of how attitudes toward security forms are modified as circumstances change.

The following terms of the Security Banknote Company convertible subordinated income debenture 5's, dated June 1, 1956, and due in 1976, illustrate the principal features of this type of security:

Interest payable . . . at 5% per annum, to extent earned; noncumulative.

. . . .

Sinking Fund—Annually, April 30, 1957–75, cash (or debentures) equal to 10% of consolidated net earnings, for redemption of debentures at 100.

. . . .

Security—not secured; subordinated to prior payment of senior indebtedness, including bank borrowings.

Dividend Restrictions—Company may not pay cash dividends on common while interest, principal or sinking fund installment is in default.

. . . .

Issued—Series A . . . in exchange for preferred at rate of $20 of debentures for each preferred share; series B issued in payment for preferred dividends in arrears.[4]

Price Range (over-the-counter bid) 1959: 86–80.[5]

---

[4] *Moody's Industrial Manual, 1960,* p. 992.

[5] Standard & Poor's Corporation, *Standard Corporation Descriptions,* P–S, August–September, 1960 (New York, 1960), p. 8853.

Note that in this particular case the bond issue is further weakened by subordination.

In recent years the Interstate Commerce Commission has authorized a number of railroads to issue income debentures for the purpose of retiring preferred or Class A common stock. The Commission commented on this trend as follows, in 1957: "There was a continuance of the trend which began several years ago for railroads to substitute interest-bearing obligations for preferred stock, with payment of interest generally contingent upon earnings, in order to reduce Federal income taxes. Interest on debentures is deductible whereas dividends on preferred stock are not."[6]

Modifications of the Distribution of Income: Stock

One of the ways in which the normal income position of preferred stock has been modified is by setting up certain conditions under which the preferred stockholder may share in income beyond the stated dividend. Such a stock is known as a *participating preferred.* The terms of the Virginia-Carolina Chemical Corporation 6 per cent cumulative participating preferred illustrate this form: "Dividend Rights—has preference over common as to cumulative dividends of 6% annually. . . . After common has received $3 per share in any fiscal year entitled to participate share for share with the common in any additional dividends in such fiscal year."[7]

It is obvious that such a feature can result in a major income concession to the preferred shareholder at the expense of the common shareholder; and for this reason, it is not found very frequently in preferred stock issues. Its presence indicates that at the time of issue the company and/or the common shareholder were in an unusually weak bargaining position.

Of more frequent occurrence is the *convertible preferred.* Since the characteristics of this security are very similar to those of the convertible bond as far as this feature is concerned, it will be discussed very briefly. Like the bond, it gives the senior security holder an opportunity to profit from his investment in the business beyond the fixed limits of his security type. To the extent that he does, it is at the expense of the common shareholder. If the security is issued as an intermediate stage in a plan for ultimate common stock financing, it

---

[6] Interstate Commerce Commission, *Seventy-First Annual Report* (Washington, D.C.: U.S. Government Printing Office, 1957), p. 57.

[7] *Moody's Industrial Manual, 1960*, p. 245.

will be necessary to include the call feature in order to be able to force conversion when the time becomes appropriate.

Typical of the terms of such an issue is Abbott Laboratories 4 per cent convertible preferred, par $100:

> Convertible into common at any time to Dec. 31, 1961 incl., on basis of 1.7 common shares for each preferred share, with no adjustment for dividends and with scrip for fractional shares. Conversion rights subject to adjustment in certain events. Right to convert preferred called for redemption prior to Jan. 1, 1962 will terminate not earlier than seventh day prior to redemption.
>
> Callable as a whole or in part on not less than 30 days' mailed notice at any time at $105 per share and dividends.[8]

It is interesting to note that the 1960 price range for Abbott Laboratories common stock was 69½–50 and for the convertible preferred, 114½–98¼. At the high for the common of 69½ the gain from conversion would have been $18 over the par value of the preferred and $13 over the call price. The high for the preferred was 114½.

Privileged Subscriptions: Rights

Whether conferred by law, corporate charter, or as a privilege extended at the discretion of management, the right to subscribe to new securities has important implications for income and potential capital gains. In many instances the right to subscribe to a given number of new securities is made at a price below the normal market price, and this means that those who hold the rights have a measurable advantage over those who do not.

It will be the primary purpose of this section to describe the effect of rights on the market price of the outstanding stock. In Chapter 23 the legal and market aspects of rights will be considered as a part of a general discussion of the raising of new equity capital.

The privilege of subscribing to new securities on favorable terms may be offered to any class of security for the purchase of the same or another class of security. The most common example, however, is a right extended to common shareholders for the purchase of additional shares of the same stock. We deal with this situation here.

We shall use as an example the National Aviation Corporation, which in 1956 offered its stockholders the privilege of subscribing to one new share for each four old shares held. In this case, one right was the privilege to subscribe to one-quarter share. In practice, while this right could be sold independently, it could only be exercised in

---

[8] *Ibid.*, p. 698.

conjunction with three other rights, to permit subscription to one share of the new issue.

If the stock is traded on an exchange, the exchange typically designates a date after which the stock will be traded free of the rights, or *ex-rights*. Until that date, trading is on a *cum-rights* basis (also termed *rights on* and *with rights*). When stock is sold cum rights, the seller of the stock agrees that the buyer is to receive, in addition to the shares of stock, any rights that have been or are being issued on that stock.

Referring again to the National Aviation Corporation illustration, stock rights to expire on May 22, 1956, were mailed to stockholders of record as of May 8, 1956. The stock was traded on the New York Stock Exchange cum rights through May 9, and thereafter on an ex-rights basis. During the ex-rights period the stock and the rights were traded separately with independent quotations.

During the time that rights are effective, any person planning to invest in the stock of the company has alternative ways to acquire it. He may buy a share on the market at the current market price, or he may buy the proper number of rights and then subscribe at the subscription price. In the latter case his total cost is the price of the rights plus the subscription price.[9] It is clear that investors will not be attracted to the new issue unless the subscription price is less than the going market price of the outstanding stock. Consequently, the setting of the subscription price contains the problem of predicting likely market prices for the security during the life of the rights. Some companies attempt to set the subscription price close to the market in order to minimize dilution. Others price the new issue well below the market in order to provide maximum inducement for use of the rights and to protect against the possibility that downward pressure on market price during the offering period will render the rights valueless.

In practice, the question of dilution of market values arises in every case because the subscription price for the new stock is at least somewhat lower than the recent market price for the existing issue. In fact, it will appear from the following discussion that the market value of a right represents (approximately but not fully) the amount of the dilution of the previous market values which is implicit in the new offering at favorable subscription prices.

Effect on Market Value of Issue of Stock at Less than Old Market Price. Perhaps the effect on market value can be pictured best by first examining the theoretical effect on market value of a *stock split;* for

---

[9] We ignore brokerage.

in a stock split the number of shares of stock is increased, but the net worth of the company does not change. From the standpoint of the stockholder, his total values remain the same; and in theory, he has gained or lost nothing as a result of the split.

For example, a 4-for-1 stock split is announced for a stock selling at 120. Since the corporation will acquire no new money as a result of the split, its stock will have gained or lost nothing in value. A total value of 120 is now represented by four shares. Hence, the new stock would be expected to sell at

$$\frac{120}{4} = 30.$$

(Further reference to the stock split will be found in Chapter 27 on refunding and recapitalization.)

Now, let us return to the National Aviation illustration of the sale of new stock. Although the old stock was selling at about $41\frac{1}{4}$ cum rights, stockholders received rights to purchase at 30 one new share for each four shares held. What dilution of market value of the old shares results from the issue at 30? In answering, let us consider a stockholder who owns four old shares. Before the stock went ex rights, his four shares represented a value of $165 ($41\frac{1}{4}$ times 4). In exercising his rights to purchase one new share, he added an investment of $30 in cash, making a total investment of $195 now represented by five shares. One new share, then, could be expected to have a value of

$$\frac{195}{5} = 39.$$

Actually, the first sale on the first day of trading ex rights was at $39\frac{1}{8}$, and the market closed at 39.

A formula incorporating this reasoning is widely used as a rough measure of the theoretical effect of issuance of stock at less than the market on the ex-rights market price of the stock. In the formula the following notations are used:

M = Market value of one share cum rights
N = Number of old shares that entitle the holder to purchase one new share
P = Theoretical market value of one share ex rights
S = Subscription price

Using the above notations, the formula is:

$$P = \frac{MN + S}{N + 1} \text{ (Theoretical Market Price after Exercise of Rights)}$$

Substituting the facts from the National Aviation illustration:

$$P = \frac{(41\frac{1}{4} \times 4) + 30}{4 + 1}$$

$$P = \frac{195}{5}$$

$$P = 39$$

Valuation of Stock Rights. If the stockholder does not care to exercise his right to purchase, at what price will he be able to sell the right in the market? Once the stock is selling ex rights, the calculation of the value of one right is relatively simple. The value of one right is the difference between the ex-rights market price of one share and the subscription price, divided by the number of rights necessary to purchase one share. In the National Aviation case the first market price on the first day of trading ex rights was $39\frac{1}{8}$. With four rights an investor could buy one share at an effective discount of $9\frac{1}{8}$, since the subscription price was 30. Hence, one right had a worth of about $2\frac{1}{4}$.

Expressed in a formula, this relation is:

$$\frac{P - S}{N} \text{(Theoretical Market Value of One Right, Ex Rights)}$$

$$= \frac{39\frac{1}{8} - 30}{4}$$

$$= 2\frac{1}{4}$$

Before the ex-rights date, when the stock is still selling cum rights, the value of one right can be predicted by use of the following formula:

$$\frac{M - S}{N + 1} \text{ (Theoretical Value of One Right, Cum Rights)}$$

Using the National Aviation illustration again, with the cum-rights market price of $41\frac{1}{4}$:

$$\text{(Theoretical Value of One Right)} = \frac{41\frac{1}{4} - 30}{4 + 1}$$

$$= \frac{11\frac{1}{4}}{5}$$

$$= 2\frac{1}{4}$$

It will now be apparent that the value of one right, in theory, will equal the anticipated dilution of market value of one old share. Hence, if brokerage fees and income tax questions involved in sale of the rights are ignored, the stockholder who sells his rights theoretically receives enough cash from the sale so as to sustain no net loss or gain in total market value of his holdings. From this point of view, a privileged subscription, if exercised or sold, prevents dilution of the *market value* of the total interests of the existing shareholders.

As a matter of interest, the following is the actual record of National Aviation Corporation common stock during the period (taken from the *Wall Street Journal*):

DATE	PRICE OF COMMON*		PRICE OF RIGHT
	Cum Rights	Ex Rights	
May 7, 1956..............	41⅜	....	...
May 8, 1956..............	41½	....	...
May 9, 1956..............	41¼	....	...
May 10, 1956..............	....	39	2⅛
May 11, 1956..............	....	38⅜	2¼
May 14, 1956..............	....	38⅜	2⅛
May 15, 1956..............	....	38¼	2
May 16, 1956..............	....	38⅜	2
May 17, 1956..............	....	38⅜	2⅛
May 18, 1956..............	....	38½	2⅛
May 21, 1956..............	....	38⅝	2¼
May 22, 1956..............	....	38½	2⅛

* Closing prices only.

The discussion above was based on an issue of common stock. In valuing rights to subscribe to issues of straight preferred stock or bonds (an event much less frequent than in the case of common stock), the ex-rights formula given above, $\frac{P - S}{N}$, may be used in all instances, since dilution is not involved. If a valuation of the rights to buy preferred stock or bonds in advance of the establishment of a market price for the issue is desired, a probable market price, P in the formula, must be assumed.

Rights offerings are generally made with the presumption that a large proportion of the new shares will be subscribed for: ninety per cent subscription is regarded by many financial analysts as the lower limit of a "successful" rights sale. Under such circumstances, the issuing company can either withhold the few unsubscribed shares from the market or sell them to the general public. In order to increase the chances that a large part of the issue will be taken up by stockholders, a number of companies offer *oversubscription* privileges, sometimes known as *the second bite*. Under this arrangement, stockholders are allowed not only to subscribe to the new issue on a prorata basis but also to oversubscribe any shares not bought on the initial subscription.

Before leaving the subject of rights, we call the reader's attention to the widespread use of the option to buy stock at a favorable price as a part of an executive compensation plan. This practice must be considered not as an aspect of the bargain for funds but rather as an aspect of the bargain for executives. Nevertheless, from a strictly financial viewpoint the effect on the common shareholders is the same as if the right to buy common stock had been extended to another group of security holders. It has been estimated that as of 1957, well over 50 per cent of the companies with common stock listed on the New York Stock Exchange offered a plan of this sort to their employees.[10] The average amount of stock set aside for this purpose was approximately 5 per cent of the shares outstanding prior to the offering.[11]

Of course, the attractiveness of such plans depends on a rising market price, and it is not surprising that some of the enthusiasm wears off in periods of recession. This was evident in the period of declining profits and uncertain market prices of stock during 1960 and extending into 1961.

C. Modification of the Distribution of Control

In Chapter 15 the normal distribution of control among the basic security types was discussed. It was brought out that normally, voting power rests in the hands of the common shareholders alone, although certain contingent voting privileges may be reserved for the preferred shareholders in event of suspension of dividend payments.

In some companies the preferred stock does have a share of the voting power at regular shareholders' meetings. The extent varies from one issue to another. The holders of Sperry Rand Corporation $4.50 cumulative preferred have full voting rights of one vote per share along with the common. The holders of Mead Johnson & Company 4 per cent cumulative preferred are entitled to one vote per share, to use these votes cumulatively in voting for directors, and on some issues, to vote as a group. Under certain circumstances, the voting power of the preferred shareholders could be a major consideration in the minds of the common shareholders and hence an important issue in setting the terms of the preferred.

It has been mentioned previously that some companies have subdivided their common stock into two classes. Usually, the primary purpose of this is to reserve the voting power for one class and use the

---

[10] J. H. Rothschild, "Financing Stock Purchases by Executives," *Harvard Business Review*, March–April, 1957, p. 136.

[11] *Ibid.*

other class as a means of raising capital from the investing public. Obviously, such nonvoting stock can be sold only to shareholders who are first and foremost investors and therefore attach only secondary importance to the voting privilege. It is a significant fact that nonvoting common stock is not accepted for listing by the New York Stock Exchange.

Although bondholders and most preferred stockholders do not have a direct voice in management, they nevertheless influence the actions of management by means of positive or negative covenants in the bond indenture or in charter provisions relating to preferred stock. Further, if the issue is in default and/or the company in bankruptcy, these investors or their representatives will have a strong influence on management decisions, and this influence may be perpetuated in a reorganization under which old securities are exchanged for new securities with voting power. The full implications of reorganization will be taken up in a later chapter.

Summary

In this and the preceding chapter, we have developed the idea of the security form as a product of the bargaining process between the corporate user of funds and those individuals and institutions which supply the funds. It has been seen how certain security features are to the advantage of the issuing company and other features are to the advantage of the security holder, and that the resultant security is basically a compromise of objectives which is acceptable to both parties to the contract. We have stressed that the fundamental give-and-take of this process is not really between management as such and a group of security holders but rather between one group of security holders and another—between the common shareholders, on the one hand, and the senior security holders, on the other.

Because of the wide variation of circumstances and objectives, it is not surprising that this bargaining process has produced a complex of special security types. We have reviewed the major variations in general use; but as we stated at the beginning of the chapter, this is by no means a catalogue of all possible types. The reader is referred to the appendix of the first edition of Graham and Dodd's *Security Analysis* for a list of illustrations of unusual variations of the common security forms.[12] This list includes such securities as bonds payable at the option of the bondholder, noninterest-bearing bonds, preferred is-

---

[12] B. Graham, and D. L. Dodd, *Security Analysis* (1st ed.; New York: McGraw-Hill Book Co., Inc., 1934), Appendix, Note 3, pp. 618–35.

sues with little or no claim as to assets, preferred stock with a mortgage lien, and common stock with a claim to income senior to another issue. The perusal of such a list brings home the importance of judging a security not by the name which the company has applied to it but rather by the specific terms which determine its true nature.

Chapter 21

The Cost of Capital

IN THIS chapter, we shall return to the three basic types of security issues, and add leases to our scope. Again, attention will be focused on the flow of funds that are called for either by contract or as a matter of policy. In Chapter 14, at page 291, we referred to these flows as "burden," and showed how to make ratios of this burden to the amounts of fund inflows developed from the operations of the business. Here, we wish to discuss another relationship: that of the burdens of a particular security to the amounts that can be raised by issuing that security, that is, to the *cost of capital*.

Introduction—and Definition

The example of a short-term loan made by a bank to a corporation can be used to show more clearly the focus of our interest and to introduce some of the quantities involved. Let us say that the XYZ Corporation needs $10,000 for a month to cover some seasonal need. A bank makes the loan, quoting the interest rate of 6 per cent per year. Following the usual practice in such short-term arrangements, the bank would *discount the loan*, deducting interest in advance. Thus, the company at the outset of the loan would have *net proceeds* of $9,950 at its disposal; and it would be required to pay $10,000 one month later, a sum which we defined in Chapter 14 as the burden of the debt.

The *cost of capital* contained in a financing arrangement may be determined in amount by finding the difference between the net proceeds actually made available to the company and the total burden incurred during the arrangement. In terms of a rate of interest, it may be defined as the rate that must be earned on the net proceeds to pro-

413

vide the cost elements of the burden at the times they are due.[1] Having
computed this rate, management may use the cost of capital to select
from among alternative financial arrangements, or to decide whether
promised gains from some operation are sufficient to justify the costs
of raising the needed funds.

Even in considering the bank loan, unfortunately, the complications begin. The cost is not the rate of 6 per cent per year, for that
rate was applied to $10,000, a sum that was not received by the bor-
rower. The net proceeds were $9,950. The cost of capital is the rate
that must be earned on this sum to provide the $50 interest that will
be due in a month: $\dfrac{\$50}{\$9,950} = 0.503$ per cent in one month, or at the
rate of 6.04 per cent per year, before tax.

Another example from short-term financing will be taken. A company can often obtain extended use of funds by paying its accounts
payable on a delayed basis. If $10,000 is owed on a 2/10, n/30
basis, the company has the option of paying $9,800 within 10 days or
$10,000 at the end of 30 days. If the second option is taken, the funds
provided are $9,800, and the cost is $200. Again, the determination
of the rate that must be earned (before tax) to produce the needed
$200 is: $\dfrac{\$200}{\$9,800} = 2.04$ per cent for 20 days, or at the rate of 37 per
cent per year.

If we consider these two examples as alternatives available to a
company, it is clear that great advantage lies in choosing the bank
loan, because of its much lower cost. Here, we see one of the important
uses of the cost-of-capital calculation, for it is a basis for a choice
among alternative ways of raising funds.

If we assume that the XYZ Corporation does not have bank credit
available, we can see another use of the computation of the cost of
capital, for it would take a most promising opportunity (or a great
necessity) to justify carrying the account payable beyond the discount
period. That is, the cost of capital can be used as a criterion in comparison with anticipated rates of profit for the acceptability of projects
requiring funds.

We now turn to a description of how the cost of capital can be determined for each of the basic financial contracts taken separately. In
doing so, we shall draw the needed quantities from the experience of
the Long Island Lighting Company, which in 1953 obtained funds

---

[1] We have worded this definition carefully so as to omit questions of the sources of
funds necessary to retire the net proceeds themselves.

from the public by using bonds, preferred stock, and common stock at various dates during the year. It is, of course, easy to determine what such figures are after the financing has taken place. The precision thus given to our figures was not present when management was making its decisions; but the reader, we feel, will have troubles enough at this introductory stage without the need to worry about the accuracy of his forecasts. Suffice it to say here that cost-of-capital figures used in planning are based on estimates, and that the results of calculations are regarded as approximations rather than precise amounts. In practice, estimates are first based on the observation of the fate of similar issues made by other companies and/or the market behavior of the outstanding securities of the particular company. Later, the estimates can be refined from the preliminary quotations that are received from potential distributors in the process of discussing an issue.

Costs of Fixed Return Types of Securities

The easiest costs to determine are those related to contracts which have the outlay fixed at the time they are issued: preferred stock, bonds, and leases. Preferred dividends cannot go above a known limit (in the usual case of a nonparticipating issue), bond interest is rigidly set so that it cannot vary up or down, and a majority of leases also call for amounts that are defined in the original contract. We shall proceed to explain how the costs of each of these types of financing can be computed, taking them in the order named above.

The principal types of cash costs associated with the acquisition of funds through financial contracts may be classified as follows:

a) Periodic payments to the contract holder in the form of interest, dividends, or rent.

b) Any payment to the distributor of the issue as compensation for his services in marketing the issue and for assuming the risks associated with a public offering. The distributor deducts from the price received from the investor an amount which he has agreed is adequate compensation and then remits the net proceeds to the company. The difference between the price to the investor and the price to the company is referred to as the *spread*.

c) Other costs incidental to the making of the contract which are paid by the issuing company, such as legal and printing costs.

d) Any payment to the contract holder at the retirement of an issue in excess of the amount originally provided by the investor. This *discount* applies only to securities which have a definite maturity, or which may be redeemed at the option of the company, and only when the issue is sold at a price less than the amount payable at retirement. This amount may be amortized over the life of the issue and considered as an addition to the periodic interest or dividend cost. According to similar reasoning, security sold at a *premium* would involve a downward adjustment of the interest or dividend cost.

1. Preferred Stock. The case of a "straight" preferred stock, one without a sinking fund, is relatively simple, for two reasons. First, the security is a fixed income type, where compensation to the investor in the form of dividend payments is rigidly limited to the amount specified at the time of issue. While this annual payment is not mandatory, as in the case of bonds, it is appropriate that management assume it to be, as has been explained before. The other simplifying feature is that the ordinary straight preferred stock does not have a fixed date for the repayment of the principal sum; therefore, the costs which may be associated with repayment (item [*d*]) are ruled out.[2]

For our purposes, it is desirable to express the cost of capital as an annual percentage outlay on the dollars provided. As the issuer views it, the dollars provided are the net proceeds available for investment in corporate activity—the sum provided by the investor, less the costs of issue, including the amount retained by the investment banker handling the issue and the expenditures incurred directly by the issuer. These are, of course, items (*b*) and (*c*) in the foregoing list.

An illustration of this process in the case of preferred stock will be helpful. The prospectus on Long Island Lighting Company's Series C preferred stock, offered during 1953, gave the following information:

Amount: 100,000 shares, par $100:
- *a*) Cumulative dividend.............................5.25%
- Price to public....................................$100
- *b*) Spread...$2
- Proceeds to company (from underwriter)............$98
- *c*) Other costs of issue paid by company...............$45,000
- Other costs as a percentage of total issue............0.45%
- Net proceeds to company.........................$97.55

It will be seen that although the public was to pay $100 per share, the company would have only $97.55 per share available for investment. For the use of this sum of money the company would pay the investor $5.25 per year. Under these circumstances, the annual cash payment, expressed as a percentage of the investable funds, would amount to 5.38 per cent; and this will be taken as the cost, on an after-tax basis:

---

[2] It is true that a redeemable preferred may be repaid eventually at the option of the management, but this would normally be a possibility so uncertain at the time of issue as to rule it out of consideration at that time.

$$\frac{\text{Payment to Holders}}{\text{Net Proceeds to Issuer}} = \frac{\$5.25}{\$100.00 - (2.00 + 0.45)} = \underline{\underline{5.38\%}}.$$

The reader already knows how to convert this figure to a before-tax basis. At a tax rate of 52 per cent, the before-tax outlay cost is 11.21 per cent.

2. Bonds. The measurement of the annual cash obligation on bonds runs in a pattern similar to that for the preferred stock but is complicated by the facts that bonds must be repaid at a specific future date and that the amount originally received by the company is likely to differ from the amount repaid to the investor at maturity. Thus, for example, if we are considering a 15-year, 3 per cent bond with a face value of $1,000, which brought the issuer $980 net, we must take into account not only the $30 annual interest payment but also the $20 which must be paid to the investor at the end of 15 years in addition to the $980 actually received and used by the company. Here, we shall first present an approximate method of calculating cost, and then describe how to use tables to get a value that takes time into account.

The method of approximation which we use is taken because its results are the closest to the time-adjusted values in the range most often encountered in connection with bond issues. For each $1,000 bond the issuer is committed to an annual interest payment of $30 cash. To this amount may be added the appropriate fractional share of the excess of the amount due at maturity over the net proceeds received—one fifteenth of $20, or $1.33, giving a total annual cost of $31.33. This approach makes the assumption that the excess of $20 is gradually built up over a 15-year period rather than provided in a lump sum at the end, but without any revenue from the fund being accumulated. The amount invested must therefore be considered not as the $980 originally provided but the average of $980 and the $1,000 built up at the end of 15 years, or $990. The approximate effective percentage cost thus becomes:

$$\frac{\$31.33}{\$990} = \underline{\underline{3.16\%}}.$$

If it happens that the amount payable at maturity is less than the net proceeds to the company at time of issue, the amount may be considered as a deduction from the semiannual interest payments and the effective percentage cost will be below the coupon rate on the bonds. In general terms, the formula is:

$$\frac{\text{Annual Interest} + \text{or} - \text{Prorated Difference between Net Proceeds and Maturity Value}}{\text{Average between Net Proceeds and Maturity Value}}$$

The calculation above is not entirely accurate, because it omits the factor of the varying values that should be given to sums of money that are transferred at various times. Fortunately, *bond value tables* have been published to which one may make reference when an exact figure is wanted. The section of a bond value table applicable to the problem above is reproduced in Table 21–1. It will be seen that for a

TABLE 21–1

THREE PER CENT BONDS

Yield to Maturity	14½ Years	15 Years	15½ Years
2.75%..........	$102.97	$103.06	$103.14
2.80............	102.37	102.44	102.50
2.90............	101.18	101.21	101.24
3.00............	100.00	100.00	100.00
3.10............	98.84	98.81	98.78
3.20............	97.69	97.63	97.57
3.25............	97.13	97.05	96.97

3 per cent, fifteen-year bond which nets the company $98 per $100 of bond, the actual cost lies between 3.1 and 3.2 per cent. The precise figure may be gained by interpolation. It is 3.169 per cent.[3]

We may now proceed to consider the case of the Long Island Lighting Company bonds offered during 1953, comparing them with the preferred stock. The facts of the issue, as given in the prospectus, follow:

```
 Total amount.....................................$25,000,000
 Term.............................................30 years
    a) Coupon rate................................3½%
       Price to public............................100.929%
    b) Spread.....................................0.719
       Proceeds to company........................100.210%
    c) Other costs of issue.......................$195,000
       Other costs as a percentage of total issue..0.780%
       Net proceeds to company....................99.430%
    d) Discount...................................0.570%
       Maturity value.............................100.000%
```

Following the method of computation suggested above, we note that the company must pay $35 of interest per year on each $1,000

---

[3] The difference between this calculation of the effective cost to the user of funds and the yield calculation of an investor may be noted. The bond above might have been sold by the underwriter to the investor at a premium—say, at $1,020. The difference of $40 was used to compensate the distributor and pay other costs. As far as the investor is concerned, the yield to him is less than 3 per cent, since he must make allowance for the fact that he will not receive $1,020 at maturity, but only $1,000. His effective return (taken from a bond table) at this price would be 2.835 per cent. It will be apparent that the difference between the yield to the investor and the cost to the company results from the use of a portion of the proceeds to cover the costs of issue.

bond and, in addition, amortize one thirtieth of $5.70—the excess of the amount to be repaid over the amount received on a $1,000 bond. Bond tables give the effective cost in this case as 3.53 per cent. Since we are dealing with a bond, this figure represents a before-tax cost. On an after-tax basis the cost is 1.69 per cent.

Readers who are watchful of details will note that we have made no allowance for the effect of periodic retirement of the bond through sinking funds, although methods do exist for this refinement. The usual calculations for the cost of bonded debt rely on bond value tables, and these are based on the assumption either that the bonds in question are not to be retired by sinking fund or (another way of saying the same thing) that sinking fund purchases and the ultimate maturity will be priced so as not to incur further cost or to create further income. For most purposes, the values given by bond value tables are sufficiently accurate.

In Chapter 14, we specified that any method of calculation of burdens and costs must give consistent results. We have achieved the desired result here; and the following table shows the cost of the preferred stock to be 3.2 times that of the bonds, whether one looks at before-tax or after-tax costs.

COSTS OF CAPITAL AS COMPUTED

	Before Tax	After Tax (52%)
Bonds	3.53%	1.69%
Preferred stock	11.21%	5.38%

3. Leases. In order to show how the cost of a lease contract may be evaluated, we must temporarily depart from the Long Island Lighting Company, and return to the case of the variety store, already used in Chapter 18. By the lease, the chain obtained assets costing $225,000, and incurred obligations to pay:

$22,035 for 10 years	$220,350
11,583 for 15 years	173,745
	$394,095

The total burden exceeds the proceeds by $169,095, which is the cost in dollar terms. The average of this cost over 25 years is $6,764 per year. The average amount provided by the lease can be approximated as $112,500, since we are told that the lessor will amortize the cost of the property over the time of the lease. An approximate rate of cost is, then:

$$\frac{6,764}{112,500} = 6.01\%.$$

Since we were told in Chapter 18 that the rate was calculated to be 6 per cent, we have a satisfactory approximation.

Coverage Requirements as Limits to Borrowing at Established Rates

If the Long Island Lighting Company, with all other things equal, had tried to raise twice as much money with its bond issue, would it have been able to obtain the same terms as to cost? Almost certainly not, since the investors would have insisted upon higher rates to compensate for higher risk. In appraising a particular security for possible investment, the investor is concerned not only with the amount of the prospective income to be derived but also with the certainty of that income. It is common knowledge that even in the case of a senior mortgage bond, the terms of which are legally enforceable, there is an element of uncertainty about the periodic interest payments and the repayment of principal at maturity. This uncertainty comes from the possibility that at some time over the life of the issue the issuing company may find itself with a cash position so weakened that it cannot fulfill its obligation to the security holder.

There are various ways in which investors may take steps to protect themselves against this risk. The primary safeguard is considered to be a demonstrated capacity to earn, in normal times, an income substantially in excess of the total contractual or assumed obligation on the securities. It is recognized that however well managed a business may be, it cannot escape the influence of a general business recession, should such occur. It is therefore necessary to be assured that the earnings available for payments to senior security holders in prosperous times are large enough so that the possible shrinkage in bad times will not endanger these payments, either in fact or in the minds of investors. Suppose it is assumed that a recession might cut net earnings available for bond interest to one half the level of prosperous times; then the ratio of such net earnings to total bond interest in normal times would have to be more than 2/1 for the bondholder to feel any real protection. This "cushion" of excess earnings capacity will be referred to in this discussion as the *earnings coverage* on a security.

It may be helpful to illustrate how these considerations apply in practice. Let us compare two railroad bonds which in several important respects seem to offer a similar investment opportunity:

1. New York, New Haven and Hartford Railroad first and refunding 4's, Series A, due in 2007.
2. Illinois Central Railroad first-mortgage 3⅜'s, Series H, due in 1989.

Although the two companies concerned are not comparable as to size, the securities have a number of aspects in common. They are both bonds, secured by a first mortgage on the same type of property, and both have relatively distant maturity dates. They are both callable at the option of the issuing company on a predetermined basis, both protected by sinking fund arrangements, and both accepted for listing on the New York Stock Exchange. However, in spite of these important similarities, *Moody's Transportation Manual* for investors, 1956 edition, rated the Illinois Central issue as an "A" bond and the New Haven issue as a "Ba" bond. The latter rating is two grades below the former (A, Baa, Ba). It is instructive to note the general statement in *Moody's Transportation Manual* concerning these ratings:

> A—Bonds which are rated A possess many favorable investment attributes and are to be considered as higher medium grade obligations. Factors giving security to principal and interest are considered adequate but elements may be present which suggest a susceptibility to impairment sometime in the future.
>
> Ba—Bonds which are rated Ba are judged to have speculative elements; their future cannot be considered as well assured. Often the protection of interest and principal payments may be very moderate and thereby not well safe-guarded during both good and bad times over the future. Uncertainty of position characterizes bonds of this class.[4]

On closer examination, the most striking difference between these two securities is in the extent to which annual earnings have exceeded bond interest. In the case of Illinois Central the ratio times fixed charges earned (before tax) was 7.2 for the year 1955.[5] In the case of the New Haven the same comparison for 1955 showed before-tax earnings only 2.0 times fixed charges.[6] The substantially better showing of Illinois Central in this regard was also borne out by a similar comparison over the most recent five-year period. It cannot be concluded, of course, that this was the only factor leading to the downgrading of the New Haven issue, but it was undoubtedly of great importance in any such appraisal.

Assuming that the market in general agreed with Moody's appraisal of the situation, we should expect the New Haven issue to be at a disadvantage in the market. Many investors who are satisfied with an A bond would not even consider a Ba bond with its "speculative

---

[4] *Moody's Transportation Manual, 1956,* p. vi.

[5] *Ibid.,* p. 151.

[6] *Ibid.,* p. 1222.

elements." The significant comparison here, in terms of future need for funds, is yield to maturity based on the current market prices of these bonds. It reveals an even greater disparity. Using the average market prices prevailing in 1955, the yield to maturity on the Illinois Central bond was 3.3 per cent and on the New Haven bond was 5.2 per cent. It is clear that in 1956, any new financing by New Haven would have been significantly more costly than it would have been for Illinois Central. Unquestionably, this higher cost was directly related to the greater risks which investors have come to associate with the weaker company.

To return to the Long Island Lighting Company example, cited earlier, earnings which merely covered the direct cash outlay of 3.53 per cent on the bonds would not be sufficient to satisfy a bond buyer's concept of a safe investment. It is clearly a part of the over-all financial obligation associated with new security issues that a business meet the minimum earnings coverage necessary to induce the bondholder or stockholder to invest at the current rate of return. This aspect is difficult to pin down quantitatively, however, because of the lack of uniformity of investment standards in the securities market. We term this kind of requirement the *coverage requirement*, and emphasize that the outlay cost of any security always has behind it a coverage requirement which is larger. Without such coverage and the assurance it gives, the specific rate of outlay cost would not have been acceptable to the investor.

For purposes of illustration, we have chosen to use the standard used by a major insurance company, because it is a standard which has actually been applied by this investor to our case in question, the Long Island Lighting Company. We emphasize that this is an example and is not intended to suggest a general rule.

For public utility bonds, the desired earnings coverage rates applied by this particular investor are measured by a times interest earned ratio of $3\frac{1}{2}$:

$$\frac{\text{Earnings before Interest and Taxes}}{\text{Interest on Long-Term Debt}} = 3\frac{1}{2}.$$

If the Long Island Lighting Company bonds are to meet this test without drawing on the general earning power of the company, the investment that will be financed by the proposed issue must earn something like three and a half times its cost—or the issue will be rated as more risky and will become more costly, if it will be sold at all. In some cases, failure to meet the standard could mean that the investors would not buy the bond on any terms. At all events, the question of earnings coverage is one that must be considered by management whenever a fixed charge type of financial contract is proposed.

Elements to Consider in the Cost of Common Equity

We have seen in the previous section how the cash outlays on senior securities can be measured precisely and expressed as a percentage of the net proceeds made available for investment. We also have just indicated the existence of not so clearly defined coverage requirements which must also be met if the issuer wishes to continue to sell these senior securities at the same quality rating.

In considering these two aspects of the financial obligation associated with senior securities, it is apparent that there is a clear line of distinction between what the security holder actually receives in earnings and the earnings he asks the company to provide as a margin of protection against the effects of adverse circumstances, protection which has the twofold significance of demonstrated "excess" earning power and a growing equity base to the extent that these earnings are reinvested.

On the surface, the relation of a corporation to the holders of common stock appears to have similar components. The common shareholder, like the preferred shareholder, receives his dividend as a cash outlay and looks to an excess of earnings per share as his assurance that this dividend will continue in the future. However, there is an all-important difference in the case of common stock, in that the excess earnings, though not received at the moment, nevertheless belong to the shareholder. They add directly to the value of his investment in the business; and if wisely reinvested, they add to his earnings (and dividends) in the future.

For this reason, most analysts agree that the value of a common stock (which has its most tangible manifestation in market price) is usually based on two components:[7] (1) an anticipated income stream which will be realized in cash (dividends) and (2) an anticipated income stream which will not be realized in cash in the normal course of events but which nevertheless is potentially realizable if properly conserved. This second component interacts on the first to the extent that it increases confidence in the continuity of the current dividend and leads to the expectation of an increase in the future. This is a

---

[7] Some analysts would state a third component: the price at which it is believed the stock will be sold later on. But is not this price an evaluation of dividends and earnings in the more distant future?

complex relationship, which varies from company to company, industry to industry, and time to time.

However, it is apparent that total earnings on common stock, as well as dividends, are important to the shareholder. This viewpoint is axiomatic in the processes for which we will now proceed to develop measurement of the cost of common equity capital. At the same time, it is important to keep in mind that the size of any dividend (in dollars and percentage pay-out) is undoubtedly of great significance in the determination of market price at any point of time. At the moment, we assume that for a given company the policy with respect to dividends is known, so that the investor can appraise its value to him. The determinants of dividend policy were discussed in Chapter 17.

In the material which follows, we regularly use a market price in our calculations. This price is sometimes derived from quotations in the stock market, sometimes from the specific terms of a proposed issue. Only the latter figure is available to a company whose stock is not traded in a market. Such *closely held* companies must, where necessary, rely upon quotations of similar securities—and this is much easier to say than to do.

Measuring the Cost of Equity Capital

In the measurement of the cost of common equity capital, it is necessary to distinguish between the two ways in which such capital enters the business and to treat each separately: (1) the sale of new common stock; and (2) *internal financing* which, in turn, is divided into (*a*) reinvested earnings and (*b*) funds related to depreciation charges. These will be discussed in order.

So far, it has been clear that the cost of capital has been described from the point of view of the issuing corporation. As we turn to considering the cost of common equity capital, we must now be more specific. The point of view necessary for the proper appraisal of the cost of this type of equity capital is that of the *existing common shareholder*. Assuming that financing is being considered prior to the decision to expand, it is clear that existing shareholders would not favor expansion unless earnings per share were at least maintained, and preferably increased. Any less favorable result would constitute a *dilution* of the values of the existing equity investment.

1. New Common Stock Issues. When we come to additional issues of common stock, the situation is complicated by the fact that changes in earnings per share may affect the price of the stock and thus the stockholders' return on their investment. If the new project will not produce on the new shares earnings per share at least equal to those already experienced for the old shares,[8] the average earnings per share after the project will fall, and the market value of the old shares may fall also (and *will* fall if the drop in E.P.S. is large). The minimum acceptable result is, therefore, one where the proportion in which total earnings increase is no less than the proportion in which total shares increase. The latter quantity, the total number of shares to be issued, is determined by the amount of money to be raised and the price per share. Since the latter is set with reference to the existing market level, we establish our criterion:

$$\frac{\text{Existing Earnings}}{\text{Existing Investment}} = \frac{\text{Increment in Earnings}}{\text{New Investment}} = \frac{\text{Earnings per share (New)}}{\text{Price (New)}}$$

This criterion has been well expressed as follows: "The cost of equity capital might well be defined as that rate of return percentage which must be earned on incremental investment in order that the market value of existing stockholders' proprietary interest in the firm be neither increased or decreased."[9]

Since the earnings/price relationship is to be the measurement of the cost of new equity capital, it is necessary to pause briefly to consider what earnings and what price should be assumed. Ideally, the earnings should be those which would be earned by the existing common shares in the future if the proposed expansion were not carried out. In practice, analysts usually choose the most recently reported earnings or use an average of recent periods. The objective is to represent the earnings level of the future, and the analyst's judgment must be relied on for the proper choice.

The calculation of cost of capital of new common stock issues may therefore be expressed in general terms by a simple formula:

Let C = Cost of capital on new common stock, on an after-tax basis.
  E = Anticipated earnings per share that would be experienced if the project were not adopted.
  Po = Price obtainable on new stock, net.

Then

$$C = \frac{E}{Po}.$$

---

[8] We are assuming that the new project does not change the risk classification of the company.

[9] Sanford L. Margoshes, "Price/Earnings Ratio in Financial Analysis," *Financial Analysts Journal*, November–December, 1960, pp. 125–30, p. 129.

The price, since we are considering what the new project must produce to keep the present shareholders where they have been, must be the net proceeds obtainable from the proposed issue. This number, too, will only be observed in the future. In practice, analysts use current market quotations, averages of recent quotations, or prices developed from a study of similar issues of other companies. It is, again, a matter of judgment.

To be more explicit, let us refer again to the case of the Long Island Lighting Company. The prospectus for a common stock issue during 1953 gave the following information:

> Amount: 685,648 shares.............................$10 par
> Price to public.......................................$16
> Spread...$0.29
> Proceeds to company.................................$15.71
> Other costs of issue.................................$128,000
> Other costs as percentage of total issue.............1.17%
> Net proceeds per share...............................$15.52
> Market price of common, 1953: 18⅜–15½, average 17

The most recent annual earnings per share figure on the outstanding common stock at this time was $1.15 per share (after taxes).[10]

To express the cost measured by a rate of return on the dollars invested, we must recognize the fact that each new share will produce only $15.52 of investable funds, and not the $17 currently quoted on the market. Consequently, the after-tax rate of return must be

$$\frac{1.15}{15.52} = 7.4 \text{ per cent}$$

in order to produce the rate desired by the existing stockholder. This is the after-tax cost of capital on a new issue of common stock of Long Island Lighting Company at this time. In terms of before-tax dollars the comparable rate of return would be 15.4 per cent (tax rate, 52 per cent).

Even the rate of return indicated will not equalize the situation for the old shareholder with respect to another important element of value to a shareholder, participation in the growth of profits. As we pointed out in describing range-of-earnings charts (Chapter 16), any increase in the number of shares reduces the rate at which an individual share participates in future growth. Therefore, unless the new project can be expected to increase the prospect of earnings growth so much that dilution will be counteracted, an expansion by the sale of new capital stock will be disadvantageous to the existing shareholders unless (*a*) further growth of earnings will be impossi-

---

[10] *Moody's Public Utilities Manual, 1954*, p. 1371.

ble without the expansion and (*b*) senior securities have been used to a safe maximum within the limits of company policy. *We cannot overemphasize this matter, which is often neglected by management.*

   2. *Internal Financing: Retained Earnings.* We now turn to another form of equity financing, the retention of earnings. From what has been said so far, one could easily infer that most of the money raised by American corporations is obtained from new security issues. In fact, however, the largest single source of funds for corporate expansion has been the funds produced by operations and retained in the business. Chart 21–1 gives the history of the years 1951–60.

CHART 21–1

SOURCES OF FUNDS FOR CORPORATE EXPANSION, 1951–60

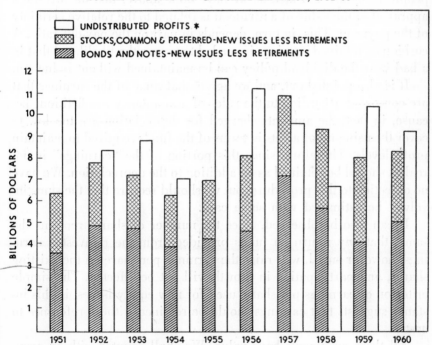

* Profits after taxes, minus cash dividends; Department of Commerce estimates.
SOURCES OF DATA: Securities and Exchange Commission, *Statistical Bulletins*, for new security issues; Board of Governors, Federal Reserve System, *Federal Reserve Bulletins*, for undistributed profits.

In view of the great importance of retained earnings as a source of corporate capital, the question whether such sums should be regarded by management as having a cost also has great importance. It is a matter about which managers and theorists have differed for many years. In the treatment which follows, we shall try to indicate the reasons why some earnings need to be retained regardless of cost. Then, as to the rest of the retained earnings, we ultimately side with the theorists who claim that a cost should be assigned to retained funds when financial policies are considered.

Practice indicates that many firms consider retained earnings to be essentially a cost-free source of funds. It becomes a well-accepted company policy to reinvest a portion of annual earnings, even though the amount reinvested apparently bears no relation to the prospective return on investment opportunities from year to year.

It is pointed out that some earnings must be retained in order to support the established appraisal of the dividend, and that—for these earnings, at least—their "cost" has no significance. Management people recognize the fact, as we have done above, that an investor's appraisal of the value of a dividend is related to the relative certainty of the payment. This, in turn, depends in part on the pay-out ratio. A cushion of retained earnings is needed to assure the likelihood that in a bad year the dividend policy can be maintained without reduction.

It is also pointed out, and we agree, that some of the earnings that are computed according to the rules of accountancy are fictitious because, in fact, the amounts charged for depreciation are too low to cover the using-up of assets in terms of the funds required to maintain profit levels. Therefore, since this portion of the "earnings" is not real, it should be retained as an addition to the depreciation. We have no objection to this procedure, but we should require that the sums involved be estimated with some care.

It can also be observed, since the number of shares remains the same, that *any* return on funds provided from the reinvested earnings, however small, will raise the earnings per share on the existing shares, and participation in growth will not be affected. The simple criterion of earnings per share, used for new equity issues, in this instance suggests that earnings should be retained without reference to cost.

All these arguments have value. We shall counter with an argument that has value on the other side, namely, that it is quite possible that the shareholder's funds might earn more if they had been put into his hands and he had invested the money elsewhere. We feel that management must view the investment in a particular business as one of several investment opportunities open to the stockholder. If the stockholder had free access, funds could be withdrawn and used wherever they could be more profitably invested. Every investment, including reinvested earnings, viewed in this way has its *opportunity cost,* that is, the income forgone by not investing elsewhere. For a fair comparison the alternate investment must be of the same quality and risk. This is best measured by the price given by the already existing shares of the company.

If there were no income tax to be paid by the investor on his receipts from dividends, we could propose the same earnings/price measurement of cost as we have just suggested for a new issue of stock, and say that management should pay out dividends if it cannot reinvest them in projects which will pay at least this rate. But in fact, the great majority of shareholders are taxed, so that the sum of earnings that can be retained in the business is greater than the sum that would remain in the investors' hands if the earnings were distributed. That is to say, the company does not need to earn as much as the shareholder in order to do as well for the shareholder's interests.

An exact analysis of this point requires consideration of the length of time the firm retains the funds, as well as of the rates of tax to which the corporation and its various shareholders are subject. It can be seen that this could be a complex problem, and we do not propose to give the details of such an analysis here. In any actual case, however, the tax position of shareholders must be considered. Wherever possible, it should be determined for the particular company under consideration. If the facts on the tax position of shareholders are not available, we suggest taking the minimum individual federal income tax rate, since all shareholders (except tax-exempt institutions) must pay at least this rate.[11] If this be done, the cost of reinvested earnings will be:

$$\frac{(0.80)(\text{Earnings})}{\text{Price}}$$

This is a very rough measure, but it does call attention to the tax position of the shareholder. It must not be forgotten.

3. *Internal Financing: Depreciation.* Our consideration of retained earnings has so far excluded those funds which are retained through depreciation charges with the purpose of restoring the original investment to liquid form. It is a mistake, however, to consider

---

[11] In our previous edition, we suggested 25 per cent, the maximum rate on capital gains. That choice came from the assumption that the shareholder could only "withdraw" funds by selling shares. Our change to 20 per cent now seems better to us, but we must admit that either figure is essentially arbitrary.

that such funds should be automatically committed to the business regardless of the return which their reinvestment brings. On the contrary, they should be regarded as funds available for alternative investment on the most advantageous basis. From the point of view of the investor, there is theoretically no reason to replace the capital of the business unless the replacement will earn at least as much as it would in an alternative investment of comparable risk. Few firms, however, assign a cost to such funds. In practice, such a procedure gives rise to almost no errors, for there are nearly always enough needs for funds that are of the "must" category to absorb the depreciation charges.

Historical Behavior of Costs of Capital

An alert financial manager will recognize that the costs of various types of securities are constantly changing. This fact can be observed not only from the terms that his company obtained whenever it did issue new contracts but also and more continuously from the behavior of the issues of his company and similar issues in the market. As was pointed out earlier, the historical costs of a particular issue are not so important to the management as the likely costs of the next issue; but costs in the near future may be inferred, as a first approximation, from the present level and historic behavior of the market. For this reason, we present in Chart 21–2 certain measures of cost since the end of the second World War.

The outstanding features of the pattern shown are that despite the continuing superiority of borrowed funds (from a cost point of view), the degree of advantage of debt over equity has been lessening because of a combination of rising interest rates and the falling earnings yield of common stocks. On the debt side the "seller's market" seems to be over; while on the equity side, hopes for participation in further higher levels have created very low costs for equity. If such hopes are ever shaken, the older "spread" of costs may return. The relative stability of the cost of preferred stocks is also worthy of note.

Summary: Costs of Individual Classes of Securities

The cost of raising funds from fixed return types of securities can be obtained from the relationship of the outlays required to support them to the net amounts obtained from these securities during the period they are outstanding, but it must be remembered that the particu-

CHART 21-2

<small>INDICATORS OF COSTS OF CORPORATE ISSUES*, 1946–60</small>

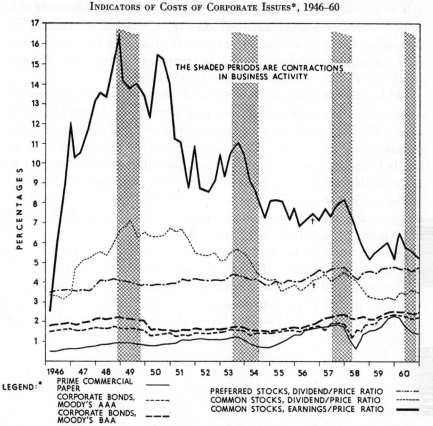

THE SHADED PERIODS ARE CONTRACTIONS
IN BUSINESS ACTIVITY

LEGEND:*

PRIME COMMERCIAL
PAPER _____

CORPORATE BONDS, _ _ _ _ _
MOODY'S AAA

CORPORATE BONDS, _ _ _
MOODY'S BAA

PREFERRED STOCKS, DIVIDEND/PRICE RATIO _ _ _ _ _

COMMON STOCKS, DIVIDEND/PRICE RATIO _ _ _ _ _ _ _ _

COMMON STOCKS, EARNINGS/PRICE RATIO ▬▬▬▬

* Interest rate on prime commercial paper, four to six months, after tax at 52 per cent; yields on corporate bonds, after tax at 52 per cent: Moody's Aaa and Moody's Baa; dividend/price ratio on Standard & Poor's Corporation's preferred stocks; dividend/price ratio and earnings/price ratio on common stock: Moody's 125 industrials to September, 1956; Standard & Poor's 90 stocks to June, 1957, and 500 stocks thereafter.

† Shift in series.

NOTE: The shaded periods are contractions in business activity.

SOURCES OF DATA USED: Office of Business Economics, Department of Commerce, *Statistical Supplements* to *Survey of Current Business*, for stock data to December, 1951; Board of Governors, Federal Reserve System, *Federal Reserve Bulletins*, for all other data.

lar cost that is actually observed depends upon the investors' quality rating of the issue. This, in part, depends upon the degree of coverage in excess of the precise burden that must be met. In this chapter, methods of determining the cost are given, but the determination of the coverage requirement is indicated only by an example.

The cost to be considered for equity capital is derived from the argument that existing stockholders will wish to avoid earnings dilution of their present shares. The earnings/price ratio thus becomes the "cost" of common stock equity. We believe that this ratio should be applied not only when new money is to be raised by the sale of shares, but also as an important consideration whenever it is to be decided how much earnings should be retained or whether depreciation funds should be reinvested. In the latter two cases, however, an adjustment should be made (favoring the retention of earnings) for the tax position of the shareholder.

Although the costs of each class of security can be determined separately, it must be recognized that there is an interrelationship among the costs of the types of capital of a particular company. If a management chooses to increase significantly the proportion of bonds in the company's capitalization, the effect will be not only to increase the cost of debt, but also—because of the increased trading on the equity—to change the cost of equity financing. Until recently, this interdependence of costs has been too much ignored. We shall have more to say of it in Chapter 30.

Among the uses for computed costs of capital are (1) selection for lowest cost among alternative ways of raising desired funds, (2) appraisal of estimated profits from a project against the cost of financing it, and (3) comparison of the cost of a proposed financing at a certain time with historical levels of cost for the type of security being studied.

PART VII

The Sources of Long-Term Corporate Capital

Chapter 22

Sources of Long-Term Capital

IN THIS chapter, we shall consider first the extent to which American corporations raise funds through the sale of new securities. Then we shall focus our attention on the markets for corporate securities. It is axiomatic in marketing that selling programs should be built on a foundation of knowledge about the potential customers. We shall present basic information about the major buyers of corporate securities, indicating the types of securities they buy and their relative importance in absorbing new issues of securities. In the following chapter, we shall discuss the major means by which corporate sellers of securities can tap these markets—the principal methods of distributing new issues and the major institutions, particularly the investment banking industry, which exist to facilitate distribution of new issues. Finally, we shall review the markets for outstanding securities and how they relate to the sale of new securities.

The Volume of Funds Raised through Sale of New Securities

Data on new issues of corporate securities in 1934 and 1938 through 1960 are presented in Table 22–1. Retirements of outstanding securities are also shown. There is much of significance to the student of finance in these data. Especially notable is the upswing in net new issues over the period from the earlier years when corporations were supplying rather than drawing long-term funds from the capital markets. In the earlier years, much of the sale of bonds was for the purpose of refunding old issues at the very low interest rates which prevailed in the late thirties and the forties. New issues peaked at almost $14.8 billion in 1958.

As can also be seen from Table 22–1, corporations have made par-

435

TABLE 22-1

Net Changes in Outstanding Corporate Securities
(In Millions of Dollars)

Year	Bonds and Notes			Stocks			Total		
	New Issues	Retirements	Net New Issues	New Issues	Retirements	Net New Issues	New Issues	Retirements	Net New Issues
1934	391	635	− 244	154	78	76	545	713	− 168
1938	2,092	1,504	588	147	166	− 19	2,239	1,670	569
1939	1,939	2,550	− 611	243	171	72	2,182	2,721	− 539
1940	2,477	2,814	− 337	324	260	64	2,801	3,074	− 273
1941	2,391	2,516	− 125	402	301	101	2,793	2,817	− 24
1942	929	1,327	− 398	222	137	85	1,151	1,464	− 313
1943	996	1,800	− 804	337	329	8	1,333	2,129	− 796
1944	2,693	3,391	− 698	731	508	223	3,424	3,899	− 475
1945	4,924	5,996	−1,072	1,533	910	623	6,457	6,906	− 449
1946	4,721	3,625	1,096	2,459	1,173	1,286	7,180	4,798	2,382
1947	5,015	2,011	3,004	1,867	512	1,355	6,882	2,523	4,359
1948	5,938	1,283	4,655	1,632	400	1,232	7,570	1,683	5,887
1949	4,867	1,583	3,284	1,865	292	1,572	6,731	1,875	4,856
1950	4,806	2,802	2,004	2,418	698	1,720	7,224	3,501	3,724
1951	5,682	2,105	3,577	3,366	667	2,700	9,048	2,772	6,277
1952	7,344	2,403	4,940	3,335	348	2,987	10,679	2,751	7,927
1953	6,651	1,896	4,755	2,898	533	2,366	9,550	2,429	7,121
1954	7,832	4,033	3,799	3,862	1,596	2,265	11,694	5,629	6,065
1955	7,571	3,383	4,188	4,903	2,216	2,687	12,474	5,599	6,875
1956	7,934	3,203	4,731	5,267	1,836	3,432	13,201	5,038	8,162
1957	9,638	2,584	7,053	4,712	1,024	3,688	14,350	3,609	10,741
1958	9,673	3,817	5,856	5,088	1,479	3,609	14,761	5,296	9,465
1959	7,125	3,049	4,076	5,730	1,809	3,922	12,855	4,858	7,998
1960	8,044	3,010	5,034	4,914	1,751	3,164	12,958	4,760	8,198

SOURCE: *Federal Reserve Bulletin*, based on Security and Exchange Commission estimates. These figures include the new securities issued by investment companies. Securities sold in the United States by foreign companies are not included. Retirements of stocks include the repurchase of their shares by investment companies ($300 million in the first nine months of 1957) and stock retired in connection with mergers, reorganizations, and mergers (almost $300 million in the first nine months of 1957). A further explanation of the way these figures are compiled is available in the monthly *Statistical Bulletin* of the SEC.

ticularly heavy use of debt securities in financing their great post-World War II expansion. In recent years, however, the sale of stocks has become more important; and in 1959, stock sales contributed 49.0 per cent of the total net inflow from sale of securities. Doubtless, the rise in the sale of stocks was due, at least in part, to the relatively high levels of common stock prices during the fifties. While the data do not separate common and preferred stocks, other sources indicate that common stocks accounted for the bulk—and in recent years the predominant portion—of the proceeds from stock sales; in the year ended June 30, 1959, common stocks represented 96 per cent of the total, preferred stocks the remaining 4 per cent.[1]

How important in recent years has the sale of new securities been to American corporations in comparison with retained earnings, depreciation, short-term borrowing, and other sources of financing? Helpful in answering this question, and thus putting sale of securities into perspective as a source of funds, are the data on corporate sources and uses of funds since World War II presented in Table 22–2. Clearly apparent from the table is the dominant importance of the operational sources, retained earnings, depletion, and depreciation. Over the full period since 1945, these particular internal sources together provided roughly three times the funds raised by corporations through *net* new security issues. The growth of depreciation to particular importance as a source of funds and the relative decline in retained earnings are also evident. Even though overshadowed by the internal sources, external financing through sale of securities did add the hardly insignificant amount of $91.0 billion to corporate coffers in the years from 1946 through 1959. It is apparent that for American business in general, the availability of outside capital on acceptable terms has been a major factor permitting expansion of activities and hence growth of the economy. Had the funds raised through sale of securities not been forthcoming, the postwar expansion of our economy would have been very much smaller.

While the data in Tables 22–1 and 22–2 give an idea of the role of sale of securities in the financing of corporations generally, it should be recognized that these are aggregate figures for corporations as a whole. As such, the aggregate figures conceal such important differences as those between various industries, between groups of companies by size, and between individual concerns. For example, the electric utility industry has made particularly heavy use of the sale of

---

[1] Securities and Exchange Commission, *Twenty-sixth Annual Report* (Washington, D.C.: U.S. Government Printing Office, 1960).

TABLE 22-2

Sources and Uses of Corporate Funds
(In Billions of Dollars)

USES	Annual Average of 1946-55	1956	1957	1958	1959	Total, 1946-59
Increases in:						
Cash and U.S. government securities	1.37	− 4.3	− 0.3	3.5	3.8	16.4
Inventories	4.38	7.6	2.1	− 3.3	5.3	55.5
Receivables	5.38	8.8	4.5	2.8	10.6	80.5
Gross plant and equipment	19.61	29.9	32.7	26.4	27.7	312.8
Other assets	0.20	3.0	1.3	0.9	4.2	11.4
Total Uses	30.94	45.0	40.3	30.3	51.6	476.6
SOURCES						
Increases in:						
Trade payables	2.84	5.5	2.4	− 1.5	6.3	41.1
Federal income tax liabilities	0.82	− 1.7	2.2	− 2.4	2.4	4.3
Short-term bank loans	1.18	2.2	− 0.3	− 2.4	2.1	14.0
Long-term bank loans	0.21 ⎫	3.2	1.4	1.4	1.7	18.5
Mortgage loans	0.87 ⎭					
Other liabilities	1.38	3.0	2.1	− 0.1	1.9	20.7
Retained earnings and depletion	8.71	10.5	8.9	6.1	9.1	121.7
Depreciation	9.05	17.3	19.1	20.2	21.5	168.6
Net new security issues*	5.55	7.9	10.6	9.5	8.0	91.0
Statistical discrepancy	0.33	− 2.9	− 2.3	− 0.5	− 1.4	− 3.3
Total Sources	30.94	45.0	40.3	30.3	51.6	476.6

* The discerning reader will note that the figures for net new security issues shown in Tables 22–1, 22–2, and 22–3 differ somewhat. The differences are due to variations in the treatment of such items as sales of securities to foreigners, sales of securities by investment companies which in turn are invested in other corporate securities, and the treatment of cash received when securities such as convertible bonds are exchanged for common stock and additional cash is paid into the company. For our purposes, we have been content to keep the tabulations in their original form. For students whose special purposes may require reconciliation of the data, we suggest reference to Irwin Friend, *Individuals' Saving* (New York: John Wiley & Sons, Inc., 1954).

SOURCE: *Survey of Current Business*, September, 1954; October, 1956; September, 1957; and October, 1960. Banks and insurance companies are not included.

new securities in financing its expansion. In recent decades the electric utilities as a group have paid out a relatively high percentage of their earnings in dividends; hence, retained earnings have been of less importance than in the case of manufacturing companies, which have made less heavy use of the capital markets through sale of stocks or bonds.

For reasons discussed in more detail later, the typical small corporation finds the problems in effective sale of securities much more formidable than does its large counterpart. Consequently, smaller concerns have relied more on internal and short-term sources than have large corporations. Indeed, the hundred largest corporations account for a very substantial portion of the sale of new securities each year. The American Telephone and Telegraph Company, and its operating subsidiaries, alone raised almost $1.1 billion through security issues in the single year 1960.

A few companies have been able to grow to great size without recourse to the sale of securities to the public. The Ford Motor Company, which from its inception through 1955 drew no funds from the capital markets through stock or bond issues, and yet amassed total assets of almost $2.6 billion, is a striking example of a large enterprise that long relied entirely on internal and short-term sources of funds for expansion. And even Ford found it necessary to finance part of the major expansion program in 1956 and 1957 through a large private placement of debt securities.

The Sources of Funds for Purchase of Corporate Securities

This chapter has been headed "Sources of Long-Term Capital." It should be emphasized that there is no single homogeneous market for new issues of corporate securities. Instead, it is more useful to think of the buyers of corporate securities as being grouped in a number of more or less tightly compartmented segments with differing investment objectives and operating under distinctive investment policies and practices. For some of the segments or individual markets, available information permits fairly precise, summary description; in other segments, few data are available, and our comments must be more general and tentative.

The savings of individuals are the most basic source of funds for investment in corporate securities. If individuals in the United States spent all their income for current consumption, few corporate securities could be sold. Indeed, in many underdeveloped countries, the inability or unwillingness of the people to forgo current consumption makes it extremely difficult for private industry to accumulate the capital necessary for large-scale and expensive industrial development. In other underdeveloped countries, such as India, the problem of raising funds for private industrial development is further accentuated by a long-standing preference on the part of many of those who have been able to save and accumulate capital for investment in gold, precious jewels, real estate, or other material wealth rather than in intangibles such as stocks and bonds of corporations.

In the United States the people turn over much of their savings to financial institutions, which in turn invest the funds entrusted to them. Thus, financial institutions, including insurance companies, savings banks, etc., are the actual buyers of many of the new securities issued by corporations. Since the financial institutions, other than commercial banks, do not create funds, they must be thought of rather as conduits or intermediaries in the flow of savings from the people into effective investment.

As we shall explain in detail later, a large and generally increasing share of the financial savings of the people reaches the capital markets *through* financial institutions. But by no means all of the savings flow into institutions for investment by them. Many individuals, particularly the more affluent, buy corporate securities for their own account.

Competing Demands for Savings

Corporations seeking capital through the sale of securities do not represent the only ultimate outlet for savings seeking investment. Instead, corporate demand for capital must compete with several other sectors of demand for the public's savings. The demand from four major noncorporate sources, as shown in Table 22–3, has resulted in strong competition for the saver's—or his institutional intermediary's—dollars in recent years.

The demand for mortgage credit to finance individuals' purchases of homes has been particularly strong. The purchase of the record-breaking volume of new homes constructed since World War II has been financed by the buyers largely through borrowing secured by mortgages on the homes. Total mortgage debt outstanding on one- to four-family homes increased from $18.6 billion at the end of 1945 to $139.1 billion on September 30, 1961.

Increasing use by consumers of instalment debt, primarily to finance the purchase of automobiles and other durable goods, has

TABLE 22-3

MAJOR SECTORS OF THE ECONOMY ABSORBING INVESTMENT AND COMMERCIAL BANK FUNDS, 1955–60*

(In Billions of Dollars)

	1955	1956	1957	1958	1959	1960 (Estimated)
Increase in mortgage debt............	16.2	14.6	12.1	15.4	19.1	15.4
Increase in consumer credit...........	6.4	3.6	2.8	0.3	6.4	3.9
Increase in net debt of state and local governments..........	3.4	3.3	4.9	5.9	5.1	4.0
Increase in publicly held debt of U.S. government and agencies................	1.6	– 6.1	– 0.0	6.2	10.3	– 2.7
Net new issues of securities by nonfinancial corporations......	6.1	7.2	9.8	8.0	6.6	6.9

* Data are from Bankers Trust Company, *The Investment Outlook for 1961* (New York, 1961).

been an important basic source of demand for credit. New borrowing by consumers has far exceeded their repayment of such debt in most recent years. The net increase in the use of credit by consumers has come to represent a significant but sharply fluctuating demand for capital. Between the end of 1945 and 1960, total consumer debt outstanding grew by almost $54 billion.

State and local governments have also stepped up their borrowing through bond sales. New public school construction and highway building are typically financed by bond issues, and the heavy activity in these two fields has been the source of much demand for long-term capital by states, cities, toll road authorities, and other public agencies. Interest income on the bonds sold by the state and local governmental units, unlike the interest on United States government bonds issued since 1941, is essentially free of federal income taxation; and this feature of "municipal securities"—the term applied to securities issued by states and any other governmental unit, other than the federal government—makes them particularly attractive to some investors.

During most of the years since 1945 the U.S. government operated at a cash deficit and issued bonds to raise funds. In other years, notably 1956 and 1960, it operated at a cash surplus and supplied funds to the capital market through retirement of debt held by the public. When the federal government and its agencies are heavy borrowers in periods when the demand for funds from other sectors also is strong, as in 1959, the pressure of total demand for funds is intense. Since financial savings tend to be relatively stable from year to year, total demand can be met only through expansion of the credit supply through the commercial banks, which have a unique capacity to create credit. If the Federal Reserve System, which controls the expansion of commercial bank credit, believes it important to restrain credit expansion for anti-inflationary or other reasons, it may allow interest rates to rise and money to become "tight." Thus, even though a sizable increase in bank lending was permitted, credit became tight and interest rates high in 1959. Lesser demands for funds in 1960, particularly from the federal government, and Federal Reserve easing of restraint contributed to much lower interest rates and easier money market conditions in the latter part of 1960.

The main point to be drawn for our purposes from the brief review of data on the demand for capital funds from various sectors of the economy is that corporations, to be successful in raising capital through the sale of securities, must compete with other major claimants for funds. When demand is great and supply is not unlimited, corporations naturally must sweeten the terms of their security wares in order to get the funds they want. At the same time, when funds are harder to get and more costly, the projects calling for more funds can be rigorously scrutinized by business managers and expansion plans curbed in order to lessen the need to raise capital funds under unattractive capital market conditions.

The Institutional Market for Corporate Securities

As we noted earlier, much of the financial savings[2] of the people flows into institutions which have the task of putting it to work. The major financial institutions fall into two main groups—the deposit type, such as commercial banks, savings banks, and savings and loan associations; and the contractual type, such as life insurance companies, corporate pension funds, and governmental unit pension funds. Estimates have placed total personal financial savings during the 1950's at $220 billion. Of this total, some 40 per cent was estimated to have flowed into deposit-type institutions, 40 per cent into the contractual type, and the remaining 20 per cent to have been invested directly in securities or through investment companies or personal trust funds.[3] Fortunately, rather reliable data are available as to how the more important institutional investors employ the funds entrusted to them, so that it is possible to assess the importance of the various institutions as suppliers of long-term corporate funds. Further, while the various individual institutions of a particular type do not follow identical investment policies and practices, there is considerable similarity among firms of each type. The various life insurance companies, for example, are subject to much the same governmental regulation and other basic circumstances bearing on the investment of funds under their control.

Institutional investors currently or potentially important as buyers of corporate securities include the following:

1. Life insurance companies.
2. Fire and casualty insurance companies.
3. Corporate pension funds.
4. State and local government retirement funds.
5. Investment companies.

---

[2] Investment of savings in tangibles, such as homes and consumer durables, is not included in "financial savings."

[3] Jules I. Bogen, "Trends in the Institutionalization of Savings and in Thrift Institution Policies," *Proceedings of 1960 Conference on Savings and Residential Financing* (Chicago: U.S. Savings and Loan League, 1960).

6. Commercial banks—as investors of deposit funds and as trustees for private trust funds.
7. Mutual savings banks.
8. Savings and loan associations.
9. Religious, educational, and charitable funds.

The Life Insurance Companies as Buyers of Corporate Securities

The life insurance companies of the country represent a large and ever-growing segment of the institutional market for corporate securities.[4] The total assets of the U.S. life insurance companies grew from $19 billion in 1930 to almost $120 billion on December 31, 1960. This great growth in assets was the result not only of the increase in outstanding policies as more life insurance was sold but, even more importantly, the accumulation of premiums paid in over a period of years before the maturing of the obligation of the insurance company to pay at the death of the insured (or maturing of annuities) on an ordinary life policy. The young man of 30, on an actuarial average, will pay into the insurance company annual premiums which the company can use over the years until his death calls for the policy to be paid. One insurance company executive has estimated that if no further policies were sold, the assets of his company would continue to increase for more than twelve years.

Due to the continued growth, stability, and predictability of their funds, the life insurance companies have been able to invest a major portion of their huge assets, which represent largely reserves held against policy obligations to millions of policyholders, without primary emphasis on liquidity. Since only a small portion of these policies is expected to mature during any year or at any single time, the insurance companies hold only a small percentage of their assets in cash and feel free to invest the bulk of their funds in income-producing securities on a long-term basis.

In their investment policies, however, the life insurance companies are subject to certain legal restrictions imposed by the states in which they operate. The restrictions are designed to insure protection of principal, and tend to limit investment primarily, although not exclusively, to low-risk debt instruments.

Table 22–4 presents a breakdown of the assets of U.S. life insurance companies as of December 31, 1940, 1950, and 1960. Especially noteworthy, along with the almost fourfold growth in assets

---

[4] The life insurance companies were estimated to hold 70 per cent of all institutional holdings of corporate debt securities in 1958.

TABLE 22-4
DISTRIBUTION OF ASSETS OF U.S. LIFE INSURANCE COMPANIES
(Dollar Figures in Millions)

	DECEMBER 31, 1940		DECEMBER 31, 1950		DECEMBER 31, 1960 (ESTIMATED)	
	Amount	Percentage	Amount	Percentage	Amount	Percentage
Cash	*	*	$ 1,005	1.6%	$ 1,332	1.1%
U.S. government bonds	$ 5,767	18.7%	13,459	21.0	6,444	5.4
Foreign government bonds	288	1.0	1,060	1.7	434	0.4
State and local government bonds	2,392	7.8	1,547	2.4	4,590	3.8
Railroad bonds	2,830	9.2	3,187	5.0	3,715	3.1
Public utility bonds	4,273	13.9	10,587	16.5	16,710	13.9
Industrial and other corporate bonds	1,542	5.0	9,526	14.9	26,715	22.3
Stocks	605	2.0	2,103	3.3	4,900	4.1
Mortgage loans	5,972	19.4	16,102	25.1	41,760	34.9
Real estate	2,065	6.7	1,445	2.2	3,780	3.2
Policy loans	3,091	10.0	2,413	3.8	5,267	4.4
Miscellaneous assets	1,977	6.3	1,586	2.5	4,070	3.4
Total Assets	$30,802	100.0%	$64,020	100.0%	$119,717	100.0%

* Included with miscellaneous assets.
SOURCE: Institute of Life Insurance, *1960 Life Insurance Fact Book* (New York, 1960) for years 1940 and 1950; estimates for 1960 made by Life Insurance Association of America from Institute of Life Insurance figures.

during the two decades, was the great increase in the life insurance companies' investment in "industrial and other corporate bonds." Included in this category are most of the life insurance term loans discussed in Chapter 13. Total corporate bond holdings amounted to more than $47 billion, or 39.4 per cent of their total assets. In addition, some of the mortgage loans represented intermediate credit to business firms.

The life insurance companies also are seen to have a significant and growing investment in common stocks.

Perhaps even more revealing as to the continuing importance of life insurance companies as buyers of corporate securities are the data on their sources and uses of funds over several years since 1954, presented in Table 22–5. These show only the *net* new funds the in-

TABLE 22-5

Sources and Uses of Funds, Life Insurance Companies, 1955–60

(In Billions of Dollars)

	1955	1956	1957	1958	1959	1960 (Estimated)
Sources of Funds:						
Increase in admitted assets*....	5.7	5.8	5.6	5.7	5.9	6.0
Uses of Funds:						
Mortgages.................	3.5	3.5	2.2	1.8	2.1	2.6
Corporate bonds.............	1.9	1.9	2.4	2.2	2.0	1.6
Corporate stocks*...........	0.1	..	0.1	0.1	0.2	0.4
All other assets..............	0.2	0.2	0.8	1.5	1.4	1.4
	5.7	5.8	5.6	5.7	5.9	6.0

* Net of appreciation or depreciation in market value.
Source: Bankers Trust Company, *The Investment Outlook for 1961* (New York, 1961), Table 12.

surance companies have to invest. Actually, their annual inflow of funds for investment is swelled as payments are received on outstanding mortgages and other debt securities, and as particular security holdings are sold, mature, or are called for redemption by the issuers. There is compelling evidence that life insurance companies will continue to grow in the future, although at a slower rate; and they should continue as a strong and relatively constant source of demand for those corporate securities which they regard as suitable for their portfolios. For certain types of corporate securities, principally high-grade debt issues, the insurance companies very probably will continue to be the *major* market. Consequently, corporate designers of a bond issue of this type must tailor the security in a way that meets the needs and tastes of the investment officials of the insurance companies, for their approval can be the *sine qua non* of a successful offering.[5]

Fire and Casualty Insurance Companies

Fire and casualty insurance companies are also important investors in corporate securities. Total assets of these companies amounted to $26.3 billion at the end of 1958, up sharply from $5.1 billion in 1940 and $7.9 billion in 1945. In general, these companies are subject to much less rigid legal restrictions in their investment policies than the life insurance companies, and they have invested relatively heavily in common stocks. A breakdown of the holdings of companies representing about 99 per cent of the industry assets showed holdings of corporate bonds of $1.6 billion, or 6.1 per cent of total assets; corporate preferred stocks of $0.8 billion, or 3 per cent; and common stocks of $7.6 billion, or 28.9 per cent. Holdings of government bonds were also large.[6]

In recent years, these companies have added to their holdings of common stock at an average rate of about $200 million a year. Additions to corporate bond holdings have been smaller but significant.[7]

Corporate Pension Funds

Corporate pension funds which accumulate funds paid in by corporate employers, and to a lesser extent by employees, are largely a post-World War II development. The assets being accumulated against present and future obligations to pay pensions to retired employees have grown from a modest figure in 1947 to an estimated $42.8 billion in 1959.[8] A significant portion of these funds, $17.5 billion at the end of 1959, was held by life insurance companies under "insured plans" and commingled for investment purposes with their other assets. A larger amount, $25.3 billion at year-end 1959, was held and administered by trustees, frequently banks, appointed for the purpose.[9] Strictly speaking, it may be inaccurate to classify

---

[5] In recent years, some of the largest life insurance companies have confined almost all their new acquisitions of debt securities to "private placements" and have bought few public issues.

[6] *Best's Fire and Casualty Aggregates and Averages* (New York: Alfred M. Best Co., Inc., 1959).

[7] Bankers Trust Company, *The Investment Outlook for 1960* (New York, 1960), Table 15.

[8] Noninsured pension plans of labor unions, educational, religious, and other noncorporate groups were estimated by the Securities and Exchange Commission to total an additional $1.9 billion in 1959.

[9] Securities and Exchange Commission, *Statistical Bulletin*, June, 1960, p. 5.

funds so managed as "institutional"; but to the extent that the pension funds are run by full-time investment managers on a continuing professional basis, in operation they are handled much like institutional funds, and so we discuss them under the institutional heading.

Most pension fund managers believe they can, like life insurance companies, invest appropriately in long-term corporate securities. The investment income of pension trusts is free of federal income tax. Table 22–6 shows the distribution of noninsured pension funds on December 31, 1959. Note the heavy emphasis on corporate securities, including common stocks.

TABLE 22–6

CORPORATE PENSION FUNDS,
DISTRIBUTION OF ASSETS, DECEMBER 31, 1959
(In Millions of Dollars)

	Book Value	Percentage of Total	Market Value	Percentage of Total
Cash.........................	$ 407	1.6%	$ 407	1.4%
U.S. government securities.....	2,148	8.5	1,998	7.1
Corporate bonds..............	12,797	50.5	11,368	40.3
Preferred stock..............	657	2.6	592	2.1
Common stock..............	7,714	30.5	12,251	43.5
Mortgages...................	576	2.3 ⎫	1,579	5.6
Other assets.................	1,008	4.0 ⎭		
Total Assets..............	$25,307	100.0%	$28,197	100.0%

SOURCE: Securities and Exchange Commission, *Statistical Bulletin*, June, 1960, p. 5.

The chief significance of the pension funds as investors in corporate securities lies not so much in the size of their present holdings as in their impressive growth in recent years and the currently large additions to their holdings through new purchases each year. The noninsured pension funds alone during the five years through 1959 added more than $6.6 billion to their holdings of corporate bonds and $5.6 billion to their investments in corporate stocks. In 1959 alone, these funds increased their corporate bond portfolio by $1.1 billion and their common stocks by $1.6 billion.[10]

Most corporate pension funds were established as a result of collective bargaining with labor unions, and pressures from unions should tend toward increasing the long-term importance of the pension funds. For this and other impressive reasons, we anticipate that the pension funds will continue to grow robustly and that they will

---

[10] *Ibid.*

represent a continuing, important source of funds for investment in corporate securities. If the trends of recent years continue, these funds will be especially important buyers of common stocks.

State and Local Government Retirement Funds

Like the corporate pension funds, the retirement funds of state and local governments are accumulated in order to meet obligations to pay pensions. The total amount of such funds at the end of 1959 was estimated at $17.2 billion. In 1960, payments into such funds and investment income were estimated to total $3.4 billion, while benefit payments amounted to only $1.3 billion. While the bulk of their assets has been invested in municipal and U.S. government bonds, $0.9 billion was added to their holdings of corporate bonds in 1960. This source of demand for corporate bonds can be expected to grow in the future.

Parenthetically, social security and retirement funds administered by the U.S. government can be acknowledged as representing a huge and growing accumulation of savings. These funds are invested exclusively in U.S. government securities. As of November 30, 1960, these funds, along with other U.S. government agency and trust funds, held $55.4 billion of U.S. government securities. This compares with a total figure for such holdings of $27 billion at the end of 1945. Since they have absorbed U.S. government bonds that otherwise might well have been sold in competition with corporate securities, these funds have had a significant, though *indirect*, effect on the markets for corporate securities.

Investment Companies

On June 30, 1960, 570 companies engaged primarily in the business of investing in securities were registered with the Securities and Exchange Commission as investment companies. Known also as "investment trusts," these firms have grown sharply in recent years, primarily through the appreciation in value of their holdings but also, in the case of the "open-end" companies,[11] through sale to the

---

[11] Investment companies are of several types, two of which, the "open-end" and the "closed-end" types, are of especial importance. The open-end companies, of which Massachusetts Investors Trust, with assets of $1,508 million on December 31, 1960, is the largest, have no fixed number of shares of common stock. Instead, they offer new common shares for sale continuously. The price of the shares is established by the current per share value of the company's assets plus a "loading" to cover sales commissions and other expenses of selling the new shares. The open-end companies typically contract to repurchase their shares at the per share asset value of the investment company on the date they are presented for redemption. In recent years the sales of new shares of the

public of their own securities—the proceeds of which are in turn invested in other corporate securities. Chart 22–1 shows the growth in the market value of their assets over recent years. The market value of the assets of the 570 registered companies amounted to some

CHART 22–1

ESTIMATED MARKET VALUE OF INVESTMENT COMPANY ASSETS
AS OF JUNE 30

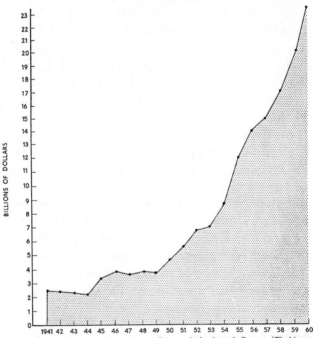

SOURCE: Securities and Exchange Commission, *Twenty-sixth Annual Report* (Washington, D.C.: U.S. Government Printing Office, 1960), p. 169.

$23.5 billion on June 30, 1960, compared with $2.5 billion on June 30, 1941.[12] In contrast to the policies of other institutional investors, American investment companies consistently have placed the bulk of their assets in corporate common stocks, primarily those of large, prospering companies—the "blue chips" of the market.

open-end companies have far exceeded the redemptions, so that the assets available for investment have grown for this reason, as well as because of market appreciation of holdings over the years.

The closed-end trusts operate with a fixed number of shares. These shares are traded on the stock exchanges or over the counter and may sell at wide discounts or premiums over their asset values. Lehman Corporation, which had assets with market values of $314 million on December 31, 1960, is an example of a closed-end investment company.

[12] Securities and Exchange Commission, *Twenty-sixth Annual Report* (1960), p. 169.

Table 22–7 gives a breakdown of the portfolio of eight important investment trusts at the end of 1948, 1952, 1956, and 1959.

TABLE 22-7

AVERAGE DISTRIBUTION OF THE PORTFOLIOS
OF EIGHT INVESTMENT COMPANIES
AT YEAR END

Type of Investment	1948	1952	1956	1959
Cash and U.S. government bonds....	15.1%	6.5%	4.9%	5.4%
Corporate bonds..................	3.7	3.1	3.7	1.8
Corporate preferred stocks.........	8.0	2.6	1.4	0.6
Corporate common stocks..........	73.2	87.8	90.0	92.2

SOURCE: Standard & Poor's Corporation, *Industry Surveys: Investment Companies,* November 3, 1960.

The leading open-end investment companies have developed aggressive sales outlets for their own securities and—barring a major, continuing decline in the market values of common stocks—should continue to represent a growing sector of demand for common stocks of higher investment quality.

The Commercial Banks

The commercial banks of the country, with over $253 billion in total assets at the end of 1960, held $61 billion in U.S. government bonds.[13] Banks have legal sanction for investment in corporate bonds of better investment quality and, at some periods in the past, have represented an important market for such corporate bonds. In recent years, faced with a strong demand for loans, the banks have been net sellers rather than buyers of corporate bonds. Near the end of 1960 the total commercial bank investment in corporate bonds amounted to approximately $3 billion, compared with $3.7 billion in 1947.[14] Only if the demand for bank loans slumps severely can the banks be expected to add significantly to their present holdings of corporate bonds.

In addition to their holdings of corporate securities in their own investment portfolios, many of the nation's banks act as trustees for various private funds and in a fiduciary capacity administer the investment funds put in their care. In their administration of personal trust funds the banks are subject to restrictions on their full freedom of investment action imposed both by certain governmental regula-

---

[13] *Federal Reserve Bulletin*, February, 1961, p. 181.
[14] *Ibid.*

tion and by the terms of many of the trust instruments under which the trusts were established.

A national survey of the assets held in personal trusts administered by banks with total trust assets of over $10 million, conducted by the Trust Division of the American Bankers Association in 1959, indicated total personal trust holdings by these banks of $57.2 billion. The distribution of the assets of these funds was as follows:[15]

(In Billions)

Common stock	$37.2
State and municipal securities	7.8
Participations in common trust funds	2.6
Corporate bonds and debentures	2.6
U.S. government securities	2.6
All other assets	1.9
Preferred stock	1.3
Mortgages	0.7
Cash	0.5
Total	$57.2

The heavy investment in common stocks and tax-free state and municipal bonds is strikingly apparent. The large investment in tax-free bonds and, to some extent, the size of the investment in common stocks reflect the fact that the trust funds typically represent assets of relatively high income groups. While the investment in common stocks of trust funds has increased sharply in recent years, the increase appears attributable much more to the rise in market values of their holdings than to new money additions to the trusts. Nevertheless, bank-administered trust funds must be recognized as the major institutional investor in common stocks.

Mutual Savings Banks

The mutual savings banks, largely concentrated in New England, New York, and Pennsylvania, had assets amounting to more than $38.9 billion on December 31, 1959. The mutual savings banks have invested primarily in home mortgage loans and in U.S. government bonds. Although subject to close legal restriction in their investment in corporate securities, a breakdown of their assets at the end of 1959 showed holdings of $4 billion in corporate bonds and $0.8 billion in corporate stocks.[16] Should the recently abundant opportunities for

---

[15] Trust Division, American Bankers Association, *The Trust Bulletin*, September, 1960, p. 14.

[16] U.S. Comptroller of the Currency, *Ninety-seventh Annual Report, 1959* (Washington, D.C.: U.S. Government Printing Office, 1960), p. 196.

investment in home mortgages decline importantly, the savings banks may well prove a more important market for corporate securities, mainly high-quality bonds of intermediate and long maturities.

Savings and Loan Associations

In recent years, savings and loan associations have been particularly effective in competing for individuals' savings. Their total assets on December 31, 1960, amounted to almost $72 billion. Regarded by many savers as the approximate equivalent of savings banks, the savings and loan associations have invested predominantly in home mortgages and to a much lesser extent in government bonds. To date, their investment in corporate securities has been negligible, but they represent a possible source of demand for corporate securities should the supply of mortgage investments available to them shrink greatly.

Religious, Educational, and Charitable Funds

The assets of the various nonprofit institutions of the country are largely invested in corporate securities. They are relatively free of legal restrictions on their investment policies, and their security holdings include substantial amounts of common and preferred stocks as well as bonds. An analysis of the investment portfolios of 64 college and university endowment funds on June 30, 1960, showed a weighted average investment of 33.4 per cent in bonds, 2.4 per cent in preferred stocks, and 53.6 per cent in common stocks. The total investment funds of these 64 institutions totaled $3.5 billion.[17]

The assets of other nonprofit organizations' total several billion dollars and also include a substantial amount of corporate equities.

The inflow of funds to the nonprofit funds is relatively slow, so that they are net buyers of corporate securities only in moderate amounts.

Summary of the Institutional Market

Before turning to a review of the noninstitutional, or individual, investor segments of the market, we can appropriately point up and summarize some key points about the institutional markets for corporate securities. We have reviewed briefly the investment practices of the institutions with important amounts of funds to invest in corporate securities along with other segments—pension funds and institu-

---

[17] Boston Fund, *A Comprehensive Study of College and University Endowment Funds, 1960* (Boston, 1960), p. 3.

tionally administered personal trust funds—of the market that are professionally managed. We have seen that the institutions, broadly considered, represent a very important market for corporate bonds. In fact, it has been estimated that 93 per cent of the total outstanding corporate bonds are held by these investors.[18] Further, the institutions are continuing to buy a dominant portion of new issues of debt securities, and there is evidence to support the view that they will continue to be the principal purchasers of new issues in the future.

In terms of segments of the institutional market, the life insurance companies (which alone hold more than half the outstanding corporate bonds), pension funds, and state and local government retirement funds are particularly heavy buyers of bonds. Fire and casualty insurance companies, savings banks, nonprofit institutions, and commercial banks, as administrators of personal trust funds, and to a limited extent for their own portfolios, represent smaller but significant sources of demand for corporate bonds.

The institutional investors represent an increasingly important market for corporate equity securities. The New York Stock Exchange estimated that institutional holdings, *excluding* bank-administered trust funds, of stocks listed on that Exchange at the end of 1959 had a value of $49.6 billion, or 16.1 per cent of the total value of $307.7 billion. The percentage had grown from 12.4 per cent in 1949.[19] Less recent but more comprehensive estimates of the Securities and Exchange Commission put the total market value of outstanding common stock of all U.S. corporations, excluding intercorporate holdings, at $252 billion at the end of 1954. The SEC further estimated institutional holdings, *including* those of pension funds and bank-administered personal trusts, at $57.8 billion, or 23 per cent of the total. In the case of preferred stocks, institutions held $8.7 billion, or 54 per cent of the $16 billion total. Individual investors held $6.9 billion, or 43 per cent of the total outstanding preferred stock.[20]

The available evidence, although unprecise, strongly suggests that institutional investors have been absorbing an increasing percentage of the new issues of equities in more recent years and that their importance as current buyers of equities is greater than that suggested

---

[18] Sherwin C. Badger, "Funds in the Stock Market," *Harvard Business Review,* July–August, 1956.

[19] *New York Stock Exchange Fact Book, 1960,* p. 29.

[20] Senate Committee on Banking and Currency, U.S. Congress, *Factors Affecting the Stock Market* (Sen. Rep. 1280, 84th Cong., 1st sess.; Washington, D.C.: U.S. Government Printing Office, 1955), p. 89.

by the breakdowns of their existing holdings, the NYSE study, or the 1954 SEC study.

The Noninstitutional Market for Corporate Securities

Now, let us turn to what can be loosely termed the "individual investor" segment of the market. As we said earlier, much investment in corporate securities is made by individuals directly, using their own funds. Unfortunately, fully reliable and detailed statistical data on this important part of the market for corporate securities do not exist; and since it is very difficult to assemble such data, the deficiency of precise information in the area will probably continue, despite some helpful studies in prospect. Consequently, the data—and the conclusions gingerly drawn—that will be presented must be regarded as tentative and highly approximate.

One inescapable characteristic of the individual investor segment is its heterogeneous nature. The investment objectives of the various individual holders of corporate securities, for example, are widely varied, running all the way from the needs of the almost impecunious widow, who desires most the protection of her small principal but who also needs income, to that of the speculator, who is willing to risk his money on the most hazardous issue in hope of large return through capital gains.

The degree of investment sophistication and skill is also extremely varied. The Kansas farmer with a large supply of extra cash from the last wheat crop obviously is a prospective investor quite different from the seasoned speculator who has survived many years on Wall Street. The diverse character of the individual market in this respect contrasts with the institutional market, in which it is presumed that most important firms have the resources and personnel for careful, informed investment management.

Now, let us consider the size of the individual market for corporate securities, looking first at data covering the absorption of new security issues by individuals in recent years. The Securities and Exchange Commission undertakes, as a part of its continuing estimates of individuals' savings, to determine annual additions to the holdings of nongovernment securities by individuals.[21] The SEC estimates, admittedly rough, of the changes in such holdings in recent years are as follows:

---

[21] These figures include purchases of investment company shares, which in recent years have accounted for a large portion of the total net additions.

Year	Net Additions (in Billions)
1952	$ 1.8
1953	1.1
1954	−0.1
1955	2.2
1956	3.5
1957	2.8
1958	2.5
1959	1.2
1960	1.4

As we have seen, individuals are believed to hold something near three fourths of all outstanding common stock, something less than half the preferred stock, and one fourteenth of the corporate bonds.

One of the more recent studies is that of the New York Stock Exchange.[22] On the basis of a study in early 1959, it concluded that some 12,490,000 individuals held shares in publicly held corporations. One out of every eight U.S. adults owned common stock. The total number of shareholders was almost double that in 1952. Geographically, shareholders represented more than 10 per cent of the population in New England and in the Middle Atlantic states, only 3.3 per cent in the South Central region.

While the total number of shareholders sounds impressive, stockholders represent just 7 per cent of the total population; in contrast, 64 per cent of the total population owned life insurance policies in 1959.

Further, the total number of shareholders includes many whose holdings are very small. Available data indicate clearly that the bulk of the stock holdings of individuals is held by a relatively small number of individuals of high income. On the basis of one such study,[23] it was estimated that in 1949, family spending units with incomes of $50,000 and over, which represented only 0.1 per cent of the family spending units in the country, held about 35 per cent of all the marketable stock owned by private investors. Further evidence of the importance of high-income groups as investors in corporate securities is shown in the brief table on page 457, taken from data in this study.

The study, while recognizing that taxes have substantially cut into the incomes of upper income groups, did not find evidence to support

---

[22] *Share Ownership in America: 1959* (New York, 1959).

[23] J. Keith Butters, Lawrence E. Thompson, and Lynn L. Bollinger, *Effects of Taxation: Investments by Individuals* (Boston: Division of Research, Harvard Business School, 1953), p. 25.

Spending Units with Income of:	Approximate Percentage of all Spending Units	Cumulative Percentage of Marketable Stock Owned by Private Investors
$50,000 and over.........	0.1%	35%
$25,000 and over.........	0.5	50
$15,000 and over.........	1.0	65
$10,000 and over.........	3.0	75

the view that these taxes prevent upper income groups from investing current savings in equity securities.

Much more recent evidence that high-income groups continue to be the major holders of corporate stocks is available in data based on income tax returns. Such data, in the form of the percentage of dividend payments received by various income groups, are given in Table 22–8. Note that taxpaying units with incomes of over $20,000 received 57.6 per cent of total dividend payments, though their total income was but 10.1 per cent of the total adjusted gross income.

Perhaps significant was the correlation of share ownership with educational achievement, revealed in the NYSE study. Of the total population of college graduates, 38.9 per cent were shareholders, while only 5.3 per cent of the adults who had not finished high school owned shares.

As might be expected, share ownership was most common among individuals in the 55–64-year age group. Of the population in this age group, 17.4 per cent owned stock.

Interestingly enough, and for whatever significance it has, women shareholders outnumbered the men, 52.5 per cent of the adult shareholders being women, mostly housewives.

Summary of Noninstitutional Market for Corporate Securities

Available data on individual investors as buyers of corporate securities are much less complete and reliable than those on the institutional investors. However, it appears clear that individual investors directly hold the lion's share of corporate common stocks and almost half of the preferred stocks. While data on the recent purchases by individuals of corporate equities are not at all precise, individuals clearly represent a highly important market for corporate equities. It does appear, however, that individuals in recent years have not stepped up their rate of acquisition of new equity issues as much as have the institutional buyers.

TABLE 22-8

Dividends and Interest Received by Individuals in Various Income Groups, as Reported in Income Tax Returns for 1958

(Dollar Figures in Millions)

Adjusted Gross Income Group	Adjusted Gross Income	Percentage of Total	Cumulative Percentage	Dividend Income (after Exclusions)	Percentage of Total	Cumulative Percentage	Interest Income	Percentage of Total	Cumulative Percentage
Under $5,000	$ 91,958*	32.7%	32.7%	$ 981	11.2%	11.2%	$1,158	31.7%	31.7%
$5,000–$10,000	121,384	43.2	75.9	1,141	13.0	24.2	938	25.6	57.3
$10,000–$20,000	39,270	14.0	89.9	1,589	18.2	42.4	708	19.4	76.7
$20,000–$50,000	18,209	6.5	96.4	2,025	23.2	65.6	543	14.8	91.5
$50,000–$100,000	6,050	2.1	98.5	1,326	15.2	80.8	191	5.2	96.7
$100,000–$500,000	3,424	1.2	99.7	1,236	14.1	94.9	105	2.9	99.6
$500,000–$1,000,000	360	0.1	99.8	174	2.0	96.9	8	0.2	99.8
$1,000,000 or more	499	0.2	100.0	269	3.1	100.0	8	0.2	100.0
	$281,154	100.0%		$8,741	100.0%		$3,659	100.0%	

* Gross income of $92,970 million less gross deficit of $1,012 million.

Source: Internal Revenue Service, U.S. Treasury Department, *Statistics of Income, 1958: Individual Income Tax Returns for 1958* (Washington, D.C.: U.S. Government Printing Office, 1960), Table 3, p. 29.

Individual investors hold a minor portion of outstanding corporate bonds and, in recent years, appear to have been unimportant as buyers of new bonds compared with the institutional buyers.

The individual investor group is heterogeneous in character. Certain general features of this market are worthy of note, however. Stock ownership, despite some broadening in recent years, remains concentrated in a modest portion of the population. Investors of relatively high incomes own a very substantial portion of the total stock held by individuals. Both men and women are important as stockholders. As might be expected, persons of relatively high educational achievement are particularly important as investors in corporate equities, as are individuals in the higher age group.

Chapter 23

Tapping the Sources of Long-Term Capital

EARLIER, WE pictured the relative importance to American corporations in recent years of capital raised through the sale of new issues of securities, and sketched in broad-brush terms the nature of the ultimate market for these securities. In this chapter, we shall discuss the major means by which corporations issuing new securities can reach buyers for their securities and thus avail themselves of long-term capital. Although numerous methods of distribution of corporate securities have been developed, our discussion will center on the few basic methods that are of particular importance.

Relation of the Markets for Outstanding Securities to the Distribution of New Issues

It is important to full understanding that the reader at this point clearly distinguishes between the primary distribution of securities— that is, the distribution of *new* issues—and transactions in the *secondary markets,* such as the New York Stock Exchange, where outstanding, or "old," issues are bought and sold. The existence of a secondary market where investors can buy and sell outstanding securities is important to the primary distribution, but the secondary markets have purposes, mechanisms, and institutions distinct from those of primary distribution. Consequently, they will be discussed separately later in this chapter.

Each new issue of securities competes, directly or indirectly, with outstanding securities for the ultimate investor's dollar. The terms and price of new offerings must be made temptingly attractive in comparison with those of outstanding securities which can be bought in the secondary markets. Furthermore, the anticipated existence of a good secondary market, in which investors can sell the

460

newly issued securities, if such appears at a future date necessary or advantageous, without undue trouble or cost, adds much to the attractiveness to buyers of a new security issue. In other words, good secondary markets lend the valuable element of potential marketability to the securities bought upon initial, primary distribution.

Major Types of New Offerings

Most new security issues fall into one of three basic types of offerings:

1. A *public offering*, in which the issue is offered for sale to the general public.
2. An *offering to security holders* of the company. Under this type of "public offering," existing security holders of the company are given prior rights, typically transferable, to subscribe pro rata to the new issue. In some cases the new issue may be taken up with existing securities exchanged as whole or part payment for the new issues. In the typical offering *not* involving exchange of shares, the corporation can offer to the general public those securities not subscribed to by existing shareholders.
3. *Private placements*, which represent the offering of an entire issue to a single or limited number of investors who buy as ultimate investors rather than for early resale.

Particularly reliable data are available for all of such placements over $1 million during the fifteen years from 1935 through 1949. Table 23–1 shows the relative importance of each major type of offering for 4,906 issues, broken down into bonds, preferred stock, and common stock. The importance of private placements in the case of new bond issues is noteworthy. Of the bonds offered to existing security holders, most were debt issues convertible into common stock or were bonds issued in exchange for old bond issues.

In sharp contrast with offerings of bonds, more than one half of the new issues of common stock were to existing common stockholders, and very few issues of new common were placed privately.

Chart 23–1 presents more recent data on the volume of bonds offered for cash sale and the relative importance in terms of dollar volume of private placements. It will be noted that private placements accounted for more than half of the total debt issues in the early years of the fifties. However, private placements failed to grow in absolute terms and, except in 1959, represented a lesser share of total debt issues in the more recent years.[1] Private placement is particularly

---

[1] For a more detailed analysis of private placements, see Avery B. Cohan, *Private Placements and Public Offerings: Market Shares since 1935* (Chapel Hill: University of North Carolina, 1961).

TABLE 23-1

NUMBER OF NEW SECURITY ISSUES BY TYPE OF OFFERING, 1935–49

	All Issues		Bonds*		Preferred Stock		Common Stock	
	Number	% of Total Number	Number	% of Total Number	Number	% of Total Number	Number	% of Total Number
Total..................	4,906	100%	3,215	100%	973	100%	718	100%
Public offerings........	2,241	45.7%	1,344	41.8%	586	60.2%	311	43.3%
Offerings to security holders...	772	15.7	88	2.7	301	30.9	383	53.3
Private placements.........	1,893	38.6	1,783	55.5	86	8.8	24	3.3

* Including bonds, debentures, notes, etc.

SOURCE: *United States of America* v. *Henry S. Morgan, Harold Stanley, et al., Doing Business as Morgan Stanley & Co., et al.,* U.S. District Court for Southern New York, Civil No. 43–757, Defendants' Preliminary Memorandum for the Court, p. 21.

CHART 23–1

PRIVATE PLACEMENT AND PUBLIC OFFERINGS OF NEW CORPORATE DEBT ISSUES

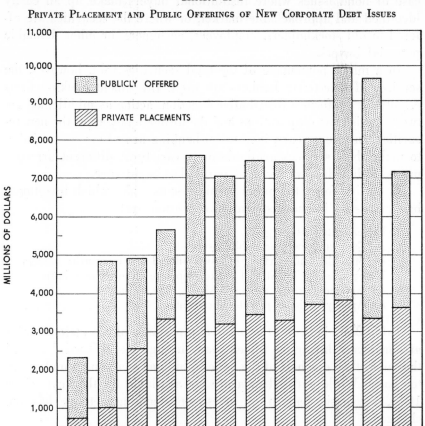

SOURCE: Securities and Exchange Commission, *Twenty-sixth Annual Report* (Washington, D.C.: U.S. Government Printing Office, 1960), p. 224.

common in the case of debt issues under $15 million. Larger issues usually are offered publicly.

The Role of Investment Bankers in Distribution of New Issues

The issuing corporation usually is free to undertake all aspects of the job of distributing its securities to investors; and a significant amount of the total new issues is, in fact, marketed by issuers without the services of middlemen in the distributive function. Direct sale to investors is particularly common in the case of new, small companies where the potential market is so local and restricted that it can be readily reached through direct solicitation. It is also common in the case of bond issues where institutional buyers make up an easily identified and approachable market, or where the securities are offered to old stockholders, employees, customers, or other definable potential buyers.

In a major percentage of the total securities sold, however, the services of investment bankers are used. Investment banking firms essentially perform a distributive function, acting as middlemen between the issuing corporations and the ultimate buyers of the new securities. In recent years, investment banking firms have been willing to make their services available on a variety of different arrangements, although several are of particular importance.

In outline form, the major arrangements under which investment bankers assist in the distributive operation are:

1. Underwritten issues
   a) Fully underwritten public issues
   b) Stand-by underwriting of issues offered first to security holders
2. Issues in which investment bankers operate on an agency basis
   a) Nonunderwritten agency basis on sales to public
   b) Agency basis on private placements

Table 23–2 indicates the relative importance of the various major arrangements during the fifteen years through 1949. It will be noted that more than one half of the issues tabulated were on an underwritten basis. While parallel data are not available for the years since 1949, the basic pattern of investment banking activity has not changed.

Underwritten Public Issues

In underwritten issues, one or a group of investment banking firms working together on an issue assure the issuing firm a definite sum of money for the issue at a definite time. The underwriting investment banking firms are willing to back their judgment as to the marketability of the issue at the proposed public offering price by agreeing to purchase the entire issue at a firm, agreed price, assuming the risks that they will be unable to resell the issue to the public. In other words, they assure, or "underwrite," the success of the issue, and add the function of risk taking to their selling function.

At this point, it is well to distinguish between underwritten issues in which the arrangements between issuer and investment bankers as to price and other key factors are arrived at by *negotiation* between the parties and those other underwritten issues in which the terms of the new security issue are drawn up by the issuer and the issue is

TABLE 23-2

NUMBER OF NEW SECURITY ISSUES BY TYPE OF TRANSACTION, 1935-49

	BONDS*		PREFERRED		COMMON		ALL SECURITIES	
	Number of Issues	% of Total Number	Number of Issues	% of Total Number	Number of Issues	% of Total Number	Number of Issues	% of Total Number
Total.........	3,215	100%	973	100%	718	100%	4,906	100%
Underwritten negotiated....	856	26.6%	706	72.6%	438	61.0%	2,000	40.8%
Underwritten public sealed bidding.......	502	15.6	89	9.1	32	4.5	623	12.7
Total Underwritten....	1,358	42.2%	795	81.7%	470	65.5%	2,623	53.5%
Nonunderwritten agency.......	32	1.0%	47	4.8%	62	8.6%	141	2.9%
Nonunderwritten, no investment banker.......	42	1.3	45	4.6	162	22.6	249	5.1
Total Nonunderwritten....	74	2.3%	92	9.5%	224	31.2%	390	7.9%
Private placement agency.......	818	25.4%	52	5.3%	6	0.8%	876	17.9%
Private placement, no investment banker.......	965	30.0	34	3.5	18	2.5	1,017	20.7
Total Private Placements	1,783	55.5%	86	8.8%	24	3.3%	1,893	38.6%

* Including bonds, debentures, notes, etc.
SOURCE: *United States of America* v. *Henry S. Morgan, Harold Stanley, et al., Doing Business as Morgan Stanley & Co., et al.*, U.S. District Court for Southern New York, Civil No. 43–757, Defendants' Preliminary Memorandum for the Court, p. 24.

placed with underwriting investment bankers on the basis of *public sealed bids.* Under the public sealed bid arrangements, commonly known as *competitive bid* deals, the issue is, in effect, put up for sale to the highest responsible bidder. Use of competitive bidding is confined almost exclusively to security issues of regulated industries or governmental units.

The negotiated arrangement is the traditional form of underwriting and is favored by investment bankers generally. It is used more often than is competitive bidding. In a negotiated underwritten public offering, the services of the investment bankers may be utilized, to the extent the issuer wishes, in every stage of the process from the design of the security through its actual distribution to the public. An investment banking firm, which will act as manager of the syndicate of banking firms it selects to assist in the underwriting and sales operation, will be chosen at a very early stage. Morgan Stanley & Company, for example, from 1935 through 1957, served as manager or comanager in offerings totaling more than $16 billion. The firm selected as manager or comanager undertakes a searching and detailed investigation and analysis of the affairs of the issuer, with especial emphasis on its current and future financing needs. Working with company officers, the managing firm attempts to work out details of an issue which effectively reconcile the objectives of the issuer and the requirements of investors under anticipated conditions upon offering of the security. Typically, the investment bankers assist corporate management in reaching decisions as to the type or types of securities to be offered, their provisions, and the timing of the offering. The banker and his counsel also help in the drafting of the registration statement and prospectus, usually required by the Securities and Exchange Commission, and in the filing of other documents necessary to qualify the issue legally for sale. Since most companies undertake public issues only infrequently, the market *expertise* of the investment bankers can be highly valuable to the issuer.

About the time the prospective new security takes tentative form, the investment banker undertakes to line up other investment banking firms to join in a "syndicate" to share the risks of underwriting and the job of selling. In a large issue the syndicate will usually include many firms. The size of the syndicate formed and the number of selling dealers enlisted tend to increase with the size of the issue. In the huge offering of Ford Motor Company common stock owned by the Ford Foundation—10.2 million shares sold the public at $64.50 for a total of $657.9 million—in January, 1956, seven firms served as comanagers of the underwriting syndicate, which was composed of 722 firms. In addition, the syndicate employed the services of 1,000 security dealers in selling the issue. The issue was quickly oversubscribed.

Firms joining the syndicate as underwriters also act as selling firms; in large deals, additional firms commonly are brought in only as selling dealers, as was the case in the Ford issue. Because the security issues often are large in relation to the capital resources of individual investment banking firms, and because it is helpful in tapping as wide a market as possible to have a number of firms with customers throughout the country, the syndicate arrangements under which various firms band together on a single issue have become typical for all but the smallest issues. The composition of the syndicates and the percentage participation of each firm differ from one issue to another, but certain firms tend to work together on many issues.

Tentative understandings as to probable price both to the company and to the public (thus approximating the anticipated "banker's spread," or gross margin of profit, on the deal) may be reached early in the discussions. Just before the registration statement becomes effective and the issue legally can be sold, definite prices and terms of the issue are established in final negotiation between bankers and issuer.

To be fully satisfactory to all concerned, such a pattern of operation requires a high degree of mutual confidence and trust on the part of all parties. One of the prime assets of a successful investment banking firm is its reputation for fair and effective operation over the years, and such reputations are jealously guarded. This feature also helps to explain why many issuing firms have developed close relationships with particular investment banking houses and continue to do business with them in successive issues over long periods of years.

The investment bankers make strenuous efforts to sell new issues quickly—both to achieve rapid turnover of their capital and to minimize the risk that a downturn in the market will leave the securities "on the bankers' shelves" at what become unattractively high prices. Despite the bankers' best efforts at close pricing, relatively minor downturns in the market can leave an issue unsold at the issue price, necessitating either sale at reduced prices or holding for an upturn in prices, which may not materialize and in any case ties up the investment bankers' capital. The spread between the price that the bankers pay the issuers and the resale price to the public is usually so small that even a small break from planned prices can result in losses to the bankers.

Sales are typically made by the manager and associated underwriters, sometimes through dealers who do not share in underwriting risks or margins. Many of the sales to institutional buyers, especially important in the case of high-grade bonds, typically are made by the manager for the account of the whole underwriting syndicate.

In compliance with regulations which control the practice, the manager for the syndicate generally is authorized to—and when the occasion requires, does—undertake buying and selling in the market designed to *stabilize* the market price of the security during the period in which the new securities are being sold by the syndicate. Profits and losses stemming from the stabilizing operations are for the account of the whole syndicate.

Important prospective buyers are supplied with copies of the prospectus describing the issue, complete except for final price and a few other terms, for their study well before the offering date. Many make their decision to buy or not, contingent on the final price, before the actual offering. Consequently, if the issue is to be a successful one, it usually "goes out the window," that is, it is entirely sold out, in a matter of hours or a few days after the initial offering—and the syndicate is quickly terminated. When sales are slow, the syndicate typically continues in operation for a longer time with sales only at the agreed, announced price. If the offering is not sold out in a few weeks, by agreement the syndicate usually breaks up, stabilization activities are abandoned, and each investment banking underwriter is free to hold or dispose of his inventory of securities as he sees fit.

For example, a syndicate headed by Morgan Stanley & Company on May 21, 1957, "won" a competitive bid for $70 million of 34-year mortgage bonds of the New York Telephone Company. Their bid was 101.113 for 4½ per cent bonds, while the next highest bid was 100.857. The offering was repriced to the public at 101.755, affording the bankers a presumed spread of $6.42 per thousand. The bond market turned soft, however, and sales were very slow. Finally, as reported in *Barron's*, June 10, 1957, "the bankers terminated their agreement Tuesday, June 4, and the bonds dropped to about 99 from the original offering price of 101.755. Since more than two-thirds of the issue was undistributed when the account broke up, the loss for the underwriters obviously was a large one." Bankers holding for a better price found little relief in ensuing weeks as the market price dropped by June 21, 1957, to 97⅞ bid 98⅜ asked.

Illustrative of a successful negotiated underwritten public offering was the sale of 300,000 shares of common stock by Owens-Corning Fiberglas Corporation in March, 1957. A syndicate of 128 firms headed by Goldman Sachs & Company, Lazard Freres & Company, and White Weld & Company was formed to buy and resell the stock. The terms of purchase from the company provided that the price to the public would be below that of the last recorded sale of outstanding common stock on the New York Stock Exchange the day before the stock was offered the public but within $1.00 per share of that price. The underwriters received as compensation a discount from the offering price of $2.25 per share, or a total of $675,000. The last sale price on the Exchange proved to be $55, and the new issue was quickly oversubscribed at the offering price of $54.25.

Underwritten Issues under Competitive Bidding

Security issues under public sealed bidding generally follow this basic pattern: The issuing firm offers an entire issue, generally of bonds or preferred stock, for outright purchase by the bidder offering the highest price—in terms of the lowest cost of money to the issuer. Bidding typically is by investment banking syndicates formed for the purpose of bidding on the specific issue. Unlike the pattern in negotiated underwritings, the investment bankers come into the picture at a late stage in the financing process. The investment bankers who bid on the issue do not act as consultants to the company in designing the issue—in fact, they are forbidden by administrative regulation to do so. The issuer and its counsel, or other expert advice, design the issue entirely by themselves and solicit by advertisement sealed bids for the definitively designed issue. (See Exhibit 23–1.)

The process of bidding and sale under competitive bidding has been described in the following terms:

Normally, numbers of bankers associate together to form accounts to bid for a specific issue. The reason for such association is the same as in the case of a negotiated transaction—to spread the risk and to accomplish distribution of the securities. After analyzing the registration statement, prospectus and other general data available as to the issuer and the issue to be offered, and after meeting with the issuer at a prebidding information session, the bankers comprised within each account meet together just before the bidding date to determine a bid. In the light of their estimates of the highest price at which the securities can be sold to the public based on then current market conditions, prices of comparable securities, and other relevant factors, each account determines the bid it will make for the entire issue. It frequently occurs that underwriters withdraw from the [syndicate] account because their views of the proper bid are lower than the bid price set by the other members of the account, or for other reasons. If the number of such "drop-outs" is large, it may be impossible for that account to submit a bid at all, in which case it disbands without further action unless other bankers will come in.

Each bid submitted indicates that the members of the account, as then constituted, offer to purchase the entire issue on a several basis[2] at the bid price.

The underwriters in the winning account then determine by themselves,

---

[2] Purchase by the underwriters on a "several basis" means that each member of the syndicate is legally obligated to the issuer to take only that portion of the issue subscribed to by it.

Southern California Edison Company

PUBLIC INVITATION FOR BIDS

for the Purchase of
$40,000,000 First and Refunding Mortgage Bonds, Series I, Due 1982

Southern California Edison Company, a California corporation (hereinafter called the "Company"), hereby invites bids, subject to the terms and conditions herein stated or referred to, for the purchase from it of $40,000,000 principal amount of its First and Refunding Mortgage Bonds, Series I, Due 1982 (hereinafter called the "Bonds"). Copies of the Statement of Terms and Conditions Relating to Bids for the purchase of the Bonds and of other relevant documents referred to therein may be examined, and copies of certain of such documents may be obtained, at the office of the Company, 601 West Fifth Street, Los Angeles, California.

Sealed written bids will be received by the Company at the office of its President, 601 West Fifth Street, Los Angeles, California, up to 9:00 A.M., California Time, on July 1, 1957, or on such later date as may be fixed by the Company as provided in the Statement of Terms and Conditions Relating to Bids.

Prior to the acceptance of any bid, the bidder or bidders will be furnished with a copy of the Prospectus relating to the Bonds as contained in the Registration Statement at the time it became effective. Bids will be considered only from persons who have received copies of the Prospectus and only if made in accordance with and subject to the Statement of Terms and Conditions Relating to Bids.

The Company hereby further advises prospective bidders that representatives of the Company, counsel for the Company, counsel for the possible purchasers, and a representative of Messrs. Arthur Andersen & Co., will be present at the office of the Company, 601 West Fifth Street, Los Angeles, California, on June 28, 1957, at 10:00 A.M., California Time, to meet with prospective bidders for the purpose of reviewing with them the information contained in the Registration Statement, in the Prospectus, in the Statement of Terms and Conditions Relating to Bids, in the Form of Bid and in the form of Bond Purchase Agreement.

SOUTHERN CALIFORNIA EDISON COMPANY
By HAROLD QUINTON,
PRESIDENT

Los Angeles, California
June 26, 1957.

and without reference to the issuer, the public offering price, the method of sale, and any concessions or reallowances, subject, where and to the extent required, to the approval of the proper regulatory authority. The difference between the public offering price and the bid price establishes the level of anticipated gross compensation for the underwriters of the issue.

The offering to the public in public sealed bidding issues usually differs from that of a negotiated underwritten public offering in the extent of distribution. Since the winning account knows that it has been successful only a very short time in advance of the public offering and has had no assurance that it would win the issue, there has been little time and no assurance of reimbursement for the advance work of educating dealers or investors in the special characteristics of the prospective issue. As a result, and in view of the fact that such issues are generally of the higher grades permissible or suitable for institutional investment, the underwriters frequently sell much of the issue in large blocks to institutions. The underwriters have no undertaking to the issuer to try to place the securities with any particular class or classes of investors or in a particular or widespread geographical area, and the cost of organizing selling efforts through dealers may not be warranted by the spread which may exist for the particular issue, so that wide distribution is often not achieved.

If the issue is successful the compensation received may (although not always, even in a successful issue) cover the function of carrying the risk of the issue, the distribution function and the services of the manager in managing the distribution. Since no services have been performed in the design of the issue, and in view of the nature of the distribution, the services of the manager are much less than in a negotiated issue and the compensation, if any, is substantially less.[3]

Use of competitive bidding has been restricted largely to firms in the public utility and railroad industries, which are required to use it by administrative agencies—chiefly the Securities and Exchange Commission, the Interstate Commerce Commission, the Federal Power Commission, and various state agencies regulating public utilities.[4] Use of competitive bidding received a great boost in April, 1941, when the SEC issued Rule U–50, which required its use, subject to certain exceptions, for issues by public utility holding companies under its jurisdiction under the so-called "Death Sentence Act" —the Public Utility Holding Company Act of 1935. In announcing the new rule, the SEC argued: "After weighing the evidence and considering all aspects of the problem, the Commission concluded

---

[3] This description is taken from the Defendants' Preliminary Memorandum for the Court in the case of *United States of America* v. *Henry S. Morgan, Harold Stanley, et. al., Doing Business as Morgan Stanley & Co., et al.,* U.S. District Court for Southern New York, Civil No. 43–757.

[4] Most new bond issues by state and local governmental units are sold to investment bankers through competitive bidding.

that there was no way short of competitive bidding that would afford it satisfactory means of determining the reasonableness of spreads [investment banker's gross margins] or the fairness of prices [of new issues bought by investment bankers], assure disinterested advice in financial matters to the companies concerned, and effectively control their dealings with affiliates."[5]

Whatever the merits of competitive bidding from the issuer's viewpoint, the investment bankers generally have taken a dim view of its merits relative to those of negotiated bidding. And it is significant that competitive bidding has been little used by issuers who are not under pressure from regulatory agencies to use it. Indeed, the record in recent years shows that public utilities that have come out, through reorganization, from under SEC jurisdiction as holding company units or subsidiaries and that had had experience with competitive bidding, have generally chosen not to use it when they subsequently have had free legal choice in the matter.

An example of the use of competitive bidding, as well as the importance of sharp timing in security issues, is provided by the *Wall Street Journal*, July 24, 1957, report of an issue by Pacific Gas and Electric Company:

> The renewed deterioration of bond market prices showed up in the bidding for Pacific Gas & Electric Company's $60 million of first and refunding mortgage bonds.
>
> The big issue went to underwriters led by First Boston Corp. and Halsey, Stuart & Co., Inc., on their bid of 99.92 for a 5% coupon—or at a borrowing cost of more than 5%.
>
> "That cost," investment bankers said, "rivals the rates charged borrowing utilities in June, when bond market prices were at a 25-year low."
>
> Bond quotations firmed up considerably from the June lows, only to deteriorate anew within the past week or so under the influence of large prospective new offerings.
>
> The First Boston and Halsey-Stuart combination is putting the new P. G. & E. bonds out for general distribution today—following compliance with Securities and Exchange Commission requirements—at 100.789 to yield 4.95% to maturity on June 1, 1989.
>
> Indications of retail interest in the issue at that price were described as "favorable."
>
> Yesterday's relatively high cost for Pacific Gas came notwithstanding the fact that the utility made the AA-rated securities nonrefundable for a period of five years.
>
> Had the issue been offered early last week, according to some authori-

---

[5] Securities and Exchange Commission, *Seventh Annual Report, 1941* (Washington, D.C.: U.S. Government Printing Office, 1942), p. 101.

ties, it probably would have gone to the public at a 4.80% yield, rather than the 4.95% that actually turned out.

They also compared P. G. & E.'s borrowing cost of more than 5% with the 4.76% Southern California Edison Co. is paying for the $40 million of bond money it raised July 1 through sale of similarly rated 4¾'s.

The lone competing bid for the new P. G. & E. 5's—99.599 on a 5% coupon—was submitted by a Blyth & Co., Inc. group.

On Pacific Gas & Electric's last bond market trip, January 22, 1957, it sold a $35 million block of 4½'s, due December 1, 1986, at 4.55%. It will put the proceeds from yesterday's 5's into its construction program.

It is interesting to note that the difference between the bids submitted by the two bidding groups amounted to $3.21 per thousand, and that the gross spread between price to the issuer and to the public amounted to $8.69 per thousand. The two managing firms of the syndicate that won the bid enlisted the participation as underwriters of thirty-seven other firms.

Investment Bankers' Activities in Nonunderwritten Public Issues

In some public issues the issuing company is willing to stand the risk of an unsuccessful offering but desires to use the services of investment bankers on an "agency" basis. Under such arrangements the investment banking firm, for a fee, typically assists the issuer in surveying and gauging the market for the issue, in the design of the security, in setting fees the issuer will pay for distribution services, and in organizing dealers to distribute the securities for the account of the issuer. Under the usual agency arrangement the dealers receive a commission based on the amount they are able to sell. The bankers may also assume greater responsibility by agreeing with the issuer that they will use their "best efforts" to sell the entire issue, and receive commissions for the sales made as a result of their efforts.

Sale of New Issues to Existing Security Holders

The existing security holders represent a significant and identifiable potential market for further issues of securities; and a substantial percentage of new issues of common stock, and of bonds and preferred stocks convertible into common stock, is offered first to existing common stockholders. Some corporations have free choice in deciding whether or not to offer new common shares first to present stockholders, but in many companies the present common shareholders possess a legal right to receive *privileged subscriptions* to new issues of common stock. The legal right to privileged subscriptions is termed a *pre-emptive right*. Where it exists, corporations have no choice but to offer new issues of securities for cash pro rata to the security holders having the pre-emptive right.

What determines whether a particular security issue has this pre-emptive right? In most cases the status of the pre-emptive right is governed by specific provisions on the subject in the charter or bylaws of the corporation. If the status of the right is not clearly established in this way, the laws on the subject of the state of incorporation must be studied. In the absence of both charter and statutory definition of the pre-emptive right, reference must be made to the common law.

A number of states have enacted specific legislation in regard to the status of the pre-emptive right for corporations incorporated under their laws. Under the statutes of many of these states, corporations are empowered to write into their charters and bylaws clauses granting, limiting, or denying the pre-emptive right to any or all classes of their securities. In the absence of charter statements, certain broad rules are stated to apply. Some states, including Indiana, California, and Delaware, have enacted legislation providing that the pre-emptive right does *not* exist unless it is specifically called for in corporate charters. For example, the California law provides: "Unless otherwise provided in the article [of incorporation] the board of directors may issue shares, option rights, or securities having conversion or option rights, without first offering the same to stockholders of any class or classes."[6]

Where the status of the pre-emptive right is not established clearly by state legislation or the terms of corporate charters or bylaws, the legal status of the pre-emptive right has been evolved from common-law decisions on the subject. The courts have recognized the fact that the issue of new stock may well mean dilution of the voting power, asset values, earning power, and market values of the holdings of existing stockholders and have concluded that the stockholders are entitled, in justice, to the protection against such a dilution of voting power and other interests afforded by the pre-emptive right. Consequently, the common-law decisions on the pre-emptive right have established the principle that a stockholder is entitled to the pre-emptive right in the absence of charter or statutory provisions to the contrary, with the following restrictions:

1. The pre-emptive right is restricted to common stockholders and applies only to common stocks or securities convertible into common stocks.

---

[6] California Civil Code, Sec. 297.

2. It does not apply to stock issued for property.
3. It does not apply to treasury stock or to stock originally authorized under the corporate charter and issued in a "reasonable time" after incorporation.

A corporation that has decided to offer a new issue of stock to its stockholders usually distributes to them purchase warrants known as *rights*. The rights state the privilege of the holder to subscribe at a specified subscription price to a stated number of the new shares. Usually, such stock purchase rights must be exercised within a limited period of time, seldom more than thirty days. Such shares as remain unsubscribed on the date the rights expire may then be offered to the public at the same or at a higher price.

In most instances the rights are freely transferable, so that a stockholder who does not care to exercise his rights can sell them to someone who does want to use them to buy the stock at the subscription price. When the issue of rights is a large one, active trading in the rights usually develops and continues until the date the rights expire. In trading, the price of "a right" is the price of the subscription privilege derived from ownership of one old share.

For example, the Philadelphia Electric Company, in June, 1957, offered 609,815 additional shares of common stock to existing shareholders on the basis of one new share for each twenty shares held of record on June 4, 1957. The last sale price of the common stock on the New York Stock Exchange on June 3, 1957, was at $38⅞. Purchase warrants, or "rights," were issued to common stockholders entitling them to buy new shares at $36.25 and twenty rights per share. As is typical, the rights were transferable, so that shareholders preferring not to subscribe for new shares could sell the rights on the New York Stock Exchange, where trading in the rights continued throughout the duration of the offering, which was announced as terminating on June 25, 1957.

During the time that rights were effective, any person wishing to invest in the stock of the company could have bought shares in the open market; or alternatively, he could have bought the necessary number of rights, twenty per share, and together with the required cash, $36.25 per share in the case of Philadelphia Electric, subscribed to the new issue. Clearly, the rights would have value and the new issue would be attractive only when the current market price was greater than the subscription price. A decline in the market price below $36.25 for a protracted period during the twenty-one-day offering period would have jeopardized sale of the new issue to the public. The setting of the subscription price, therefore, in such offerings to stockholders involves prediction of likely market prices for the security during the life of the rights. Some companies attempt to set the subscription price close to the market; others price the new issue well below the market in order to provide maximum inducement for use of the rights and successful sale of the issue. In the Philadelphia Electric case, market prices for public utility common stocks declined generally during the rights offering period, and on June 24 the common stock sold as low as 36¼ and rights sold at ⅟₁₂₈. A total of 541,937 shares were taken up by exercise of the rights, leaving 67,878 to be taken up by the investment bankers.

In offering securities to existing shareholders, the issuing company frequently elects to dispense entirely with the services of investment bankers and absorb any risks that market declines will cause the offering to fail. In other cases, as was the fact in the Philadelphia Electric offering, the issuer employs investment bankers on a "stand-by underwriting" basis. That is, the underwriters guaranteed Philadelphia Electric a definite amount for the entire issue by agreeing to stand by during the subscription period to purchase unsubscribed shares, at a predetermined price, whatever the market price for the securities at that time. In the Philadelphia Electric instance, the eighty-six underwriters agreed to buy all unsubscribed shares at the subscription price. The underwriting fee was set at a minimum of $96,046, plus 70 cents a share for any shares purchased by the bankers through the exercise of warrants and for unsubscribed shares taken by them. The underwriters agreed to share with the company net profits, if any, realized on sales of unsubscribed shares.

Relatively seldom are nonconvertible bonds and preferred stocks offered through rights to existing shareholders of sizable concerns. As indicated above, this method is quite important in the sale of common shares or securities convertible into common stock.

Private Placement of New Security Issues

As was shown in Table 23–1 and Chart 23–1, it has become common for industrial concerns to sell entire issues of debt securities and, to a much lesser extent, of preferred or common stock to a single or limited number of investors who buy as investors rather than with intention of early resale. This practice has been made possible by the importance of institutional investors, primarily life insurance companies, as buyers of corporate securities. As was noted in the preceding chapter, the life insurance companies have had huge sums to invest in corporate bonds. There are advantages to both issuer and investing institution in direct negotiation leading to private placement. Usually, the need to go through the registration and other procedures required by the SEC for public issues is avoided, along with the need for underwriting, thus reducing both the time and the expense necessary in the issue. Further, in private placements the terms of the security can be worked out over the conference table in direct negotiation between issuer and investors, and subsequent changes in the security contract are relatively easily accomplished once the parties agree to them.

The insurance companies, in return for the advantages direct placement affords issuers, usually expect a higher return (one half of 1 per cent or more) on the securities bought directly than on comparable issues bought on public sale or in the market. They also may be able to insist upon redemption premiums or other features more favorable to them as investors than would have been necessary in a public sale of the securities.

Investment bankers frequently act as agents for the issuers in giving advice in the design of issues for private placement, and in locating and negotiating with the institutional buyers. Naturally, their fees as agents normally are much less than their charges as underwriters of issues for public sale.

Direct Sale to Employees, Suppliers, or Other Special Groups

Although the total amount of new issues sold to employees and other special groups is not such as to make it a major means of raising capital, it does deserve brief mention. Many companies make stock available to key employees on an option basis, and some have special plans on a continuing basis to permit employees to buy new shares. Usually, the motives of the issuer in such security issues are not primarily financial—that is, not primarily to raise capital—but rather to provide additional incentive compensation or to encourage or cement employee loyalties to the company. In a few instances, however, amounts of capital raised thereby have been quite consequential—as in the case of American Telephone and Telegraph Company, where instalment payments by employees buying common shares amounted to $269 million in 1960.

During the 1920's a number of companies, especially public utilities, made strenuous efforts to sell securities to employees and to customers, largely with the aim of increasing the good will of these groups toward the companies. Many found, however, that subsequent declines in the market values of the securities sold these groups resulted in ill will rather than good feeling toward the company. Another objection to this practice is grounded in the fact that employees are, in effect, being asked to compound their risks when they are asked to invest their savings in the same enterprise on which they are dependent for a livelihood.

Costs of Sale of New Security Issues

So far, we have spoken of the costs of getting a new issue of securities issued and sold only with reference to individual cases. Fortunately, considerable data are available which permit a useful general review of the costs to issuers connected with the sale of new issues.

In Table 23–3, we present data on the total costs of sale as a percentage of total proceeds of securities offered the general public. Some form of underwriting was typical of these issues, and the figure for "compensation" covers the payments to investment bankers for underwriting and/or selling services.

One of the striking features to be noted from the data is the relatively low issue costs of debt securities sold to the public in comparison with the cost of sale of common stock. In all size groups, bonds were sold at lower costs of issue and sale than were common stocks. Costs of preferred stock sale fall between those of bonds and common, tending to be closer to the costs of bonds than of common stock.

Reference to similar material on issue costs for earlier years, not presented here, indicates no marked trend in costs of issue through public sales since World War II except for a tendency for costs of small issues of common stock to increase. Comparison with data for the decades of the twenties and thirties shows that costs of sale for the post-World War II years were significantly lower than for the earlier decades.

Why are the costs of sale of common stock so much higher than those for bonds? A basic reason is the difference in the nature of the markets. As indicated in the preceding chapter, a large percentage of the new bond issues is sold to the relatively concentrated, easily reached institutional market. In the case of common stock a much higher percentage must be placed with the diffuse individual buyer market. Hence, typically, it is much easier and cheaper for investment bankers to sell bonds than common stocks.

Generally, more selling effort is required in common stocks than

TABLE 23-3
COSTS OF SALE AS PERCENTAGE OF PROCEEDS*
Securities Offered General Public†
in Selected Years: 1951, 1953, 1955

SIZE OF ISSUE (IN MILLIONS OF DOLLARS)	BONDS, NOTES, AND DEBENTURES			PREFERRED STOCK			COMMON STOCK		
	Compensation	Other Expenses	Total Costs	Compensation	Other Expenses	Total Costs	Compensation	Other Expenses	Total Costs
Under 0.5	.....	.....	.....	.....	.....	.....	20.99%	6.16%	27.15%
0.5–0.9	7.53%	3.96%	11.49%	8.67%	3.96%	12.63%	17.12	4.64	21.76
1.0–1.9	5.80	2.37	8.17	5.98	2.09	8.07	11.27	2.31	13.58
2.0–4.9	2.37	1.41	3.78	3.83	1.05	4.88	8.47	1.50	9.97
5.0–9.9	1.01	0.82	1.83	2.93	0.79	3.72	5.31	0.86	6.17
10.0–19.9	0.88	0.64	1.52	2.40	0.52	2.92	4.20	0.46	4.66
20.0–49.9	0.85	0.48	1.33	2.84	0.35	3.20	4.98	0.38	5.37
50.0 and over	0.88	0.32	1.19	2.12	0.38	2.51	.....	.....	.....

* Data on compensation do not include the ultimate burden involved in the granting to underwriters of additional but contingent compensation in the form of options or warrants to purchase common stock at what may prove to be bargain prices. Options are particularly common in the case of small issues of common stock.

† Only securities registered with the Securities and Exchange Commission are included. Bank stocks and railroad equipment trust certificates are the major types of public sales excluded.

SOURCE: Securities and Exchange Commission, *Cost of Flotation of Corporate Securities, 1951–1955* (Washington, D.C.: U.S. Government Printing Office, June, 1957).

for bonds, where institutional buyers pretty much decide for themselves whether or not to purchase. Except in the case of "hot" issues the investment bankers have to "sell" new issues of common stock aggressively. Further, their selling largely takes the form of recommending the issue to their customers as a "good buy." For their efforts and for "putting on the line" their own reputations as shrewd analysts of value, they expect more compensation.

It will be noted also from Table 23–3 that the percentage costs of sale of securities are very much higher for small issues than for large. The costs of selling small issues of common stock are particularly high in comparison with those of large issues. There are several reasons for the higher costs of smaller issues. First, many of the costs of investment bankers in investigating an issue, in preparing an issue for sale, and in selling it are relatively fixed. Since the absolute amount of the costs does not increase proportionately as the amount of the issue is increased, the costs in percentage terms of the smaller issues are much greater. In addition, the larger issues tend to be of firms that are well known to investors and hence require less selling effort. Institutional buyers are more likely to represent an important potential market, easily reached, in the case of issues of strong, large companies. The investment quality of the security generally *tends* to be higher with size of the issuer. Small issues of companies with uncertain futures tend to involve considerable price risk to investment banker-buyers. Again, when an investment banker with a fine reputation takes on the job of selling the securities of a small, little-known firm, the banking firm is selling its reputation as much as or more than that of the issuing firm—so the banker expects a compensating margin for his contribution and risks.

A brief explanation of the nature of issue costs to the issuer other than compensation to investment bankers is appropriate here. The SEC has estimated the expenses of issue, other than compensation, for an "average debt issue" of $15.5 million at about $110,000, broken down as follows:

Legal fees	$16,700
Printing and engraving of the bonds, prospectus, etc.	30,500
Accounting fees	5,300
Engineering fees, etc.	9,100
Federal and state stamp taxes and fees	21,400
Trustees' fees	16,300
SEC fees	1,600
Miscellaneous costs	9,900

In sales of common and preferred stocks, trustees' fees are avoided, but costs in each of the other categories are typically incurred.

As will be seen from Table 23–4, the costs of issuing common stock through first offer to existing shareholders typically are smaller than those of common stock sold to the general public. The chief saving is in the compensation paid investment bankers. As we have seen, in some offerings to stockholders, stand-by underwriting is avoided altogether. Where used, stand-by underwriting fees and

TABLE 23–4

Costs of Sale as Percentage of Proceeds*

Registered Common Stock Offerings through
Rights to Existing Stockholders, 1955

Size of Issue (in Millions of Dollars)	Compensation†	Other Costs	Total Costs
Under 5.0.............	3.81%	1.81%	5.33%
5.0–19.9.............	4.24	2.48	7.26
20.0–99.9.............	2.48	1.04	3.45
100.0 and over........	1.50	0.85	2.82

* Median percentages in each size group.
† Primarily to investment bankers for stand-by underwriting and services in aiding the sale.
Source: Securities and Exchange Commission, *Costs of Flotation of Corporate Securities, 1951–1955* (Washington, D.C.: U.S. Government Printing Office, June, 1957).

other investment banking charges typically are smaller than in the case of underwritten issues sold to the general public.

The costs of placing security issues privately, which include the fees paid to investment bankers when they are used as agents, are very much smaller than the costs involved in either sales to the public or sales to stockholders through rights issue. Cost data for a large number of such issues are given in Table 23–5.

TABLE 23–5

Costs of Sale as Percentage of Proceeds*

Securities Placed Privately in Selected Years:
1951, 1953, 1955

Size of Issue (in Millions of Dollars)	Bonds, Notes, and Debentures†	Preferred and Common Stock
Under 0.3....................	1.49%	1.25%
0.3–0.4.....................	1.06	0.13
0.5–0.9.....................	0.83	0.53
1.0–1.9.....................	0.59	0.61
2.0–4.9.....................	0.43	0.50
5.0–9.9.....................	0.34	0.38
10.0–19.9...................	0.32	0.14
20.0 and over...............	0.22	...

* Median percentages in each size category.
† Data are drawn from 1,846 issues of bonds, notes, and debentures and from 108 issues of preferred and common stock.
Source: Securities and Exchange Commission, *Cost of Flotation of Corporate Securities, 1951–1955* (Washington, D.C.: U.S. Government Printing Office, June, 1957).

We should caution the reader that the "costs of sale," as we have discussed them here, include only the costs of getting the new issue out and sold. They do not include the continuing costs associated with the issue once it is outstanding. Thus, the concern that must pay a higher interest rate on bonds sold privately than it would have had to pay on bonds sold to the public may well use up in higher interest costs over a period of years any savings in issue costs achieved through private placement.

The Secondary Markets for Corporate Securities

As we indicated earlier, the existence of good markets where investors can buy or sell outstanding securities has an *important, though indirect,* effect on the ability of corporations to raise new capital through the sale of securities. In this section, we shall briefly review the secondary markets for corporate securities.

The Organized Security Exchanges. Much of the secondary trading in corporate securities takes place on organized security exchanges such as the New York Stock Exchange (NYSE). The exchanges essentially provide central market places where individual and firm members execute buying and selling orders for securities admitted for trading. Member brokers act primarily as agents of customers wishing to trade particular securities, executing buying or selling orders in their behalf. In return for executing the orders and related services, the broker charges a commission, the amount of which is determined by reference to a standard schedule of fees established by the exchange.

Trading on the organized exchanges is conducted on what can be termed a "two-way auction" basis. Members with buy orders compete with each other to purchase the shares at the lowest possible prices. At the same time, sellers compete to get the highest possible price. A transaction is made when the highest bidder and the lowest offerer get together. The prices at which sales are made are recorded and immediately publicized. Consequently, the prices for exchange transactions reported in the newspaper represent actual transactions, and the person for whom orders to buy or sell are executed can assure himself that the prices reported to him by his broker represent reasonable prices, given the state of the market at the time of the transaction.

Obviously, the exchange and its member brokers do not create the prices at which securities are traded; instead, the prices arrived at by buyer and seller are the reflection of relative supply and demand for the security at the time it is traded.

Issuing firms must take the initiative in getting their securities listed for trading on the exchanges. To qualify its securities for listing, the corporation must meet certain requirements of the exchange and of the SEC. The NYSE requires that the concern be a going business with substantial assets and earning power. The company's stock should have sufficiently wide distribution and potential activity that a reasonable auction market may be expected to develop; as indication of this, it should have a minimum of 1,500 stockholders, who hold at least 400,000 shares. In addition, the company must conform to various SEC or stock exchange rules requiring independent outside audit, publication of financial statements, etc. The other exchanges also have rules relative to the listing of stocks for trading but, in addition, permit trading in stocks not fully listed under certain conditions, which include the permission of the SEC. There has been a marked tendency over the years toward stricter requirements for listing.

In mid-1960, 1,317 issuing companies had 1,531 stocks, common and preferred, and 1,137 bond issues listed for trading on the NYSE. In addition, some 1,500 other stocks were admitted to trading on other registered exchanges, either on a listed or on an unlisted basis.

Twelve stock exchanges registered with the SEC and subject to its regulations account for virtually all the trading on exchanges. Table 23–6 shows the volume of stock traded on each of the registered exchanges in 1960. The dominant position of the NYSE, where 84 per

TABLE 23–6

SALES OF STOCKS ON REGISTERED EXCHANGES DURING 1960*

Exchange	Market Value (in Millions)	Percentage of Total
New York..................	$37,960	83.9%
American..................	4,176	9.2
Midwest..................	1,235	2.7
Pacific Coast..............	881	2.0
Philadelphia-Baltimore......	471	1.1
Boston...................	272	0.6
Detroit...................	155	0.3
Cincinnati................	35	0.1
Pittsburgh................	28	0.1
Salt Lake.................	3	....
Spokane..................	2	....
San Francisco Mining.......	1	....
	$45,219	100.0%

*The Chicago Board of Trade, a registered securities exchange, had no trading in securities in 1960.
SOURCE: Securities and Exchange Commission, *Statistical Bulletin*, February, 1961.

cent of the trading in stocks on exchanges took place, will be noted. The importance of New York City as a trading center for stocks is also readily apparent. The NYSE and the American Stock Exchange (formerly the N.Y. Curb Exchange), also located in the New York City financial section, together accounted for 93 per cent of all stock trading on exchanges.

What is the extent of market turnover for all stocks listed on the New York Stock Exchange? The total market value of all equity shares listed on the NYSE was $307.7 billion on December 31, 1959, and $307 billion on December 31, 1960. The market value of shares traded in 1960 was $38 billion, or 12.4 per cent of the average market value of the listed shares. Total value of all bonds listed for trading on the NYSE at the end of 1960 amounted to $108.3 billion; but trading in bonds on the NYSE was very light, only $1.6 billion in 1960, most of the trading in bonds being done in the over-the-counter market, discussed later. In other words, the NYSE is a very important market for stocks and relatively unimportant for bonds.[7]

Like the organized exchanges, the over-the-counter markets perform the basic economic function of promoting liquidity—or more accurately, transferability—for investors in securities. In contrast to the exchanges the over-the-counter markets do *not* represent auction markets where buying bids and selling offers of many customers are brought together. Instead, prices are arrived at by negotiation between dealers and between dealers and investors. In this trading the dealers act as principals for their own accounts rather than as broker-agents for customers. Publicity of prices is limited to the furnishing of bid and asked quotations rather than the reporting of actual sales prices. Many over-the-counter dealers specialize in a limited number of selected issues and "make a market" for these securities by carrying an inventory of the securities and standing ready to buy or sell the securities to customers or other dealers.

Let us review how an order might well be handled for purchase of an over-the-counter security. Suppose you wished, on April 5, 1961, to buy 100 common shares of Republic Natural Gas Company, a medium-sized natural gas and oil-producing firm. Since there is fairly active trading in this stock, you noted in the morning *Wall Street Journal* that data on the current market for this stock are available under the headings, "Over-the-Counter Markets," "National Mar-

---

[7] Securities and Exchange Commission, *Statistical Bulletin*, February, 1961.

ket," and "Industrial and Utility Stocks." Data are prefaced with the notation: "The following bid and asked quotations from the National Association of Securities Dealers, Inc. do not represent actual transactions. They are a guide to the range within which these securities could have been sold (indicated by the 'bid') or bought (indicated by the 'asked') at the time of compilation. The 'National' list is composed of securities which have a wide national distribution." Having been cautioned that the quotations provide a guide only as to the price at which you can expect to buy Republic, you noted that Republic common was listed as 33¼ bid, 35⅝ asked (dollars per share).[8] Suppose you lived in Tucson and dealt with the local office of Hemphill Noyes & Company—a large firm with offices in twenty-eight cities. If you wished definitely to buy, provided you had to pay no more than 35⅝, the local office of Hemphill Noyes would take your order on that basis. Since the firm operates as an over-the-counter dealer as well as a broker on national exchanges, it is possible that they carry an inventory of Republic and can sell you shares out of their inventory. More likely, they do not and would consult data which provide quotations and indicate the twenty-odd dealer firms which customarily make a market in Republic, and ask for firm offers on 100 shares from several of these firms. If they accepted the lowest offer—say, 34—and bought as your agent, they would charge you $34 a share plus a regular brokerage commission. Had Hemphill Noyes made a market in Republic shares and carried a dealer's inventory in these shares, they would likely have priced the shares to you at 34¼ or 34⅜—or whatever amount above the prevailing dealer's market price they regarded as providing an appropriate dealer's margin. In this case the report of the transaction to you would make clear that the transaction was with them as principal. Since they make their profit as principal, no brokerage commission is charged. If you did not have confidence that the Hemphill Noyes offer would be a good one, you would be free to ask them only for a quotation and could seek quotations from other firms.

What securities are traded over the counter? The answer is a bit involved. A very important segment of the market is composed of United States bonds. Although some U.S. issues are listed on the NYSE, an overwhelming percentage of total trading in governments is car-

---

[8] In actual fact, the published offering quotation usually is significantly higher than the figure at which over-the-counter shares can be purchased. In other words, the actual market spreads between bid and offered are not so wide as the published quotations suggest.

ried on in the over-the-counter markets, with seventeen dealer firms handling the bulk of the volume. Trading in U.S. bonds is very heavy. In the early weeks of 1961, *daily* trading in U.S. government securities in the over-the-counter markets ran between $1.2 and $1.7 billion, or about six times the value of stocks traded on the New York Stock Exchange during this period of active stock trading.[9] Traded over the counter exclusively are the bonds of some 150,000 state, municipality, school district, and other local governmental units, known as *municipals*. A number of dealer firms specialize in municipals, a few firms dealing exclusively in them. It is interesting to note that commercial banks have authority to act as dealers in government bonds and in certain classes of municipal bonds, and a few large commercial banks are among the leading dealer firms in this activity. Trading in corporate bonds is also accomplished mainly in the over-the-counter markets, although many are listed on the NYSE.

The common stocks of commercial banks are traded only in the over-the-counter market, and the shares of insurance companies are predominantly traded in the over-the-counter market. The industrial and utility issues traded over the counter are typically those of small or medium-sized companies whose securities are narrowly distributed and whose trading is relatively inactive. Since the securities of a large number of the corporations in the country are so characterized, the total number of issues of corporate stocks traded in the over-the-counter market in the course of a year is large. The National Quotation Bureau, a private concern circulating quotations for over-the-counter stocks, reported about 26,000 security issues carrying over-the-counter quotations in its October, 1960, volume, which is a cumulative record covering a period of years. The daily quotation sheets of the Bureau carry some 6,500 stocks, about 10 per cent of which are listed on a U.S. or Canadian stock exchange. That many of these are small or closely held is suggested by SEC estimates in 1960 that there are about 3,500 U.S. corporations, exclusive of investment companies, with three hundred or more stockholders each, whose stocks are traded only over the counter. These stocks were estimated to have a total market value in 1959 of about $66 billion. This figure included bank stocks valued at $17.5 billion and insurance stocks at $11.8 billion.[10]

In addition to the trading in corporate stocks not admitted for

---

[9] *Boston Herald*, March 31, 1961, based on Federal Reserve Bank of New York data.

[10] Securities and Exchange Commission, *Twenty-sixth Annual Report* (1960).

trading on organized exchanges, there is considerable trading over the counter in stocks that are also traded on the exchanges. Many large blocks of listed stocks are traded in negotiated deals off the exchanges, despite efforts of the exchanges to develop specific techniques for handling effectively large block transactions on the exchanges.

The total dollar volume of trading in corporate stocks in the over-the-counter market unquestionably is large, but the amount is difficult to estimate. One estimate,[11] reached with considerable effort, put the total dollar volume of trading in outstanding corporate stocks in the over-the-counter markets in 1949 at about one half of the volume traded on the exchanges, or roughly one third of all trading in corporate stocks that year. The same author noted "a strong upward trend from 1920 to 1951 in the relative importance of the over-the-counter market."[12]

A Look at the Firms Doing Business in the Primary and Secondary Security Markets

The piecemeal references to financial houses in this chapter, variously speaking of "investment bankers," "brokers," "broker-dealers," "traders," etc., has probably been confusing to the reader. At this point, clarity may be served by a recapitulation of the major functions served by financial houses and a brief elaboration of their patterns of operation.

We have at various points identified several major functions performed by financial firms:

1. Participation as underwriters of new issues and related activity in selling new issues.
2. Selling of new issues without underwriting participation.
3. Brokerage activity as agents, for a commission, in the buying and selling of outstanding securities.
4. Trading as principals in the buying, holding for trading, and selling of securities in the over-the-counter market.

Not noted earlier are additional roles assumed by many firms. For example, some firms invest in securities for continued holding as investors rather than for early resale. Related but distinct are the activities of some firms in trading for their own account for short-run gains. This may take the form, for example, of arbitraging—taking

---

[11] Irwin Friend, *Activity on Over-the-Counter Markets* (Philadelphia: University of Pennsylvania Press, 1951), p. 9.

[12] *Ibid.*, p. 10.

advantage of aberrations of the market which present opportunities for profitable two-way simultaneous transactions in equivalents, in which one security is bought and its equivalent sold at about the same time, as in the case of stock purchase rights and the security they can be used to buy.

Some large firms, such as Merrill Lynch, Pierce, Fenner & Smith, or Carl M. Loeb, Rhoades & Company, although best known as brokers, actually are engaged in all the major types of activity summarized above. Other firms specialize, many exclusively, in performing one of the above functions. Thus, Morgan Stanley & Company specializes in underwriting and, indeed, in the management of underwriting syndicates; while Aubrey G. Lanston & Company, Inc., operates as a dealer in U.S. government and federal agency bonds in the over-the-counter market.

Since a very large percentage of the firms are engaged in some form of over-the-counter trading, data on the 3,000-odd firms operating as registered security dealers in 1949 are rather comprehensive. Operating with a combined capital of over $700 million in the fiscal year 1948–49, all registered security firms participating in any over-the-counter business grossed approximately $450 million. An estimated $130 million should be deducted, as it represents total exchange commissions earned by the large number of concerns which are members of the exchanges as well as over-the-counter dealers. The remaining $320 million gross income was divided as follows:[13]

1.	From underwriting	$ 85,000,000
2.	From over-the-counter transactions in outstanding securities	140,000,000
3.	From service fees	35,000,000
4.	From interest and dividends	40,000,000
5.	From nonsecurity sources	20,000,000
		$320,000,000

[13] G. Wright Hoffman, *Character and Extent of Over-the-Counter Markets* (Philadelphia: University of Pennsylvania Press, 1952), p. 2.

Chapter 24

The Nature and Effects of Government Regulation on Long-Term Finance

IN CONSIDERING the subject of long-term corporate finance, it is necessary to take account of the very considerable influence which government has come to exert on this aspect of business activity. This influence has always existed in some degree because of the fact that the corporation is a creature of the state and derives its characteristics from a charter issued in accordance with the provisions of state company laws. As indicated in a previous chapter, the charter includes the authorization to issue securities in specified amounts and of a specified character. However, the control exerted by government through the laws of incorporation is in the main more potential than actual, and it has been through other devices and in other ways that the real teeth of state and federal intervention have been displayed.

Except for the railroads, most of the effective regulation in this area had its origin in the collapse of the stock market in 1929 and in the severe depression which followed in the early thirties. This sharp and unhappy experience caused the federal government to make a major effort to restore some measure of prosperity and to correct the abuses which in its judgment had brought on this situation. The widespread collapse of confidence was nowhere more apparent than in the financial aspects of the economy, and direct governmental action here came early and took a vigorous form. From the nature of this action, certain objectives were apparent. One was to modify the form of certain key financial institutions—notably, the commercial banks and the securities exchanges—with the intention of eliminating the weaknesses which had led to their breakdown under pressure and contributed to the general decline in economic activity and employment. Another objective was to protect the investor, particularly the small-scale unsophisticated investor, from what were considered to be unnecessarily severe losses in the collapse of stock market values. Beyond this, there was the intention of restoring the investors' confidence in the securities markets, so that savings would again flow into productive activity. Still another objective, which appeared in regard to certain key industries such as the public utility industry, was that of protecting the public as consumers against the actual or potential decline in efficiency and increase in costs resulting from weaknesses in or abuses of corporate financial policy.

Federal Regulation of New Issues

The principal federal agency for achieving these objectives has been the Securities and Exchange Commission, established in 1934. Under the authority of a series of acts passed between 1933 and 1940, the Commission was empowered to regulate a wide variety of matters bearing on long-term corporate finance.[1] The first in this series was the Securities Act of 1933, which was designed to regulate the issuance of new corporate securities. The basic aims of the legislation have been to eliminate misrepresentation, to assure a full disclosure of pertinent information on new security issues, and to have this information in the hands of the investor before he makes a commitment to buy. The Act requires registration with the SEC of all securities offered for sale to the public through the mails or "other instrumentalities of interstate commerce." Apart from securities which are issued entirely on an intrastate basis, there are two noteworthy aspects of the market which are outside the scope of this regulation. The first is that relating to small issues—issues of less than $300,000 do not have to be registered.[2] Also excluded are those issues which are placed privately. Of an estimated total of $10,159 million of new corporate securities offered for cash sale in the United States in 1960, $3,503 million were sold privately rather than by public offering.[3]

---

[1] The Commission's *Twenty-fifth Annual Report* (Washington, D.C.: U.S. Government Printing Office, 1959), for the fiscal year ended June 30, 1959, pp. xiii–xxxix, reviewed at some length the causes, objectives, and principal features of the statutes under which the Commission acts. The Commission's rules are found in the *Code of Federal Regulations*, Title 17, Chap. II.

[2] This does not mean, however, that small issues are beyond the scope of the powers of the SEC under the Act.

[3] Securities and Exchange Commission, *Statistical Bulletin*, February, 1961, p. 3.

Companies which issue securities coming under the provisions of the Act must file a registration statement containing certain specified information on the prospective issue. This statement must be accompanied by a copy of the prospectus to be issued to investors, which must also contain this same basic information. The information requested covers a variety of subjects, including the financial history of the company, particulars about the holdings of the major stockholders, details of outstanding securities, the purposes of the issue, the proposed offering price, and underwriter's commissions and discounts and other expenses of the offering. The registration statement and the prospectus are reviewed by the Commission to determine whether all material facts have been disclosed. If the Commission is satisfied on this point, the registration will be allowed to become effective; but if not, amendments or additions will be requested. The SEC is empowered to issue a *stop order* either before or after the registration becomes effective if it is apparent that the circumstances under which the securities are being offered to the public are contrary to the Act. In the event of continued violation of the Act the Commission may request a court injunction. It is to be noted that the responsibility of the Commission does not extend to the consideration of investment quality and the risk to the investor; these are matters which remain the responsibility of the investor himself.

The median lapse of time between the date of filing a registration statement and the date it became effective, for registrations which became effective during the 1960 fiscal year, was estimated by the SEC at forty-three days.[4] This interval was originally intended as an opportunity for the public to become adequately informed on the issue before it was offered for sale. In practice, the time is taken up with the analysis by the SEC of the registration statement and prospectus, the preparation and delivery of a *letter of comment*, and the filing of amendments. Once the registration becomes effective, the issue may be offered to the public subject to the provision that each investor must be supplied with a copy of the prospectus.

There are, of course, significant benefits to corporate enterprises generally resulting from government pressure for honest reporting of the facts about new security issues. Publicity under the auspices of a disinterested agency builds public confidence in the securities markets and strengthens the demand side by reducing the chance of misrepresentation or fraud. On the other hand, such measures have

---

[4] Securities and Exchange Commission, *Twenty-sixth Annual Report* (1960), p. 31.

their price—not only in the time and expense of formal registration but, more importantly, in introducing an element of rigidity in the procedure of issue at a point where maximum flexibility is desired. In a highly volatile securities market, time is of the essence in assuring a successful sale, in terms of both volume and price. It is only fair to say, however, that the Commission is fully conscious of this problem and does its best to reduce to a minimum its interference with the normal processes of the market.

The provisions of the Securities Act are supplemented by the Trust Indenture Act of 1939. This Act was brought into being in order to improve the provisions of bond or other debt indentures concerning the protection of bondholders in event of default. The scope of the regulation is similar to that of the Securities Act, extending to all bonds or other debt securities offered for sale to the public through the mails or other channels of interstate commerce. Issues of less than $1 million principal amount are exempted. Primary attention is given to the role of the trustee. It was the intention of the legislation to make certain that the trustee is completely independent of the indebted company or the underwriter and acts with a sense of responsibility to the bondholder. To this end the Act requires that the indentures of all issues coming within its scope be submitted to the Securities and Exchange Commission. Before an issue can be offered for sale, the Commission must rule that the indenture qualifies as being in conformity with the provisions of the Act. This procedure ties in to the registration procedure under the Securities Act, and registration will not be permitted to become effective without a favorable ruling on the indenture.

State Regulation of Security Issues

Prior to the enactment of the Federal Securities Act, many states had laws on the statute books relating to the sale of securities. The primary purpose of these laws was to prevent the sale of fraudulent security issues to unsuspecting investors. They came to be known as *blue-sky laws*, as descriptive of the extravagant and unfounded representations made by the promoters of such securities.

The immediate pressure for federal regulation in this area came from the market collapse of the thirties, but behind this lay a general dissatisfaction with state regulation. The laws were not uniformly good, nor was the enforcement uniformly effective. Of greater significance, however, was the basic inadequacy of intrastate law in combating what was basically an interstate and even at times an international problem. The misuse of securities markets did not stop at state borders. As a consequence, federal regulation, once in existence, rapidly assumed a dominant role.

Regulation of the Securities Markets

1. The Organized Exchanges. The second major piece of legislation administered by the SEC is the Securities Exchange Act of 1934. This Act was designed to complement the regulation of the purchase and sale of new securities. The basic objective has been to assure a market free from manipulation and abuse, and also to provide the information on issues being traded which is necessary to reasoned investment decisions. In this, as in other areas of government regulation, the exercise of control presupposes a large measure of self-regulation by the parties concerned—in this case, through the rules and regulations of the securities exchanges and of the National Association of Securities Dealers, Inc.

The Act requires that all national exchanges be registered with the SEC. In the year 1960, thirteen exchanges were so registered. Their names and relative importance were indicated in a previous chapter. Through the registration statement the Commission and the public are informed on such matters as rules, trading practices, and membership requirements. Any changes made subsequent to registration must be reported. In addition, the Act requires registration of all securities listed for trading on these exchanges. This procedure provides a body of basic information on these securities which must be kept current. Failure to provide this information or to comply with the Act or the rules of the Commission may bring denial or suspension of trading privileges. This threat is a powerful weapon against dishonesty in the national securities markets on the part of the security issuer.

The Act also contains provisions which enable the SEC to take aggressive action against manipulative practices in the nation's securities markets. The Commission is continuously on the alert for evidence of such practices in the over-the-counter markets as well as in the organized exchanges. It is authorized to instigate private investigations, may subpoena relevant material, and may take testimony under oath. Action to stop any undesirable practices may be taken directly by the Commission or through the courts. A phase of this activity is the supervision of what is termed *stabilization*. This is the practice, on the part of those who are selling a new issue, of repurchasing varying amounts of the securities in order to maintain a stable market price through the offering period. The SEC is charged with the very difficult task of drawing the distinction between the acceptable practice of adjusting temporary price inconsistencies during the offering period and the maintenance of an artificially high initial price leading to damaging price declines when the support is withdrawn.

One of the abuses which the Securities Exchange Act was designed to eliminate is the misuse of a position of influence for personal gain on the part of corporate officers, directors, and major shareholders. The primary regulating device here is the requirement that such individuals (including all shareholders holding more than 10 per cent of a listed stock) report to the Commission their holdings of securities in the company concerned and report any subsequent changes in these holdings. Such information is made available to the public. In addition, the Act provides for the recovery by the issuing company of profits realized by an "insider" in the purchase and sale of securities of the company within a period of six months. The intention here is to prevent the use of inside information for personal gain by such individuals.

The SEC has also been concerned with the matter of corporate control. As we have seen previously, the large-scale corporation generally draws its equity funds from a large number of shareholders. Although, as owners, they represent the ultimate control in the corporation, many of these shareholders are not in a position to attend the annual shareholders' meeting. The only alternative, if their vote is to be exercised, is to designate someone who will be in attendance as their proxy.

Possible abuse of the proxy device arises because shareholders are often indifferent or ill-informed on management matters. It has become common practice for the existing directors regularly to solicit the proxies of the shareholders and for many shareholders either to sign these as a matter of course or to ignore their vote entirely. In this way the existing management can often perpetuate itself indefinitely without ever really rendering full account to the shareholders who elect them (directly or by default).

As a part of the general objective of developing a well-informed investing public, the federal securities laws require that certain relevant information be made available to shareholders when companies solicit proxies, consents, and authorizations. Such requirements encourage a responsible shareholder group and provide it with the basis upon which informed action can be based. This proxy material must be submitted to the SEC at least ten days in advance of the solicitation. The SEC also provides for a means whereby a modification of the proposals or counterproposals may be brought before the shareholders as a group in the event that some shareholders disagree with the management position.

This is an appropriate point at which to raise the issue of one of the most publicized phenomena of current business life—the proxy fight. To the extent that shareholders become alerted to their actual or potential influence as the electors of top management, with or without the assistance of the SEC, the possibility that the existing management may be challenged from without grows in significance. In recent years, there have been some spectacular battles between the established board of directors and a rival individual or group seeking to take its place. Both groups actively solicit the proxies of the masses of independent shareholders in advance of the annual meeting at which directors are elected. Depending on the form of voting used by the corporation, the persuasiveness of the rival parties, and the size of the "independent vote," the "outsiders" may fail completely, elect a minority of directors, or sweep the "old guard" out of office. The outcome may be highly uncertain until the vote has been actually counted.

To the disinterested observer, the event of a proxy fight raises some significant questions. On the one hand, the fact that it can happen may help to keep the management alert and responsive to the interests of the shareholders. It provides an occasion on which shareholders are made very conscious of their responsibilities as the ultimate authority in the business. It is entirely possible that the existing management should be replaced. On the other hand, the experience can be seriously damaging to the morale and efficiency of the business as a whole. Competent management, as well as incompetent management, may be challenged in this way, and by outsiders whose capacities and motives may be in doubt. Many shareholders are not really equipped to choose. We leave the reader to consider for himself the merits of the existing state of corporate control and of the regulations designed to protect it.

2. *The Over-the-Counter Market.* Regulation of the over-the-counter markets takes the form of supervision of the activities of brokers and dealers and of their association—the National Association of Securities Dealers, Inc. By requiring the registration of all brokers and dealers using the mails or other means of interstate commerce in any dealings in securities which come under its control, the

SEC is able to inform itself of their activities and, if necessary, use its powers to eliminate unlawful or undesirable practices. The Commission has the authority to prevent brokers and dealers from entering or continuing in interstate security dealings by refusing or revoking their registration and by suspending or expelling them from membership in the NASD and the national exchanges. Such action may be taken where the broker or dealer is found by the SEC to be guilty of "misconduct."

The following statistics for the fiscal year 1960 give some indication of the extent of SEC action in this regard:[5]

Effective registration of brokers and dealers at end of last fiscal year (1959)..	4,907
Proceedings pending at the start of the fiscal year to:	
Revoke registration..	53
Revoke registration and suspend or expel from NASD or exchanges...	39
Deny registration to applicants...........................	6
	98
Proceedings instituted during fiscal year to:	
Revoke registration..	46
Revoke registration and suspend or expel from NASD or exchanges...	36
Deny registration to applicants...........................	12
	94

As part of its regulatory powers the Commission can make periodic and special examinations of the books and records of brokers and dealers. Such examinations are in addition to those that are made by other public regulatory agencies, by exchanges, or by dealer associations. Acts of misconduct are illustrated in such practices as the taking of secret profits or unreasonable pricing (out of line with the market).

In addition to its control over individual dealers, the SEC also exerts control over national securities associations, which at the present time means the National Association of Securities Dealers, Inc. By requiring the Association to register with the SEC and report regularly on its rules and membership action, the Securities Exchange Act puts the Commission in the position of being able to determine whether the Association's activities are in accord with the letter and spirit of the Act. Since it has authority over both rules and

---

[5] Securities and Exchange Commission, *Twenty-sixth Annual Report* (1960), pp. 89 and 91.

membership, the SEC has all the power it needs to enforce compliance with its decisions.

Investment Companies and Advisers

Because of the complexities involved in the selection of a group of securities for investment, many investors feel incapable of making their own selections. In these circumstances, the investor may seek the advice of a professional investment counselor or may side-step the problem entirely by placing his money in the hands of an investment company, which then applies its own investment standards and policies. In either case the inexperienced investor is potentially at the mercy of the adviser or the investment company. The opportunities for misuse of this position of trust in the past have been considered so significant that the federal government has enacted legislation which empowers the SEC to oversee these activities. This legislation is the Investment Advisers Act of 1940 and the Investment Company Act of 1940.

The basic objective of the Investment Advisers Act is to assure that those who seek investment counsel get advice which is honestly given and free from the influence of self-interest on the part of the adviser. To this end the Act prohibits practices which may be construed as fraud or deceit, requires advisers to reveal any personal interest they may have in the securities in question, and prohibits certain financial arrangements which might bias the advice given to the client. On the other hand, the Act does not require the SEC to assume any responsibility for the professional competence of the adviser or the soundness of the advice given, nor does the SEC assume such responsibility. The legislation fits the general regulatory pattern of getting the important facts out in the open and then leaving the investor to use them as he wishes and to make his own decisions.

As of June, 1960, there were 570 investment companies registered under the Investment Company Act with an estimated asset value of $23.5 billion.[6] Obviously, the managements of these companies exercise control over a major segment of the investment market and hold the fortunes of a great many investors in their hands. In the early days of investment company growth, serious abuses of management responsibility developed, which contributed to the heavy losses and investment company liquidations of the early thirties.

---

[6] *Ibid.*, p. 168.

This led to federal government action aimed at eliminating the hazards of ownership of investment company stock other than those inherent in the investment process itself. In addition to the requirement of registration, which provides the SEC with a tool of control and brings important facts of company operation out into the open, the regulation has the further objectives of strengthening the control of the shareholders over company policy, assuring the integrity of management by prohibiting or supervising practices which would give rise to a conflict of interest between management of the investment companies and their shareholders, and improving the capacity of such companies to survive recessions by regulating the issuance of senior securities. Of particular interest is the close watch kept by the SEC on transactions between the company and its directors and officers. Another possible conflict of interest is minimized by the rule that underwriters, investment bankers, and brokers may not hold a majority position on the boards of directors of investment companies.

SEC Requests for Further Powers

Since the securities markets are by nature a highly dynamic institution, the regulatory agency must be sensitive to change if it is to be successful. It is not surprising, therefore, that the SEC makes proposals from time to time for the amendment or extension of the legislative framework upon which its powers depend.

Some of the many proposals made by the Commission from year to year relate to minor matters of clarification and regulation. Other proposed changes are of a more fundamental nature. Thus, for example, among the proposals supported by the Commission during the fiscal year 1959 were the following:[7]

1. A proposal to amend the Securities Act of 1933 to increase from $300,000 to $500,000 the size of offerings which may be exempted from registration.
2. Proposals to amend the Securities Exchange Act of 1934 (a) to authorize the Commission to suspend or withdraw the registration of a securities exchange when it has ceased to meet the requirements of its original registration and (b) to prohibit trading in the over-the-counter market for limited periods when the public interest and the protection of investors so requires.
3. Proposals to amend the Investment Company Act of 1940 (a) to require investment companies to make formal statements of basic in-

---

[7] Securities and Exchange Commission, *Twenty-fifth Annual Report* (1959), pp. 9–14.

vestment objectives, which could not be changed without stockholder consent, and (b) to strengthen the provisions requiring a minimum number of independent or nonmanagement directors.

It is very informative to review these proposals made or supported by the Commission, since they provide a measure of the trend of thinking of those responsible for federal regulation.

Government Regulation of Corporate Financial Policy

The regulation which has been outlined up to this point has been concerned with the development of a sound market for new and outstanding securities which is free from manipulation and deceit and in which the investor's basic rights are assured and his decisions informed. It is likely that most businessmen would agree that such regulation is desirable and that, on balance, it has facilitated the task of raising long-term funds for the legitimate business enterprise. Of course, it is inevitable that regulation will interfere with the free process of the market to some extent, and this may be counted as the cost to be set off against the gains from such regulation. In the main, however, government regulation of the securities markets has only touched the fringes of the corporation's financial activities and has not constituted a serious encroachment on freedom of action in corporate financial policy. There is, nevertheless, an area of government regulation which does invade what is normally considered the private area of internal financial policy, and it is this with which we shall now be concerned.

The Role of the SEC under the Public Utility Holding Company Act

The Public Utility Holding Company Act was passed in 1935 in an effort to put a stop to certain corporate practices which had had free play in the electric utility industry during the preceding decade. By means of the parent-subsidiary device and the creation of nonoperating (holding) companies, which existed merely as a means of concentrating the ownership of operating companies, vast electric utility pyramids were developed, with control concentrated in the hands of a relatively few men. Because of the widespread indifference of investors to their ownership responsibilities, it was possible for determined individuals to gain voting control of a utility with a comparatively small investment and then proceed to issue large quantities of nonvoting senior securities. With the funds so produced, the utility in question could then be used as a base for the acquisition of voting control in other utilities; and they, in turn, would become the means of bringing more companies within the orbit of the central organization. Such pyramiding of control was theoretically without limit, and so it must have appeared to those who attempted to use it for personal gain.

In an industry which by its very nature has distinct monopolistic characteristics, the integration of a number of operating companies and the concentration of control in the hands of a few at the top of the pyramid presented the federal government with a challenge it could not ignore indefinitely. While it was recognized that integration per se was not a bad thing, these practices had in some cases resulted in serious abuses of the consumer and the investor. In these situations, efficiency of operating companies became a secondary consideration; corporate funds and corporate earnings were drained off to purchase stock in other companies; and top-heavy capital structures were created which became a burden to earnings and a threat to solvency. Companies and managements were linked together where there was no conceivable economic advantage to be gained.

The public utility holding company having had more than a decade in which to develop its maximum potential, drastic governmental action was required to check and reverse the trend. The authority for this action was contained in the Public Utility Holding Company Act of 1935, which conferred almost unlimited powers on the Securities and Exchange Commission, the agency which was to administer the Act. The regulation was limited to electric and gas utilities, and covered both the holding companies themselves and their operating subsidiaries. The SEC was given the power to require holding companies to divest themselves of subsidiaries which, in the opinion of the Commission, were not an integral part of a geographic and economic unit. As the result of such action, 924 electric, gas, and nonutility subsidiaries, with combined assets valued at about $13 billion, were separated from holding company systems during the period June 15, 1938, to June 30, 1960. As of June 30, 1960, there remained in existence 18 active registered holding company systems involving a total of 172 system companies.[8]

The continuing task of simplifying public utility systems has been paralleled by efforts to simplify the capital structures of the remaining holding companies and their operating subsidiaries. Through a gradual process of retirement and consolidation of issues,

---

[8] Securities and Exchange Commission, *Twenty-sixth Annual Report* (1960), pp. 130–32.

it was intended that the confusing maze of senior security issues characteristic of these systems in the twenties would be replaced by an uncomplicated and clear-cut bond, preferred stock, common stock relationship. Important as this simplification process was for public utility financing, it represented only a part of what has amounted to total supervision of long-term financial practices and policies by the SEC. A detailed study of the standards which have guided the SEC in this regard is of real significance far beyond the public utility industry itself. It provides a sample of what government regulation can mean in the area of corporate finance. It is a measure of the attitudes and thinking of this administrative body, which is accepted by many as the "financial conscience" of the nation. Because of the great influence of the SEC in the general securities markets, the criteria of sound corporate finance it applies directly to one important industry "affected with the public interest" may well have an indirect but significant impact on corporate practices generally.

Debt/Equity Balance

In setting standards of sound financial practice for electric and gas utilities, the SEC has had as one of its major preoccupations the debt/equity balance in the capital structure. Its concern in this regard derived from the fact that many of the companies which the Commission set out to regulate had a capital structure so top-heavy with senior securities that it threatened profitability, stability, and even solvency. The severe depression of the thirties demonstrated that even a public utility could experience a significant shrinkage in earnings and that the consideration of safety of investment in both the bonds and the stocks of such companies required a limitation on the proportion of securities bearing a fixed commitment to the investor. A further reason for such a limitation was to provide for some reserve of borrowing power in anticipation of future financing and the need for flexibility in the timing of new issues.

An expression of this general objective and its hoped-for results is found in the Commission's annual report for 1950:

. . . By insisting that parent holding companies undertake common stock financing periodically to match increases in system debt financing, the Commission seeks to prevent a return of the high-leveraged, unwieldy structures which led to the legislation it now administers. Many holding companies have recognized their responsibilities in this respect and a number . . . have already reached a point where the market receptivity to their common stock offerings is almost comparable with that accorded to the stock of good quality operating companies.[9]

The standards which have been evolved in this regard have taken various forms, but all have the common objective of keeping senior securities within "reasonable" limits. The most common form is in terms of a maximum percentage of debt in the capital structure. An indication of SEC thinking is found in a decision on an issue of debentures by the Columbia Gas System, Inc., in 1949. A report of this decision by the Commission reads, in part, as follows:

> The indenture . . . permits the company to issue debt to the extent of 60 percent of its total capitalization. Columbia Gas indicated that while . . . a debt ratio of not more than 50 percent is desirable, it felt that . . . additional borrowing capacity might be necessary in periods of heavy construction which would temporarily bring the debt ratio above this level. The Commission recognized the desirability of such flexibility. . . . It indicated, however, that it considered 50 per cent to be the desirable proportion of debt for the system and noted that its approval was not to be construed as an indication that the issuance of debt to the full limit permitted by the indenture would be approved under all circumstances.[10]

Limitations on debt have also been expressed in terms of earnings coverage—the extent to which earnings available for the payment of fixed charges should exceed these fixed charges. The annual report of the Commission for 1947 expressed such a standard in an unusually general and unqualified form. The statement of this and other standards was preceded by these significant remarks:

> During recent years the Commission has evolved comprehensive protective provisions relating to bonds and preferred stock. . . . The extensive refunding program of the last few years has accelerated the pace at which these provisions have been put into effect. However, because many operating companies are being removed, under section 11, from the jurisdiction of this Commission, much of the prospective new financing . . . will not contain these provisions unless they are accorded the support of other regulatory bodies as well.[11]

The report then proceeds to set up certain standards, among which is found the following relating to earnings coverage: "Issuance of additional bonds is also conditioned upon the adequacy of the earnings coverage for the entire amount of bonds to be outstanding. This coverage is computed on the basis of earnings before income taxes

---

[9] Securities and Exchange Commission, *Sixteenth Annual Report* (1950), p. 104.

[10] Securities and Exchange Commission, *Seventeenth Annual Report* (1951), p. 95.

[11] Securities and Exchange Commission, *Thirteenth Annual Report* (1947), p. 88.

and a coverage of at least two times is usually required."[12] It must be noted that these standards were prefaced by a statement which emphasized the need for flexibility in individual cases and also for continuous re-examination. Nevertheless, it does indicate a standard which has evolved from experience and which has widespread application.

The use of debt has also been limited by a standard expressed in terms of the value of new property acquisitions financed by this (and other) means:

> The issuance of additional bonds is limited to 60 percent of the cost or fair value of net bondable additions to fixed property. While the Commission endeavors to limit the amount of debt initially outstanding to 50 percent of new fixed property, the standard of 60 percent with reference to additional bonds is designed to give the issuer sufficient flexibility to meet future emergencies while at the same time requiring it to provide a reasonable proportion of junior capital in meeting its growth requirements.[13]

Because of the heavy preponderance of fixed assets in the asset structure of public utilities, the above standard bears a close similarity to the standard cited earlier in the Columbia Gas case.

An additional means by which the equity base may be strengthened is through the control of dividend policy and retention of earnings:

> As an additional means of protecting senior security holders, the Commission has continued to insist upon suitable restrictions on the payment of dividends where common stock equity was considered inadequate. For example, in the case of *Western Light & Telephone Co.* the declarant agreed that—"If at any time the aggregate of the common stock and surplus . . . is or becomes less than 20 percent of the total capitalization, dividends on common stock in any fiscal year shall be limited to 50 percent of net income available . . . and whenever such ratios shall be 20 percent or more but less than 25 percent, then not more than 75 percent of the earnings accumulated . . . shall be used therefor. No dividends shall be paid on common stock which will reduce such ratio to less than 25 percent.[14]

Likewise, standards with regard to sinking fund provisions on bond issues may be used to reduce gradually the outstanding debt, relying on retained earnings or new stock offerings to maintain the level of investment. The Commission's views have been stated as follows:

---

[12] *Ibid.*

[13] *Ibid.*

[14] Securities and Exchange Commission, *Twelfth Annual Report* (1946), p. 77.

The primary function of a sinking fund is to improve the ratio between debt and net property. . . . The Commission ordinarily requires a sinking fund of 1 percent of the largest principal amount of the issue at any time outstanding; where the initial ratio is unfavorable, this percentage is increased.[15]

In these various ways the SEC has sought to force the electric and gas utility industry to accept a set of objective yardsticks by which to measure the limits of a sound and, at the same time, flexible debt/ equity balance in the capital structure. For those utilities which come directly under the regulatory powers of the Commission, such standards virtually become "law," since their acceptance by the utility is a prerequisite to Commission consent to reorganization plans, new security issues, and new indentures. This control is made complete through authority over short-term borrowing as well. For example, ". . . the Commission approved a credit agreement under which Middle South [Utilities, Inc.] may borrow up to $15 million from banks. . . . However, no loan renewal may be made . . . without further application to the Commission. . . . These loans are to be subsequently replaced with permanent financing."[16]

Financial Flexibility

As previously indicated, one of the objectives of the Commission in limiting the use of senior securities was the establishment of a "reserve" of borrowing power which would give the companies concerned a desired degree of flexibility in the timing of new issues. "Public utilities, unlike most other industries, are usually faced with the problem of expanding plant facilities in periods of depression as well as prosperity. A high degree of financial flexibility is therefore essential in order to insure maintenance of adequate service to consumers."[17] In order to add to this flexibility, the SEC has insisted that all new issues of senior securities have a redemption clause, so that the issuer is not unavoidably bound to a given amount of debt for the life of the issue. This policy is seen in the following quotation: ". . . in the light of its [the SEC's] established policies under which it has almost uniformly required that senior securities be fully redeemable at the option of the issuing company upon payment of a reasonable premium."[18] It will be recalled that in the chapter on the

---

[15] Securities and Exchange Commission, *Thirteenth Annual Report* (1947), p. 89.

[16] Securities and Exchange Commission, *Eighteenth Annual Report* (1952), p. 118.

[17] Securities and Exchange Commission, *Seventeenth Annual Report* (1951), p. 105.

[18] Securities and Exchange Commission, *Twenty-first Annual Report* (1955), p. 54.

bargain for funds, we noted a growing resistance to this clause on the part of investors.

Cost of Financing

Another set of standards which has been developed for utility financing has had as its objective the minimization of costs in the issuance of new securities. The most widely publicized Commission ruling in this connection has been its insistence, in the large majority of cases, on competitive bidding by investment houses seeking to handle new utility issues. Studies undertaken by the SEC have satisfied it that this results in a significantly improved price to the issuing company as compared with private negotiation of issues. The results were reported, in part, as follows:

> It was anticipated that the use of competitive bidding would bring about a reduction in underwriting costs or "spreads," and this expectation has been amply fulfilled. A study of underwriting spreads prevailing during the 5-year period ended January 1, 1940, revealed that slightly over one-half of the 159 utility mortgage bond issues studied had been sold on the basis of a 2-point spread; in only four cases was a smaller spread found. The average spread for these 159 issues, which had been sold by traditional methods of private negotiation, was 2.49 points. . . .[19]

This statement was followed by a table showing what was termed "the sharply contrasting picture" of spreads under competitive bidding during a five-year period ended June 30, 1949. The figures indicated that out of 179 issues, only eight showed spreads of 1.25 or over and that over half the issues were sold with spreads of 0.75 or less.[20] As we have noted previously, the preference of the SEC for competitive bidding is not necessarily shared by the issuing companies.

The objective of greater economy in financing has been one of the reasons why the Commission has encouraged the application of the pre-emptive right and rights offerings in further issues of outstanding stock. A new issue which is taken up largely if not entirely by the existing shareholders minimizes or eliminates the services and costs of the investment banker as "middleman." This policy has been expressed as follows: "It is, and has long been, our opinion that when holding companies and public utility companies subject to our jurisdiction sell additional shares of common stock, their own interests, as well as the interests of their common shareholders are,

---

[19] Securities and Exchange Commission, *Fifteenth Annual Report* (1949), p. 88.
[20] *Ibid.*, p. 89.

absent special circumstances, best served by allowing common share-holders the right to purchase their proportionate shares of the new issue."[21]

Further, the Commission has reported, with apparent approval, a trend away from the underwriting of rights offerings as, presumably, an avoidable cost:

> Probably the most significant development in this group of issues was the growing importance of the non-underwritten rights offering. Only five offerings . . . were made with the aid of firm underwriting commitments. Four issues . . . were offered without underwriting, but had the benefit of dealer solicitation. The remaining five rights offerings . . . were sold without the benefit of underwriting or dealer solicitation assistance. All five were subscribed in percentages ranging from 106 to 188. In each of these cases the oversubscription privilege made an important contribution to the success of the sale.[22]

The attitude of the SEC on the matter of rights offerings has been subject to some modification in recent years. During 1952 a study of recent rights offerings was undertaken; and shortly after this was completed, the following statement was made: ". . . it is our view that, while there are many advantages to a rights offering, these advantages are not so conclusive as to warrant a strict policy in favor of rights. . . . Accordingly it will be the policy . . . not to insist upon a rights offering where management can make a showing that an underwriting by competitive bidding without an offer to stockholders would be preferable."[23]

Preferred Stock

Although the Commission has been primarily concerned with the control of debt in public utility capital structures, it has also developed a set of standards for preferred stock. Preferred stock has presented a special problem because of its somewhat paradoxical position halfway between a fixed charge security and a true equity security. The opinions of the Commission reflect the difficulty of a satisfactory classification for the stock, at one time treating it as a part of equity capital and at another time treating it as a senior security which has a fixed claim on earnings and which results in a mandatory drain on cash. This conflicting interpretation is seen in the following com-

---

[21] Securities and Exchange Commission, *Holding Company Act Release No. 9730*, as quoted in the Commission's *Eighteenth Annual Report* (1952), p. 128.

[22] Securities and Exchange Commission, *Seventeenth Annual Report* (1951), p. 109.

[23] Securities and Exchange Commission, *Nineteenth Annual Report* (1953), p. 78.

mentary of the Commission, made in 1948, regarding an observed trend toward sinking funds as a requirement of new preferred issues:

> Since institutions were no longer under any particular pressure to buy preferred issues, they were in a position to demand certain concessions in the terms of security. In this way the sinking fund came into use in connection with utility preferred stocks. These provisions were initially set up on a 2 percent basis. . . . Thus preferred stock ceases to be permanent capital . . . [the sinking fund] places an additional cash requirement upon the issuer and has undoubtedly led some companies to seek other means of financing.
>
> The declining interest in preferred stock has rendered more difficult the problem of maintaining an adequate proportion of equity security in the capital structure.[24]

In spite of the inference in the above quotation that preferred stock normally lies on the equity side of the debt/equity balance, the Commission has formulated standards which treat preferred stock as a senior security akin to bonds. Note the following decision which applied to a convertible preferred issue:

> Subsequent to this offering [the New England Electric System] submitted a general financing program proposing the sale of $7,500,000 of convertible preferred stock and $5,000,000 of debentures by the parent company. . . . the Commission found that the proposal was faulty in failing to provide for additional common equity to balance the large amount of senior securities proposed to be issued. It indicated that a minimum acceptable position might be reached if the $7,500,000 now proposed to be raised through convertible preferred stock were raised instead through the sale of additional common shares.[25]

The idea of preferred stock as a senior security and therefore subject to limited usage in the interests of financial safety and flexibility is well established in certain SEC standards, notably in the one cited on page 503 regarding dividend policy and in the minimum proportions for common stock and surplus. (From our treatment of preferred stock in earlier chapters the reader will be aware that we share this view.) A rule similar to the one cited for the maintenance of a minimum cushion of common equity in the capital structure was included in a list of specific provisions prepared by the Commission to be included in corporate charters of utilities about to issue new preferred stock.[26] Another rule in the same list requires that preferred

---

[24] Securities and Exchange Commission, *Fourteenth Annual Report* (1948), p. 78.

[25] Securities and Exchange Commission, *Sixteenth Annual Report* (1950), p. 95.

[26] Securities and Exchange Commission, *Holding Company Act Release No. 13106* February 16, 1956, p. 3; found in *Federal Register,* Vol. XXI (February 28, 1956), p. 1288.

stocks be redeemable at the option of the issuer, thus again recognizing the need for flexibility in the use of a semifixed security type.[27]

Financial Planning

A natural by-product of the SEC's careful probing of utility capital structures has been an emphasis on careful planning for future needs. Where it appears necessary, the Commission insists on a forecast of future capital expenditures and a plan for financing these expenditures which preserves the desired balance of debt and equity sources. Recognizing the long-term growth characteristics of the utility industry and the uncertainties of the capital market over the years, the Commission has stressed the desirability of a margin of borrowing power in existing capital structures as a necessary prerequisite to financial planning and to the appropriate timing of new issues.

An example of the role of the Commission in the area of financial planning is seen in the following SEC commentary:

> . . . Before granting approval of $18,000,000 of bank borrowings . . . the Commission . . . gave careful consideration to the over-all financing program of [American Gas and Electric Co.] . . . and devoted particular attention to the responsibility and intentions of the holding company to preserve the balance of underlying equity in the system.
>
> American, in response to this inquiry, placed before the Commission the details of its 3-year construction and financing program. . . . The Commission observed that the financing program ". . . appears feasible and sound in the light of the standards of the Act."[28]

Shareholders and Management

In its efforts to strengthen the financial structure of the electric and gas utility industry, the SEC aims to benefit directly or indirectly all who are associated with the industry, including the stockholders. In a sense the Commission has been attempting to protect ownership from its own shortsightedness and mismanagement. Of course, the existence of the large numbers of shareholders who do not have any effective voice in management decisions leads to the conclusion that special safeguards are necessary if their somewhat defenseless position is not to be abused. In line with this the SEC has advocated a number of corporate practices which are designed either to strengthen the voice of the shareholders or to protect them where they are voiceless.

---

[27] Securities and Exchange Commission, *Holding Company Act Release No. 13106*, p. 2.

[28] Securities and Exchange Commission, *Sixteenth Annual Report* (1950), p. 88.

As a protection for preferred shareholders, the SEC has presented the following provision for inclusion in corporate charters as a part of a formal statement of policy on preferred stock:

> If and when dividends on any series of the preferred stock shall be in arrears in an amount equal to four full quarter-yearly payments or more per share, the holders of all series of the preferred stock voting together as a class shall be entitled to elect the smallest number of directors necessary to constitute a majority of the full board of directors until such time as all dividend arrears on the preferred stock shall have been paid or declared and set apart for payment.[29]

As a means of giving a voice to minority groups of common shareholders, the Commission has advocated the adoption of cumulative voting rules for the election of directors of electric and gas utilities. Commission rules have also included protection of preferred shareholders against the creation of additional securities with an equal or prior claim without the consent of a majority of the preferred shareholders, and it has also encouraged the use of the pre-emptive right as a means of protecting the common shareholder against some of the effects of dilution.

The Role of the SEC under Chapter X of the Bankruptcy Act

In one sense the powers of the SEC to regulate corporate financial policy by direct intervention in the policy-making process are confined entirely to a relatively small segment of business, namely, the electric and gas utility industry. However, they have considerably broader implications. To the extent that the Commission's standards become formalized and are known and accepted by the investing public, they may become the model for investment standards in other industries.

There is also another way in which the Commission makes its influence on financial policy felt beyond the limits of the public utility industry. Under the provisions of Chapter X of the Bankruptcy Act, the SEC may act in an advisory capacity in proceedings leading to the reorganization of corporations in bankruptcy. The specific nature of this activity of the SEC will be treated in some detail in Chapter 27 on corporate reorganization. At this point, it is sufficient to note that there is a natural carry-over of concepts and standards developed in the public utility field into the more diversified applications of the bankruptcy courts.

---

[29] Securities and Exchange Commission, *Holding Company Act Release No. 13106,* p. 3.

It is also interesting to note that in practice the role of the SEC under the Bankruptcy Act has not been the passive one which might be inferred from an "advisory" role. Rather, it has assumed the role of "watchdog" and moves with obvious determination when the situation appears to warrant its participation. During the 1960 fiscal year the Commission participated in fifty-two proceedings involving the reorganization of eighty companies with aggregate assets of $567 million.[30] The fact that the Commission has welcomed this broadening of its influence is evident in its reports on this aspect of its operations. The following statement appeared in the Commission's annual report for 1951 in regard to a particular court decision: "The case is of particular significance in the field of bankruptcy reorganizations because of the clear statement of the important weight which should be accorded advisory opinions of the Commission."[31]

Regulation by Other Federal Agencies

In view of the unusual lengths to which the regulation of long-term finance in the electric and gas utility field has gone under the control of the Securities and Exchange Commission, it is significant to compare federal regulation in other public utility industries. In particular, a comparison can be made with the regulation of telephone companies under the Federal Communications Commission and of railroads under the Interstate Commerce Commission.

The telephone industry presents a sharp contrast. Despite the fact that interstate communication facilities are operated by a comparatively small number of companies, these companies have been free from any direct regulation of financial policies by their federal regulatory agency, the Federal Communications Commission. The FCC is not empowered to do so. On the other hand, they are subject to indirect influence from state rate-making bodies. However, this influence is not to be compared with what we have observed in the regulation of public utility holding companies, where private enterprise is still paying the price of the sins of the past and experiencing the momentum of an alert and well-established regulatory authority.

Perhaps a more meaningful comparison is that with the railroad industry. Here, the regulatory agency, the Interstate Commerce Commission, was given the power to regulate the issuance of new securities by the railroads, and we have a history of such regulation dating back to 1920. The activities of the ICC in this regard present some

---

[30] Securities and Exchange Commission, *Twenty-sixth Annual Report* (1960), p. 153.

[31] Securities and Exchange Commission, *Seventeenth Annual Report* (1951), p. 133.

significant contrasts to the activities of the SEC under the Holding Company Act. While the ICC has concerned itself with a number of basic aspects of railroad finance, the regulation has been substantially less comprehensive and shows a disinclination to become involved in the more intimate details of financial policy. In line with this, there has been a noticeable reluctance to dictate specific rules of financial conduct which would standardize financial behavior throughout the industry.

The following brief survey of the major issues which the ICC has raised in its supervision of the issuance of new railroad securities will suggest the nature of these differences in approach. One of the primary concerns of the Commission, which reflects the financial condition of many segments of the industry, has been to avoid or reduce overcapitalization. The desired objective is to have a full value of tangible assets standing behind every dollar of outstanding securities. This is achieved by requiring that new issues of securities represent actual expenditures. A related requirement is that the Commission will set the minimum price at which new issues will be sold. In this way the Commission seeks to assure that the issue will produce the maximum of funds possible under the circumstances.

With the exception of these two aspects of railroad finance, neither of which would appear to infringe on the freedom of action of management to any serious extent, the Commission generally takes a more flexible position and is more inclined to "suggest" than to "require." On the subject of competitive bidding the ICC has backed away from a universal requirement. Although it has required competitive bidding on interest-bearing securities, the Commission has clearly recognized that exceptions are often justified. This is seen in the following statement:

. . . On May 8, 1944 we made a report [on proceedings 257 I.C.C. 129] stating our conclusions. . . . We found that there are many situations in which it would be undesirable and even impracticable to sell railroad securities at competitive bidding; that any requirement that railroad securities be sold at competitive bidding should make provisions for exemption of certain classes of securities . . . and that, subject to such exemptions, the scope of mandatory competitive bidding should be expanded so as to cover interest-bearing obligations generally.[32]

Prior to this, competitive bidding had been mandatory only for equipment trust certificates.

Perhaps the most significant area of intervention by the ICC has

---

[32] Interstate Commerce Commission, *Fifty-eighth Annual Report* (Washington, D.C.: U.S. Government Printing Office, 1944), p. 15.

been in regard to debt/equity proportions in the capital structure. Here, its actions are in sharp contrast to those of the SEC, reported earlier in this chapter. Note the general tone of the following statement: "It is our view that railroads with weak financial structures, and those just emerging from receivership or reorganization proceedings . . . should be encouraged to use their earnings . . . to build up and improve their property, retire their funded debt, and create corporate surpluses in amounts sufficient to meet their emergency needs, support their borrowing powers, and afford insurance against obsolescence."[33]

The principal means by which the ICC has attempted to bring about a more conservative capital structure in railroads has been through the sinking fund requirement, initiated in 1933. In 1936 the Commission reported on this requirement as follows: "In all cases where we have been called upon to approve the actual issue of bonds we have insisted that the applicant make provision for the retirement of all or a part of the bonds before maturity and have required that sinking funds be provided, unless good and sufficient reasons appeared for not doing so."[34]

It is undoubtedly true, of course, that the more restrained regulation of the ICC has been conditioned by the characteristics of the industry and also by the fact that its responsibilities were only in part financial. On the matter of the balance of debt and equity in the capital structure, for example, the Commission has considered it a fact of life in the railroad industry that improvement in the ratio through new equity issues is often out of the question:

> Few railroads are in a position to reduce their indebtedness through the sale of capital stock. Most railroads must look entirely to their earnings for necessary funds. . . .
>
> At present a large proportion of the outstanding railroad bonds can be bought at large discounts. This affords a most favorable opportunity to eliminate debt and to cut fixed charges. . . .
>
> In our last report we again discussed the importance of debt reduction. We suggest that the present favorable earnings be used as largely as is practicable for that purpose. We are convinced that both the public interest and the interests of the carrier shareholders will in the long run be served by that policy.[35]

It is apparent that under these circumstances, the Commission feels that all it can or should do is to suggest and encourage action toward the desired objective.

---

[33] Interstate Commerce Commission, *Fiftieth Annual Report* (1936), p. 19.

[34] *Ibid.,* p. 17.

[35] Interstate Commerce Commission, *Fifty-sixth Annual Report* (1942), p. 29.

Before we leave this subject, it is interesting to note that the ICC in recent years has permitted the substitution of income bonds for preferred stock as a means of reducing the tax burden on the railroads concerned.[36] This reflects the general trend away from preferred stock as a source of funds and the growing respectability of the income bonds as a security combining the flexibility of equity capital with the tax advantage of debt.

Summary

In this chapter, we have been considering the various ways in which government, particularly the federal government, exercises an influence over the long-term financing of private enterprise. It will now be apparent that government regulation has extended far beyond its initial objectives of protecting the unsophisticated investor from fraud and his own ignorance. Much of this necessary kind of regulation continues today. It is, however, in the area of regulation of long-term financial policy where the most significant recent developments have come. In focusing on the detailed regulations of the SEC and other federal agencies, we have attempted to serve two purposes: (1) to present for consideration and discussion a set of specific standards of financial practice which have been imposed on private enterprise on an industry-wide basis and which have implications for business generally, and (2) to illustrate what government intervention can mean in restricting the area of decision making in long-term finance.

---

[36] Interstate Commerce Commission, *Seventy-third Annual Report* (1959), p. 65.

PART VIII

Financing Growth and Readjustment

Chapter 25

Financing the New Small-Scale Enterprise

IN FINANCING the new small-scale business enterprise, certain variations in the financial problems and practices occur which are peculiar to a business at this stage of its development. This chapter is designed to bring out the nature and significance of the more important of these variations. A primary objective will be to draw a distinction between the problem of smallness in business and the often related but different problems of newness, inexperience, and incompetence.

Chapter 28, on the subject of liquidation, provides some statistics on the formation of new business units (see Chart 28–1, page 581). In view of the large numbers of new businesses being formed, it is obvious that each year a substantial percentage of the business owner-manager population is going to be preoccupied with the special problems of a business in formation. When these figures are considered in relation to those on business termination, it is also apparent that a great many businessmen cope with these problems unsuccessfully. A recent study on business turnover was that prepared by the Department of Commerce relating to the postwar period 1946–54.[1] This study indicated that about half of the businesses formed in this period were sold or liquidated within two years. Only one in every three survived a four-year life, and only one in every five survived for ten years. The Department of Commerce figures suggest that the turnover is greatest in the retail trade, where only three out of five survived beyond the first year and only one in six reached an age of ten years.[2]

---

[1] "Age and Life Expectancy of Business Firms," *Survey of Current Business*, December, 1955, pp. 15–19.

[2] *Ibid.*, p. 15.

Statistics such as these, which have been available and widely circulated for many years, are not likely to encourage an attitude of optimism toward new businesses on the part of those who are asked to supply capital to such businesses. Of course, aggregate statistics cannot provide a satisfactory basis for judgment in the individual case. Unfortunately, however, a new business is by definition a business without a record of performance by which potential can be measured; consequently, there is little if any basis for differentiating it from what is assumed to be typical. A new and small business must have some unusual appeal before it can be considered an exception from the general expectation of great risk and probable failure, an expectation which continues to be supported by experience even in times of high-level prosperity.

Newness as a Financial Problem

A new business which is well conceived and well planned possesses certain inherent competitive advantages. At the same time, the fact of its newness may have significant financial disadvantages. One of these comes in financial planning. The starting point of any program for the financing of a business is a careful estimate of requirements. The usual starting point in business forecasts is the record of the immediate past, modified for foreseeable variations during the forecast period. Without the advantage of a period of actual performance upon which to base assumptions, it is exceedingly difficult to anticipate such vital information as the amount and timing of customers' orders, credit experience with customers, and profit margins with the degree of accuracy necessary to make the forecast useful. The possibility of substantial errors of forecast is great. Unfortunately, the spirit of optimism which is a necessary accompaniment of new ventures in business tends to produce underestimates rather than overestimates of the needed funds.

Take, for example, the problem of forecasting the absorption of funds into working capital in a business manufacturing children's clothing which is commencing its first season of operations. First, there is the problem of customers' orders—amount and timing. Typically, samples would be made up in advance of the season and shown to buyers. Then comes a waiting period while buyers delay their commitments as long as possible as a precaution against sudden changes in consumer buying. The manufacturer may lay in cloth in expectation of the hoped-for sales, but the question is: How much? What kind and grade of material? What colors? To misjudge in any direction may mean that funds are unnecessarily tied up in unusable inventory. Even if he judges correctly, he does not wish to invest earlier than necessary, since the cost of funds is a function both of the amount and of the period of time over which it is needed. On the other hand, to invest too late may mean that inventory is not available at reasonable prices and/or that delivery dates cannot be met.

Eventually, the actual buying time arrives, and orders are placed by various customers within a matter of weeks in varying amounts and with varying delivery dates. Even this does not completely answer the question of sales volume, since there remains the possibility of reorders of successful items at a later date. The anticipation of demand in such an industry is difficult even for a business of long standing, but it becomes an almost impossible task for a new one. Added to this are the uncertainties of the production process. The costs and capacities of workers and machines individually and as a productive unit are to a considerable extent unknown until an actual run has been experienced. Workers prove incapable of their jobs, machines break down, scheduling proves inefficient and must be changed. An interruption at one point may well affect the whole operation. The usual result is more money invested for a longer period of time than was anticipated.

When the garments are finally produced and the order shipped, there comes a further waiting period over which the new manufacturer has little control—the time it takes for each customer to get around to paying his bills. Here, some information may be available on the experience of others; but there is no way of knowing how the customer will view this particular supplier, particularly when it is obvious that he is anxious to build up business. Every additional day that a customer uses the manufacturer as a source of short-term funds (by delaying payment) means another day during which the manufacturer is prevented from using those funds for a new cycle of working capital investment, and therefore means a net addition to his total financial need.

To the inherent difficulty of forecasting the need for funds may be added another problem. New businesses frequently involve new and inexperienced management. Since the idea which sparks the drive for independence in business normally grows out of experience in areas other than finance, the basic problem of forecasting the need for funds is often complicated by a lack of understanding of the means by which business transactions are translated into financial terms. Errors in projecting needs which result from inexperience are particularly common in the calculation of absorption of funds into working capital as production and sales develop.

Incompetence in the financial area may not be disastrous. The effects of ignorance depend on the nature and magnitude of the errors, the circumstances which may either magnify or cushion the effects, and the rapidity with which management can recognize and correct its mistakes. On the other hand, managerial incompetence is considered to be the primary cause of failure among new and small businesses. In Chapter 28, we cite the study of Dun & Bradstreet in reference to this. It is difficult in practice to separate incompetence in the financial area from incompetence in other areas of managerial responsibility, since most important decisions have their financial implications. Thus, "receivables difficulties" may have resulted from overenthusiastic selling, inadequate credit control, or an inability to anticipate the working capital requirement of credit to customers. There is no doubt, however, that the typical manager of a new business is much better prepared for his responsibilities in the areas of production or sales than he is in finance.

The disadvantage of newness is also to be found in relations with suppliers of capital. For those suppliers who are motivated by purely business considerations (as distinct from friends and relatives who play an important part in financing many new ventures), the principal guide to future performance is again the record of the immediate past. In the absence of operating statements, balance sheets, and credit and other records which lend some degree of objectivity to a judgment of future prospects, the prospective creditor or shareholder lacks a firm basis for the assumption of the very considerable risks involved. The inevitable result is that many sources, particularly institutional sources, refuse to assume these risks or insist on protective provisions such that the extent of their participation is seriously limited. Thus, a bank may be prepared to make a limited short-term loan, provided it is well protected by high-grade collateral with a value substantially in excess of the amount of the loan. A loan which is only a fraction of the value of inventory or accounts receivable will not solve the working capital problem of a new and growing business.

One business source of capital which frequently departs from the attitude suggested above is trade credit from suppliers. Primarily because suppliers wish to develop new customers, they often show a very tolerant attitude toward the new business, provided the management gives evidence of good faith in its dealings. In this regard, openness about financial difficulties in discussions with suppliers often yields better results than secretiveness. It is because of this policy on the part of suppliers that trade credit ranks as one of the major sources of short-term funds in new and small businesses. It is unfortunately true that many new businesses under financial pressure will abuse trade credit, going on the assumption that the supplier will not get tough because he is anxious for business and will wait for his money (and even ship more inventory on credit) when a bank or finance company would not.

A partial substitute for lack of a performance record in the new business is to have management which has had a record of satisfactory performance in other business situations. If such is the case, the persons in question know and are known by suppliers of debt and equity capital, and may be able to overcome their suppliers' natural reluctance by the confidence they personally inspire. Confidence inspired by individuals must, of course, be supported by early indications of strength in the new venture.

As a result of one or more of these disadvantages of newness, the founder of the new business may well find himself in an unusually weak bargaining position until such time as he is able to give clear proof of profit potential. If the founder needs further capital in the intervening period (which may last several years) and is not able to supply it himself or obtain it through normal channels such as trade credit, he may not be able to obtain the extra funds except on unfavorable terms. On the one hand, he himself is committed to the business and cannot withdraw at this stage without the chance of serious loss. On the other, there is little by which calculating investors can be attracted to the business except by the enthusiasm of those who need the money. The prospective creditor or shareholder is in a position to drive a hard bargain.

The Related Problem of Smallness

In the large majority of cases the new business is also a small business—small in the sense that the entire responsibility of management rests on one or two men. How far this statement is true can be seen from Table 25–1, which shows a breakdown of the annual increment of new businesses by size, measured in terms of number of employees. The figures indicate that about 99 per cent of all new businesses have fewer than twenty employees at the time of their origin and that 86 per cent have fewer than four employees. Thus, consideration of the problems peculiar to the new business must be sup-

TABLE 25-1

Number of New Businesses in the United States, by Size of Firm, 1945-55

(Thousands of Businesses)

Year	Total of All Industries	Breakdown by Number of Employees			
		0-3	4-7	8-19	20 or More
1945.................	422.7	372.1	33.1	12.3	5.3
1946.................	617.4	533.0	56.5	20.9	7.1
1947.................	460.8	397.6	43.1	15.3	4.9
1948.................	393.3	337.7	38.3	13.0	4.3
1949.................	331.1	286.9	30.4	10.3	3.6
1950.................	348.2	298.3	34.3	11.7	3.9
1951-55 (total).......	1,798.0	1,560.9	161.0	55.0	21.1

Source: *Survey of Current Business*, May, 1954, Table 6, p. 20, for 1945-50; and September, 1959, Table 4, p. 18, for 1951-55.

plemented by a consideration of those associated with smallness of scale of operations.

One of these problems is the highly personal character of businesses of the size indicated above. The business typically stands or falls on the experience, intelligence, and initiative of one man. This can be a very real asset, and it is this which makes the small business so well suited to certain types of business activity. It can also give rise to difficulties. A business at this stage is merely an extension of an individual's personal activities, and its business decisions—particularly financial decisions—may be strongly influenced by purely personal considerations. So, for example, a failure to use debt in the capital structure may result from a deeply rooted personal feeling against borrowing in general, although the circumstances of the business may indicate that a limited use might be highly desirable and financially sound. In the larger business with a management group and possibly with a separation of ownership and management, personal considerations are more likely to be subordinated to the common goals of the business.

The attitude of suppliers of capital may be influenced adversely by the fact of one-man management. The possibility of death or withdrawal of this individual presents a risk of major proportions. Here, insurance can be of some help, but continuity of the business as a profitable unit independent of particular persons is much to be desired in financial contracts. The corporate form provides the legal fiction of continuity of life, but it becomes a reality only through the development of a competent and reliable management group capable of reproducing itself.

Another aspect of one-man management is the pressure of time which frequently bears down on one individual who is attempting to discharge all the demands made on him as owner-manager as well as to perform the many operating tasks which others in the business are not capable of doing. The inevitable result is to give low priority to those things which appear to him to be less important at the moment, less interesting, or by nature more postponable. Financial matters often fall into this category. Insufficient time is given to keeping informed on the financial implications of action, to careful projection of needs, and to the cultivation of sources of capital so important in the rather informal capital market in which the small business often operates.

This raises another aspect of the small-scale business—the peculiarities of its market for funds. Since the depression of the thirties, the organized capital market has been under attack for being insensitive to the needs of small business. There are good and obvious reasons why financial institutions are likely to be less interested in the small business than in the large business. Banks and insurance companies have a primary responsibility to depositors and policyholders to maintain high standards of safety in their investments. The record of solvency in small business has not been encouraging; and while this does not mean that large-scale business is necessarily a safer investment, these investors tend to be wary of heavy involvement in new and small-scale businesses. Further, there is the obvious point that the return to be derived from the small account is less interesting than that from the large account, particularly in view of the relatively fixed costs of servicing the account. It is for this reason that the machinery which has been developed in the capital market for such tasks as the marketing of securities is primarily designed for the larger sums required of large-scale enterprise.

This does not mean that a small business cannot satisfy its need for funds in the normal capital market. Many mature and profitable small businesses are more than adequately supplied in this way. What it does mean is that the small-scale businessman may have to spend considerable time and effort cultivating this market before the desired results are obtained.

New businesses are typically small for two reasons: The scale may be that which is best suited to the particular activity, or the resources of the founders are such that a larger and more efficient scale is not possible at the outset. Through either ignorance, impatience, or sheer venturesomeness, many businesses are started on a scale far below that which the industry and the market require as a prerequisite for permanence, stability, and profitability. For such a business, rapid growth is vital to survival. There is a great sense of urgency to obtain the break-even point of profitability in the shortest possible time; and if the business has promise, there may be the opportunity to grow as rapidly as financial, physical, and human capacities permit. It is not unusual to find a business in its early years doubling or tripling sales volume from one year to the next. Such a rate of growth gives the business an almost insatiable appetite for new capital. Until it reaches and passes the break-even point, however, the business has little appeal to outside investors and little, if any, throwoff of funds from internal sources. Operations in this early period may actually constitute an additional drain on funds because of a net excess of costs over revenues. A business in these circumstances has little staying power, and the slightest reverse creates a major financial crisis.

The Sources of Funds for New Enterprise

In many respects, the financing of a new small-scale business is no different from that of business in general. By calling attention to certain peculiarities which have widespread occurrence among such businesses, there is a danger of leaving the impression that they exist in a financial world of their own. On the other hand, it is important to be alerted to the fact that certain variations in the normal pattern of business finance can be traced to the age and size of the business unit.

The primary source of equity capital in the new small-scale business is the personal savings of the founders and the earnings of the business. In a study made by the Office of Business Economics of the Department of Commerce of the initial financing of wholesale and retail businesses, it was found that two thirds of the total investment came from personal savings.[3] Further, it was indicated that in the sample under consideration, 45 per cent of the firms financed the initial investment entirely through savings. Chart 25–1 shows the sources of the initial capital for the sample of retail businesses. In many cases the personal savings of the founder were supplemented by the personal savings of relatives and friends. The comparative importance of this source reflects a desire for independence of ownership and control, and also the basic difficulty of raising initial capital from impersonal sources except on a relatively minor scale and only when the owners are themselves heavily committed.

The other side of the same picture is the very minor role played by

---

[3] "Capital Requirements of New Trade Firms," *Survey of Current Business*, December, 1948, pp. 19–20.

CHART 25-1

Sources of Initial Investment Funds—600,000 Retailers
Period of Origin: 1945–47*

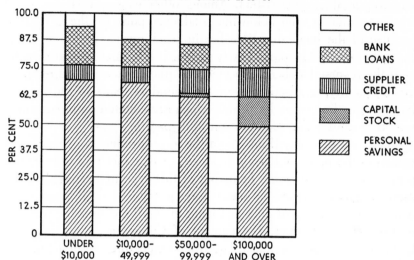

* Office of Business Economics, Department of Commerce, "Capital Requirements of New Trade Firms," *Survey of Current Business*, December, 1948, Table 1, p. 23.

public offerings of stock. The study quoted above showed that for businesses with sales up to $50,000, this source was practically non-existent. In businesses with sales over $100,000, it provided a modest 13 per cent of the total. This situation exists primarily for two reasons. One is the widespread reluctance among founders of new businesses to share the hoped-for profits and control of the business. The other is that public offerings of stock involve considerable overhead-type costs, as well as substantial risks, which make the costs of flotation of new and small issues almost prohibitive. A study made by the Securities and Exchange Commission for the years 1951, 1953, and 1955 of costs of flotation of new issues of common stock for cash sale through investment bankers showed that for issues under $500,000, commissions and discount averaged 20.99 per cent of gross proceeds and other expenses averaged 6.16 per cent, giving a total cost of 27.15 per cent. On the other hand, issues of $2 million to $5 million cost 8.47 per cent in commissions and discount and 1.50 per cent in other expenses, totaling 9.97 per cent of gross proceeds.[4]

The remaining means by which the owner-manager can contribute to the capital of the business is by plowing back all earnings of the

[4] Securities and Exchange Commission, *Cost of Flotation of Corporate Securities, 1951–1955* (Washington, D.C.: U.S. Government Printing Office, June, 1957), Table 1, p. 37.

business except for a modest salary. Unfortunately, it is often true that the earnings of a business in the early years, when need is greatest, are small or nonexistent. Among other causes, this may result from a volume of sales below the break-even point for the industry or because of the inevitable time lag in reaching maximum efficiency. This situation will be particularly serious if it has not been anticipated or if the reverse has been expected and plans made accordingly. All too frequently, the optimism of the founders leads to the hope of large profits immediately, profits which are counted on to contribute essential capital for stabilization and growth.

Whatever one may think about the appropriateness of trading on equity in the new small-scale business, it is a fact that debt capital plays a major role in the financing of this type of business. This is supported by the figures on retail stores previously cited (page 525). A more recent study of debt financing in small business by the Office of Business Economics, Department of Commerce, gives more detailed information which bears out what others have observed in individual cases.[5]

This study gives information on the financing of newer firms with respect to both funds obtained and funds not obtained. The figures in Table 25–2 are for the year 1954. It can be seen that the primary demand, whether satisfied or not, was for debt capital. It is interesting to note, however, that the businesses concerned had better success in obtaining debt capital than equity capital.

The same study provided an analysis of the character of the loans sought and obtained by these newer firms. The statistical data are shown in Table 25–3. Certain features stand out. One is the dominant place of banks as a source of loan funds and the very minor role played by other established financial institutions, such as insurance companies. Another feature is the absence of collateral in over 50 per cent of the loans made. It is also significant that, with respect to the duration of the loan, most of the loans obtained were of the seasonal type, but most of the unsatisfied need for debt capital was in the categories of one to three years and longer. Finally, it is perhaps not surprising to find that the loans wanted but not obtained were for larger amounts than was the case for loans obtained.

The importance of trade credit as a source of funds for the new and small business has already been mentioned. The magnitude of its contribution to small businesses in general is indicated in Chart 25–1.

---

[5] See "External Financing of Small- and Medium-Size Business," *Survey of Current Business*, October, 1955, pp. 15–22.

TABLE 25–2

CAPITAL FINANCING BY NEWER FIRMS* FOR YEAR ENDED JUNE 30, 1954

(Per Cent)

All Firms—Total	*100.0%*
No outside funds wanted	46.8
Outside funds wanted	53.2
Obtained all funds wanted	25.3
Did not obtain all funds wanted	27.9
Obtained some funds	19.2
Obtained no funds	8.7
Aggregate Demand—Total	*100.0%*
Loans	87.0
Equity	13.0
Funds Obtained—Total	*100.0%*
Loans	92.0
Equity	8.0
Funds Wanted but Not Obtained—Total	*100.0%*
Loans	74.0
Equity	26.0
Loan Demand—Total	*100.0%*
Obtained	75.0
Not obtained	25.0
Equity Demand—Total	*100.0%*
Obtained	45.0
Not obtained	55.0
Aggregate Demand—Total	*100.0%*
Obtained	71.0
Not obtained	29.0

* Newer firms defined as firms with one or more paid employees, which started new businesses after March, 1951.

SOURCE: Office of Business Economics, Department of Commerce, "External Financing of Small- and Medium-Size Business," *Survey of Current Business*, October, 1955, pp. 18–19.

The place of trade credit in the financing of a particular business depends on its particular group of suppliers, the customary credit terms of the industry, and the general state of the market. As a source of short-term debt capital, trade credit has a special appeal not only because of its magnitude but also because of the comparative flexibility in the enforcement of credit terms by suppliers.

A development in recent years that may hold considerable significance for new and small-scale businesses is the interest shown by insurance companies and some other lenders in an equity type of participation as a part of a loan agreement. The option to purchase a block of common stock at a favorable price is regarded as an inducement to make a loan that would otherwise be considered unattractive at fixed interest rates within the customary range. This suggests a possible formula whereby some conservative financial institutions which are not now considered as a primary source of capital for small business may be induced to divert some funds into this market. So far,

TABLE 25-3

Statistics on Loans Obtained and Not Obtained by Newer Firms*
for Year Ended June 30, 1954

| | Source of Loans | | | Type of Collateral Required | | | | |
	Bank	Individual†	Other‡	None	Current Assets	Equipment	Other Fixed Business Assets	Personal and Other
All firms	68.8%	15.7%	15.5%	54.1%	11.1%	14.8%	11.5%	8.5%
Construction	70.5	13.4	16.1	50.4	10.6	12.0	18.4	8.6
Manufacturing	67.9	12.2	19.9	53.5	10.0	22.3	12.3	1.9
Wholesale trade	70.6	16.4	13.0	60.0	20.7	9.0	4.8	5.5
Retail trade	67.7	18.7	13.6	54.7	8.3	14.8	8.9	13.3

Duration of Loans

| | Loans Obtained | | | | Loans Not Obtained | | | |
	90 Days or Less	91–364 Days	1–3 Years	3 Years or More	90 Days or Less	91–364 Days	1–3 Years	3 Years or More
All firms	43.5%	19.1%	30.0%	7.4%	3.2%	9.2%	52.8%	34.8%
Construction	40.1	24.4	25.6	9.9	1.2	11.0	63.4	24.4
Manufacturing	45.1	20.0	28.8	6.1	2.4	7.1	47.6	42.9
Wholesale trade	62.6	16.3	18.4	2.7	6.3	12.5	40.6	40.6
Retail trade	37.5	16.1	38.2	8.2	4.3	7.4	50.0	38.3

Median Amount of Borrowed Funds

	Obtained	Wanted but Not Obtained
All firms	$ 4,500	$10,000
Construction	5,000	10,000
Manufacturing	7,300	10,000
Wholesale trade	10,000	15,000
Retail trade	3,100	7,000

* Newer firms defined as firms with one or more paid employees, which started new businesses after March, 1951.
† Partner, corporate official, acquaintance, or relative.
‡ Insurance companies and other financial institutions, supplier, equipment dealer, factor, government, and other.

Source: Office of Business Economics, Department of Commerce, "Financing of Small and Medium Size Business," Survey of Current Business, October 1955.

however, loans of this type form a very modest part of the portfolios of the lending institutions making use of them.

A point which has been observed to be significant to many new and small businesses is the time and effort required in the cultivation of capital sources. When a business must supplement regular sources such as trade credit and bank loans by recourse to the secondary capital market of relatives, friends, business acquaintances, customers, finance companies, and the like, there are very few reliable guides. Each source must be explored carefully and exhaustively to pin down the precise terms upon which the money will be made available. Even when terms are established, the reliability of the lender may be in doubt, especially if the agreement extends over a considerable period of time. In such situations the negotiations for capital can consume a great deal of time and effort, and the task cannot be delegated by the owner-manager.

Special Assistance to Small Businesses

The widespread acceptance of the idea that small business is confronted with unusual problems peculiar to it has resulted in efforts (on the part of government and private agencies) to diminish or eliminate these problems. For many years, government has assumed the role of custodian of the competitive system, and one of the key elements in such a system is a business climate favorable to the formation of new competitive units where the need exists. It is natural, therefore, that the government would take it upon itself to keep the opportunities for new and small business alive. Whether or not such governmental activities are appropriate may be open to debate; but they are a fact of life for small businesses, a vital fact for many, and must therefore be taken into account.

All levels of government have hastened to pay at least lip service to the needs of small business, but the most noteworthy service has been that offered by the federal government. The principal agency for this activity is the Small Business Administration. The work of the SBA has very significant financial implications for the small business which seeks and qualifies for its assistance. One of the responsibilities of the SBA has been to assist small businesses in getting their share of government contracts. This is done by acting as a source of information for government purchasing agencies, as well as potential suppliers, by certifying businesses as being financially and technically competent to undertake government contracts, and by helping to form production pools.

The SBA is also authorized to assist in the financing of small business either by making direct loans or by participating with banks or other private credit institutions. The loan may be for the purpose of financing plant and equipment or working capital. There are a number of restrictions as to the circumstances under which a loan will be made, one of which is that all other reasonable sources, internal and external, must first be exhausted. The SBA is a lender of last resort— a possible alternative to the high-cost secondary money market so frequently used by small businesses.

Some statistics on SBA loans will give a more precise idea of the nature and extent of this activity.[6] From the beginning of its loan program through June 30, 1960, the SBA approved 20,362 business loans for a total of $955 million. This is exclusive of disaster loans. Approximately 79 per cent of loans to manufacturers for the six months ended June 30, 1960, were to companies with fewer than 50 employees, and only 1 per cent were to companies with 250 or more employees. About 20.5 per cent of the loans approved for the six months through June 30, 1960, were for less than $10,000, and 74.7 per cent were for less than $50,000. About 2 per cent exceeded $250,000. The purposes of these business loans were as follows:

Working capital. 28.0%
Construction of facilities. 29.1
Consolidation of obligations. 29.9
Equipment. 13.0

The first edition of this book, published in 1958, noted the small number of SBA loans in trouble at that time. In the period since then, the numbers have increased substantially. As of June 30, 1960, there were 532 loans in liquidation status, and 522 loans had payments delinquent in excess of sixty days. Only $2,000,644 of principal, however, had been charged off thus far by the SBA on a total of 192 loans.

A third function of the SBA is to provide financial counseling and other management and technical assistance where it is needed and requested. The criteria as to what businesses may qualify for these various forms of assistance are not completely rigid. The business must be independently owned and operated and not dominant in its field. For contract assistance a firm with fewer than 500 employees is small. The measure for financial assistance is more complex. In any

---

[6] Small Business Administration, *Fourteenth Semiannual Report for Six Months Ending June 30, 1960* (Washington, D.C.: U.S. Government Printing Office, 1960), pp. 27–71.

manufacturing industry a firm with fewer than 250 employees is small, and a firm with more than 1,000 employees is considered large. For companies between these limits, acceptability varies with the industry. A retail business with annual net sales of $1 million or less is considered small-scale, and in wholesaling the limit is set at $5 million. It is clear that these limits in terms of number of employees and sales volume are arbitrary, but it is also clear that a line must be drawn at some point.

In 1958 the SBA was made the channel through which a new form of federal assistance became available to small business. In this year the Small Business Investment Act was passed. This Act provided for the licensing and incorporation of investment companies to supply equity as well as debt capital to small business. Minimum initial capital required for such an investment was $300,000, half of which might be provided by the federal government through a long-term loan and at least half by private investors through the purchase of stock. The effect of the Act was to encourage private investment in small business and to recognize the critical need for equity funds as well as debt capital. The very considerable interest in this new development is seen in the fact that as of January 31, 1961, 177 small business investment companies had been licensed, with combined capital of $166 million.[7]

Another and quite different means by which governments have sought to assist small-scale business is through relief from taxation. The primary tax on business income is the corporate income tax. Since many small and new businesses are not incorporated, they escape this tax. Whether or not this is an advantage depends on circumstances. The owner escapes the business income tax but must pay the personal income tax on all business income, whether withdrawn or not. The problem comes down to a comparison of corporate and personal income tax rates for the sums involved.

Within the federal corporate income tax, there is presently a degree of relief for the small business in the breakdown between the so-called "normal" 30 per cent tax and the 22 per cent surtax, which applies only to income in excess of $25,000. For the very small corporation the advantage of this provision can be significant. It is interesting that, to date, tax concessions of this type have been solely in terms of size of a business (measured by taxable income) rather than some combination of size and age of the business. There is reason to

---

[7] Investment Division, Small Business Administration, mimeographed release dated January 31, 1961.

believe that if tax relief is justified in the broad economic sense, it would be for the new business rather than the small business as such. Greater competitive stimulus might well result from substantial but temporary relief for the new business rather than permanent shelter for the small business.

Some indication of government thinking on the subject of taxation and small business is seen in the following excerpt from a speech by the Undersecretary of the Treasury in 1953:

> The broad objective of providing a tax system under which small business will flourish has three major aspects: First, small business must be permitted to grow. An ample supply of available funds from the business' own earnings and from outside sources is essential to finance expansion. In this connection the structure and rates of the corporate and individual income taxes, the definition of income, the allowable deductions and the treatment of undistributed corporate income are all of great importance. Second, the continued independent existence of established small business must be encouraged. Those features of the law and regulations which relate to financing the estate taxes due when important members of the business die are of particular interest. The tax effect of the recapitalization which occurs in connection with the partial withdrawal of investment of the original owners is also of special importance. The third major approach . . . is concerned primarily with lightening the burden of the compliance for small business through simplification of the tax laws and regulations and improvement in administrative attitudes. . . .[8]

While generally less ambitious in scope, state and local governments have also established programs in aid of the small-scale business. Such programs generally have the twofold objective of helping existing businesses to become more efficient and profitable and of attracting new business ventures, large and small, to a particular area. For many years, New York State has been one of the leaders in encouraging better-informed and better-qualified small business management. Through various publications the State Department of Commerce gives general advice on starting and operating small business, specific counsel and information on the operation of forty different types of small businesses, such as restaurants and electrical appliance stores, a variety of pertinent business statistics for the state as a whole and by districts, and other information which is not readily available to the small-scale operator. In addition, personal counsel is available through regional offices of the Department and by the operation of regional workshops and forums.

---

[8] From a speech by Marion B. Folsom before the House Committee on Small Business, May 21, 1953, as quoted in the *Journal of Accountancy*, July, 1953, p. 106.

As a general rule, state and local governments refrain from becoming involved in financial assistance to small business. They have, however, lent encouragement to the establishment of an institution of some real significance in this respect—the business development corporation. These corporations have as their primary objective the encouragement of industrial growth in an area, working on the assumption that one of the chief obstacles, particularly for smaller businesses, is a lack of medium- and long-term debt capital. An example of this type of institution is the Massachusetts Business Development Corporation. Its capital is derived from loans from banks with which it is associated and from the sale of stock. Its loans vary in amount from $2,500 to $600,000, with 80 per cent under $150,000. Interest charges are in the area of 6 per cent per annum. At the end of 1959 the MBDC had outstanding or undisbursed loan commitments totaling $6,113,-450. The loans were primarily of a long-term character, with maturities ranging to ten years. For the most part, they were secured by one or more of the following types of collateral: first or second real estate or chattel mortgages (usually not including inventories), assignments of life insurance policies, and guaranties. In six years of operation the MBDC approved a net amount of $14,820,000 (125 loans) in long-term financing. The Corporation itself disbursed or committed to disbursement $11,480,534; participating banks supplied $3,339,466.[9]

At the present time the presence of various governmental and private agencies in the small business capital market has not made any radical change in the general financial position of the new and small business. However, for particular businesses, they have often meant the difference between continued operation and liquidation. Further, they appear to have become a permanent part of the financial scene.

The Conservation of Scarce Funds

Because the typical new and growing enterprise is faced with a persistent shortage of funds, which places serious restrictions on management's freedom of action, it is necessary not only to explore all possible sources of capital but also to consider ways and means of making available funds go as far as possible. In every business, there are certain physical facilities, stock-in-trade and personal, and other services which must be provided in order to operate at all. On the other hand, these requirements normally have some element of flexi-

---

[9] Massachusetts Business Development Corporation, *Seventh Annual Report* (December 31, 1959).

bility, and there may be two or even several ways of providing some requirement, which have significantly different financial implications. Hard-pressed small business managers must of necessity use as much persistence and originality in managing the productivity of each dollar raised as they do in raising it.

Without attempting to provide a complete catalogue of the ways in which the business investment dollar may be made to go farther, the job of conservation can be illustrated by reference to several approaches which are in common use by small business managers. The investment in the physical facilities necessary for a given scale of operations may be minimized as follows:

1. Rent factory or store space, and rent equipment rather than purchase. Store or office space is usually easier to find on a rental basis than is factory space because the former is a more standardized commodity. The opportunity for rental of machinery and equipment depends a great deal on the industry, since practices differ. The shoe industry is one example of an industry where rental is generally accepted and widely used.

2. Purchase secondhand rather than new machinery and equipment. The availability of good secondhand equipment varies with the degree of standardization of the equipment to be used and the size and character of the industrial area in which the new business is to be located. For example, it is quite feasible to pick up suitable secondhand equipment for a garment factory in the New York City area, where the industry is well established.

3. Purchase an existing business in financial difficulties. The opportunity to begin business in this way depends a great deal on the patience and flexibility of the individuals involved and the timing of the misfortunes of others. The individual who cannot or will not delay his start and who is strongly wedded by experience or prejudice to one line of activity is unlikely to find a favorable opportunity just when he wants it.

4. Build rather than buy ready-made. Many small business owners have saved scarce dollars by undertaking to construct their own physical facilities and, at least to some extent, make their own equipment. The possibilities here obviously depend on the capacities of the people involved and the nature of their business.

5. Assemble rather than manufacture. It is very common to find new businesses in the manufacturing area doing what is essentially an assembly operation. This helps to minimize the initial investment in plant and equipment. As they prosper and grow, they tend to take on more and more of the manufacturing, with the timing largely influenced by the growth of their financial resources.

6. Substitute labor for equipment. The initial financial burden in a new business may be minimized by purchasing only that equipment which

is absolutely necessary and using labor wherever possible. Labor-saving equipment may then be added at a later date as funds permit.

In other ways the basic investment in working capital may be reduced by:

1. Keeping inventory down to what is absolutely necessary for continuous operation—and running some risk of inability to meet customer orders or of work stoppages.
2. Handling product lines which are available on favorable credit terms and avoiding lines which are not.
3. Restricting sale to those customers who are prepared to pay cash on delivery or within a brief credit period.
4. Scheduling production so as to produce salable products in the shortest possible time. The objective here is to produce an account receivable in the shortest possible time. Efficient production scheduling is not necessarily based on individual customers' orders, but it may be forced into this pattern if the need for release of cash is great.
5. Operating in whole or in part as a subcontractor to a larger business which may be willing to ease the financial burden by such means as supplying the raw materials for the operation out of its own inventory.

These devices are examples of what may be termed legitimate efforts to pare down the financial requirements of the business. It must be added that under extreme financial pressure, businesses sometimes resort to tactics which have a similar end result but which hardly qualify as sound financial practice. One of these is to abuse trade credit by allowing obligations to remain outstanding well beyond the limits set by the supplier. This practice is based on the assumption that because the supplier wants the business, he will not react by cutting off the supply and enforcing payment. A little experimentation along these lines shows up the soft spots. Another practice is to rely on the "float" of issued but uncashed checks to extend the usefulness of the bank account. Checks may be issued without being covered at the moment by cash in the bank in the hope that they will not be cashed immediately and that, by the time they are, deposits will have covered the amount. It is hardly necessary to say that this kind of "shoestring" financing is at best a questionable device for getting over the occasional tight spot and cannot be a part of a sound long-run financial policy.

In a review of the various ways of effecting some reduction in the need for funds during the initial stages of business life, it becomes apparent that the ultimate financial implications are not always the same. Four distinctly different effects can be observed:

1. A genuine reduction in the capital required to conduct the business —as illustrated by the purchase of assets at distress prices or the sale of products for cash rather than on extended credit terms.
2. Illusory economies of capital which simply defer the outlay—as illustrated by the purchase of secondhand plant or equipment which requires drastic overhaul or replacement in the near future.
3. The exchange of one financial problem for another—principally the exchange of a large initial outlay for a series of smaller payments over a period of time. This is illustrated by the "rent versus buy" alternative and the substitution of labor for machinery.
4. A reduction in the initial capital required in exchange for some loss of efficiency and profitability. This is seen in the subcontracting of aspects of a manufacturing process, in small and frequent purchases of raw materials, and in the scheduling of production in terms of orders rather than economical runs (when these conflict).

In taking a course of action which serves to postpone an expenditure or changes its form from a lump sum to a series of smaller payments, the business manager is primarily buying time. Such a step may be based on a careful projection of the future financial position of the business or may merely reflect an impatience to get under way and a blind optimism that things will work out somehow if only a start is made. If, as often happens, the shortage of funds is solved by "economies" which reduce efficiency, increase costs, and lower profit margins, the business manager may merely be postponing the evil day. The immediate financial relief is bought at the cost of lower profits in the future—profits which are a vital source of funds for consolidation and expansion. The hazards of such an approach to a shortage of capital are heightened by the fact that many men new to the role of the independent business operator may be ignorant of the effect on profit or, if aware of this possibility, are unable to assess its magnitude and tend to ignore it.

Summary and Conclusion

In this chapter, we have outlined some of the financial problems and practices commonly associated with the new and small-scale business. It would be unfortunate if, in doing so, we overstated the differences between small-scale and large-scale business. In fact, businesses on both sides of this rather arbitrary classification are faced with the same basic financial problems involved in planning, raising, managing, and conserving the capital necessary to carry on their activities. In general, the approach and analysis to the problems we have described throughout this book can be applied with equal advantage to both small-scale and large-scale business. Thus, for example, the usefulness of a detailed cash budget has nothing to do with the size of the operation.

It is true, of course, that much of our discussion, particularly as it relates to long-term finance, has been in terms which are more familiar to the large business. Even here, however, the careful reader will observe that, for example, the public stock offerings and privately placed bond issues of the multimillion-dollar corporation have their modest counterpart in the equity and debt arrangements of the one-man business and present the same basic questions as to the proper apportionment of risk, income, and control. Similar parallels could be drawn in regard to such problems as capital budgeting, the bargain for funds, and income administration. It was the major purpose of this chapter to assist the reader in making the necessary modifications of his analysis when dealing with a new or small-scale business problem.

Chapter 26

The Financial Aspects of Business Mergers

Definition of Terms

The term *merger* implies a combination of two or more formerly independent business units into one organization with a common management and ownership. In business practice the term is loosely used to cover a variety of legal and financial devices by which this union of ownership and management is achieved. Other terms—*consolidation, amalgamation, acquisition*—are used in a similar context, and the lines of distinction are often unclear. Since an event of this sort has major legal implications, it might be helpful to begin with the legal concept.

Formal statutory provision for corporate mergers is to be found in the corporation laws of the various states. To choose a prominent example, the corporation law of the state of New York makes specific provision for both mergers and consolidations. According to this law, a *merger* takes place when Company A, owning at least 95 per cent of the stock of Company B, makes formal application to the Department of State for a merging of the assets and liabilities of the two companies and such application is approved. Company B, as a corporate entity, goes out of existence in the process. Provision is made for the appropriate treatment of any minority interest. A *consolidation,* on the other hand, covers the situation where two or more companies make formal application to join together either under a new corporate form or under the corporate form of one of the combining companies. Such application must be backed by the affirmative vote of the holders of at least two thirds of the shares of each corporation involved. Here again, provision is made for those shareholders who formally protest the decision within the stated time limit.[1]

---

[1] See *The Corporation Manual* (1959 ed.; New York: U.S. Corporation Co., 1959), Vol. II, New York, pp. 59–66.

In contrast with the rather narrow and precise legal definition, we have the relatively loose and all-inclusive concept of a merger as used by the Federal Trade Commission. With an obvious interest in the monopolistic implications of mergers, the FTC is concerned with any act which causes the disappearance of a formerly independent business. It prefers to use the term *acquisition*, which includes "all business and corporate organizational and operational devices and arrangements by which the ownership and the management of independently operated properties and businesses are brought under the control of a single management."[2] Accordingly, this term includes mergers which are defined as acquisitions of large companies, as contrasted with those where the acquired company is small compared to the acquiring company. In this sense, mergers are numerically less important than acquisitions.

Within the framework of this book, we are primarily concerned with the financial implications of mergers. Thus, definitions which are useful for legal or regulatory purposes are not completely satisfactory for our purposes. A statutory merger of Company A with Company B, where A already owns 100 per cent of the stock of B, is largely a legal formality with no major financial implications at this time. Similarly, there could be acquisitions which appeared highly significant to the FTC, in terms of potential control of output or markets, which do not give rise to major financial problems for the businesses concerned. It will therefore suit us best to use an all-inclusive definition of a merger and ignore those forms which are of a non-financial character. Such a broad definition was suggested at the outset: the concept of a merger as a union of two or more independent business units into one organization with a common ownership and management.

The Merger Movement

What is termed *the merger movement* refers to the periodic rise and fall in the number of mergers taking place, roughly corresponding to cyclical swings of prosperity and depression. The Federal Trade Commission has brought up to date a statistical study of mergers which was begun by the Temporary National Economic Committee. A graph showing the number of mergers taking place in the years from 1919 through 1960 is reproduced in Chart 26-1. As indicated by the FTC, certain limitations of the study make the absolute figures unduly conservative, but the relative changes in merger activity are

---

[2] Federal Trade Commission, *Report on Corporate Mergers and Acquisitions* (Washington, D.C.: U.S. Government Printing Office, May, 1955), p. 8.

unmistakable. As can be seen, the first wave of merger activity came following World War I, to be followed by a second peak in 1929—an all-time high. The third upsurge came toward the end of World War II, subsiding in 1948 and 1949, to be followed by another increase in activity which had not as yet subsided by the final date of the study. As of the present moment (1961), substantial numbers of

CHART 26-1

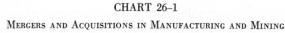

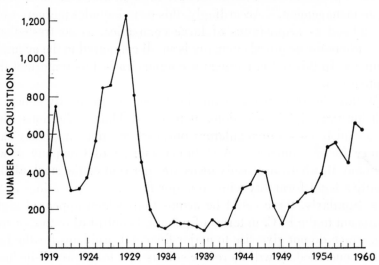

SOURCES: Federal Trade Commission, *Report on Corporate Mergers and Acquisitions* (Washington, D.C.: U.S. Government Printing Office, May, 1955), Appendix Table 1, p. 33, and annual press releases. This series covers only mergers and acquisitions listed from *Moody's Investors Service* and *Standard Corporation Records*, and includes only mergers actually consummated. It covers only part of the mergers and acquisitions now reported by the Federal Trade Commission, but it is carried on to keep up the data started by the Temporary National Economic Committee.

mergers are still taking place, in spite of rumblings from federal regulatory bodies, which read into the trend monopolistic implications.

A significant rise in the number of mergers such as we have experienced in recent years naturally leads to questions as to why mergers take place. In a broad sense the answer lies in the fact that mergers are basically a form of expansion and therefore it is to be expected that periods of prosperity would be accompanied by increased merger activity. This, however, is not particularly informative in arriving at the answer as to why a decision was made to merge companies A, B, and C at some particular point in time.

On the subject of causes of corporate mergers the studies which have been conducted[3] reveal that there may be several factors in a given situation and that it is often difficult to rank these in order of importance. It is also pointed out that there are at least two sides to every merger, and the reasons for acquiring a company may be very different from the reasons for offering the company for acquisition. As mentioned above, the primary drive on the part of the acquiring company is the desire for expansion and the conclusion that this can be done more effectively by purchasing a going concern than by internal growth. Such expansion may be encouraged by the existence of surplus funds. It may take the form of expanded capacity in existing product lines, integration back toward basic raw materials or forward toward the production of the ultimate end product, diversification of product lines, acquisition of marketing facilities, or any other form which expansion of corporate activities may suggest. There may be the expectation of improved competitive position, higher gross earnings or lower costs, improved financing, or better management. It may be possible to achieve these advantages more rapidly and with greater assurance through merger than through the development of additional facilities within the acquiring company.

The Butters-Lintner study indicates that the primary reasons for the sale of the business being merged fall into three basic categories: management considerations, investment considerations, and taxation.[4] Under the heading of management considerations are the problems of weak management, death or impending retirement of key personnel, and internal disputes. There are many such situations where the best alternative appears to be to sell out if a favorable price can be obtained. Investment considerations include the desire to make the most of an investment opportunity by selling when its value is considered to be at a maximum, and the desire to become less vulnerable to risk through greater diversification.

The tax implications of corporate mergers appear to relate almost entirely to the interests of those who are selling out. Although there often is a tax advantage for a profitable company in absorbing an unprofitable one with a record of recent losses which can be used as a tax offset, the study previously mentioned did not find this to be a significant motivation for purchase. On the other hand, tax considerations

---

[3] See J. K. Butters and J. Lintner, *The Effects of Taxation on Corporate Mergers* (Boston: Division of Research, Harvard Business School, 1951); also Federal Trade Commission, *op. cit.*

[4] See Butters and Lintner, *op. cit.*, esp. chap. viii, pp. 201–32.

were found to be of considerable importance in the sale of closely held companies. One of these is the desire to liquidate in advance of the death of the principal owner, so that the cash will be available to pay the estate tax. For the man whose resources are tied up in one company which is without a public market for its stock, the risks of financial embarrassment to his heirs and of loss in a forced sale of the business after death are very real. The other important tax consideration on the part of those whose business is being merged concerns the basis upon which the profits of a business are to be taxed at the time they are withdrawn. If profits are withdrawn as dividends, they are taxed as personal income, and the rate can be as high as 91 per cent, depending on individual circumstances. If the profits are successfully reinvested in the business and the business is ultimately sold, they are reflected in the selling price and are withdrawn as a capital gain, taxable at a maximum of 25 per cent. If the merger is effected by a tax-free exchange of stock in the acquired company for stock in the surviving company, then the tax is avoided entirely at that point of time.

As mentioned previously, there are often several factors which provide the justification for a merger of two companies. For our purposes the quest to determine which of these factors is the most important in a given situation is not particularly necessary or useful. It is important, however, to recognize when financial considerations are involved—the present and future demand for funds, profitability, cash savings, marketability of securities, to name some of the more common ones—and to evaluate their significance as objectively as possible.

The Procedure of Mergers

We have already mentioned the formal procedures which have been prescribed by state law for the effecting of corporate mergers and consolidations. Such *statutory mergers,* as they are called, represent one of the ways in which businesses are brought together under common management and ownership. The steps taken under company law for the dissolution of the merged company may in fact be merely giving formal recognition to a union which has been in effect for some years. It is the purpose of this section to describe how mergers commonly come about and how the financial aspects are worked out.

Mergers may be initiated by either of the parties to the merger or by an outside organization such as an investment banking firm which sees in it some direct or indirect advantage to itself. Negotiations may be conducted between or among the top managements concerned or directly with the owners. At times, top management may be deliberately by-passed where it is expected to be antagonistic to the change. The most frequently used procedure for bringing ownership and management together is for one company to acquire ownership of all or a substantial portion of the voting stock of the other. In the initial stages, therefore, the company to be merged retains its identity, and the two companies are in a parent-subsidiary relationship. This relationship may continue for a very brief period or sometimes for years before actual merger takes place. If the acquiring company does not gain 100 per cent ownership in the original transaction, it may find it necessary or desirable to add to its ownership before initiating merger proceedings. Even if it has the majority necessary to vote approval of the merger by the company to be merged, it may wish to reduce further the minority interest, which will have to be reimbursed in cash at an arbitrated price. As previously indicated, in order to bring about a statutory merger under New York State law, the acquiring company must own at least 95 per cent of the stock. In the meantime, the fraction of the stock originally acquired may be quite sufficient to operate the two companies as if they were parts of a single organization.

The voting stock of the company to be merged may be acquired in several ways. It may be obtained in a private negotiation between the acquiring company and a single owner or small group of owners. In the case of a publicly owned company the stock may be purchased gradually on the open market at the market price in effect at the time. It may be purchased by a public offer to buy all or a stated number of shares of the company at a price which is usually above the market price. This offer may be made with or without the knowledge and blessing of the management of the company to be merged. As an alternative to the payment of cash for the stock, the acquiring company may offer its own stock in exchange at a ratio which is expected to be attractive. In this way the shareholders of the merged company become shareholders of the surviving corporation. Apart from the possible advantages of the exchange itself, there may be considerable attraction in becoming a part of a larger and more diversified organization.

The other alternative to the acquisition of the stock of a going concern is to purchase its assets. This might appear to be a more direct and therefore more satisfactory procedure for the acquiring company, since the ultimate purpose in acquiring stock is to have the use of these assets. Instead of the shareholders receiving the payment directly, the acquired corporation receives it and ultimately disburses it to the stockholders as a liquidating dividend when they dissolve the company. The acquiring company is thus relieved of the formal merger proceedings and the problems of minority interests. However, in practice, the purchase-of-stock route often proves to be the quicker and more effective procedure, as evidenced by its use in a majority of cases. Where there is an established market price for the stock, the key problem of valuation is greatly simplified. Further, the purchase of stock is a way of by-passing antagonistic management, and it may be done with a minimum of publicity through the impersonal medium of the stock market.

When a company is acquired through the purchase of stock, the acquiring company indirectly takes on responsibility for its liabilities as well as its assets, since it has assumed the responsibilities of ownership. When a direct purchase of assets is made, there is no necessity for the acquiring company to assume the liabilities as well, although this may be a part of the deal, especially where the merged company is in a weakened financial condition.[5] Otherwise, the company concerned is simply converting earning assets into cash, and it retains responsibility for discharging its own obligations before it is dissolved and any cash disbursed to its shareholders.

As an illustration of the varied procedures in corporate mergers, we may use the experience of one company, Textron Inc., during the year 1956. The annual report of the company for that year reported the following acquisitions:

> On April 2 we acquired all the stock of General Cement Mfg. Company of Rockford, Illinois on a part fixed price and part contingent installment purchase plan. This division manufactures radio, television, and electronic parts and tools, liquid cements and certain chemicals.
>
> On April 2 we purchased on a part fixed price and part contingent installment purchase plan all the stock of Benada Aluminum Products Company of Girard, Ohio. This division is a leading producer of extruded aluminum products consisting primarily of storm windows, doors, awnings, and siding.
>
> On April 2 we purchased for cash and short term notes all the assets, subject to certain liabilities, of Myrtle Point Veneer Company, Norway, Oregon, and on June 20, for preferred stock, the assets, subject to certain liabilities, of Bandon Veneer and Plywood Association, Bandon, Oregon. Both these plants have been integrated with Coquille Plywood Division.
>
> On April 20 we acquired for cash substantially all the assets, subject to certain liabilities, of Campbell, Wyant and Cannon Foundry Company of

---

[5] Federal Trade Commission, *op. cit.*, p. 101.

Muskegon, Michigan. C.W.C. is a leading producer of alloy iron and steel castings for the automotive, railroad, agricultural implements, refrigeration, marine and other industries.

On May 1 we acquired for cash all the stock of Carolina Bagging Company, Henderson, North Carolina, as an addition to the F. Burkart Manufacturing Company Division to supplement its six other plants with an operation in the rapidly-growing South-East.

On June 29 we purchased for cash all the assets, subject to liabilities, of Hall-Mack Company of Los Angeles, California, and at the same time we acquired the business of its affiliate, Peat Manufacturing Corporation of Norwalk, California. Hall-Mack manufactures and distributes a distinctive line of bathroom accessories and fixtures.

On July 10 the company purchased the S.S. LaGuardia, which has since been rechristened the S.S. Leilani. This is a 18,500 ton, single class, tourist passenger liner with accommodations for about 650 persons. She has been bare boat chartered to Hawaiian Steamship Company, Limited on a long term net lease over which all costs and responsibilities of operation are borne by Hawaiian Steamship. Regular sailings between the West Coast and Honolulu started February 5, this year. Three quarters of the purchase price and reconstruction costs have been paid for through non-recourse mortgage notes held or insured by the government.

On August 31 we acquired, on a common stock for assets basis, the business of the Federal Leather Company (now Federal Industries) of Belleville, N. J. Federal Industries manufactures vinyl resin coated fabrics for automotive interiors, as well as for use in railway cars, planes and ships, and for luggage, handbags, shoes, furniture upholstery and wall coverings.[6]

The Problem of Valuation

When two or more independently owned businesses are merged, a problem of valuation is inevitably involved. If it is done by the purchase of stock or of assets, the cash equivalent must be established. If the merger is accomplished by an exchange of stock, then the relative value of each component part must be determined in order to find the share which each of the formerly independent stockholder groups will have in the surviving corporation. It will be apparent that this valuation will be the key issue in negotiations between or among the parties to the merger. It is appropriate, therefore, that we take up the problem of the valuation of a going business concern in some detail.

It should be noted that while valuation is of special significance in business mergers, this is not by any means the only situation in which this problem arises. The question of the value to be placed on a going business, either as a whole or on a fraction thereof (a share or block of shares), also comes up in the pricing of new issues of securities; in

---

[6] Textron Inc., *Annual Report, 1956*, p. 4.

the purchase, sale, taxation, or pledge of existing securities; in re-capitalization; and in reorganization and liquidation. Because of this, the following discussion of valuation should be read not only in relation to the question of mergers but also in terms of its wider application to these other situations.

Kinds of Value

The term *value* is used in economic, business, and legal phraseology with a wide variety of meanings. Some of the many kinds of value confronting the student of finance are *assessed value* for purposes of property taxation; *condemnation value* awarded as payment in takings by right of eminent domain; *book value,* as derived from accounting statements; *reproduction value* of existing fixed tangible business assets; *going-concern value* of assets of at least potentially profitable business enterprises; *liquidating value* of assets on dissolution of a business; *collateral value,* representing the amount that may be borrowed on the pledge of an asset; *fair value,* used as a base for public regulation of utility rates; *sales value,* representing the anticipated realizations upon sale under various conditions; *market value,* usually determined from actual prices, or bids and offerings in some sort of "market" (which implies the existence of potential buyers and sellers), though it may be imputed by estimate; and *fair market value* that adds to the concept of market value the assumption of the existence of a large number of buyers and sellers and sometimes the assumption that those buyers and sellers are well informed and entirely rational in their evaluations. The value derived under this last assumption is also called *intrinsic value* or *investment value,* distinguishing it from market price.

Despite the variety of the concepts of value indicated above, most of the methods of security valuation fall into three main categories: those based on the capitalization-of-earnings concept, those that emphasize asset values, and those that stress actual or imputed market prices. The outlines of each major approach will be drawn in succeeding pages. For purposes of simplicity, each approach will be discussed in terms of the valuation of a single share of stock. It will be apparent that whether we are placing a value on the business as a whole or on a fractional interest in the business, the concepts will be the same, and there will be a direct relationship between the two.

The reader will soon become aware of the fact that there is no single, always reliable method of determining *the* value of a business or its securities that can be applied to all situations. Often, several methods of getting at an answer, or various combinations of methods, will be useful in a particular situation. Further, it must be emphasized that the purpose of the particular valuation and the point of view of the evaluator will strongly influence the selection of approach. Typically, valuations are undertaken for a definite purpose and from a definite point of view, and the choice of approach and the final appraisal will inevitably reflect that purpose and point of view. For example, a businessman who is considering the purchase of the majority stock of a street railway company with intentions of liquidating the company for the scrap value of its property would obviously approach the problem of placing a dollar value on the stock differently from an investor who plans to acquire the stock for the income it may produce from continued operation.

The Capitalized Earnings Approach

The capitalized earnings approach to the evaluation of common stocks rests on the philosophy that the current value of property depends on the income it can be made to produce over the years. Hence, it is argued, ownership shares in the assets of a business concern are properly valued on the basis of the earning power of the business. It is the earning power that will provide income to the shareholder, and it is income that he values rather than the physical assets themselves. The basic validity of the concept that value rests on earning power, or potential earning power, is seldom challenged. It is in the application of the concept to actual situations that major questions arise.

In other chapters of this book, particularly the later chapters, which deal with capital budgeting, the reader is introduced to the idea and method of establishing a present value for a stream of earnings (or savings) extending into the future. In those chapters, however, we are primarily concerned with the internal investment opportunities commonly available to a going concern in a period of growth. The required investment is generally taken as given, and the question is one of determining the time-adjusted rate of return to be realized from the expected earnings or savings. This is then compared to a standard set by the company's cost of capital or some other criterion.

The problem we now take up is largely an extension of this line of reasoning, although the form of the question has changed. Attention shifts from the determination of an expected rate of return on a given investment of capital to the determination of what this investment of capital should be. From the point of view of the one acquiring the investment, the question is: What is the maximum amount I am willing to pay for this stream of earnings? From the point of view of the one selling the investment, the question is: What is the maximum amount I can reasonably expect to get for this stream of earnings? Unlike the capital-budgeting problems, the problem we are now considering involves an investment which is an entire business entity (or group of entities); consequently, the "earnings" in this case are the total net profits of the business (after taxes).

There are two basic problems involved in arriving at an earnings valuation of a business. One of these is the determination of the annual earnings (or earnings per share) which the business can be expected to produce in the future. The other basic problem is the determination of the rate of return to be applied to these earnings. We shall discuss these in order.

Estimate of Earnings. Before considering the problem of estimating earnings, we should note another difference between our analysis here and our capital budgeting problems. There, specific investment opportunities are considered to have an income stream of limited duration. A business entity, on the other hand, must, in the absence of evidence to the contrary, be considered as having an unlimited future; therefore, its income stream must be treated as if it will continue to infinity. Thus, it is natural that we think of earnings figures in terms of earnings per unit of time—the amount per year.

The task of arriving at a reasonable estimate of future earnings is not an easy one. The analyst knows that the profits of a particular concern will be influenced by movements of the economy as a whole, by conditions within a particular industry, and by the effectiveness of the individual company within its industry. Taking General Motors Corporation as an example, the future of GM will clearly be affected by conditions of world economy, of national economy, of the industry, and of the competitive effectiveness of GM within the industry.

In practice, an analyst seldom has the time and resources to undertake a complete weighing and cataloguing of all the factors that will bear on future profits of a particular company. Usually, the analyst works from the basis of earnings reported by the company for recent years, adjusting the figures upward or downward in accordance with his appraisal of the total effect of factors he thinks will affect the fortunes of the company. Although future earnings may be expected to vary from year to year, it is usually considered impractical to attempt a precise forecast of annual variations for many years into the future. What is commonly done is to forecast smooth trends—upward, level, or downward. Not infrequently, the forecast is simply that of average earnings over the years.

Let us assume that the analyst, either as a result of a painstaking and reasonably complete consideration of the various factors that may effect General Motors' profitability or as a result of a "horseback estimate" by way of a quick mental adjustment of recent earnings figures, forecasts earnings of $3.00 a share. How much is the probable earnings stream of $3.00 per share of General Motors stock worth? What value should be placed on a share of this stock?

Rate of Capitalization. The assumption that the earnings of a business will continue at a constant amount per year to infinity simplifies the mechanics of our calculation of the value of this income stream. Starting with an earnings figure arrived at after deducting depreciation charges which provide for the maintenance of the original investment fund, all we need is a simple percentage relationship between the amount to be invested and the earnings per year. Expressed in terms of our example above, if we know the percentage rate of return which it is reasonable to expect from an investment in General Motors—say 8 per cent—then the value of a share of GM stock is simply:

$$\frac{\$3.00}{0.08} = \$37.50.$$

Reversing this, we are saying that an investment of $37.50 in GM stock will bring an earnings return on investment of 8 per cent per annum if the expected $3.00 a year is in fact realized. The earnings valuation of GM as a whole would then be $37.50 times the number of common shares outstanding.

However, all this is deceptively simple; and in fact, the determination of the appropriate rate of return—or *capitalization rate,* as we call it—is the most difficult and subjective aspect of the problem.

In general, the selection of a rate of capitalization is determined by the relative certainty of the estimated earnings actually being realized. The more certain the prospective buyer is that the earnings will materialize, the more he will pay for the claim to the earnings. On the other hand, where uncertainty is great—or in other words, where the risk is believed high—the buyer will insist on a high rate of return. For example, in the case of a small concern producing a highly competitive item of uncertain demand, the buyer of stock may insist on a price which will yield a return of 25 per cent on his investment.

That is, he would capitalize estimated earnings of $5.00 a share at 25 per cent and reach a valuation of $20 for one share of the stock:

$$\left(\frac{\$5.00}{0.25} = \$20.00 \right)$$

Another commonly used way of expressing this is to say that the risk justifies a value of "four times earnings."

If, however, the business in question were a very stable one with every prospect of steady earnings at the $5.00 level, the buyer might well be willing to accept a capitalization rate as low as 5 per cent, in which case he would value one share of stock at $100:

$$\left(\frac{\$5.00}{0.05} = \$100 \right), \text{ or "twenty times earnings."}$$

An alternative reason for applying a low capitalization rate would be a strong and sustained upward trend in earnings, one classic example of this being International Business Machines.

In the example of the high-risk situation above, the analyst might prefer to adjust for the risk by writing down the estimate of earnings to, say, $2.50. To the extent that he has thus made allowance for the risk factor through a conservative estimate of earnings, a duplicate allowance for the uncertainty would not be made through the capitalization rate. In other words, if the earnings estimate were written down from $5.00 to $2.50 to allow for the risk, then a capitalization rate of 12½ per cent rather than 25 per cent would be in order.

Since the factors that go to determine the risk in a particular situation are complex and the weighing of them is a matter of judgment, it is apparent that the selection of a capitalization rate appropriate to the risk is subjective. It is also clear that a small change in the rate of capitalization applied will make a substantial change in the final valuation figure. In practice, many analysts tend to classify industries by groups and to develop rules of thumb governing appropriate rates, however questionable on theoretical grounds. Thus, for many years, it was widely felt that the more stable industrials with good prospects were "worth" about ten times conservatively estimated earnings.

The question of what importance, if any, should be attached to the disposition of earnings as between dividends and retained earnings has been raised before and will be reviewed again briefly in this context. The reader might well point out that the preceding approach makes no distinction between the two alternative uses of earnings; as a result, the approach contains the implicit assumption that a dollar of retained income is as valuable to the investor as a dollar received in the form of a dividend. If the analyst is not prepared to accept this assumption, and many are not, then presumably a company's dividend policy must be taken into account as an additional factor affecting the value of its common stock. On this point, Graham and Dodd write: "Our conclusions [in a preceding chapter] were that dividends were basically the most important single factor in valuation from the standpoint of the ordinary public stockholder; that earnings were chiefly important because of their bearing on present and future dividends; and that average market prices were influenced (and properly so) to a preponderant degree by the company's pay-out policy."[7]

In countering this argument, supporters of the capitalization-of-earnings approach might point out that not all American concerns have an established dividend policy under which a definite percentage of earnings is paid out as dividends over the years. Numerous factors influence the policy of boards of directors with respect to dividends; consequently, it is extremely difficult to estimate the percentage of earnings that will actually be disbursed as dividends in the future. The analyst might also argue that the directors would not vote to retain the earnings in the business unless they believed the funds could be profitably employed and that the reinvestment would ultimately lead to higher dividend payments. If the stockholder is forced to sell, it is argued that his investment will have gained in value by reason of the reinvested earnings, and he will be able to realize on the gain in the form of a higher price when he sells. Polaroid Corporation might be cited as an example: The company has shown profits since 1949, increasing from $1.63 a share on 404,375 shares (disregarding preferred arrearages) in 1949 to $2.26 a share on 3,866,000 shares in 1960. Cash dividends paid over this period, unadjusted, were 25 cents in 1952, 50 cents in 1953–56, and 20 cents in 1957–60. Stock dividends were paid as follows: 50 per cent in 1954, 50 per cent in 1956, and 300 per cent in 1957. The market price of Polaroid common stock reached a range of 261¾–163¼ in 1960, a price level which is obviously in response to earnings and earnings trends, and not to dividends.[8]

Analysts will undoubtedly continue to disagree about the logic of

---

[7] B. Graham and D. L. Dodd, *Security Analysis* (3d ed.; New York: McGraw-Hill Book Co., Inc., 1951), p. 586 (by permission). The authors' suggested formula for estimating the value of railroad and industrial common stocks is as follows: VALUE = EARNINGS MULTIPLIER × (EXPECTED DIVIDEND + ONE-THIRD EXPECTED EARNINGS) (p. 454).

[8] *Moody's Industrial Manual, 1960*, pp. 379–80; and *Moody's Investors Service, 1961*.

the capitalization-of-earnings approach, for the problem has no simple answer. If there is a trend of opinion at the present time, however, it appears to be in the direction of giving special consideration to the dividend factor.

Asset Approaches to Valuation

Several methods of valuation can be termed *asset approaches,* since they center attention more on the assets to which the shares of stock have claim than on income data. Among the more significant of these concepts of value are book value, reproduction value, and liquidation value.

As the terminology suggests, *book value* is derived from the asset values shown on the company's own books and presented in its most recent balance sheet. The excess of assets over debts represents the accounting net worth of the business and hence the book value of the stockholder's investment. Where preferred stock is outstanding, a value for the preferred shares must, of course, be deducted to determine the net worth applicable to common. The net worth available to common stock divided by the number of common shares outstanding yields book value per share.

Many refinements on this direct method of computing book value are in use. Some analysts prefer to exclude from net worth some or all of such intangible assets as good will, patents, bond discount, organization expense, and deferred charges. Others analyze reserve accounts and add to net worth those reserves which are felt to be essentially segregations of surplus. A few inject a measure of the capitalized earnings approach by allowing good will (or even adding it when none is shown on the books) if the earnings have been large enough to support a contention that the concern has a "going-concern" value in excess of the stated value of the tangible assets.

Despite the variance in method of computation, book values are relatively easily and simply determined. To the unsophisticated, they are exact and clear cut and, until relatively recent times, were widely accepted as standards of security value.

The student of accounting, however, will immediately recognize the fact that the figures for book value for a particular company will be influenced by the accounting policies of that company. The variations between companies in accounting for current assets are relatively small. The lack of standardization of accounting practice is particularly significant in the valuation of fixed assets and in the treatment of intangibles such as patents and good will. Hence, a concern with a rigorous depreciation policy would show lower net fixed assets and thus lower book values than would a similar concern that had charged less depreciation. When book values are used in valuing the security of one company against that of another, the analyst must attempt the often difficult task of reconstructing reported figures so as to get them on a comparable basis.

Even if a concern follows "conventional accounting practice" in all respects, it will arive at its balance sheet values by reference to conventions rather than sheer logics of value. Hence, inventories are generally carried at cost or market, whichever is lower. More important, fixed assets are typically carried at historical cost less depreciation rather than at current values.

An even more important weakness than the influence of vagaries of accounting convention and practice is the failure of the book value approach to give consideration to the earning power of the assets as the real test of their worth. For example, the Coca-Cola Company of Delaware reported earnings averaging $6.79 per share of common stock over the ten years ended 1959. Yet, the net tangible assets per share in 1959 only amounted to $42.15 per share.[9] Clearly, the book figures, even with the inclusion of the good will on the books of the company, are no reasonable indication of the worth of the Coca-Cola stock. On the other hand, there are companies—for example, certain railroads—where book values substantially overstate the worth of the company if earnings are taken as the standard.

Book values are most useful in appraising companies whose assets are largely liquid and subject to fairly accurate accounting valuation (i.e., banks, investment trusts, and insurance companies); but even in these instances, book values used alone are seldom reliable standards of value.

Reproduction value, or the cost of reproducing the assets of a concern at current prices, is of significance mainly in the case of public utilities, where it sometimes becomes a factor in the determination of rate schedules by governmental regulatory bodies. As a single standard of value, it is seldom used. A major objection lies in the inescapable fact that the typical business is much more than the sum of its physical assets. While costs of replacing physical properties can be calculated with some exactness by painstaking appraisal, the cost of duplicating the business organization, its experience, know-how, and reputation, apart from the physical assets, is most difficult of determination.

When physical assets are the principal things of value to a concern,

---

[9] *Moody's Industrial Manual, 1960,* pp. 1031–32.

however, and when they can be readily reproduced, the cost of reproducing the assets will tend to serve as a ceiling on valuations reached
by other methods. For example, in the case of a concern the principal
asset of which is a residential apartment house, few buyers would pay
more for the shares of the apartment house concern than the cost of
erecting and getting into operation a similar apartment house, regardless of the earnings of the present concern.

On the other hand, *liquidation values* tend to put a floor under valuations reached from other approaches, since there are many firms
which will purchase concerns when valuations placed on the business
become so low as to create an opportunity for worth-while profits
through their liquidation. During depression periods, when earnings
are low or nonexistent for a number of firms, liquidation values may
become widely significant.

It might be noted at this point that even in the liquidation approach
the valuation of the assets is based indirectly on their potential earning capacity. Unless they are to be sold for scrap value, the assets will
ultimately find a market in someone who feels that he can use the assets effectively—that is, make them earn him a profit.

In certain cases in which the business as a whole is being valued, a
combined capitalized earnings and asset approach may be appropriate. The appraiser may find, after valuing the shares on the basis of
the earning power of the business, that the concern owns certain assets
which may be sold or distributed to security holders without impairing the earning capacity of the company. Unneeded cash, government
securities, or unused plant may fall in this category. These "extra"
assets may properly be valued without reference to the earning
power of the business, and their net realization value added to the
capitalized earnings value in the final determination of the worth of
the stock. This is known as the *redundant asset* method.

Conversely, when additional investment by the purchasers is
needed in order to realize the estimated earning power, the additional
investment required may appropriately be subtracted from the value
arrived at by capitalized future earnings based on the assumption that
the additional investment will be made.

Market Value Approach

Another major approach to value looks to the prices set for the security in actual transactions between buyer and seller—to "the
bloodless verdict of the market place." Proponents of this approach
argue that actual market prices are set by buyers and sellers acting in

basic self-interest. Thus, they are appraisals of supposed experts who are willing to support their opinions with cash. Therefore, it is maintained that the prices at which sales take place are practical expressions of value which are definitely to be preferred to theoretical views of value.

Supporters of market price as a standard argue that the market price at any particular time reflects the value of the security sold in relation to all other securities or opportunities for investment and that all values are basically relative. Hence, the price of a security in a free market serves as an effective common denominator of all the current ideas of the worth of a security as compared to other investment opportunities. Also, market price is a definite measure that can readily be applied to a particular situation. The subjectivity of other approaches is avoided in favor of a known yardstick of value.

Whatever truth is embodied in these arguments, there are many problems in applying market price as a standard of value. In the first place, recent market prices are available for the common stocks of only the larger American companies. In the period July, 1957–June, 1958, there were 940,147 corporate income tax returns filed for active corporations.[10] Yet, even in 1960, only 2,307 issuing companies had securities listed on national registered exchanges.[11] Further, "listing" does not in itself create an active group of buyers and sellers, and many listed stocks are traded on a very desultory and infrequent basis.

Where there are few prospective buyers and sellers for a security, a "thin market" is said to exist. Markets are particularly thin for many securities traded in the over-the-counter market, where one will often find such wide spreads between bid and asked prices as "16 bid, 19 asked." The release of a relatively small number of shares on such a thin market may be enough to depress market prices substantially. Further, the market price for a particular stock on a given date may be influenced by artificial means. Stabilization, or price-support activity, is legal in a number of instances and is typical during the period in which a new issue is being marketed by the underwriters.

Another question often arises in the valuation of large blocks of

---

[10] Internal Revenue Service, U.S. Treasury Department, *Statistics of Income, 1957–58: Corporation Income Tax Returns* (Washington, D.C.: U.S. Government Printing Office, 1960), p. 3.

[11] Securities and Exchange Commission, *Twenty-Sixth Annual Report* (Washington, DC.: U.S. Goverment Printing Office, 1960), p. 246.

securities. Recorded sales prices for the date in question may be based on the sale of one or two hundred shares. Is it fair and appropriate to apply the price set on a small scale to a large block of shares?

A more basic objection frequently raised is the contention that the market itself tends to exaggerate major upward and downward movements in stock prices. For example, it is argued that speculative influences pushed common stock prices for certain widely traded stocks in the historic boom of 1929 far beyond "reasonable" levels. Conversely, it is claimed that prices in 1932 were so depressed by purely psychological factors and by technical pressures for liquidity as to be manifestly poor standards of long-run value. Other, though perhaps less dramatic, examples could be cited from more recent experience of market and individual company price fluctuations.

Partially in answer to some of the objections above noted, the theory of *fair market value* or *intrinsic value* has been developed. Under this approach, fair market value is the value at which a sale would take place if there were willing buyers and willing sellers actually in the market, each equipped with full information on the security and prepared to act in an entirely rational manner. This concept does meet most of the objections stated; yet, per se, it raises a need for other standards of valuation than market quotations and suggests recourse to something like capitalized earnings as a more valid appraisal of "intrinsic worth."

At any rate, largely because of their ease of application, market prices are widely used by the courts and by tax authorities, although not to the exclusion of other standards where they are deemed appropriate. Regardless of theoretical weaknesses of market price as a measure of intrinsic value, where a market price exists for even one share of stock, it will inevitably affect the appraisal of a prospective buyer or seller, however large the potential transaction. The seller will, in ordinary human nature, hesitate to take a price much less than the price label established in the market, and the buyer will resist evaluations substantially higher than the market quotations.

Valuation in Practice

These three approaches to valuation represent attempts to remove the problem from the realm of personal opinion and to place it on an objective basis. In this respect, they are only partially successful; and in each, some element of individual judgment remains. It must be remembered, also, that in mergers and in most other valuation situations, the final determination of value is a part of a bargaining process and that a compromise value is therefore likely to result. In such cases, it would be largely a matter of coincidence if the agreed-on value corresponded exactly to that indicated by any of the objective approaches. This does not mean that they are therefore of no value in practical situations, for they will normally play a significant role in setting rational limits within which the negotiated value will fall. It is not surprising to find that each party to the negotiation will champion the method of valuation most favorable to its interests.

A study of the bases of valuation used in corporate mergers during the years 1953–54 indicated that present and future earnings were of "overwhelming importance."[12] At the same time, it indicated that book values were comparatively unimportant, except in cases where liquidation was a definite possibility. These conclusions are helpful in suggesting the nature of recent precedent in the "court" of corporate practice. In addition, they lend support to the observation that a negotiated price does not necessarily imply one based on nonrational considerations. It must not be interpreted, however, to mean that capitalized earnings value will, or even should, govern every valuation decision. Each case must be considered on its own merits. Without a careful analysis of the particular circumstances, there is no way of distinguishing the exception from the rule.

The Effect of Mergers on the Capital Structure of the Acquiring Corporations

In some cases a merger is effected by the formation of a new corporation, which takes over the assets and liabilities of the merged companies and issues new stock in exchange for the old. In most cases, however, one of the companies involved survives the merger by "buying out" the others. It is important to note the possible effects of a merger on the capital structure of the acquiring company. Unlike internal growth, which tends to be gradual, growth by merger comes suddenly and often in relatively large "bites," and this may give rise to some manifestations of financial indigestion.

One of these may be a significant shift in the debt/equity balance. If the acquiring company does not possess adequate amounts of surplus cash, it will be necessary either to sell new securities in order to provide cash or to issue new securities for purposes of an exchange. In either case the former balance of debt and equity is likely to be changed and normally in the direction of increased equity. Offsetting

---

[12] C. C. Bosland, "Stock Valuation in Recent Mergers," *Trusts and Estates*, June, July, and August, 1955.

this, at least in part, will be the assumption of the liabilities of the merged company by the acquiring company. The net effect and its significance will depend on several factors, among which will be the capital structures of the companies being merged, the price paid for the acquired company, and its size relative to the acquiring company.

There are other aspects as well. It is often the case that the earning capacities of the companies being merged differ significantly as to the certainty of annual profits. The merger may serve either to increase or to decrease the risk inherent in the acquiring company and thus to cause investors to revise their concepts of margins of safety in the market price/earnings relationship. There is also the related question of the effect on earnings per share and dividend policy. The immediate effect on the E.P.S. of the old shareholders of the acquiring company depends directly on the earnings of the newly acquired assets and the price that was paid for them either in cash or by exchange of stock. A factor which is usually somewhat uncertain at the outset is the added earnings or savings which may be generated by the merger itself. If the two companies have had different dividend policies, at least one of the shareholder groups will experience a change in dividend pay-out following the merger, since it is obvious that all must be treated alike.

It should also be noted that there are significant organizational and managerial problems in harmonizing the internal financial operations on such matters as cash balances and liquidity and credit policy. Of course, some of these problems can be worked out gradually, but it should be apparent that the formal aspects of a corporate merger are only the beginning of the process of full and effective integration.

Chapter 27

Refunding and Recapitalization

IN CONSIDERING the management of long-term finance, it is natural that our attention should have been concentrated on the issuance of securities for the purpose of acquiring new capital. This is a primary concern of both new and growing businesses. In prosperous times the purpose of raising new money is the dominant one in corporate security offerings, as is shown by the following table:[1]

PROPOSED USES OF ESTIMATED NET PROCEEDS FROM
OFFERINGS OF CORPORATE SECURITIES
(In millions)

	1957	1958	1959	1960
Total Net Proceeds.........	$12,661	$11,372	$9,527	$9,936
New money................	*$11,784*	*$ 9,907*	*$8,578*	*$8,905*
Plant and equipment......	9,040	7,792	6,084	5,711
Working capital..........	2,744	2,115	2,494	3,194
Retirement of securities.....	214	549	135	282
Other purposes............	663	915	814	750

However, as the table indicates, there are other reasons why corporations issue securities. For the more mature business, there is likely to come a time when new securities will be issued not to add to the funds invested but rather to replace some portion of the existing investment. When a new issue of securities is sold to a new group of security holders and the proceeds are applied to the retirement of an existing issue of securities, the company is said to be engaged in *re-financing.* The most common form of refinancing is the sale of a new bond issue to replace an existing bond issue, and this is known as *re-*

---

[1] Securities and Exchange Commission, *Statistical Bulletin,* January, 1958, p. 9; January, 1960, p. 11; February, 1961, p. 5.

559

funding the debt. There are also those situations where a group of existing security holders accepts a new issue in voluntary exchange for the issue it now holds. This process of modifying the capital structure is referred to as *recapitalization,* to distinguish it from refinancing.

In our discussion in this chapter, these distinctions will be preserved, although in practice, new financing, refinancing, refunding, and recapitalization may be linked together in some degree in one operation. For example, a new issue of securities may be in part new money and in part refinancing. Similarly, the refunding of a bond at maturity may be accomplished in large measure by the existing bondholders taking new bonds in exchange for the old, thus coming under the definition of recapitalization. However, the problems associated with each of these types of capital structure changes are sufficiently different to warrant separate treatment.

Refunding

The reader is now well aware that a corporate bond involves the contractual obligation to repay the face value of the bond in cash at a fixed maturity date. The setting of the life period of a bond is determined more by convention than by the issuer's long-range plans. At the time of issue the conditions and needs 15 or 20 years hence cannot be foreseen with any degree of accuracy. Thus, it will normally be mere coincidence if the maturity date coincides with a time when disinvestment or a change in the debt/equity balance is desired. On the contrary, it will frequently be true that a business finds it continues to need the funds supplied by the bondholders and is confident that the existing debt/equity balance is one that can and should be preserved.

Under these circumstances, the company will desire to refund the old issue. The normal procedure is to create a new issue of bonds approximately equal in amount to the maturing issue and offer these to the bondholders in exchange for the old bonds. The bondholders are, of course, entitled to receive cash and will be paid in cash if they so desire. On the other hand, it is likely that if they have been satisfied with the bonds of this company up to the present, they too will be interested in continuing the investment. Provided the new bonds are offered on terms which are attractive to the investors, a large percentage of them are likely to take advantage of the exchange. The balance can then be paid off in cash provided by the sale of the unexchanged refunding bonds.

It will be most unlikely that the refunding bonds will contain precisely the same terms as the bonds they are replacing. Both the company and the investment market are likely to have changed significantly between time of issue and time of maturity. Whether the net result will run toward more favorable terms for the issuer or for the bondholder depends on the individual circumstances. Normally, it is to be expected that the financial condition of a successful and profitable business would improve over a period 15 or 20 years to the point where the company's bargaining position in the market would be reflected in an upgrading of its bonds. Thus, it might be expected that the new bonds could be offered at a lower interest rate or with other terms more favorable to the issuer. On the other hand, the company must reckon with the general market trends and with the general demand for and supply of investable funds at the time of maturity. It may well be that a weakness in the market at that time could more than offset any improvement in the company's financial position and risk status.

It would appear that the refunding process is one which involves considerable hazard for the issuing company and, at the same time, one in which the outcome is largely outside the discretion of management. It is quite conceivable that a large bond issue could come due in a very soft bond market, which would make it very difficult to refund except, perhaps, on unfortunate terms. It would also appear that there is little management could do about this, in view of the fact that it cannot influence the timing of refunding or the market conditions.

In practice, both the hazard and the limitation of management discretion may be considerably reduced. In various ways the amount of the debt may be substantially diminished by the time of ultimate maturity. As previously mentioned, many bond issues today carry sinking fund provisions which make retirement of a substantial portion of the debt prior to maturity mandatory. Further, there is nothing to prevent a company from acquiring its own bonds on the open market at any time before maturity, with or without a sinking fund provision, thus reducing the outstanding obligation.

Equally important in this regard is the call provision. The call feature is now "standard equipment" on public utility issues, owing to the insistence of the Securities and Exchange Commission, and it is also widely used in industrial bonds. It is the call feature which makes refunding a matter for managerial discretion, since it enables management to choose its own time for refunding, within the broad limits of the life of the issue. If management chooses to perpetuate its debt, it will attempt to use the call feature so as to take advantage of market conditions which give the company its greatest bargaining strength. It will be apparent that this is no simple problem, since it involves an appraisal of future market conditions over a period of several years. Because the call provision may be exercised at any time during the life of the bond, early or late, the company may consider a refunding operation at any time it feels that the terms of borrowing can be significantly improved.

CHART 27–1

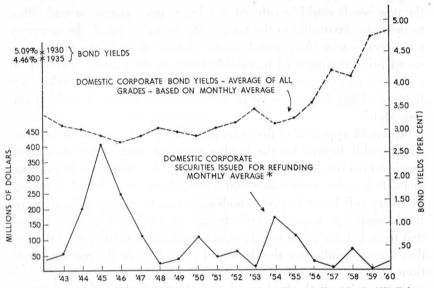

5.09% ⊹ 1930 ⎫ BOND YIELDS
4.46% ⊹ 1935 ⎭

DOMESTIC CORPORATE BOND YIELDS – AVERAGE OF ALL
GRADES – BASED ON MONTHLY AVERAGE

DOMESTIC CORPORATE
SECURITIES ISSUED FOR REFUNDING
MONTHLY AVERAGE *

* Data for refunding issues through 1955 from the *Commercial and Financial Chronicle;* for 1956–60 from the Securities and Exchange Commission.
    SOURCES: For bond yields, U.S. Department of Commerce, Office of Business Economics, *Business Statistics, 1959 Edition, A Supplement to the Survey of Current Business* (Washington, D.C., 1959), p. 101; *Survey of Current Business,* March, 1960, p. S–20, and February, 1961, p. S–20. For refunding issues, U.S. Department of Commerce, Office of Business Economics, *Business Statistics, 1957 Edition* (Washington, D.C.), p. 94; Securities and Exchange Commission, *Twenty-Sixth Annual Report, Fiscal Year Ended June 30, 1960,* p. 237, and *Statistical Bulletin,* February, 1961, p. 5.

The most significant incentive in the refunding of callable bonds is to gain a better (lower) interest rate for the issuer. Apart from changes in the investment quality of the company's bonds, there are cyclical shifts and trends in the general structure of long-term interest rates which may make refunding at lower rates possible. Chart 27–1 shows the year-by-year changes in corporate bond yields from 1942 through 1960 and the volume of refunding of corporate security issues. It will be seen that there is a significant inverse correlation between changes in long-term interest rates and the timing of refunding issues. The tremendous upsurge of refunding in the period 1944 through 1947 is largely explained by the fact that in this period, interest rates were lower than they had been since the twenties. The comparable figure for average corporate bond yields in 1935 was 4.46 per cent and in 1930, 5.09 per cent. This, coupled with the fact that it was a period in which businesses were looking forward to post-war financial needs, brought a volume of refunding of record proportions. It will also be noted that in subsequent years a significant downturn in interest rates brought a revival of refunding, and an upturn choked it off again.

An example of refunding in the 1954–55 period is the case of Food Fair Stores, Inc.[2] On September 1, 1954, Food Fair Stores offered a $20 million debenture issue at par, carrying a 3⅜ per cent coupon rate and due on September 1, 1974. The main purpose of this issue was to refund a $12.5 million issue of sinking fund debentures sold only a year and a half earlier (February 1, 1953), which carried a 4 per cent coupon rate and was due on February 1, 1973. The new issue would also enable the company to repay a bank note and add to its working capital. It is apparent that the primary incentive for refunding was the saving of ⅜ per cent on the interest rate over the remaining life of the old issue (eighteen and a half years), a saving which appeared attractive even though calling the old bonds at this early date required a maximum call premium of 3¼ per cent on the principal amount.

It is important to be able to calculate the interest savings realized in such a refunding process. This will be illustrated with reference to the Food Fair Stores example. Conservative practice suggests that these savings be considered over the remaining life of the old bond issue. An approximate basis of comparison is in terms of annual dollar amounts:

ANNUAL SAVINGS, 18½-YEAR PERIOD, NET OF TAXES

Savings:
Annual coupon, old 4's	$500,000
Annual coupon, new 3⅜'s	421,875
Gross Gain per Year	$ 78,125

Costs:
Share of call premium, old 4's	$253,906
Share of underwriting costs	156,250
Share of legal and other costs	46,875
One month's interest, old 4's*	41,600
	$498,631
Amortized costs (498,631 ÷ 18½)	$ 26,953
Net savings before taxes	$ 51,172
Less: Taxes at 52%	26,609
Net Annual Savings after Taxes	$ 24,563

* New bonds issued on September 1, 1954; old bonds retired on October 1.

[2] Information obtained from *Moody's Industrial Manual, 1954*, p. 1401; *1955*, p. 152; and company prospectus.

A more precise method of calculation takes into account the different periods of time at which money is spent and received. The total outlay made at the time of refunding is shown above as $498,631. The annual inflow over eighteen and a half years is the savings in interest of $78,125. Present value tables (see Chapter 29 for discussion of present value tables) show us that the rate of return which would equate this stream of savings to the total outlay cost is approximately 14 per cent. Another way of saying this is that an investment now of $498,631 in the refunding issue will bring in a return through the reduced coupon rate of 14 per cent (before taxes). It may be assumed that this "investment" opportunity looked more attractive to Food Fair Stores, Inc., at this time than any alternative use of the required funds.

Other Forms of Refinancing

Refinancing is not confined to debt, nor is it confined to replacing one security form with another issue of the same form. Thus, in addition to the objective of obtaining funds on more favorable terms, refinancing may also be concerned with a readjustment of the debt/equity balance because of a shift in the proportions of bonds and equity securities. It may be helpful to illustrate some other types of refinancing.

During the period of heavy refunding in the middle forties a number of companies took advantage of the favorable capital market to refinance preferred stock which had been issued under less favorable circumstances. This opportunity fell to those companies which were fortunate enough to have preferred stock with the call provision. One such company was Liquid Carbonic Corporation, which had a 4½ per cent cumulative preferred stock callable at any time at 107 plus dividends. These securities were retired in February, 1946, and the funds were provided by a new preferred issue (also callable) bearing a dividend rate of 3½ per cent and sold at 100.[3]

An example of refinancing involving a change of form is found in the case of Sterling Drug, Inc.[4] In April of 1955 the company sold $25 million of sinking fund debentures, 3¼'s due in 1980, for the primary purpose of redeeming the outstanding 3½ per cent preferred stock. It is interesting to note that since the rates were almost identi-

---

[3] *Moody's Industrial Manual, 1945,* p. 471; *1946,* p. 108.
[4] *Ibid., 1956,* p. 2011.

cal, the main advantage was to be derived from the fact that the interest charges were deductible for tax purposes.

A change in the opposite direction is illustrated by the action of Sylvania Electric Products, Inc., in October, 1945.[5] In that year, Sylvania called for redemption a 3¼ per cent sinking fund debenture issue, due in 1957 and callable at 102½, and replaced the funds by the sale of a $4.00 cumulative preferred stock at 104. The company's annual report for 1945 had this to say about the refinancing: "The sale of preferred stock in 1945 took advantage of favorable market conditions and left the Company free of bonded indebtedness. This action assures greater flexibility when additional financing is again desirable."

Recapitalization

The term *recapitalization* normally refers to the voluntary exchange of one security for another. While the term is broad enough to cover a variety of different exchange combinations, certain forms of recapitalization have been more common than others, and these will be given special attention in this section. The use of the adjective *voluntary* is designed to exclude from the discussion those exchanges which take place under conditions of bankruptcy and receivership where the choice on the part of the existing security holders can hardly be described as free. Such exchanges of securities will be discussed in Chapter 28, which deals with this subject.

It is general knowledge that the terms of a legal contract are binding during the life of the contract and that they cannot be changed without the full and free consent of both parties. For a corporate issuer to attempt to modify the terms of a bond, or to make a substitution of a new security without the bondholders' consent, would not only be without legal foundation but would also justify a legal action on the part of the bondholders for enforcement of the original contract and recovery of damages, if any. While equity securities do not have the same rigid form as the bond, the holders of these securities are also protected by law and the courts in the fulfillment of whatever terms may be attached to these securities. Preferred stock certificates normally specifically prohibit the company from modifying the prior position of the stock without the consent of the shareholders. (See Chapter 19.) Since common stock is the voting stock, it is normally

---

[5] *Ibid., 1945*, p. 1094; *1946*, p. 1198.

considered that the power to elect the board of directors is sufficient protection of the best interests of this stockholder group. The one specific right which may be attached is the pre-emptive right, which is intended to protect the individual shareholder against dilution of the voting privilege and of the value of his investment. In addition to this, corporation law normally provides for the protection of the shareholder in the event of an exchange of stock under a merger. (This was the subject of Chapter 26.)

Thus, through the common law of contract, state corporation laws, charter provisions, and company bylaws, it has become generally accepted that recapitalization of a solvent company must be with the consent of the security holders concerned. This presents a phase of the problem which was absent in the cases of refinancing previously discussed. By exercising the call provision, the company legally discharged its obligation to the old security holders and replaced them with a new group of security holders who were prepared to accept the terms of the new issue. In such cases, there was no need to consult the holders of the redeemed securities.

In order to keep recapitalization in perspective, it should be borne in mind that the typical industrial corporation has a relatively simple capital structure made up of some combination of bonds, preferred stocks, and common stocks, and that if this structure is changed at all by recapitalization during the life of the corporation, it is only at infrequent intervals and under unusual circumstances. The problems of recapitalization under the more common of these unusual circumstances will now be taken up.

Preferred Stock Arrearages

Under the provisions of a cumulative preferred stock, no dividends may be paid on common stock unless and until all dividends, present and past, have been paid on the preferred stock. A brief and temporary lapse in preferred dividends for a portion of a year or even a year or two will not present an impossible hurdle to future common dividend payments and may provide the company with the necessary flexibility to meet a tight cash position. However, there are those situations where the break in preferred dividends has been so long and the arrearages have become so great that it is highly unlikely, if not impossible, that the common shareholder will receive a dividend in the near future, even though normal earning capacity has been restored.

A case in point is that of the Ward Baking Company.[6] In 1945 the company had the following capital structure:

1. $7.00 cumulative noncallable preferred, par $50. .255,808 shares
2. Class A common, no par...................... 82,975 shares
3. Class B common, no par.....................500,000 shares

In the years since 1938, when this capital structure was set up, the company had been unable to pay preferred dividends. As a result, arrearages on the preferred had accumulated to $57.30 per share by April 3, 1945. (This included a certain carry-over from a previous preferred issue.) The annual preferred dividend amounted to $1,780,656, as compared to total net profit after taxes in 1944 of $1,-300,000. Under these circumstances, there appeared to be little prospect of ever being able to pay off the accumulated arrearages and therefore an equally slim chance of paying common dividends.

In such a situation the only hope of the common shareholder is for a recapitalization which removes the arrears and places preferred and common dividends on a basis which is realistic in terms of the company's earning capacity. Unless this occurs, there can be no real future for the common stock, either in income or in capital gains. Since this cannot take place without the consent of a majority of the preferred shareholders (usually 66⅔ per cent), there must be some reason why the preferred shareholders would accept the inevitable "watering-down" of their position. The recapitalization will not of itself produce larger net profits, and they already have a well-established priority on whatever is earned.

They will recognize, however, that in the process of accumulating arrears, a time will come when the prospect of common dividends is so remote that the incentive to pay up the arrears loses much of its impact. When this occurs, the advantage of the cumulative preferred position largely disappears. If this is recognized by the preferred shareholders, they also will be looking for a way of restoring the incentive to pay regular dividends, and they are ready for a compromise. Naturally, whatever plan is proposed must be adapted to the special circumstances of the company and will reflect the relative bargaining strength of the preferred and common shareholders.

In the Ward Baking Company case the following exchange of stock was approved by both preferred and common shareholders on September 16, 1945:

---

[6] *Ibid.*, *1944*, p. 1287; *1945*, p. 1684; *1946*, p. 1442.

Old	*New*
1 Share $7 Preferred	$25 of 5½% subordinated debenture due 1970 ¼ share 5½% cumulative preferred stock, par $100 2½ shares common
1 Share Class A Common	1 share common 1 warrant to buy ½ share of common at $12.50. Valid April, 1947 —March, 1951
1 Share Class B Common	Warrant to buy ½ share common at $12.50. Valid April, 1947— March, 1951.

The application of this plan produced the following capital structure:

1. Subordinated debenture 5½'s, due 1970.........$6,395,200
2. 5½ per cent cumulative preferred, par $100...... 6,395,200
3. Common, par $1.00........................... 722,495

The total par value here is approximately equal to the total stated value of the previous capitalization.

How did the various classes of stockholders fare in this recapitalization? If the exchange is considered as of a date prior to its implementation, the problem is more difficult than it is after the exchange is made and a market price for the new securities is established. One approach would be to compare the previous paper claims of the preferred shareholders (approximately $108 per share) with the par value of the securities received in exchange ($52.50). Another more subjective but perhaps more meaningful comparison would be to compare the securities held by the three shareholder groups before and after the exchange and the features of each. In this regard, we note particularly the reduction in the rate of return and the transformation of the old preferred shareholder into a split personality—part bondholder, part preferred shareholder, part common shareholder. There was the added protection of a bond, offset by the more speculative position of a common stock. The Class A common shareholder was to remain a common shareholder but was now to share this position with the preferred shareholders, who would own the majority of the stock. Somewhat offsetting this was the modification of prior claims and the elimination of the legal obstacle to dividends. The Class B common shareholder was to be left only with the right to buy a share of stock in the future, a right which had no value unless the price rose (or was expected to rise) above $12.50.

We may also view the exchange in terms of the claim on earnings. Assuming 1945 net profit after taxes of $1,122,000, the total annual claims of the old $7.00 preferred exceeded this ($1,780,000) and so left nothing for the common shareholders. The prior claim of the new debentures plus new preferred is now to be reduced to $700,000. With the tax allowance on the debenture interest taken into account, this leaves $561,300 for the common shareholders. Roughly 89 per cent will now stand to the credit of the old preferred shareholders and the balance to the credit of the 82,975 shares which the old Class A shareholders receive under the plan.

After the exchange was approved and carried out, we have the verdict of the market to add to our analysis. The market values of the old securities in 1944 and 1945 were as follows:

	1944	1945
$7.00 preferred (par $50)..........	62–45	70–57¾
Common A.....................	11⅞–8	14–9⅜
Common B.....................	2⅛–1½	2¾–1½

It should be noted that in paying the price it did for the preferred, the market was well aware of the arrears. The market values of the new securities in 1945 and 1946 were as follows:

	1945	1946
Debentures.................	109–100	110½–103
5½% preferred.............	105½–91¾	107⅞–100
Common...................	16⅜–8¾	18¾–11⅞
Warrants..................	8½–3½	9⅛–4¼

The change in the market value of one old share compared with its equivalent in new securities is seen below:

	Market Value before Exchange, 1945	Market Equivalent after Exchange, 1946
Preferred...............	70–57¾	101–80 (approx.)
Class A common.........	14–9⅜	27⅞–12⅛
Class B common.........	2¾–1½	9⅛–4¼

As a matter of incidental interest, it may be added that the price range of the common during the period of the warrant option was as follows:

1947	19⅞–10¾
1948	16⅞–10½
1949	17½–12
1950	20⅜–14½
1951	21⅝–17⅛

As of 1960 the Ward 5½ per cent preferred was selling at 89½–81⅝ and the common at 15¾–9½. Regular dividends have been paid on the preferred stock since date of issue. Dividends on the common stock have been paid as follows:

1945	0.15	1955	1.25
1946	1.25	1956–57	1.00
1947	1.35	1958	0.50
1948	1.85	1959	0.20
1949–53	2.00	1960	0.60
1954	1.80		

It is left to the reader to decide whether the recapitalization plan for the Ward Baking Company was an equitable one for all concerned. Without the benefit of hindsight the decision is not an easy one to make.

In a case of voluntary recapitalization, there is a question of what becomes of the stockholder who refuses to go along with the proposal. As a general rule, it takes only two thirds of the stockholder group to approve a plan to change the form of the security. This may leave a substantial minority of dissenters. Of course, even those who vote against the plan may ultimately accept it and tender their stock for exchange. Provision must be made, however, for those who stand firm. Corporation law normally provides that such dissenting stockholders must be paid off in cash at a price to be set by independent appraisal or arbitration. It should now be apparent that there is no quick answer to this problem; therefore, the value which is finally set as a basis for compensation may be truly independent or merely a compromise between extreme positions.

Stock Splits

A *stock split* is a type of recapitalization designed to increase the number of shares outstanding. There is also a *reverse split,* in which the number of shares outstanding is reduced. In a stock split the shareholders receive more shares of the same class of stock (for example, 1½ to 1, or 2 to 1) for each old share previously held. Thus, the number of certificates of ownership outstanding is increased by a multiple without any change taking place in the total value of the investor's holding. It will be apparent, however, that the one thing that is affected is the value of one share. Since no new funds have been added and nothing has happened to the basic determinants of the value of the business as a result of this exchange of paper, reason would suggest that the value of one share after a stock split will be that fraction of the value before the split which is the inverse of the increase in the number of shares. If it is a 3-for-1 split, for example, three new shares for one old, then the value of the new shares would be one third the value of the old shares, so that the total valuation of the stock after the split is exactly equal to the total valuation before the split.

The reason usually advanced for a stock split (or stock "split-up") is that of providing a broader and more stable market for the stock. It is argued that a larger volume of lower priced securities should make for a more continuous market and therefore one which is less subject to erratic fluctuations. The pressure for a stock split is usually found in a company which has demonstrated consistent profitability over a number of years. As a result of this, the market price of the stock has appreciated considerably. There may be a feeling that the price of the stock has moved out of the price range of many investors and that this is detrimental to the future growth of the stock. In fact, it is often seen that the number of shareholders increases after a split.

Although it is not always explicitly stated, there is often the additional hope that the market reaction to the split will be irrational to the extent of giving the three new shares a combined market value in excess of one old share. As a result, some capital appreciation will have been realized by the holders of the old shares. The one valid reason for expecting such a result holds if the old stock has been somewhat undervalued in a market which is "narrower" because of its relatively high price. This line of reasoning would argue that the split restores the stock to the full impact of market demand and to a "proper" valuation.

Whether or not stock splits actually increase the over-all market valuation is a hotly debated issue. This would seem to be a debate easily resolved by reference to the facts of market price. However, the problem is one of isolating the effects of the split from the many factors which can have a cause-and-effect relationship with market price. Those who see a capital gain advantage can point to cases where a higher over-all valuation obtained after the split; but to prove the precise cause is difficult, if not impossible. Those who oppose the stock split claim that if there is any benefit at all, it is only a temporary one resulting from speculative activity. It should be noted that when a company splits its stock, it is usual to make a parallel downward adjustment in the per share dividend, so that the total payment is the same as before.

The problem may be illustrated by the case of the American Telephone and Telegraph Company. Between 1936 and 1959 the common stock of A.T.&T. did not sell below $100, and there was a steady upward trend, which brought the price to the 224–65 range in early 1959. In recent years, there had been strong pressure on management to split the stock, pressure which management resisted. This activity culminated in a vote on the issue in 1957, at which time the split was rejected by a substantial majority. At the annual meeting of the previous year, 1956, the president of the company commented on the stock split proposal, in part, as follows:

> When there is an announcement of a stock split, the price of stock goes up, there isn't any question about that at all. You will get a flurry in the stock market and a rise in the price of the stock. But if there is no substantial dividend increase . . . at the time of the stock split, or shortly thereafter, that stock goes down in the market. And in almost every case it goes down below where it was before. . . . So I think if the telephone company were to split without a dividend increase, you would see our price go up on the market temporarily. That would benefit some people who bought our stock on a short-term basis. It would not benefit you people that want to keep your stock on a permanent investment.[7]

In 1959, however, the management suddenly reversed its position, split the stock 3 for 1, and increased the cash dividend. The following explanation of the change was given by the president at the annual meeting in 1959: "Conditions have changed from two years ago. The Company has consistently opposed a stock split with no dividend increase, and at the time referred to an increase could not be justified. Recently our growth in share owners has slowed down—it is important to encourage more people to invest in the business—an increased dividend is needed to maintain investors' confidence—and the Company's improved financial situation permits us to pay it. . . ."[8]

---

[7] American Telephone and Telegraph Company, *Report of the Annual Meeting of Share Owners, April 18, 1956,* pp. 7–8.

[8] American Telephone and Telegraph Company, *Report of the Annual Meeting of Share Owners, April 15, 1959,* p. 12.

Stock Dividends

An alternative to the stock split as a means of increasing the number of shares outstanding is the stock dividend. The number of shares in a company could be doubled without an increase in the funds invested in one of two ways: (1) by subdividing the item Capital Stock so as to have twice as many shares representing the same total nominal or par value as shown on the balance sheet; and (2) by declaring a 100 per cent dividend in stock, issuing each shareholder one new share for each share now held and transferring from the Earned Surplus account to the Capital Stock account an amount equal to what is now in that account.

The difference in accounting procedure may be illustrated. Suppose a company to have the following net worth:

```
Capital stock:
    Common, $10 par, 100,000 shares............... $1,000,000
Earned surplus................................    3,000,000
                                                 $4,000,000
```

After a 2-for-1 split, this would appear as follows:

```
Capital stock:
    Common $5.00 par, 200,000 shares.............. $1,000,000
Earned surplus................................    3,000,000
                                                 $4,000,000
```

After a 100 per cent stock dividend the net worth would show as follows (using par value as a basis for the transfer):

```
Capital stock:
    Common $10 par, 200,000 shares............... $2,000,000
Earned surplus................................    2,000,000
                                                 $4,000,000
```

While the accounting procedure is different and the balance sheet will appear differently in each case, the net effect is the same, namely, to double the number of shares by a paper transaction with no increase in funds invested or in earning capacity as a result of these changes. Thus, a stock dividend can be a means of bringing about this type of recapitalization without the trouble of arranging for the exchange of stock, provided, of course, that the authorized capital stock permits and earned surplus is large enough to cover the transfer.

Since it has been argued in terms of logic that a stock split should bring a reduction in per share market value which is exactly the inverse of the increase in the number of shares, so it would appear to follow that a stock dividend will bring a similar lowering of market price. If all that has happened as a result of the dividend is that the shareholders hold twice as many certificates as before, each certificate should be worth one half of what it was worth before the dividend with no net increase in the total market valuation of the company. An important distinction must be made, however, between the large-scale stock dividend, illustrated above, which is basically a stock split in a different form, and the small-scale stock dividend which is in the range of 1 per cent, 2 per cent, or 5 per cent of the outstanding stock.

Stock dividends on a modest scale have become quite popular with management in recent years. In some companies, such dividends have been issued as a supplement to cash dividends on a regular basis over a period of several years. The reasoning usually advanced for such stock dividends is that in this way, management is recognizing the shareholders' additional contributions through retained earnings in a tangible form which can be either retained or sold, as the individual shareholder chooses. The inference is that the declaration of the stock dividend has, in and of itself, added something to the value of the shareholder's existing investment. Thus, if he sells the stock received as a dividend, the remaining investment will be as valuable as it was before the stock dividend.

The facts of the situation run contrary to this argument. If any value has been added, it is the result of the earnings which have been realized and retained, and this will be reflected on the balance sheet and in the market price of the existing shares without any assistance from the formalities of a stock dividend. Rationally, the effect of a small stock dividend should be the same as that of a large one—simply to spread existing values over a larger number of shares, thus reducing value per share in exact proportion to the increase in the number of shares. Each shareholder is left exactly as he was before, with the exception that he has more pieces of paper to store in his safety deposit box. If he sells the shares received as a "dividend," he is in fact liquidating a portion of his investment. This is not "income" but rather a conversion of principal into cash.

Having recognized this basic point, we can now proceed to note how a stock dividend may have some real meaning and value to the shareholder. It will be recalled in the reference to the American Telephone and Telegraph Company that the president qualified his criticism of a proposed stock split in saying "if there is no substantial

[cash] dividend increase." In the case of a stock split or large stock dividend, it would be an unusual company which could maintain the per share cash dividend paid before the split or stock dividend. However, in the case of a small stock dividend of, say, 2 per cent or 5 per cent of the outstanding issue, it is quite possible that the company could maintain the existing per share cash dividend, thus increasing the dollar dividend pay-out in the period following the stock dividend payment.

Thus, if a person held 100 shares and was receiving a $2.00 per share cash dividend, a 5 per cent stock dividend would give him 105 shares and a total cash dividend in the following year of $210 rather than $200. A number of companies which have a stable cash dividend policy declare periodic small-scale stock dividends with this in mind. The stock dividend becomes, in effect, a promise of increased cash dividends in succeeding years. Of course, the same result could be obtained by raising the cash dividend on the old number of shares.

Thus, the small periodic stock dividend may have real future value in the eyes of the shareholder; and this, coupled with the conflicting evidence regarding the reaction of the market price, gives the stock dividend considerable appeal among shareholders. In addition, for management, there is a possible advantage in a lower market price and a wider and more stable market for the stock.

Conversion as an Aspect of Recapitalization

Significant changes in the capital structure can be effected by the exercise of the conversion privilege attached to bonds or preferred stock. However, unlike the forms of recapitalization already mentioned, conversion is not initiated by management at a time of its own choosing but rather is at the discretion of the security holder, if and when the price is "right." These forms are similar in that they involve a voluntary exchange of securities and bring about the replacement of one type of security by another of distinctly different form. The factors involved in conversion have already been discussed in Chapter 20.

While it is true that management cannot "make" a favorable market price or decide for the shareholder whether he wants to be in a preferred position or a common equity position, it can nevertheless have a great deal to do with the decision and timing of conversion. By setting a time limit on conversion, by setting a conversion price which is close to the market at the time of issue, and particularly by having a call provision in the senior security, management is in a position to precipitate a mass conversion at an early date. The one thing it cannot do is guarantee a rising market price for the common stock. Many issues of convertible senior securities are sold by companies which have a definite plan for forcing conversion—recapitalizing—at the earliest favorable opportunity.

Other Forms of Recapitalization

As in the case of refinancing, recapitalization can take many forms, and it would be a mistake to focus on the more common forms of recapitalization to the exclusion of other possibilities. Since this is a voluntary process, recapitalization can take any form agreed upon by the security holders concerned and sanctioned by law. Two interesting variations in recapitalization beyond those already mentioned are illustrated in this section.

On December 14, 1950, the shareholders of the Diamond Match Company approved the following exchange of stock:[9]

For Each Old Share—	Shareholder Obtained—
6% cumulative preferred $25 par. Noncallable. Participating, share for share, with common in excess of 6% up to a maximum of 8% total dividend (600,000 shares).	1. One share of $1.50 cumulative preferred, nonparticipating, callable at $34, par $25 (600,000 shares) 2. ³⁄₁₀ share of common.

It is apparent that while the basic preferred dividend remained at $1.50 per share, other significant advantages were gained by the company and the common shareholder through the exchange. These were the elimination of the participating feature and the addition of the call feature. As the president stated it in the annual report for 1950: "The purpose of the plan was to simplify the Company's capital structure and to provide flexibility in financing future capital requirements. As an inducement to accept the modification of their rights, the preferred shareholders were given some participation in the common stock issue."

An exchange of preferred stock for a more senior security, an income debenture, is illustrated in the experience of the Minneapolis-Moline Company. On May 28, 1956, the company offered the following exchange to the holders of its $5.50 first preferred stock:[10]

[9] *Moody's Industrial Manual, 1957*, p. 1495.
[10] *Ibid.*, p. 125.

For Each Old Share as Follows—	Shareholders to Receive $100 Principal Amount of—
$5.50 cumulative first preferred $100 par, callable at 100, voting (one vote per share). Sinking fund. Market price range, 1955: 93½–82.	6% subordinated income debentures. Interest payable from available income or surplus. Cumulative, callable at 105 (to 1957). Sinking fund. Convertible into common at $23 per share for first five years, $30 per share for next five years. Maturity, 1985.

The proxy statement for the annual meeting of shareholders of January 31, 1956, indicated that the exchange proposal was subject to a favorable ruling by the Internal Revenue Service regarding the deductibility of debenture interest as an expense. It also indicated that that the exchange was part of a plan to eliminate the preferred stock in anticipation of possible new issues of voting preferred in the future. This exchange offer was to expire on January 31, 1957.

In addition to the $5.50 preferred the company had outstanding a $1.50 cumulative convertible second preferred, par $25. There were 71,763 shares of this stock outstanding on October 31, 1956. On December 10, 1956, the company offered these shareholders an exchange for the new debentures on the basis of $110 of debentures for four shares of stock. The offer was to expire on January 31, 1957. Both offers were subsequently extended one month. This voluntary exchange of securities reduced the first preferred from 78,925 to 18,302 shares and the second preferred to 50,811 shares.

The Position of the Individual Shareholder in Voluntary Reorganization

It is generally true that the changes in the form or character of securities which we have been discussing are initiated by management, with or without pressure from the common shareholders. In a broad sense the recapitalization may work to the benefit of all security holders; but more often than not, it is designed to further the plans of management and to be of direct benefit to the common shareholders. While it is true that the plan for recapitalization must have the consent of a majority of the shareholders affected, the individual shareholder may find that his decision is not as "voluntary" as the term *voluntary recapitalization* implies.

Let us take the example of a preferred shareholder who has been offered a subordinated debenture in exchange for the stock he now holds. Normally, such an exchange offers the shareholder certain benefits as compensation for what he may be giving up. However, since the proposal comes from those who favor it, it is likely that the potential disadvantages will not be presented as forcefully as the potential advantages. It may be that if the disadvantages are significant, there will be organized opposition among the preferred shareholders presenting the other side of the case. More commonly, however, the shareholder makes his decision alone, without knowledge of the viewpoint of other preferred shareholders. If he votes against the proposal and is in the minority, he may feel he has no choice but to go along with the exchange, since the new security will be senior to the one he now holds. Thus, in his mind the choice may be viewed as being between the lesser of two evils; whatever happens, he will not be as well off as before the exchange.

Of course, such a possibility is inherent in the standard terms of preferred stock permitting recapitalization in the face of a substantial minority dissent (as much as 33⅓ per cent of the outstanding shares). Thus, it may be argued that this is one of the risks involved in being a preferred shareholder, which the investor should recognize when he buys the stock.

Recapitalization and the Bargain for Funds

We have now seen that there are a number of ways in which a business corporation may modify its capital structure from time to time. The usual methods by which this comes about and the immediate and potential benefits have been illustrated. It is clear that the basic objective of refinancing and recapitalization is to improve the position of the company and (usually) its common shareholders through a modification of the terms of the existing security forms.

Properly considered, these activities on the part of the issuing company are a continuation and extension of the bargaining process we discussed in Chapters 19 and 20. It is generally true that in the process of refunding, refinancing, or recapitalization, the gains or improvements realized by the company and its common shareholders are at the expense of other classes of security holders. Such changes would not be initiated by the company unless an advantage, through a change in the market and/or the bargaining strength of the company, was anticipated. On the other hand, it must also be true that if there is to be a change at all, it must be generally acceptable to the other security holders and realistic in terms of existing market conditions.

Chapter 28

Business Failure: Liquidation versus Reorganization

THE DECISION to terminate a business venture may be reached under a variety of circumstances and for a variety of reasons. It is customary to associate terminations with *failure*—with *insolvency* and *bankruptcy*. While insolvency and bankruptcy will be a primary concern of this chapter, it is necessary to keep in mind that many businesses are terminated while they are still quite solvent and even profitable. Disregarding personal reasons, which are of considerable importance as a cause of termination in closely held businesses, the circumstances surrounding the decision may vary considerably. In the financial sense a specific business is an investment opportunity to be considered in relation to other alternatives. It may cease to be the most attractive alternative long before profits turn into losses. In a sense, it has failed if and when this fact becomes apparent. However, in everyday business usage, we apply the term *failure* only to those cases of termination where it is financially impossible to continue normal business activities. Dun & Bradstreet, Inc., the primary source of statistics on business failures, uses the term to mean "a concern that is involved in a court proceeding or a voluntary action that is likely to end in loss to creditors."[1] It is in this sense that we shall be using the term in this chapter.

Before proceeding, it is necessary to explain the meaning of two other terms which are used in conjunction with failure—*insolvency* and *bankruptcy*. In normal usage, insolvency means inability to meet

---

[1] Office of Business Economics, Department of Commerce, *Business Statistics, 1959 Edition: A Supplement to the Survey of Current Business* (Washington, D.C., 1959), p. 211.

579

contractual financial obligations as they come due. Thus, inability to make an interest payment on a bond issue on the due date is evidence of insolvency. The Federal Bankruptcy Act defines the term somewhat differently in Section 1 (19): "A person shall be deemed insolvent . . . whenever the aggregate of his property . . . shall not at a fair valuation be sufficient in amount to pay his debts."[2] It is to be noted that an element of judgment is introduced, since "fair value" must be established.

Like the term *failure,* common usage has given the term *bankrupt* a number of shades of meaning. In the more precise legal sense, however, the word refers to a person who has become involved in the legal proceedings of a bankruptcy court and who has been adjudged bankrupt by that court. At a later point, we shall take up more specifically what this implies; but at this point, it is sufficient to realize that the term is somewhat narrower than either failure or insolvency. To refer again to Dun & Bradstreet's usage of the term *failure,* it includes "All industrial and commercial enterprises which are petitioned into the Federal Bankruptcy Courts . . . also included . . . are concerns which are forced out of business through such actions in the State courts as foreclosure, execution, and attachments with insufficient assets to cover all claims as well as voluntary discontinuances with known loss to creditors and voluntary compromises with creditors, where obtainable."[3]

Business Population Statistics

Statistics of business population help to set business failure in perspective. Chart 28–1 shows the total business population of the United States for the years 1940 through 1960. It also shows (1) the number of new firms[4] coming into existence each year; (2) the number of firms discontinued each year (for any reason, including failure); and (3) the number of transferred business, which include changes in ownership and changes in legal form. It will be noted that during World War II the number of discontinuances exceeded the number of new firms, with a resultant decline in the total of firms in operation. Also, in recent years, discontinuances have approached equality

---

[2] *United States Code: 1952 Edition* (Washington, D.C.: U.S. Government Printing Office, 1953), Title 11, Bankruptcy, Sec. 1 (19).

[3] Office of Business Economics, Department of Commerce, *loc. cit.*

[4] A *firm* is defined as "a financially responsible business organization under one management with an established place of business and may control one or more plants or outlets." Includes all nonfarm businesses but excludes professional practices. (*Loc. cit.*).

with new formations, resulting in a more or less stabilized business population.

One conclusion from these statistics is that discontinuances represent a significant fraction of the total business population—approx-

CHART 28–1

BUSINESS POPULATION, 1940–60

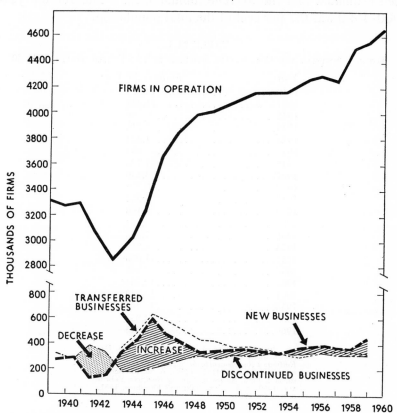

* Transfers include firms undergoing a change of ownership or a change of legal form.

SOURCE: Office of Business Economics, Department of Commerce, *Business Statistics, 1959 Edition, A Supplement to Survey of Current Business* (Washington, D.C., 1959), pp. 26–27, for 1940–55 and all figures for transfers; *Survey of Current Business,* May, 1960, p. 13, for 1956–59.

imately 7.5 per cent in the year 1959. At this rate the total business population turns over once every fourteen years. When we add to this the turnover of ownership, as represented by transfers, the figure approaches 15 per cent a year. These figures may be compared with the statistics of failure shown in Table 28–1. Since the original source of these data was Dun & Bradstreet, these are failures which involved loss or potential loss to creditors. By comparison, failures in this sense have been relatively insignificant in recent years—approximately 0.53 per cent of the total population in the year 1960.[5] Even in the depths of the depression of the thirties the failures only reached the 32,000 level (1932), as compared with 15,445 in 1960. It has been estimated that the average annual failure rate for the years 1900–1960 was 0.7 per cent of the total population.[6]

TABLE 28-1

TOTAL INDUSTRIAL AND COMMERCIAL FAILURES IN THE UNITED STATES, 1940–60

Year	Failures for Year
1940	13,620
1941	11,844
1942	9,408
1943	3,216
1944	1,224
1945	804
1946	1,128
1947	3,480
1948	5,256
1949	9,252
1950	9,168
1951	8,064
1952	7,608
1953	8,868
1954	11,088
1955	10,968
1956	12,684
1957	13,740
1958	14,964
1959	14,053
1960	15,445

SOURCE: Office of Business Economics, Department of Commerce, *Business Statistics, 1959 Edition: A Supplement to the Survey of Current Business* (Washington, D.C., 1959), p. 28, for figures through 1958; *Survey of Current Business*, February, 1960, p. S–5, for 1959; and February, 1961, p. S–5, for 1960.

The obvious conclusion from a review of these statistics is that the subject of this chapter, narrowly defined, is a problem experienced by only a small minority of business owners and managers. However, the statistics also bring out that in a broader sense the liquidation or sale of a business under unfavorable circumstances is a much more common occurrence. Further, as statistics of actual failures and terminations, they understate the number of times the prospect of liq-

---

[5] Small Business Administration, *Fourteenth Semiannual Report, for the Six Months Ending June 30, 1960* (Washington, D.C.: U.S. Government Printing Office, 1960), p. 12.

[6] *Ibid.*

uidation has entered the minds of management as a very real alternative, under distressing circumstances which were later proved to be temporary.

The Causes of Business Failure

It is a question as to how much can be said usefully by way of generalization on the causes of failure in business. The best-known continuing study of causes of business failure is that made by Dun & Bradstreet. For the year 1960 the following breakdown of apparent causes was given:[7]

		Percentage of Total Failures
Inexperience, incompetence*		90.8%
Inadequate sales	48.8%	
Heavy operating expenses	5.7	
Receivables difficulties	8.9	
Inventory difficulties	7.0	
Excessive fixed assets	6.6	
Poor location	2.3	
Competitive weakness	23.0	
Other	4.2	
Neglect		3.2
Fraud		1.7
Disaster		1.1
Reason unknown		3.2
		100.0%

* Note that there is some duplication in the percentages under this heading.

A more significant set of ideas on business failure is found in Kaplan's book on small business[8] and is summarized below:

1. Deficiencies in management combined with unfavorable external circumstances
2. Lack of preparation in organizing the business
3. Weaknesses in financial management
4. Preoccupation with business details
5. Personality difficulties
6. Severe competition
7. External factors beyond the influence of management

It is probably a mistake to try to establish a single dominant cause of failure in each case, as is attempted in the Dun & Bradstreet studies. Invariably, there are several facets to each case of failure, and an attempt to say which is primary tends to lead one into a "chicken and egg" type of dilemma. This is especially apparent

[7] *Dun's Review and Modern Industry*, March, 1961, p. 13.

[8] A. D. H. Kaplan, *Small Business: Its Place and Problems* (New York: McGraw-Hill Book Co., Inc., 1948), pp. 66–68 (by permission).

in the so-called "financial" causes of failure. An analysis of unsuccessful businesses shows evidence of such weaknesses as insufficient working capital, overextension of credit, overinvestment in inventory, excessive debt, and excessive withdrawals of profits. Yet, each of these may be traced back at least one step: for example, insufficient working capital to lack of intelligent planning, overextension of credit to a tough competitive situation, or overinvestment in inventory to a misjudgment of future trends in demand. They may also be interrelated: for example, a possible relationship between excessive debt, excessive withdrawals of profits, and insufficient capital.

It is not the intention here to suggest that it is either impossible or undesirable to search for causes of failure, even though to the parties involved in liquidation, this research may appear purely academic. In a broad sense, it is desirable in order that there may be a useful transfer of experience regarding avoidable hazards. In the specific case, it may also be of vital importance. When a business is to be reorganized rather than liquidated, it is obvious that the new company must know—and as far as possible, correct—the mistakes of the past in order to have any prospect of surviving. For these purposes, it is important to know all the important contributing factors.

Insolvency without Bankruptcy

It is a rare case where a healthy business is turned into a bankrupt one over night. It is more usual to find that insolvency (the inability to meet obligations as they come due) is the termination point of a period of struggle to preserve profitability and solvency which has lasted for months or years. During this period the business has gradually exhausted the various means of preserving solvency, in the vain hope that a turning point would be reached.

If a business is experiencing a gradual depletion of its resources resulting from an inability to show a profit, it is likely to turn to any one of a number of courses of action which will enable it to stay in operation. Setting aside the alternative of direct negotiation with creditors for the moment, the more common courses of action for this purpose are summarized below:

1. Convert nonessential assets into cash (what is considered "essential" depends on the severity of the situation). For example:
   a) Sale of idle plant and equipment
   b) Scaling-down of inventory
2. Cut back or defer all payments which are not absolutely required by contract, e.g.:

    a) Defer accounts payable
    b) Cut preferred and common dividends
3. Replace debt of imminent maturity with debt of more distant maturity, particularly by recourse to the high-cost finance company type of loans.
4. "Extract" new capital from those who have a reason for preserving the company's existence—officers, shareholders, suppliers, and customers.

For some companies, any or all of these steps may serve to preserve the company long enough to enable it to reverse the trend and establish itself on a sound financial footing. For others, they will prove to be only temporary expedients which merely postpone the day of reckoning.

If and when the time comes that a business finds it impossible to continue to meet its obligations on time, even after the kind of emergency action suggested above, the only remaining hope for preserving the business lies in a direct appeal to the creditors in the expectation of some concessions from the rigid terms of the existing contract. The prospects for a permanent or even temporary solution by this means depend very much on all the circumstances of the case. If the debtor continues to hope for a change of fortune, he may seek an *extension* on any or all of his obligations. Extensions usually involve a plan of repayment as well as a postponement of the due date. Apart from humanitarian considerations, there may be valid reasons why creditors, in their own self-interest, may be willing to accept less than that to which they are legally entitled. Formal bankruptcy proceedings are costly and time-consuming, and there is strong likelihood that they will not produce full satisfaction of claims. On the contrary, liquidation under court supervision is almost certain to involve loss to at least some of the creditors. In addition, there is the unpleasant publicity associated with bankruptcy proceedings, which is avoided by creditors and debtors alike if at all possible. Thus, if the creditor has any reason to share the hope of the debtor for an improvement in his circumstances and trusts his basic integrity, he may be willing to go along with the arrangement and may in the long run be better off by so doing.

Another alternative, which usually has less appeal for the creditors, is what is termed a *composition*. The composition is an agreement which takes the form of a legal contract, whereby the debtor pays an agreed-upon percentage of what he owes, and this is accepted by the creditors in full discharge of the debt. The debtor is then free to pursue his normal business activities. Such an arrangement may appeal to creditors, particularly suppliers, who have an interest in preserving the business of the debtor and see no hope of its getting out from under the existing debt. Except where the provisions of Chapter XI of the Bankruptcy Act (which will be discussed in the following pages) apply, the composition must be purely voluntary on the creditors' part. Once accepted, however, the arrangement is final. Because of this finality, it is normally less desirable from the creditors' point of view than the extension, though it may still be preferable to liquidation in bankruptcy.

These arrangements may be carried out in an informal manner where the creditors are few in number and/or can be readily brought together for united action. The detail of the arrangement may be worked out by direct negotiation with the creditor or a creditors committee or through the services of a trustee or outside agency such as a credit bureau. There is no necessity for court proceedings in order that any agreement shall be binding on all who willingly participate. At the same time, any creditor who refuses to go along with the arrangement must be satisfied according to the terms of his original contract, or the debtor runs the risk of his filing a petition for bankruptcy proceedings. Satisfaction in full of certain creditors' claims may be a part of any agreement that is worked out.

Arrangements may also be worked out within the framework of the courts under the provisions of the Federal Bankruptcy Act. Under Chapter XI of the Act, formal provision is made for court supervision of arrangements between a natural person or corporation and unsecured creditors. Arrangements between corporations and secured creditors come under the reorganization provisions of Chapter X, whereas such arrangements on the part of natural persons are covered by Chapter XII of the Act. The provisions of the Act apply whether or not the debtor is involved in bankruptcy proceedings at the time of the petition. Very briefly stated, the procedure involves a petition by the debtor for consideration of a specific plan for extension or composition. Upon receipt of the petition the court will bring the creditors together for consideration of the proposal. In the process, arrangements are made for any supervision of the assets of the debtor and for verification of the claims of the creditors. Unanimous acceptance by the creditors is desired but is not a prerequisite for confirmation of the proposal. An application for confirmation made by the debtor and backed by acceptance in writing by a majority of the creditors may be approved by the court if in its judgment the proposal is "fair and equitable and feasible" and in the best interests of all concerned. The arrangement will then apply to all creditors alike. Section 771 states: "The confirmation of an arrangement shall discharge a debtor from all his unsecured debts and liabilities provided for by the arrangement, except as provided in the arrangement. . . ."

In considering insolvency without bankruptcy, mention should be made of the role of the *creditors committee*. It sometimes happens that creditors may be willing to work out an arrangement which will preserve the business of the debtor on condition that a creditors committee is allowed to play an active, if not dominant, role in management during the period of rehabilitation. The desire for a part in management may stem from a lack of confidence in existing management with respect to either its ability or its willingness to fulfill its obligations. Any arrangement of this type must be consented to by the existing ownership, but in view of the unpleasant alternatives the wishes of the creditors are likely to be recognized. Once the claims of the creditors have been fully satisfied, they will withdraw, and full control will return to those who own the company.

In these various ways a business which becomes insolvent may avoid bankruptcy and liquidation. Obviously, this cannot be accomplished without the consent, if not the active support, of the creditors. Generally speaking, creditors heartily dislike liquidation as a means of realizing their claims and will give serious consideration to any alternative which offers real hope of ultimate return of their investment.

Corporate Reorganization

With the exception of adjustments under Chapter XI of the Bankruptcy Act mentioned previously, the means of preserving insolvent businesses covered so far take place outside a court of law. Such procedures are well suited to smaller businesses where ownership as well as creditors' claims are concentrated in the hands of a few, thus making informal negotiation a practical possibility. In the case of larger corporations the involvement of large numbers of shareholders and creditors makes a formalized procedure supervised by a court of law almost mandatory.

We have noted that Chapter XI of the Bankruptcy Act provided for court supervision of arrangements in the case of insolvent corporations or individuals whose obligations were entirely unsecured. It was the intention of the Act that wherever possible the rehabilitation of insolvent businesses would take place under the provisions of this chapter. However, in those corporations which have secured as well as unsecured debt, rehabilitation must take the form of reorganization under the provisions of Chapter X. Apart from the matter of secured versus unsecured debt, the distinction between an arrangement and a reorganization under the Bankruptcy Act is not a sharp one. Both involve a reconsideration and adjustment of creditors' claims. However, the application of Chapter X is confined to corporations and deals specifically with the problem of groups of owners (shareholders) as well as groups of creditors.

The term *reorganization*, as applied to business corporations, means a reconstruction of the financial structure, particularly the debt/equity relationships, in order to permit the resumption of normal business activity. It generally involves a more radical readjustment than does the recapitalization of solvent companies, described in an earlier chapter. Further, corporate reorganization, taking place under court jurisdiction, loses some of the voluntary aspects which are inherent in recapitalization.

The initial step in corporate reorganization under Chapter X is the filing of a petition to reorganize with the appropriate federal court. The petition may be filed by the insolvent business or by its creditors. It is not essential that the business be involved in bankruptcy proceedings at the time of the petition. If and when this petition is approved by the court, procedure under Chapter X then takes precedence over any other action. Section 548 states: "Until otherwise ordered by the judge, an order approving a petition shall operate as a stay of a prior pending bankruptcy, mortgage foreclosure, or equity receivership proceeding, and of any act or other proceeding to enforce a lien against the debtor's property."

Following approval of the petition the judge will proceed to appoint a *trustee* for the property of the debtor, except in cases where the indebtedness is less than $250,000, where he may choose to continue the debtor in possession. The primary function of the trustee is to assemble the facts of the various claims against the corporation and to take the initiative in preparing a plan of reorganization. In the process of preparing a plan, the trustee will hear proposals which creditors and/or shareholders may wish to make. At this stage, there is no certainty that a workable plan of reorganization will be forthcoming. It is the responsibility of the trustee to explore all possibilities, but the Act anticipates that a plan may not be forthcoming by providing that the trustee "shall prepare and file a plan, or a report of his reasons why a plan cannot be effected" (Section 569). In the case where the debtor is continued in possession, the court may appoint an individual known as an *examiner*, who will perform the duties otherwise undertaken by the trustee.

When the plan of reorganization submitted by the trustee has been prepared, the court then calls a hearing of shareholders and creditors so that the judge may consider any objections or amendments. In the case of companies where the schedule of indebtedness exceeds $3 million, the judge must submit the plan to the Securities and Exchange Commission for its consideration and recommendations. In the case where indebtedness is less, submission to the SEC is optional; and in any case, its recommendations are advisory only.

Following initial hearings on the plan and the receipt of the report of the SEC, if any, the court will transmit the plan it has approved to the creditors and shareholders. The court may then confirm the plan if and when it is accepted (in writing) "by or on behalf of creditors holding two-thirds in amount of claims filed and allowed of each class" (Section 579). When confirmed by the court, the plan becomes binding on all, including the dissenters. If the company involved has not been found to be insolvent, the plan must also be approved by shareholders holding a majority of the stock.

Fairness and Feasibility in Reorganization

The primary responsibility of the court in giving its approval to a plan of reorganization is to assure that the plan is "fair and equitable and feasible" (Section 621 [2]). It is inevitable that the new capital structure will change somewhat the claims the various classes of investors have in the business and the value of such claims. In a sense, it may be said that certain of these investors will be arbitrarily dispossessed of values which were theirs by legal right (although the real substance of such values may have been lost in the deterioration preceding bankruptcy). It is obvious, then, that the court has a serious responsibility in formulating the new capital structure embodied in the reorganization plan, with little guidance to be found in the words *fair* and *equitable*. It is also necessary that the court give consideration to the *feasibility* of the plan. There is little point to reorganization unless the financial burden imposed by the new capital structure is one which makes possible a permanent return to solvency.

It has already been noted that in seeking a solution to this problem, the court is assisted by the trustee, the advice of shareholders and creditors, and in some cases by the SEC. In order to get a clearer idea of what is implied by the terms *fair, equitable,* and *feasible,* it is helpful to refer to some of the published statements of the SEC in regard to those reorganization proceedings in which it has participated. In Chapter 24, on government regulation, mention was made of the fact that although the role of the SEC is advisory only, the Commission has performed its functions with considerable vigor and made the most of its opportunities in seeking the adoption of reorganization principles it considered proper.

On the question of fairness the Commission has expressed its views from time to time. The objective of fair and equitable treatment of investors is obviously at the heart of the whole program of the SEC activities, so that the extension of this interest to include bankruptcy is a natural one. On this point the stand of the SEC is clear, as reflected in the following statement:

> Basic to the Commission's approach to questions involving the fairness of reorganization plans under Chapter X is the fixed principle, firmly established by Supreme Court decisions, that full recognition must be accorded to claims in the order of their legal and contractual priority either in cash or in the equitable equivalent of new securities and that junior claimants may participate only to the extent that the debtor's properties have value after the satisfaction of prior claims or to the extent that they make a fresh contribution necessary to the reorganization of the debtor.[9]

This is the rule known as the rule of *absolute priority.* It will be noted, however, that a question of judgment comes in through the use of the term *value.*[10] The reader is already well aware of the different approaches which may be taken in arriving at the valuation of a business, and of the absence of universal standards. The position taken by the SEC on this point is again quite clear: "Concomitant to this rule [the rule of absolute priority], it is clear that a sound valuation of the debtor is essential to provide a basis for judging the fairness as well as the feasibility of proposed plans of reorganization. The Commission has continued to urge that the proper method of valuation for reorganization purposes is primarily an appropriate capitalization of reasonably prospective earnings."[11] Thus, the Com-

---

[9] Securities and Exchange Commission, *Seventeenth Annual Report, 1951* (Washington, D.C.: U.S. Government Printing Office, 1952), p. 130.

[10] Some observers have commented that while the law appears to be rigid on the rule of absolute priority, its operation in effecting actual reorganizations does not always bear this out. The result in such cases may be more accurately described as the application of *relative priority*—where priority is still recognized but not to the point of excluding junior claims from receiving some consideration.

[11] Securities and Exchange Commission, *Eighteenth Annual Report* (1952), p. 156.

mission endorses a forward-looking concept of value, as opposed to the alternatives of book or liquidating value, but one which is at the same time highly subjective, particularly under these circumstances.

In the application of the rule of absolute priority the SEC has under certain circumstances sought to draw a distinction between shareholders who have a voice in management and those who have not: "In connection with the fairness of plans . . . the Commission has been concerned with situations where mismanagement or other misconduct on the part of a parent company or a controlling person required that the claim of such person be subordinated to the claims of the public investors or that participation be limited to cost. Such matters must be given full consideration since they form an integral part of the concept of the 'fair and equitable' plan."[12]

As a part of its concern with fair treatment of investors, the Commission makes a practice of reviewing the charter of the reorganized company. Its announced standards with regard to the provisions of such charters show a close similarity to those developed for public utilities under the Holding Company Act, as might be expected. This is seen in the following statement:

> Frequently, the plan of reorganization contains provisions relating to the terms to be incorporated in corporate charters, bylaws, trust indentures, and other instruments. . . . the Commission pays careful attention to these matters and endeavors to obtain the inclusion of protective features and safeguards for investors. Among numerous other matters, the Commission has urged and generally favored provisions for cumulative voting for directors, pre-emptive rights for stockholders, provisions making lists of stockholders available for inspection, the ratification by stockholders of the selection of auditors, and, in certain instances, a limitation upon compensation for management. . . . Unless justified by the special and unusual circumstances of the case, the Commission has opposed the voting trust because it disenfranchises stockholders. . . .[13]

The SEC's stand on the feasibility of reorganization plans has at least as important a bearing on corporate financial policy as does its stand on fairness. In view of the fact that bankruptcy and reorganization involve such a diverse group of businesses and industries, it is not to be expected that the Commission would come up with as precise a set of standards as those applied to the electric and gas utilities. At the same time, however, the thinking of the Commission is obviously influenced by the general concepts of appropriate financial

---

[12] Securities and Exchange Commission, *Fifteenth Annual Report* (1949), p. 144.
[13] *Ibid.*, pp. 146–47.

practice developed in and for its public utility work. This is to be seen in the following statement of considerations which the Commission takes into account when assessing the feasibility of a plan of reorganization:

> . . . In order to assure a reorganization which will not result in the debtor's return to Chapter X because of financial difficulties, the Commission gives a great deal of attention to the various factors affecting feasibility. Generally speaking these factors involve the adequacy of working capital, the relationship of funded debt and the capital structure as a whole to property values, the type and characteristics of the securities to be issued, the adequacy of corporate earning power to meet interest and dividend requirements, the possible need for capital expenditures, and the effect of the new capitalization upon the company's prospective credit.[14]

It is interesting to note that the interest of the Commission does not necessarily cease when it has stated its views on the plan of reorganization. In this regard the Commission has had the following to say: "The Commission's interest in the entire reorganization process includes not only the consummation of the plan and the winding up of the affairs of the trusteeship (which may occur many years after a plan has been consummated) but may also extend to the execution of the terms of the plan by the reorganized company."[15]

Liquidation

At the outset of this chapter, it was pointed out that the termination of a business either through sale as a business unit or through sale of its several assets separately is not necessarily an event forced on the owners by insolvency. In many cases, liquidation takes place with no loss to creditors or even to owners. Ideally, investment in a business which has failed to come up to expectations should be withdrawn long before profits have turned into losses and the assets have become so depleted that creditors, as well as owners, fail to recover their investment.

It is a fact, however, that it is not always easy to find a market for an unsuccessful business or its assets. It is also true that many businessmen, once committed to a course of action, will pursue it unswervingly, despite the odds, holding to the hope that next year will somehow be different. Such businessmen do not stop until they have either succeeded or literally run out of cash. With creditors pressing

---

[14] Securities and Exchange Commission, *Eighteenth Annual Report* (1952), p. 156.
[15] Securities and Exchange Commission, *Sixteenth Annual Report* (1950), p. 128.

for payment and no cash either to pay them off or to finance further sales, there is no alternative but to liquidate.

Liquidation may be *voluntary* or *involuntary*. That is to say, it may be initiated by the owners of the business, or it may be initiated by one or more creditors with valid and unsatisfied claims against the business. It may take the form of an informal settlement between owners and creditors in which the assets are sold and the proceeds distributed among the creditors. It may also take the form of a more formal assignment of assets to a third party, a trustee, who liquidates and distributes the proceeds. The assignee may be any person or organization willing to perform the function and acceptable to the creditors, for example, a lawyer or a credit bureau. The great advantage of these informal arrangements is their relative speed, efficiency, and economy.

It is important to note, however, that for informal liquidation to work, the debtor must be trusted by the creditors, and the creditors must be in general agreement among themselves. According to bankruptcy law, an assignment on behalf of creditors is an act of bankruptcy, and any dissatisfied creditor may institute formal court bankruptcy proceedings in spite of whatever informal arrangement may be in process. The owners of the business may also petition for court action. Although there are state bankruptcy laws as well, we shall confine our attention here to the Federal Bankruptcy Act of 1898, as amended, to illustrate what is involved in formal liquidation under court supervision.

Before we do so, however, it will give some perspective if we review a few statistics on the federal bankruptcy courts.[16] During the year ended June 30, 1959, a total of 100,672 bankruptcy cases, personal and business, were commenced in federal courts. Of this total, only 11,729 were business bankruptcies, and 10,436 of these were voluntary. In view of the number of business discontinuances and failures cited earlier, it can be seen that most liquidating businesses manage to avoid the federal courts in the process.

One good reason for doing so is seen in the court statistics of the drain on the bankrupt's assets resulting from the court proceedings and related expenses, over and above payments to creditors. This is well illustrated in Chart 28–2. Although the figures relate to all bankruptcies, business and nonbusiness, they have very real significance

---

[16] U.S. Administrative Office of the United States Courts, *Tables of Bankruptcy Statistics* (Washington, D.C.: U.S. Government Printing Office, June 30, 1959), p. 2.

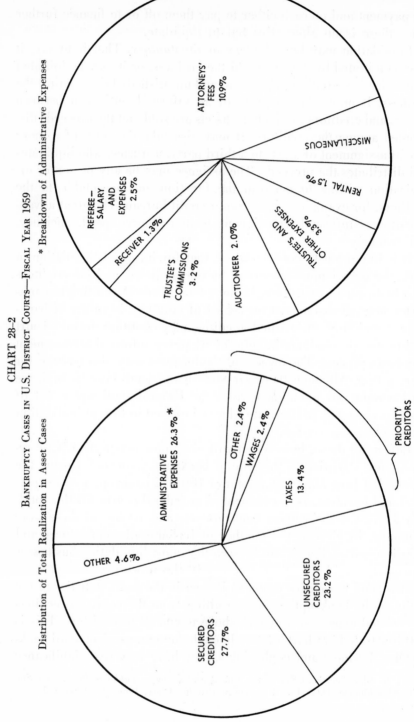

CHART 28-2

BANKRUPTCY CASES IN U.S. DISTRICT COURTS—FISCAL YEAR 1959

Distribution of Total Realization in Asset Cases

* Breakdown of Administrative Expenses

ADMINISTRATIVE EXPENSES 26.3% *

OTHER 2.4%

WAGES 2.4%

TAXES 13.4%

PRIORITY CREDITORS

UNSECURED CREDITORS 23.2%

SECURED CREDITORS 27.7%

OTHER 4.6%

ATTORNEYS' FEES 10.9%

MISCELLANEOUS

RENTAL 1.5%

TRUSTEE'S AND OTHER EXPENSES 3.3%

AUCTIONEER 2.0%

TRUSTEE'S COMMISSIONS 3.2%

RECEIVER 1.3%

REFEREE— SALARY AND EXPENSES 2.5%

SOURCE: U.S. Administrative Office of the United States Court, *Tables of Bankruptcy Statistics* (Washington, D.C.: U.S. Government Printing Office, June 30, 1959), Charts 3 and 4.

for business. From these diagrams, it can be seen that in the year 1959, 26.3 per cent of the total realization from assets in these cases went to pay the expenses of the proceedings themselves.

The procedures in bankruptcy center around the basic tasks, namely, the preservation of asset values pending liquidation, conversion into cash as rapidly as possible, and the distribution of cash through what are called liquidating dividends to creditors whose claims have been established, recognizing whatever priorities may exist. In this, the court is assisted by a *referee,* who oversees the administrative details, such as preparing lists of assets and creditors, declaring liquidating dividends, and so forth; and by a *trustee,* whose primary duty is to "collect and reduce to money the property of the estates." The general creditors will be represented by a creditors committee in any negotiations between them and the court or its representatives. Secured creditors will not be a part of this activity unless it is apparent that their claims will not be satisfied from the specific assets which have been pledged. To the extent that they do remain unsatisfied, they become general creditors for the balance.

The creditors of a bankrupt business normally fall into three general categories: (1) priority creditors, (2) secured creditors, and (3) unsecured or general creditors. The Bankruptcy Act states that certain creditors, called priority creditors, are entitled to prior payment in full before any liquidating dividends are distributed to other creditors. The principal priority claims, in their order of priority, are (Section 104):

1. The costs and expenses of preserving the estate
2. Wages earned within three months, up to $600 per claimant
3. Federal, state, and local taxes
4. Debts given priority by federal or state law—e.g., rent to a landlord

The general unsecured creditors will therefore rank after these priority claims as well as after secured creditors with respect to those assets which have been pledged. It can be readily seen why unsecured creditors may find themselves in the position of receiving only a fraction of their legitimate claims.

The adjudication of a person as bankrupt by the court constitutes an application for a discharge of his debts except in the case of a corporation, when an application for discharge may be filed within six months of adjudication. Provided the bankrupt has not been granted a previous discharge within a six-year period and has not engaged in fraudulent acts or acts contrary to the provisions of the Act, the court will grant the discharge. Section 35 (*a*) states: "A discharge in bankruptcy shall release a bankrupt from all of his provable debts, whether allowable in full or in part . . . ," with the following exceptions:

1. Taxes
2. Certain civil or criminal liabilities
3. Claims not scheduled in time for proof and allowance, through no fault of the creditor
4. Claims created through fraud, etc.
5. Wages
6. Moneys held on behalf of employees as a bond

Failure as a Management Problem

At the beginning of this chapter, we drew a distinction between the concept of failure as it is usually presented, with its attendant distress and loss to owners and creditors, and the termination of and/or withdrawal of investment from a business because it has failed to meet the original expectations of its owners. It is true, of course, that once a business has reached the point of insolvency, the initiative shifts from its owners to the creditors or the courts. When a business has reached this stage, management, if it has any role at all, becomes more of a participant than a dominant force directing events.

If, however, management is able to recognize the hard facts of an unfavorable business environment before it has exhausted its resources in a vain attempt to overcome this environment, then it is in a position to retain the initiative. This, of course, is easily said and unusually difficult to do. On the one hand, the handwriting on the wall may only be partially apparent, even to the unbiased observer. This uncertainty about the future becomes the basis for continued hope for recovery. On the other hand, businessmen, being human, become emotionally involved in the situation and personally identified with their particular business ventures so that, like the captain steeped in naval tradition, they would never consider abandoning a sinking ship. It is also true that there are situations where, however willing the management may be to abandon ship, it may be impossible to withdraw without heavy losses.

Nevertheless, there are many situations where a realistic look at the facts in the early stages of decline and a willingness to admit defeat will enable the owners to minimize their losses and shift what remains of their investment to a more promising opportunity. This also implies a full discharge of obligations to creditors and the preservation of the intangible but valuable asset of a good credit record.

PART IX

The Analysis of Long-Term Investment Opportunities

Chapter 29

Time Adjustment

WE HAVE already said that the problems of the financial manager center around the flows of funds in a firm, as they take place from time to time. Here, we want to turn our attention to the effect of the variable of time upon the values to be assigned to funds flows. Many decisions involve in some way a comparison of the usefulness of receiving or paying funds at one time rather than another, and we need a means of evaluating the effect of the time span involved. The procedure of *time adjustment* provides a consistent and accurate means for the needed evaluation.

One basic assumption must be made before application of the mathematical procedure, which involves nothing more than compound interest. We assume that a firm always can find some way to invest funds to produce some net gain, or *rate of return.* The rate may be very low, as when funds are temporarily placed in short-term treasury bills, or it may be as high as the gain from some new product greatly in demand. In fact, if a firm does not act to obtain some return from the use of its funds, we speak of the *opportunity cost,* which is the loss of revenue because an opportunity was not taken. Therefore, since there can always be earnings from the investment of funds, we can say as a general rule that whenever a business has a choice of the time when it will obtain certain funds, the rule should be "the sooner, the better." This point will be familiar to readers of earlier chapters.

The first step to an understanding of time adjustment is to relate the amounts involved to one another along a scale of time. The time is divided into periods (e.g., days, months, years), and a particular point in time is selected as the starting point from which the effect of compound interest on the funds will be regarded. This time is named the *focal date*. Periods later than this date are designated by the plus sign, periods earlier by the minus sign, and the focal date is designated by zero. To the mathematician, it is unimportant what actual time is chosen as the focal date. The financial analyst can choose any date, past or present, most convenient for his purposes. In fact, for many problems of financial planning, it is convenient to have the focal date in the future, usually the date at which a specific sum will be received or paid, or at which a certain periodic flow of funds will terminate.

It is necessary to calculate the changing values of flows of funds as they occur both before and after the focal date. We first turn to *compounding*, that is, the subsequent growth in the value of funds initially invested at the focal date, because this process is one with which most readers will be familiar from such well-advertised operations as savings accounts on which interest is compounded. We shall then turn to *discounting*, which looks in the other direction from the focal date along the time scale.

Compounding

There are three quantities necessary for the calculation:

1. *The Rate of Return.* In the following exposition, to show the effects of different rates, we shall use two that are well within the range of business experience.
2. *The Amount of Funds in Question.* It is convenient to use the sum of $1.00 to develop the formulas, since if one knows how the values of this sum are affected by time, one can compute the values of any other sum by simple multiplication.
3. *The Length of Time from the Focal Date.* This may be measured in days, weeks, etc., so that for the sake of generality, one refers to the *period* rather than to some specific unit of time. One warning is necessary here. The rate of return used must be stated consistently with the actual length of the time period. Thus, 6 per cent per year becomes 0.5 per cent per month, and so on.

The growing amount that will be found at later times from an investment of $1.00 at the focal date is referred to as the *compound amount* (of a single sum). Interest is computed on the original sum and then added to the original sum at the end of the first period. The new and larger principal is then the base for the interest calculation in the second period, and so on. Jumping over the detailed mathematics, we can turn to any set of tables for business computations, among which we shall find values for the compound amount of a single sum invested at a given time. See Table 29–1 for a portion of such a table.

TABLE 29–1
COMPOUND AMOUNT OF $1.00

Periods	Rate 4%	Rate 10%
0.................	1.000	1.000
+1.................	1.040	1.100
+2.................	1.082	1.210
+3.................	1.125	1.331
+4.................	1.170	1.464
+5.................	1.217	1.611

Discounting

The process of compounding discloses how the value of an investment made at the focal date grows in later time. We now turn to *discounting*, a process which looks at times preceding the focal date and answers the question: How much must be invested before the focal date to produce a desired sum at the time of the focal date?

The answers to such questions are determined by using the reciprocals of the values in the table of compound amounts, for the reasons exemplified in the following instance. Take 4 periods and 4 per cent. Table 29–1 shows that if $1.00 is compounded for this time and rate, it will increase to $1.17. To have only $1.00 at the end of four periods of compounding, we obviously need to invest less than $1.00. The calculation is :

$$\frac{1.000}{1.170} = \frac{x}{1.000}$$
$$x = 0.855$$

present value

The number so produced is known as the *present value* (at the selected time and rate) which will produce $1.00 at the focal date. The term *discounted value* is also used, although less frequently.

Since present values are often used in financial calculations, a table of present values is provided in this book (Table A, at page 930). For convenience, we reproduce a portion of it in Table 29–2.

Having shown how to evaluate a sum both before the focal date (by discounting) and after the focal date (by compounding), we are in a position to picture the changing value of the sum of $1.00 at the time of the focal date over a time scale. This is presented graphically in Chart 29–1, where the figures from Tables 29–1 and 29–2 are used.

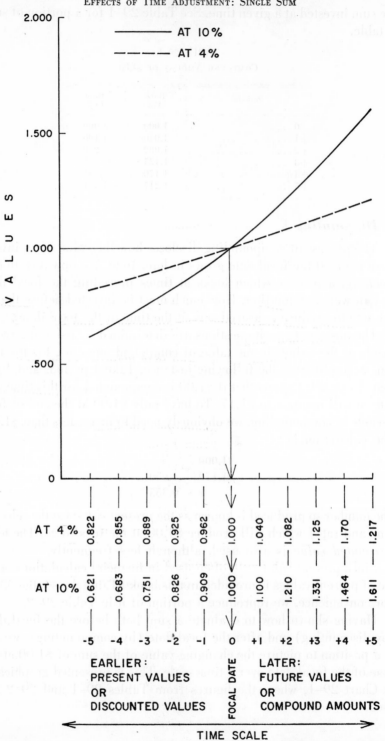

CHART 29–1

EFFECTS OF TIME ADJUSTMENT: SINGLE SUM

——————— AT 10%

– – – – – AT 4%

VALUES

2.000

1.500

1.000

.500

0

| AT 4% | 0.822 | 0.855 | 0.889 | 0.925 | 0.962 | 1.000 | 1.040 | 1.082 | 1.125 | 1.170 | 1.217 |

| AT 10% | 0.621 | 0.683 | 0.751 | 0.826 | 0.909 | 1.000 | 1.100 | 1.210 | 1.331 | 1.464 | 1.611 |

-5 -4 -3 -2 -1 0 +1 +2 +3 +4 +5

EARLIER:
PRESENT VALUES
OR
DISCOUNTED VALUES

FOCAL DATE

LATER:
FUTURE VALUES
OR
COMPOUND AMOUNTS

TIME SCALE

TABLE 29–2
PRESENT VALUE OF $1.00

Periods	Rate 4%	Rate 10%
0	1.000	1.000
−1	0.962	0.909
−2	0.925	0.826
−3	0.889	0.751
−4	0.855	0.683
−5	0.822	0.621

The basic relationships to be observed are simple but very important:

1. The value of a sum invested at any time grows as time passes.
2. The necessary investment to produce a future sum decreases as the time to produce it is increased.
3. Both these effects are magnified as the rate of return increases.

Examples of Compounding and Discounting

We shall now present two simple examples of how problems of compounding and discounting arise in business, and briefly indicate the nature of their solution.

Example 1. A firm with a major debt maturity at the end of two years sets aside $500,000 for investment in tax-exempt bonds at 4 per cent to help meet the maturity. How much will be available from this source when the debt matures?

The problem is one of compounding. The focal date is the present, and the period is two years. From Table 29–1, we find 1.082 as the compound amount of $1.00 at 4 per cent. Multiplying by $500,000 gives us $541,000, which is the sum that will be on hand.

Example 2. A factor often given importance when a firm is deciding whether to own or lease land and buildings is the residual value of the property that the firm would own if it bought rather than leased. Suppose that a certain property, now costing $1 million, is expected to be worth $2 million after allowance for taxes on the capital gain at the end of 25 years. How much importance should this terminal value have on a decision now?

The problem is one of discounting. The concept of opportunity cost also enters. Let us assume that the firm averages 10 per cent return (after taxes) on assets invested in the business. One way to obtain $2 million at the end of 25 years is by holding the real estate. An alternative way would be to invest some funds now and use them at 10 per cent to produce $2 million. What present investment at 10 per cent will produce $2 million at a focal date 25 years hence? From Table A (page 930), we find that the present value of $1.00 at 10 per cent after 25 periods is 0.092. Multiplying by $2 million, we obtain $184,-000. Thus, the desired value can be obtained either by using $184,-000 in the business, allowing profits to compound, or by spending $1 million to buy the property. The possibility of error in overvaluing the expectation of remote capital gains is shown by this example. It is particularly serious when high rates of return are available from funds used otherwise in the business.

Finding the Rate of Return

There is another use to which tables of present values are often put in financial work. Given values at two dates, one is sometimes required to find the rate of return that will produce a desired change in value. Using the figures from Example 2 above, the problem can be stated as follows: At what rate of return will $1 million grow to $2 million in 25 years?

The focal date is the end of the 25-year period, when the present value table expects $1.00 to be paid. Converting the data from the actual case therefore requires division of the initial and terminal values by $2 million:

$$\frac{2,000,000}{2,000,000} = 1.000$$

and

$$\frac{1,000,000}{2,000,000} = 0.500.$$

The question has become: At what rate of discount will 0.50 become 1.00 at the end of 25 periods?

Looking at the table of present values at page 930 and going across the line for 25 periods, we find:

```
Periods........................25
Rate 2%........................0.610
Rate 4%........................0.375
```

By the process of interpolation,[1] we find the answer, which is 2.9 per cent (much lower—and therefore less desirable—than the use of funds to produce 10 per cent).

[1]
$$
\begin{array}{ll}
2\% = 0.610 & 2\% = 0.610 \\
4\% = 0.375 & x = 0.500 \\
\hline
2\% = 0.235 & \boxed{0.110}
\end{array}
\quad \frac{110}{235}\,(2\%) = x = 0.9\%
$$

Annuities

Our explanation of the effects of time on the value of funds has so far dealt only with single sums. That is, we have confined ourselves to watching the growth in value of a single investment, once it is made. We now turn to what is perhaps more frequently experienced in business, namely, the receipt or payment of a series of sums periodically over a stated number of time periods. Examples are rent and the flow of funds attached to a tax shield arising from depreciation.

There is much similarity between the mathematics already used and that which is necessary for *annuities,* as this type of periodic payment is termed by mathematicians. The focal date, however, takes on a new meaning, which the conventions of financial mathematics make even more complex. If one is looking into periods following the focal date, that date is the beginning of the first period of the annuity. In this case the applicable value at the focal date is zero, for the first payment of the annuity will take place only at the end of the first time period. If one is looking at times which are earlier than the focal date, however, the focal date is defined as the end of the last period, just after the moment of the final payment of the annuity. Again, the value is zero.

We shall introduce the annuity tables in the same order as before; that is, we first look ahead in time to consider the *compound amount* of an annuity, and then back to consider the *present value* of an annuity.

Compounding

Any annuity can be separated into a series of single payments and evaluated by the table of compound interest already described.

Suppose $1.00 is to be received at the end of each period, and that each $1.00 is to be invested at compound interest. How much will be the amount of the annuity a specified number of periods after the focal date? Let us take 4 per cent and five years. The answer can be built up from Table 29–1, of compound amount, as follows:

```
  $1.00 received at time +1 at 4% for 4 years becomes.............1.170
   1.00 received at time +2 at 4% for 3 years becomes.............1.125
   1.00 received at time +3 at 4% for 2 years becomes............1.082
   1.00 received at time +4 at 4% for 1 year becomes.............1.040
   1.00 received at time +5 at 4% for 0 year becomes.............1.000
      Total Value, Amount of Annuity.......................5.417
```

From this example, we can see that a table of the desired values for annuities can be obtained by accumulating values from compound interest tables. See Table 29–3 for a brief portion of such a table.

TABLE 29–3
AMOUNT OF ANNUITY OF $1.00 PER PERIOD

Periods	Rate 4%	Rate 10%
0....................	0	0
+1....................	1.000	1.000
+2....................	2.040	2.100
+3....................	3.122	3.310
+4....................	4.246	4.641
+5....................	5.416*	6.105

* The difference between this figure and 5.417, the amount of annuity given above, is due to rounding.

The question answered by such a table is: How much will the periodic receipt of $1.00 grow if all payments are held at compound interest at a specified rate and for a specified number of periods? In business terms, we are dealing with an annuity that is to be received.

Discounting

We now look at an annuity that is being paid out by the business, asking the question: How much must be invested in period $-n$ at the specified rate to permit the payment of an annuity of $1.00 per period, leaving nothing at the focal date? As before, this can be broken down into separate payments, which can be evaluated from the table of the present value of single sums. Let us take 4 per cent and five years once more. Table 29–2 can be used.

> At the beginning of period −5:
> it takes 0.822 to produce $1.00 in 5 years,
> it takes 0.855 to produce $1.00 in 4 years,
> it takes 0.889 to produce $1.00 in 3 years,
> it takes 0.925 to produce $1.00 in 2 years,
> it takes 0.962 to produce $1.00 in 1 year.
> Total 4.453, Value of Annuity at Period −5

This example shows how the desired present values of annuities can be obtained by accumulating values from the table of the present values of a single sum. Such a table has been included in this book as Table B at page 931; but for convenience, we reproduce a portion in Table 29–4.

TABLE 29-4

PRESENT VALUE OF $1.00 RECEIVED PERIODICALLY

FOR *n* PERIODS

Periods	Rate 4%	Rate 10%
0...................	0	0
−1...................	0.962	0.909
−2...................	1.886	1.736
−3...................	2.775	2.487
−4...................	3.630	3.170
−5...................	4.452*	3.791

* The difference between this figure and 4.453, the value
of the annuity given above, is due to rounding.

When we were dealing with the changing values of a single sum over time, we ended our explanation with a diagram. A similar one, Chart 29–2, can be presented for annuities, although the situation is more complex. The reader will note, in studying the charted annuities, that the values get larger as one proceeds in either direction from the focal date. This is because of the periodic payments of $1.00 that are involved. The reader will also note here, as in the more simple case, that changing the rate of return has considerable influence on the values, especially as time becomes more remote. In each instance the higher the rate, the greater the advantage to the user of the funds. That is, if 10 per cent is applied, an annuity will cost less, or produce more, than if a lower rate were applied.\

Before we leave the subject of the present values of annuities, we shall describe in another way the operation of the investment of $4.452 at 4 per cent to permit paying $1.00 per year for five years. This will not add to the theoretical structure, but it will picture the process in a way that is more useful in financial thinking.

At the beginning of year −5, invest $4.452.
At the end of year −5, take interest of $0.178, and withdraw $0.822.
At the beginning of year −4, remainder invested becomes $3.630.
At the end of year −4, take interest of $0.145, and withdraw $0.855.
At the beginning of year −3, remainder invested becomes $2.775.
At the end of year −3, take interest of $0.111, and withdraw $0.889.
At the beginning of year −2, remainder invested becomes $1.886.
At the end of year −2, take interest of $0.075, and withdraw $0.925.
At the beginning of year −1, remainder invested becomes $0.961.
At the end of year −1, take interest of $0.038, and withdraw $0.962.
There is a difference between $0.962 and $0.961, because of the use of abbreviated tables. Ignoring this, we can see that the annuity ends with the final payment of $1.00.

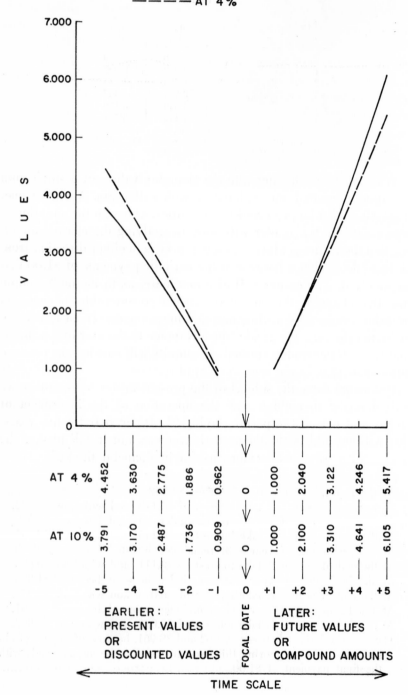

CHART 29-2
EFFECTS OF TIME ADJUSTMENT: ANNUITY

———— AT 10%

– – – – AT 4%

From this table, it can be seen that a company can receive $1.00 a year for five years with an initial investment of $4.452, if the interest rate is 4 per cent. It can also be seen, however, that the initial investment of capital is consumed in the process. It is of great importance to recognize that the table does *not* say that if the rate of return is 4 per cent, the annuity will go on without reducing principal. If the principal is to be preserved, its withdrawals must not be consumed, but invested elsewhere. Also, if 4 per cent is to continue to be obtained from the use of funds, the new investment opportunities must yield this rate.

Examples Using Annuities

As before, we conclude our explanation of the derivation of tables of compound amount and present value for annuities with examples taken from business situations.

Example 1. A firm which is considering setting up a pension fund determines that it can afford to set aside for this purpose $100,000 a year for 10 years. It is advised that a trustee can earn 4 per cent (tax exempt) with such moneys. How much will have been accumulated after 10 years?

The problem is to evaluate an annuity of $100,000 whose focal date is the present, whose period is 10 years, and whose rate is 4 per cent. Tables of compound amount (not available in this book) give a factor of 12.006 under these conditions. Multiplying by $100,000 gives the desired answer, which is $1,200,600.

Example 2. Analysis of a certain investment project indicates that it will produce $50,000 a year, before taxes, for 10 years. How much could the company justify investing in this project if other investments are available at 4 per cent? At 10 per cent?

The problem is the evaluation as of now of an annuity whose focal date is 10 years from the present. Using Table B at page 931, we find the present value factor for 10 periods to be 8.111 for 4 per cent, and 6.145 for 10 per cent. Multiplying by $50,000, we find $405,550 for 4 per cent and $307,250 for 10 per cent. These are the sums that could be invested at the specified rates to produce $50,000 a year for 10 years.

Example 3. Taking the figures as developed in Example 2, assume that the firm finds that $350,000 is required as an investment to establish the project. Since this number is more than the present value at 10 per cent, the firm should not undertake the project if it has other opportunities on which 10 per cent can be earned. The firm should, however, consider the project an excellent one if the alternative opportunities are offering 4 per cent return.

Finding the Rate of Return

One last step in the use of present value tables will be illustrated here. Given the periodic amount of an annuity and the original investment, what is the rate of return? Using the figures from Example 3, above, what rate of return will produce a 10-year annuity of $50,-000 from the investment of $350,000?

The focal date is the end of the 10-year period, when the last payment will be received. The present value table is based on annuities of $1.00 per period, so the figures in the actual case must be converted by dividing through by $50,000:

$$\frac{50,000}{50,000} = 1.000$$

and

$$\frac{350,000}{50,000} = 7.000.$$

Looking at the table of present values of an annuity at page 931, and going across the line for 10 periods, we find:

```
Periods........................10
Rate 6%......................7.360
Rate 8%......................6.710
```

By interpolation, the answer can be computed. It is 7.1 per cent.

Amortization of Loans

With increasing frequency in business practice, the terms of payment of long-term loans are designed so that the lender makes a *level payment* of the same sum each time, the sum being large enough to cover the interest due and leave a balance to be applied to the reduction of the principal. Most of each earlier payment is consumed by interest, while the greater part of each later payment goes to reduce the remaining principal. Our example at page 607 can be taken as an instance of the process, where the debt was $4.452 and the level payment was $1.00.

It is convenient to have a table for the principal of the debt expressed as $1.00, so that the needed periodic payments for specified periods and rates can be determined more easily from the amount of the loan. Such tables are available. The values are the reciprocals of those in the table of the present value of an annuity, and the desired answers can be determined from Table B according to the following example:

A corporation borrows $5,000,000 for 20 years at 6 per cent. What is the level of payment that will pay principal and interest on an annual basis?

From Table B, we find the present value of an annuity of $1.00 for 20 years at 6 per cent to be 11.470. Dividing $5 million by 11.470, we obtain $435,920, the desired amount.

Chapter 30

The Appraisal of Capital Investment Opportunities

Introduction

As has been indicated, part of the total responsibility of management in handling flows of funds in a firm is to see to it that acquisitions are made when they are needed to further the goals of the firm. Decisions for capital investment are made contemporaneously with other financial decisions, such as the dividends to be paid, the amounts of working capital to carry, and so on. These have been the subject of much discussion elsewhere in the book. In this chapter, we shall discuss how management determines the amount of funds it should use in investment projects. This area is still in development; the "best" theories are still subject to further refinement. Nevertheless, much that is useful has already been agreed on and can be presented here.

More important than purely financial considerations, of course, is the flow of ideas and suggestions from which projects may be developed. They will come from time to time from all levels of responsibility in an organization if it is sensitive to opportunities—from workers and foremen for projects that increase productivity, from plant engineers and others in contact with technical developments inside and outside the firm, from the sales department, from top management. The first task of a management is to stimulate such a flow of ideas and to prevent their being cut off from consideration by rigid rules or by unimaginative persons at intermediate levels in the organization. To handle such a flow of ideas, at least two administrative procedures are necessary. There must be rules for preliminary screening of projects, to select those deserving of further study. Then, as promising ideas are accumulated, there must be a more precise scheme for the study of individual projects, including some way of ranking them in the order of their desirability.

Any project must be studied from many points of view, any one of which might be the most important in a particular case. The availability of personnel, the need for specialized know-how, the extent of the market, the possible reactions of competitors are only a few of the many factors to be studied. We are well aware of their diversity and importance. On the other hand, we feel that the question of the financial profitability of a project is always important, and we propose to show how this profitability can be estimated, for use with the other criteria that need also to be considered.

In contrast to our feeling that is is important to assign quantities to the elements of every investment project, we must admit that various field studies of actual business decision making show that a majority of managements do not make their selections with so much care. In particular, we can refer to the field survey made by one of the authors of this book in 1958, in which it was found that managements tend to divide proposals into two groups. The first group includes all projects which will continue the company in its established business, increase its efficiency, and help it to hold its accepted "market share." "Normal growth" is included in this group. Such projects as new facilities for warehousing, cost-reducing equipment, and "normal" increases in capacity would come into this group. The second group contains projects outside the area that has become the accepted one for the particular management.

The finding of the field research is that projects in the first group are given far less searching analysis of a financial (return on investment) nature than are projects in the second group. That is, a project believed to be in the natural course of development is often undertaken without any test of whether its profitability is as great as that of a project in a less familiar area. There are many reasons for this expression of preference on the part of management; yet, there is a growing group of observers and managers who feel that *all* projects should be studied for their likely financial return, as well as other matters. In what we shall say below, we are trying to increase the size of this group.

Criteria for the Selection of Investment Proposals

The logical model on which the procedures we shall describe are based is this: A firm will have a financial criterion, or *cutoff point,* which establishes a standard of desirability that projects must meet.

There is diversity of practice in the choice of such a criterion, with the following being most frequently encountered: (1) a total-sum-of-money standard; (2) a liquidity standard, saying that the investment in a project must be returned in liquid form within a specified time period, often referred to as the payback period; (3) a rate-of-return standard, related to the present earning power of the assets used in the firm or some other level deemed desirable; (4) a cost-of-capital standard, related to the existing securities of the company or some other measure of financial cost.

After the firm has chosen its criterion, each project must be analyzed by a procedure which will measure the desirability of the project according to the selected criterion, and also its desirability in comparison with competing projects. In this way, projects can be ranked according to their desirability from the financial point of view; and the ultimate *capital budget,* or listing of the expenditures for approved projects, can be drawn up with this ranking available for consideration. The methods of analysis to be described and the criteria just mentioned are related as follows:

Cut-off Criterion	Calculation Required
1. Total sum of money	1. The amounts of funds required
2. Liquidity	2. The "payback"
3. Rate of return on assets, etc.	3. The return on the investment in
4. Cost of capital	the project, measured by:
	a) Approximate method
	b) Time-adjusted method:
	1. Index of desirability, or
	2. Internal rate of return

To have the basic information for each project in order to compute the needed number to compare with any of the cutoff points in use, four quantities must be estimated. We shall first discuss them in general terms and then present an example. They are (1) the amount of the capital investment required, (2) the change which is anticipated in the funds flows of the firm as the result of the project, (3) the times at which funds can be expected to flow in or out, and (4) the anticipated length of life.

The Amount of Investment Required

It is important to note that in arriving at the figure for investment outlay, business practice differs somewhat. For present purposes the best approach includes all movements of funds, whether in or out, caused by the project. Not only the cash outlays associated with the initial price but also such items as transportation costs and installation costs must be included. Also (although frequently forgotten), there must be a determination of the addition to permanent working capital necessary to support the output of the new assets at the desired capacity. This may include, for example, the added inventory related to a machine and the added accounts receivable related to the estimated increase in sales. Such sums usually are not needed before the machine is ready for operation.

If, say, a new machine has been intended as a replacement for an existing machine still in productive employment, certain variations in the calculation would occur. On the outlay side, it would be necessary to add change-over costs and to subtract any scrap value in the old machine. There would be no substantial change in working capital needs unless there were differences in capacity. Here again, we need a figure for the net addition to invested funds, which will certainly be different from the figure that the accountant will put on the books as the capital value of the new fixed asset.

After determination of the net outflow of funds required to establish the project, an estimate should be made of the net inflow of funds which may be expected from salvage operations at the time the project is terminated. Nondepreciable assets, such as items of working capital, should preserve their value during the project, and one can set down a salvage value equal to the initial investment. For depreciable assets the salvage value will normally be much less than cost; and since whatever is received will be an inflow at the end of the project, the present value will be low. In fact, scrap values are usually so uncertain and so small in terms of present value that it is often better to ignore them when studying a project. In only a small number of cases, especially those where great appreciation in price can be expected (as might in rare instances be true of strategically located real estate), will salvage values of depreciable assets play a part of any importance when the initial decision is being made.

The Change in the Income of the Firm

The second quantity, at once the most important and the most difficult to estimate, is the result of the operations of the project, expressed in inflows and outflows of funds by periods during the life of the project. The desired quantity is not an accounting figure. It is the difference between what the total funds received by the business would be if the project is not adopted and what the firm is expected to receive if the project is adopted. Costs of financing, such as interest or dividends, are excluded because we shall treat the means of financing as separate from the project itself. In this way the benefit of the project ex financing can be compared with the cost of the financing, whenever means of financing are to be considered.

Our definition of the measure of funds to be provided has included in the ordinary list of projects for study those which are undertaken by the firm in order to preserve its existing earning power. Take, for example, a necessary replacement for a machine whose continued use would make operations in its production line inefficient or impossible. The replacement may be analyzed by a figure which shows the difference between the loss that could be incurred (through breakdowns, etc.) by continuing to use the old machine and the gain (perhaps no more than before) that will be experienced if the machine is replaced.

The Times at Which the Benefits Are to Be Received and the Costs Are to Be Paid Out

Many investment projects cannot be expected to produce funds at an even rate over the length of life which it is reasonable to assume for their use. In early years a project is often slow in coming into profitability if only because a growing market has been anticipated and the demand has yet to be experienced. There is also in the early part of a project's life a period of the collection of know-how, during which income is often reduced for some time. Later, toward the close of its life, a project can be expected to produce somewhat less than it did at the beginning, because of increased maintenance if nothing else.

The use of the more rapid depreciation methods now available under the tax laws also creates inequalities in the after-tax funds flows in different years. Such possibilities of irregular amounts of flows increase the work of evaluating the amounts anticipated at various periods of time.

Similarly, the expenditures necessary to create the project are not always made at a single time or in equal amounts. Construction costs, for example, are usually paid out as the work is completed, and working capital to support the project is not needed until operations begin. Some payments, such as major overhauls, may occur well along in the life of the project.

Although reasonable amounts of effort should be made to estimate inflows and outflows accurately for specific time periods, it is often sufficient (where approximating methods are to be used) to treat all capital expenditures as if made at the start of the project, and to use an average figure for the inflows. It is, however, very desirable to be able to describe irregularities and their timing at least in general terms as a supplement to the averages.

The Anticipated Length of Life

The fourth quantity to be estimated is the total time the project is expected to be productive. Although it is to be expected that the working capital portion of a proposed investment project can be considered to be a permanent investment, not depreciating in value as time goes by, the major portion of most investment projects is to be expended for productive equipment. All such equipment becomes valueless over time. By the term *economic life,* we refer to the period over which the equipment (or other investment) remains economically superior to alternative equipment that might be purchased for the same purpose —the period before it becomes obsolete. It is often difficult to estimate this time; yet, the effort must always be made, since the period of time within which a project must justify itself is extremely critical. An estimate based on the experience of persons who have spent considerable time in the business is often more useful than some technical estimate by either an engineer or a tax accountant.

Thus, there is uncertainty both in estimating income in years far removed from the time of making the forecast and in estimating the length of the economic life of productive assets. These combined uncertainties lead many firms to select for application as a general rule some term of years within which a project must justify itself—leaving possible gains in later years to be hoped for but not relied upon. Some analysts refer to this terminal date as a *horizon*—a happy choice of terms, since we are dealing with operations requiring foresight.

Here again, experience is usually the ultimate guide. One can merely ask that those who have experience use it as carefully as possible. Too many managements use horizon times which are arbitrarily shorter than experience would seem to justify, as shown by the continued desirability of many projects years after the horizon has been passed. However, we can expect to find a horizon time often used in practice, and to find it essentially an arbitrary figure.

Presentation of Funds Flows over Time

We now proceed to an example which can give more precise meaning to the general statements just made. The first project we shall describe is a small addition to factory equipment to permit increased production of a product in high demand. The cost of the machinery,

installed, is $92,650. Its scrap value at the end of its usefulness is esti-
mated to be $15,000. It is estimated that net working capital must be
increased by $12,000 to support the increase in sales. The cost of the
machine must be paid in equal instalments, one half during the year
of installation, the other half during the first year of operations. The
needed working capital can be provided over three years as sales increase.

On a funds basis the annual gain from operations is estimated to
be $14,400 in the first year, $18,000 in the second, and $24,000 there-
after. The most advantageous tax life of the project is seven years, and
the economic life is ten years.

From the foregoing information the accompanying table of funds
flows has been derived (Table 30–1). The form has been set up to
show explicitly the computation of the tax shield from depreciation
(which is computed on the sum-of-digits basis without regard for salvage). That is, income tax is first computed as if no depreciation were
to be taken, and the tax shield is separately computed and used to reduce the effect of the "gross income tax." The exact form to be used
is, of course, not mandatory; it will depend on the nature of the project and the taste of the analyst. Table 30–1 also shows the net income
expected from the project according to the rules of accountancy.

Data from a table such as the one we present can be used to calculate for each particular project a figure which measures the desirability of the project against the criterion which the firm has decided
to use. We shall proceed to show how this can be done for each of
the four types of criteria mentioned above.

Application of Criteria

1. Total Sum. The first criterion mentioned was a total sum of
money, set by management as the limit to expenditure in a certain
time period. A number of reasons can be cited to explain why such a
limit may be set. Field studies indicate that a great many managements have decided never to undertake outside financing, which
means that retained earnings set a limit to new investments. Still other
firms (erroneously, in our opinion) use the annual charge for depreciation as their limit, especially in allocating funds among departments or sections of the business. Other firms seem to set amounts for
capital investments as an extension of recent trends in the company's
experience, perhaps with some adjustment for the state of depression
or recovery.

Whenever there is a total limit set as a sum of money, there will

TABLE 30-1

Presentation of Funds Flows
Capital Investment Project

	Sign*	Year of Construction −1	Years of Operation										Total All Years	Average Year
			+1	2	3	4	5	6	7	8	9	10		
Capital Investment:														
Depreciable..........	− −	$46,325											$ 92,650	
Nondepreciable.......	−	4,000		$ 4,000	4,000								12,000	
Subtotal............	−	$50,325		$ 4,000	$ 4,000								$104,650	
Salvage:														
Depreciable..........	+ +											$15,000	$ 15,000	
Nondepreciable.......												12,000	12,000	
	+											$27,000	$ 27,000	
Operations:														
Funds inflows, net† ...	+		$ 14,400	$ 18,000	$ 24,000	$ 24,000	$24,000	$24,000	$24,000	$24,000	$24,000	$24,000	$224,400	
Gross income tax, 52% ..	−		7,488	9,360	12,480	12,480	12,480	12,480	12,480	12,480	12,480	12,480	116,688	
Depreciation‡	0		(23,162)	(19,853)	(16,545)	(13,236)	(9,927)	(6,618)	(3,309)				(92,650)	$(9,265)
Tax shield, 52%	+		12,044	10,324	8,603	6,883	5,162	3,441	1,721				48,178	4,818
Total.............			$ 18,956	$ 18,964	$ 20,123	$ 18,403	$16,682	$14,961	$13,241	$11,520	$11,520	$11,520	$155,890	$15,589
Accounting net income§ ..	0												(63,240)	(6,324)

* Plus sign indicates funds to be received; minus sign indicates funds to be paid out; zero with figures in parentheses indicates a quantity not representing a flow of funds.
† Exclusive of financing costs.
‡ All nonfunds expenses to be entered here. Depreciation computed on sum-of-digits basis without regard for salvage.
§ Annual details omitted, as they depend on method of depreciation selected for reporting purposes.

still remain the problem of selecting projects in the order of their desirability; in fact, the problem may become very acute. There will be a tendency to discard projects of a novel character. Even so, the basic problem of ranking can be solved only in financial terms by the use of one or another of the remaining criteria, to which we now turn.

2. *The Payback Period.* As usually defined, the payback period is the period within which the project is expected to produce enough funds to restore the total depreciable cost associated with it, if it earns no taxable income and all the funds are devoted to retirement. In other words, this criterion poses the question: "How soon can we get back our investment in depreciable assets if all the funds inflow of the project is devoted to this purpose and tax liabilities are ignored?" The period is usually computed without allowance for any costs required by financing.

Looking at Table 30–1 giving our example, we see that the total cash outflow for depreciable assets is $92,650. Offsetting this is the funds inflow, which will amount to $80,400 in four years, with $24,000 expected in the fifth year. Thus, the *payback* of this project is about 4½ years, as it is usually calculated.

Some firms use a payback criterion exclusively in selecting investment projects. The justification might be expressed in these words: "The future is too uncertain. Let's confine ourselves to short periods. Once we have our money back, all further gains are gravy."

Let us look at the payback figure a little more closely. We see that if the project operates as planned for 4½ years, and then suddenly becomes worthless, the firm will have its investment back. Payback ratios do not tell us how the funds might actually be regained if, say, depreciation were charged as planned and taxable income were reported from the beginning. This is in itself a weakness of the criterion. In our example, we can see that our best estimate, taking all factors into account, is that five years would elapse before funds inflows exceed $92,650. We can refer to such a calculation as a "realistic" payback.

The greatest weakness of the payback period as an investment criterion is that it does not recognize the duration of anticipated earning power. As applied to the figures in our example, the criterion would give the same result regardless of the duration of earnings beyond five years. We think this omission is so great that payback cannot be used as a sole criterion for investment analysis.

The matter of prompt return of invested funds is, however, not one that can be ignored completely, for the funds so received can be invested elsewhere to produce new earnings while the original project continues to operate. We can see the value of realistic payback (computed from the best estimates of funds flows including all factors) as a supplement to the more important criteria to which we now turn.

3. Rate of Return on the Investment (Approximate Method). The last two of the four criteria we named above are expressed as desired rates of return. The method of computation used on the figures for the project must therefore produce a rate for comparison. The approximate method gives an *average-rate-of-return* figure, which is sufficient for many projects but is not suitable where there is a close competitor in some other project or where the rate is close to the cutoff point. In such cases the more accurate method, to be described in the last section of this chapter, is indicated.

The approximate method assumes that it is not important when the income of the project will be received, that is, that a dollar of inflow or outflow in any year is worth as much as in any other year. On this assumption the rate of return for our example is:

$$\frac{\text{Average Net Income}}{\text{Average Investment}} = \frac{6{,}324}{12{,}000 + 15{,}000 + \frac{1}{2}(92{,}650 - 15{,}000)} =$$
$$9.6\% \text{ after taxes}$$

The reader should note that the investment in the amount of depreciable assets not salvaged is divided in half. This is because the value of this investment declines to zero during the ten-year period, so that on an average basis, only half the investment is used.[1]

A figure of this nature can be used to rank this project in the order of its desirability when compared with other projects. In this connection, we can see the usefulness of a realistic payback calculation as a supplementary criterion. If two projects, one of which is our example, promise a return of approximately 10 per cent after taxes, the preference should usually be given to the one which will more quickly return funds for other purposes. The weight to be given to this secondary consideration will depend upon the rate of profits the management believes can be earned in the future, but it is almost always in favor of the project promising more rapid liquidation.

The rate of return promised by the project is also used for compari-

---

[1] In our first edition, we adopted the view of Professor Gordon that it would be better to put the gross investment in the denominator. We now prefer to average the depreciable assets, as we find that this formula gives better results with the majority of actual instances. For the argument the other way, see M. J. Gordon, "The Payoff Period and the Rate of Profit," *Journal of Business,* October, 1955, pp. 253–60 (Chicago: University of Chicago Press).

son with the rate of return chosen by the firm for its cutoff point. For instance, if this firm insists that projects return 15 per cent after taxes because the investments now in use give this return, our project will fail to meet the test. If, on the other hand, the firm has decided to maximize its gains, and the cost of capital is 9 per cent, the project is (by a small margin) desirable for adoption.

Choice of Cutoff Rate

The choice of the rate which is to be the cutoff point is obviously important. A rate which reflects the historical level of profitability of the business is clearly the most popular among practicing managers. Where new projects are tested according to existing levels, there is obviously a tendency for future profit levels, as measured, to stabilize or grow. Such a condition is satisfying to many managers and investors. Such ratios are used as profits to total assets at net book value, profits to total assets at gross book value, profits to total assets adjusted to replacement levels, profits to net assets. Net assets may be found by deducting from total assets the current liabilities and (usually) any intangible assets. Net assets, thus defined, are equivalent to the capitalization of the company. This ratio of profits to net assets is sometimes referred to as *profits on capitalization* or *return on invested capital*. It is the ratio we prefer in this group.

On the other hand, most economists and a growing number of managers realize that such a standard as the retention of past averages will not serve to maximize gains. A "marginal" analysis, as performed at many points in economic theory, will show that projects should be accepted as long as they promise a rate of return that will exceed the cost of financing. The needed figure for "cost of capital" is estimated in a number of ways, as discussed briefly below.

The difference may be illustrated as follows. Assume a company with a capitalization of $1 million and profits of $120,000 (12 per cent) after taxes. The cost of capital for the company is 8 per cent, also after taxes. This capitalization and profit can be expected to continue. Projects for expansion have been analyzed, with rates of return as follows:

Project	Capital Amount	Profit after Taxes	Rate of Return
A........................	$25,000	$3,750	15%
B........................	25,000	3,250	13
C........................	25,000	2,500	10
D........................	25,000	2,250	9

The results of using a 12 per cent and an 8 per cent cutoff point are as follows:

	12% Cutoff	8% Cutoff
New investment......................	$50,000	$100,000
Profit from new investment.............	$ 7,000	$ 11,750
Cost of raising new funds..............	4,000	8,000
New profit allocable to old capitalization...	$ 3,000	$ 3,750
Return on total investment.............	12.100%	11.977%
Return on old capitalization...........	12.300%	12.375%

This example shows that the profits for the existing owners of the firm will be maximized by accepting all projects with returns above the cost of new capital. One very important condition exists, which is that the cost of capital has been properly estimated with consideration of the effect of increasing investments upon the cost itself. If so, the new investor is getting what he wants, and the management is maximizing the results from the owner's point of view within the conditions thus established.

4. *Cost of Capital.* In Chapter 21, we presented ways of computing the cost of capital for the various elements of a company's capitalization. It is now necessary to suggest a way of combining these costs into a single figure, which can be used as the "cost of capital" for the analysis described above. Before we proceed with our analysis, however, our readers should be made aware of the fact that a precise statement of the combined cost of the various forms of capital is a task of unusual complexity and one which continues to occupy the attention of experienced financial theorists and practitioners. Many aspects are still the subject of debate in financial journals, and the last word has yet to be written. We present here an approach to this subject which we consider to satisfy current theory and to be meaningful in practice.

Our problem, then, is to identify the cost of capital and provide a means of measurement which can be compared with the expected rate of return on new investment opportunities. Since we have expressed the latter as an annual percentage after taxes, but before the costs of financing, the cost of capital should be expressed on an after-tax basis.

At first glance a table of the supply of our funds (for this is a typical supply-demand analysis) would be made up by listing each possible security issue in order of increasing costs. Bonds of various types would normally be the least expensive on such a list, preferred stocks would usually follow, and common stock would be expected to be the most costly type of new issue. Funds generated internally by the operations of the firm would be included also, with their cost measured in some way by comparison with the alternative gain of using these funds outside the business.

Such a table would tend to lead to the maximum use of low-cost instruments, such as bonds, a practice which, if not restrained, could ultimately be very damaging to the interests of the owners because of the degree of risk that such financing would create. Any scheme of ranking capital costs must deal with this problem. We propose to do so by using a weighted average of the costs of individual parts of the capitalization, a procedure which will permit maximization of the value of the equity interest in the long run.

For most companies, any particular financing should be regarded as a part of a continuing program. If we assume for the moment that a business has a satisfactory balance among its securities, then new debt cannot be contemplated at a certain time without the definite expectation that new equity will be provided later (from reinvested earnings and otherwise) in order to restore and preserve the balance in the capital structure. From the long-range point of view, relatively low-cost debt goes hand in hand with high-cost equity capital in the proportions set by business experience and the standards of investors. If the proportions for a certain firm were to be altered significantly, both the cost of debt and the cost of equity would change.

A failure to recognize this principle may lead to mistakes in investment planning, as in the following illustration. Suppose a management considers that the ideal proportion of debt for its firm is at or near 30 per cent of total permanent capital and that the current securities market is unusually receptive to a new bond issue. If the projects for expansion are related solely to the cost of the bond issue used to finance them, it might appear that any investment which earns over, say, 2½ per cent after taxes would result in a net gain in earnings per share and therefore would be financially acceptable to the shareholders. The new bond issue, however, may push total debt up to or beyond the upper limit of risk, so that the next round of expansion would necessarily be financed by common equity capital at a cost made higher by the new element of risk. If the same short-run approach were then taken, new investment would have to earn a very high rate in order to add anything to the earnings per share of the existing shareholders. An investment yielding less than this would be rejected. This piecemeal analysis could result in acceptance of a 5 per cent addition to the earning assets of the business at one stage and the rejection of a 15 per cent addition a year or two later.

A more rational long-range approach to the setting of minimum earnings standards for new investment would be to calculate *an average cost of new capital,* weighted according to the proportions of debt to equity which preserve the desired balance. Before one can compute the weighted average cost, as we suggest must be done, one must have some idea of the proportions of the various sources which the particular company will use. Ideally, each firm should consider the proper balance of income, risk, and control for the nature of the company and its particular stockholders. The costs of the permissible securities would then be combined according to the proportions indicated by this analysis.

Few such studies have been made explicitly, but most firms do have a pattern for the proportions of the various sources of capital. The patterns can be derived from the financial statements of the firms and the records of recent financing. In the Long Island Lighting Company (to return to the example used in Chapter 21), the amounts of debt and equity financing (measured by the net proceeds of its issues) in 1953 were roughly as follows:

Bonds	$24,857,500
Preferred stock	9,755,000
Common equity capital	10,641,257
	$45,253,757

Let us assume, for the sake of our example, that the management of the Long Island Lighting Company considers this to be a balance appropriate to the company's circumstances and one which it wishes to preserve in future financing. This then provides us a source of the weights to be used for bonds and preferred stocks in the average cost calculation. It leaves unanswered the cost of the new equity investment, because internal funds were also used.

Since we concluded that retained earnings had a cost below new stock issues, it would appear advantageous to use as much of our annual earnings as possible in providing the common equity capital required to preserve this balance. This raises questions of dividend policy. At this point, we merely assume that the dividends are a given amount and that therefore the contribution of earnings to new financing will be whatever the company is able to earn over and above these dividends, the remainder of the equity being supplied by new common stock issues. Recent experience of the company gives some indication that about 16 per cent of the total will be supplied by retained earnings and depreciation. This gives us the remaining piece of information needed for the calculation of Long Island Lighting Company's average cost of capital at this point of time. The calculation is shown in Table 30–2.

TABLE 30–2

LONG ISLAND LIGHTING COMPANY
Cost of Capital, 1953

	Amount Provided (A)	Percentage of Total (B)	After-Tax Cost (C)	Weighted Amount (B × C)
Raised by:				
Bonds............	$24,857,500	45.91%	1.69%	77.59
Preferred stock....	9,755,000	18.02	5.38	96.95
Common stock....	10,641,257	19.65	7.40	145.41
Internal funds:				
Earnings retained..	2,340,449 ⎫			
Depreciation and	⎬ 16.42	5.92*	97.21
amortization.....	6,549,791 ⎭			
	$54,143,997	100.00%		417.16
Weighted average....				4.17% after tax

* (7.40)(0.8) = 5.92

The reader will recognize the danger in assuming that the proportions of new financing provided by various sources in the past necessarily coincide with what these proportions will be or should be in the future. On the other hand, an alert management will have recognized the basic characteristics of risk in the industry in which it operates, and this awareness tends to be reflected in the existing debt/equity balance of the company. Thus, for example, relatively stable industries, such as the one to which Long Island Lighting belongs, show an average proportion of senior securities substantially higher than those of industries exposed to a more variable earnings experience.

Assuming, then, that the proportions used in the calculations above are considered appropriate and that a "marginal approach" is to be used, the cutoff point suitable for planning the capital budget of this company is 4.17 per cent after taxes.

In order that a firm may avoid the dangers of becoming committed to certain investment opportunities with relatively low return to the exclusion of later opportunities offering a higher return, it is suggested that all investment opportunities should earn at least the weighted average cost of capital. It follows that each financing decision, whether it be to sell bonds, preferred stock, or common stock, or to retain earnings, will be regarded as one of a series that includes both debt and equity capital. At any point in time the current condition of the market and the expectation as to future trends will determine the specific security to be used. If the market is judged accurately, this will keep the average cost of capital for the desired mix of sources at a minimum. In particular, the issuing company should aim to time its issues of high-cost equity capital to coincide with periods of peak market price, thus minimizing the number of shares issued.

The Use of Time-Adjusted Figures

As has been indicated, the approximate method of computing a rate of return is sufficient for most projects. Signs of a need for increased accuracy are an indicated rate of return near to a cutoff criterion rate, or a pattern of cash flows that is irregular from year to year, especially if the irregularities occur in the earlier years.

If it is decided to improve the estimate by the use of time adjustment, the first step is the scheduling of funds flows in a manner similar to that in Table 30–1. A good deal of work lies behind such a table, and it will be recognized that the basic figures for flows of funds are merely "best estimates."[2]

The next steps involve evaluating the funds according to their present values. Before we perform these steps on the figures in the example, however, we shall develop a more simple example to explain the logic behind the work.

Suppose some one offers to pay you $1,000 five years from now. How much would you pay for the promise now? You would not know until you discovered at what rate of return you could invest your funds at equal risk. Suppose you discover that 4 per cent can be obtained equally safely by investment in corporate bonds or otherwise. The present value table (Table A, page 930) tells you that $822 will grow to $1,000 in five years.

With this background, knowing that you have the alternative of investing $822 now to obtain $1,000 in five years, you turn to bargaining with the offerer. If you find he wants $810 for his promise, you

---

[2] To those who are interested in the application of the mathematics of probability to the development of estimates, we wish to point out that the "best estimate" may itself be regarded as the *result* of thinking in terms of probability, though the alternate values and their weights are often not explicitly expressed by the person doing the estimating.

should accept because of the lower initial investment required by his proposition. If he wants $830, do not accept, because you have a better alternative.

Suppose further that someone else offers you $500 in six years, for the price of $375. This is the present value of the payment we are offered. We may assume the same risk characteristics for this offer as in the previous one. The investment to receive $500 in six years at 4 per cent is $395, according to Table A. This proposal, therefore, is also attractive. But is it more or less attractive than the one for $1,000 in five years?

Projects of different lengths or involving different quantities can be compared by making a ratio, called an *index of desirability*, between the present value of the investment and that of the flow of funds from operations. If the ratio is greater than 1.00, a project is desirable because the capital invested will produce more by undertaking the project than if it were invested otherwise to produce the chosen rate of interest. The higher the ratio, the more desirable the project. We present here the pertinent facts for our two examples, showing that the second is the better project as far as the rate-of-return criterion is concerned:

Promise	Offer (A)	Alternative (B)	Index of Desirability C = B/A
$1,000 in five years..........	$810	$822	1.01
500 in six years..........	375	395	1.05

We do not know the rate of return offered by the two projects, but we do know that each is better than 4 per cent, and we have a way of knowing that one is better than the other. Applying this scheme of analysis to funds flow tables like the one we have been using in our example, we have the following rules: (1) Compute the present value of the flow of funds representing capital value and salvage. The resulting number corresponds to what we have just described as an offer. (2) Compute the present value of the flows of funds from operations. This number represents the amount we should have to invest to achieve the same return in some alternative use. (3) Divide item 2 by item 1. If the result is greater than 1.00, the project satisfies the criterion. The desirability of projects may be ranked according to the size of this index number.

In the case of our more complex example, as appears in Table 30–3, it is first necessary to establish present values for the various outflows and inflows, dividing them into two groups: those associated with the investment, and those associated with the operations of the project. At first we select two rates. One is 10 per cent, the rate which we shall assume is the cost of capital for the company. The other is 15 per cent, the previously assumed average return on the investments the company has already made. The application of the appropriate values from Table A gives the needed present values, from which indices of desirability have been calculated.

At the 15 per cent rate, we are told that an investment of $96,044 in this project will produce the same flows of funds as would result from an investment of $84,213 in some project yielding 15 per cent. This is not a worthwhile project, if in fact we can invest elsewhere at 15 per cent. At 10 per cent, on the other hand, we can see that $100,878 would be needed to produce the estimated flows, and the project which requires $92,588 is acceptable.

Although we have gone far enough to find the answer as to whether the project meets the criterion selected by management, another step is of interest. Let us compute the present values and the related indices of desirability at some rate higher than 15 per cent, say 25 per cent, and at some rate lower than 10 per cent, say 8 per cent. This work has been done in Table 30–3. Chart 30–1 can then be drawn, showing how the index of desirability changes as the criterion rate is altered. It will be seen, as is to be expected, that the desirability of this project is greater when the criterion rate is low; but the principal advantages of the chart lie in its assistance in telling us the index at any rate of capitalization we choose, and enabling us to determine easily the rate at which the index has the value of 1.00. It is at 11.7 per cent (instead of the approximate rate of 9.6 per cent found on page 621), and this rate, where the present values of the two streams are equal, is known as the *internal rate of return.*[3]

The Uncertainty Factor in Estimation

One can always question the accuracy of estimates of the various quantities which must be used in an analysis to determine the promised rate of return. The future is inherently uncertain. For this reason, it may be decided to limit the extent of refinement of the quantitative

---

[3] In our first edition, we presented a trial-and-error method for obtaining the internal rate of return, and did not describe the ratio of desirability. Subsequent studies have indicated that under certain factual conditions, there can be two points that will give an internal rate. The graphic method using several values is therefore safer, and the whole procedure is less laborious. See R. I. Reul, "Profitability Index for Investments," *Harvard Business Review*, July–August, 1957, pp. 116–32.

TABLE 30–3

EVALUATION OF FUNDS FLOWS

Capital Investment Project

Year	Flows from Table 30–1	Factor for 10%	Present Value at 10%	Factor for 15%	Present Value at 15%	Factor for 25%	Present Value at 25%	Factor for 8%	Present Value at 8%
−1	−46,325	1.100	−50,957	1.150	−53,274	1.250	−59,706	1.080	−50,031
+1	−50,325	0.909	−45,745	0.870	−43,783	0.800	−40,260	0.926	−46,601
2	− 4,000	0.826	− 3,304	0.756	− 3,024	0.640	− 2,560	0.857	− 3,428
3	− 4,000	0.751	− 3,004	0.658	− 2,632	0.512	− 2,048	0.794	− 3,176
10	+27,000	0.386	+10,422	0.247	+ 6,669	0.107	+ 2,889	0.463	+12,501
	Investment		−92,588		−96,044		−101,685		−90,735
+ 1	18,956	0.909	+17,231	0.870	+16,492	0.800	+15,165	0.926	+17,553
+ 2	18,964	0.826	15,664	0.756	14,337	0.640	12,137	0.857	16,252
+ 3	20,123	0.751	15,112	0.658	13,241	0.512	10,303	0.794	15,978
+ 4	18,403	0.683	12,569	0.572	10,526	0.410	7,545	0.735	13,526
+ 5	16,682	0.621	10,360	0.497	8,291	0.328	5,472	0.681	11,360
+ 6	14,961	0.564	8,438	0.432	6,463	0.262	3,920	0.630	9,425
+ 7	13,241	0.513	6,793	0.376	4,979	0.210	2,781	0.583	7,720
+ 8	11,520	0.467	5,380	0.327	3,767	0.168	1,935	0.540	6,221
+ 9	11,520	0.424	4,884	0.284	3,272	0.134	1,544	0.500	5,760
+10	11,520	0.386	4,447	0.247	2,845	0.107	1,233	0.463	5,334
	Operations		+100,878		+84,213		+62,035		+109,129
	Index of Desirability	1.09			0.88		0.61		1.20

analysis or, alternatively, to allow a margin for error in the form of an adjustment to the calculated rate. Thus, a company that has selected 12 per cent as its cutoff rate will perhaps accept a "sure thing" at that rate, while requiring that a risky project promise 20 per cent.

Professor Joel Dean has suggested the following four-part classification which is very useful in dealing with the problem of uncertainty.[4] We are glad to accept it, while adding a fifth. The distinctions among the classes are based upon differences in certainty of estimating the basic data to appraise the desirability of the investment. As Dean says, ". . . it is important to note that most capital expenditures have mixed objectives . . . and thus do not fit neatly into any single category."

1. *Replacement investments*, where the new project is proposed to replace an existing investment, perhaps simply because of wearing out, but more often because of technical obsolescence. Savings in cost are usually anticipated. Estimates of the net flow of funds for the investment and of the savings are usually accurate enough to be used.

2. *Expansion investments*, where increased earnings rather than

---

[4] Joel Dean, *Capital Budgeting: Top-Management Policy on Plant, Equipment, and Product Development* (New York: Columbia University Press, 1951), chap. v.

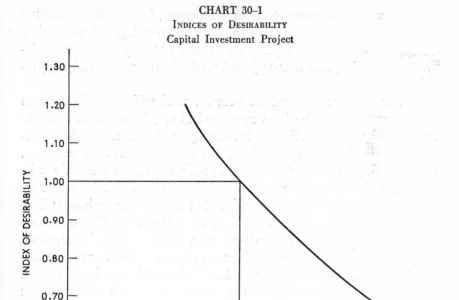

CHART 30–1
INDICES OF DESIRABILITY
Capital Investment Project

INDEX OF DESIRABILITY

RATE OF CAPITALIZATION (PER CENT)

reduced costs are anticipated. If the demand for the new capacity is real, estimates in this area are also reliable.

3. *Product line investments,* where improvements to existing products or new products are planned but the demand is not assured. In this area the uncertainties of estimation are much greater, and judgment must have great weight. In no area is this more true than that of maintaining competitive position.

4. *Strategic investments,* where the benefits are so spread through the firm that their effect on income is almost impossible to measure. Examples of such projects would be a new locker room for the staff, air conditioning, or new elevators in a store. For most such projects the numerical procedures described in this chapter cannot be applied, although the relevant quantities should be estimated to the extent possible.

5. We would add a category, *Contractual Change,* where most of the flows of funds are determined by contracts, and alternatives are to be considered. For example, the exact terms and times of payment

under construction contracts, loan agreements, leases, etc., often play a major part in the choice of a project or its financing. Whenever they do appear, the relevant figures are usually not only easily determinable but precise, and time-adjusted methods are particularly appropriate.

If management followed the practice of classifying its investment opportunities along the lines suggested above, it would be likely to establish different cutoff rates for each grouping to reflect the different levels of uncertainty involved. The measurement of uncertainty, however, is a very difficult task. As a result, such rates are likely to be determined subjectively rather than objectively. There is more than one way of approaching this problem in practice. The authors believe that a sensible procedure would be to use a single cutoff rate for new investments which are of a similar nature (replacement of equipment, normal market expansion). This rate might well be the average cost of capital, which reflects the risk level inherent in the firm's normal business activity. For investments which are clearly of a different risk classification, the company would establish other cutoff rates relative to this basic rate of return, adjusting them up or down, depending on whether the risk appears above or below that of the accustomed area of investment.

Cases

Case 1

Weber Markets, Inc.

In JUNE, 1956, Mr. G. C. Scarlatti, general manager of Weber Markets, Inc., was considering an offer of Elgar Fisheries Company to sell 10,000 cases of frozen fish sticks at a substantial discount provided that Weber Markets would make payment for and accept delivery of the entire shipment by June 30. A smaller discount was offered if the delivery and payment were made during July.

Weber Markets, Inc., operated a chain of 34 supermarkets in a major northwestern city and its suburbs. The company had been founded in 1925 with the opening of a single small food store. From time to time, other units had been added until 73 stores were in operation in 1937. All but three of these were small combination grocery and meat markets with an average area of less than 2,000 square feet. In these stores, customers were served by clerks who waited upon them from behind counters.

Beginning in 1936, certain significant changes in the company's operations were initiated in keeping with trends in the retail food industry. No new small units of the traditional type were opened. Additions to the chain took the form of large supermarkets.

Together with the construction of supermarkets, a policy of gradually closing the small stores was adopted. The result was a decrease in the number of units in the chain, from 73 in 1937 to 34 in 1956.

Later, larger amounts of space had been used for frozen foods. By 1953, frozen food display cases extended along the entire length of the two sides of each market. The meat department and checkout counters occupied the back and front of the store, respectively.

In 1948, the company had reached a decision to integrate its operation vertically by constructing its own warehouse to service the chain. A modern, centrally located, one-story building with an area of 300,000 square feet had been completed in 1950, and a fleet of six trucks had been acquired for distribution purposes. A feature of the warehouse was a large freezer room for the storage of frozen foods. It covered 25,000 square feet of land at the rear of the warehouse.

On June 1, 1956, Weber Markets, Inc., held cash and government securities totaling $2,860,000. Of these funds, $2,000,000 was earmarked for initial costs in connection with the construction of five new supermarkets, scheduled to begin during the summer, and was thus unavailable for other purposes. The company had a $500,-000 line of credit with Rainier-Hood National Bank, of which $84,-000 was drawn down on June 1, 1956. This loan carried interest at 6%. Additional borrowings could be made at the same rate, and it was likely that the bank would agree to a loan substantially in excess of the $500,000 credit line. The bank expected that any loan of this type be paid up during at least one month of the year, although this requirement had been waived on one occasion in the past. The company had no plans to sell new issues of securities during 1956 or 1957.

Elgar Fisheries Company supplied fresh, frozen, and processed fish to food jobbers and directly to large retailers. It operated a fleet of seven fishing vessels in the waters off the northwestern United States. The bulk of its fish, however, was purchased from independent fishermen at public auctions in seaport towns. In recent years, the processed fish segment of its business had grown rapidly to a point where it accounted for over 70% of total dollar volume in 1955.

By far the most important item in the Elgar line of processed fish was a relatively new item, fish sticks. These were breaded, precooked fillets of cod, haddock, or ocean perch. They were frozen and packed ten to a package. Following the introduction of this product in late 1953, national sales had increased quickly, aided by extensive promotion by processors made possible by their margins, which averaged approximately 31% of the wholesale price. By 1955, industry production exceeded 65 million pounds, or over six times the rate of production in late 1953. The number of producers of fish sticks had increased in the same period from 13 to 55. Subsequently, several smaller firms had dropped out of the fish stick business as national consumption appeared, at least temporarily, to level off. Between December, 1953, and January, 1956, the wholesale price of fish sticks in the Northwest had declined from

$4.75 per case to $3.85 per case. By June, 1956, this price had re-covered to $4.25 per case.

An increasingly pressing problem to Elgar Fisheries was the seasonality of its fish stick business. The fish were caught and proc-essed mainly in the late spring and summer months. On the other hand, the periods of peak consumption of this product occurred in October and during the Lenten season. Accordingly, Elgar was faced with the problem of financing the purchase, processing, and stocking of fish sticks for several months before sales to retailers and jobbers took place in any volume. It was the practice of most of Elgar's customers, including Weber Markets, Inc., to buy fish sticks on a "hand-to-mouth" basis; that is, purchases were made in relatively small amounts shortly in advance of need. The usual terms of sale were cash within 24 hours of delivery. Elgar therefore rented storage space for its summer production of fish sticks in a commer-cial frozen storage warehouse located near its processing plant at a rate equivalent to an annual charge of $2.50 per square foot.

In order to finance the production and carrying of its fish stick inventory, Elgar borrowed seasonally from its bank of account, Evergreen Trust Company. Interest at the rate of 6% was charged by the bank on such borrowing. During 1955, these bank loans had reached a peak of $3,400,000.

In an effort to alleviate its problems of seasonality with respect to fish sticks, Elgar's management had decided early in 1956 to offer a 14% discount to customers willing to pay for and accept delivery on "large orders" of fish sticks during the month of June. "Large orders" were defined as orders of 10,000 cases or above. A discount of 10% was to be offered for purchases during July.

Accordingly, on June 10, 1956, Mr. Franck, Elgar's sales man-ager, had called upon Mr. Scarlatti and offered to sell 10,000 cases or more of frozen fish sticks at $3.655 per case, provided that delivery was accepted and payment made by Weber Markets before June 30, 1956. This price represented a 14% discount from the prevailing wholesale price of $4.25. A price of $3.825 was of-fered if payment and delivery were made before July 31.

In considering these offers, Mr. Scarlatti recalled that Weber Markets' sales of fish sticks in 1955 had amounted to 11,200 cases. There were presently 200 cases on hand. Gross profit on this item had averaged 30% of wholesale price. He estimated that the storage of 10,000 cases would require 5,000 square feet of warehouse freezer space. Checking with the chief accounting officer, Mr. Scar-latti learned that total costs attributed in 1955 to the 25,000 square foot warehouse freezer area had been $56,000, or $2.24 a square foot. At no time during 1955 had more than 75% of the capacity of the freezer area been utilized; and under current plans, apart from the possible use for frozen fish sticks, increased utilization in 1956 appeared unlikely.

With this information at hand, Mr. Scarlatti was considering how to use it in reaching a sound decision on the Elgar proposal. Mr. Scarlatti knew that Elgar rented frozen storage space. Consequently, he was also considering the likelihood that Mr. Franck would be willing to negotiate a somewhat larger discount than 14%.

As he turned to the figure work which he felt would be helpful, Mr. Scarlatti decided that he would use 1955 sales data as if they would apply to 1956 and early 1957.

Exhibit 1

WEBER MARKETS, INC.
MONTHLY SALES OF FISH STICKS IN 1955

	Cases	Cumulative %
January	810	7.2
February	1,520	20.8
March	2,490	43.0
April	1,710	58.3
May	820	65.6
June	150	67.0
July	90	67.8
August	60	68.3
September	220	70.3
October	1,630	84.8
November	930	93.1
December	770	100.0
Total	11,200	

Exhibit 2

WEBER MARKETS, INC.
COST OF FISH STICK SALES, MONTHLY, 1955*

	Cases	Average Wholesale Price	Cost
January	810	$4.56	$ 3,693.60
February	1,520	4.48	6,809.60
March	2,490	4.42	11,005.80
April	1,710	4.35	7,438.50
May	820	4.41	3,616.20
June	150	4.27	640.50
July	90	4.33	389.70
August	60	4.25	255.00
September	220	4.10	902.00
October	1,630	4.12	6,715.60
November	930	4.01	3,729.30
December	770	3.90	3,003.00
Total	11,200		

* It may be assumed that purchases and sales were made in the same month.

Case 2

Herber Silver Company

On the morning of December 10, 1950, Mr. William Elting, treasurer of the Herber Silver Company and a member of the executive committee of company officers, learned that the production superintendent, Mr. Alfred Sims, had decided to recommend at the next executive committee meeting a new method of production scheduling calling for a steady rate of output throughout the forthcoming year. The company was currently scheduling production at varying rates, a little ahead of seasonal sales requirements. Mr. Sims believed that the change would lower costs, assure prompt deliveries, and reduce employee turnover. Mr. Sims had not considered the financial implications of his proposal, and Mr. Elting decided to study how this proposed change would affect the company's finances in 1951.

Mr. Sims, the production superintendent, had proposed the change in policy because he believed that it would be desirable to eliminate the strains on production caused by the seasonal demand for sterling flatware. In slack periods, the company had often operated its plant only 24 hours a week on a one-shift basis. On the other hand, during the peak production season, it had been necessary for the company to re-employ old or hire new workers, and to work more than 40 hours a week at overtime rates to meet sales demands. It was becoming increasingly difficult to tempt back old employees after layoffs, and training new employees was expensive. Although it was difficult to estimate the cost savings involved in level production, Mr. Sims believed the overtime premium payments during 1950, which were $37,000, would represent the minimum level of possible savings.

The Herber Silver Company, located in a small New England city, was a well-known producer of sterling flatware. The company currently had a line of 15 active pattern designs. The company's sales experience showed that changes in the popularity of established patterns had been evolutionary in nature, thus making it possible to predict how long the demand for various patterns would justify their manufacture.

Nevertheless, detailed sales forecasting had always presented a difficult problem for the Herber Silver Company. Most sales of flatware were direct to retail outlets, both jewelry and department stores. Sales volume had fluctuated widely as a result of the many economic factors which tended to influence the retail outlets' willingness to purchase sterling flatware. For instance, although late in 1949, sales estimates for the early months of 1950 had been made carefully, Mr. Elting recalled that sales had been much less than had been anticipated. However, a buying spurt following the outbreak of the Korean War had pushed company sales for the entire year to an unanticipated record high. Deliveries had fallen behind orders, and friction had developed with some retailers. Sales information for 1950 is summarized in Exhibit 1.

According to a report from an independent economic consultant, sales volume for 1951 was expected to be higher than in 1950, since consumer incomes were still growing and retail outlets' inventories appeared to have been depleted, judging by the size of recent orders. This report agreed with field reports from company salesmen and officers, and the sales department had projected monthly sales estimates for 1951, as shown in Exhibit 2. These sales estimates had been agreed upon as the basis for planning for the year by all departments.

Production schedules for seasonal operations customarily had been made four times a year. For example, in the latter part of the third quarter of 1950, a final monthly sales estimate for the first quarter of 1951 had been prepared by the sales department. This estimate had then been converted into pattern and piece requirements. In this quarterly procedure, adjustments were made in the production figures to allow for any changes in the inventory level that had resulted from previously inaccurate sales estimates.

The proposed method of level production differed from the seasonal scheduling procedure in several respects. During the latter part of each year, a sales estimate covering a 12-month period beginning April 1 of the following year was to be prepared. The production process itself took an average of seven weeks to complete. To be able to meet orders promptly, it was found that sterling flatware production should be completed and put into finished goods inventory three weeks before shipment was anticipated. Thus, actual production of sterling flatware was scheduled to start ten weeks before the estimated date of shipment. However, planning production schedules twelve weeks in advance of sales requirements was necessary to allow sufficient time for raw material scheduling as well as manufacturing. Therefore, during each week of operations beginning January 1, $\frac{1}{50}$ of the sales estimate for the year starting April 1 would be scheduled (the plant shut down two weeks in July for vacations). While the dollar value of production was to be leveled in this way, the scheduling department could vary pattern and piece quantities.

Mr. Elting had previously made a financial budget for 1951, a procedure which required the assignment of production costs by months and the projection of inventories at the end of each month. These projections are shown in Exhibit 3. When Mr. Elting received Mr. Sims's schedule of manufacturing inputs under the level production plan, he converted this plan into a schedule of additions to inventory, as shown in Exhibit 4. The estimates in Exhibit 4 were based on the following facts and assumptions with reference to the elements of total manufacturing costs: materials, labor, and manufacturing overhead.

Silver was the primary raw material. Using a recent quoted price of 80 cents per ounce, Mr. Elting thought that silver would average 68% of the total cost to manufacture sterling flatware in 1951. Because a silver supplier was located nearby, deliveries could be obtained daily against schedules, so practically no inventory of this material was kept on hand.

Other materials amounted to 6% of total manufacturing costs. These materials were purchased frequently, so variations in raw inventories for this type of goods could be considered negligible. Materials other than silver were charged into process the day production was started in the factory.

In percentage terms, labor costs varied almost directly with production volume, and were distributed relatively evenly over the period of production. Currently they amounted to 11% of total manufacturing costs. Variable overhead expenses ran at about 10% of total manufacturing costs.

Fixed manufacturing overhead expenses were estimated at $30,-000 per month in 1951, which would be 5% of manufacturing cost at the volume anticipated.

The total manufacturing cost, totaling 100% as outlined above, was expected to approximate 65% of sales in 1951. These percentages did not include the savings expected by Mr. Sims. Selling and administrative overhead expenses were budgeted at $231,000 per month during the forthcoming year. This expense amounted to 25% of expected sales volume for 1951.

Payments of cash for the expenses listed above were not scheduled in Exhibit 4 because Mr. Elting felt that the time lags involved were not important enough to justify adjusting for them. The times involved were: Silver was purchased for cash on delivery ("spot cash"). Other materials were paid for net, end of month. Payroll payments were made the week after the labor was obtained. Variable overhead was usually paid for in the month it was used. Fixed overhead was paid irregularly, some in the month after use, and some on an annual prepayment basis.

The Herber Silver Company had borrowed heavily in the past from the Security National Bank of Boston, and was in debt at the end of November, 1950. Mr. Elting believed the Security National Bank would be willing to loan the company additional funds at an interest rate of 3% per annum in 1951. Bank borrowings were generally reduced to the lowest level during November and December of each year.

Exhibit 1

HERBER SILVER COMPANY

RECORD OF MONTHLY ORDERS AND SHIPMENTS, 1950
(Dollar figures in thousands)

	Orders Unfilled Beginning of Month	Orders Entered Current Month	Orders Shipped ("Sales")	Unfilled Orders End of Month
January	$120	$ 491	$ 319	$292
February	292	501	516	277
March	277	513	566	224
April	224	392	390	226
May	226	449	421	254
June	254	554	598	210
July	210	479	282	407
August	407	1,022	715	714
September	714	773	711	776
October	776	839	1,131	484
November	484	977	956	505
December	505	.......Not yet available.......		

Exhibit 2

HERBER SILVER COMPANY

SALES ESTIMATES

MONTHLY, DECEMBER, 1950—MARCH, 1952
(Dollar figures in thousands)

	Estimated Monthly Sales	Cumulative Total Sales from April, 1951
December, 1950	$ 680	...
January, 1951	520	...
February	790	...
March	820	...
April	990	$ 990
May	770	1,760
June	720	2,480
July	660	3,140
August	940	4,080
September	880	4,960
October	1,600	6,560
November	1,320	7,880
December	990	8,870
January, 1952	550	9,420
February	770	10,190
March	880	11,070

Exhibit 3

HERBER SILVER COMPANY

PROJECTED INVENTORY ESTIMATES FOR SEASONAL PRODUCTION
MONTHLY, DECEMBER, 1950—DECEMBER, 1951
(Dollar figures in thousands)

	1950 Dec.	1951 Jan.	Feb.	Mar.	April	May	June	July	Aug.	Sept.	Oct.	Nov.	Dec.
Manufacturing costs incurred in month:													
Raw materials and materials put into process													
Silver..............	$ 357	$ 517	$ 354	$ 284	$ 384	$ 476	$ 374	$ 272	$ 763	$ 459	$ 376	$ 287	$ 358
Other materials.........	32	46	31	25	34	42	33	24	67	41	33	25	32
Direct labor.........	43	75	64	53	50	80	61	32	110	88	72	62	44
Variable manufacturing overhead.	39	68	58	48	45	73	56	29	100	80	66	56	40
Fixed manufacturing overhead into process......	30	30	30	30	30	30	30	30	30	30	30	30	30
Total additions to inventory........	$ 501	$ 736	$ 537	$ 440	$ 543	$ 701	$ 554	$ 387	$1,070	$ 698	$ 577	$ 460	$ 504
Add: *Opening inventory*........	1,721*	1,780	2,178	2,201	2,108	2,008	2,209	2,296	2,254	2,713	2,839	2,376	1,977
Total inventory during month........	$2,222	$2,516	$2,715	$2,641	$2,651	$2,709	$2,763	$2,683	$3,324	$3,411	$3,416	$2,836	$2,481
Deduct: *Cost of goods sold*.......	442	338	514	533	643	500	467	429	611	572	1,040	859	643
Closing inventory........	$1,780	$2,178	$2,201	$2,108	$2,008	$2,209	$2,296	$2,254	$2,713	$2,839	$2,376	$1,977	$1,838

* The company maintained an inventory of out-of-style patterns amounting to approximately $300,000 in order to fill replacement orders.

Exhibit 4

HERBER SILVER COMPANY
ADDITIONS TO INVENTORY, OR
TOTAL MANUFACTURING COSTS TO BE INCURRED UNDER LEVEL PRODUCTION
MONTHLY, DECEMBER, 1950—DECEMBER, 1951
(Dollar figures in thousands)

Work-Weeks in Month	Silver	Other Material	Direct Labor	Variable Manufacturing Overhead	Fixed Manufacturing Overhead	Total Additions to Inventory
4.......December, 1950..........	$357	$32	$43	$39	$30	$501
5........January, 1951.............	489	43	77	70	30	709
4.......February.................	392	35	60	55	30	572
4.......March...................	392	35	63	57	30	577
4.......April....................	392	35	63	57	30	577
5.......May.....................	489	43	79	73	30	714
4.......June....................	392	35	63	57	30	577
2.......July....................	196	18	31	29	30	304
5.......August..................	489	43	79	73	30	714
4.......September...............	392	35	63	57	30	577
4.......October.................	392	35	63	57	30	577
5.......November...............	489	43	79	73	30	714
4.......December...............	392	35	63	57	30	577

Case 3

The Hintz Company

On May 10, 1954, Mr. Samuel Hintz, president of The Hintz Company, noted that the company's accounts receivable balance had increased to $93,000 as of April 30, 1954. Since this was $19,000 higher than it had been on March 31, 1954, Mr. Hintz decided to investigate the reasons for the increase to see whether it might have significance in determining the company's future plans.

The Hintz Company, located in New York City, manufactured baseball, basketball, and other athletic uniforms. The company's 20 employees cut and sewed fabrics to color and size specifications. The uniforms were sold directly to retail sporting goods shops in the New York metropolitan area. As there were several other small manufacturers of uniforms in New York City, competition for the business of these retail outlets was keen.

Since Hintz's founding in 1946, it had operated profitably, and sales volume had reached a peak of $350,000 in 1951. In the fall of 1952, sales failed to recover from the seasonal low of the summer months. In July, 1953, when a new sales manager, Mr. Katz, was employed, sales volume began improving. By May, 1954, Mr. Katz had secured 50 new accounts for the company.

After reading trade papers, Mr. Hintz believed that the prospects of the athletic uniform market looked promising for the remainder of 1954. It was reported that there were a large number of newly organized athletic teams in the New York area and that schools and other regular purchasers were buying new uniforms more frequently. Since Mr. Katz's more detailed experience in the market tended to confirm this information, Mr. Hintz was looking forward to the best year in the company's history. On this basis, he projected sales and profits by months for the remainder of 1954 as follows:

	Sales	*Profit before Taxes*
May	$ 50,000	$ 4,000
June	40,000	2,000
July	40,000	2,000
August	40,000	2,000
September	50,000	4,000
October	55,000	5,000
November	60,000	6,000
December	60,000	6,000
Total	$395,000	$31,000

Hintz's customers were, for the most part, small sporting goods stores. Of 450 accounts, only six purchased more than $10,000 worth of uniforms in a year. Most of the remainder made periodic purchases of approximately $100 per order. Hintz sold on terms of net 30, but only the large stores paid consistently within 60 days of billing. Bad debt losses were 1% of sales in 1953. A substantial portion of the retail stores' sales of athletic uniforms was made to schools that paid their accounts slowly, and Hintz's collections also tended to be slow. Mr. Hintz believed that many of the smaller stores were operated without adequate capital investment.

Mr. Katz received a salary of $6,000 and a 2% commission on his personal sales. He sold one third of the company's accounts as well as supervising the company's two other salesmen. Each salesman was paid a straight commission of 5%. No attempt was made to charge a salesman for bad debt losses resulting from his sales efforts.

Neither Mr. Hintz nor the company's bookkeeper, Mr. Stein, had abundant time to devote to credit management. As a result, the following general policies had been established for guidance in credit matters. Before selling to a new account, a company salesman, on the basis of his observations at the store, was expected to appraise the storekeeper's character and abilities, and to judge the financial condition of the store as best he could. If these appeared satisfactory, a line of credit of $200 was extended to the store. After a year, a salesman was authorized to increase the line of credit to $500 if the store had made all its payments within 90 days of billing. After two years of satisfactory credit experience, open lines of credit were granted when necessary. If a specific case warranted exception to these rules, Mr. Hintz reviewed the information available and made the final decision.

Billings were prepared by Mr. Stein when shipment was made. If payment was not received within 60 days, a form letter was sent to the customer calling his attention to this omission. After 90 days, a warning letter was sent, requesting payment within 10 days. Mr. Hintz phoned all store owners who had not made payment within 100 days of billing; and unless he received a firm promise for immediate remittance, he threatened to turn the account over to his lawyer. If payment was not received after 120 days, the receivables were given to a law firm for collection, and the account was written off as a bad debt.

On April 30, 1954, $2,200 in outstanding receivables were in the hands of lawyers pending settlement. Legal fees on these collections amounted to 25% of the amount collected or $50, whichever was the larger. Mr. Hintz considered the company fortunate if it received as much as 50% on a receivable after it had been turned over to a law firm. In several instances, final settlement took as long as one year.

Although sales tended to fluctuate from month to month, Mr. Hintz maintained raw material and finished goods inventories at even levels. As the company's production facilities were adequate to support a substantial increase in sales volume, no additions to fixed assets were contemplated. Mr. Hintz noted that with the exception of the bank loan, current liabilities tended to remain relatively constant.

On May 10, 1954, when Mr. Hintz received the April 30, 1954, balance sheet shown in Exhibit 1, he was disturbed by the sharp increase in accounts receivable. He thought several questions important: (1) whether the increase indicated larger bad debt losses might be incurred in the future; (2) whether the current policies of credit administration needed alteration; and (3) whether the receivables balance might increase in the future to the point where the company would require more funds from the bank. To help answer these questions, he had requested Mr. Stein to prepare the information contained in Exhibits 2 and 3. Profit and loss statements are given in Exhibit 4.

Exhibit 1

THE HINTZ COMPANY

BALANCE SHEETS, DECEMBER 31, 1952–1953; APRIL 30, 1953–1954
CHANGES IN BALANCE SHEET AMOUNTS, SELECTED PERIODS

(Dollar figures in thousands)

| | *Balance Sheets* | | | | *Changes* | |
	Dec. 31 1952	April 30 1953	Dec. 31 1953	April 30 1954	Dec. to April 1953–1954	April to April 1953–1954
ASSETS						
Cash	$10	$10	$10	$ 4	$ −6	$ −6
Accounts receivable (net)	41	37	68	93	+25	+56
Inventory	23	22	25	22	−3	−
Total current assets	$74	$69	$103	$119	$+16	$+50
Machinery and equipment (net)	20	20	19	19	−1	−1
Other assets	4	3	4	3	−1	−
Total assets	$98	$92	$126	$141	$+15	$+49
LIABILITIES						
Accounts payable	$20	$19	$ 21	$ 21	$ −	$ +2
Taxes payable	4	−	4	5	+1	+5
Accrued payroll	6	8	5	8	+3	−
Bank loan	−	−	25	32	+7	+32
Total current liabilities	$30	$27	$ 55	$ 66	$+11	$+39
Common stock	35	35	35	35	−	−
Surplus	33	30	36	40	+4	+10
Total liabilities and net worth	$98	$92	$126	$141	$+15	$+49

Exhibit 2

THE HINTZ COMPANY

SUMMARY OF TRANSACTIONS IN ACCOUNTS RECEIVABLE, JANUARY, 1953—APRIL, 1954

(Dollar figures in thousands)

1953	Accounts Receivable Beginning	Sales (+)	Collections (−)	Bad Debts (−)	Accounts Receivable Ending	Collection Period (Days)
January	$41.5	$ 30.6	$ 30.7	$0.5	$40.9	34*
February	40.9	32.4	37.1	0.6	35.6	40*
March	35.6	24.1	21.4	0.6	37.7	44*
April	37.7	26.3	26.4	0.6	37.0	43*
May	37.0	25.4	24.7	0.6	37.1	38*
June	37.1	22.0	28.0	0.7	30.4	40*
July	30.4	24.6	22.7	0.5	31.8	47*
August	31.8	27.6	17.7	0.5	41.2	47*
September	41.2	24.6	23.1	0.5	42.2	48*
October	42.2	31.7	28.0	0.4	45.5	60*
November	45.5	30.1	13.3	0.5	61.8	60*
December	61.8	38.2	31.2	0.5	68.3	73†
Total	$41.5	$337.4	$304.3	$6.3	$68.3	
1954						
January	68.3	33.7	40.8	0.5	60.7	51*
February	60.7	38.1	28.4	0.6	69.8	58*
March	69.8	45.8	41.0	0.5	74.1	53*
April	74.1	54.9	35.1	0.6	93.3	55*
Total 1954 to date	$68.3	$172.5	$145.3	$2.2	$93.3	65†

* Based on most recent 60-day sales period.
† Based on year, or year to date.

Exhibit 3

THE HINTZ COMPANY

ANALYSIS OF COLLECTIONS, APRIL, 1953–1954, AND ACCOUNTS RECEIVABLE,
APRIL 30, 1953–1954

(Dollar figures in thousands)

Month of Sale	Age April 30 (Days)	Amount of Sales 1953	1954	Amount Collected in April 1953	1954
Collections in April					
April........	0–30	$26.3	$54.9	$ 1.0	$ 2.7
March.......	31–60	24.1	45.8	2.1	5.5
February.....	61–90	32.4	38.1	22.7	26.3
January......	91–120	30.6	33.7	0.6	0.5
Earlier.......	121+	....	....	0.0*	0.1*
				$26.4	$35.1

				Amount of Outstanding Receivables by Month of Sale	
Age of accounts receivable on April 30					
April........	0–30	26.3	54.9	$25.3	$52.2
March.......	31–60	24.1	45.8	9.5	37.7
February.....	61–90	32.4	38.1	2.0	2.7
January......	91–120	30.6	33.7	0.2	0.7
Earlier.......	....	....	....	0.0*	0.0*
				$37.0	$93.3

* Charged off, in hands of attorneys.

Exhibit 4

THE HINTZ COMPANY

PROFIT AND LOSS STATEMENTS

(Dollar figures in thousands)

	Year		Four Months Jan.-Apr.	
	1952	1953	1953	1954
Sales...................................	$335	$338	$114	$173
Cost of goods sold........................	213	215	75	120
Gross profit.............................	$122	$123	$ 39	$ 53
General selling and administrative expenses............................	101	103	36	40
Bad debt loss............................	3	3	1	1
Operating profit........................	$ 18	$ 17	$ 2	$ 12
Provision for taxes......................	4	4	0	3
Net profit..............................	$ 14	$ 13	$ 2	$ 9
Dividends..............................	10	10	5	5
Retained earnings......................	$ 4	$ 3	$ (3)	$ 4

Case 4

James W. Saxton Company

THE James W. Saxton Company, manufacturer of fine home furniture in Rocky Mount, North Carolina, distributed its products directly
to department stores, independent home furnishing retailers, and a
few small regional furniture chains. Early in April, 1951, the credit
manager of the Saxton Company, Mr. Frank Preston, received from
his assistant, Mr. Richard Rossi, pertinent information on two accounts in Missouri—Bauman's, Inc., of St. Louis, and Vardon's Emporium of Kansas City. Mr. Rossi believed changes in these companies warranted Mr. Preston's attention.

Bauman's retailed quality home furnishings from four locations, one in the downtown section of St. Louis and the others in
nearby suburban areas. The company also manufactured custom
upholstered furniture on special order. Since Bauman's handled
a complete line of home furnishings, sales were fairly steady
throughout the year and were approximately 75% for cash and 25%
by 30-day charge or 12-month instalment terms. Instalment terms
called for 25% down and the balance in equal monthly payments
over a 12-month period.

The store had been established in 1915 as a partnership and was
incorporated in 1946. In June, 1950, two of the four original partners
sold their shares in the company to the two remaining owners.

Bauman's had been a customer of the Saxton Company since
1918 and had previously handled its affairs in a most satisfactory
manner. Vardon's Emporium was a comparatively new customer of
Saxton's, having been sold since 1946. A medium-sized department
store in downtown Kansas City, it was well known for its extensive
lines of home furnishings. Its account with Saxton's had been satisfactory through 1950.

Both accounts were sold on terms of 1/10, net 30 and, although not discounting, had been paying invoices promptly until December, 1950. Mr. Preston had previously established a $10,000 limit on Bauman's and a $15,000 limit on Vardon's.

The Saxton Company advertised its lines nationally and attempted to maintain intensive coverage of trading areas by distributing through stores strategically located within a particular marketing area. Beginning in 1949, activity in the furniture market had become sufficiently spotty that quality of product and service were not the only bases for competition among manufacturers for outlets. Credit terms and financing of dealers became equally important; thus, the Saxton Company, in Mr. Preston's words, was "backed into the position of supporting numerous customers in order to maintain adequate distribution for its products."

Because of this requirement for the extension of fairly liberal credit, Mr. Preston had since 1949 adhered strictly to a policy of obtaining current reports on the financial status of customers. These reports, obtained as annual balance sheets and profit and loss statements, for customers that were considered satisfactory risks, were supplied directly by the customers. Under certain circumstances, wherein Saxton's was working very closely with a particular customer who was trading actively on a small investment, Mr. Preston received quarterly and at times monthly statements in order "to keep on top" of the credit situation.

In early April, 1951, Mr. Richard Rossi, assistant credit manager of the James W. Saxton Company, received the annual reports of Bauman's, Inc., and Vardon's Emporium. After reviewing these statements and checking the accounts receivable ledger for both customers, Mr. Rossi felt that the accounts should be reviewed by Mr. Preston. Accordingly, he furnished Mr. Preston with the information found in Exhibits 1 through 5.

When reviewing the accounts, Mr. Rossi kept in mind that 1950 had not been a particularly good year for retail furniture stores. It was generally known that stores such as Vardon's, carrying low-priced furniture lines, were the first to suffer the declines which had come in the late summer and early fall. This situation was followed by signs of a relaxing demand for furniture of higher quality and higher price toward the end of 1950. The drop in volume and the subsequent price cutting hit the profit margins of some retailers to such an extent that their losses in the latter part of the year equaled or more than offset profits gained in the earlier part of the year.

In the early months of 1951 the "softness" of the furniture business continued. Although there was no severe drop in the buying of furniture at the retail level, there was an indication that "scare" buying and purchasing in anticipation of potential shortages had been curtailed. Accordingly, retail stores reduced orders of new lines and reorders of established lines in February, March, and April. Throughout the country, orders for shipment in April were down about 30% from March; March had itself shown a drop of about 10% from February. Thus, credit managers among furniture manufacturing concerns were placed in the unhappy position of trying to please sales managers who wanted to maintain volume while they were aware that the shipment of furniture to customers who had already overextended their financial positions was potentially dangerous in such a period.

Exhibit 1

JAMES W. SAXTON COMPANY

Bauman's Inc., Balance Sheets as of January 31, 1949–1951

(In thousands of dollars)

ASSETS	1/31/49	1/31/50	1/31/51
....	$ 14	$ 11	$ 8
ounts receivable, net..	231	261	268
ntory..	304	303	304
Total current assets.....................................	$549	$575	$580
l...	59	59	59
dings, fixtures and equipment..............................	225	228	263
ess: Reserve for depreciation................................	31	48	66
buildings, fixtures, and equipment..........................	$194	$180	$197
stment..	11	11	11
from stockholders...	....	36	48
rred charges..	7	3	3
Total assets...	$820	$864	$898
LIABILITIES			
ounts payable...	$144	$145	$154
es payable—employees......................................	12	13	13
mated federal income tax....................................	11	....	....
rent maturities on long-term debts...........................	26	60	37
cellaneous accruals...	36	34	11
Total current liabilities..................................	$229	$252	$215
es payable—bank*...	91	150	145
rtgage notes payable.......................................	376	375	438
erred stock—5% noncumulative.............................	32	32	32
mon stock...	60	60	60
ital surplus...	....	....	19
ied surplus...	32	5ᵈ	11ᵈ
Total liabilities..	$820	$865	$898

ᵈ Deficit.
* Secured by pledged accounts receivable.

Exhibit 2

JAMES W. SAXTON COMPANY

INCOME STATEMENTS OF BAUMAN'S, INC., FOR YEARS ENDED JANUARY 31, 1949–1951
(In thousands of dollars)

	1/31/49	1/31/50	1/31/
Sales	$1,945	$1,583	$1,5(
Less returns and allowances	175	186	12
Net sales	$1,770	$1,397	$1,3£
Cost of goods sold	1,077	854	8£
Gross profit	$ 693	$ 543	$ 5£
Less operating expenses	595	515	4£
Operating profit	$ 98	$ 28	$ £
Other income	67	11	1
Net after other income	$ 165	$ 39	$ £
Other deductions	40	41	£
Net profit (loss) before tax	$ 125	$ (2)*	$ (
Dividends paid	$ 35	$ 35	....

* Parentheses denote losses.

Exhibit 3

JAMES W. SAXTON COMPANY

VARDON'S EMPORIUM—BALANCE SHEETS AS OF JANUARY 31, 1950–1951
(Dollar figures in thousands)

ASSETS	1/31/50	1/31/
Cash	$ 123	$ 7
Notes and accounts receivable[p]	917	88
Inventory	895	82
Tax carryback claim	......	7
Total current assets	$1,935	$1,8£
Fixed assets, net	244	22
Leasehold improvements, net	598	57
Cash value life insurance[p]	47	4
Investments	9	
Notes receivable—officers and employees[p]	18	2
Prepaid and deferred items	25	2
Total assets	$2,876	$2,76

LIABILITIES		
Notes payable—Industrial Finance Corporation	$ 885	$ 71
Accounts payable	407	44
Miscellaneous accruals	98	11
Total current liabilities	$1,390	$1,27
Common stock	570	57
Surplus	916	91
Total liabilities	$2,876	$2,76

[p] Pledged to secure 30-day renewable notes to Industrial Finance Corporation.

Exhibit 4

JAMES W. SAXTON COMPANY

VARDON'S EMPORIUM—INCOME STATEMENTS FOR YEARS ENDING JANUARY 31, 1950–1951
(Dollar figures in thousands)

	1/31/50	1/31/51
ross sales	$5,210	$4,828
Less: Returns and allowances	478	369
et sales	$4,732	$4,459
ost of goods sold	2,975	3,064
ross profit	$1,757	$1,395
perating expenses	1,499	1,630
perating profit	$ 258	$ 235ᵈ
Adjustments:		
Elimination—reserves for inventory losses	...	135
Reduction—bad debt reserve	...	18
Tax carryback	...	84
Federal income tax	108	...
et before dividends	$ 150	$ 2
ividends paid	100	1
et to surplus	$ 50	$ 1

ᵈ Deficit.

Exhibit 5

JAMES W. SAXTON COMPANY

AGING OF ACCOUNTS RECEIVABLE BALANCES
AS OF MARCH 31, 1951

Due from	Prior	Dec.	Jan.	Feb.	Mar.	Totals
Bauman's, Inc.	.....	$5,803.14	$ 913.30	$3,524.37	$1,028.01	$11,268.82
Vardon's Emporium	$380.84*	4,883.96	1,025.55	4,352.00	9,124.77	19,767.12
	(October)					

* Represents invoice on disputed shipment; customer claimed damaged merchandise.

Case 5

The Case of the Unidentified Industries

DESPITE variations in operational and financial policies and practices and in operating results between firms in the same industry, the nature of the industry has an important impact on the general patterns of the need for funds (asset allocation), the methods of meeting these needs, and the financial results of most firms in the industry. Presented in Exhibit 1 are balance sheets, in percentage form, and selected ratios drawn from the balance sheets and operating statements of eight firms in eight different industries. Recognizing the fact of certain differences between firms in the same industry, each firm whose figures are summarized is broadly typical of those in its industry.

See if you can identify the industry represented. Then, be prepared as best you can to explain the distinctive asset structures and ratios of each industry.

1. Electric utility
2. Railroad
3. Automobile manufacture
4. Basic chemicals
5. Apparel manufacture
6. Tobacco manufacture
7. Aircraft manufacture
8. Retail grocery chain (leasing most of store premises)

Exhibit 1

THE CASE OF THE UNIDENTIFIED INDUSTRIES

Balance Sheet Percentages	A	B	C	D	E	F	G	H
Cash and marketable securities	28.4	5.4	1.9	2.2	3.7	8.2	17.2	5.9
Receivables	3.8	12.4	4.2	6.6	2.8	31.8	2.6	24.6
Inventories	13.3	17.0	3.1	81.4	1.4	46.2	36.1	47.4
Other current assets	0.6	...	0.2	0.3	0.2	0.5	1.0	1.1
Plant and equipment (net)	39.4	62.5	88.7	8.4	69.9	13.1	42.1	20.2
Other assets	14.5	2.7	1.9	1.1	22.0	0.2	1.0	0.8
Total Assets	100.0	100.0	100.0	100.0	100.0	100.0	100.0	100.0
Notes payable	...	6.5	2.4	6.9	...	16.5	...	4.7
Accounts payable	9.4	3.5	2.5	0.1	3.5	25.6	16.5	11.1
Accrued taxes	12.0	5.5	3.6	6.7	1.2	1.7	13.3	4.0
Other current liabilities	3.5	4.1	2.8	3.7	0.9	9.4	...	3.3
Long-term debt	6.4	20.0	40.5	18.7	41.3	11.8	16.5	13.0
Other liabilities	...	0.1	0.9	...	5.2	...	1.1	0.1
Capital stock and capital surplus	14.4	49.8	37.0	32.4	28.1	20.1	16.0	14.2
Retained earnings and surplus reserves	54.3	10.5	10.3	31.5	19.8	14.9	36.6	49.6
	100.0	100.0	100.0	100.0	100.0	100.0	100.0	100.0

Profit and Loss Percentages								
Net revenues	100.0	100.0	100.0	100.0	100.0	100.0	100.0	100.0
Operating costs and expenses	85.8	82.3	85.4	79.1	85.4	97.8	97.0	93.5
Operating profit	14.2	17.7	14.6	20.9	14.6	2.2	3.0	6.5
Net nonoperating expenses	5.8	8.8	2.2	11.8	13.1	1.4	1.7	3.1
Net Income	8.4	8.9	12.4	9.1	1.5	0.8	1.3	3.4

Selected Ratios

	A	B	C	D	E	F	G	H
$\dfrac{\text{Current Assets}}{\text{Current Liabilities}}$	1.85	1.77	0.82	5.19	1.42	1.63	1.90	3.44
$\dfrac{\text{Cash, Marketable Securities, and Receivables}}{\text{Current Liabilities}}$	1.30	0.91	0.53	0.56	0.91	0.75	0.66	1.33
$\dfrac{\text{Total Debt}}{\text{Total Assets}}$	0.313	0.397	0.527	0.361	0.521	0.650	0.474	0.362
$\dfrac{\text{Net Sales}}{\text{Total Assets}}$	1.37	0.82	0.34	1.44	0.42	2.71	5.52	1.57
$\dfrac{\text{Net Profits}}{\text{Total Assets}}$	0.12	0.07	0.042	0.08	0.006	0.02	0.07	0.05
$\dfrac{\text{Net Profit}}{\text{Total Net Worth}}$	0.17	0.12	0.086	0.12	0.013	0.06	0.15	0.08

Case 6

Renaldo Supply Company

THE Renaldo Supply Company of Watertown, Massachusetts, was formed in 1940 as a wholesale distributor of plumbing and heating fixtures and supplies. Throughout the period of World War II, the company grew slowly but steadily.

With greater availability of materials in the postwar period, Renaldo's volume of business expanded rapidly. During 1948 the company experienced a sales volume of nearly $1 million, the largest up to that time. During the latter part of that year the company's officers found it necessary to rent additional warehouse space to handle its rapidly increasing inventory. This arrangement was found to be so cumbersome and expensive that the management of the Renaldo Company decided to construct on its property a new building which would permit the storage of larger inventory and also afford room to display a completely equipped kitchen and a completely equipped bathroom, thus attracting some retail sales. All sales were made on credit terms of net 30.

When the financial statements for the year 1948 were completed during the second week of January, 1949, the president, Gino Renaldo, and treasurer, Carley Malden, of the Renaldo Company visited the Watertown Commercial Bank and Trust Company, where the company had banked for five years. This was, however, the first time the company officers had asked for a loan. They discussed with Mr. John Vreeland, a loan officer, methods of financing the expansion of the company's fixed assets. Mr. Vreeland was shown the 1948 financial statements and the estimated statements for the year 1949, giving effect to the acquisition of larger facilities (see Exhibit 1).

Based on these financial statements and his general knowledge of the business, Mr. Vreeland agreed to lend $75,000 to help finance the construction and to finance the normally experienced seasonal increase in sales during the spring and early summer. The loan was established on a three-year basis, calling for repayment of $25,000 each year, beginning with a $25,000 payment January 31, 1950.

From time to time throughout the spring of 1949, officers of the Renaldo Company stopped in to see Mr. Vreeland to report progress on construction, which was completed in early April. Upon the occasion of further visits throughout 1949, the officers reported expanding sales and profits.

On January 15, 1950, the banker received the following letter from the treasurer of the Renaldo Company:

DEAR JACK:

I am pleased to enclose our statements for the year ended December 31, 1949 [see Exhibit 2]. You will, of course, be interested to learn that sales thus far this year are running slightly ahead of those of a year ago.

I don't believe you have looked in on our new facilities other than when we had our grand opening last April. I hope you can find time in the near future to pay us another visit.

Cordially yours,

(*Signed*) CARLEY MALDEN

Exhibit 1

RENALDO SUPPLY COMPANY

BALANCE SHEETS AS OF DECEMBER 31

ASSETS	Actual 1948	Forecasted 1949
Cash	$ 27,700	$ 25,000
Receivables, net	62,000	71,200
Inventory*	166,000	183,400
Current assets	$255,700	$279,600
Fixed assets	57,700	72,700†
Less: Reserve for depreciation	32,200	10,500†
Net fixed assets	$ 25,500	$ 62,200
Deferred charges	7,200	7,800
Total assets	$288,400	$349,600
LIABILITIES		
Accounts payable	$ 21,900	$ 20,900
Miscellaneous accruals	4,100	3,500
Provision for federal income tax	25,800	39,800
Current liabilities	$ 51,800	$ 64,200
Capital stock (par $100)	100,000	100,000
Earned surplus	136,600	158,600
Total liabilities	$288,400	$322,800
Funds needed		26,800
		$349,600

* Inventory as of December 31, 1947, was $139,800.
† After write-off during 1949 of fully depreciated old building carried at $25,000.

PROFIT AND LOSS STATEMENT FOR YEARS ENDED
DECEMBER 31

	Actual *1948*	*Forecasted* *1949*
Net sales..............................	$970,400	$1,164,500
Cost of sales*.........................	630,800	733,600
Gross profit............................	$339,600	$ 430,900
Operating expenses†...................	271,700	326,100
Operating profit.......................	$ 67,900	$ 104,800
Federal income tax (38%)...............	25,800	39,800
Net profit after tax....................	$ 42,100	$ 65,000
Dividends paid........................	28,000($28 per share)	43,000($43 per share)
Net earnings retained..................	$ 14,100	$ 22,000

* Purchases during 1948 were $657,000; they were estimated at $751,000 for 1949. Terms were generally n/10 and n/30..
† Includes depreciation of $1,600 in 1948, and $3,300 estimated for 1949.

Exhibit 2

RENALDO SUPPLY COMPANY

ACTUAL BALANCE SHEET, DECEMBER 31, 1949*

ASSETS		LIABILITIES	
Cash............................	$ 26,700	Accounts payable.................	$130,100
Receivables, net..................	86,800	Miscellaneous accruals.............	5,600
Inventory........................	314,400	Provision for federal income tax.....	42,100
Current assets.................	$427,900	Bank loan, current.................	25,000
Fixed assets......................	90,600	*Current liabilities*............	$202,800
Less: Reserve for depreciation.....	10,900	Bank loan due after one year........	50,000
	$ 79,700	Capital stock (par $100)...........	100,000
Deferred charges..................	7,600	Earned surplus....................	162,400
Total assets.................	$515,200	*Total liabilities*..............	$515,200

PROFIT AND LOSS STATEMENT
FOR YEAR ENDED DECEMBER 31, 1949*

Net sales..	$1,583,200
Cost of sales†......................................	1,052,800
Gross profit..	$ 530,400
Operating expenses‡................................	419,500
Operating profit....................................	$ 110,900
Federal income tax (38%)............................	42,100
Net profit after tax.................................	$ 68,800
Dividends ($43 per share)............................	43,000
Earnings retained in business........................	$ 25,800

* As enclosed in letter of January 15, 1950.
† Purchases during year were $1,201,200.
‡ Includes depreciation of $3,700.

Case 7

Clarkson Lumber Company

FOLLOWING a rapid growth in its business during recent years, the Clarkson Lumber Company in the spring of 1940 anticipated a further substantial increase in sales. Despite good profits, which were largely retained in the business, the company had experienced a shortage of cash and had found it necessary to borrow $48,000 from the Suburban National Bank. In the spring of 1940, additional borrowing seemed necessary if sales were to be increased and purchase discounts taken. Since $48,000 was the maximum amount which the Suburban National would lend to any borrower, it was necessary for Mr. Paul Clarkson, proprietor of the Clarkson Lumber Company, to look elsewhere for additional credit.

Through a personal friend who was well acquainted with one of the officers of a large metropolitan bank, the Northrup National Bank, Mr. Clarkson obtained an introduction to the officer and presented a request for an additional bank loan of $80,000. Consequently, the credit department of the Northrup National Bank made its usual investigation of the company for the information of the loan officers of the bank.

The Clarkson Lumber Company was founded in 1930 as a partnership of Mr. Clarkson and Mr. Henry Stark, a brother-in-law of Mr. Clarkson. Six years later Mr. Clarkson bought out Mr. Stark's interest and continued the business as sole proprietor.

The business was located in a suburb of a large midwestern city. Land and a siding were leased from a railroad. Two portable sheet metal storage buildings had been erected by the company. Operations were limited to the wholesale distribution of plywood, moldings, and sash and door products to lumber dealers in the local area. Credit terms of net 30 days and net 60 days on open account were usually offered customers.

Sales volume had been built up largely on the basis of successful price competition made possible through careful control of operating expenses and by quantity purchases of materials at substantial discounts. Almost all of the moldings and sash and door products, which amounted to 40% and 20% of sales, respectively, were used for repair work. About 55% of total sales were made in the six months from March through August. No sales representatives were employed, orders being taken exclusively over the telephone. Annual sales of $313,646 in 1935 and of $476,275 in 1936 gave net profits of $32,494 and of $34,131, respectively. Comparative operating statements for the years 1937 through 1939 and for the three months ending March 31, 1940, are given in Exhibit 1.

Mr. Clarkson was an energetic man, 39 years of age, who worked long hours on the job, not only handling management matters but also performing a large amount of the clerical work. Help was afforded by an assistant who, in the words of the investigator of the Northrup National Bank, "has been doing and can do about everything that Mr. Clarkson does in the organization."

Other employees numbered 14, of whom 11 worked in the yard and 3 drove trucks. Mr. Clarkson had adopted the practice of paying union dues and all social security taxes for his employees; in addition, bonuses were distributed to them at the end of each year. In 1939 the bonus amounted to 40% of annual wages. Mr. Clarkson was planning to incorporate the business in the near future and to sell stock to certain employees.

As a part of its customary investigation of prospective borrowers, the Northrup National Bank sent inquiries concerning Mr. Clarkson to a number of firms which had business dealings with him. The manager of one of his large suppliers, the Barker Company, wrote in answer:

> The conservative operation of his business appeals to us. He has not wasted his money in disproportionate plant investment. His operating expenses are as low as they could possibly be. He has personal control over every feature of his business, and he possesses sound judgment and a willingness to work harder than anyone I have ever known. This, with a good personality, gives him an excellent turnover; and from my personal experience in watching him work, I know that he keeps close check on his own credits.

All of the other trade letters received by the bank bore out the statements quoted above.

In addition to the ownership of his lumber business, Mr. Clarkson held jointly with his wife an equity in their home, which was mortgaged for $12,000 and which cost $20,160 to build in 1927. He also held a $16,000 life insurance policy, payable to Mrs. Clarkson. Mrs. Clarkson owned independently a half-interest in a home worth about $8,000.

The bank gave particular attention to the debt position and current ratio of the business. It noted the ready market for the company's products at all times and the fact that sales prospects were particularly favorable. The bank's investigator reported: ". . . it is estimated sales may run from $1,280,000 to $1,600,000 in 1940." The rate of inventory turnover was high, and losses on bad debts in past years had been quite small. Comparative balance sheets as of December 31, 1937, through 1939 and as of March 31, 1940, are given in Exhibit 2.

The bank learned, through inquiry of another wholesale lumber company, that the usual terms of purchase in the trade were 2%. 10 days after arrival. Suppliers took 60-day notes when requested but did this somewhat unwillingly.

Exhibit 1

CLARKSON LUMBER COMPANY

OPERATING STATEMENTS FOR THE YEARS ENDING DECEMBER 31, 1937, THROUGH 1939 AND FOR THE THREE MONTHS ENDING MARCH 31, 1940

(Dollar figures in thousands)

	1937	1938	1939	1st Quarter 1940
Net sales	$740	$880	$1,179	$310*
Cost of goods sold:				
Beginning inventory	111	97	141	180
Purchases	611	846	1,069	336
	$722	$943	$1,210	$516
Ending inventory	97	141	180	244
Cost of goods sold	$625	$802	$1,030	$272
Gross profit	$115	$78	$149	$38
Operating expenses	38	48	73	20
Net operating profit	$77	$30	$76	$18
Add: Purchase discounts taken	5	5	5	0.6
	$82	$35	$81	$19
Deduct: Sales discounts allowed	16	18	28	8
Net profit†	$66	$17	$53	$11*
Drawings by proprietor	.....	.....	$28	$6

* In the first quarter of 1939, net sales were $252,000 and net profit was $13,000.

† This item is stated before any provision for federal income tax liabilities. As distinct from corporations, no federal income taxes are levied on the profits of proprietorships and partnerships, as such. The owners of a proprietorship or partnership, however, must include in their personal income their proportionate share of such profits and must pay taxes on them at the regular personal income tax rates.

Exhibit 2
CLARKSON LUMBER COMPANY
Comparative Balance Sheets as of December 31, 1937, through 1939, and as of March 31, 1940

ASSETS	1937	1938	1939	March 31 1940
Cash	$ 56	$ 282	$ 3,560	$ 1,338
Accounts receivable—net of reserve for bad debts	57,322	89,387	109,686	128,893
Inventory	97,005	141,416	179,557	243,658
Total current assets	$154,383	$231,085	$292,803	$373,889
Property—net of reserve for depreciation	5,963	7,608	11,430	10,361
Deferred charges				2,594
Total assets	$160,346	$238,693	$304,233	$386,844

LIABILITIES	1937	1938	1939	March 31 1940
Notes payable—bank				$ 48,000
Notes payable—employees for bonuses				4,840
Notes payable—Henry Stark	$ 32,000			
Notes payable—trade				65,767
Accounts payable	57,460	$136,723	$173,439	138,336
Accrued expenses		3,440	7,194	902
Total current liabilities	$ 89,460	$140,163	$180,633	$257,845
Net worth	70,886	98,530	123,600	128,999
Total liabilities	$160,346	$238,693	$304,233	$386,844

Case 8

Union Paint and Varnish Company

ON APRIL 14, 1952, in Los Angeles, Mr. Robert Maple, the credit manager, and Mr. Harry Hill, the regional manager of the Union Paint and Varnish Company, met with Mr. Sidney G. Snider, president of Suburban Auto Stores Corporation, to discuss possible credit arrangements for sales of Union products to Suburban. After extensive discussion concerning the current financial position and future prospects of Suburban, Mr. Snider asked if Mr. Maple would approve three-year terms on an initial order, amounting to some $35,-000, for a basic inventory of the complete line of Union products. If such an arrangement could be made, Mr. Snider also wanted to know upon what credit basis "fill-in" orders to replace goods sold could be placed.

Union Paint (see Exhibit 1 for 1951 financial statements) was operating near capacity in the spring of 1952, but with the anticipated return to a "buyers' market," Union began to prepare for increasingly keen competition. Accordingly, Union was aggressively seeking new outlets through which to sell the company's expanding volume. In this connection, Mr. Hill had pointed out that Suburban, whose account he had sought for several years, had an excellent reputation for being an aggressive merchandising organization; he stressed to Mr. Maple the fact that Union's weakest market coverage was "right in its own backyard," Los Angeles.

For about a year the sales department had been pursuing a nationwide promotional and merchandising program addressed to consumers. In addition, missionary salesmen worked to develop new dealerships, which frequently were excellent market outlets but were financially undercapitalized. Although typical terms to retail accounts were 1/10, n/60, terms up to five years had been granted to enable new accounts of this type to purchase permanent display and backup stock. Such arrangements were believed necessary to get adequate market coverage and to continue large volume operations.

Mr. Hill told Mr. Maple of the opportunity at Suburban on April 2, 1952. The previous day, Mr. Hill had visited the offices of Suburban and talked with Mr. Snider, its president. Mr. Snider had said that he desired a three-year payment plan to enable him to acquire the initial stock. Mr. Hill had replied that he could make no commitment, but believed that an extended payment plan could be arranged to cover the initial stock of paints and varnishes.

After this meeting, Mr. Hill concluded that Suburban could now be sold, and thought that steps should be taken promptly to "sew up" the potential account, for he realized that Union's competitors might also recognize Suburban's readiness to drop its present line. He asked Mr. Maple to act as promptly as possible to determine the credit standing of Suburban. Mr. Maple ordered a credit agency report and called his company's bank of account, Golden Gate Trust Company, in San Francisco, requesting information regarding Suburban.

On April 7, Mr. Maple received the credit report (see Exhibit 2) and a phone call from John Farmer, an officer of the bank, who reported that the company was indebted to three Los Angeles banks for a total of $345,000, each bank participating equally. These loans, he said, were unsecured but endorsed by Mr. Sidney Snider, president of Suburban. Mr. Farmer stated that the loans, which had been made on a 90-day renewable basis, matured on March 31, 1952, but that a temporary extension on a demand basis had been granted to permit the corporation to raise approximately $150,000, the estimated amount which Suburban had lost through operations for the fiscal year ended January 31, 1952. Although no specific time limit had been set for raising the $150,000, it was generally understood that this was to be accomplished by the end of May, 1952. The banks were not willing to comment on how long they would continue "to go along with" Suburban. Such action appeared to depend upon the company's ability to raise funds from outside sources to replace the operating loss.

The total cash balance among the three banks was reported to be slightly more than $60,000 at the moment. A few trade creditors in 1952 indicated a slow manner of payment which had not been experienced previously. All, however, considered Suburban a desirable account.

Suburban's inventory position in March was reported to be in excess of $1 million despite vigorous attempts to liquidate a surplus of television sets and major appliances in late 1951. The banks were reported to be dissatisfied with this inventory, having concluded that substantial investment rested in types of goods which were moving too slowly. Furthermore, Mr. Farmer stated that the banks were unhappy about a new store opened in November, 1951, when funds were known to be needed to bolster a weak working capital condition. Nevertheless, Mr. Farmer added that the three banks unanimously agreed that they held the Suburban management in high regard as an aggressive merchandising organization.

On Tuesday morning, April 8, Mr. Maple met with Mr. Hill and Union sales manager, Mr. Joseph Carton, to discuss Suburban as a potential account. Mr. Maple said that it appeared to him inadvisable to make a definite decision regarding a deferred payment plan with Suburban until its financial status, especially the relationships with the banks, could be clarified.

Mr. Carton reported that he had learned that Suburban was interested in changing its line of paints because it was dissatisfied with the selling arrangements made by its current supplier, another nationally known manufacturer. Suburban was required to purchase paint products on a consignment basis, a procedure that was both bothersome and embarrassing.

Mr. Carton was anxious to get a decision on this account because he estimated, based on Suburban's sales of paint products in past years, that Union's sales should run in excess of $150,000 annually. He re-emphasized that all Suburban's sales would be in territory new to Union, since only a few small hardware stores were handling Union's line in Los Angeles.

Mr. Hill commented that, although Mr. Snider had not mentioned it, he had learned through others in the trade that two other national paint manufacturers were currently attempting to sell Suburban Auto Stores their complete line. He further noted that Dun & Bradstreet, Inc., had rated the firm AA1 on January 16. Mr. Maple replied that nevertheless the company was short of working capital, was at that time negotiating with its banks regarding future loans, and that the Dun & Bradstreet report did not reflect the as yet unpublished January 31, 1952, statement.

The credit department of Union Paint and Varnish Company had classified its accounts in three categories: (A) well-financed customers—virtually no risk of loss; (B) moderately financed customers—average risk of loss; and (C) financially weak customers—great risk of loss.

As of April 1, category C accounts totaled nearly $440,000 for

accounts sold on regular terms. In addition, about $75,000 of $750,-
000 receivables on extended terms (averaging three years) were in
category C. Since Mr. Maple believed that the proposed account
would be in the C group, he pointed out to Messrs. Carton and Hill
that a decline in general business activity might bring substantial bad
debt losses. The fact that Union's bad debt losses had been less than
one half of 1% of credit sales since 1945 did not measure possible
losses in a depression.

Mr. Carton quickly countered that since about one fifth of the company's total expenses continued regardless of sales, he was obliged
continually to get more volume in order to spread those fixed charges
as thinly as possible. Thus, Union had to take certain calculated risks
to break into the Southern California market, where there was potentially great volume. Finally, Mr. Carton said that even if Suburban
resulted eventually in a loss, in the meantime enough volume could
well have been accomplished to more than offset the loss.

On April 10, Mr. Hill, at the request of Mr. Maple, had visited
two of Suburban's banks of account to get the most recent information on the company. Officers in both banks expressed considerable
faith in the management of Suburban. They indicated that, although
the company had suffered a loss of more than $100,000 as a result of
a drop in television and major appliance sales, this was typical of the
retail trade during 1951. Both officers told Mr. Hill that they were
willing to continue accommodating Suburban at least until July of
1952, when they could review operating results for the first six
months of the year.

On April 11, Mr. Hill, concerned about the possibility of losing a
large potential customer, arranged for Mr. Maple to visit Mr. Snider
on the 14th in Los Angeles. At this meeting, Mr. Snider showed Mr.
Maple summary figures as of January 31, 1952, stating that he wished
to keep the statement confidential until it was made public in about a
week. These figures are shown below:

SUBURBAN AUTO STORES CORPORATION
BALANCE SHEET AS OF 1/31/52

Cash	$ 64,975	Due banks	$ 345,000
Accounts receivable	102,695	Accounts payable	347,645
Inventory	1,227,760	Reserve for taxes	32,555
Total current assets	$1,395,430	Other current liabilities	117,875
Equipment, fixtures	185,725	Total current liabilities	$ 843,075
Prepayments	23,000	Reserve	64,170
Total assets	$1,604,155	Net worth	696,910
			$1,604,155

Mr. Snider said that although the television inventory had reached a high point during the last year of $500,000, the inventory position in April amounted to only $125,000. He also stated that the gross profit on television sales throughout the country dropped considerably between 1950 and 1951. For Suburban, this drop was from 22% to 16%, thus causing a $148,000 loss in spite of the fact that sales volume and gross profit on most other items sold by the company remained at very even levels. It was Mr. Snider's opinion that rapid progress could be made, since the newest store of the chain was just getting established.

Mr. Snider asked Mr. Maple whether three-year terms might be given his company on an initial order of about $35,000. He said he understood that fill-in orders were usually offered on a 1/10, n/60 basis. It was his estimate that Suburban should be able to do an annual volume with Union of over $200,000 if such terms were offered.

Exhibit 1

UNION PAINT AND VARNISH COMPANY

BALANCE SHEET AND INCOME STATEMENT FOR YEAR ENDING DECEMBER 31, 1951

(Dollar figures in thousands)

BALANCE SHEET

CURRENT ASSETS		CURRENT LIABILITIES	
Cash	$ 14,991	Accounts payable	$ 5,675
Accounts receivable* (net)	22,317	Federal and state income taxes	10,790
Inventories	35,777	Miscellaneous accruals	1,516
Total	$ 73,085	Current portion term loan	1,725
		Total	$ 19,706
Real estate, plant and equipment	61,188		
Less: Reserve for depreciation	25,659	Term loan—banks†	14,950
	$ 35,529	Common stock	29,587
Prepaid and deferred charges	1,641	Surplus	46,012
Total assets	$110,255	Total liabilities	$110,255

* Bad debt reserve, $601,831.

† Term loan with five banks at 3%, payable at rate of $1,725,000 each January 15 to 1961, when final payment is $2,875,000.

INCOME STATEMENT

Net sales	$262,801
Cost of sales	214,282
Gross profit	$ 48,519
Selling, general and administrative expense	30,224*
Operating profit	$ 18,295†
Provision for federal income taxes	8,314
Net profit	$ 9,981

* Includes $152,725 for bad debt expense.

† Total costs were composed of approximately 20% fixed costs, with 80% variable with volume of production.

Exhibit 2

UNION PAINT AND VARNISH COMPANY

WEST COAST CREDIT REPORTS, INC.

October 15, 1951

Suburban Auto Stores Corporation   Los Angeles, California

Sidney G. Snider—*President and Treasurer*

Jack Binstein—*Exec. Vice President*

Laura B. Goode—*Secretary*

SUMMARY

CORPORATION FORMED 1932; HOLDS A PROMINENT POSITION LOCALLY IN RETAIL TRADE. OPERATIONS HAVE SHOWN A PROFITABLE TREND IN RECENT YEARS ON AN EXPANDING VOLUME. FINANCIAL STATEMENTS OF JANUARY 31, 1951, SHOWED TANGIBLE NET WORTH $855,000 AND A GENERALLY SATISFACTORY FINANCIAL CONDITION. SUBSTANTIAL UN-SECURED BANK ACCOMMODATION AVAILABLE, WITH ACTIVE USE MADE OF BORROWING FACILITIES. TRADE PAYMENTS SATISFACTORY.

PERSONNEL

Sidney G. Snider, born 1898, married; started business in this line in 1921 with his older brother, Julius Snider, operation under the trade name of Julius Snider Company, Inc. On May 4, 1932, a 50% settlement was made with creditors on an indebtedness of $168,000. Julius Snider Company, Inc., continues active in the automobile supply line with Julius Snider, President and Treasurer, and Sidney G. Snider as Executive Vice President of this corporation.

Jack Binstein, born 1906, married; was elected Executive Vice President in June, 1949. He was formerly employed as an accountant for the company.

Laura B. Goode was appointed Secretary of Suburban Auto Stores in 1947, having been employed by Sidney Snider as his personal secretary since 1936.

HISTORY

INCORPORATED: Under California laws, October 10, 1932, as a new business. *Authorized Capital Stock:* 250,000 shares of Common Stock.

General Background Information: From its inception, this organization grew rapidly, opening new stores from time to time; and by the end of the fiscal year of 1941, the chain operated a total of 32 stores. During the war years, 17 of these stores were closed as the results of war shortages. In the postwar period, 5 of the original stores have been enlarged and modernized and 4 stores added. Until 1941, the company was engaged exclusively in the retailing of automobile accessories and equipment. Since 1942, new lines have been added from time to time, so that the automotive merchandise now constitutes less than 50% of the total volume. Merchandise now carried includes radios, television sets, major electrical appliances and minor appliances, work clothes and related apparel, hardware, housefurnishings, unpainted furniture, house paints, glassware, automobile supplies, tires and accessories, batteries and supplies, toys, luggage and sporting goods.

Locations: All the store locations are leased. Executive offices are maintained at South Flower Street, Los Angeles, where the corporation leases approximately 50,000 square feet of floor space.

Number of Employees: Total 335 employees.

Terms of Sale: Cash sales account for approximately 95% of total volume, this percentage including instalment sales, which are financed by a bank, without recourse. Suburban receives full cash payments from the bank as soon as the latter has approved credit for the account. The remaining 5% of sales are on a deferred payment plan, payments being scheduled up to a period of three months, with notes on certain sales being secured by a chattel mortgage on automobiles. This paper is carried by Suburban.

COMPARATIVE FINANCIAL STATEMENTS

	Jan. 31, 1949	*Jan. 31, 1950*	*Jan. 31, 1951*
Cash	$ 121,305	$ 130,361	$ 157,402
Accounts receivable	49,628	49,128	86,598
Inventory	1,291,778	1,293,516	1,347,799
Total current assets	$1,462,711	$1,473,005	$1,591,799
Equipment, fixtures	132,574	144,712	129,578
Prepaid and deferred	22,005	29,775	24,048
Total assets	$1,617,290	$1,647,492	$1,745,425
Due banks	$ 345,000	$ 345,000	$ 345,000
Accounts payable	285,963	323,615	291,062
Reserve for taxes	120,518	96,295	101,835
Television service contract	......	44,759	75,183
Customers' deposits	......	14,778	19,864
Total current liabilities	751,481	824,447	832,944
Reserve unrealized profit on instalment sales	51,633	41,700	57,524
Common stock	433,838	400,833	394,422
Surplus	380,338	380,512	460,535
Total liabilities	$1,617,290	$1,647,492	$1,745,425
Net sales	$6,800,228	$7,304,935	$8,292,551
Net Profit*	......	......	......
Dividends*	......	......	......

* Not made public.

GENERAL COMMENTS

Management has declined to furnish complete operating particulars, but points out that during fiscal year ended January 31, 1951, company realized satisfactory profit from operations. This profit was offset to a large extent through inventory writedowns.

Financial condition at January 31, 1951, continues to show relatively large current debt as the result of transacting a sizable volume in relation to net working capital, but at the same time the figures reflect a favorable improvement over the preceding year.

Notwithstanding the fact that company trades quite actively in relation to the net investment, it has been able to finance operations and to meet maturing obligations in a satisfactory manner by reason of the fact that fully 95% of sales are on a cash or close to cash basis, plus the fact that substantial bank lines are utilized in order to enable the company to carry representative lines of merchandise at each of its stores. During periods of lower than average inventories (which usually occur in the early months of the calendar year), bank loans are rotated in order to give each bank a full cleanup. During the remaining months of the year, full use is made of borrowing facilities at all of the company's banks.

Television service contracts payable, amounting to $75,183 at January 31, 1951, are liquidated at monthly intervals during the life of each service contract, which runs for a period of one year.

Reserve for unrealized profit on instalment sales, $57,524, is a surplus reserve transferrable to earned surplus on a percentage basis, upon collection of each monthly payment on respective instalment basis.

BANKING RELATIONS

Accounts are maintained at three local banks. Satisfactory average balances are reported. Accommodation is granted on corporate note, endorsed by Sidney G. Snider. In addition, one of the banks also discounts customers' paper on a nonrecourse basis. Active use is made of loan facilities, but each of the banks was given a full cleanup during the current year.

CREDIT INTERCHANGE BUREAUS
OF THE
NATIONAL ASSOCIATION OF CREDIT MEN

Central Offices
512 Arcade Bldg.
St. Louis 1, Mo.

Report on   SUBURBAN AUTO STORES CORP.   Los Angeles, California
South Flower Street
Los Angeles County

March 16, 1952

The accuracy of this Report is not guaranteed. Its contents are gathered in good faith from members and sent to you by this Bureau without liability for negligence in procuring, collecting, communicating or failing to communicate the information so gathered.

Business Classification	How Long Sold	Date of Last Sale	Highest Recent Credit	Now Owing Including Notes	Past Due	Terms of Sale	Dis-counts	Pays When Due	Days Slow	Comments
SOUTHERN CALIF. 220–2										
AutoA	yrs.	1–52	12,310	5,900		2-10 EOM		x		
Hdwe.	yrs.	12–51	1,855	712	712	2-10-30	x		30	Slower
Inds.	1 yr.	12–51	26,475	12,575		60-1-10		x		
Tool	yrs.	1–52	175			2-10-30		x		
I & S	2 yrs.	1–52	19,400	7,300		Special		x		
Elec.	yrs.	11–51	28,940	1,940		2-10-30			30	
Elec.	yrs.	12–51	1,940	1,940	1,940	2-10-30			45	
AutoA	10–51	1–52	1,058			2-10	x			
Chem.	yrs.	12–51	838	838		2-10px	x	x		
Rdo.	yrs.	12–51	8,125	1,550	1,550	2-10 EOM			60	
Equip.	6–51	11–51	3,084	1,550	1,550	3-5px			90	
Tex.	yrs.	10–51	24,600	18,600	16,500	2-10 EOM				
NORTH & CEN-TRAL CALIF. 221–14										
AutoA	yrs.	1–52	28,375	28,375	500	2-10 EOM	x	x	30	First time slow
Elec.	10–51	12–51	940			5-10-30			30	
Hdwe.	yrs.	10–51	19,529	19,529		2-10-30				
Plstc.	yrs.	12–51	7,500	7,500		2-10px		x		
Rbr.	yrs.	1–52	22,478	22,478		Regular		x		

Business Classification	How Long Sold	Date of Last Sale	Highest Recent Credit	Now Owing (Including Notes)	Past Due	Terms of Sale	Dis-counts	Pays When Due	Days Slow	Comments
ARIZONA 222–12										
Chem.	yrs.	9–51	250			2–10px		x		
Elec.	yrs.	11–51	24,490			2–10–30		x	30	
Equip.	6–51	1–52	2,845	2,845	2,845	2–10px			45	
ROCKY MTS. 223–106										
Chem.	yrs.	11–51	28,464	28,464	6,464	2–10–30			60	Slower
AutoA	yrs.	10–51	21,495	21,475	21,475	2–10–30			90	First sale
Elec.	1–52	1–52	7,050			2–10–30	x			
I & S	yrs.	1–52	22,310			2–10 EOM		x		
Inds.	yrs.	11–51	27,400			Special		x		
CHICAGO 223–18										
Elec.	yrs.	12–51	490	490	490	2–10 EOM		x	45	
Hdwe.	yrs.	1–52	26,400	12,400		2–10–30		x		
Hdwe.	yrs.	1–52	9,410	9,410		2–10–30				
Equip.	6 mos.	9–51	3,000					x	45	
Tool	yrs.	1–52	18,650	18,650		2–10–30				
CLEVELAND 223–28										
Elec.	12–51	1–52	5,100	5,100		2–10–30	x	x	30–60	
Chem.	yrs.	9–51	3,400			2–10–30				
TOLEDO 223–19										
Rbr.	yrs.	12–51	23,540	18,500	12,500	Regular		x	90	
Rbr.	yrs.	1–52	7,500	7,500		2–10px				
NEW YORK–PHILADELPHIA 224–225										
Elec.	1–51	12–51	16,538	8,538	3,540	2–10–30			45	
Chem.	yrs.	1–52	250				x	x		
Tex.	yrs.	1–52	1,812	800		2–10–30	x			
Hdwe.	yrs.	12–51	6,540							

BU 95 LM

Case 9

Bedrock Life Insurance Company

"JOHN, I'm flying to Chicago late this afternoon. I understand the J. I. Case annual report just came in and that they showed a big loss last year. Dig into the report for me and summarize the highlights. As you know, we own a few of their debentures. I expect to be talking with some bankers who are close to the Case situation, so point up any questions I ought to ask them. Please come on up with what you've got on Case by 4:00 o'clock."

With these instructions from his boss, an investment officer of Bedrock Life Insurance Company, John Stahley, a young investment analyst, turned to the assignment. The material in Exhibits 1 through 6 is excerpted from the published annual reports of J. I. Case Company for 1959 and 1960.

Exhibit 1

BEDROCK LIFE INSURANCE COMPANY
J. I. CASE COMPANY—
REPORT TO STOCKHOLDERS, 1959*

Fiscal 1959 established a new level in your company's volume of sales and, for the second consecutive year, broke all previous sales records in the J. I. Case Company's 117-year history.

This continued upward trend in sales was evident in practically every phase of our operation, and was particularly pronounced in the greatly expanding sales of our construction, roadbuilding, and materials handling wheel and crawler tractors and equipment. By the end of the 1959 fiscal year, the Case Industrial Division, which was established early in 1957 as an outgrowth of the merger with American Tractor Corporation, had grown into one of the major sales and profit-producing segments of our operation.

In this period of less than three years, Case sales of construction, roadbuilding and materials handling equipment increased to over $63 million, or

* SOURCE: J. I. Case Company, *Annual Report, 1959*, p. 2.

678

Exhibit 1—Continued

better than 30% of the company's total volume. Even more significant, however, is the future outlook of this division which, at the end of the 1959 fiscal
year, ranked among the ten largest in the industry.

Earnings in fiscal 1959, and for the past three years in a row, have exceeded our rate of sales growth. This underlines the soundness of your management's long-range growth policy, which is based on the three-phase
sequence of new product engineering, higher sales, and greater profits. This
fundamental business philosophy is particularly well tailored to the J. I.
Case Company, whose domestic and overseas manufacturing facilities include the manufacture of our own engines, transmissions, forgings, castings,
hydraulics and other major components. It is expected that these integrated
facilities will make it possible to substantially increase our production and
sales in ensuing years. . . .

Exhibit 2

BEDROCK LIFE INSURANCE COMPANY

J. I. CASE COMPANY—
PART I: PRESIDENT'S LETTER, 1960*

DEAR FELLOW STOCKHOLDERS:

The fiscal year ended October 31, 1960 was a critical period in the history
of your Company. A major program was undertaken toward putting J. I.
Case on a firm financial basis. Financial highlights of the year follow:

The consolidated income statement showed a loss of $39,814,973. A tax
loss carry-forward of $25,000,000 resulted from the loss that can be applied
against earnings of future years.

The loss had an adverse effect on net working capital which was $10,-
771,948 at year-end, compared with $59,033,807 a year earlier.

To provide necessary funds the Company increased its bank loans to $82,-
279,457 at the end of the year, compared with $36,803,707 a year earlier.
Short-term indebtedness of J. I. Case Credit Corporation was $62,364,992 at
the end of the year, compared with $105,404,730 at the end of the previous
year. Part of this reduction was made possible by the placement early in the
year of $20,000,000 of 15-year notes with four institutional investors. The
total short-term indebtedness of both Companies was $144,644,449 on Octo-
ber 31, 1960, compared with $142,208,437 at the previous year-end.

On the positive side, retail sales (as measured by wholesale settlements)
were at $168,834,000, compared with $174,941,000 for the previous year.
From the retail standpoint the 1960 fiscal year was the second best in your
Company's recent history. This was achieved in spite of serious shortages
of certain products during our fall selling season due to strikes at two of
our plants.

Reducing dealer inventories and wholesale accounts receivable was the
first task undertaken by the undersigned after being elected chief executive
officer of your Company in the early part of the year. The continuous
build-up of inventory in the hands of our dealers was halted and substantial

---

* SOURCE: J. I. Case Company, *Annual Report, 1960.*

Exhibit 2—Continued

progress was made in reducing unsold stock in the field to manageable proportions.

As evidence of the progress made in moving dealer inventories, wholesale accounts receivable of Case at the end of 1960 were reduced to $20,731,528 from $33,848,705 at the previous year-end. The Wholesale receivables of Case Credit, which represent inventories in the hands of our dealers, were reduced during the year to $87,350,692 from $112,828,374. The total reduction in the aggregate was $38,594,859, as compared with an increase of approximately $89,000,000 in the previous three years.

This reduction in dealer inventories was the result of a two-point program. First, sales efforts were concentrated on helping our dealers move their inventory through the promotion of retail sales. This involved additional selling expenses which were charged to 1960 operations. Second, production and shipments to dealers were limited to levels which would permit a significant reduction. Since certain costs and expenses continue regardless of plant activity, the reduced production level and the strikes at two of our plants had a severe effect upon income. Sales of the Company to its dealers were $127,041,387 during 1960, compared with $200,582,136 for the previous year. A major part of our loss in 1960 may be attributed to these factors.

The progress made during the year in correcting our distribution problems enabled us to commence production for fiscal 1961 two months earlier than usual. This accounts for the higher factory and branch year-end inventories which were $65,869,426 compared with $56,660,373 a year earlier. As a result, new equipment will be available to our dealers in time for the selling season.

Development Expense Re-evaluated

Since 1957, major product development costs have been charged off over a two-year period. In 1960 we returned to our former practice of charging these costs to operations as incurred. Consequently, we absorbed in this year all of this year's charges in addition to those unamortized in previous years.

Marketing Organization Strengthened

In a major move the Company established an overall marketing division, encompassing all phases of our marketing activities. We have also re-oriented our sales program to place major emphasis on retail sales. The potential for specific products will be explored by market research in advance of the selling season. These are fresh concepts which are expected to increase the effectiveness of our product development, production and sales effort.

On October 7, 1960, Mr. A. Earl Lee was elected Vice President, Marketing, to supervise and co-ordinate all of the Company's marketing activities. Mr. Lee was previously Manager, Marketing and Economics Research North American Operations, for a leading manufacturer of agricultural machinery.

Credit Corporation Position Improved

J. I. Case Credit Corporation, a wholly-owned subsidiary, continues to operate at a profit. It improved its receivable and working capital position significantly.

Wholesale receivables were reduced from $112,800,000 to $87,350,000.

Exhibit 2—Continued

Retail receivables, which are the most profitable for the Corporation, remained steady at $99,000,000, compared with $100,700,000 a year ago.

Summing Up

While ample dealer stocks are necessary for adequate retail movement of goods and will be maintained, wholesale sales are budgeted in relation to retail requirements to allow for still further reductions in dealer inventories.

With much of the correction behind us, production will more nearly approximate our sales level. This will enable better production scheduling and more efficient operation. Additional study is being given to measures designed to further reduce costs and otherwise improve efficiency of manufacturing operations.

Tighter budgetary controls have been put into effect and should reduce expenses.

New products introduced are proving very popular.

In summation, the 1960 fiscal year bore the impact of adjustments deemed necessary by the management. The financial results are disappointing. We believe, however, that the course of action started in 1960 will prove to be in the best interest of stockholders. In the light of corrections made and progress to date, your management is optimistic about the future of the Company. We urge you to study the detailed presentation of our overall operations on the following pages.

WM. J. GREDE, *President*

January 19, 1961

PART II: YEAR IN REVIEW*

OPERATING RESULTS

The loss for the year after tax credit was $39,814,973 as compared with a reported net profit in the prior year of $6,200,111. Following is an analysis of the causes for this difference.

(In Millions)

Unusual costs attributable to reduced wholesale sales volume of $73,000,000 and reduced production level of $65,000,000 (including the estimated effects of strikes at Racine and Bettendorf plants)	$29.9
Non-recurring charges:	
Increase in research and development expense, primarily as a result of change in accounting policy to write-off such expense as incurred (before adjustment for related taxes on income)	5.5
Other, principally special allowances to move dealer inventories and losses on liquidation of receivables	8.7
Adjustment of carrying value of investment in French subsidiaries	6.0
Added costs during 1960 such as increases in interest and selling expenses	8.9
Difference in taxes on income	(13.0)
Total	$46.0

* SOURCE: J. I. Case Company, *Annual Report, 1960*, pp. 5–6.

Exhibit 2—Continued

J. I. CASE CREDIT CORPORATION

Earnings of J. I. Case Credit Corporation in 1960 were $2,233,105 as compared with $2,033,813 in the previous year. This subsidiary provides credit facilities for our dealers and retail customers.

OVERSEAS SUBSIDIARIES

The operations of the French manufacturing subsidiaries of the Company resulted in a loss in 1960 of $4.0 million which, when added to the prior year's losses, substantially eliminates the underlying equity. This loss of equity has been recognized by a charge against earnings of J. I. Case Company in 1960. The French operation is a serious problem and is presently the subject of intensive study. However, it now appears that the operation will be continued without substantial further loss.

J. I. Case International, S. A., and the other overseas subsidiaries, namely, J. I. Case Company, Limited (Britain), J. I. Case do Brasil (Brazil), and J. I. Case (Australia) Pty. Ltd., showed sales increases and were, in the aggregate, profitable operations in 1960.

DIVIDENDS

Under the provisions of the bank Credit Agreement dated September 15, 1960, payment of dividends on the Company's 7% Cumulative Preferred stock and the 6½% Second Cumulative Preferred stock is restricted to consolidated net income earned after October 31, 1960. As previously announced, in order to conserve working capital, the Directors of the Company did not declare the dividend on the Preferred Stocks which would have ordinarily been paid on January 3, 1961.

ENGINEERING AND NEW PRODUCT DEVELOPMENT

Recognizing its importance to the future of the Company, product development and engineering in the agricultural, construction and materials handling lines of equipment is continuing. A steady flow of new products will be introduced in the years ahead.

MANAGEMENT

On February 1, 1960, Wm. J. Grede, Director since 1953, was elected President. On December 19, 1960, Mr. Grede was also elected Chairman of of the Board, succeeding John T. Brown who was elected Vice Chairman of the Board. Mr. Grede was formerly President of Grede Foundries, Inc., of Milwaukee, Wisconsin. He is a member of the Board of the Federal Reserve Bank of Chicago and a former President of the National Association of Manufacturers.

On August 15, 1960, William Ewing, a limited partner of Morgan Stanley & Co., retired as a Director of the Company after serving in that capacity for forty years, and H. Edward Vollmers, a general partner in the firm of Morgan Stanley & Co., was elected a Director. Mr. Vollmers was elected a member of the Executive Committee of the Board on September 1, 1960.

Exhibit 2—Continued

INDUSTRY TRENDS

With the upward trend in gross farm income in the later months of 1960, it would appear that the retail farm equipment market will be moderately improved in 1961. Current estimates are that farmers' cash receipts were fractionally above the $33.8 billion received in 1959, with increased volume offsetting price declines. The U.S. Department of Agriculture has reported that 1960 crop production was at an all-time high. Historically, increased sales of farm equipment have followed a good crop year.

Man-hour productivity has increased 120% in agriculture since 1940, compared with a 50% increase in industry as a whole. This has been achieved through increased use of chemical fertilizer and increasing mechanization. This latter trend provides a substantial replacement market as well as a steady demand for additional equipment.

In the construction field, highway contract awards have increased throughout 1960, and this should have a salutary effect on the sale of industrial equipment. Housing starts in 1960 fell 17% below the level of 1959, which depressed machinery sales related to residential building. The easing of credit during the past year has not yet significantly affected the demand for housing, and an upturn will depend on general economic developments. The latest government estimates indicate total new construction of all types will be up 4%.

Exhibit 3

BEDROCK LIFE INSURANCE COMPANY
J. I. CASE COMPANY AND CONSOLIDATED SUBSIDIARY COMPANIES
Statement of Operations and Accumulated Earnings
Retained for Reinvestment in the Business
for the Years Ended October 31, 1960 and 1959
(Dollar figures in thousands)

	1960	1959
Gross sales, less returns and allowances	$127,041	$200,582
Cost of goods sold, selling and distribution, and administrative expenses (including depreciation of $5,094,743 in 1960 and $5,069,291 in 1959)	159,481	182,706
(Loss) or income from operations	$(32,440)	$ 17,876
Other credits:		
Income of J. I. Case Credit Corporation, before taxes on income	4,833	4,384
Interest and finance charges earned	1,687	1,310
Miscellaneous	368	234
	$(25,552)	$ 23,804
Other charges:		
Finance charges less interest received from J. I. Case Credit Corporation	8,991	6,535
Interest paid	5,557	4,304
Provision for losses of nonconsolidated French subsidiaries (Note 4)*	5,965	. . . .
	$ 20,513	$ 10,839
(Loss) or income before taxes on income	$(46,065)	$ 12,965
(Credit) or provision for taxes on income:		
Federal	(6,550)	6,450
State and foreign	300	315
	$ (6,250)	$ 6,765
Net (loss) or income for the year	$(39,815)	$ 6,200
Accumulated earnings retained for reinvestment in the business at beginning of year	54,111	49,097
	$ 14,296	$ 55,297
Dividends paid in cash on:		
7% cumulative preferred stock—$7 per share	650	650
6½% second cumulative preferred stock—$4.55 per share	546	536
	$ 1,196	$ 1,186
Accumulated earnings retained for reinvestment in the business at end of year (Note 7)*	$ 13,100	$ 54,111

* The notes referred to in this exhibit are reproduced at the end of Exhibit 4.
SOURCE: Adapted from material in J. I. Case Company, *Annual Report, 1960*.

Exhibit 4

BEDROCK LIFE INSURANCE COMPANY
J. I. CASE COMPANY AND CONSOLIDATED SUBSIDIARY COMPANIES
Statement of Financial Condition,
October 31, 1960 and 1959
(Dollar figures in thousands)

ASSETS

	1960	1959
Current Assets:		
Cash	$ 13,240	$ 11,991
Notes and accounts receivable:		
Customers:		
Notes	6,230	5,545
Accounts	14,501	28,304
Estimated doubtful accounts	(1,000)	(500)
Sundry receivables	1,234	1,651
Claim for refund of income taxes (Note 3)	4,563	......
Due from J. I. Case Credit Corporation	4,732	13,358
Inventories:		
Industrial at average cost, not in excess of market; agricultural at cost, on "last-in, first-out" basis. "LIFO" inventories were $17,750,000 below current cost at October 31, 1960, and $18,000,000 below current cost at October 31, 1959	65,869	56,660
Prepaid expenses	1,264	1,520
Total current assets (Note 2)	$110,633	$118,529
Investments and Other Assets:		
Investment in J. I. Case Credit Corporation, at equity in underlying net assets (see accompanying financial statements)	52,162	44,929
Investment, advances, and current accounts receivable—French subsidiaries, less provision for losses of $5,965 in 1960 (Note 4)	793	737
Deferred engineering and product development costs (Note 5)	......	4,141
Other deferred charges	584	562
Miscellaneous	2,453	1,395
	$ 55,992	$ 51,764
Properties, at cost:		
Land	2,460	2,256
Buildings, plant, and equipment	83,674	81,063
	$ 86,134	$ 83,319
Accumulated depreciation	45,425	43,277
	$ 40,709	$ 40,042
Excess of Cost of Assets Acquired Over Assigned Value Thereof (Note 6)	11,546	11,946
	$218,880	$222,281

LIABILITIES

	1960	1959
Current Liabilities:		
Notes payable to banks (Note 7)	$ 82,279	$ 36,804
Accounts payable	8,046	13,391
Accrued liabilities	8,159	4,838
Federal and other taxes on income (Note 3)	539	3,680
Current portion of long-term debt, less cost of debentures held in treasury	838	782
Total current liabilities (Note 2)	$ 99,861	$ 59,495
Deferred Income Taxes	......	2,350
Long-Term Debt:		
Twenty-five year 3½% sinking fund debentures, due February 1, 1978, less amount due within one year	20,955	22,023
5½% subordinated debentures, due 1983, convertible into common stock until October 15, 1968, at $22.75 of debentures for each share	20,130	20,130
Purchase money real estate mortgages payable	1,122	477
	$ 42,207	$ 42,630
Stockholders' Equity:		
Capital:		
7% cumulative preferred stock—authorized, 101,825 shares of $100 par value each; issued, 92,906 shares	9,291	9,291
6½% second cumulative preferred stock—authorized, 1,300,000 shares of $7 par value each; issued, 1,198,895 shares	8,392	8,392
Common stock—authorized, 4,000,000 shares of $12.50 par value each; issued, 2,863,193 shares in 1960 and 2,862,189 in 1959 (Note 8)	35,790	35,777
Capital contributed by stockholders in excess of par value	10,238	10,234
	$ 63,711	$ 63,694
Accumulated earnings retained for reinvestment in the business (Note 7)	13,101	54,112
Total Stockholders' Equity	$ 76,812	$117,806
	$218,880	$222,281

SOURCE: Adapted from material in J. I. Case Company, *Annual Report, 1960.*

Exhibit 4—Continued

J. I. CASE COMPANY AND CONSOLIDATED SUBSIDIARY COMPANIES
Notes to Financial Statements*

Note 1—BASIS OF CONSOLIDATION:

The consolidated financial statements include J. I. Case Company and all its subsidiary companies except J. I. Case Credit Corporation for which separate financial statements are presented herewith, French subsidiaries commented upon in Note 4, and merchandising subsidiaries which are not significant.

Note 2—NET ASSETS IN FOREIGN COUNTRIES:

Net assets in foreign countries at October 31, 1960 amount to $16,109,-517, consisting of net current assets of $11,792,689 and branch house property and other assets of $4,316,828. These net assets are widely distributed throughout Canada, Australia, South America, Europe, England and other countries.

Net current assets in foreign countries have been converted into United States dollars at free rates or other appropriate rates in effect on October 31, 1960. Other assets have been converted at rates in effect at the time of the expenditures.

Note 3—FEDERAL INCOME TAXES:

Operations for 1960 gave rise to a claim of $4,563,429 for refund of 1957–1959 federal income taxes and to a loss carry-over of approximately $25,000,000 which may be used to reduce taxable income for the years 1961–1965 inclusive.

With respect to prior years' federal income taxes, there are unsettled questions with Treasury Department representatives concerning the appropriate costing of inventories commencing with the 1947 fiscal year. Provision has been made in the accounts for additional taxes which will result from agreed upon adjustments to prior years' taxable income but no provision has been made for additional taxes or interest which may result from any restatement of the inventories. It is believed that the ultimate determination with respect to the unsettled questions will not have a material effect upon the net financial position of the company. It is anticipated that no additional taxes for prior years or interest thereon will be paid during the 1961 fiscal year.

Note 4—INVESTMENT IN AND ADVANCES TO FRENCH SUBSIDIARIES:

The amounts invested in and advanced to the French subsidiaries to October 31, 1960 have been written off since their operating losses, principally in the 1960 fiscal year, have substantially eliminated any equity applicable to such amounts. Many of the costs contributing to these losses were the result of problems which in large part have been overcome and it is believed that future operations can be conducted without substantial loss. The company has made additional advances of $1,350,000 to these subsidiaries since Oc-

---

* SOURCE: J. I. Case Company, *Annual Report, 1960*, p. 10.

Exhibit 4—Continued

tober 31, 1960. During 1959 the company guaranteed $3,700,000 of the French subsidiaries' debt. At January 11, 1961, there was a remaining contingent liability under these guarantees of $2,470,000.

Note 5—ENGINEERING AND PRODUCT DEVELOPMENT COSTS:

In 1960 the company adopted a policy of charging all engineering and product development costs to expense as incurred, a change from its previous policy of deferring major costs relating to products scheduled for future production and amortizing those costs over the two years following the year in which they were incurred. Such costs in the amount of $4,140,964 (included in cost of goods sold), deferred at the beginning of the year, less related deferred income taxes of $1,933,165 (included in credit for taxes on income), were also charged to expense in 1960.

Note 6—EXCESS OF COST OF ASSETS ACQUIRED OVER ASSIGNED VALUE THEREOF:

"Excess of cost of assets acquired over assigned value thereof" resulted from the merger of American Tractor Corporation into J. I. Case Company on January 10, 1957 and is being amortized over a 20-year period. Under the plan of amortization, $400,000 was charged to operations in 1960.

The litigation instituted by a J. I. Case Company stockholder against the Company and several of its directors seeking to have the merger with American Tractor Corporation declared illegal and void is still pending. The original action was dismissed on the Company's motion by the United States District Court for the Eastern District of Wisconsin. The plaintiff was subsequently permitted to amend his complaint, but the amended complaint does not substantially change the nature of the action and the Company is still of the opinion that the action is without merit. Several motions including a motion to dismiss the amended complaint are presently pending.

Note 7—CREDIT AGREEMENT AND DIVIDEND RESTRICTIONS:

J. I. Case Company and J. I. Case Credit Corporation have entered into an agreement with certain banks covering the period ending September 1, 1961, whereby the banks agree to make loans to the companies from time to time up to the aggregate principal amount of $178,380,000, of which $95,-105,000 is normally available to J. I. Case Company and $83,275,000 is normally available to J. I. Case Credit Corporation. If either company is not using all of its normal commitment, certain additional amounts as set forth in the agreement may be available to the other company. Interest at $5\frac{1}{2}\%$ ($5\frac{3}{4}\%$ in Canada) is payable on the unpaid principal amounts of the loans. During the period of the agreement, neither company may declare or pay cash dividends without the prior written consent of the banks, except that J. I. Case Company may declare and pay dividends on its preferred stocks provided the aggregate amount of all dividends on such stocks does not exceed consolidated net income after October 31, 1960.

The Board of Directors did not declare the regular quarterly dividends on both classes of preferred stock ordinarily payable in January 1961.

Exhibit 4—Continued

In addition to restrictions under the credit agreement, various covenants restricting the payment of cash dividends on common stock are included in indentures relating to the long-term debt under which no amount of accumulated earnings retained for reinvestment in the business at October 31, 1960 was available for the payment of dividends on common stock.

Note 8—STOCK OPTION PLAN:

Under the terms of a stock option plan, the company reserved 250,000 shares of its authorized but unissued common stock for issue to officers and other management employees of the Company and its subsidiaries at not less than the market price of the common stock on the date such options were granted. The options become exercisable after eighteen months of continued employment and terminate ten years from the date granted, unless employment shall previously terminate as provided in the plan. In 1960 options for 29,000 shares were granted, options for 35,700 shares were cancelled and options for 1,000 shares were exercised. At October 31, 1960 a total of 172,100 shares of common stock were issuable under options (of which options for 137,100 shares were exercisable) at prices ranging from $10.125 to $24.25 per share, aggregating $2,969,238.

Exhibit 5

BEDROCK LIFE INSURANCE COMPANY
J. I. CASE CREDIT CORPORATION
Statement of Income and Accumulated Earnings
for the Years Ended October 31, 1960 and 1959
(Dollar figures in thousands)

	1960	*1959*
Income:		
Financing charges to parent company, principally on wholesale notes receivable	$10,256	$ 8,095
Earned finance charges on retail notes receivable	7,161	5,601
Other	396	248
	$17,813	$13,944
Operating expenses:		
Interest expense	10,547	7,942
Provision for possible losses on notes receivable	1,987	1,307
Other	446	311
	$12,980	$ 9,560
Income before provision for taxes on income	4,833	4,384
Provision for or in lieu of taxes on income (Note 1)	2,600	2,350
Net income for the year	$ 2,233	$ 2,034
Accumulated earnings:		
Beginning of year	2,929	895
End of year (Note 2)	$ 5,162	$ 2,929

Note 1—FEDERAL INCOME TAXES:

The income and expenses of J. I. Case Credit Corporation will be included in a consolidated federal income tax return filed by the parent company for the 1960 fiscal year and no tax will be payable because of the loss of the parent company. However, J. I. Case Credit Corporation made a provision in lieu of taxes in an amount approximately equivalent to the taxes that would have been payable on a separate company basis. This amount is being paid to the parent company on the normal due dates of the tax.

Note 2—CREDIT AGREEMENT AND DIVIDEND RESTRICTIONS:

See Note 7 of Notes to Financial Statements of J. I. Case Company.

Note 3—LONG-TERM NOTES PAYABLE:

	October 31,	
	1960	*1959*
Long-term notes payable comprise:		
5⅝%, due May 1, 1973, payable $1,000,000 annually begining in 1964	$25,000,000	$25,000,000
5¾%, due May 1, 1974, payable $1,000,000 annually begining in 1965	25,000,000	25,000,000
6¼%, due February 1, 1975, payable $1,000,000 annually beginning in 1966	20,000,000	....
	$70,000,000	$50,000,000

SOURCE: J. I. Case Company, *Annual Report, 1960*, p. 11.

Exhibit 6

BEDROCK LIFE INSURANCE COMPANY

J. I. CASE CREDIT CORPORATION

Statement of Financial Condition,

October 31, 1960 and 1959

	1960	1959
ASSETS		
Cash...	$ 19,698	$ 18,299
Notes receivable:		
Wholesale, including approximately $13,000 and $26,000, respectively, due after one year...........................	87,351	112,828
Retail, including approximately $51,000 and $56,000, respectively, due after one year..............................	99,001	100,715
	$186,352	$213,543
Unearned finance and insurance charges.....................	(11,896)	(12,599)
Allowance for losses.....................................	(2,250)	(2,000)
	$172,206	$198,944
Other assets...	1,508	1,844
	$193,412	$219,087
LIABILITIES AND STOCKHOLDER'S EQUITY		
Short-term notes payable (Note 2)*..........................	$ 62,365	$105,405
Accrued interest, etc......................................	207	78
Due to J. I. Case Company.................................	4,731	13,358
Federal and other taxes on income (Note 1)*.................	316	2,011
Amounts withheld from dealers.............................	3,632	3,307
Long-term notes payable (Note 3)*..........................	70,000	50,000
Total liabilities......................................	$141,251	$174,159
Stockholder's equity and subordinated notes:		
5¾% subordinated notes payable, due March 1, 1975.........	22,000	22,000
Capital stock..	25,000	20,000
Accumulated earnings retained for reinvestment in the business (Note 2)*...	5,161	2,928
	$ 52,161	$ 44,928
	$193,412	$219,087

* See notes at foot of Exhibit 5.
SOURCE: J. I. Case Company, *Annual Report, 1960*, p. 11.

Case 10

Larabee Company

ON JANUARY 6, 1947, Mr. John Larabee, the owner and manager of a small retail store specializing in children's clothing and accessories, was engaged in preparing a cash budget for the first six months of 1947. The budget was being prepared at the request of Mr. Wilbert Walker, an officer of the Security National Bank, where the Larabee Company maintained a deposit and borrowing account. Mr. Larabee had recently called on Mr. Walker to talk over his plans for the spring season and to make sure that the bank would continue to supply the necessary credit to meet the needs of the company. After reviewing the balance sheet of the company as of January 1, 1947, as shown in Exhibit 1, and discussing Mr. Larabee's expectations as to purchases and sales of merchandise during the next six months, as shown in Exhibit 2, Mr. Walker expressed the opinion that it would be easier to visualize the company's probable needs for credit if Mr. Larabee would draw up a cash budget. In reply to Mr. Larabee's question as to just what he meant by "cash budget," Mr. Walker explained that what he had in mind was a statement of expected cash receipts and payments for each of the next six months. Mr. Larabee agreed to draw up such a statement and to return for further discussion based on the statement.

Mr. Larabee had opened the store in the latter part of 1943. Since his personal capital had been limited, he had been forced to borrow heavily and to limit sales to a cash basis. Sales had expanded rapidly, with corresponding increases in investment in inventory. In 1946, net sales had amounted to $181,800, net profit before federal income taxes $17,158, and net profit after taxes

691

$11,740. Since the store was not incorporated, the net profit was taxed as personal income.

During the first three years of operation, Mr. Larabee had aimed at building a clientele of steady customers who would patronize the store because they expected good quality at a reasonable price and not primarily because they were attracted by the promotion of special items at exceptionally low prices. As part of this program, he eliminated price appeal from all his advertising and emphasized the quality and service to be obtained at Larabee's. His chief competition came from department stores and specialty stores which carried children's wear in addition to other apparel. Since these stores offered charge accounts to their customers, Mr. Larabee had decided that he must offer similar arrangements. Therefore, he decided to make allowance in his cash budget for the probable effect of offering 30-day open charge accounts. He estimated that if he offered 30-day open charge accounts to his customers, 5% of his sales would be charge sales in January, 10% in February, 13% in March, 16% in April, 18% in May, and 20% in June. According to department store figures in the *Federal Reserve Bulletin* for December, 1946 (p. 1406), the average ratio of collections during a month to accounts receivable at the beginning of the month had been approximately 60% during the first 10 months of 1946.

The usual terms for Larabee's purchases of merchandise were 8/10 E.O.M.,[1] and such terms could be applied to the $12,600 accounts payable shown on the January 1 balance sheet. The other accounts payable shown on the balance sheet represented various obligations other than the purchase of merchandise and were payable at face value in January. The "Notes payable—bank" were due February 1. The bank had been extending credit on 30-day notes at 6% annual interest and renewing them as necessary. Mr. Larabee expected this practice would be continued.

The social security and withholding taxes of $412 were due in January.

Mr. Larabee had estimated his 1946 income tax at $100 and had paid three quarterly instalments of $25 each on March 15, June 15, and September 15, 1946. Another $25 instalment was due on January 15. On January 1, 1947, he estimated his final tax for 1946 at $5,418. Therefore the amount payable on March 15 would be

---

[1] The term "8/10 E.O.M." meant that an 8% cash discount would be allowed for payment within 10 days after the end of the month in which the invoice was dated.

$5,418 less $100. Currently, Mr. Larabee estimated his quarterly payments for 1947 income tax at $1,350. Two of these would be paid on March 15 and June 15.

Mr. Larabee's merchandise plans for the spring season had been made on the assumption that all sales would be made for cash. Although he believed that offering charge accounts might bring about a greater increase in sales than the 20% planned in the budget, he believed that the magnitude of the increase was so uncertain as to make it unwise to increase his budget. Among the important factors considered in the preparation of the merchandise budget was the fact that Easter fell on April 6 in 1947. Mr. Larabee's contemplated purchases and his estimated sales through June are shown in Exhibit 2.

Since Mr. Larabee had all his money invested in the business, he found in necessary to withdraw cash for his personal use each month. He estimated that these withdrawals would be approximately $350 per month during the first six months of 1947.

Mr. Larabee had made a table of expenditures as shown in Exhibit 3. This budget included certain items calling for cash outlay during the period. Included in the various breakdowns of outlay for January were the amounts shown on the January 1 balance sheet as "Other accounts payable" and "Social security and withholding tax." The expense budget did *not* include anticipated income tax payments, Mr. Larabee's withdrawals, or anticipated payments for merchandise.

In view of the difficulty of estimating accurately the small amount that would be paid the bank as interest, the banker, Mr. Walker, had suggested that the outlay for bank interest not be included in the calculations. Mr. Larabee accepted this suggestion. All other foreseeable outlays, as indicated, would be included.

Working from this material, Mr. Larabee then developed the cash budget shown in Exhibit 4. At that point, Mr. Larabee settled to the task of reviewing the budget he had prepared, as he wanted to be sure it depicted with reasonable accuracy the maximum credit needs his business would be likely to encounter during the six months. If not, he wanted to modify the budget in a way that would bring the anticipated needs to light.

Exhibit 1

LARABEE COMPANY

BALANCE SHEET

As of January 1, 1947

ASSETS

Current assets:

Cash	$ 4,930	
Deposits for utilities	105	
Inventory, December 31, 1946, at cost	37,143	
Total current assets		$42,178

Fixed assets:

Fixtures and equipment	$ 3,268	
Automobile	1,528	
Total fixed assets		4,796
Total assets		$46,974

LIABILITIES

Current liabilities:

Accounts payable—merchandise, at billed cost	$12,600	
Other accounts payable	820	
Social security and withholding tax	412	
Notes payable—bank	3,750	
Income tax for 1946*	5,343	
Total current liabilities		$22,925
Net worth as of January 1, 1946	$17,033	
Profit for period	11,740	
	$28,773	
Withdrawals	4,724	
Net worth as of January 1, 1947		24,049
Total liabilities		$46,974

* Due March 15, 1947, except for $25 due January 15.

Exhibit 2

LARABEE COMPANY

PLANNED PURCHASES AND SALES OF MERCHANDISE

	Planned Sales	Planned Purchases at Billed Cost
January	$ 9,500	$ 3,821
February	12,000	15,925
March	22,000	13,325
April	17,000	9,555
May	17,000	7,020
June	13,500	6,175
	$91,000	$55,821

Exhibit 3

LARABEE COMPANY

PARTIAL CASH DISBURSEMENT BUDGET FOR PERIOD ENDING JUNE 30, 1947

	Jan.	Feb.	Mar.	April	May	June	Total
Payroll	$1,400	$1,600	$2,000	$1,800	$1,800	$1,600	$10,200
Rent	400	400	400	400	400	400	2,400
Advertising	150	400	800	600	600	400	2,950
Supplies	150	200	350	250	200	150	1,300
Other	700	600	800	700	700	500	4,000
Total	$2,800	$3,200	$4,350	$3,750	$3,700	$3,050	$20,850

Exhibit 4

LARABEE COMPANY

WORK SHEET—DISBURSEMENTS

	Dec.	Jan.	Feb.	Mar.	April	May	June
Merchandise bought	$12,600	$ 3,821	$15,925	$13,325	$ 9,555	$ 7,020	$ 6,175
Less: 8/10 E.O.M. discount	1,008	306	1,274	1,066	764	562	494
Net amount due on merchandise	$11,592	$ 3,515	$14,651	$12,259	$ 8,791	$ 6,458	$ 5,681
Payments of accounts payable		11,592	3,515	14,651	12,259	8,791	6,458
		Receipts					
Total sales		$ 9,500	$12,000	$22,000	$17,000	$17,000	$13,500
Cash sales		9,025	10,800	19,140	14,280	13,940	10,800
Credit sales		475	1,200	2,860	2,720	3,060	2,700
Accounts receivable at beginning of month			475	1,390	3,416	4,086	4,694
Add: Credit sales during month		475	1,200	2,860	2,720	3,060	2,700
		$ 475	$ 1,675	$ 4,250	$ 6,136	$ 7,146	$ 7,394
Less: Collections during month (60% of beginning A/R)			285	834	2,050	2,452	2,816
A/R outstanding E.O.M.		$ 475	$ 1,390	$ 3,416	$ 4,086	$ 4,694	$ 4,578
		CASH BUDGET					
Cash receipts:							
Cash sales		$ 9,025	$10,800	$19,140	$14,280	$13,940	$10,800
Collection of A/R			285	834	2,050	2,452	2,816
		$ 9,025	$11,085	$19,974	$16,330	$16,392	$13,616
Cash disbursements:*							
Payments of accounts payable		$11,592	$ 3,515	$14,651	$12,259	$ 8,791	$ 6,458
Other cash disbursements		2,800	3,200	4,350	3,750	3,700	3,050
Income tax payments, 1946 tax		25		5,318			
Income tax payments, 1947 tax				1,350			1,350
Personal withdrawals		350	350	350	350	350	350
Cash disbursed during month		$14,767	$ 7,065	$26,019	$16,359	$12,841	$11,208
Change in cash during month		−5,742	+4,020	−6,045	−29	+3,551	+2,408
Cumulative change		−5,742	−1,722	−7,767	−7,796	−4,245	−1,837

* Excludes renewal of bank loans and interest on bank loans.

Case 11

Power Mowers, Inc.

IN EARLY January, 1957, Mr. Harold Harman, treasurer of Power Mowers, Inc., was working on a loan request to be presented in the following week to the company's bank of account, Hudson-Security Bank. Mr. Harman had to determine how large a loan to ask for, as well as the duration and type of the loan, and to appraise the likelihood of the bank's granting the loan.

Power Mowers, Inc., was a manufacturer of power lawn mowers for home and institutional use. The company had been founded in 1946 and had experienced a rapid growth in sales. Operations had been profitable in each year since 1948. Recent balance sheets and income statements are shown in Exhibits 1 and 2. Power Mowers, Inc., distributed its products through appliance and general line wholesalers and sold directly to large retailers. In addition, approximately 10% of annual production was sold under contract to a major mail-order house.

The power mower industry had become highly competitive in postwar years. There were over 200 manufacturers of power mowers in the country, but approximately 40 of them accounted for nearly 90% of industry sales in 1956. Numerous firms had failed in the past few years; and competitive conditions, if anything, were expected to intensify during the next few years.

During the last three years, Power Mowers, Inc., had undertaken a major expansion and modernization program aimed at providing the efficient production facilities that management considered vital to the company's survival in view of the competitive situation. Plant capacity had already been increased to a point sufficient to handle a volume of $25 million per year in anticipation of rapid growth in the demand for power mowers. It was expected that the company's expansion program would be completed in March, 1957, with the installation of new equipment costing $400,000.

The expansion program had been timely, inasmuch as forecasts indicated a 20% increase in the demand for power mowers in 1957. The management of Power Mowers, Inc., estimated that company sales would reach $18 million in 1957, an increase of approximately 21% over 1956 volume. Further sales growth of between $1 million and $2 million per year was expected in 1958–60.

The company's sales, like those of the industry as a whole, were highly seasonal. Over two thirds of annual sales commonly were made during the first six months of the year. Exhibit 3 shows the forecasted monthly pattern of sales in 1957 based upon the sales pattern of previous years. On the other hand, production was generally held relatively steady throughout the year. This policy was necessary to retain and give regular employment to the highly skilled workers required in the company's manufacturing operations. In 1956, the company had been able to maintain production at nearly an even rate throughout the year.

Power Mowers, Inc., had borrowed seasonally from Hudson-Security Bank for several years. These loans had been made under a line of credit arranged annually in January. The bank required that the loan be completely repaid and "off the books" for at least one month during the year.

In previous years, Power Mowers, Inc., had not experienced difficulty in obtaining seasonal loans and meeting loan requirements. Hudson-Security Bank had always readily granted the company's seasonal needs, which in 1956 had amounted to $3.5 million at the peak. Normally, the company began borrowing in early January and repaid its loans by mid-July.

However, in 1956 the company had been unable to liquidate its loan until mid-September and by late October had again required bank funds. At the end of 1956, the bank loan outstanding amounted to $1,620,000. Although the bank had not hesitated to extend this credit, its officers expressed disappointment at not being given greater forewarning of the continued need, particularly at a time when bank credit was in tight supply. They suggested that it would be helpful if Mr. Harman could plan his requirements during 1957 more carefully.

Mr. Harman was also disturbed by the unexpected increase in borrowing and what it might mean in terms of future requirements.

Therefore, he began collecting data that might prove helpful in making his plans for 1957.

The company's nominal terms of sale were net 30 days. However, for competitive reasons, these terms were not strictly enforced, and invoices frequently were outstanding for considerably longer periods. Moreover, seasonal swings were experienced in collections, owing to fluctuating cash requirements of customers. Projected accounts receivable balances by months for 1957 are shown in Exhibit 3. In making these projections, Mr. Harman took into account the facts that additional smaller customers were expected to be added and that existing accounts were growing somewhat more lax in their payment schedules. The effect of these factors was difficult to calculate precisely; however, Mr. Harman included in his accounts receivable estimates some allowance for a probable slowing of payments.

Production was scheduled to be level throughout 1957 except for the two weeks beginning Monday, August 5, and Monday, August 12, when it was planned to shut down the plant for the annual paid-for vacation period. Materials purchases were scheduled at $750,000 per month, except for August, when purchases of $500,000 were scheduled. The company purchased its materials on terms of net 30 days. Depreciation expense of $500,000 was forecast for the year. Disbursements related to other overhead and labor were planned at $500,000 per month throughout 1957. Operating expenses were estimated at a total of $912,000 in 1957. Disbursements for operating expenses were expected to run fairly evenly throughout the year. Under current tax regulations, the accrued taxes outstanding on December 31, 1956, of $646,000 would be due and payable in equal instalments of $323,000 in March and June of 1957. In addition, payments each equal to 15% of the estimated federal income taxes on 1957 income were due in September and in December, 1957.

The new equipment, costing $400,000, was to be delivered in March. It would be paid for in four equal monthly instalments, beginning in March. Other smaller and recurring equipment expenditures were forecast at $20,000 per month throughout 1957.

In 1957, sales were forecast at $18 million, cost of goods sold at $14.9 million and operating expenses at $912,000. Mortgage loan interest of $172,000 was also anticipated. Profits before taxes were estimated at $2,016,000. Mr. Harman based his plans upon the expectation that a tax rate of 50% would apply during 1957.

In 1953, Power Mowers, Inc., had borrowed $4 million from a

life insurance company under a 16-year mortgage loan secured by the entire plant and equipment. This loan was repayable in equal semiannual instalments in June and December in each year. Interest at the rate of 5% per annum on the unpaid balance was also payable at these dates. In his financial forecasting, Mr. Harman planned to treat differently the interest payments on the mortgage loan and on the bank loan. The two mortgage interest payments, totaling $172,-000, due in 1957, would be shown separately in the cash flow and income projections. In contrast, bank loan interest payments had been roughly estimated and included in the total operating expense estimate of $912,000.

In 1956, the company had raised its annual dividend to stockholders to $1 per share, payable semiannually in March and September. Mr. Harman knew that the directors of Power Mowers, Inc., would be extremely reluctant to reduce the dividend as they wished to enhance the investment standing of the stock with a view to possible future equity financing. The directors regarded the company as too little known to sell stock at the present time. However, they hoped that another two or three years of profitable operation and growth might make an equity issue feasible.

As chief financial officer of the company, Mr. Harman had given considerable thought to the optimum cash position of his company. He had concluded that a cash balance of at least $500,000 should be maintained at all times. Furthermore, he believed that the deposit balances of $500,000 or more would satisfy the increasingly strong insistence of the bank that large business borrowers maintain substantial deposit balances at the bank.

On the basis of the plans outlined above, Mr. Harman asked an assistant to prepare a monthly cash flow forecast for 1957, which he hoped would indicate the amount and timing of the bank credit that Power Motors, Inc., would require. He also asked his assistant to prepare an estimated balance sheet for the company as of December 31, 1957. He suggested that his assistant assume no change in "other assets" or "miscellaneous accruals" from their year end, 1956, levels.

Exhibit 1

POWER MOWERS, INC.
BALANCE SHEETS AS OF DECEMBER 31, 1954–1956
(Dollar figures in thousands)

	1954	1955	1956
Cash	$ 3,188	$ 729	$ 508
Accounts receivable	1,170	1,292	1,680
Inventory	1,972	2,280	2,960
Total current assets	$ 6,330	$ 4,301	$ 5,148
Plant and equipment (net)	6,341	8,483	9,439
Other assets	302	355	370
Total	$12,973	$13,139	$14,957
Bank loan	—0—	—0—	1,620
Accounts payable—trade	690	720	780
Reserve for federal income taxes	472	583	646
Miscellaneous accruals	79	121	138
Mortgage, current	250	250	250
Total current liabilities	$ 1,491	$ 1,674	$ 3,434
Mortgage payable	3,750	3,500	3,250
Common stock (500,000 shares @ $12.00 par)	6,000	6,000	6,000
Earned surplus	1,732	1,965	2,273
Total	$12,973	$13,139	$14,957

Exhibit 2

POWER MOWERS, INC.
INCOME STATEMENTS, 1954–1956
(Dollar figures in thousands)

	1954	1955	1956
Net sales	$11,546	$12,791	$14,822
Cost of goods sold*	9,875	10,870	12,372
Gross profit	1,671	1,921	2,450
Operating expenses	727	755	834
Profit before taxes	944	1,166	1,616
Federal income taxes	472	583	808
Net profit	472	583	808
Common dividends	350	350	500
Retained earnings	122	233	308

* Includes straight-line depreciation of:
  1954........$355
  1955........$370
  1956........$470

Exhibit 3

POWER MOWERS, INC.

ESTIMATED MONTHLY SALES AND MONTH-END
ACCOUNTS RECEIVABLES FOR 1957

(Dollar figures in thousands)

	Net Sales	*Accounts Receivable End of Month*
January	$ 1,240	$2,610
February	1,750	3,290
March	2,470	4,730
April	2,550	5,720
May	2,850	6,180
June	1,610	5,240
July	1,340	3,300
August	1,120	2,730
September	640	1,820
October	600	1,310
November	630	1,320
December	1,200	1,980
	$18,000	

Case 12

Trivett Manufacturing Company (A)

In July, 1946, Eldon Brigham, treasurer of the Trivett Manufacturing Company, was reviewing the working capital position. It was his custom to calculate working capital needs for the next six months in January and July of each year and to formulate plans for meeting such needs.

The Trivett Manufacturing Company, which had been founded in 1934, operated a small machine shop in a Philadelphia suburb. The company had originally manufactured lapping plates and made gauges and special tools on order. In 1941 a newly designed industrial stapling machine was added to its line.

Operating losses and poor financial management had kept the company in financial difficulty during the greater part of its early history. Matters were made worse by a conflict which developed between the common and preferred stockholders. Inability of these two groups to agree had prevented the taking of corrective measures.

In the spring of 1942, this situation came to the attention of Mr. Brigham, a businessman who specialized in rehabilitating financially weak concerns. He analyzed the company and found that it had in its employ a number of skilled machinists and possessed good equipment suitable for precision work. Mr. Brigham was also impressed by postwar prospects for the company's stapling machine, which was far superior to competitive products. As a result of his analysis, Mr. Brigham concluded that with competent management the company could be operated profitably. The two stockholding groups were approached, and an agreement was worked out whereby Mr. Brigham became, in effect, head of the company. For his efforts, he was to receive a fixed salary plus a percentage of profits. Mr. Brigham, who

703

was an officer of a number of other concerns, was to devote only part of his time to the Trivett Manufacturing Company.

During the war, Mr. Brigham concentrated on obtaining fixed fee Army contracts for the manufacture of precision instruments. Because of rigid economies which he instituted, these contracts proved highly profitable, even after renegotiation. Wartime profits and Mr. Brigham's skillful financial management soon rehabilitated the company. By the end of 1944 the deficit accumulated during many years of unprofitable operations had been eliminated.

The ending of hostilities in August, 1945, brought cancellation of the company's Army contracts. Mr. Brigham immediately took steps to curtail overhead and administrative expenses, but he retained the company's skilled machinists.

Sales and production efforts were concentrated on the industrial stapling machine. Prewar prices on the company's lapping plates had been about 50% less than for standard makes. As a result, the prices which the Office of Price Administration would permit the company to charge currently were set at a level that Mr. Brigham considered too low. Until a better price could be obtained, he did not intend to manufacture plates. Furthermore, since there was sharp price competition for gauge and tool work in the locality after V–J Day, Mr. Brigham decided that no effort should be made to seek this type of business for the time being.

Demand for the stapling machines was good. Monthly shipments during the first half of 1946 averaged about 75 units priced at $200 each. More units could have been sold and shipped, but Mr. Brigham did not wish to risk overextending the company while conditions were so unsettled.

Balance sheets and operating statements for 1944, 1945, and the first six months of 1946 are shown in Exhibits 1 and 2.

Early in May an invitation was received to bid on an Army contract for the manufacture of 301 gun sights. Mr. Brigham thought that a good profit could be made on the sights, and so he decided to submit a bid. His first bid of $720 a unit was rejected, but a second bid of $615 was accepted. One "pilot" sight was to be produced during August for the purpose of testing design and production methods. It was to be retained at the plant but invoiced on September 1 at $615. This experimental unit was to be manufactured from materials on hand. Direct labor for this model was estimated at $500. The lessons learned during the making of the first unit were expected to enable the company to start gun sight production at full scale about

September 1. Production was expected to be maintained at a fairly constant rate until November 30. Delivery of the sights was to start the first week in October and was to be made at the rate of 100 units a month during October, November, and December.

Estimated per unit direct costs of producing the gun sight were as follows: labor, $242; material, $128.

In addition to the estimated direct labor cost of $242 per unit, Mr. Brigham estimated that the build-up of the additional labor force needed for gun sight production would require $2,500 in extra wage expense during August. Similarly, $3,000 of additional wage expense was budgeted for December so as to permit less abrupt reduction of the work force upon completion of the contract. Virtually all of the $3,000 would be paid out in the first three weeks of December.

To insure against delays in delivery, Mr. Brigham intended to keep a minimum of one month's supply of raw material for the gun sight on hand at all times during the production period. Work-in-process inventory for gun sight production was expected to average $20,000 during the period of full-scale production. The great majority of the company's purchases were made on terms of net 30, and invoices were paid promptly when due. Wages were paid every Friday.[1] The production process from raw material to finished product was estimated to take a month. The Army would accept shipments in lots of 25 units, and payment would be received about 60 days after shipment.

Estimated per unit direct costs of producing the stapling machine were as follows: materials, $40; labor, $36. A minimum inventory of a three months' supply of raw material was currently considered necessary because of unsettled conditions. Work-in-process inventory for stapling machine production was expected to continue at the present level. All current inventory was usable. The length of the production process was four weeks. Units were shipped as soon as produced, and terms of sale were net 30. The company had a backlog of orders for 350 machines. Production and shipments, however, were expected to continue at the rate of about 75 units a month through the first quarter of 1947.

Monthly indirect expenses were currently running as follows: depreciation, $540; other factory overhead, $3,500; administration, $2,350. Tooling for the gun sight contract started in July. During

---

[1] There were four paydays in July, five in August, four each in September and October, five in November, and four in December. At each payday, wages were paid for the current week.

July and August, tooling expenses and experimental manufacture of the pilot gun sight were expected to increase factory overhead by about $1,200 a month. Starting in September, when full-scale production of the gun sight was to begin, factory overhead was expected to become about $4,500 a month until the end of November. Administration expense was expected to increase to about $3,000 a month from September 1 to the end of December.

The Army contract had made necessary the purchase of $2,000 of special tools. Delivery of these tools was expected in August; payment terms were C.O.D. Upon completion of the contract, these tools would be scrapped. An additional $5,000 might also have to be spent for the replacement of old machinery which appeared to be nearing the end of its useful life. There was no way of knowing, however, when this machinery would finally break down. Mr. Brigham was confident that he could find replacements within a few days in the event of an emergency. The machinery to be retired was fully depreciated.

Mr. Brigham worked out a tentative purchase schedule for the various material requirements. The schedule is reproduced as Exhibit 3. It shows the amounts of purchases in the months that they were expected to be booked.

The company maintained a small deposit account with a local bank and kept the remainder of its cash in an account with the Fourth National Bank of Philadelphia. The company had originally banked with the Farmers and Merchants Bank, a small local institution, from which it had borrowed from time to time during the war to help finance production on government contracts. Toward the end of the war, however, Mr. Brigham sensed that Mr. Appleseed, the bank's president, was becoming apprehensive about lending money to the company. Mr. Brigham attributed this reluctance to the fact that Mr. Appleseed had had little experience in lending money to industrial concerns; the greater portion of the bank's commercial loans were to local storekeepers. Therefore, Mr. Brigham withdrew his account from the bank. A small account was opened at another local bank, and the remainder of the company's funds were deposited with the Fourth National Bank of Philadelphia, a medium-sized bank with a legal loan limit of $150,000. Mr. Brigham had discussed the company's prospects in general terms with the bank's officers on a number of occasions, but he had never requested a loan.

Mr. Brigham considered his current cash balance of almost $28,-000 to be in excess of operating needs. He was willing to reduce cash to a minimum of $5,000. No dividend payments were scheduled for the remainder of 1946.

It was Mr. Brigham's policy not to plan more than six months in advance, since he believed that it was impossible to predict with any accuracy what was going to happen for a longer period. The company's plans for the first half of 1947 would be made in the light of conditions as they developed and of the company's prospective financial condition at the end of 1946.

Exhibit 1
TRIVETT MANUFACTURING COMPANY
BALANCE SHEETS

ASSETS	Dec. 31, 1944	Dec. 31, 1945	June 30, 1946
Current assets:			
Cash	$ 12,982	$ 16,066	$27,753
Accounts receivable, net	48,107	29,583	19,593
Inventory	45,514	34,016	......
Raw material	......	......	13,134
Work in process	......	......	6,636
Prepaid items	725	1,179	325
Total current assets	$107,328	$ 80,844	$67,441
Fixed assets:			
Property account	$ 46,507	$ 47,153	$47,776
Less: Reserve for depreciation	14,534	19,916	21,057
Property account, net	$ 31,973	$ 27,237	$26,719
Total assets	$139,301	$108,081	$94,160
LIABILITIES AND CAPITAL			
Current liabilities:			
Accounts payable	$ 27,668	$ 17,338	$ 9,066
Accrued liabilities	9,592	1,836	4,777
Reserve for previous year's federal taxes	8,172	4,891	12,095*
Reserve for current year's federal taxes	8,451	24,649	4,486†
Accrued taxes	6,381	2,736	1,812*
Total current liabilities	$ 60,264	$ 51,450	$32,236
Fixed liabilities:			
Due officers	13,834	......	......
Due U.S. government on contract advances	21,996	......	......
Capital:			
Preferred stock, 6%	21,000	21,000	21,000
Common stock, $100 par	17,000	17,000	17,000
Surplus	5,207	18,631	23,924
Total liabilities and capital	$139,301	$108,081	$94,160

* Payable in equal instalments, September 15 and December 15, 1946.
† Payable in equal instalments, March 15, June 15, September 15, and December 15, 1947.

Exhibit 2

TRIVETT MANUFACTURING COMPANY

OPERATING STATEMENTS

	Year 1944	Year 1945	6 Months Ending June 30, 1946
Sales, net	$282,888*	$331,575*	$86,966
Cost of sales:			
Material	$ 36,548	$ 97,065	$21,680
Direct labor	116,366	85,758	15,279
Depreciation	6,515	5,382	3,242
Factory overhead	52,842	47,940	20,514
Gross profit	$ 70,617	$ 95,430	$26,251
Less: Administration expense:			
Shipping expense	$ 9,561	$ 5,886	$ 235
Selling expense	10,442	7,480	......
Other expense	31,533	43,300	14,775
Net operating profit	$ 19,081	$ 38,764	$11,241
Other charges	308	521	......
Net gain before federal taxes	$ 18,773	$ 38,243	$11,241
Less: Federal taxes	8,450	24,183	4,486
Net profit	$ 10,323	$ 14,060	$ 6,755

* After adjustment for renegotiation.

Exhibit 3

TRIVETT MANUFACTURING COMPANY

TENTATIVE SCHEDULE OF PURCHASES

July–December, 1946

	July	Aug.	Sept.	Oct.	Nov.	Dec.
Raw material—stapler	....	$ 1,994	$ 3,000	$ 3,000	$3,000	$3,000
Raw material—gun sight	....	12,800	12,800	12,800	.....	.....
Special tools—gun sight	....	2,000	.....	.....	.....	.....
Total	....	$16,794	$15,800	$15,800	$3,000	$3,000

Replacement machinery........$5,000 (uncertain date)

Case 13

Trivett Manufacturing Company (B)

IN JULY of 1946, Mr. Lyman Huffman, a vice president and loaning officer of a medium-sized Philadelphia bank, the Fourth National Bank, had a visit from Mr. Eldon Brigham, treasurer of the Trivett Manufacturing Company. Mr. Brigham explained that his firm had recently received a contract for the manufacture of 301 gun sights for the U.S. Army. The contract was to be completed within six months, and the work on the contract would be in addition to the company's regular production of a line of stapling machines.

According to a projected income statement for the next six months, which Mr. Brigham brought with him, the contract promised to be very profitable. However, much additional working capital would be needed to finance the operations of the company during the period. Speaking from a schedule of anticipated cash receipts and expenditures for each of the last six months of 1946, Mr. Brigham explained that according to his estimates, as much as $100,000 might be required to complete the order as planned. Such a large loan would be required for only a brief time, Mr. Brigham felt. As work on the order was completed and payments began to come in from the Army, the company's cash position would improve, and repayment of the loan could begin. Mr. Brigham estimated that repayment could be completed by the end of February, 1947.

Since money was not needed at once, Mr. Brigham asked that the company be granted a line of credit under which the company could borrow, as needed, up to $100,000 on short-term notes.

After looking over the June 30 balance sheet of the company, Mr. Huffman observed that $100,000 was a very large loan for a small company. Mr. Brigham seemed somewhat annoyed at this comment and replied that he thought this was just the kind of self-liquidating loan proposition that commercial banks liked. He added that he had recently been approached by a finance company which would be very happy to have this business. Mr. Huffman quickly said that the Fourth National Bank had always held the reputation of being a progressive bank and that the bank was definitely interested in Mr. Brigham's request. On the other hand, he felt that the bank owed a real obligation to its many depositors to protect their funds. Accordingly, he asked Mr. Brigham to leave with him the pro forma statements and cash budget he had prepared, so that he and other members of the bank's loan committee could study the proposal. He promised that Mr. Brigham would hear from him within a few days. After a brief discussion, Mr. Brigham asked Mr. Huffman to telephone him if the material raised any questions which he might answer.

Mr. Huffman was somewhat familiar with the affairs of the Trivett Manufacturing Company, since he had talked about the company in general terms with Mr. Brigham on several occasions after the company had opened a deposit account something more than a year before. He had formed a rather favorable impression of Mr. Brigham and the company, and a review of the brief file that had been built up on the company indicated that it paid its bills promptly and enjoyed a good reputation in trade circles.

Mr. Huffman's responsibilities as the loaning officer responsible for the Trivett account included all necessary analysis and investigation of the credit; decision on the terms of a loan, including collateral, maturity, and interest; and oral presentation of his recommendations before the bank's loan committee. This group, made up of senior officers, sometimes reviewed a proposal thoroughly through their questioning and discussion.

Case 14

Sprague Machine Tool Company

On September 20, 1951, Mr. Harry Greenwood, vice president of the Wolverine National Bank of Detroit, was examining the company's credit file on Sprague Machine Tool Company, a customer located in a nearby small city. Renewal of a $350,000 loan made to that company was to be considered by the loan committee the next day, and Mr. Greenwood was reviewing what had happened since the bank had taken on Sprague's account, so that he could decide what action he should recommend to the committee. The note had originally been a nine-month loan made in December, 1950, but the Sprague management was requesting a 90-day extension.

Since its establishment in 1900, Sprague had successfully weathered the cyclical fluctuations characteristic of the machine tool manufacturing business. Its peak production had been achieved during World War II, sales reaching $7,300,000 in 1943. From that year, however, sales had declined, reaching a low of $1,765,000 in 1947, and the sales volume had been below $3,000,000 in each subsequent year through 1948. Sprague had come out of World War II with a strong working capital position; with volume reduced in subsequent years, it had had no need to borrow prior to December, 1950.

Mr. Greenwood recalled that in December, 1950, Mr. Robert G. Murray, president of Sprague, requested a loan of $350,000 to assist in purchasing the stock interests of several dissident stockholders. While Sprague Machine Tool Company at that time had some excess cash over that required for normal operations, even more cash was required for the stock purchase, and Mr. Murray had, therefore, requested the Wolverine National Bank to lend Sprague Machine Tool Company $350,000 for a period of nine

711

months. To justify the credit, Mr. Murray had submitted a monthly forecast of shipments for 1951 (Exhibit 1) and a balance sheet dated November 30, 1950 (shown in the first column of Exhibit 2). The Wolverine National Bank had agreed to make the loan, and in December, 1950, the company had retired 24,300 shares of its $10 par value stock purchased from its stockholders at an aggregate cost of $936,100. After this, there remained several hundred stockholders.

After the loan was made, Mr. Murray regularly sent the bank profit and loss statements and balance sheets. Mr. Greenwood selected the figures given on Exhibits 2 and 3 for use in his analysis.

The company manufactured machine tools which were sold to several metalworking industries but principally to automobile manufacturers and some aircraft manufacturers. These products were largely made to order; their sales prices ranged from $20,000 to $500,000 per installation. Sprague's selling terms were 30 days net. Occasionally, a customer placing a large order would make Sprague an advance payment to help finance the construction of the machines involved, which covered periods up to five or six months for some of the more complex types of machines. Upon completion and shipment of orders against which advances had been obtained, Sprague deducted the amount of the advance from the amount billed the customer.

On September 19, 1951, Mr. Greenwood had received a letter from Mr. Murray requesting a 90-day extension of Sprague Machine Tool Company's note. Mr. Murray's letter commented at some length on the company's financial condition and stated that the management expected to be able to pay off the note in full within 90 days. Mr. Murray's letter is set forth in full as Exhibit 4.

Exhibit 1

SPRAGUE MACHINE TOOL COMPANY
SHIPMENTS AT SELLING PRICE
(Dollar figures in thousands)

1951	As Forecast December, 1950	Actual	As Forecast September, 1951
Jan.	$434	$287	
Feb.	624	224	
Mar.	545	622	
Apr.	351	522	
May	431	291	
June	493	540	
July	496	241	
Aug.	599	169	
8 months' total	$3,973	$2,896	
Sept.	433		$721
Oct.	449		435
Nov.	437		468
Dec.	766		655

Exhibit 2

SPRAGUE MACHINE TOOL COMPANY
BALANCE SHEETS
(Dollar figures in thousands)

	11/30/50	12/31/50	3/31/51	6/30/51	7/31/51	8/31/51
Cash.	$ 855	$ 155	$ 214	$ 507	$ 652	$ 602
Accounts receivable, net.	415	664	657	631	423	228
Inventories.	867	883	1,158	1,092	1,208	1,588
Total current assets	$2,137	$1,702	$2,029	$2,230	$2,283	$2,418
Fixed assets.	$1,301	$1,301	$1,301	$1,302	$1,302	$1,308
Less: Reserve for depreciation.	998	1,002	1,011	1,018	1,018	1,022
Net fixed assets.	$ 303	$ 299	$ 290	$ 284	$ 284	$ 286
Prepaid expenses.	21	20	13	8	8	14
Total assets	$2,461	$2,021	$2,332	$2,522	$2,575	$2,718
Notes payable—bank.	...	$ 350	$ 350	$ 350	$ 350	$ 350
Accounts payable.	$ 116	117	227	133	207	316
Accruals.	140	249	283	179	148	137
Reserve for federal taxes*—1950.	138	154	108	63	63	63
—1951.	...	...	112	218	242	277
Customer advance payments.	280	280	280	522	522	522
Total current liabilities.	$ 674	$1,150	$1,360	$1,465	$1,532	$1,665
Common stock.	380	137	137	137	137	137
Surplus.	1,407	734	835	920	906	916
Total liabilities.	$2,461	$2,021	$2,332	$2,522	$2,575	$2,718

* 1950 Federal Income Taxes Payable in 1951: 30% of total on each of March 15 and June 15; 20% of total on each of September 15 and December 15.
1951 Federal Income Taxes Payable in 1952: 35% of total on each of March 15 and June 15; 15% of total on each of September 15 and December 15.

Exhibit 3

SPRAGUE MACHINE TOOL COMPANY

Income Statements

(Dollar figures in thousands)

	Year Ending 12/31/50	1950 Dec.	Jan.	Feb.	Mar.	Apr. 1951	May	June	July	Aug.	Eight Months Ending 8/31/51
Net sales..............	$2,618	$517	$287	$224	$622	$522	$291	$540	$241	$169	$2,896
Cost of sales*..........	1,684	374	158	123	454	379	189	399	170	92	1,964
Gross profit...........	$ 934	$143	$129	$101	$168	$143	$102	$141	$ 71	$ 77	$ 932
Selling and administration expenses....	564	107	49	32	97	83	47	68	40	31	447
Net profit before taxes........	$ 370	$ 36	$ 80	$ 69	$ 71	$ 60	$ 55	$ 73	$ 31	$ 46	$ 485
Provision for federal and state taxes....	154	16	41	35	36	29	28	46	24	36	275
Net profit.............	$ 216	$ 20	$ 39	$ 34	$ 35	$ 31	$ 27	$ 27	$ 7	$ 10	$ 210
Dividends paid.........	$ 14	....	$ 7	....	....	....	....	....	$ 21	....	$ 28

* Includes depreciation charges of $28,000 in 1950, $4,000 in December, and $3,000 per month in 1951.

Exhibit 4

SPRAGUE MACHINE TOOL COMPANY

DEARBORN, MICHIGAN

September 18, 1951

MR. HARRY GREENWOOD, VICE PRESIDENT

WOLVERINE NATIONAL BANK

DETROIT, MICHIGAN

DEAR MR. GREENWOOD:

I enclose the company's August 31 financial statements. While our cash balance currently is $602,000, you will note that we have an obligation to a customer for cash advances of $522,000, and we expect to ship this order over the next two months. With respect to our note for $350,000 due September 25, we request that you renew our loan for another 90 days. At the end of that period, as you can see for yourself, we expect to be able to have enough cash on hand to retire our obligation in full.

For the past month or more, we have been producing at capacity and expect to continue at that rate through the end of the year. On August 31, our backlog of unfilled orders amounted to about $5,500,000. Our shipment schedule has been upset, particularly the last month or two, because we have had to wait on our suppliers for shipment of electrical control mechanisms; at August 31, we had seven machines with an accumulated cost of about $440,000 completed except for the installation of these electrical components. The components were finally received last week and will enable us to complete a number of machines in the next few days. The remainder of our work in process will probably stay at present levels for the foreseeable future because of our capacity rate of production. Our finished goods inventories are negligible at all times, since we ship machines within a day of completion.

We bought raw materials beyond our current needs in July and August to be assured of completing our orders scheduled to be shipped by December 31. Our purchases were $220,000 in July and $330,000 in August. We have, therefore, accumulated about $140,000 worth of scarcer components above our normal raw material inventories. The extra $140,000 will be used up by the end of the year, bringing our raw material inventories back to normal levels for capacity production. Because we have bought ahead this way, we expect to cut our purchases to about $200,000 a month in each of the four remaining months of 1951.

Our revised shipment estimates are as follows:

	(at selling prices)
September	$ 721,000
October	435,000
November	468,000
December	655,000
	$ 2,279,000

The shipment estimates include the $700,000 order for the Giant Automobile Company. We are now scheduled to ship against this order as follows: September $280,000, October $280,000, November $140,000. Since we obtained a $522,000 advance from Giant on this order, we will be due nothing on these shipments until their $522,000 credit with us is exhausted.

You will probably note the decline in our accrued expenses. As I mentioned to you last month when you visited us, we have been paying off commissions due our two principal salesmen (who are also large stockholders in the company). Last year when we needed funds to redeem part of our capital stock, these men agreed to defer their commissions until the funds could more easily be spared. In August, we paid off the last of these back commissions. This has been the principal cause of the decline in this item, which normally does not change much from month to month. Our outlay each month for all expenses other than materials should be around $136,000. This assumes that accruals will stay about the same as on August 31.

The business which we expect to ship in the next four months is on our books on profitable terms. While our profit, as you know, varies with the item involved, our engineering estimates indicate we will probably make a net profit (before taxes) of about 15% of sales on these items. Unfortunately, we shall be working mostly for Uncle Sam—we have already exceeded our excess profits tax credit and as a result our profits earned during the next four months will be taxed at 77% (normal tax plus excess profits tax).

We have spent very little on new equipment in the last eight months. We will avoid buying new equipment in the next four months, unless breakdowns make it necessary to replace existing equipment.

Our profits for the year to date have been quite satisfactory, and toward the end of December we plan to pay a dividend to our stockholders. Our dividend disbursements in 1951 have been quite modest so far, and we want to be sure that those stockholders who stood by us last December have no cause to regret their action. Under the circumstances, we feel that a $50,000 dividend payable in December is the least we can do in view of our high earnings.

If there is anything further you need to know, please do not hesitate to write or phone.

Sincerely yours,

ROBERT G. MURRAY

President

Case 15

Troy Company

EARLY in September, 1950, Henry May, senior loan officer of the Empire State Trust Company of Albany, New York, was reviewing a request from the Troy Company for a 90-day unsecured loan in the amount of $125,000. The Troy Company manufactured metal novelties for sale to chain stores, department stores, and organizations promoting "home club plans." Ordinarily, sales were level throughout the year except for a Christmas seasonal period lasting from September through the middle of December. In the summer of 1950, however, the Troy Company received several large orders from well-known soap manufacturers for novelties to be used as premiums for advertising purposes. As of September 1, the company sales were running about $200,000 a month.

For many years the metal novelties trade had been a cyclical business, enjoying very profitable operations during periods of general prosperity and experiencing extremely poor results during periods of general depression or recession. Relatively little capital was required to enter this industry; hence many companies were modestly capitalized. This fact served to accentuate the troubles of the industry in years of limited business activity, and the turnover of firms in the industry during such years was large. As a consequence of the cyclical nature of this business, prices in the industry were volatile, especially during prosperous years when the over-all supply of metals was tight.

George Riley, president and general manager in 1950, had purchased the Troy Company in 1934. He operated the business as an individual proprietorship until 1940, at which time he incorporated it. During this seven-year period the volume of operations fluctuated considerably; and the concern suffered a severe financial deterioration for the first five years, partly recovering during 1939 and 1940.

718

At incorporation, new funds were injected into the business; and then, after an undistinguished performance for about 18 months, the company began to make progress in both sales and earnings as a result of war contracts.

When its war contracts were canceled in 1945, the Troy Company returned immediately to the manufacture of consumer products. The line of goods made by the company, however, did not receive the ready acceptance which the management anticipated. Heavy losses were incurred during 1946 and 1947. In 1948 the company restyled its products and began an intensive sales promotional campaign. Shortly after this merchandising reorganization, operations returned to a profitable basis. Although dividends had not been paid since 1945, prior to that time a substantial proportion of earnings had been paid in dividends.

Early in August, 1950, several suppliers of the Troy Company notified the management that in view of the increasing defense production and the shortage of critical metals, their ability to supply the needs of the Troy Company after September 30 would be limited. Immediately, Troy placed large orders for raw materials to be delivered throughout August and September. As of August 31, total inventory amounted to more than $300,000.

In view of the unusually heavy summer season resulting from the large sales to soap manufacturers, William Riley, treasurer of the Troy Company, arranged in late July with John Clark, loan officer of the Troy County Bank, a $70,000 unsecured loan which was to be repaid in instalments of $10,000 each month, beginning November 15, 1950. The proceeds of this loan enabled the company to pay promptly bills that matured in August. However, when Mr. Riley reviewed the outstanding payables as of August 31, he realized that the immediate cash resources of the company were insufficient to meet these obligations, all due within 30 days. The board of directors thereupon authorized Mr. Riley to negotiate a larger loan with the Troy County Bank.

When Mr. Riley approached Mr. Clark for an additional loan, Mr. Clark was sympathetic but explained that the current loan in the amount of $70,000 was very near the legal loan limit of his bank. He suggested that through his bank an introduction be arranged to Mr. May, the senior loan officer of the Empire State Trust Company in Albany, a correspondent of the Troy County Bank. Mr. Riley agreed with this plan, and a meeting was arranged.

At the meeting with Mr. May, Mr. Riley explained his company's problem and requested an unsecured loan for $125,000. Mr. May replied that, before he could give a definite answer with regard to the loan, he would need additional information. He asked Mr. Riley if the Troy Company was working on any defense contracts. Mr. Riley replied that his company had been wholly engaged with civilian orders and so had not yet sought defense work.

During the interview, Mr. May explained to Mr. Riley that the Empire State Trust, like many other city banks at that time, was "pretty well loaned up." Mr. May added that his bank nevertheless was always interested in sound loan proposals. He requested from Mr. Riley recent financial statements and a letter setting forth pertinent information regarding expected operations to the year end.

After the interview Mr. May ordered a credit report on the Troy Company and received the report presented in Exhibit 3. A few days later he received the letter that he had requested of Mr. Riley. The letter read as follows:

September 11, 1950

Mr. Henry May, Vice President
Empire State Trust Company
Albany, New York

Dear Mr. May:

I submit the following information in support of our request for an unsecured loan in the amount of $125,000 for 90 days. Since we have several trade obligations maturing shortly, we therefore request that the loan be made effective September 15.

We have enough orders on hand from our present customers to insure operations at capacity through November 30. Hence, sales for September, October, and November should approximate $200,000 monthly. We expect that December sales will run about $160,000.

We enclose our recent financial statements that you requested. [See Exhibits 1 and 2.] You may be interested to know that our inventory, as of August 31, was composed of:

Raw materials and supplies	$175,000
Work in process	80,000
Finished goods	50,000

Additionally, we have ordered raw materials and supplies to be delivered during the month of September in the amount of $75,000. Most of these materials were purchased on net 30-day terms. Although our suppliers have not indicated how much material they will be able to ship us during the months of October, November, and December, we are relatively certain that receipts of raw materials and supplies during this period will average about $40,000 monthly. If more material is available, we shall endeavor to procure it in order to operate at capacity during 1951; assuming we continue at capacity output, our work in process and finished goods inventories should hold at about August 31 levels.

During September we expect to collect from the approximate $220,000 of accounts receivable about $190,000. As for collections during the remainder of the year, we can estimate only on the basis of past years' experience. Accordingly, we anticipate that we shall collect during October 90% of the total accounts receivable outstanding at the beginning of the month. During November and December, collections should run about 80% of receivables outstanding at the beginning of the month. Incidentally, you may be interested in the breakdown of accounts receivable as of August 31:

Current............................	$186,000
Up to 30 days slow....................	11,000
31 to 60 days slow....................	7,000
Over 60 days slow....................	16,000

Our "other income" is from royalties and generally amounts to $7,000 monthly.

The operating efficiency that we demonstrated during the first seven months of this fiscal year is typical of what we should be able to do for the remainder of the year. Even during December, when our sales will have dropped from capacity operations, our cost of goods sold should run about 65%. As for the make-up of the cost of sales, our recent experience indicates 40% for raw materials, 37% for direct labor, and 23% for factory overhead.

Selling, general, and administrative expenses should continue about $35,000 per month in spite of possible fluctuations in sales volume.

No expansion of productive facilities is planned, but one of our die-casting machines, purchased secondhand for $12,000 during the war and fully depreciated by 1948, has practically worn out. We have ordered a replacement, on which delivery is promised this month. The machine will cost $30,000, payable on delivery. Depreciation expense, which is included in the 23% factory overhead estimate, will run about $2,000 per month, including charges on the die-casting machine replacement.

Although payments on a loan to us from the Troy County Bank are supposed to begin in November, Mr. Clark intimated to me that payments can be deferred until your loan is repaid.

The mortgage of $42,000, secured by all our fixed assets, is held by an individual. The repayment schedule calls for an annual repayment of $2,000 plus interest due May 15.

Finally, since we are confident that our operations for the rest of the year will be as profitable as those experienced to date, and since no dividends have been paid since 1945, we expect to pay a token $25,000 in dividends in December.

Sincerely yours,
TROY COMPANY

(*Signed*) WILLIAM RILEY, *Treasurer*

Exhibit 1

TROY COMPANY
INCOME STATEMENTS
(In thousands of dollars)

	Year Ending December 31, 1948	Year Ending December 31, 1949	Eight Months Ending August 31, 1950
Net sales	$833	$1,646	$1,072
Manufacturing cost*	640	1,171	683
Gross profit	$193	$ 475	$ 389
Selling, general and administrative expenses	148	362	234
Operating profit	$ 45	$ 113	$ 155
Other income	...	1	46
Profit before taxes	$ 45	$ 114	$ 201
Federal income tax	12	43	77
Balance to surplus	$ 33	$ 71	$ 124

* Includes depreciation expenses as follows:
Period ending 12/31/48—$11,000
Period ending 12/31/49— 16,000
Period ending 8/31/50— 14,000

Exhibit 2

TROY COMPANY
BALANCE SHEETS
(In thousands of dollars)

ASSETS	December 31, 1948	December 31, 1949	August 31, 1950
Cash	$ 7	$ 57	$ 15
Accounts receivable, net	95	210	220
Inventories	21	41	305
Marketable securities	5	16	14
Current assets	$128	$324	$554
Fixed assets (subject to mortgage)	76	167	167
Less: Reserve for depreciation	31	47	61
Net fixed assets	$ 45	$120	$106
Prepayments	1	1	1
Total assets	$174	$445	$661

LIABILITIES			
Accounts payable	$ 89	$165	$196
Notes payable—bank	8	29	70
Estimated federal income tax	12	43	99*
Miscellaneous accruals	28	56	22
Mortgage—current	...	2	2
Current liabilities	$137	$295	$389
Mortgage due after 1 year	...	42	40
Total liabilities	$137	$337	$429
Capital stock	67	67	67
Surplus	d(30)	41	165
Total liabilities	$174	$445	$661

* August, 1950, figure includes $22,000 taxes due on 1949 income and payable in $11,000 instalments on September 15 and December 15, 1950.
d = deficit

Exhibit 3

TROY COMPANY
CENTRAL CREDIT REPORTING SERVICE

July 6, 1950

TROY COMPANY

PRINCIPALS: George J. Riley, President, and General Manager.
William C. Riley, Treasurer.

DIRECTORS: The officers of the firm together with Harold J. Riley.

ANTECEDENT
INFORMATION: This business was started in 1934 by George J. Riley, who operated as an individual until the company was incorporated in 1940.

George J. Riley—1910; single; holds 1,015 shares of the 1,344 shares outstanding. After finishing college, was employed by his father, Harold J. Riley, in the H. J. Riley Manufacturing Company, manufacturers of costume jewelry. In 1934 George Riley left the employ of his father to start this business with a capital of $8,000 given him by his parents. He is reported to have inherited in the late '30's $50,000, a sizable portion of which he is reported to have invested in the business.

William C. Riley—1914; married; brother of president. Also employed formerly by father. In 1938 parents are reported to have given him an undisclosed sum of capital with which he entered the business of manufacturing metal novelties. The business was unsuccessful, and in 1942 he made an assignment for the benefit of creditors. Creditors declined to report the amount of assets and liabilities when the assignment was made.

Harold J. Riley—1875; married; father of George and William Riley. Principal stockholder of the H. J. Riley Manufacturing Company which reported in 1948 a tangible net worth of $76,000. This individual is not active in the subject company, and the extent of his stock interest is not known.

FINANCIAL
INFORMATION: The company sells on terms of net 30 to variety chain stores and department stores. Two salesmen are employed and 40 factory employees. Company produces fairly steadily throughout the year except for a fall season when retail stores buy for the Christmas season. Trade sources reveal that the president, George J. Riley, is considered the principal owner of the business, which in the past has had "an up-and-down record." During 1948 Jack Donovan, formerly with Special Sales Company, was hired as sales manager and is credited with having sparked the sales success of the subject company.

On June 30, 1950, subject company's past and present suppliers were circularized, with the following experiences reported:

Highest Credit Balance	Current Balance	Current Balance Overdue	Terms	General Manner of Payment	Sold Since
25	—		Net 30	Prompt	July, 1949
850	250		Net 30	"	1940
32,000	25,700		Regular	"	Years to date
300	—		Net 30	"	Feb., 1949
200	75		Net 30	"	Mar., '48 to date
25	—		Net 10	"	1949 only
150	150		Net 30	Prompt-slow-10	July 1949 to date
7,200	7,200		Net 30	Slow 15–30	Aug., '49 to date
4,500	—		Net 30	" 30	1946 to Oct. 1949
600	400		1% 10–30	" 60	Sept. 1949
300	—		Net 30	" 60	April 1949
125	—		1–10 n 30	" 60	Nov. '48 to Sept. '49
10,000	9,700	4,400	Net 30	" 90	Mar. 1949
1,800	1,200		Net 30	" 90	July 1949

Two others sell on cash or COD

Financial Statements
Does not supply financial statements to the usual sources.

Case 16

Storkline Shops

In early January, 1958, Mr. Barnes, the president of a small bank in Houston, Texas, was reviewing the latest loan request from Storkline Shops, a chain of retail stores specializing in maternity clothes and accessories. Mr. Barnes had handled the Storkline account since Mr. Richard Klein, owner and president of the business, first approached the bank in August, 1955, requesting $15,000 to finance the fall's seasonal needs. The initial loan request had been granted, and since that time the firm had experienced a persistent and increasing need for funds. This need had been met in part by the bank; and in early January, 1958, the proprietorship was borrowing $30,000. From the granting of the initial request to the present time, Storkline Shops had been in steady debt to the bank. Mr. Klein's most recent request was for an additional $10,000 to finance "unexpected inventory requirements" in the coming weeks. Before reaching a decision on this latest request, Mr. Barnes wanted to review developments in the account since it was opened in August, 1955.

Establishment of Storkline Shops—August, 1954

Mr. Klein founded Storkline Shops in the fall of 1954 with an initial investment of $15,000. Though he had no direct experience in the retailing of women's clothing and accessories, he had extensive experience in the merchandising and distribution of various other consumer goods. This experience, at both retail and wholesale levels, was gained with numerous companies throughout the Southwest. Deciding to enter a retail business of his own, he surveyed the many available alternatives and selected the maternity clothes line because he believed there was a unique and unfilled demand for a specialty shop in this field.

726

Mr. Klein started his business by opening three shops in the Houston area. Within the next six months, he added five more shops, one in Houston and four in other large Texas cities. Mr. Klein performed all the buying for his shops by visits to Eastern fashion shows. He also planned all the merchandising, pricing, and advertising programs for the chain as a whole, as well as working out in detail the specific interior design and merchandising plans for each shop location. Each shop was staffed by one or two women, selected by the owner himself for their experience, appearance, and sales ability. Storkline shops owned no store locations; each store was leased on a two- to three-year basis at annual rentals averaging about $3,300.

As was typical in the ladies' ready-to-wear business, sales mounted seasonally during the spring and during the fall. Sales were on a cash-and-carry basis, and there was little investment in fixed assets. The main investment of the business was in retail inventory; a broad line of clothing and accessories had to be maintained to service the seasonal buying habits and changing fashion requirements of customers. In preparation for peak selling seasons, retail inventories were usually built up by March 15 and September 30 of each year. Mr. Klein also carried a line of accessories in his chain of stores, with such items amounting to approximately 15% of retail sales and inventory value. Most maternity garment makers sold to Storkline on terms 8/10 E.O.M. or a negotiated net price due 10 days E.O.M. Accessories were typically purchased on terms ranging from 2/10, net 30 to 8/10, net 30.

The Initial Loan—August, 1955

In his initial request for a loan in August, 1955, Mr. Klein reported that his operations were very satisfactory for the first six months of 1955 and submitted to the bank his most recent operating statement and balance sheet (see Exhibits 1 and 2). These early operations were attributable primarily to the first three Houston stores, as the other stores had been in operation for only two or three months. In addition to his proprietorship in Storkline Shops, Mr. Klein owned a building in the Houston area with a market value of $60,-000, against which he had a mortgage of $40,000. He also had other miscellaneous assets of an approximate value of $15,000. Mr. Klein emphasized the unique appeal of a maternity wear specialty shop and the limited competition in this line of retailing. After some study, Mr. Barnes decided that his bank could accommodate the young and growing organization and granted the company a $15,000 loan, with the understanding that it was to be repaid by the end of 1955. Recognizing Mr. Klein's aggressiveness and zest for expansion, Mr. Barnes obtained his assurance that he would open no new outlets without first consulting the bank.

Developments during the First Six Months of 1956

On a visit to the bank in January, 1956, Mr. Klein brought with him the company's financial statements for the full year 1955 (see Exhibits 1 and 2). Mr. Klein explained that the year-end inventory was $8,000 greater than anticipated because sales in November and December had not been up to expectations. Looking ahead to the first half of 1956, Mr. Klein expected that sales would reach $223,000, earnings before drawings and taxes would be $35,000, and the inventory would peak in March at about $75,000 and be reduced to $29,000 by June 30. Though the loan balance as of the end of the year had remained at $15,000, as shown in Exhibit 3, it was paid down to $10,000 on January 2. In order to pay personal income taxes coming due, Mr. Klein requested renewal of the $10,000 and that an additional $10,000 be loaned to the proprietorship. Based on his six-month estimates, Mr. Klein felt there would be no problem in paying all indebtedness by June 30. Mr. Barnes granted this loan request with the understanding that a cleanup would be accomplished as planned.

During the following month, Mr. Klein again visited the bank and requested an added $5,000. The proprietor of Storkline Shops reported that he had opened an additional Houston store during the latter part of January and was interested in another location in a Dallas suburb. He wanted the added $5,000 to purchase the inventory presently stocked at this suburban location and to take over operation of the shop. Mr. Klein said that his earlier estimate of net profits for the first six months of 1956 now appeared very conservative. The request for an additional $5,000 was granted, but Mr. Barnes cautioned that the notes had to be paid by June 30 and no new shops were to be added until figures for the first half of the year were available.

Developments during the Last Six Months of 1956

By late July, the chain of stores and locations had increased to 13 with an aggregate annual lease expense on these locations amounting to approximately $39,000. In a visit to the bank during July, Mr.

Klein stated that the minimum basic inventory to support the present sales level of his company amounted to about $50,000. Though the business was unable to clean up its bank debt by June 30, it had been able to meet $9,000 of a $10,000 note, and thus had reduced the loan balance to $16,000 by June 30 (Exhibit 3).

Financial statements for the first six months of operations in 1956 were received by the bank in mid-September (see Exhibits 1 and 2). Shortly afterward, Mr. Klein requested a renewal of the $16,000 loan and asked for an additional $9,000 to finance the rising seasonal inventory, which he estimated would reach $75,000 at the end of September (see Exhibit 2). He reported that profits before drawings for July through October were running some $5,000 to $8,000 per month. Mr. Barnes granted the request for additional funds on a promise that a cleanup would be made before December 31.

Developments during the First Six Months of 1957

In early January, 1957, Mr. Klein again visited the bank, bringing an estimated balance sheet as of the end of 1956. Though his inventory had been up to about $87,000 at the end of October, Mr. Klein believed he had reduced it to about $56,000 by the end of the year. A year-end audit was currently under way in each store. Though he had been unable to clean up his bank debt, as earlier arranged, Mr. Klein pointed out that his profits had been better than expected, and that net working capital had increased since June 30 by $18,000. Mr. Klein also volunteered information about the small manufacturing operation he had started in late 1956 in order to reduce his cost of purchases. The proprietor said that he was doing his own design and cutting work but that sewing was being contracted with a local concern. Mr. Klein estimated that during the fall of 1956, his manufacturing operation netted about $3,700 before drawings and taxes. The proprietor said he planned to manufacture only for the retail side of his business and that he hoped to provide perhaps three fifths of his retail needs for spring sales from this source. Since he was doing this manufacturing, he would need to borrow earlier than would have been necessary with a pure retail operation. As a result, the proprietor wanted to renew the outstanding $10,000 note and to borrow an additional $10,000 to finance the purchases of the piece goods inventory. Since Mr. Klein had continued to generate a growing profit, Mr. Barnes granted this request for funds.

In mid-February, 1957, the bank received the operating and financial statements for 1956 (see Exhibits 1 and 2), accompanied by a memo from Mr. Klein that he had opened up three new locations, one in Houston and two in suburban areas of other Texas cities, bringing the total number of locations to 16. After discussing the 1956 results with Mr. Barnes a few days later at lunch, Mr. Klein asked for an additional $15,000 to finance peak inventory needs for the spring season. He reported that his present inventory amounted to about $80,-000, of which $50,000 was staple retail merchandise. The added $15,000 would bring borrowings to a new high of $35,000 (see Exhibit 3), but Mr. Klein believed this amount was required to get over the seasonal hump. With the agreement that all notes would be repaid by June 30, the request was granted.

In mid-April, Mr. Klein called to report that his three-month operations to March 31 had been very successful; sales had been $155,000, and profits before drawings and taxes were $11,700. Of this profit, $2,000 was from retail operations and $9,700 from manufacturing. Retail sales for the coming three months were estimated at $180,000, which, in combination with tight control of purchases, would draw down retail inventory to $60,000 by June 30. Upon inquiry, Mr. Klein said that his present inventory amounted to $101,000, of which $17,000 was in piece goods (see Exhibit 2). Mr. Klein said that he still believed there would be a cleanup of his notes by June 30, 1957, as agreed to earlier.

Developments during the Last Six Months of 1957

In July, 1957, Mr. Barnes noted that Storkline had reduced its notes only to $15,000 at midyear (see Exhibit 3). In discussing the plans for the fall season with Mr. Klein in early September, Mr. Barnes learned that the company had now expanded to 18 locations and operations for the fall season were mounting. Retail sales for August had reached about $40,000; and for September and October together, Mr. Klein expected volume to reach $100,000. Mr. Klein said he was also selling manufactured products to a few select, outside customers. Mr. Klein expected his retail inventory to peak by the end of August, and a request for an additional $5,000 was granted. Financial statements for the seven months ending July 31 were recorded during this visit (see Exhibits 1 and 2).

In mid-October, the bank received a financial statement as of September 30, indicating inventory had mounted to $130,900, of which $98,600 was in retail goods (see Exhibit 2). Mr. Klein appended a note to this statement, stating that he expected his retail inventory to be reduced to $65,000 by the end of the year.

In talking with Mr. Barnes in mid-December, Mr. Klein argued that a $65,000 minimum inventory level was unrealistic for the present size of his business. Mr. Klein considered a more appropriate figure to be in the vicinity of $90,000. During this visit, Mr. Klein requested an additional $10,000 loan to finance the acquisition of piece goods inventory for the manufacturing operations and early purchasing for spring retail needs. Mr. Klein emphasized how very profitable the manufacturing operations were becoming, and considered this part of his business to have special promise. Storkline's proprietor assured Mr. Barnes that the $10,000 note, bringing the company's indebtedness to $30,000, would be adequate for seasonal requirements, and the request was granted.

The Latest Request—January, 1958

In mid-January, 1958, Mr. Klein brought to the bank a report of his five-month operations since August 31, 1957, and a year-end balance sheet (see Exhibits 1 and 2). In discussing future operations, Mr. Klein predicted that the manufacturing side of the business would have sales of $300,000 during the first six months of 1958. Storkline's spring line was being very well received, and many additional customers were actively interested in purchasing the line. He said he was now manufacturing 60% of his own requirements, in addition to selling to a few leading department stores and chains. He added that he was able to do a much larger volume in the manufacturing side of the business than at present, but that in compliance with the bank's suggestion he was moving slowly in accepting orders from outside concerns. He further reported that although national retail sales of maternity clothes during 1957 had dropped some 20% from the 1956 level, Storkline Shops had maintained sales at the 1956 level. Because of the exceptional progress since the beginning of his business in 1954, and the co-operation the bank had given him throughout that period, Mr. Klein hoped that the bank would be pleased to meet his current needs. In this regard, the proprietor wanted an additional $10,000 to finance payment of some maturing bills for piece goods.[1] Mr. Klein believed that he would have no difficulty in completely liquidating his bank

---

[1] Garment makers usually purchased piece goods on terms of 2/10 E.O.M. or on the basis of a negotiated price due net 60.

debt by midsummer. Whereas in previous years his profits had depended heavily upon the retail side of the business, Mr. Klein pointed out the keen buyer interest and lucrative profits being generated in the designing and manufacturing operation. He added in parting that the added credit would very much improve his ability to repay all notes by midsummer. Since total loans of $40,000 would permit expansion of the highly profitable manufacturing operations, Mr. Klein thought that the cash generated from these operations in the next six months would be more than enough to liquidate all bank debts.

Exhibit 1

STORKLINE SHOPS

OPERATING DATA FOR SELECTED PERIODS

(Dollar figures in thousands)

	First 6 Months 1955	12 Months 1955	First 6 Months 1956	12 Months 1956	First 7 Months 1957		Last 5 Months 1957	
					Retail	*Manufacturing*	*Retail*	*Manufacturing*
Net sales	$107.5	$260.1	$199.0	$425.7	$283.0	$ 96.0†	$231.1	$117.0‡
Cost of goods sold	58.0	135.0	107.2	226.1	n.a.	n.a.	115.0	75.0
Gross profit	49.5	125.1	91.8	199.6	n.a.	n.a.	116.1	42.0
Operating expenses*	37.2	97.1	77.7	163.4	n.a.	n.a.	85.1	17.0
Net profit	12.3	28.0	14.1	36.2	13.8	17.4	31.0	25.0
Withdrawals during period	6.2	8.5	6.2	18.5	...	$20.3	...	...
Reinvestment of withdrawals, end of period	6.0	1.0	0.1	13.1	...	...	$3.0	...
*Includes: Depreciation	n.a.	3.4	n.a.	6.9	n.a.	...	n.a.	...
Store rentals	n.a.	15.2	n.a.	37.5	30.4	...	26.0	...

† $3,000 to outside customers in the first seven months of 1957.

‡ $47,000 to outside customers in the last five months of 1957.

Exhibit 2

STORKLINE SHOPS

SELECTED BALANCE SHEETS

(Dollar figures in thousands)

ASSETS	Audited 6/30/55	Audited 12/31/55	Audited 6/30/56	Estimated 9/30/56	Audited 12/31/56	Estimated 4/15/57	Audited 7/31/57	Estimated 9/30/57	Estimated 12/31/57
Cash	$ 4.6	$ 8.6	$10.9	$16.0	$ 4.4	$ 6.0	$ 8.4	$ 14.0	$ 8.0
Accounts receivable	...	...	...	...	2.8	...	2.2	8.3	30.1
Inventory									
Retail	27.0	48.2	57.9	75.0	64.5	84.0	77.2	99.9	105.0
Piece goods	...	...	...	...	1.0	17.0	25.0	31.0	41.0*
Current assets	$31.6	$56.8	$68.8	$91.0	$ 72.7	$107.0	$112.8	$153.2	$184.1
Machinery, fixtures, equipment (net)	13.6	17.7	20.7	n.a.	30.6	n.a.	32.3	31.2	35.0
Miscellaneous assets	2.1	2.7	7.7	n.a.	4.1	n.a.	4.1	4.3	2.1
Total assets	$47.3	$77.2	$97.2	n.a.	$107.4	n.a.	$149.2	$188.7	$221.1
LIABILITIES									
Notes payable—bank	...	15.0	16.0	25.0	10.0	35.0	15.0	20.0	30.0
Notes payable—others	3.1	1.1	2.6	...	1.7	...	...	...	...
Accounts payable	10.7	11.0	22.2	26.0	15.1	22.0	35.2	42.6	40.1
Accruals	2.7	4.9	3.2	2.0	4.5	3.0	12.0	14.5	11.0
Current liabilities	$16.5	$32.0	$44.0	$53.0	$ 31.3	$ 60.0	$ 62.2	$ 77.1	$ 81.1
Net worth	30.8	45.2	53.2	n.a.	76.1	n.a.	87.0	111.6	140.0
Total liabilities	$47.3	$77.2	$97.2	n.a.	$107.4	n.a.	$149.2	$188.7	$221.1
Data received and recorded by the bank	8/16/55	1/25/56	9/13/56	9/21/56	2/17/57	4/18/57	9/2/57	10/11/57	1/13/58

* Includes $15,000 finished goods held by manufacturing operation against firm orders.

Exhibit 3

STORKLINE SHOPS
RECORD OF BALANCE OF NOTES PAYABLE—BANK
(End of month)
(Dollar figures in thousands)

	1955	1956	1957
January	—	$20	$20
February	—	25	35
March	—	25	35
April	—	25	35
May	—	25	25
June	—	16	25
July	—	16	15
August	$11	16	15
September	15	25	20
October	15	25	20
November	15	16	20
December	15	10	30

Case 17

Santos Coffee Company

EARLY in July, 1947, Mr. John Richards, a credit officer of the Free State Bank of Baltimore, Maryland, was considering what action the bank should take regarding a large unsecured loan to the Santos Coffee Company. In recent months a series of undesirable developments in connection with the loan had convinced Mr. Richards that the present situation was highly unsatisfactory from the bank's viewpoint. It seemed to him that unless the loan could be covered by adequate security, the bank would have to insist on payment of the loan, even though such action might result in liquidation of the company. Since the company owned little real property, the only possible collateral was the company's accounts receivable and inventory.

The Santos Coffee Company had been founded in 1929 by four salesmen who had worked previously for a large coffee roasting firm in Baltimore. The new company operated as an importer, roaster, and wholesaler of coffee.

The company customarily ordered its principal raw material, green coffee in bean form, from Brazilian exporters. Shipment was made from Santos, the principal coffee exporting port of Brazil. The method by which payment for the coffee was accomplished is outlined as follows: When a shipment was loaded aboard ship, the Brazilian exporter drew a draft on the Santos Coffee Company for the agreed dollar value of the shipment. The draft usually called for payment "on sight," that is, within three days after presentation of the draft to the company. With "shipping papers"[1] attached, the draft was then deposited for collection by the Brazilian exporter at its bank. This bank forwarded the draft and attached papers to its correspond-

---

[1] Consisting typically of invoices, ocean bill of lading, marine insurance certificates, and consular certificates.

ent bank in the United States, which in turn sent it on to the Free State Bank, which paid the draft as instructed by the Santos Coffee Company. Upon payment of the draft, the Free State Bank turned over the shipping papers to Santos, so that it could claim the coffee upon arrival in Baltimore.

Soon after the Santos Coffee Company moved its account to the Free State Bank in 1934, it arranged to borrow up to $30,000 from the bank to meet drafts for shipments of coffee. As the bank advanced the funds to pay for a particular shipment, it prepared a demand note for the amount of the advance. Papers accompanying the note gave the bank legal title to the coffee until the note was paid. Although the bank held title to the coffee, it released the coffee to the company for storage under a legal arrangement known as a "trust receipt." It was the customary practice of the company to pay the note secured by a particular shipment of coffee when it removed that coffee from storage for processing. Each trust receipt identified the particular shipment involved by reference to distinctive marks on the coffee bags in that shipment.

During the 10 years from 1934 to 1944, the company's sales gradually increased, and the amounts of money advanced for the company by the bank against coffee also increased. The bank also made additional unsecured advances to the company on a demand basis from time to time. By 1944, total advances to the company amounted at times to as much as $40,000. Since the company continued to show modest profits and sales increased somewhat, and since the company had only small debts owing to other creditors, the bank had taken no steps to see that the company was fully carrying out its obligations under the trust receipt arrangements. For example, the bank made no inspections of the inventory outstanding under the various trust receipts to make sure that it could be readily identified and that the company had reported promptly all withdrawals from storage. In the absence of these precautions, the bank regarded the advances against coffee under the trust receipts as, in fact, unsecured loans.

In 1944, Mr. John Stone, who had served as president of the company since its inception, died. Mr. Stone was succeeded by Mr. R. H. Sager, formerly sales manager for the company. At the time, the bank was somewhat concerned about the future management of the company, since all of the remaining officials were experienced primarily in the sales aspects of the business. Operations continued satisfactorily, however, and a profit of more than $5,000 was recorded in 1945. Late in 1945 the bank learned that Mr. Pierre LeBlanc, one of the salesmen, had purchased Mr. Stone's shares of common stock from his estate. This gave Mr. LeBlanc 385 shares out of the total of 890 shares outstanding. Consequently, Mr. LeBlanc assumed direction of the company with the title of vice president and general manager.

Under Mr. LeBlanc's leadership the company undertook a program of aggressive sales promotion. Sales were made principally to independent retailers and to restaurants and hotels. In 1946 the company had more than 3,400 accounts in Maryland, the District of Columbia, Virginia, and southern Delaware. Late in 1946, subsequent to the removal of OPA price restrictions on coffee, there was a sharp increase both in the price of green coffee and in the company's selling prices. However, the increase in prices accounted for only a portion of an increase in net sales from $432,000 in 1945 to $781,000 in 1946. Profits increased from $5,472 to $9,537.

During the latter part of 1946 the bank agreed to increase the amount of credit granted to the company in view of the increased working capital requirements as a result of higher sales and higher prices. A tentative maximum line of credit of $80,000 was established.

Early in January, 1947, Mr. LeBlanc requested that the line of credit be increased further. He explained that the company was currently spending large amounts on advertising and expected a further increase in sales. Mr. Richards had agreed to the increase in the line of credit in late 1946 to $80,000 with considerable reluctance, since he felt that the additional sales should more properly be financed by increased capital investment by the owners. Therefore, he declined to advance the line beyond $80,000 but promised to lay the matter before the officers' loan committee of the bank.

Shortly thereafter, in late January, 1947, Mr. Richards had a telephone call from an officer of the Chesapeake Trust Company, who informed him that the Santos Coffee Company had opened a borrowing account with the Chesapeake Trust Company in the fall of 1946 and was currently borrowing some $35,000 from that bank. The other banker expressed some dissatisfaction with his new account, particularly when Mr. Richards told him that this was the first news the Free State Bank had that Santos was borrowing from another bank. Shortly thereafter the Free State Bank received a copy of the audited annual report as of December 31, 1946, which confirmed the fact of outside borrowing. The balance sheet of the company on December 31 showed "notes payable to banks" of $105,000. Since $70,000 was outstanding from the Free State Bank, $35,000 was apparently owing the Chesapeake Trust on that date. Other payables also showed a substantial increase over the 1945 figures. Accordingly, Mr. Richards asked Mr. LeBlanc to come in and see him. In an ensuing discussion, he expressed dissatisfaction with Mr. LeBlanc's action in borrowing from another bank without informing the Free State Bank. He further stated that the Free State line of credit of $80,000 was based on the assumption that the company would not borrow from any other bank. He stated flatly that if Mr. LeBlanc did not accept this arrangement, he would have to pay off all the Free State loans and seek other banking accommodations. Mr. LeBlanc agreed to pay off the loans from the Chesapeake Trust Company and to reduce the scale of his operations so that $80,000 would be sufficient bank credit for the company's needs.

Despite the previous understanding, Mr. LeBlanc soon requested a temporary increase in the loans above $80,000 on the ground that he needed at least 2,200 bags of coffee in stock to meet his sales requirements and that the financing of this much inventory, together with the other needs of the business, would require an increase in the loan above $80,000. Mr. Richards replied that $80,000 was the bank's top limit and suggested that the company build up its capital through earnings and through the sale of preferred stock. Mr. LeBlanc agreed to undertake to find additional capital.

Early in May a representative of the bank visited the company and made a brief inspection of the inventory. A classification of the inventory of the company on April 30 was obtained. This was as follows:

	Thousands of Dollars
Green coffee	37.6
Roasted coffee	12.6
Tea	15.9
Groceries and miscellaneous supplies	6.8
Manufacturing supplies	38.6
	111.5

Upon inquiry it was learned that the manufacturing supplies consisted largely of glass containers, which had been purchased in quantity during a shortage period. Very recently, adequate supplies of tin containers had become available. Since tin containers were regarded as much more satisfactory, the company had shifted back to use of tin. There were more than five carloads of surplus glass containers. When pressed for an appraisal of the value of these containers, Mr. LeBlanc conceded that a loss of as much as $14,000 might be expected when they were sold.

In addition, it was learned that recent operations of the company had not proved profitable, although sales were large. In another conversation with Mr. LeBlanc, based on this information, Mr. Richards urged him to reduce the currently large expenditures for advertising and to try to reduce the loan to $55,000. Mr. LeBlanc agreed to do so. He also agreed to make available to Mr. Richards the financial statements of the company as of June 30 as soon as they were available.

Copies of the balance sheet and profit and loss statement for the first six months of the year were received by the bank on July 10. (See Exhibits 1 and 2.) Mr. Richards found the statements highly disturbing. Net working capital amounted to only $39,000, compared with total debt of $140,000. In addition, although the first half of 1947 had been a period of general prosperity and good corporate earnings, the Santos Coffee Company showed a loss of $34,000 for the period. At this stage, Mr. Richards was convinced that drastic action was necessary if the bank's interests were to be fully protected and possible loss prevented. While he was determining what action to recommend to the officers' loan committee, he received a call from Mr. Sager, one of the original founders of the firm and the manager during the year intervening between the death of Mr. Stone in 1944 and Mr. LeBlanc's assumption of the job late in 1945. Mr. Sager informed Mr. Richards that the stockholders had determined that a change in management was desirable. Mr. LeBlanc had agreed to resign as general manager and to resume his old duties as salesman. Mr. Sager was assuming the job of treasurer and with other stockholders would assume active management of the company. He agreed that the affairs of the company were in poor shape but expressed the strong hope that the bank would give the new management a chance to pull the company out of its current difficulty. He explained that the large expenditures for advertising had been terminated, that pressure was being put on overdue accounts receivable, that the recent practice of cutting profit margins to get additional sales would be stopped, that salaries were being reduced, and that every step to conserve funds was being taken. He asked Mr. Richards to tell him within a few days what the bank would do in regard to meeting the credit needs of the company.

Mr. Richards was impressed with the earnestness of Mr. Sager's appeal and with his apparent grasp of the management mistakes which appeared to be the cause of the company's difficulties. In view of all the facts, however, Mr. Richards decided that the Santos Coffee Company account should no longer be carried on an unsecured basis. In general, the Free State Bank had followed a policy of trying to work out of difficult situations, where there seemed a reasonable opportunity to do so, rather than forcing liquidation of borrowing customers.

Mr. Richards first centered his attention on the possibilities of securing a pledge of accounts receivable. In order to get a better idea of the company's accounts receivable, a representative of the bank was asked to undertake an aging of the accounts outstanding on June 30. He reported that the company had several thousand accounts, so that the average balance and the individual invoices were small. Of the $75,000 of receivables outstanding on June 30, $52,000 were current or no more than 30 days overdue. Of the remaining $23,000, $15,000 of the accounts were over 90 days overdue. Returns and allowances were very small.

Mr. Richards next focused his attention on the value of the company's inventory as collateral. Upon investigation he found that the green coffee used by the company consisted primarily of common grades of Brazilian coffee for which there was a continuous and rather wide market in Baltimore and in the neighboring cities. At any one time, part of the coffee was in ocean transit to the company. Green coffee actually on hand, preparatory to being roasted, was stored in vacant space in the building which the company rented. The company felt that it was essential to carry a substantial supply of green coffee, either on hand or en route to it, in order to insure no interruption in its supplies. Such a supply would at current prices amount to between $35,000 and $55,000 in total value. As a part of the retrenchment program, the new management planned to concentrate on the sale of coffee, reducing the June 30, 1947, inventory in tea and other lines.

Upon investigation, Mr. Richards verified his opinion that coffee in the green state could be held for many months without substantial deterioration, provided clean, dry storage was available and no other commodities of strong aroma were stored near by. He also investigated recent movements in green coffee prices. The results of the investigation of prices are shown in Exhibit 3. Mr. Richards learned that the government of Brazil, the country which accounted for more than 70% of world production of coffee, had for a number of years made strenuous efforts to maintain the price of coffee at what it considered reasonable levels. These efforts largely took the form of restriction on coffee exports so that they did not exceed world demand. When necessary, substantial stocks had been destroyed in Brazil in order to reduce supply in the world market. Consequently, some observers currently felt that the Brazilian government would take energetic steps to try to prevent any substantial decline from the current high prices.

Mr. Richards also investigated the possibility of getting a secured position in regard to the green coffee which would be unquestionably valid against general creditors in the event of bankruptcy of the firm. The trust receipt method of taking security on the coffee left some doubts on this score. He learned that there was an independent public warehouse across the street from the building in which the company operated, which had surplus space available at reasonable charges. He then conceived the following plan for loaning against the inventory: When drafts covering the new shipments of coffee were received, the bank would advance the agreed loan value, and Santos Coffee would supply the balance necessary to meet the drafts. Immediately, trust receipts describing the bags in the shipment would be prepared and executed by the company. Thus, the bank would have a secured position on the coffee while it was in transit. Marine insurance would be carried and made out so as to recognize the bank's security interest in the coffee in transit. When the coffee arrived in Baltimore, it would be moved immediately to the public warehouse. The warehouser would issue a warehouse receipt naming the bank as owner of the coffee. The warehouse receipt would be held by the bank, which would then return the trust receipt to the company. When the company needed the coffee for roasting, it would pay the bank the full amount of the loan advanced against the coffee. Thereupon, the bank would direct the warehouse company to release the coffee to Santos.

Such a procedure, Mr. Richards felt, would insure that the bank could properly identify the security back of the inventory loan and establish beyond challenge the bank's ownership of the coffee. The warehouseman was bonded to perform his duties properly; and the coffee, while in the warehouse, would be covered by fire and other insurance. The proposed procedure would involve some expense and trouble for the company, since it now stored its green coffee in otherwise useless space in its rented building. The company would be required to pay the storage charges of the bonded warehouse and, in addition, would incur expense for trucking and handling charges in and out of the warehouse.

After careful study, Mr. Richards concluded that the bank could probably escape with little or no loss if it demanded payment of its loans now and liquidation of the company resulted. Therefore, the major alternatives now open to the bank seemed to boil down to the following:

1. Demand payment of the loans.
2. Continue to loan to the company reasonable amounts on the basis of a pledge of accounts receivable.
3. Continue to loan to the company by advancing reasonable amounts of funds against drafts for shipments of coffee only if the coffee was moved into the public warehouse immediately upon arrival and warehouse receipts pledged as security for the loan.
4. A combination of 2 and 3.

Exhibit 1

SANTOS COFFEE COMPANY

BALANCE SHEETS

(Dollar figures in thousands)

	Dec. 31 1944	Dec. 31 1945	June 30 1946	Dec. 31 1946	June 30 1947
Cash	$ 21	$ 12	$ 14	$ 12	$ 16
Accounts receivable, net	37	47	62	87	75
Inventory	46	65	97	129	88
Total current assets	$104	$124	$173	$228	$179
Machinery and fixtures, net	7	13	18	17	18
Other notes and accounts receivable	2	2	2	2	2
Goodwill	28	28	28	28	28
Prepaid expenses	1	1	2	2	3
Total assets	$142	$168	$223	$277	$230
Notes payable—trade	...	...	...	...	$ 10
Notes payable—banks	$ 21	$ 28	$ 37	$105	74
Accounts payable—trade	2	11	48	26	46
Accrued expense	1	5	3	13	4
Reserve for taxes	4	4	7	4	6
Total current liabilities	$ 28	$ 48	$ 95	$148	$140
Common stock ($100 par)	89	89	89	89	89
Surplus	25	31	39	40	1
Total liabilities	$142	$168	$223	$277	$230

Exhibit 2

SANTOS COFFEE COMPANY

INCOME STATEMENTS

(Dollar figures in thousands)

	Year 1944	Year 1945	6 Months 1946	Year 1946	6 Months 1947
Net sales	$310.7	$431.8	$323.7	$780.7	$361.7
Gross profit	55.5	84.2	75.1	180.9	67.2
Administrative and selling expense	51.7	78.4	60.3	161.9	97.2
Operating profit	3.8	5.8	14.8	19.0	30.0*
Other income (purchase discounts)	1.2	2.8	0.9	1.4	0.2
Charges against income	4.8	3.1	7.3	10.9	4.2
Net income	0.2	5.5	8.4	9.5	34.0*
Common dividends	0.9	...	...	...	4.0

* Loss.

Exhibit 3

SANTOS COFFEE COMPANY

AVERAGE SPOT PRICE OF COFFEE IN NEW YORK*

(In cents per pound)

	Jan.	Feb.	Mar.	April	May	June	July	Aug.	Sept.	Oct.	Nov.	Dec.
1937	11.3	11.8	11.2	11.2	11.7	11.7	11.6	11.4	11.4	11.5	9.4	8.8
1938	8.6	8.1	7.5	7.3	7.6	7.4	7.6	7.9	7.8	8.0	8.1	8.0
1939	7.7	7.8	7.4	7.2	7.3	7.4	7.3	7.6	7.7	7.8	7.4	7.3
1940	7.5	7.4	7.3	7.3	7.2	7.3	7.0	6.8	6.8	7.0	7.2	7.4
1941	7.8	8.3	9.0	9.9	10.8	11.5	12.2	13.4	13.4	13.2	13.1	13.3
1942†	13.4	13.4	13.4	13.4	13.4	13.4	13.4	13.4	13.4	13.4	13.4	13.4
1943†	13.4	13.4	13.4	13.4	13.4	13.4	13.4	13.4	13.4	13.4	13.4	13.4
1944†	13.4	13.4	13.4	13.4	13.4	13.4	13.4	13.4	13.4	13.4	13.4	13.4
1945†	13.5	13.6	13.6	13.6	13.6	13.6	13.6	13.6	13.6	13.6	13.6	13.6
1946†	13.4	13.4	13.4	13.4	13.4	13.4	20.6	22.1	22.1	24.1	26.3	26.4
1947	26.9	27.2	27.7	25.8	23.7	25.3	...	...	...	...	...	...

* Santos No. 4. Source: Bureau of Labor Statistics.

† United States price controls on coffee were in effect during 1942–1946.

Source: *Commodity Year Book, 1948,* "Coffee," p. 165.

Case 18

Custom Plastics, Inc.

IN THE last week of July, 1956, Mr. Stanley Ebanson, vice president and loan officer of the Tradesman National Bank of Milwaukee, was introduced to Mr. Charles Miller, newly elected president of Custom Plastics, Inc. Mr. Miller, who with an investment group had purchased control of Custom Plastics two months earlier, was requesting short-term credit accommodation for the company from the Tradesman Bank. Though Custom Plastics was an old and reputable firm in the custom molding field, the company had suffered financial difficulties since 1953. In view of the company's continuing management and operating problems, the former owners accepted the offer of Mr. Miller's group to acquire immediate control of the company and pay out the former owners over a five-year period. The company had been extended short-term bank credit for many years by the Manufacturers Bank; but by mutual agreement between the former owners, Mr. Miller, and the officers of the Manufacturers Bank, the new president was to arrange the company's short-term credit needs with a new financial institution as soon as possible.

Custom Plastics was a manufacturer of custom molded plastic products. Manufacturing facilities were located in Milwaukee, Wisconsin, where the company leased a four-story plant for $50,000 per year, the current lease to expire in 1958. The company employed about 300 personnel and currently was operating on a two-shift basis. Custom Plastics was equipped with a complete line of molding machines, both compression and injection, capable of producing items of all sizes and shapes typically required by an industrial customer. Though the machinery was old and less efficient than new equipment on the market, the management believed the company's technical and engineering skills were of greater importance to profitable operation.

As was typical for a custom molder, Custom Plastics helped design a plastic product, obtained the specially cut mold from a local toolmaker, and manufactured the end product in its own molding machines. The company had a wide reputation for its ability successfully to undertake tricky mold design and product manufacturing assignments. The full cost of mold design and purchase was borne by the customer and paid to Custom Plastics in the initial purchases of the special plastic item. Custom Plastics was fully responsible for the quality of a finished plastic component, and most customers had rigid inspection procedures and quality standards. To obtain physical custody of a mold, the customer was required under a "mold contract" to pay Custom Plastics an additional 30% over the reimbursement price previously agreed to and paid Custom Plastics in the initial purchases.

In 1952, the company entered the plastic dinnerware business under a design and brand name licensing agreement with a nationally known designer. The line of dinnerware provided about 20% of the total sales volume in 1955. Two separate sales forces were maintained to contact the company's 175 customers, no one of which accounted for more than 10% of the company's volume. On the other hand, the list of the company's 15 most important customers in 1954 accounted for over half of that year's volume and included large, nationally known manufacturing, service, and retail distribution companies, each with a top credit rating.

Having been founded in 1905, Custom Plastics had "grown up" with the plastics industry and over the years had established a reputation for quality and service. Except during the depression years, the financial position of the company had always been healthy and operations profitable. Ownership was concentrated in the Saunders family; the senior member of the family had been active in the company management until the late 1940's. Though in many years a high proportion of earnings was paid out in dividends, the owners had retained adequate working capital and had established a substantial equity in the business as of the end of 1952.

During 1952, the production manager died; in his long association with the company, this man had become a key figure in the control and profitability of the manufacturing process. In his absence, cost control procedures were relaxed, and cost estimates and pricing decisions were less firmly based on adequate information. In an effort to lessen the impact of pricing decisions based on underestimated costs, material specifications were side-stepped, and some customers began to reject and return merchandise. At the same time, the co-ordination between engineering and production personnel began to weaken. Finally, productivity and morale among the employees reached a low point after a profit-participation plan promised them over the years was withdrawn from consideration in mid-1953. This incident, in combination with generally deteriorating morale conditions in the plant, led to a four-month strike in the early part of 1954 and continued management-labor friction thereafter.

As a result of these management and operating complications taking effect in 1953, the company's net profit before federal income tax fell from $238,000 in 1952 to a loss of $91,000 in 1953 (Exhibit 1). In 1954, the company suffered heavy losses due to a large reduction in revenues and excessive costs due to the strike and the heavy, unexpected returns of merchandise. At the time, however, the magnitude of these losses was not clearly known because of faulty accounting procedures in effect at the company.

During this period, financial strain developed, and the company began to rely heavily on trade and bank credit. Since the late 1940's, the company had been borrowing from the Manufacturers Bank moderate amounts, $10,000–$50,000, on unsecured notes to finance working capital needs arising from slight seasonality or unusually large orders. As the unfavorable operating results and the heavy demand for funds developed in late 1953, the management arranged a line of credit with the bank, pledging as security the company's accounts receivable in bulk. The bank agreed to loan up to 90% of the receivables balance. During the same year, added reliance was placed on trade credit, with trade payables increasing from $85,000 at the end of 1952 to $205,000 at the end of 1953 (Exhibit 2). Of this amount, $107,000, which was payable to five important suppliers, was placed on a deferred basis in early 1954 and secured by a chattel mortgage on certain machinery and equipment. Repayment of these notes in 18 monthly instalments with interest at 4½% was to commence in January, 1956. These financing arrangements permitted the company to remain current on new material purchases during 1954 and early 1955.

Owing to turnover in management personnel and almost complete loss of accounting and manufacturing cost control, the extent of the losses taking place in 1954 and early 1955 was not fully recognized until mid-1955. Upon the recommendation of the Manufacturers Bank, the owners of the business discharged the accounting manager and replaced him with an experienced C.P.A. After a thorough audit, losses before taxes in 1954 were calculated to have been $495,000, of which some $150,000 had been obscured by a failure to reflect returns and allowances as deductions from outstanding accounts receivable and from the period's sales. Losses for the first four months of 1955 were estimated at $85,000 before taxes.

When the scope of unprofitable operations became clear, the owners of the company decided to sell their interest in Custom Plastics rather than attempt its rehabilitation. This decision was stimulated, at least in part, by the vigorous suggestion of the bank, and by the recommendation of the five trade-note creditors, whose prospects of receiving payment on schedule seemed dim. While the owners were looking for a buyer, losses mounted to $109,000 before taxes by the end of 1955 (Exhibit 1). Working capital was squeezed to a minimum, and cash was drawn down to below $5,000. By the end of 1955, the Saunders family had invested an additional $53,000 in the company on unsecured notes, with the hope of tiding operations over until a buyer with an acceptable plan of purchase could be located. As the Saunders family wanted to withdraw entirely from the operations of the company, it expected a prospective buyer to pay out these notes as a part of the purchase plan. The deferred notes due trade creditors starting January, 1956, were renegotiated in late 1955 to postpone the payment schedule six months. At the same time, it again was becoming difficult to pay for current purchases.

Based on the unfavorable disclosures in 1955 regarding the company's receivables, the Manufacturers Bank asked Custom Plastics to pledge the cash surrender value of life insurance on certain officers and to give a chattel mortgage on the machinery not mortgaged to trade creditors as additional security behind its loan. In addition, the bank raised the interest rate from 5% to 6% on its loan and required the Saunders family to subordinate the company debt held by them to the bank obligations. Also, the bank became much more selective in the receivables against which it would lend, accepting only receivables under 60 days of age of the better credit risks. Finally, the bank hinted to Mr. Saunders that it would terminate its credit to the firm unless a prospective buyer of the business would be willing to bring substantial new equity funds into the company. Upon the completion of transfer of ownership to the new owners, the bank considered its obligation to the Saunders family and the company had been fulfilled and thought a fresh look by a new creditor might be beneficial to all parties.

In early 1956, Mr. Charles Miller, the president of Louisville

Desk Company, a small but prosperous manufacturer of metal furniture, became acquainted with Custom Plastics' situation and went to Milwaukee to investigate the company. Mr. Miller had a varied background in investment banking and light industry and with the aid of a group of friends had purchased the Louisville Desk Company in 1948. Though this company had a record of unprofitable operations and poor future prospects, Mr. Miller quickly revived the organization, reorganized its management, shifted product emphasis, and within a few years had built it into a quite successful small enterprise. Having completed this task, he sold his interest in the company at a substantial capital gain and was again looking for a "sick" company to purchase and rehabilitate.

Through the early months of 1956, Mr. Miller investigated the Custom Plastics operation rather thoroughly. Convinced that the company's former profitability could be restored under new ownership and management, he arranged in May, 1956, to buy the company, with payment over a five-year period. The Miller syndicate first purchased $150,000 of newly issued debentures, convertible into a new and second series of common stock. These debentures were secured by a second mortgage on all machinery and by an assignment of the company's mold contracts. Notes payable to the former owners of $53,000 were retired with cash received from the sale of the first $50,000 in new debentures. The existing and first series of common stock was placed in a voting trust with syndicate members as trustees. In each of the next five years, 15% of the company's after-tax profits in each year were to be used to repurchase this stock for cancellation, with the proceeds going to the former owners. Any stock not repurchased by the fifth year was automatically transferred to the company and canceled. Furthermore, the total of the five annual repurchase transactions was limited to $98,000. In summary, the obligation under this agreement was contingent upon profits and limited in aggregate amount and period of liability. The monthly balance sheet and operating statements of the company throughout the period of and following the negotiations are shown in Exhibits 3 and 4.

Though Mr. Miller brought additional funds into the Custom Plastics business and presented a plan for regaining profitable operations, the Manufacturers Bank decided to terminate its lending relationship with the company. Upon assumption of control of Custom Plastics, Mr. Miller had quickly organized a board of directors from among prominent Milwaukee businessmen, one of whom was the treasurer of an equipment manufacturer in Milwaukee. This new director was very impressed with the plans and managerial skill of Mr. Miller, and he offered his assistance to Mr. Miller in finding new credit accommodations for the company. As his company was an important depositor at the Tradesman National Bank and had a long and successful relationship there, the new director introduced Mr. Miller to Mr. Stanley Ebanson, a vice president and loan officer at this bank.

At a meeting with Mr. Ebanson in early August, 1956, Mr. Miller outlined his program for rehabilitating Custom Plastics. In order to utilize the full capacity of the machinery and to push operations well above a break-even level, Mr. Miller believed that sales volume had to be increased quickly. Mr. Miller thought break-even operations currently would result at a sales level of $200,000 per month; and to surpass this level, he intended to push aggressively for new business as well as regain the confidence and orders of lost customers. Though the backlog of orders stood at about $400,000, it consisted of many older and less profitable orders which had been deferred by the previous management in order to process the more profitable, cash-generating orders. Many customers, promised delivery in March, had not received shipment in July, and Mr. Miller considered it vital that this work receive first priority. To encourage salesmen to push profitable new projects, the president was offering bonuses for selected types of orders. In addition, he was personally trouble-shooting problems of rejections and returns which were causing direct losses and poor customer relations. Finally, selective price increases were being made to some customers who had been receiving merchandise on unreasonably good terms.

The second part of Mr. Miller's program was designed to increase the company's gross margin. Whereas the company's margin had been running from 10% to 14%, the industry range was 15% to 18%. The margin on the dinnerware line was about 23%. In reviewing the manufacturing costs, Mr. Miller was especially concerned with the low worker productivity at Custom Plastics. He intended gradually to put in a piecework system wherever possible, and some incentives had already been installed and well received by the employees. To assume much of the direct control of manufacturing operations which he was presently handling, the new president had just hired an able and experienced production manager from a competing molding firm. This new man would be expected to work quickly in expediting old orders, accurately estimating costs on new business and making sound pricing recommendations, increasing labor and machinery productivity and worker morale, and reducing wastage of raw materials.

Mr. Miller expected that operations in July and August would probably show a loss, due primarily to the backlog of unattractive orders which he had inherited. He believed September and October would be break-even months, and profits could be expected in October and thereafter. The new president said that if sales of $200,000 to $250,000 per month could be reached and gross margins increased as planned, the earnings of the company could be restored to 1951-52 levels. He hoped to have his accounting people make a more thorough cost study of the industrial versus the dinnerware lines; his own tentative studies indicated the profits from the dinnerware line were being offset by the losses in the industrial line. Mr. Miller pointed out also that the company had a federal income tax loss carry-over in the next four years of over $500,000 and that no taxes would have to be paid on earnings in this amount made during that period.

In light of these plans, Mr. Miller asked the Tradesman Bank to loan Custom Plastics 80% on net receivables up to a loan limit of $200,000. The company would pledge these assets, maintain accurate aging records, adequately provide for returns and adjustments, screen new credit with care (but with full knowledge of the need for additional business), and present the bank with timely monthly reports of the condition of receivables and the month's operating results. Mr. Miller planned to redeem the cash proceeds of the life insurance to supplement working capital. Pointing out the substantial investment he and his associates already had placed in Custom Plastics, Mr. Miller said he would not consider personally endorsing the company's bank indebtedness. The president added that the company's five main trade creditors were confident of the company's future because they agreed again to defer their notes, now totaling $98,000, and accept repayment at about $5,000 per month (including interest) beginning in September and extending for 22 months.

Mr. Ebanson was impressed with Mr. Miller's seeming insight into the problems at Custom Plastics. From the Louisville banker who was closely familiar with Mr. Miller's handling of the Louisville Desk situation, Mr. Ebanson received a strong recommendation of the new president of Custom Plastics. Mr. Miller was described as unimpeachable in integrity, venturesome in spirit, able to accomplish plans and deal with emergencies, and frank and open in his relations with creditors. Also, the associates of Mr. Miller were reputable businessmen, well-known in their separate communities and fields. Finally, although money and credit conditions were currently tight, the Tradesman Bank was actively interested in seeking new customers and establishing relationships which would prove attractive in the long run.

As Mr. Miller would want to know in a day or so whether the Tradesman Bank would be able to meet the company's loan request, Mr. Ebanson set about immediately to evaluate the company's financial needs and the basis, if any, upon which the Tradesman Bank would be willing to accommodate Custom Plastics.

Exhibit 1

CUSTOM PLASTICS, INC.

OPERATING STATEMENTS, 1951–1955

(Dollar figures in thousands)

	1951	1952	1953	1954	1955
Gross sales	$2,051	$2,335	$2,306	$1,687	n.a.
Returns and allowances	$137	$168	$ 50	$239	n.a.
Amortization of dies	22	48	3	2	n.a.
Discounts	17	19	14	15	n.a.
	176	235	67	256	
Net sales	$1,875	$2,100	$2,239	$1,431	$1,944
Materials	$601	$477	$692	$556	n.a.
Direct labor	372	462	513	385	n.a.
Indirect labor	223	261	328	278	n.a.
Overhead	278	318	366	316	n.a.
	1,474	1,518	1,899	1,535	
Gross profit	$ 401	$ 582	$ 340	$(104)	182
Officers' salaries	$ 53	$110	$115	$111	n.a.
Sales salaries and commissions	130	119	192	192	n.a.
Other general and administrative	92	133	169	106	n.a.
	275	362	476	409	300
Operating profit	$ 126	$ 220	$ (136)	$ (513)	$ (118)
Other income—net	33	18	45	18	9
Net profit before tax	$ 159	$ 238	$ (91)	$ (495)	$ (109)
Federal income tax	34	165	(90)	(75)	n.a.
Net profit after tax	$ 125	$ 73*	$ (1)	$ (420)	n.a.

* After renegotiation.

Exhibit 2

CUSTOM PLASTICS, INC.

BALANCE SHEETS AS OF DECEMBER 31

(Dollar figures in thousands)

	1950	1951	1952	1953*	1955*
ASSETS					
Cash	$ 59	$ 52	$163	$116	$ 3
Accounts receivable	114	164	199	321	198
Inventory	201	271	219	265	192
Total current assets	$374	$487	$581	$702	$393
Machinery and equipment, net	146	131	117	129	94
Cash value life insurance	28	29	30	31	34
Miscellaneous receivables	4	6	18	25	6
Secret process	27	27	27	27	...
Total fixed assets	$205	$193	$192	$212	$134
Total assets	$579	$680	$773	$914	$527
LIABILITIES					
Notes payable—banks	$ 45	$ 25	...	$125	$212
Notes payable—equipment	8	...	...	...	...
Notes payable—vendors	124	...	...	...	63
Accounts payable	...	70	$ 85	205	172
Accrued taxes	...	50	75	67	...
Other accruals	30	44	58	60	75
Total current liabilities	$207	$189	$218	$457	$522
Notes payable—equipment	...	...	...	...	7
Notes payable—vendors	...	...	...	...	44
Notes payable—officers	...	...	...	...	53
Total long-term liabilities	...	...	...	...	$104
Common stock	$263	$263	$263	$263	263
Earned surplus	109	228	292	193	(362)
Total net worth	$372	$491	$555	$456	$(99)
Total liabilities	$579	$680	$773	$913	$527

* No data available for 1954.

Exhibit 3

CUSTOM PLASTICS, INC.

MONTHLY OPERATING STATEMENTS, 1956

(Dollar figures in thousands)

	Jan.	Feb.	Mar.	April	May	June
Net sales	$140	$191	$200	$192	$195	$173
Material	n.a.	n.a.	n.a.	n.a.	68	60
Direct labor	n.a.	n.a.	n.a.	n.a.	43	38
Indirect labor	n.a.	n.a.	n.a.	n.a.	34	32
Overhead	n.a.	n.a.	n.a.	n.a.	29	28
Cost of sales	$127	$157	$168	$167	$174	$158
Gross profit	$ 13	$ 34	$ 32	$ 25	$ 21	$ 15
Officers' salaries	n.a.	n.a.	n.a.	n.a.	3	5
Other general and administrative	n.a.	n.a.	n.a.	n.a.	19	21
Operating expense	$ 25	$ 22	$ 23	$ 23	$ 22	$ 26
Operating profit	(12)	12	9	2	(1)	(11)
Other income—net	3	1	2	1	6	2
Net profit before tax	(9)	13	11	3	5	(9)

Exhibit 4

CUSTOM PLASTICS, INC.
MONTH END BALANCE SHEETS, 1956
(Dollar figures in thousands)

ASSETS	Feb. 29	March 31	April 30	May 29	June 30
Cash	$ 1	$ 6	$ 5	$ 9	$ 26
Accounts receivable	198	224	178	162	160
Inventory	186	209	222	238	230
Current assets	$385	$439	$405	$409	$416
Machinery and equipment, net	89	87	90	89	89
Cash value life insurance	34	34	34	34	34
Prepaid expenses	31	34	35	23	30
Fixed assets	$154	$155	$159	$146	$153
Total assets	$539	$594	$564	$555	$569
LIABILITIES					
Notes payable—bank	$176	$202	$156	$128	$111
Notes payable—vendors	63	58	83	83	56
Accounts payable	184	204	203	172	131
Other accruals	97	102	118	102	77
Customer advances	16	18	20	7	...
Current liabilities	$536	$584	$580	$492	$375
Debentures	...	...	...	50	150
Notes payable—officers	54	53	53	...	...
Notes payable—vendors	38	35	6	31	74
Notes payable—equipment	6	6	6	6	6
Long-term liabilities	$ 98	$ 94	$ 65	$ 87	$230
Common stock	263	263	263	263	263
Earned surplus	(358)	(347)	(344)	(287)	(299)
Net worth	$(95)	$(84)	$(81)	$(24)	$(36)
Total liabilities	$539	$594	$564	$555	$569

BREAKDOWN AND AGING OF ACCOUNTS RECEIVABLE—JUNE 30, 1956

Type	Amounts	Current	Last Month	Previous Month	Prior Months
Industrial	$113	$ 79	$24	$ 8	$ 2
Dinnerware	47	27	7	3	10
	$160	$106	$31	$11	$12

Terms: Industrial.........1%—10; net 30
Dinnerware.........2%—E.O.M.

Case 19

The Dunning Cabinet Company

On September 3, 1950, Mr. Dunning, 68-year-old president and sole owner of The Dunning Cabinet Company, called on Mr. Vines, vice president and loan officer of the Jefferson National Bank of Richmond, Virginia, to discuss the renegotiation of a $140,000 term loan arranged in March, 1950, to finance the expansion of the Dunning Company's plant capacity.

The Dunning Cabinet Company, located in Roanoke, Virginia, manufactured wooden television cabinets against firm orders on hand. It was not a large producer and was best suited for production runs of about 5,000 units. Its high-priced, quality cabinets were sold to large manufacturers of television sets for their console models.

The Jefferson National Bank, a medium-sized bank with a legal loan limit of $1,000,000, was actively attempting to build a reputation as a progressive bank. To help achieve this goal, the bank's loan officers were encouraged to use originality, whenever the risks did not seem insurmountable, in arranging suitable credit for companies that showed promise of developing into good accounts. It was hoped that, by extending credit to companies in situations where other banks might be hesitant in offering support, sound bank-customer relationships would be established that would prove beneficial to the bank over the long run.

In March, 1950, Mr. Dunning was contemplating a $140,000 addition to the company's single-story plant which would double its production capacity. The company's customers were pressing for production many times the operating capacity of a $1,000,000 annual sales volume. In the period from January 21, 1950, to March 15, 1950, orders totaling $3,700,000 from six major television set manufacturers were declined. These represented initial orders only; and

Mr. Dunning estimated that if these orders had been accepted, repeat business would have easily tripled these initial orders.

When Mr. Dunning visited the small Roanoke bank where the company had maintained its account since 1932, he was informed that a $140,000 loan was above the bank's legal limit. Although the loan officer of the local bank expressed his willingness to introduce Mr. Dunning to a loan officer at a large metropolitan bank in Washington, D.C., Mr. Dunning preferred to see Mr. Vines, whom he had known casually for several years. When he went to the Jefferson National Bank on March 17, 1950, to discuss the required loan, Mr. Dunning brought the balance sheets and income statements reproduced in Exhibits 1 and 2.

While at the bank, Mr. Dunning told Mr. Vines that the company had always operated profitably since its founding in 1932 and that it had never failed to have a substantial backlog of firm orders from at least one radio or television set manufacturer during its entire history. Mr. Dunning thought that the company's trade reputation was excellent and that with adequate production facilities the Dunning Company could easily double its sales volume. Since a number of the company's expenses such as sales and administration were fixed, he believed that the proposed expansion would more than double profits and would pay for itself within a little more than a year's time. He foresaw no problems in doubling plant capacity, for there appeared to be an ample supply of skilled woodworking labor in the Roanoke area. However, to finance the plant expansion, Mr. Dunning estimated the company would require a two-year loan of $140,000. He also thought additional funds would be needed to increase the working capital to a level that would support the expected increase in sales volume.

Subsequent to Mr. Dunning's visit, Mr. Vines made several checks with television manufacturers regarding Dunning's trade reputation. A typical response was: "We feel very close to Dunning and think highly of them. They are reliable in their dealings, and Dunning makes a high-quality, high-price article that cannot be obtained in the mass production cabinets usually put out by larger woodworking concerns. Our purchasing department is highly pleased with Dunning's performance and as long as we need cabinets, we will give Dunning consideration." These sources also confirmed newspaper articles which predicted that television sales would continue to grow in the foreseeable future. The Dunning Company's previous bank of account, which was not a correspondent bank of Jefferson, informed Mr. Vines that the company in recent years maintained a moderate five-figure bank account and properly attended to small seasonal loans which were required occasionally.

In reviewing the balance sheet and income statements provided, Mr. Vines noted that the company had nearly doubled its sales volume within the last three years without creating financial imbalance. Whereas only $12,000 principal repayments were required on the $78,000 first mortgage on the company's plant, the outstanding balance had been reduced by $24,000 in 1949. On the whole, Mr. Vines was impressed with Mr. Dunning as an individual, and an examination of the company's financial development in recent years strengthened his confidence.

When Mr. Vines visited the Dunning plant in late March, 1950, he noted that the production process was orderly and inventories appeared well controlled. He was favorably impressed with several younger officers he met during his tour.

On March 30, 1950, Mr. Vines completed a two and one-half year term loan agreement for $140,000 with the Dunning Company. In addition, a $160,000, 4%, open line of credit was extended to cover increased working capital requirements. When the loan agreement was signed, Mr. Vines briefly discussed the covenants of the term loan with Mr. Dunning.

Bearing interest of 4½%, the term loan was to be repaid in quarterly amounts of $16,000 beginning February 28, 1951, with the final maturity on February 28, 1953. Prepayments without penalty were permitted in whole or in part at any time prior to final maturity date and would be applied against instalments due in inverse order. However, there was a ¼% penalty fee if the loan was repaid by means of outside financing. The positive and negative covenants of the term loan agreement are set forth below:

Positive: The company agrees to . . .
1. Maintain net working capital of greater than $100,000 after excludcluding the current portion of the term loan from current liabilities.
2. Supply the bank with monthly balance sheets and income statements.

Negative: The company will not without prior permission from the bank . . .
1. Merge; consolidate; sell; or lease any asset.
2. Create a pledge or mortgage against any asset with the exception of the present $78,000 first mortgage on the "old" plant.
3. Replace or acquire more fixed assets in any year than can be purchased from the annual depreciation allowance, except for the proposed plant expansion totaling $140,000.
4. Pay dividends.

5. Purchase securities other than U.S. government bonds.

6. Repurchase the company's capital stock.

7. Increase the salaries of the company's officers.

Subsequent to the signing of the loan agreement, Mr. Vines received the monthly financial statements reproduced in Exhibit 3. As developments in the account seemed normal, he found no reason to inquire further about Dunning's progress. On August 31, he had noted that $80,000 of the term loan had been borrowed by the company but that its deposit balance exceeded $60,000.

On September 3, 1950, Mr. Dunning came to the bank to inform Mr. Vines of a change in the company's expansion plans. Instead of rebuilding the plant for a total capacity of $2,000,000 sales volume, the enlarged plant would increase production capacity to an annual sales volume of $3,500,000. This change, Mr. Dunning explained, had been forced by increased pressure from the company's customers for more cabinets. Construction was well under way, and Mr. Dunning expected the new plant to be completed by the end of 1950. He said that $53,000 of the building program had been paid, but that construction costs were now estimated at $470,000. Because the $140,000 term loan was inadequate to meet the new requirements, Mr. Dunning requested that the bank negotiate a new loan for $400,-000 to replace the original loan.

Sales during the first six months of 1950 had been $679,000, with profits before taxes equal to $123,000. In July, despite closing the plant for a two-week vacation, sales had amounted to $83,000, and Mr. Dunning estimated August volume was $138,000. Sales for the last four months of 1950 were estimated at $700,000. Of this amount, he had accepted firm orders as follows:

September	$146,000
October	232,000
November	171,000
December	28,000

By the end of September, he expected to be fully committed for the remainder of 1950. Sales in 1951 were expected to approximate the plant's capacity of $3,500,000. Although a portion of the new plant was already in operation, Mr. Dunning was still turning down orders at the rate of $800,000 per month.

Mr. Dunning estimated that profits before taxes would continue at the level of 18%, the actual results for the first six months of 1950. Income taxes payable in 1951 were estimated at 42%. He anticipated the unused $160,000 line of credit extended by the bank would adequately cover the expected increase in working capital requirements.

Mr. Vines was shocked by the action taken by Mr. Dunning, particularly in view of the fixed asset covenant in the original term loan. When asked about this restriction, Mr. Dunning said he had forgotten about it. Mr. Vines replied that such negligence was certainly not conducive to good bank-customer relations. However, he reluctantly agreed to consider a new term loan agreement.

When Mr. Vines inquired about the effect on the company's business of the Korean conflict, which had begun in June, Mr. Dunning said that it did not appear likely there would be any major cutback in television production. If there was a cutback, however, he was not much concerned, since the company had sufficient woodworking business to operate the plant 24 hours a day during the last war. Mr. Dunning expected to do as well during the Korean War if it became necessary to convert to war production in the future.

After Mr. Dunning had left, Mr. Vines phoned several of Dunning's customers to determine the company's outlook. A typical response was: "We consider Dunning an important supplier of high-quality cabinets. They are fine people to deal with; and if war or another unexpected economic development does not interfere with production of television sets, we expect our orders with Dunning will undoubtedly run higher in 1951. However, they are not one of our major suppliers due to their inability to produce in volume. In the event of an all-out war necessitating a cutback or discontinuance in television production and a resumption of war orders requiring woodworking jobs, Dunning will receive consideration."

With this information at hand, Mr. Vines began reviewing Dunning's financial requirements to determine whether the bank should grant the request for a $400,000 term loan.

Exhibit 1

THE DUNNING CABINET COMPANY
SELECTED BALANCE SHEETS
(Dollar figures in thousands)

ASSETS	December 31, 1947	December 31, 1948	December 31, 1949	February 28, 1950*
Cash	$ 19	$ 22	$ 25	$ 40
Accounts receivable	62	30	62	56
Inventory	114	144	147	98
Total current assets	$195	$196	$234	$194
Plant and equipment (net)	210	254	279	285
Other assets	6	3	6	6
Total assets	$411	$453	$519	$485
LIABILITIES				
Accounts payable	$ 14	$ 33	$ 53	$ 18
Taxes payable	53	22	43	43
Accrued payables	22	39	30	17
Total current liabilities	$ 89	$ 94	$126	$ 78
Mortgage	108	108	84	78
Common stock (800 shares—par value $25)	20	20	20	20
Surplus	194	231	289	309
Total liabilities and net worth	$411	$453	$519	$485

* Unaudited.

Exhibit 2

THE DUNNING CABINET COMPANY
INCOME STATEMENTS
(Dollar figures in thousands)

	1946	1947	1948	1949	Jan. and Feb. 1950
Sales	$505.0	$716.2	$778.5	$981.9	$181.4
Cost of goods sold*	338.9	499.5	598.4	754.2	
Gross profit	$166.1	$216.7	$180.1	$227.7	
Operating expenses	89.4	91.0	121.8	123.5	
Operating profit	$ 76.7	$125.7	$ 58.3	$104.2	
Other income (net)	0.6	2.9	2.1	0.8	
Profit before taxes	$ 77.3	$128.6	$ 60.4	$105.0	20.0
Taxes	32.3	53.2	21.8	43.2	
Net profit	45.0	75.4	38.6	61.8	
Dividends	0	0	2.0	4.0	

* Includes depreciation of:
  1946 .... $12,000
  1947 13,000
  1948 15,000
  1949 15,000

Exhibit 3

THE DUNNING CABINET COMPANY
SELECTED UNAUDITED BALANCE SHEETS
(Dollar figures in thousands)

ASSETS	March 31, 1950	April 30, 1950	May 31, 1950	June 30, 1950	July 31, 1950
Cash	$ 25.8	$ 25.6	$ 22.2	$ 10.7	$ 18.2
Accounts receivable	102.6	114.3	106.4	60.3	73.6
Finished goods	10.3	10.1	2.2	1.9	1.8
Work-in-process	20.8	19.7	22.4	120.1	138.5
Raw materials	48.9	85.4	111.4	42.3	37.5
Supplies	4.3	3.9	9.5	11.3	14.3
Total current assets	$212.7	$259.0	$274.1	$246.6	$283.9
Net plant and equipment	282.9	290.4	293.8	316.7	331.5
Other assets	5.3	7.2	6.8	6.6	6.5
Total assets	$500.9	$556.6	$574.7	$569.9	$621.9
LIABILITIES					
Accounts payable	$ 29.5	$ 39.0	$ 45.1	$ 27.5	$ 23.7
Taxes payable	26.4	26.4	26.4	17.6	17.6
Accrued payables	17.6	18.6	24.0	20.4	20.2
Total current liabilities	$ 73.5	$ 84.0	$ 95.5	$ 65.5	$ 61.5
Mortgage	78.0	78.0	72.0	72.0	72.0
Term loan					40.0
Common stock—(800 shares— par value $25)	20.0	20.0	20.0	20.0	20.0
Surplus	329.4	374.6	387.2	412.4	428.4
	$500.9	$556.6	$574.7	$569.9	$621.9
Sales	$108.0	$143.8	$ 96.9	$148.8	$ 83.0
Profit before taxes	20.2	45.2	12.6	25.2	16.0

Case 20

Community National Bank

IN MID-FEBRUARY, 1956, Mr. Paul Thompson, vice president of the Community National Bank of Pasadena, was considering whether the bank should make a term loan to Specialty Models, Inc., a small local manufacturer of precision-machined metal products, and upon what conditions and terms the granting of the loan should be contingent. The company had requested $65,000–$50,000 in a term loan and $15,000 in a real estate mortgage. From a conference with Mr. Stanley Edmonds, treasurer of Specialty Models, Inc., and from financial statements submitted by him, Mr. Thompson had pieced together the following information about the company.

Specialty Models had been organized as a partnership by Mr. John Rodney and Mr. Harold Morton early in 1948. From the outset the partnership specialized in custom and job order precision machining which required unusually close tolerances, specialized machinery, and skilled craftsmanship. Both the founders worked full time during the day in a local tool company where they had been employed as machinists for many years. In the evenings and over week ends, however, they worked in the basement of Mr. Rodney's house, making parts and components of integrating "gyros," gun sights, miniature hydraulic valves, precision gear boxes, and other related products necessary to the manufacture of electronic systems. Specialty Models did most of its work either for local electronics companies or for local branches of national companies. Almost all the finished products into which Specialty Models components would fit were manufactured on government contract.

With the rapid growth of sales in the first two years of business, more space and equipment became necessary. The partnership therefore purchased a one-story block plant and moved there early in

765

1950. At this time the partners gave up their other jobs in order to devote full time to Specialty Models. Also, the partnership hired Mr. Stanley Edmonds to handle administration of the office, supervise purchasing, and carry on outside sales work. Mr. Edmonds had a diversified background in technical development work and in the production, purchasing, and mechanical engineering associated with specialized instruments and precision-machined components.

In July, 1952, Mr. Morton died suddenly. From that time until the end of 1953, work continued while Mr. Rodney negotiated with the Morton estate for the purchase of Morton's share in the partnership. At the outset the parties to the negotiation held widely divergent views as to the value of Morton's share. Relations became increasingly strained; but in mid-December, 1953, it was agreed that Specialty Models, a new proprietorship under Mr. Rodney, would assume an indebtedness of $50,000 to the Morton estate. Of this amount, $9,000 was to be paid immediately, and the balance of $41,000 was to be paid by Specialty Models over a four-year period. Soon after the conclusion of this agreement, Specialty Models was incorporated, with Mr. Rodney becoming president and Mr. Edmonds treasurer of the new corporation. Balance sheets for selected dates from June 30, 1952, through December 31, 1955, are given in Exhibit 1.

Sales increased consistently in the period from 1948 through 1950 and then jumped from $98,500 in 1951 to over $250,000 in 1952 and 1953. Net profits before taxes in these years varied widely both in dollars and as percentages of sales (see Exhibits 2 and 3). For 1952, profits were originally reported at $74,500; but late in 1953, when faulty inventory costing procedures had been corrected, it was discovered that $27,200 of this amount was actually attributable to operations in 1949 and 1951.

In 1954, sales fell off approximately 15% from the 1953 level. Although receivables had been reduced during 1954 by some $16,000, the funds released were needed for the purchase of additional machinery. Under these circumstances, the combined impact of payments to the Morton estate and periodic reduction of the real estate mortgage became very burdensome. The payments were met promptly; but in the aggregate, they amounted to more than the year's net profit after taxes. Mr. Rodney and Mr. Edmonds believed that the purchase of additional machinery was imperative, since the range of machining assignments which the company could accept would then be broadened and the company's future profit potential would improve markedly. Mr. Edmonds therefore undertook early in 1955 to explore ways of refinancing the Morton estate notes and, at the same time, bringing new funds into the business. He and Mr. Rodney believed that a $50,000 term loan would serve the needs of the business.

Mr. Edmonds first approached the company's local bank of deposit. After reviewing the company's record and its plans for purchases of additional machinery, the bank declined to grant the requested term loan of $50,000. Some six months later, in telling a friend about this "turndown" by the local bank, Mr. Edmonds was advised that the Small Business Administration (SBA) might be willing to grant the company the loan it was seeking.

Checking with the SBA in September, 1955, Mr. Edmonds found that the agency was willing to consider a loan request. During the next two months the SBA looked into the operations of Specialty Models, Inc. By late October, sales for the year to date had amounted to approximately $180,000 and net profit after taxes to about $6,000. The company had sixteen active accounts, of which five were responsible for nearly 75% of sales. In talking with the SBA officials, Mr. Edmonds pointed out that the purchase of some new machinery would enable the company to accept profitable new business and, at the same time, make cost savings on existing types of work. He estimated that with the new machinery in operation, profits after taxes for 1956 and subsequent years might reach $18,000.

In the last week of October, 1955, the SBA agreed to make Specialty Models, Inc., a five-year, 6% term loan of $50,000, repayable in monthly instalments of $833 plus interest. As a condition of the loan the SBA stipulated that a note due to an equipment company be subordinated to the SBA loan and that no retirement of the principal of this note be made until the SBA loan was fully repaid. Specialty Models, Inc., and the equipment company both agreed to this condition, although reluctantly. The balance sheet of Specialty Models, Inc., following the acceptance of the SBA loan and the repayment of the Morton estate notes is that shown for December 31, 1955, in Exhibit 1.

Almost immediately the management of Specialty Models became dissatisfied with the terms of the SBA loan. In the first place, Mr. Rodney could see no reason why the company had been required to ask one of its equipment suppliers to subordinate his note. He believed that this arrangement was unfair to the dealer, and he instructed Mr. Edmonds to continue the repayment of this note despite the subordination agreement with the SBA. Also, the annual repayment to the SBA of $10,000 in monthly instalments was just as burdensome as the previous payments to the Morton estate. Furthermore, Mr. Rodney was of the opinion that the existing real estate loan of $10,600 was not fully utilizing the security value of the property; according to a real estate appraiser, the property had a current market value of approximately $25,000. Finally, Mr. Edmonds advised Mr. Rodney that the company needed additional machinery beyond that previously contemplated, as well as added working capital funds to finance new business.

Through a friend, Mr. Rodney arranged to visit the Community National Bank in early February, 1956, and to discuss the financial problems of Specialty Models, Inc., with Mr. Thompson, one of the vice presidents. On his visit to the bank, Mr. Rodney recited his dissatisfaction with the existing SBA arrangement and asked the Community National Bank to grant the company a $50,000, seven-year term loan and a $15,000 mortgage on its real estate. With these funds, Specialty Models, Inc., proposed to retire the SBA loan and the current real estate mortgage and to bolster its working capital. Mr. Rodney expressed a willingness to accept reasonable stipulations as to working capital, added indebtedness, and dividends and to back the loan with the personal guaranty of both corporation officers. Also, Specialty Models would move its deposits to the Community National Bank.

Upon investigation, Mr. Thompson found that Mr. Rodney's personal net worth, apart from his investment in Specialty Models, was $10,300, represented primarily by his residence, and that Mr. Edmonds' outside net worth, also in his residence, was $18,900. Specialty Models held as beneficiary a term life insurance policy on Mr. Rodney in the face amount of $55,000. From people familiar with the local precision-machining industry, Mr. Thompson learned that the company had an excellent reputation in the trade for its ability to handle unusually demanding work. Its work force of more than twenty highly skilled machinists was considered outstanding. The company's machinery was the finest available and, though crowded into the company's block plant, it was apparently well maintained. The book value of unencumbered machinery was approximately $45,000, and the current market value was approximately the same.

Although Mr. Thompson recognized that a loan to Specialty Models, Inc., might appear to be somewhat venturesome, he was mindful that the Community National Bank had been attempting in recent years to broaden its industrial lending. Many of the bank's loans were secured by marketable securities, and many others also had relatively low risk characteristics. The bank currently had unused lending capacity and especially wanted to cement relationships with industrial borrowers whose accounts held promise of attractive development in the long run. By tradition, the bank was prepared to work closely with its customers in the solution of their individual problems of financial management.

Exhibit 1

SPECIALTY MODELS, INC.
SELECTED BALANCE SHEETS
(Dollar figures in thousands)

ASSETS	June 30 1952	Dec. 31 1952	Dec. 31 1953	Jan. 4 1954	Dec. 31 1954	Dec. 31 1955
Cash	$ 22.4	$ 2.4	$ 4.9	$ 4.9	$ 9.0	$ 8.8
Accounts receivable (net)	18.1	37.2	33.3	33.3	16.9	26.2
Due from employees	...	...	...	...	0.6	0.2
Work in process	31.5	31.4	18.6	18.6	19.3	12.0
Prepaid expenses	0.2	0.3	1.0	1.4	1.3	1.2
Total current assets	$ 72.2	$ 71.3	$ 57.8	$ 58.2	$ 47.1	$ 48.4
Net fixed assets	55.5	54.1	63.2	63.2	79.4	89.0*
Goodwill	...	...	21.0	21.0	21.0	21.0
Total assets	$127.7	$125.4	$142.0	$142.4	$147.5	$158.4
LIABILITIES						
Accounts payable	22.7	32.0	9.3	9.3	7.4	10.2
Mortgage payable—current	...	...	...	...	2.2	2.2
Due to Morton estate—current	...	...	10.3	10.3	10.3	...
SBA term loan—current	...	...	...	...	...	10.0
Due to officers	2.5	2.0	28.9	17.5	17.0	...
Reserve for taxes	...	...	...	...	6.0	5.0
Equipment notes—current	1.4	1.0	7.3	11.7	11.2	...
Other accruals	0.4	3.6	3.4	3.4	3.6	2.5
Total current liabilities	$ 27.0	$ 38.6	$ 59.2	$ 52.2	$ 57.7	$ 29.9
Equipment notes deferred	...	...	...	...	...	12.5
Mortgage payable	8.3	8.5	12.7	12.7	9.4	8.4
Due to Morton estate	...	...	30.7	30.7	20.3	...
SBA term loan	...	...	...	...	...	38.9
Total long-term liabilities	$ 8.3	$ 8.5	$ 43.4	$ 43.4	$ 29.7	$ 59.8
Preferred stock	...	...	...	7.0	12.5	13.0
Common stock	...	...	...	39.8	39.8	39.8
Earned surplus	...	...	...	...	7.8	15.9
Partnership equity	92.4	78.3	39.4	...	...	...
Net worth	$ 92.4	$ 78.3	$ 39.4	$ 46.8	$ 60.1	$ 68.7
Total liabilities	127.7	125.4	142.0	142.4	147.5	158.4

* Land and building ... $ 28.7
  Machinery ... 84.1
  Other ... 9.0
  $121.8
  Less depreciation ... 32.8
  Net fixed assets ... $ 89.0

Exhibit 2

SPECIALTY MODELS, INC.

SALES AND NET INCOME, 1948–1955

(Dollar figures in thousands)

		Net Income*	
Year	*Sales*	*Dollars*	*Percentage of Sales*
1948	$ 27.3	$ 8.9	32.6%
1949	42.5	13.4	31.5
1950	76.6	41.5	54.2
1951	98.5	14.6	14.8
1952	261.1	47.3	18.1
1953	254.2	12.9	5.1
1954	216.8	14.4	6.6
1955	247.7	12.8	5.2

* Before individual or corporate income taxes.

Exhibit 3

SPECIALTY MODELS, INC.

INCOME STATEMENTS FOR 1952, 1954, AND 1955

(Dollar figures in thousands)

	1952		*1954*		*1955*	
Net sales		$261.1		$216.8		$247.7
Cost of goods sold		195.6		186.0		217.1*
Gross profit		$ 65.5		$ 30.8		$ 30.6
Expense						
Selling and distribution	$ 8.1		$ 3.0		$ 4.5	
Administrative	10.1	18.2	13.4	16.4	8.3	12.8
Operating profit		$ 47.3		$ 14.4		$ 17.8
Less: Other expenses		...		...		5.0
Net profit before taxes		$ 47.3		$ 14.4		$ 12.8

* Includes depreciation of $8.9.

Case 21

The Sabbath Container Company

IN NOVEMBER, 1952, Mr. Callahan, treasurer of The Sabbath Container Company, was considering the question of how best to determine the relative costs and advantages of two alternative methods of financing the company's expansion program, the sale of bonds or common stock. The question had been precipitated by a disagreement among the company's directors at a recent meeting. Following the meeting, Mr. Callahan had been asked by Mr. Rocco, the president of the company, to assess the logic of the arguments presented by the various directors, and outline a position to be taken by the company's management at the directors' meeting the following month.

The Sabbath Company manufactured containers for industrial and commercial use. Although the level of sales and profits fluctuated considerably with the level of business activity, the company's operations had been profitable in almost all years. Originally founded in 1896 to manufacture kerosene cans, the company's product line had changed considerably over the years; metal snuffboxes, cigarette "flat 50" tins, and a variety of other containers had proved profitable. During World War II, the company had concentrated its efforts in the manufacture of first-aid kit containers for the armed forces. Currently a considerable volume of sales was being obtained from the manufacture of small aluminum cans for the shipment of delicate instruments, particularly those used in aircraft. The company also had contracts to supply several pharmaceutical firms with tins for pills and small bandages. The latter line had contributed a needed element of stability to demand.

Management had customarily followed the policy of avoiding long-term debt. Apart from war periods, when working capital requirements had been unusually heavy, the company had met its needs by retained earnings, supplemented from time to time by short-term bank loans. In 1952, the capitalization of the company consisted of common stock and surplus, with no fixed indebtedness of any sort.

Although descendants of the founders still retained sizable holdings, ownership of the stock was widely distributed; there was no dominant interest, and the shares, which were traded "over the counter," were transferred infrequently.

Late in 1952, the management of the Sabbath Company decided that a small plant in Los Angeles, which had been acquired in 1932, should be modernized and enlarged. In recent years, this plant had proved inadequate to meet the rising demand for aluminum containers for aircraft instrument firms, and it had become clear that fundamental changes were required. Management estimated that the larger plant and additional working capital needed to finance expanded operations would require $10,000,000 in new funds. Originally it had been planned to provide these funds from retained earnings, but a general increase in working capital requirements and a lowered balance of earnings after higher income and excess profits taxes made this plan inadvisable. It was therefore planned to seek capital from outside sources.

The proposed investment was expected to net $2,000,000 in annual earnings before interest and taxes as soon as the plant was in operation. The added investment would increase the tax base of the corporation for purposes of excess profits tax computation, so that it was assumed that the 1951 over-all tax rate of 58% would apply also to the added income from the new investment. Consequently, the net incremental income after taxes was forecast at 8.4%, or $840,000.

A preliminary investigation of the price record of Sabbath common stock led Mr. Callahan to the opinion that, barring a general market decline, common stock could be sold to the public through investment bankers at $26.50 per share. After underwriting expenses and other fees, net proceeds to the company would be $25 per share. Thus, if common stock were used, the proposed financing would require the issuance of 400,000 shares.

For some years, both Mr. Rocco and Mr. Callahan had been disappointed in the market prices of Sabbath common stock (see Exhibit 1). For this reason, they had decided to re-examine the company's established policy of avoiding long-term debt. Circumstances had changed, and they believed that a new policy might be justified by the prospect of more stable future earnings. Inquiry in financial circles established the likelihood that the company could raise $10,-

000,000 through the sale of bonds. It appeared that the interest rate on a 15-year issue would be 4%. If such securities were sold directly to insurance companies or other institutional investors, they undoubtedly would insist upon some sinking fund arrangement. It seemed likely that they would require retirement of at least $500,000 of the issue annually, leaving $2,500,000 outstanding at maturity. While such terms would create a sizable annual requirement for cash, they were regarded by the company's management as about as good as could be expected.

In view of the tax deductibility of bond interest and the current income tax experience of 58%, the 4% rate was regarded by Mr. Callahan as the equivalent of 1.68%. In contrast, he considered that the stock at $25 per share and a $2 dividend rate would cost the company 8%. This comparison made the bond issue seem very desirable to Mr. Rocco.

Early in November, 1952, Mr. Rocco decided to submit the expansion proposal to the Sabbath board of directors for its formal approval. The proposal to increase the Los Angeles plant had been discussed previously by the board; after reconsidering it briefly, the board voted unanimously to authorize the president to go forward with the project, assuming satisfactory financing could be arranged. At this point, Mr. Rocco decided to sound out board sentiment to see if the possibility of debt financing as an alternative to common stock financing should be explored further. He presented the cost comparison given above. Somewhat to his surprise and concern, an active and at times acrimonious discussion developed, in which all of the directors participated.

Mr. Rocco was immediately challenged as to the cost of the bond issue, since his figure did not include the annual payment to the sinking fund. One director figured this as 8% of the average size of the bond issue over its 15-year life; to him, the cost of the stock issue was less than that of the bonds. Furthermore, he emphasized the cash outlay called for in the bond program and the $2,500,000 maturity. The use of debt thus added risks to the company, and he argued that this would make the common stock more speculative and cause greater variation in its market price.

Another director argued for a stock issue because "simple arithmetic" showed that the company could net 8.4%, or $840,000, per year after taxes on the new investment. Yet if 400,000 shares of common stock were sold, the dividend requirements at the current rate of $2 per share would equal only $800,000 per year. Since there was no thought that the $2 dividend rate should be changed, he could not see how the sale of the new common hurt the interest of present stockholders. Further, if there were any immediate sacrifice, he argued that it would be overcome shortly as the expansion of the company continued. Under such circumstances, there could be no thought of the bond issue, for it would place much greater obligations on the company.

On the other hand, one director argued vigorously that common stock was a "giveaway" at $25. He pointed out that the retention of a substantial percentage of past profits in the business had built up the book value of the stock to roughly $45 last December and $47 in November. Moreover, this value substantially understated the true worth of the business because at today's prices the company could not begin to replace properties and inventories at balance sheet cost. He concluded that the sale of common stock at $25 would give new buyers a substantial part of the value held by the company's present stockholders.

Two other directors agreed that the sale of stock at this price would dilute the value of the stock, but they measured the dilution in terms of earnings per share rather than book or market value. At the level of earnings currently anticipated, about $13,000,000 before interest or income taxes, they maintained that income per share of existing common stock would be diluted to $3.03 per share, if common stock were sold to net $25. In contrast, these directors asserted that the sale of bonds would raise earnings per share to $3.78. These directors said it was unimportant that the annual sinking fund would amount to $0.36 per share.

As discussion of these and other arguments related to cost of financing continued well past the usual hour for adjournment with no signs of developing agreement, Mr. Rocco finally interrupted the discussion to explain that he had not expected the board to go this far into the matter at this meeting. "Obviously," he said, "management must do more thinking about this matter of the costs of the two financing methods." He promised that a careful review of the costs aspects, including all those raised by the directors, would be prepared before the next meeting of the board, and asked that decision on the matter be held over. The directors agreed to this proposal, and the meeting was thereupon adjourned.

Exhibit 1

THE SABBATH CONTAINER COMPANY

SELECTED INCOME AND DIVIDEND DATA, 1945–1952
(Dollar figures in thousands)

	Net Sales	*Income before Taxes*	*Income after Taxes*	*Income Per Share*	*Dividends Per Share*	*Market Prices Per Share of Common Stock* High	*Market Prices Per Share of Common Stock* Low
1945	$ 83,562	$ 9,150	$2,366	$1.69	$1.20	$29⅝	$19⅜
1946	51,434	4,742	2,802	2.00	1.20	40	21¾
1947	81,503	7,225	3,844	2.75	1.20	27⅛	18¼
1948	89,822	9,560	5,071	3.62	1.20	25¼	16¾
1949	70,662	4,100	3,109	2.22	1.20	19⅛	15½
1950	77,736	5,802	3,495	2.50	1.20	22½	17
1951	105,640	10,790	4,464	3.19	2.00	26¾	24
1952	.....	....	....	...	2.00*	28½†	23⅞†

* Annual rate.
† To November 6 (November 5 prices were 28⅜–28¼).

Exhibit 2

THE SABBATH CONTAINER COMPANY

SUMMARY BALANCE SHEET

DECEMBER 31, 1951

(In thousands of dollars)

Assets:

Cash	$ 8,924
Accounts receivable	15,146
Inventory	32,492
	$56,562
Plant	18,821
Goodwill	5,000
Other	3,676
Total assets	$84,059

Liabilities:

Accounts payable	$ 8,888
Accrued federal taxes	5,831
Accrued expenses	5,995
	$20,714
Common stock ($10 par)	14,000
Surplus	49,345
Total liabilities	$84,059

Case 22

Dedham Hotel Corporation

In July, 1959, the management of the Dedham Hotel Corporation was studying three alternative arrangements for financing an addition of forty-two units to its property, Hotel 128. The cost of building such an addition was estimated at $240,000. The alternatives being considered for raising the funds were as follows:

1. Sale of approximately 10,000 shares of Dedham Hotel Corporation common stock at an estimated price of $24 a share.
2. Sale of $240,000 of 20-year debentures, payable in full at the end of the period (no sinking fund) and bearing 6% interest, payable annually. As an added inducement to investors, ten shares of the company's common stock would be issued cost-free with each $1,000 debenture purchased.
3. An increase of $140,000 in a first mortgage outstanding against the property, and an unsecured $100,000 loan from a trust company. The first mortgage would be increased from $460,000 at 6% on the unpaid balance, principal and interest payable in equal monthly amounts over the next 13 years beginning in July, 1960, to $600,000 at 6½% on the unpaid balance, principal and interest payable in equal monthly amounts for a 15-year period. The unsecured loan ($100,000) from a trust company would bear interest at 6% on the full amount, principal and interest payable in equal monthly amounts for a period of 13 months.

Background

Hotel 128 was a motel of contemporary architectural design situated at the intersection of Routes 1 and 128 in Dedham, Massachusetts. It comprised 101 air-conditioned rooms, a lobby, swimming pool, main dining room and kitchen, cocktail lounge, large ballroom, smaller dining rooms for private gatherings, and other related accommodations. It was the principal and only revenue-producing

777

asset of the Dedham Hotel Corporation, and had been in operation for just over one year—since June, 1958.

The motel's history dated back to December, 1956, when the Dedham Industrial Commission, composed of town officials and one member each from the chamber of commerce, the board of trade, a realty firm, and the New Haven Railroad, had sponsored a dinner to promote the idea of building a hotel on Route 128 in Dedham. The commission, whose function was to bring in selected industries without changing the residential character of the community, had invited to the dinner a group of hotel and real estate developers, among whom was Mr. Arthur L. Lee, representative of a large hotel chain. Sufficiently impressed by the commission's presentation of a need for a hotel in the area, particularly to accommodate customers and representatives of companies located in the Dedham industrial center, Mr. Lee tried to interest his firm in the project. When the hotel chain did not respond favorably, Mr. Lee decided to undertake the project himself.

In early 1957, he proceeded to interest a group of other young men (most were in their thirties) with whom he was personally acquainted, including John D. Young, an investment banking house broker; John J. Flynn, the Dedham controller; Patrick Grant, a certified public accountant; William B. Tyler, an attorney; and H. Holten Wood, a member of an investment management firm. The members of this group combined their efforts to study the prospects and organized to build a hotel in Dedham. Traffic was counted, and companies in the area were interviewed in an effort to predict the demand; interviews were conducted to sample the interest of investors; locations were checked for availability and convenience; architects were retained to prepare preliminary sketches; an option was taken on the land selected; construction and furnishings estimates were made; pro forma income statements were drawn up.

On May 23, 1957, convinced of the potential profits of the enterprise and with the preliminaries behind them, the promoters held a press conference at a well-known hotel in Boston and announced their decision to go ahead. A number of prominent citizens and investors from the Dedham community were invited to the conference, where plans, sketches, and estimates were revealed.

During the months that followed the press conference, until construction was begun on October 4, 1957, Mr. Lee and his associates in the venture completed their plans. They engaged architects to make final drawings, solicited bids on construction, raised the necessary funds, and consummated financial arrangements. Construction was completed in the spring of 1958, and Hotel 128 opened for business on June 13.

Financing Arrangements

The Dedham Hotel Corporation obtained its first money from the promoters by issuing to them a total of 1,000 shares of common stock at $10 a share. To provide the rest of the "promotion" money required by the project, a plan was then drawn up which potential investors received enthusiastically in the preliminary surveys and at the press conference. It consisted of combined issues of twenty-year, 6% debentures and common stock. Investors would be offered 10 shares of stock with each $1,000 debenture purchased. The common stock would carry the same stated value per share ($10) as the stock issued to the promoters. Since a selling price of $1,000 was set for each unit, composed of a $1,000 debenture and 10 shares of common stock, the debentures were, in effect, issued at a 10% discount from face value. The debenture issue had no sinking fund requirement.

A debenture issue of $400,000 was sold by September, 1957; and the proceeds, which had been placed on a "called as needed" basis, were fully realized in early 1958. In accordance with the objectives of the promoters, the issue was sold to 123 individual investors, all residents of the Dedham community.

During the summer of 1957 the promoters approached several savings banks and commercial banks in a search for first-mortgage money. The institutions were not interested in providing funds on this basis. The promoters then turned to a large life insurance company, which agreed to furnish $500,000 on a first mortgage with interest at 6% on the declining balance. Principal and interest were to be amortized in equal monthly payments over a fifteen-year period. On the basis of this commitment a large Boston bank agreed to furnish up to $500,000 of construction money at 6% per annum, plus a 1% fee ($5,000). The insurance company drew up a mortgage, assigned it to the bank during the period of construction, and later obtained a reassignment by taking the bank out when construction was completed.

To round out the major financing needs, the promoters searched for second-mortgage money, and found an individual investor with substantial funds available for purchasing second mortgages. The investor advanced $200,000, bearing interest at 6% on the unpaid balance. The face amount of the second-mortgage liability assumed for this money, however, was $236,000. Principal was payable at the rate of $3,000 a month for thirty-five months, with a balloon payment of $131,000 due in the thirty-sixth month. Interest was payable monthly. Under the terms of this mortgage, payment of principal could be delayed up to six months, but the full amount of delayed payments would be due and payable at the end of the delay period.

As the project progressed, it was discovered that the original financing arrangements were inadequate to cover fully the cost of construction, furnishings, and equipment. The remainder of necessary funds was raised from several sources. For example, the contractor agreed to carry $30,000 of construction costs for one year at 6% ; Mr. Lee put up $26,500 of his own money on a five-year note at 6% ; part of the furniture, fixtures, and equipment was financed on time payments.

The following figures summarize the original financing of the land, motel, equipment, and furnishings:

SOURCES OF FUNDS

Stock purchased by promoters*	$ 9,000
Sale of 20-year debentures	400,000
First mortgage	500,000
Second mortgage, net received in cash	200,000
Note payable—officer	26,500
Note payable—contractor	30,000
Note payable—supplier (furnishings and equipment)	40,000
	$1,205,500

* One of the promoters received 100 shares of stock as partial consideration for a temporary advance of funds to purchase the building site.

The Decision to Build an Addition

During its first complete year of operations, ended June 30, 1959, Hotel 128 exceeded the promoters' expectations. Although net profit was somewhat nominal in relation to total investment, it was considered unusual that this kind of project had shown a profit during its first year. Despite heavy charges for organization and start-up in June of 1958, only a small deficit remained as of June 30, 1959. Gross revenues for the year exceeded earlier estimates by about 12%. Room rentals (on 101 bedrooms) averaged approximately $3,060 a unit; and revenues on banquet facilities, dining room, and cocktail lounge averaged approximately $4,475 on a rental unit (bedroom) basis. Telephone, valet services, and other miscellaneous revenues totaled approximately $22,000, or $218 a unit. (See Exhibits 1 and 2 for statements of financial condition and operations.)

On the basis of recent demand for accommodations, Mr. Lee was confident that existing facilities would show an increase in revenues and profits in the year ahead. He estimated that average annual revenue from rentals would be at least $3,820 a unit and that average revenue, on a rental unit basis, from dining room, cocktail lounge, and banquet facilities would be $4,920, increases of 25% and 10%, respectively. Departmental expenses and cost of sales were expected to rise proportionately with increases in revenue, and general expenses and fixed charges were expected to be about the same in total.

Most important to the financial success of the operation was the motel's ability to generate cash. Depreciation and other noncash charges, added to profits, resulted in a substantial cash flow during the first year. This enabled the corporation to meet its financial obligations with little or no difficulty. Exhibit 3 presents a cash earnings statement for the year ended June 30, 1959, and estimated cash earnings for the year ending June 30, 1960.

Prompted by results of the first year and expectations for the second, the promoters began considering an addition to Hotel 128. A count taken by Mr. Lee revealed that 400 to 500 people were being turned away each week. On this basis, it was decided that demand would support an addition of 42 rental units, and estimates and plans were drawn up. It was expected that construction would begin some time in the fall of 1959 and that the new units would be completed in May or June of 1960.

The promoters then turned to the question of financing. Approximately $30,000–$40,000 was needed, of course, for furnishings, fixtures, and equipment. This probably would be financed on time payments through a local bank or trust company. An adjoining acre of land was purchased for the addition at a price of $41,000, one third down and the balance payable over a two-year period, with interest at 6% on the unpaid balance. The remaining problem was how to raise the estimated $240,000 to pay for the building.

A key factor in the decision was the average rate of occupancy that could be expected. Mr. Lee thought that the over-all average was certain to decline, at least temporarily, when the addition was finished. The number of people being turned away weekly, however, led him to believe that a decline in average occupancy would be small and only temporary. He estimated that after completion the average would be about 15% less than otherwise during the first month, 10% in the second month, 7% in the third, with a return to normal expected in the fourth or fifth month.

Great interest in Hotel 128 had been expressed by many persons who were now seeking an opportunity to acquire an equity interest in the corporation. Mr. Lee thought that the possibility of raising funds through a sale of common stock would be rejected early, however, owing to the dilution involved for existing stockholders who did not invest more. Members of the promoting group who were connected with the investment banking field believed that a price/earnings ratio of 10/1 on the year's projected earnings was probably an upper limit. On this basis a common stock issue of at least 10,000 shares, at a price of approximately $24 a share, would be required to raise $240,000.

The promoters were confident that a new twenty-year debenture issue, plus stock, could be sold to raise the money. In fact, part of a new issue could be sold to the original investing group, a number of whom had expressed a desire to invest more on the same basis as the original issue. This method of raising the money, however, would also involve a dilution of the equity interest held by those who did not invest more. The promoters wanted to avoid any dilution, if possible, but were ready to accept it if the risks and costs of the alternatives were determined to be too great.

The insurance company holding a first mortgage on the property was approached to see what amount it would be willing to furnish. It agreed to raise the balance outstanding on the mortgage ($460,000) to $600,000, and to start the fifteen-year amortization period running anew. The interest rate on the unpaid balance, however, was to be increased from 6% to 6½% on the full amount of the mortgage. To complete the financing, a trust company agreed to provide the additional $100,000 for thirteen months. Interest would be computed at 6% on the full amount for the entire period. Principal and interest would be payable in equal monthly amounts.

Exhibit 4 is an amortization schedule of long-term financial obligations, including current maturities, at June 30, 1959. Exhibit 5 presents an incremental cost and amortization schedule for each of the debt alternatives under consideration for financing the addition.

Mr. Lee thought that one final factor must be given some consideration before a decision was reached. The promoters were so enthusiastic about the results of the entire undertaking that they were thinking of starting a chain of motels. Since this appeared to be a distinct possibility for the future, it was important not to restrict flexibility unnecessarily by any action taken at this time.

Exhibit 1

DEDHAM HOTEL CORPORATION

BALANCE SHEET, AS OF JUNE 30, 1959

ASSETS

Cash..		$ 43,660
Accounts receivable, trade............................$	16,328	
Less: Reserve for doubtful accounts......................	1,127	15,201
Accounts receivable, other..............................		1,095
Inventories, at lower of cost or market....................		9,741
Prepaid expenses..		8,079
Real estate tax suspense deposit (tax liability funded to date, funds invested in commercial paper)..................		16,000
Total Current Assets.............................		$ 93,777
Noncurrent investment and receivable.....................		250
Plant and equipment, at cost............................$1,169,691		
Less: Reserves for depreciation...........................	46,728	1,122,963
Deferred charges..		99,318
Total Assets....................................		$1,316,308

LIABILITIES

Bank loan..		$ 4,200
Accounts payable, trade.................................		71,854
Accounts and notes payable, other.......................		40,383
Accrued liabilities:		
State and local taxes..................................$	21,189	
Other...	12,336	33,525
Mortgage payments, due within one year..................		58,302
Total Current Liabilities.........................		$ 208,264
Noncurrent liabilities:		
Notes payable for equipment, due after one year...........$	5,713	
Note payable, officer, due August 16, 1963................	26,500	
First mortgage payable, due after one year (Note 1).......	460,105	
Second mortgage payable, due after one year (Note 2).....	170,000	
6% debentures, due October 15, 1977...................	400,000	$1,062,318
Stockholders' equity:		
Capital stock (authorized 10,000 shares, no par value; issued, 5,000 shares)...............................$	50,000	
Deficit...	(4,275)	45,725
Total Liabilities...............................		$1,316,308

Note 1. First mortgage loan, 6%, is payable in monthly instalments of $4,220 on account of interest and principal.

Note 2. Second mortgage loan is payable in monthly instalments of $3,000 on account of principal until August, 1961, when balance of $131,000 is payable. Interest at 6% is payable monthly.

Exhibit 2

DEDHAM HOTEL CORPORATION

INCOME AND DEFICIT STATEMENT
FOR THE YEAR ENDED JUNE 30, 1959

Revenue from sale of rooms, food and beverages, and other hotel income............................			$784,105
Departmental salaries and wages, cost of sales, and other expenses..............................			468,190
Departmental gross profit..........................			$315,915
General expenses:			
Administrative................................	$78,802		
Advertising and promotion......................	24,023		
Heat, light, and power..........................	23,169		
Repairs and maintenance........................	14,542	$140,536	
Fixed charges:			
Real estate tax................................	$15,000		
State tax......................................	1,100		
Insurance.....................................	8,959		
Interest.......................................	70,766		
Amortization of debt discount....................	14,428		
Depreciation..................................	46,728		
Amortization..................................	6,243	163,224	303,761
Income before federal income taxes.................			$ 12,154
Federal income taxes (none required because of net operating loss carry-forward).................			...
Net income for year..............................			$ 12,154
Deficit, June 30, 1958............................			(16,429)
Deficit, June 30, 1959............................			$(4,275)

Exhibit 3

DEDHAM HOTEL CORPORATION

CASH EARNINGS STATEMENTS

	Year Ended June 30	
	1959	1960 (*Estimated*)
Net income before interest and federal income taxes..................................	$ 82,920	$126,000
Less: Federal income taxes (adjusted for loss carry-forward)...........................	...	23,000
	$ 82,920	$103,000
Noncash charges:		
Depreciation..............................	46,728	45,000
Amortization of debt discount...............	14,428	13,000
Amortization of organization and financing expenses.............................	6,243	6,500
Net cash earnings before interest and after taxes*..........................	$150,319	$167,500
Interest charges deducted for purposes of tax computation.....................	$ 70,766	$ 66,000

* Cash available for interest payments, debt repayment, and other purposes.

Exhibit 4

DEDHAM HOTEL CORPORATION

AMORTIZATION SCHEDULE OF MAJOR LONG-TERM FINANCIAL OBLIGATIONS, INCLUDING CURRENT MATURITIES, AT JUNE 30, 1959

(Dollar figures in thousands)

Year Ending June 30	Note Payable to Officer		First Mortgage		Second Mortgage		Debentures		Total			
	Principal	Interest	Principal	Interest	Principal	Interest	Principal	Interest	Principal	Interest	Cash Outlay Before Tax	Cash Outlay After Tax*
1960		$1.6	$22.3	$28.3	$36.0	$11.4		$24.0	$58.3	$65.3	$123.6	$91.0
1961		1.6	24.3	26.3	36.0	9.2		24.0	60.3	61.1	121.4	90.9
1962		1.6	25.8	24.8	134.0	1.3		24.0	159.8	51.7	211.5	185.7
1963		1.6	27.3	23.3				24.0	27.3	48.9	76.2	51.8
1964	$26.5	0.2	28.8	21.8				24.0	55.3	46.0	101.3	78.3
1965			30.8	19.8				24.0	30.8	43.8	74.6	52.7
1966			32.8	17.8				24.0	32.8	41.8	74.6	53.7
1967			34.3	16.3				24.0	34.3	40.3	74.6	54.5
1968			36.8	13.8				24.0	36.8	37.8	74.6	55.7
1969			38.8	11.8				24.0	38.8	35.8	74.6	56.7
1970			41.2	9.4				24.0	41.2	33.4	74.6	57.9
1971			43.8	6.8				24.0	43.8	30.8	74.6	59.2
1972			46.2	4.4				24.0	46.2	28.4	74.6	60.4
1973			49.2	1.4				24.0	49.2	25.4	74.6	61.9
1974								24.0	...	24.0	24.0	12.0
1975								24.0	...	24.0	24.0	12.0
1976								24.0	...	24.0	24.0	12.0
1977								24.0	...	24.0	24.0	12.0
1978							$400.0	7.0	400.0	7.0	407.0	403.5
Total	$26.5	$6.6	$482.4	$226.0	$206.0	$21.9	$400.0	$439.0	$1,114.9	$693.5	$1,808.4	$1,461.9

* Tax rate assumed at 50%

Exhibit 5

DEDHAM HOTEL CORPORATION

INCREMENTAL COST AND AMORTIZATION SCHEDULE—COMPARISON
OF ALTERNATIVE DEBT-FINANCING PLANS

(Dollar figures in thousands)

Year Ending June 30	Principal	*Alternative 2* *New Debenture Issue**		
			Cash Outlay	
		Interest	Before Tax	After Tax†
1961................		$ 14.4	$ 14.4	$ 7.2
1962................		14.4	14.4	7.2
1963................		14.4	14.4	7.2
1964................		14.4	14.4	7.2
1965................		14.4	14.4	7.2
1966................		14.4	14.4	7.2
1967................		14.4	14.4	7.2
1968................		14.4	14.4	7.2
1969................		14.4	14.4	7.2
1970................		14.4	14.4	7.2
1971................		14.4	14.4	7.2
1972................		14.4	14.4	7.2
1973................		14.4	14.4	7.2
1974................		14.4	14.4	7.2
1975................		14.4	14.4	7.2
1976................		14.4	14.4	7.2
1977................		14.4	14.4	7.2
1978................		14.4	14.4	7.2
1979................		14.4	14.4	7.2
1980................	$240.0	14.4	254.4	247.2
Total..........	$240.0	$288.0	$528.0	$384.0

* Twenty-four hundred shares of common stock would be issued with the new debentures.
† Tax rate assumed at 50%.

Exhibit 5—Continued

Alternative 3

Year Ending June 30	New First Mortgage Principal	New First Mortgage Interest	Loan from Trust Co. Principal	Loan from Trust Co. Interest	Principal	Total Interest	Cash Outlay	Cash Outlay under Existing First Mortgage	Net Cash Outlay Before Tax	Net Cash Outlay After Tax†
1961	$ 24.6	$ 38.2	$ 92.3	$6.0	$116.9	$ 44.2	$ 161.1	$ 50.6	$110.5	$101.5
1962	25.8	37.0	7.7	0.5	33.5	37.5	71.0	50.6	20.4	14.1
1963	28.2	34.6			28.2	34.6	62.8	50.6	12.2	6.5
1964	30.0	32.8			30.0	32.8	62.8	50.6	12.2	6.7
1965	31.2	31.6			31.2	31.6	62.8	50.6	12.2	6.3
1966	34.2	28.6			34.2	28.6	62.8	50.6	12.2	6.8
1967	36.0	26.8			36.0	26.8	62.8	50.6	12.2	6.9
1968	38.4	24.4			38.4	24.4	62.8	50.6	12.2	6.9
1969	41.4	21.4			41.4	21.4	62.8	50.6	12.2	7.4
1970	43.8	19.0			43.8	19.0	62.8	50.6	12.2	7.4
1971	46.8	16.0			46.8	16.0	62.8	50.6	12.2	7.6
1972	50.4	12.4			50.4	12.4	62.8	50.6	12.2	8.2
1973	53.4	9.4			53.4	9.4	62.8	50.6	12.2	8.2
1974	56.4	6.4			56.4	6.4	62.8	....	62.8	59.6
1975	59.4	3.4			59.4	3.4	62.8	....	62.8	61.1
Total	$600.0	$342.0	$100.0	$6.5	$700.0	$348.5	$1,048.5	$657.8	$390.7	$315.2

Case 23

The Standard Oil Company of Ohio

In July, 1951, Mr. Wolf, vice president (finance) of the Standard Oil Company of Ohio, was reviewing the company's financial plans for the remainder of 1951, 1952, and 1953. A recent report of the company's Financial and Budget Committee, of which Mr. Wolf was chairman, had indicated that the planned capital expansion program, together with expected investments in affiliates and desired increases in inventories and receivables, would in these three years require funds to the extent of approximately $150,000,000. Mr. Wolf thought that about $101,000,000 could be generated internally over the period through the retention of earnings, the noncash charges against income, and sales of assets. Of the remaining $49,000,000 a reduction in the company's cash position would provide $24,000,000. The balance of $25,000,000 would be raised through a two-step program of new financing, about half in late 1951 or early 1952, and the residual amount in late 1952.

The company's long-term growth plans indicated a continuing need for outside funds to supplement those internally generated from operations. New facilities for which firm commitments were planned during this three-year period would not all be completed by the end of 1953. It was anticipated that about $16,000,000 of such commitments would be carried over into 1954. Therefore it appeared likely that additional financing might be required early in 1954 if these plans proceeded without interruption or revision.

The stated maximum planned capital expenditures for the three-year period did not all represent firm commitments; they might be revised downward if changed economic conditions, material shortages, or other industry factors dictated a "stretchout," or a termination of the expansion program. On the other hand, unforeseen requirements as great as $10,000,000 might arise at any time for the construction or acquisition of facilities essential to maintain the company's competitive position in any of the several divisions of its operations.

The Standard Oil Company of Ohio, with its subsidiaries, was a "fully integrated" operation; i.e., engaged in all branches of the oil industry: production, transportation, refining, and marketing. The latter activity, carried on under the brand name "Sohio," was concentrated in Ohio, although some marketing activities under another brand name extended to parts of West Virginia, Michigan, and Indiana.

Until 1935, the company had been engaged primarily in refining and marketing operations. Subsequently, these activities had been expanded, and the company had as well embarked on a large program of construction and acquisition of interests in pipe lines carrying crude oil and refined products, and in crude-oil producing properties. From 1935 to the end of 1946, $144,000,000 had been invested by the company to further its integration and expansion program. Capital expenditures during this period had been $123,000,000; increases in working capital and other assets had amounted to $21,000,000. Funds for the program had been obtained as follows:

Retained earnings	$ 27,000,000	19%
Additional common and preferred stock	27,000,000	19
Additional long-term debt	16,000,000	11
Depreciation, depletion, and amortization	61,000,000	42
Other sources, including sale of property	13,000,000	9
	$144,000,000	100%

In 1947, the company's integration and expansion program was accelerated, additional funds amounting to $14 million being provided by the sale of 584,117 shares of common stock at a price of $23.75 per share. During the following year, 1948, the company borrowed $35 million from a group of institutional investors, issuing 20-year, 3% unsecured debentures. This loan carried with it a provision for a sinking fund of $1 million annually from 1953 to 1958; $2 million a year from 1958 to 1967, with the balance due in 1968. The funds thus made available were used in part to retire an outstanding $14 million of unsecured debentures due in 1962, and the balance was applied to cover requirements of capital expenditures and additional working capital. Balance sheets and income statements for the years 1946–50 are presented in Exhibits 1 and 2.

On June 30, 1951, the outstanding long-term debt was $38 million, of which $35 million represented the debentures sold in 1948 and the balance consisted of miscellaneous loans and notes with maturities of five years or less. In 1951 the company had long-term leases of office space and certain marketing properties with annual rentals of approximately $1,100,000 for each of the succeeding five years, declining thereafter.

In June, 1951, Mr. Wolf had projected the company's cash requirements and possible sources of funds for 1951–53, as shown in Exhibit 3. These figures did not reflect the changes in interest and/or dividend payments which would result from the new financing, since no decision as to the method of financing had at this time been reached.

In contrast to the uncertainty of estimating expenditures for fixed assets, Mr. Wolf was satisfied with the reliability of estimates of working capital requirements, which were based on a forecast of the physical volume of sales. (See Exhibit 4.) Sales in terms of units were subject to relatively accurate projection; dollar volumes, however, fluctuated beyond the control of the company, owing to changes in selling prices. Some costs, particularly wage and salary rates, were not variable. Thus, although physical output could be predicted with reasonable success, an accurate estimate of net income was difficult; for this reason, Mr. Wolf decided that the safest assumption was that the expected increase in revenue resulting from larger unit sales volume would offset any unfavorable variations in selling prices, costs, and taxes. He therefore used the 1950 net profit figure of $30,870,000 before taxes ($20,200,000 after taxes[1]) as a basis for calculating projected earnings, subtracting the 1950 dividend payments of $8,000,000 to arrive at his reinvestable earnings estimate of $12,200,000 for each of the three years.

The company's balance sheets (Exhibit 1) showed the following capital structure on December 31, 1950, compared with other large petroleum companies:

Type of Financing	Sohio Millions	Sohio	Industry*
Funded and long-term debt (includes			
Sohio notes payable)	$ 37	18%	16%
Preferred stock	24	12	1
Common stock and surplus	145	70	83
Total capital structure	$206	100%	100%

* Composite of 30 integrated and semi-integrated oil companies.
  Source: Petroleum Department, Chase National Bank of New York, *Financial Analysis of Thirty Oil Companies for 1950* (New York, 1951).

---

[1] Taxes paid in 1950 included $9,700,000 federal income tax, as well as excess profits taxes of $850,000 and state income taxes of $100,000. Companies in the oil production industry typically pay lower rates of income taxation than industrials generally.

In July, 1951, Mr. Wolf was considering four alternative methods of financing the initial requirement of $13,000,000 which were open to him: (1) privately placed debentures, (2) preferred stock, (3) convertible preferred stock, (4) common stock.

1. Privately Placed Debentures. Mr. Wolf believed that it would be possible for the company to issue $13,000,000 of unsecured, 20-year, 3½% debentures to institutional investors. Interest payments would be $455,000 in the first year. Recently, Mr. Wolf had noted that institutional lenders had a greater demand for loans from good borrowers than they had funds; for this reason the interest rates, though still comparatively low in view of tax considerations, were higher than at any time during the past 15 years. The cost of placing such an issue was, however, very attractive; it was estimated that legal fees and other expenses would amount to only $50,000. Chart 1 presents the interest rates on high-grade, unsecured debentures for the previous 10 years, compared with the yield on the outstanding Sohio debentures.

Mr. Wolf noted the restrictive provisions that had accompanied recent privately placed debenture issues: (1) Net tangible assets were usually required to be three times the outstanding long-term debt of the borrowing company, and (2) complete amortization of the debentures must be completed by maturity through equal annual repayments on the principal. Mr. Wolf thought it likely that Sohio would have to accept substantially the same terms; if $13,000,000 were borrowed under these conditions, the company would have to begin annual repayments of principal amounting to $650,000 in 1952. The currently outstanding debenture issue contained no restrictions on the total amount or type of debt permitted, and Mr. Wolf did not wish to accept any limitations that might narrow future financing alternatives.

2. Preferred Stock. The company's stockholders had previously authorized the issuance of $13,000,000 of $100 par preferred stock with seniority equal to the outstanding issue; these shares were as yet unissued. The outstanding preferred was yielding about 4% on its current market price, and Mr. Wolf believed that a new cumulative $4 preferred issue could be sold at $100 per share to the public. New preferred dividends would total $520,000 per year; and as with the outstanding issue, a 2% sinking fund provision totaling $260,000 annually would be required. Underwriting fees were estimated at $2 per share, and other expenses would approximate $70,000.

3. Convertible Preferred Stock. It was also possible for Sohio to issue $13,000,000 of $100 par value convertible preferred stock

Chart 1

THE STANDARD OIL COMPANY OF OHIO

AVERAGE YIELDS OF MOODY'S INDUSTRIAL Aa BONDS

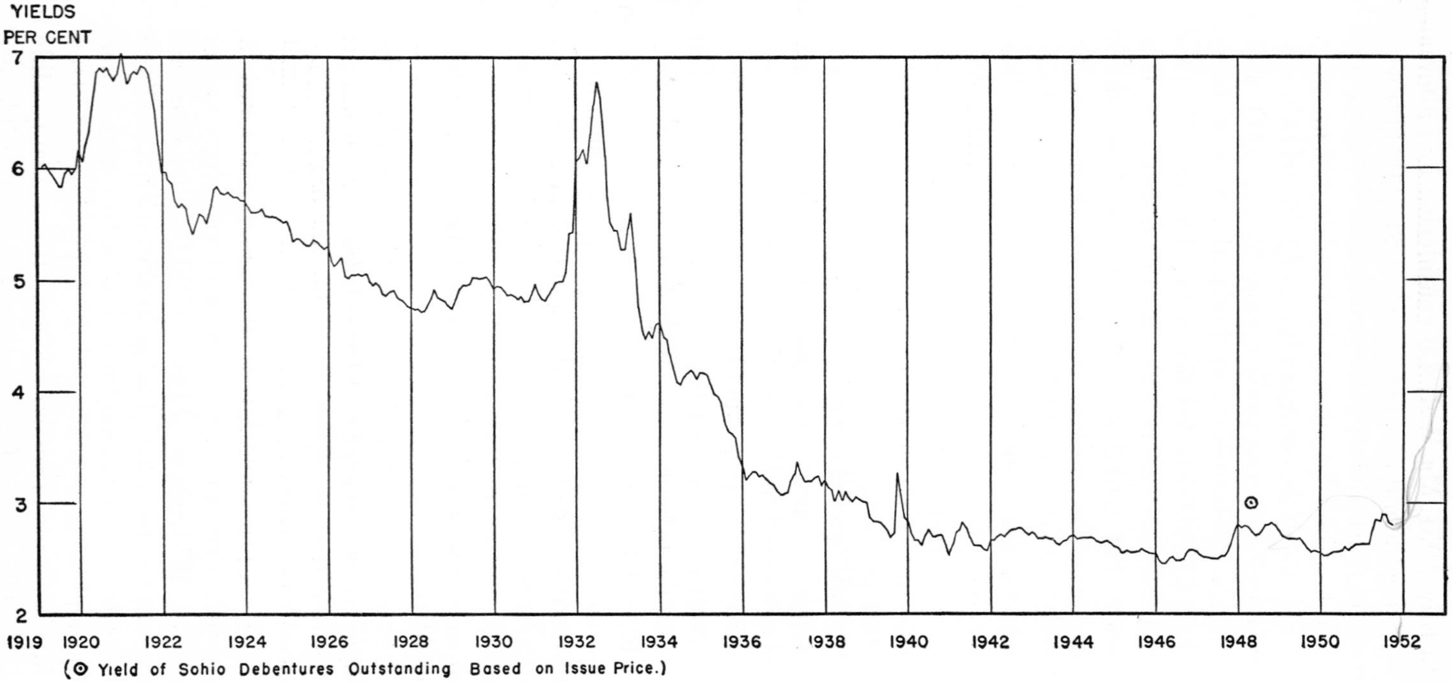

YIELDS
PER CENT

(⊙ Yield of Sohio Debentures Outstanding Based on Issue Price.)

without additional stockholder authorization. The dividend rate on such an issue would probably be $3.25 per share, or a total of $422,-500 per year. Mr. Wolf thought that the conversion ratios should be based on a price 7% higher than the current market price of the common stock. Using the current price of $35.00, the conversion price became $37.45 per share, or a ratio of 2⅔ to 1. He also thought that the issue should be callable at $103. Mr. Wolf did not want to issue convertible preferred stock unless he had a reasonable assurance that the stock would be converted within 18 months; otherwise, he thought, this additional senior security might interfere with the favorable terms expected in the next financing steps.

Under the Ohio law, common stockholders had mandatory pre-emptive rights on all new issues of common stock or issues of any security convertible into common stock. Subscription rights would be given to existing common stockholders for a period of at least 15 days. Mr. Wolf believed, on the basis of recent issues of other companies, that there would be a stand-by underwriting fee of $1 per share and an additional charge of $1 per share for those shares not taken up under the pre-emptive provisions. Other expenses would be approximately $85,000.

4. Common Stock. Mr. Wolf felt that the issuance of additional common stock was a necessary step in any long-range program, though the possibilities of placing a large issue at this time seemed uncertain. In 1947, when common stock had last been issued, the subscription price discount to stockholders had been 16% under the current market price; Mr. Wolf believed that under present conditions a much smaller discount, possibly as low as 12½% and certainly no higher than 15% would be possible. To obtain the required amount of capital, an issue of about 433,000 shares, at $30 per share, would be necessary. Mr. Wolf also knew that common stock was the most expensive form of security to issue; underwriters had told him that fees would be 85 cents per share on a stand-by basis, with an additional charge of 65 cents per share for those shares not bought under pre-emptive rights. Other expenses were estimated at no less than $85,000.

With regard to current stock market conditions, Mr. Wolf had noted that oil stocks had, in the past two years, increased in price faster and to a greater extent than the market in general, though the market had gone up 60% in the same period. (See Chart 2.) Market prices for Sohio's common stock for the previous two years are also presented in Chart 2.

Mr. Wolf also knew that it would take at least two months from

Chart 2

THE STANDARD OIL COMPANY OF OHIO

COMPARATIVE MARKET PRICES OF COMMON STOCKS

(Ratio scale)

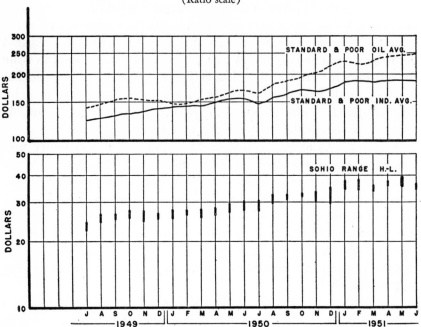

the time of a decision to issue any of the securities, with the possible exception of the privately placed debentures. Registration, underwriting, and the rights periods would produce a minimum "lead time" of 60 days, during which time market conditions might change substantially.

The company had established a regular common stock cash dividend rate which, in the judgment of the directors and based on future earnings prospects, could be maintained throughout the foreseeable future. This rate was $2 per share annually. In February and in May, 1951, the board of directors had considered raising the dividend rate. At these meetings, no action had been taken; however, Mr. Wolf thought it probable that such an increase might be approved before the end of 1951. He did not think, on the other hand, that the quarterly dividend rate would be increased by a greater amount than 10 cents per share during the next two years.

Exhibit 1

THE STANDARD OIL COMPANY OF OHIO

BALANCE SHEETS 1947–1950

(All figures in thousands of dollars)

	Dec. 31			
	1947	1948	1949	1950
ASSETS				
Cash	$ 17,657	$ 40,305	$ 32,922	$ 41,258
Accounts receivable (net)	28,453	34,555	31,467	35,247
Inventory	28,413	42,313	32,983	35,240
Total Current Assets	$ 74,523	$117,173	$ 97,372	$111,745
Other investments	8,744	3,206	3,614	3,124
Net fixed assets	101,377	112,937	128,822	136,024
Prepaid expenses	3,348	4,073	4,154	4,566
Total Assets	$187,992	$237,389	$233,962	$255,459
LIABILITIES				
Accounts payable	$ 30,212	$ 38,353	$ 29,544	$ 33,582
Other payables	1,670	1,403	1,011	803
Accrued taxes payable	6,690	10,181	9,628	15,070
Total Current Liabilities	$ 38,572	$ 49,937	$ 40,183	$ 49,455
3% debentures due 1963 (sinking fund effective 1948)	14,000	.....	.....	.....
3% debentures due 1968 (sinking fund effective 1953)	.....	35,000	35,000	35,000
Long-term notes payable	2,258	1,694	1,543	2,089
Capital stock:				
Preferred	25,841	25,304	24,767	24,229
Common	35,136	35,815	35,832	36,515
Earned surplus	72,185	89,639	96,657	108,171
Total Liabilities	$187,992	$237,389	$233,962	$255,459

Exhibit 2

THE STANDARD OIL COMPANY OF OHIO

INCOME STATEMENTS 1948–1950

(Dollar figures in thousands)

	1948	1949	1950
Net sales	$ 245,157	$ 219,011	$ 248,985
Cost of goods sold:			
Material, labor, overhead, administration, and sales expense	$ 190,604	$ 172,330	$ 195,284
Depreciation and depletion	12,482	12,326	15,099
Total cost of goods sold	$ 203,086	$ 184,656	$ 210,383
Operating income	$ 42,071	$ 34,355	$ 38,602
Other income	3,891	2,391	5,646
Total income	$ 45,962	$ 36,746	$ 44,248
Other expenses:			
Interest	$ 1,081	$ 1,315	$ 1,170
Rent	600	750	1,100
Taxes (not income)	3,972	4,465	4,870
Nonproductive expense	6,525	8,014	6,230
Total other expenses	$ 12,178	$ 14,544	$ 13,370
Net profit before income tax	$ 33,784	$ 22,202	$ 30,878
Income tax	10,000	6,060	10,650
Net income	$ 23,784	$ 16,142	$ 20,228
Preferred dividends	$ 940	$ 926	$ 911
Common dividends	5,692	7,148	7,149
Number of common shares, Dec. 31	3,581,535	3,583,213	3,615,562
Dividend per share	$1.625*	$2.00	$2.00*
Earnings per share	$6.39	$4.26	$5.30
Sinking funds—preferred stock (number of shares retired)	5,372	5,372	5,372

* Plus 2% stock dividend.

Exhibit 3

THE STANDARD OIL COMPANY OF OHIO

PROJECTION OF CASH REQUIREMENTS AND SOURCES
1951–1952–1953
(Dollar figures in millions)

REQUIREMENTS

	1951	1952	1953	*Total*
Plant and properties	$40.0	$47.9	$48.6	$136.5
Other long-term requirements (investments in affiliates, retirement of long-term debt, sinking-fund provisions)	3.6	0.4	2.7	6.7
Working capital requirements (expected increase in accounts receivable and inventory)	6.5	. . .	0.3	6.8
Total	$50.1	$48.3	$51.6	$150.0

SOURCES

	1951	1952	1953	Total
Generated internally:				
Retained net income	$12.2	$12.2	$12.2	$ 36.6
Noncash charges (depreciation, depletion)	16.5	18.5	19.6	54.6
Sale of assets	3.1	2.0	2.0	7.1
Short-term loans	1.0	0.8	0.8	2.6
Reduction of cash holdings	17.3	6.7	. . .	24.0
Net amount to be supplied through new financing	. . .	8.1	17.0	25.1
Total	$50.1	$48.3	$51.6	$150.0

Exhibit 4

THE STANDARD OIL COMPANY OF OHIO

PROJECTIONS OF THE PHYSICAL VOLUME
OF SALES, 1951–1952–1953
(Figures in millions of gallons)

1950 (actual) 1,580
1951 1,722
1952 1,742
1953 1,838

Case 24

Price Textiles, Inc.

IN PREPARATION for a board of directors meeting on June 5, 1952, Mr. Daniel Randall, treasurer of Price Textiles, Inc., had decided to recommend the payment of the regular quarterly dividend, totaling $41,000, to the holders of the company's 4½% cumulative preferred stock. He had yet to decide what dividend, if any, should be paid to the company's common stockholders in the second quarter of 1952.

Price Textiles operated several cotton and rayon textile mills in four northern states. Like many other textile companies, it had experienced a number of difficult years during the 1930's. It had staved off insolvency only by means of strong bank support. Profits improved later, were high during World War II, and had remained high through 1950.

Following World War II the company's management had taken several actions to improve the company's ability to produce efficiently and to strengthen the company's financial position. In 1946 a new issue of cumulative preferred stock provided funds to retire outstanding bank loans of $5,400,000. From 1946 through the first 16 weeks of 1952, $14,700,000 had been spent by the company in modernizing productive facilities. In addition, $21,600,000, largely written off as expense, had been used to repair existing machinery, buildings, and equipment. The capital expenditures and a working capital increase of $15,500,000 had been financed largely through retained earnings. Exhibits 1 and 2 present the company's balance sheet and income statements for selected years from 1945 to March 22, 1952.

In April, 1951, the company's profits began to decline. Increased wages, declining textile prices, and smaller quantities sold had adversely affected Price Textiles' profits over several months, as shown in Exhibit 3. From April, 1951, to June, 1952, spindle hours per workday declined 40%, loom hours fell off 35%, and total yards produced dropped 30%. By the beginning of May, 1952, order backlogs had shrunk 70%, and on June 1 the company had almost no business booked for the third quarter. On June 5, 1952, Mr. Randall felt that there had been little to indicate any immediate recovery from what he still expected to be a short-run rather than a long-term decline in sales.

With regard to the prospects for the textile industry in 1952, Standard and Poor's *Industry Surveys* carried the following article on May 15, 1952:

. . . textile production in the first quarter of 1952 held at about the same rate as in the final quarter of 1951. . . . A further drop in output is expected in the second quarter as the result of additional cutbacks made in April and seasonally slow demand.

. . . .

The favorable outlook for consumer income, and the probability of greater spending for soft-good lines, point to better business for retail stores later this year. While retailers are likely to be conservative in making forward commitments, inventory positions should permit somewhat more active orders for textile producers during the final half of 1952.

With inventories at most other trade levels in fairly good balance, improved ordering by retailers should stimulate greater activity within the textile industry. More active demand would lift prices from their current depressed levels.

The survey said the following about Price Textiles' prospects:

Although earnings were down in the first quarter of 1952, gradual improvement in Price Textiles' profits is likely, particularly in the final half, and 1952 earnings may not be too far below 1951 earnings. Dividends will probably hold at $0.40 per share in the second quarter. . . .

As indicated in Exhibit 4, dividend payments on the common stock by the company had varied considerably in the past. From December, 1946, to December, 1950, the company had paid a "quarterly" dividend of $0.30 per share, with extras during the course of each year. In 1951 a dividend of $0.70 per share was paid in each of the first three quarters of the year, plus an extra dividend of $0.40 per share in March. The dividend was reduced to $0.50 per share in the last quarter of 1951 and to $0.40 per share in the first quarter of 1952. Each dividend, when announced, was called a "quarterly" dividend or an "extra" dividend. Although the company had carefully avoided any statements which might imply that a minimum dividend rate would be maintained whenever possible, Mr. Randall felt that some stockholders had come to regard the $0.30 dividend as regular.

Mr. Randall had already decided to recommend the payment of the regular quarterly dividend on the company's 4½% cumulative preferred stock, which had been kept current since its issue in 1946. Although this issue had an obligatory sinking fund of $216,000 per year, the company had already bought and retired enough preferred stock to cover the sinking fund through 1955.

Price Textiles' common stock was owned by 8,203 individuals in most of the 48 states. On the other hand, studies of the stockholder list indicated that many stockholders were employees and local businessmen. Management holdings were not significantly large. The influence of the only large stockholder, Mr. Gustaveson, is discussed below.

In late 1950 a small group of Southern textile manufacturers headed by Mr. Arthur Gustaveson had attempted unsuccessfully[1] to secure enough Price Textiles' common stock to elect a representative to the board of directors. Mr. Gustaveson and his associates had purchased on the open market 132,700 shares of Price Textiles, or about 17% of the outstanding stock. Price Textiles' stock was not listed on any exchange; however, it was actively traded in the over-the-counter market. In December, 1950, Mr. Gustaveson failed in an attempt to secure an additional 220,000 shares when Price Textiles' stockholders rejected his exchange offer of shares in Mr. Gustaveson's Southern textile companies. The company had actively opposed this exchange offer because management believed that the election of the proposed director would benefit neither the company nor the communities in which Price Textiles operated plants. Although unsuccessful, Mr. Gustaveson intimated he might again enter the open market to increase his holdings in Price Textiles.

In the 1951 annual report the company said to its stockholders: "Your loyal support has been one of our strong assets. This loyalty has been rewarded by increasing dividends—a return for the funds which have been so necessary in Price Textiles' expansion program." The company also pledged to its stockholders "to continue its policy of reinvesting earnings for plant improvements so that the company might continue to grow."

The 1950 annual report to the company's stockholders had explained the company's reinvestment of earnings as follows:

In 1950 we spent $1,740,000 for new machinery and equipment. The money used to purchase this required equipment came from our profits. If

---

[1] The company's charter did not provide for cumulative voting in the election of directors.

we had made no profits we would have had to borrow money to purchase this equipment, which we believe is necessary to guarantee a permanent future investment for our stockholders. Next year we plan to spend $1,500,-000 on machinery if our earnings provide the cash necessary to pay for it.

Because new equipment has increased so much in price, ordinary depreciation will not provide sufficient funds to replace worn-out equipment when the need arises. We have set aside part of the 1950 profits in a reserve account, thus recognizing the inadequacy of present depreciation rates.

Furthermore, additional funds are needed to finance the increased working capital requirements resulting from higher prices and larger inventories.

Mr. Randall felt that two of the seven members of the board of directors, who were investment bankers, might be especially inclined to oppose a reduction in the dividend rate below $0.30 a share. However, a recent report from one of the over-the-counter dealers handling transactions of Price Textiles' common stock ventured the opinion that the market might already have discounted the possibility of lower dividend payment in the second quarter. In May, 1952, other cotton and rayon textile manufacturers were priced on the market to yield about 7%, based on current dividend rates. Market price ranges for Price Textiles' common stock in 1948 to June 2, 1952, are shown in Exhibit 5.

Mr. Randall felt that dividend action of other textile companies might temper or accentuate the market's reaction to any change in the the dividends paid by Price Textiles, Inc. Exhibit 6 presents recent dividend action taken by several major textile companies.

On March 5, 1952, the company had to resort to borrowing for the first time in five years. It obtained $1,800,000 from the Allen National Bank of Boston on a 3%, 90-day unsecured note. Although Mr. Randall had negotiated a 90-day renewal of the note, he hoped to begin retiring this debt before the new maturity date. If necessary, Mr. Randall believed Price Textiles could borrow several million dollars more, since the company had a strong current position and no long-term debt. He thought that additional borrowings might increase the interest rate slightly. Furthermore, if additional borrowing was necessary, he believed it would be desirable to extend repayments over a longer period than 90 days.

The only sources of cash that Mr. Randall could be assured of during the next three months other than borrowing would be from profits, if any materialized, and from depreciation, if earned; this would run at the rate of $66,000 for each four-week period. There might also be a cash gain of about $30,000 for each four-week period as a result of writing off prepaid expenditures against income.

On June 4 the company had a book cash balance amounting to $2,880,000. The company had accrued state and city taxes of $1,040,000, payable on June 15, and accrued annual vacation pay of $560,000, due employees on June 27. Outstanding commitments for new capital assets to be purchased in the next three months totaled $60,000. No new orders for machinery had been placed during the last seven or eight months, and management had made every effort to curtail expenditures other than those incident to normal operating experience. Federal income tax payments of $460,000 were payable on the fifteenth of September and December.[2] The finished goods inventory had remained at about the same level through 1952. Work-in-process inventories were down, reflecting the lower production levels in 1952; and Mr. Randall felt that as much as $1,800,000 of additional cash would be necessary to finance increased work-in-process inventories and accounts receivable should a rapid and substantial pickup in orders develop. The increase in total inventory between December 31, 1951, and March 22, 1952, was largely the result of forward purchases of cotton. No reduction in this raw material inventory was likely until September.

Technological improvement in textile machinery had been rapid after World War II. Recently one leading textile machinery manufacturer had placed on the market a revolutionary new spinning frame, and other textile machinery companies were continuously developing new machines and new techniques. Although the company's modernization program had been completed, the management of Price Textiles, Inc., realized that additional expenditures would be necessary in the future to keep their company competitive. Mr. Randall believed these expenditures would be resumed at the high level of the previous few years as soon as operations became profitable enough to finance them.

In an effort to reduce labor costs, the company had reopened discussions of its labor contract in late April, 1952. The company officials had argued that the current $0.30 per hour wage differential between their company and southern companies had seriously affected the company's ability to operate profitably. Mr. Randall estimated that each $0.01 reduction in hourly wage rates would save the com-

---

[2] Mr. Randall decided it would not be advantageous to deduct the income tax carry-backs, resulting from the company's recent losses, from the current income tax liability because subsequent profits might offset these losses. If the company's operations for the year resulted in a net loss, it would receive a tax rebate check in 1953. Thus, for short-run planning purposes, Mr. Randall considered that net losses before taxes represented the actual cash drain on the company.

pany $160,000 per year before taxes. With lower costs, he believed the company could compete more favorably for textile orders and thus increase sales volume. Management argued that this would allow them to begin rehiring workers previously laid off. The union opposed any reduction in wages, and the dispute had been submitted to an arbitration board. The company did not expect to know until late June how much, if any, reduction in the $0.30 per hour wage differential the arbitration would grant.

The question of moving entire mills to the South was under study. Mr. Randall did not know what the outcome of this study would be; but should the company decide to move even one mill to the South, he believed relocation expenses would be several million dollars.

Exhibit 1

PRICE TEXTILES, INC.

SELECTED BALANCE SHEETS
(Dollar figures in thousands)

ASSETS	1945	Dec. 31 1949	1950	1951	Mar. 22 1952
Cash...	$ 2,462	$ 3,144	$ 1,789	$ 2,566	$ 2,701
U.S. treasury notes (in excess of tax liability)........	232	245	284	.....	.....
Accounts receivable..............................	1,045	4,713	6,355	6,460	4,666
Inventories......................................	8,694	17,872	18,946	20,037	22,790
Prepaid expenses................................	.....	348	456	485	786
Total current assets...............	$12,433	$26,322	$27,830	$29,548	$30,943
Land, building, and machines (net)................	5,908	13,686	14,549	15,204	15,817
Other assets....................................	497	113	93	62	69
Total assets................	$18,838	$40,121	$42,472	$44,814	$46,829

LIABILITIES	1945	Dec. 31 1949	1950	1951	Mar. 22 1952
Accounts payable and accruals....................	$ 2,120	$ 3,041	$ 3,175	$ 1,494	$ 2,901
Provision for federal income tax (less U.S. treasury notes)..	.....	.....	.....	3,210	2,234
Total current liabilities............	$ 2,120	$ 3,041	$ 3,175	$ 4,704	$ 5,135
Notes payable—bank.............................	5,400	.....	.....	.....	1,800
Reserve for property replacement.................	10	1,142	1,426	1,560	1,560
Preferred stock (par value $100)..................	.....	3,956	3,741	3,650	3,650
Common stock (783,000 shares)...................	10,242	10,242	10,242	10,242	10,242
Earned surplus..................................	1,066	21,740	23,888	24,658	24,442
Total liabilities...............	$18,838	$40,121	$42,472	$44,814	$46,829

Exhibit 2
PRICE TEXTILES, INC.
Selected Income Statements
(Dollar figures in thousands)

	1946	1947	1948	1949	1950	1951	Jan. 1–Mar. 22 1952
Gross income	$58,050	$76,822	$84,904	$66,433	$76,589	$72,192	$15,574
Cost of goods sold:							
Materials					40,358	38,671	9,019
Wages and salary					25,224	24,653	5,627
Depreciation					790	846	204
Other					1,824	1,955	449
Total cost of goods sold	$46,240	$61,395	$68,878	$61,195	$68,196	$66,125	$15,299
Profit before taxes	$11,810	$15,427	$16,026	$ 5,238	$ 8,393	$ 6,067	$ 275
Federal taxes	4,666	6,027	6,107	2,058	3,569	3,115	133
Income tax return						440	......
Net income	$ 7,144	$ 9,400	$ 9,919	$ 3,180	$ 4,824	$ 3,392	$ 142
Distribution of net income:							
Preferred stock dividends	$ 84	$ 220	$ 194	$ 181	$ 171	$ 166	$ 41
Common stock dividends	940	1,835	2,819	1,408	2,232	2,340	317
Reserves	882	1,243	1,123	283	283	134	......
Retained in business	5,238	6,102	5,783	1,308	2,138	752	(216)
Total dividends as percentage of net income	14%	22%	30%	50%	50%	74%	252%

Exhibit 3

PRICE TEXTILES, INC.

SALES AND INCOME DATA
(Dollar figures in thousands)

Four-Week Period Ending	Sales	Income (or Loss) before Tax	Income (or Loss) after Tax
March 24, 1951	$7,590	$1,055	$506
April 21, 1951	5,151	458	221
May 19, 1951	6,037	812	392
June 16, 1951	5,539	512	245
July 14, 1951	4,448	219	104
August 11, 1951	4,426	258	122
September 8, 1951	3,868	120	54
October 6, 1951	4,145	125	67
November 3, 1951	4,949	153	74
December 1, 1951	5,763	(46)	(23)
December 29, 1951	4,960	121	61
January 26, 1952	5,220	164	84
February 23, 1952	5,324	141	70
March 22, 1952	5,001	(39)	(19)
April 19, 1952	4,692	(113)	(52)
May 17, 1952	5,217	(720) *	(360)

* This figure includes an inventory write-down of $540,000. A semiannual physical inventory and adjustment of inventory values to cost or market, whichever is lower, indicated that market values were $540,000 less than shown on the perpetual inventory record.

Exhibit 4

PRICE TEXTILES, INC.

COMMON STOCK DIVIDENDS PER SHARE
1946—MARCH, 1952

Period		Dividends/Share
1946		$1.20
1947		2.40
1948		3.60
1949		1.80
1950		2.85
1951 First quarter	$1.10	
Second quarter	0.70	
Third quarter	0.70	
Fourth quarter	0.50	
Total 1951		3.00
1952 First quarter	0.40	

Exhibit 5

PRICE TEXTILES, INC.

Market Price Ranges for Price Textiles' Common Stock
1948—June 2, 1952

	High	Low
1948	$22\frac{7}{8}$	$13\frac{7}{8}$
1949	$17\frac{1}{2}$	$12\frac{1}{4}$
1950	$39\frac{3}{4}$	$15\frac{7}{8}$
1951	$49\frac{1}{2}$	33
1952		
January	$33\frac{1}{2}$	29
February	$31\frac{5}{8}$	$28\frac{5}{8}$
March	$31\frac{3}{4}$	29
April	29	$24\frac{3}{8}$
May	$31\frac{5}{8}$	$22\frac{1}{2}$
June 2, 1952	$25\frac{1}{4}$ (asked)	$24\frac{3}{4}$ (bid)

Exhibit 6

PRICE TEXTILES, INC.

RECENT DIVIDEND ACTION TAKEN BY OTHER
MAJOR TEXTILE PRODUCERS

Company	Date	Dividend per Share	Date	Dividend per Share
American Woolen Company	2/20/52	passed	5/20/52	passed
Bates Manufacturing Company	1/16/52	$0.20	4/16/52	$0.15
Berkshire Fine Spinning Assoc.	3/1/52	0.35	6/2/52	0.25
Burlington Mills	1/24/52	0.25	4/25/52	0.25
Cone Mills	2/5/52	0.40	4/1/52	0.40
Fruit of the Loom	1/10/51	2.00	1/17/52	1.00
Gustaveson Textiles	1/15/52	0.25	4/15/52	passed
Pacific Mills	1/21/52	0.50	4/21/52	0.50
Pepperell	1/31/52	1.25 *	4/24/52	0.75
J. P. Stevens	1/8/52	0.50	4/10/52	0.50
Textron	12/12/52	0.50	3/12/52	0.25

* Includes $0.50 extra.

Case 25

Lesmer Electronics Corporation

ON JANUARY 26, 1956, the board of directors of Lesmer Electronics Corporation was to meet to declare the quarterly dividend on the common stock. Two years earlier, the same board had voted to reduce the quarterly rate from 50 cents to 25 cents per share and to supplement these payments with an annual stock dividend of 5%. The president of the company, Mr. R. K. Patterson, had been the prime advocate of the change on the grounds that the lower cash distribution was better suited to both the needs of the rapidly growing company and the desires of its stockholders. A minority of the directors had dissented from this view, however, and periodically since had proposed the restoration of the 50-cent dividend. The president, in a memorandum to the directors in mid-January, 1956, indicated that he hoped the forthcoming meeting would lead to a unanimous viewpoint on the company's future dividend policy.

Lesmer Electronics Corporation was a medium-sized manufacturer of a variety of specialized electronic products, most of which were developed by the company's research department. Its growth since 1950 had been both rapid and steady, stemming from the defense requirements of World War II and the Korean situation, the postwar development of television, and latterly the specialized applications of electronics to business data processing. Sales, earnings, and other financial data for 1945 through 1955 are given in Exhibit 1.

The board of directors formulated the major policies and programs of the company. The board was composed of the president, four vice presidents, and four outside directors. The latter were all active officers of large, noncompeting industrial firms. They had been invited by Mr. Patterson to serve on the Lesmer board and had done so for periods extending from six to eleven years. The directors as a group owned almost 7% of the outstanding common stock as of December 31, 1955.

Apart from the directors' holdings, no stockholder of record owned more than 2% of the outstanding stock. There were over 6,200 stockholders at the end of 1955, which was a record high for the company. Stockholders were geographically dispersed and comprised both individual and institutional investors. The company did not have a stock purchase program for its employees, but did have a stock option plan for its key officers. Under the provisions of this plan, an aggregate of 25,000 authorized but unissued shares were reserved for the participants at a price equal to 95% of the market price on the date the option was granted. The options had been granted in May, 1953, when the stock was selling at $50 and could be exercised at any time within the following five years.

The board had authorized management to use various methods of financing the company's decade of substantial growth. Two issues of the common stock, which had been listed on the New York Stock Exchange in 1943, were sold to the public. The first offering, in March, 1946, was 30,000 shares, issued at $36⅝ per share with net proceeds to the company of $1,006,000. The second issue was made in January, 1951, when 100,000 shares were sold at $45 to provide the company with $4,180,000. Both issues had been underwritten and were quickly sold.

A second avenue of financing which the management followed was the private placement of debentures in 1950 and 1954. Prior to 1950, the company's policy had been to incur no long-term debt. The officers relinquished this policy, however, when they realized that its consequence would be the indefinite postponement of various projects that promised returns of more than 10% after taxes. Accordingly, the company arranged the placement with the Hamilton Life Insurance Company of a $5 million, 4% debenture issue with a full sinking fund of $250,000 per annum commencing in 1951 and terminating in 1970. Management negotiated a second placement of a $5 million debenture issue in June, 1954. On this occasion, the terms were 4½% and payments to the sinking fund were deferred until 1959, when yearly amounts of $250,000 would commence. The 1954 debenture issue restricted the company in paying cash dividends on the common stock to "an amount no greater than the aggregate amount of net income after December 31, 1953, plus $2 million."

Management utilized stringent controls over the working capital employed by the company, as a further method of facilitating its growth. Since 1950, various improvements of the inventory control system had permitted the company to reduce its inventory requirements relative to sales to a level which management regarded as the absolute minimum. Similarly, the cash position of the company had been reduced to a reasonable working balance.

Although the various measures mentioned above aided significantly in financing the company's growth, the major sources of funds in the postwar period were depreciation and the retention of earnings. The company's depreciation policy was to depreciate its assets, both for accounting and income tax purposes, over the shortest period of time and on the most favorable basis permitted by the Internal Revenue Service. The company's policy on earnings retention, of course, was the complement of its dividend policy.

Dividend Policy through 1953

Although the directors of the company had not formulated a definite dividend policy prior to 1954, a number of practices had gradually evolved. Foremost of these was the practice of changing dividend payments roughly in proportion to changes in earnings. The directors desired to distribute about 30 to 40% of earnings in any single year. These payout ratios had become accepted as being fair to the stockholders in view of opportunities for profitable investment of almost any amount of retained earnings. Although this practice determined the general level of dividend payments, one other consideration influenced the specific amounts and timing of payments within the year. The directors would not increase the amounts of quarterly payments unless they believed the earnings position of the company could support the higher payments within the desired payout ratio range in future years. Therefore, in years such as 1947 and 1950, a portion of the total payments represented a year-end "special" dividend. Despite this approach, the directors had never formally represented the quarterly payments as constituting a "regular" rate, since they had desired to retain maximum flexibility in dividend determination. Exhibit 2 presents information on the company's earnings, dividends, and stock prices from 1945 to 1955.

Dividend Policy Change, January, 1954

At the meeting of the board on January 24, 1954, the directors voted to reduce the quarterly dividend payment from 50 cents to

25 cents per share and to supplement this payment with a 5% stock dividend. This action culminated discussions which had extended over several months about the best manner to finance the company's future growth.

Commencing in 1953, the company had accelerated its expansion program in order to participate fully in the greatly enlarged markets for its electronic and specialized data-processing equipment. Capital expenditures in that year had exceeded $4 million and final authorizations for 1954 were almost $7 million. Moreover, management's estimates indicated that the demand for the company's products probably would double by 1960 and that, to satisfy this rate of growth, expenditures beyond 1954 might well range from $6 million to $9 million per annum.

This great increase in the need for funds had not, of course, been unforeseen. Mr. Patterson already had received the assurance of Hamilton Life that they would be willing to purchase a $5 million debenture issue in 1954. The projected cash budget, in summary, for 1954 was as follows:

Estimated Receipts

Debentures	$ 5,000,000
Earnings	4,000,000
Depreciation	2,200,000
	$11,200,000

Estimated Expenditures

Capital expenditures	$ 6,800,000
Increased working capital requirements	2,600,000
Sinking fund	250,000
Dividends, at 1953 level	1,100,000
	$10,750,000
Uncommitted funds, Dec. 31, 1954	$ 450,000

Despite the surplus of funds indicated by the cash budget for 1954, Mr. Patterson believed that immediate action should be taken to conserve funds for the expansion program. Accordingly, he moved that the quarterly dividend be reduced to 25 cents per share. He said that these lower payments would increase the uncommitted funds at the end of 1954 to about $1 million, but that this amount and more would be needed in subsequent years to finance the company's growth.

In particular, Mr. Patterson believed that the company likely would have to issue common stock within the next few years, because it already would have drawn heavily on debt financing. Previous issues of common had been at prices substantially below the January, 1954, price range of $60 to $63 per share. With further substantial growth in earnings probable, he thought that the amount of future common stock issues should be minimized and should occur at the latest possible dates, so that the benefits of further capital appreciation would accrue largely to present stockholders. An immediate reduction in cash dividends would be in accord with this objective.

An opposing viewpoint was expressed by another director, Mr. F. B. Kugel, himself the president of a large machinery equipment company. He believed that a reduction in the quarterly cash dividend, unlike that of the year-end dividend, would be interpreted by the investment community as the signal of major financial difficulties in the company. The price of the common stock, therefore, in his opinion would decline. A lower market price in turn would adversely affect the company when it went to the market in later years, by requiring the sale of a greater number of shares to realize any needed amount of funds. He proposed, as an alternative, the continuation of the existing 50-cent rate, and the granting to stockholders of pre-emptive rights on all future equity financing, so that their share in the company's growth need not diminish.

Mr. Patterson conceded that the market might react adversely to the proposed dividend reduction, but believed that any such a decline would be short-lived. As soon as investors could see that the company's program continued to be sound and successful, their confidence in the company would be fully restored. He also argued that the possibility of the temporary market reaction was an added reason for reducing the dividend now, so the market would be back to normal before any common stock was issued.

As for pre-emptive rights on future issues, Mr. Patterson said that this approach was less desirable than a dividend reduction because of the impact of personal income taxes on stockholders. If the company halved the cash dividend rate, the whole $550,000 of added retention would be available for investment. On the other hand, if it paid this sum to stockholders, perhaps only $300,000 would be left in their hands, for use in exercising rights, after they had paid their tax bill at the marginal tax rates.

Finally, Mr. Patterson said that the use of a stock dividend to supplement the lower cash dividend would be of considerable consequence to those stockholders who needed income from their investments. If the board voted the 5% stock dividend, as he advocated, and the market price remained around $60 per share, stockholders could realize about $3.00 on each share owned by selling their stock dividends. This sum, moreover, would be subject only to the capital gains tax rates. Thus, under the new policy a stockholder could both obtain and retain more cash than he could have under the previous policy.

Although Mr. Kugel and two other directors believed that Mr. Patterson had overstated the advantages of the new policy, they agreed to vote for its adoption, at least for a trial period. Accordingly, the board unanimously voted a 25-cent cash dividend per share and a 5% stock dividend, both payable to stockholders of record on February 25, 1954. They further authorized Mr. Patterson to announce as the reasons for the change in policy, the needs for the expansion program and the benefits to stockholders of the stock dividend.

Further Developments, 1954–1955

Following the announcement of the new dividend policy, the market price of Lesmer common stock declined from 59¾ to 46⅝ and then began to rally. By December, 1955, the price had risen to 80⅞. Exhibit 3 shows the annual market prices and other data for Moody's 125 Industrial Stocks and also for companies comprising Standard and Poor's Index of Radio, Television and Electronics Companies. Exhibit 4 gives the monthly market prices for Lesmer common stock and these two indexes.

The company received criticism of the new policy from some stockholders, either through letters or through casual personal talks with directors. One investment fund, which sold its holdings of 1,000 shares in February, 1954, wrote that it "could not justify holding the stock at its lower yield." Other stockholders commended the company for instituting stock dividends, but stated that the $2.00 cash dividend should not have been reduced. Some cited the 15% payout ratio in 1954 as being "by far the lowest in your industry." Many of these protesting stockholders attributed the initial decline in market price to the dividend reduction and some complained later that Lesmer common stock had not participated fully in the unprecedented bull market of 1955.

These views were shared on the board by Mr. Kugel and, at times, by two other directors. In July, 1954, Mr. Kugel urged the board to restore the 50-cent quarterly payment, in order to bolster the depressed market price. At that time, however, the other directors felt that the new policy had not yet had time to work itself out. Quarterly payments of 25 cents in cash were continued through 1954 and 1955 and a 5% stock dividend was voted in January, 1955.

In October, 1955, Mr. Kugel again proposed the restoration of the 50-cent payment and, on that occasion, was supported by two others. He contended that the preliminary cash budget for 1956 indicated the need for some external financing, probably common stock. Although Lesmer common had risen substantially since 1953, Mr. Kugel believed that even greater appreciation should have resulted, in view of the general market rise and the outstanding sales and earnings records of Lesmer in 1954 and the first half of 1955. Furthermore, a study of the stockholders' list had indicated that less than 10% of shareholders had sold their stock dividends, thus suggesting that stock dividends were generally not an effective means of supplementing cash income.

Mr. Patterson agreed with Mr. Kugel that a common stock issue might be necessary in 1956, and, if not, almost certainly would be in 1957, in view of the foreseeable needs for funds and the reluctance of the board to incur further long-term debt in the near future. He said, however, that his previous position on minimizing the amounts of such financing remained unchanged and that he was not at all sure that the market price would rise significantly if the old policy were restored. At any rate, he urged the directors to defer consideration of a major change in dividend policy until January, 1956, when the final budget for 1956 and the long-range forecasts for 1957–1960 would be available. This viewpoint gained general acceptance and the board then voted a 25 cents per share quarterly dividend.

Board Meeting, January, 1956

About one week prior to the meeting of the board on January 26, 1956, each director received a copy of the 1956–1960 cash budget for his study. A summarized version of that document was as follows:

CASH BUDGET, 1956–1960
(Dollar figures in millions)

	1956	1957	1958	1959	1960
Estimated expenditures					
Capital expenditures	$ 7.50	$ 7.50	$ 7.50	$ 8.00	$ 8.00
Net working capital requirements	2.00	2.00	2.00	2.50	2.50
Sinking fund requirements	.25	.25	.25	.50	.50
Dividends, at 105% of previous year	.65	.68	.72	.76	.80
	$10.30	$10.43	$10.47	$11.76	$11.80
Estimated receipts					
Earnings	$ 5.20	$ 5.50	$ 6.00	$ 6.50	$ 7.00
Depreciation	2.90	3.30	3.70	4.20	4.80
	$ 8.10	$ 8.80	$ 9.70	$10.70	$11.80
Net need	$ 2.20	$ 1.63	$ .77	$ 1.06	$ 0

Accompanying the budget was an explanation of the assumptions on which it had been constructed.

1. Dividends have been projected on the assumption that annual payments will continue at $1.00 per share with a 5% stock dividend. No allowance has been made for the dividend requirements arising from issues of common stock, if any, during this period.
2. Sinking fund projections are based solely on the requirements of the outstanding debenture issues. No allowance has been made for sinking fund requirements arising from debenture placements, if any, during this period.
3. Capital expenditures and net working capital requirements have been projected on the basis of a 60% increase in sales from 1955 to 1960.
4. Earnings have been projected for somewhat less than a 60% increase to allow for starting-up costs, promotion, and other initial expenses associated with increasing sales.
5. Net needs are calculated as the difference between estimated expenditures and receipts, there being no uncommitted funds available at January 1, 1956.

Accompanying the cash budget was a memorandum from Mr. Patterson to the directors. In it, he stated his hope that the forthcoming board meeting would lead to general agreement on a dividend policy for the company to follow in the years ahead.

Exhibit 1

LESMER ELECTRONICS CORPORATION

SELECTED FINANCIAL DATA, 1945–1955

(Dollar figures in thousands)

Year	Sales	Net Income after Taxes	Depreciation	Net Working Capital	Capital Expenditures	Common Stock Cash Dividends	New Financing
1945	$14,498	$ 586	$ 440	$ 2,537	$1,382	$ 354	
1946	12,302	513	526	2,519	1,716	354	$1,006
1947	21,159	1,808	655	2,912	1,047	476	
1948	29,864	1,757	813	3,745	1,261	476	
1949	32,920	2,150	938	5,106	985	725	
1950	54,683	3,411	1,067	8,552	4,898	1,134	5,000
1951	62,417	3,419	1,181	12,594	3,382	1,106	4,180
1952	58,962	3,452	1,652	13,840	2,556	1,106	
1953	63,896	3,778	1,959	13,997	4,170	1,106	
1954	69,551	4,165	2,240	17,608	6,963	581	5,000
1955	81,178	5,093	2,547	17,894	6,494	610	

Exhibit 2

LESMER ELECTRONICS CORPORATION

SELECTED DATA ON THE COMMON STOCK,* 1945–1955

					Market Price				
Year	*Earnings per Share*	*Dividends per Share*	*Book Value per Share*	*Number of Shares Outstanding (In Thousands)*	*High*	*Low*	*Average of Monthly Prices*	*Price/Earnings Ratio, Based on Ave. Mo. Price*	*Yield, Based on Ave. Mo. Price*
1945	$1.45	$ .80	$16.31	423	33⅜	16⅝	27	18.7	3.0%
1946	1.12	.80	18.07	453	38½	21⅜	28	25.3	2.8
1947	3.97	1.20	20.84	453	27⅝	19¾	23	5.9	5.2
1948	3.86	1.20	23.50	453	30¼	24⅞	24	6.2	5.0
1949	4.74	1.60	26.64	453	37⅛	21	26	5.5	6.2
1950	7.51	2.50	33.18	453	46⅞	26⅝	37	4.9	6.7
1951	6.19	2.00	39.89	553	53¾	39½	45	7.2	4.4
1952	6.08	2.00	43.97	553	56⅝	38⅛	46	7.6	4.3
1953	6.81	2.00	48.78	553	63½	42¼	51	7.5	3.9
1954	7.15	1.00+5%	52.90	581	67¾	46⅝	56	8.0	1.8
1955	8.32	1.00+5%	57.85	610	84⅜	62¼	76	9.1	1.3

* Per share data are as calculated at year end and have not been adjusted to reflect the 5% stock dividends in 1954 and 1955.

CASH DIVIDENDS PAID BY QUARTERS, 1945–1955

	1Q	*2Q*	*3Q*	*4Q*	*Year End*	*Total*
1945	$.20	$.20	$.20	$.20	—	$ .80
1946	.20	.20	.20	.20	—	.80
1947	.20	.20	.30	.30	$.20	1.20
1948	.30	.30	.30	.30	—	1.20
1949	.40	.40	.40	.40	—	1.60
1950	.40	.40	.40	.50	.80	2.50
1951	.50	.50	.50	.50	—	2.00
1952	.50	.50	.50	.50	—	2.00
1953	.50	.50	.50	.50	—	2.00
1954	.25	.25	.25	.25	—	1.00
1955	.25	.25	.25	.25	—	1.00

Exhibit 3

LESMER ELECTRONICS CORPORATION

MOODY'S COMMON STOCK AVERAGES, 125 INDUSTRIAL COMPANIES
AS AT DECEMBER 31, 1945–1955

Year	Market Price per Share	Price Earnings Ratio	Yield
1945	$ 43.94	16.15	4.00%
1946	49.84	14.12	3.75
1947	46.10	8.67	5.06
1948	47.50	6.76	5.87
1949	46.88	7.10	6.82
1950	57.83	6.84	6.51
1951	70.72	9.60	6.29
1952	75.63	10.53	5.55
1953	76.05	9.86	5.51
1954	95.81	11.43	4.70
1955	130.66	12.43	3.93

RADIO, TELEVISION, AND ELECTRONICS COMPANIES

	Standard and Poor's Price Index* (1935–1939 = 100)	Average Price-Earnings Ratio of Stocks in Index†	Average Yield of Stocks in Index‡
1945	168.0	20.4	2.5%
1946	164.1	17.6	3.1
1947	111.3	7.0	5.9
1948	140.7	6.5	5.3
1949	139.9	8.2	5.6
1950	199.5	5.1	5.9
1951	237.4	6.8	5.5
1952	296.1	9.0	5.0
1953	285.2	8.0	5.4
1954	332.8	10.2	5.5
1955	454.1	11.4	4.3

* Index includes 11 stocks between 1951 and 1955, 5 between 1945 and 1950.

† Simple average of price-earnings ratios, as reported by Value-Line of companies included in Standard and Poor's price index. Companies with deficits were omitted in computing the average for years in which deficit occurred: 2 companies in 1945; 1 in 1948 and 1952; 2 in 1955.

‡ Simple average of dividend yields, as reported by Value-Line. Companies which did not pay dividends are omitted in years when dividends were passed; 1 company in 1946–1947, 1949 and 1951–1955.

Exhibit 4

LESMER ELECTRONICS CORPORATION

RANGE OF MARKET PRICES OF LESMER ELECTRONICS CORP. COMMON STOCK, STANDARD & POOR'S PRICE INDEX OF RADIO, TELEVISION AND ELECTRONICS
COMPANIES AND MOODY'S PRICE INDEX OF 125 INDUSTRIAL COMPANIES, 1945–1955

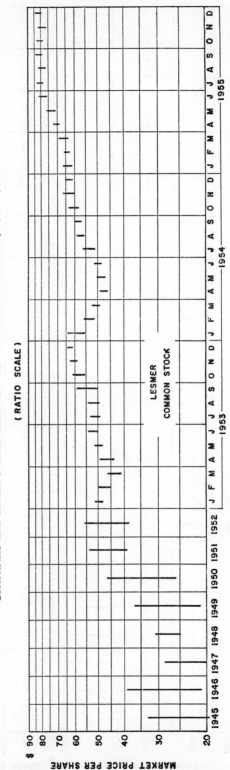

Exhibit 4 —Continued

Case 26

Ten-Pin Bowling Enterprises, Inc.

IN THE spring of 1960, three students in their final year at the Harvard Business School decided to develop a forty-lane bowling establishment. For financing the bowling equipment and accessories, they considered the following alternatives:

1. Purchase all equipment and accessories on a conditional sales contract.
2. Lease the pinspotters, and purchase all other bowling equipment and accessories on a conditional sales contract.

Building space was to be leased and a snack bar concession granted under either alternative. It was anticipated that the concessionaire would supply equipment for the snack bar.

Earlier in the year the promoters had elected, in partial fulfillment of course requirements, to make a study of a bowling alley as a new enterprise. The results of their study were so encouraging that they decided to take advantage of the opportunities that seemed to exist in the bowling alley business. Since none of the promoters had any personal cash resources, the alternatives for financing the enterprise were limited to those requiring a minimum of initial cash investment.

The promoters selected a location for the bowling alley in a community of about 100,000 population, a few miles north of Boston, Massachusetts. Building space of 32,000 square feet in a shopping center currently under construction would be available for lease at an annual cost of $1.75 a square foot. The lease would run for a ten-year period, with a ten-year renewal option.

Two bowling equipment manufacturers were the principal sources of equipment and accessories. Both manufacturers would sell all equipment and accessories, exclusive of automatic pinspotters, on conditional sales contracts, at an approximate cost of $4,200 a lane.

The contracts would require a 25% down payment and payment of the balance over five years.

One manufacturer sold automatic pinspotters as well as equipment on conditional sales contract. The cost of a pinspotter was $8,100. A minimum down payment of $500 would be required on each one; the balance would be paid at the rate of $0.12 a line bowled, with an annual minimum of $1,200 a pinspotter. The other manufacturer offered each pinspotter on an annual lease basis of $0.10 a line for the first 10,000 lines bowled, $0.08 for the next 5,000 lines, and $0.06 for each subsequent line. An installation charge of $500 a pinspotter was required under this arrangement. Both manufacturers insisted on approving the selected location before making equipment available on these terms.

Initial cash investment thus would be the same under either alternative. Exhibit 1 is a schedule of estimated cash investment requirements under each alternative.

To raise the necessary cash funds for the project, the promoters drafted a proposal for presentation to prospective investors, as follows:

Investors would supply $80,000 cash in exchange for $80,000 of 7% subordinated debentures of the firm. In addition, the investors would receive 400 shares of common stock (40% of the total outstanding) at no extra cost. The debentures would be retired at the rate of $10,000 a year, starting at the end of the second year of operations; they would, however, be subject to call at par in five years from date of issue or at any time thereafter.

The promoters would receive 600 shares of common stock (60%) in exchange for $30,000 payable to the firm within five years. Each promoter would receive 200 shares; each would owe the firm $10,000. One promoter would become the full-time, salaried manager of the enterprise. The other two would find work in Boston, and would work at Ten-Pin Bowling Enterprises in their off hours and on week ends at no cost to the firm.

Members of an investment group, with whom one of the promoters was personally acquainted, had been approached and expressed an interest in providing the initial cash investment on the terms proposed.

From the promoters' point of view, one factor would have substantial influence in a final choice of financing arrangements. The entire estimated life of the project was 10 years. The promoters' plan of action, however, called for a sale of their interest in the enterprise for capital gains in five years. The choice of financial arrangement would thus largely depend on prospects for the greatest return to them at the end of this period. Since earnings and cash flow patterns under the two alternatives would differ significantly over the entire estimated life, the promoters were uncertain regarding an appropriate method of comparison for decision purposes. Exhibits 2 and 3 present estimated earnings and cash flows under the alternatives considered. The difference in estimated earnings before interest, lease payments, and taxes under the two alternatives results from differences in depreciation charges, property taxes, and insurance.

Before reaching a decision, the promoters consulted a man with considerable experience in the bowling alley business. After reviewing the study and earnings projections, the consultant suggested that a level of 15,000 lines per alley a year was more in accordance with his experience than the 20,000 lines projected. Under this assumption, annual earnings before interest, lease payments, and taxes would be reduced approximately $100,000 in each case; debt retirement on pinspotters under Alternative 1 would then be approximately $72,000 annually for 4¼ years; lease payments on pinspotters under Alternative 2 would be $56,000 annually.

These observations were somewhat disturbing to the promoters. They thought that it would be advisable to determine what effect these changes would have on earnings and cash flow patterns of the alternatives before making a choice.

Exhibit 1

TEN-PIN BOWLING ENTERPRISES, INC.

SCHEDULE OF ESTIMATED CASH INVESTMENT

ALTERNATIVE 1

Automatic pinspotters* ($500 down payment × 40).	$20,000
Other bowling equipment and accessories† ($4,200 × 40 × 25% down).	42,000
Organization and other miscellaneous expenditures.	15,000
Operating cash balance.	3,000
Estimated Cash Investment.	$80,000

* Payment of balance required at a rate of $0.12 a line bowled, with an annual minimum of $1,200 a pinspotter.
† Payment of balance required in five equal annual instalments.

ALTERNATIVE 2

Automatic pinspotters* ($500 installation charge × 40).	$20,000
Other bowling equipment and accessories† ($4,200 × 40 × 25% down).	42,000
Organization and other miscellaneous expenditures.	15,000
Operating cash balance.	3,000
Estimated Cash Investment.	$80,000

* Lease payments required on each pinspotter at an annual rate of $0.10 a line for the first 10,000 lines bowled, $0.08 a line for the next 5,000, and $0.06 for each subsequent line.
† Same as alternative 1.

Exhibit 2

TEN-PIN BOWLING ENTERPRISES, INC.

ESTIMATED EARNINGS AND CASH FLOW UNDER ALTERNATIVE 1

(Dollar figures in thousands)

	1	2	3	4	5	6	7	8	9	10	Total
Earnings before interest, lease payments, and taxes*	$235.0	$244.0	$253.0	$262.0	$271.0	$283.0	$292.0	$301.0	$310.0	$319.0	$2,770.0
Less: Interest on debentures	$ 5.6	$ 5.6	$ 4.9	$ 4.2	$ 3.5	$ 2.8	$ 2.1	$ 1.4	$ 0.7	$	$ 30.8
Interest on other debt†	25.8	18.5	11.3	4.0	1.5	....	....	....	....	....	61.1
Lease payments on building	56.0	56.0	56.0	56.0	56.0	56.0	56.0	56.0	56.0	56.0	560.0
	$ 87.4	$ 80.1	$ 72.2	$ 64.2	$ 61.0	$ 58.8	$ 58.1	$ 57.4	$ 56.7	$ 56.0	$ 651.9
Earnings before taxes	$147.6	$163.9	$180.8	$197.8	$210.0	$224.2	$233.9	$243.6	$253.3	$263.0	$2,118.1
Taxes (at 50%)	73.8	81.9	90.4	98.9	105.0	112.1	116.9	121.8	126.6	131.5	1,058.9
Earnings after taxes	$ 73.8	$ 82.0	$ 90.4	$ 98.9	$105.0	$112.1	$117.0	$121.8	$126.7	$131.5	$1,059.2
Depreciation and amortization	92.7	83.7	74.7	65.7	56.7	44.7	35.7	26.7	17.7	8.7	507.0
Cash flow from operations	$166.5	$165.7	$165.1	$164.6	$161.7	$156.8	$152.7	$148.5	$144.4	$140.2	$1,566.2
Debt retirement: 7% debentures	$	$ 10.0	$ 10.0	$ 10.0	$ 10.0	$ 10.0	$ 10.0	$ 10.0	$ 10.0	$	$ 80.0
Pinspotters	95.9	95.9	95.9	16.3	....	....	....	....	....	....	304.0
Equipment and accessories	25.2	25.2	25.2	25.2	25.2	....	....	....	....	....	126.0
	$121.1	$131.1	$131.1	$ 51.5	$ 35.2	$ 10.0	$ 10.0	$ 10.0	$ 10.0	$	$ 510.0
Net cash flow	$ 45.4	$ 34.6	$ 34.0	$113.1	$126.5	$146.8	$142.7	$138.5	$134.4	$177.1‡	$1,093.1‡

* Annual charges for property taxes and insurance under Alternative 1 would exceed similar charges under Alternative 2 by approximately $11,000.
† Effective interest cost of 6% assumed on time payment purchase contracts for pinspotters, equipment, and accessories.
‡ Net salvage (or resale) value of equipment estimated at 7.5% of original cost and included in tenth-year figure ($36.9).

TEN-PIN BOWLING ENTERPRISES, INC.

ESTIMATED EARNINGS AND CASH FLOW UNDER ALTERNATIVE 2

(Dollar figures in thousands)

					Year						
	1	2	3	4	5	6	7	8	9	10	Total
Earnings before interest, lease payments, and taxes	$305.1	$308.0	$311.3	$314.3	$317.4	$323.5	$326.5	$329.6	$332.6	$335.7	$3,204.0
Less: Interest on debentures	$ 5.6	$ 5.6	$ 4.9	$ 4.2	$ 3.5	$ 2.8	$ 2.1	$ 1.4	$ 0.7	$	$ 30.8
Interest on other debt*	7.6	6.0	4.5	3.0	1.5						22.6
Lease payments on building	56.0	56.0	56.0	56.0	56.0	56.0	56.0	56.0	56.0	56.0	560.0
Lease payments on pinspotters	68.0	68.0	68.0	68.0	68.0	68.0	68.0	68.0	68.0	68.0	680.0
	$137.2	$135.6	$133.4	$131.2	$129.0	$126.8	$126.1	$125.4	$124.7	$124.0	$1,293.4
Earnings before taxes	$167.9	$172.4	$177.9	$183.1	$188.4	$196.7	$200.4	$204.2	$207.9	$211.7	$1,910.6
Taxes (at 50%)	83.9	86.2	88.9	91.5	94.2	98.3	100.2	102.1	103.9	105.8	955.0
Earnings after taxes	$ 84.0	$ 86.2	$ 89.0	$ 91.6	$ 94.2	$ 98.4	$100.2	$102.1	$104.0	$105.9	$ 955.6
Depreciation and amortization	33.6	30.7	27.4	24.4	21.3	15.2	12.2	9.1	6.1	3.0	183.0
Cash flow from operations	$117.6	$116.9	$116.4	$116.0	$115.5	$113.6	$112.4	$111.2	$110.1	$108.9	$1,138.6
Debt retirement: 7% debentures	$	$ 10.0	$ 10.0	$ 10.0	$ 10.0	$ 10.0	$ 10.0	$ 10.0	$ 10.0	$	$ 80.0
Equipment and accessories	25.2	25.2	25.2	25.2	25.2						126.0
Net cash flow	$ 92.4	$ 81.7	$ 81.2	$ 80.8	$ 80.3	$103.6	$102.4	$101.2	$100.1	$108.9	$ 932.6

* Effective interest cost of 6% assumed on time payment purchase contract for equipment and accessories.

Case 27

Head Ski Company, Inc.

In late February, 1960, Mr. Thomas Long, a partner in the Baltimore investment banking firm of Robert Garrett & Sons,[1] was nearing a decision on the price at which Robert Garrett would offer to underwrite and sell publicly a certain number of shares of the common stock of the Head Ski Company (HEAD). Since December, 1959, Mr. Long had been negotiating with Mr. Howard Head, president and chief stockholder of HEAD, in an attempt to arrive at the most suitable plan for the first public offering of that company's stock. The proposed offering would total approximately $280,000. Since the size of the offering was less than $300,000, HEAD would be exempt from a complete and costly Securities and Exchange Commission registration requirement. The company desired to raise approximately $162,000 in net proceeds (after underwriting commissions) to supplement existing working capital. In addition, certain selling stockholders wished to raise $90,000 in net proceeds through a secondary offering; thus, the proposed new issue would include both a corporate and a secondary offering of HEAD's common stock. It was Mr. Long's responsibility to determine the number of new shares to be issued by the company, the number of shares to be sold by the selling stockholders, and the price at which Robert Garrett & Sons would be willing to underwrite and offer to the public the Head Company stock.

The Company

The Head Ski Company was founded in Baltimore, Maryland, in 1947 by Mr. Howard Head, then 32 years old, and was operated as an individual proprietorship until 1953. Between 1947 and 1950, Mr. Head concentrated on the development of a ski radically different

---

[1] In this case, names of officers of Robert Garrett & Sons have been disguised.

from the traditional hickory skis in wide use at that time. By 1950 the Head ski had been developed—a composite design of aluminum alloy, plastic, steel, and wood. Head skis were placed on the market during the 1950 winter skiing season. Their acceptance was immediate; sales rose from 300 pairs in the 1950–51 skiing season to 8,000 pairs in 1954–55 and 33,000 in 1958–59. During this period the demand for Head skis consistently outstripped the company's production capabilities. By 1959, Head skis had developed a wide reputation in the United States, Canada, and abroad as strong, lightweight, and easily maneuverable skis, suitable for experts as well as beginners. Mr. Head estimated that sales during the 1959–60 season would approximate 40,000 pairs of skis.

HEAD currently manufactured and sold two models—the "Standard," retailed at $89.50, and the "Vector," which sold for $107.50. The Vector model was introduced in 1959 for use by more experienced skiers. With the increased interest in racing arising out of the 1960 Winter Olympics, HEAD accelerated its work on the development of an international racing ski. Three Olympic skiers visited the company after the winter games to assist on this project, and won several international races on Head skis late in the 1960 skiing season. Mr. Head thought that a product line which included a racing ski as well as the Standard and Vector models would enable Head to serve most classes of skiers.

Currently, the company employed 140 people in a new 27,000 square foot plant constructed in 1959 near Baltimore; the new facilities would accommodate an annual production level of up to 160,000 pairs of skis. Although Mr. Head had designed the original Head ski, the company currently employed six engineers and technicians who assisted Mr. Head in the research and development of new products and in refinement of existing products. Sixty-five per cent of present sales were made in the United States and Canada through five hundred franchised dealers selected for their wide experience in the sale of skis and ski equipment. One distributor in Switzerland accounted for 30% of HEAD's total sales; this dealer had established subdistributorships for sales throughout Western Europe. The remaining 5% of the company's sales were to other countries outside of Europe and North America. HEAD rigidly enforced the retail prices on its Standard and Vector model skis in order to eliminate the possible unfavorable aspects of price cutting on its product line.

The competition for Head skis came from the manufacturers of traditional hickory skis and the makers of other metal-plastic composite skis. Traditional hickory skis had for many years enjoyed popularity in the inexpensive ski field and as special purpose racing skis. The volume of sales achieved by HEAD, however, indicated that the Head design was continuing to overtake major parts of the hickory ski market. The success of the Head design had also promoted the establishment of a number of manufacturers of metal-plastic composite skis both in the United States and abroad. Mr. Head had patented certain aspects of the Head ski, but his patent protection could not prevent the development of slightly different competitive designs. This competition, however, had not prevented HEAD from selling all the skis it could produce prior to the move to its new plant in 1959. Mr. Head estimated that the second largest metal ski manufacturer produced approximately 20% of HEAD's volume, and that the volume of all such manufacturers was approximately 50% of that of HEAD.

Financial History

The company was incorporated in 1953; at that time, Mr. Head was issued 900 shares of cumulative preferred stock and 825 shares of common stock in exchange for assets valued at $90,825. Later in 1953 the requirements for additional working capital to finance expanding production levels resulted in the addition of $60,075 in equity funds through the private sale of 600 shares of cumulative preferred stock and 675 shares of common. In 1955, $7,500 was raised through the private sale of 50 shares of cumulative preferred stock and a like amount of common stock. These capital additions represented the extent of equity financing in HEAD's growth from 1947 to early 1960. As of April 25, 1959, HEAD's capital stock consisted of 1,550 shares of cumulative preferred and 1,550 shares of common stock. Changes in the company's capital accounts between April, 1959, and January, 1960, reflected the retirement of the preferred with accumulated dividends and the no-par value common stock in exchange for new shares of $1.50 par value common stock (Exhibit 1). Currently, Mr. Head owned 57.6% of HEAD's outstanding common stock.

Other than by the additions to equity capital between 1953 and 1955, HEAD's growth had been financed entirely out of retained earnings and short-term bank borrowings. By the nature of its business, HEAD's sales and heavy shipments out of inventory began in August and September, reached peak levels in October and November, and declined gradually to the end of its shipping season in early March. In the past a substantial portion of the company's seasonal cash requirements had been provided through an unsecured line of credit from a Baltimore bank. Borrowing normally began in August, peaked in December, and declined thereafter to complete pay-out by the end of March. Because of its rapid growth in sales, HEAD's credit line had increased each year since 1953 and reached a high of $450,000 in December, 1959; at that time the company's accounts receivable totaled $690,000 and inventories $263,000.

With sales showing no tendency of leveling off, Mr. Head anticipated that the company's need for bank credit would continue to increase. Earnings retention during the next few years appeared insufficient to meet expected increases in working capital requirements, and he estimated that the company would require credit accommodations of between $700,000 and $750,000 within the next two or three years. In early December, 1959, when HEAD's borrowing had reached $450,000, its bank had stated that that level represented the reasonable maximum credit the bank would be willing to extend on the basis of the company's net worth. HEAD's net worth was then slightly over $500,000, and the bank had been following a policy of placing an upper limit on the company's credit of slightly less than its net worth. At that time, HEAD's banker suggested that additional equity capital would not only strengthen the company's working capital position but also provide a larger equity base, and one upon which the bank would be willing to increase its maximum credit line to the company.

The Proposed Common Stock Offering

It was on the basis of the preceding considerations that Mr. Head approached Mr. Long of Robert Garrett & Sons early in December, 1959. The two men quickly agreed that the sale of common stock would provide the most practical method of raising additional capital. The alternative of raising debt capital was clearly undesirable in view of HEAD's seasonal borrowing requirements and was considered inappropriate in view of the need for larger amounts of permanent capital. Mr. Head was also averse to selling preferred stock, since the company had just recently retired the 1,550 shares of preferred that had been outstanding since 1956. Mr. Head was receptive to Mr. Long's suggestion that a public offering of HEAD's stock would satisfy the objectives of raising new capital and would also facilitate, for the first time, a trading market in the company's stock. The two previous stock sales in 1953 and 1955 had been private sales to a limited number of investors who had not traded actively in the stock. Between December, 1959, and February, 1960, negotiations between Mr.

Head and Mr. Long were continued on the assumption that HEAD's new capital would be raised through a public stock offering underwritten by Robert Garrett & Sons.

A preliminary consideration in establishing the size of the proposed offering was the amount of capital that HEAD would need in order to raise its borrowing capacity from $450,000 to the $700,000–$750,000 range. The company's net worth of $534,000 on January 2, 1960 (Exhibits 2 and 5) reflected an addition to retained earnings from net profits since April 25, 1959, of $62,500. Mr. Head estimated that total net earnings for the year ended April 30, 1960, would approximate $75,000. This would be lower than the $95,000 earned in 1959, despite an increase in sales, because HEAD had experienced nonrecurring expenses associated with the move to its new plant and with the development of the Vector model ski. Since HEAD paid no dividends on its outstanding common stock, estimated earnings of $75,000 for fiscal 1960 would produce a net worth on April 30, 1960, of approximately $546,000 (exclusive of the proposed offering). In discussing these projections with the company's commercial bank, Mr. Head was informed that the addition of between $160,000 and $170,000 in equity funds would enable the bank to increase HEAD's line of credit to a maximum of $700,000.

Mr. Head and Mr. Long next discussed the possibility of including a secondary offering by the existing stockholders in the proposed new issue. This appeared to be an attractive opportunity in light of the relatively small amount of capital required by the company for corporate use. A secondary offering would increase the size of the issue and make more shares available for sale; it was hoped that such a plan would stimulate increased trading activity in the stock among a wider group of investors.

An important consideration relative to a combined corporate and secondary offering involved the expense to HEAD of registering a new issue with the SEC. Mr. Head desired to keep this expense as small as possible. Under the terms of the Securities Act of 1933, a public security offering was exempt from full registration requirements if the aggregate amount of the issue offered to the public did not exceed $300,000. Mr. Long estimated that such an exemption in the case of HEAD's proposed offering would save the company between $5,000 and $10,000. According to HEAD's legal advisers, an additional consideration under such a partially exempt registration was that a secondary offering would be limited to $100,000.

On the basis of the preceding factors, Mr. Head and Mr. Long decided to limit the combined corporate and secondary offering to less than $300,000. Tentative agreement was also reached on a 10% underwriting commission to Robert Garrett & Sons as compensation for accepting the responsibility of buying and then reselling HEAD's stock to security dealers and to the public. With these stipulations as guide lines, the two men were able to define within fairly narrow limits those portions of the proceeds from the proposed issue to be allocated to the company, to the selling shareholders, and to underwriting commissions. The size of the issue would be approximately $280,000; $162,000 would represent net proceeds to the company, $90,000 would go to the selling shareholders, and $28,000 would represent the 10% underwriting commission.

By late February, 1960, the remaining issue of major importance concerned Mr. Long's recommendation to Mr. Head as to the price at which Robert Garrett & Sons would offer to sell HEAD's stock to the public. The determination of the offering price would enable Mr. Long to calculate the number of new shares to be offered by the company and the shares to be sold by the selling shareholders in arriving at the total offering price of $280,000. Mr. Head had contacted the company's major stockholders, and each had agreed to sell the same percentage of his stock ownership as the percentages sold by the other members in arriving at the gross figure of $100,000 under the secondary offering. Conceivably, Mr. Head's ownership in the company could fall below 50% after the proposed new issue, depending upon the offering price of the stock. The offering price would, in turn, determine the number of shares to be sold by Mr. Head as part of the secondary offering and the dilution in his stock ownership resulting from the new corporate issue. Mr. Head did not consider such a possibility a major drawback to the proposed offering; he indicated that he would continue to receive the backing of the present stockholders and that the combined holdings of this group would represent well over 50% of the stock outstanding subsequent to the issue. (Exhibit 3 describes HEAD's common stock and the rights associated therein.)

An important factor relative to Mr. Long's pricing recommendation to Mr. Head concerned HEAD's past earnings record (Exhibits 4 and 5). Potential investors would, as one method of evaluation, concern themselves with the offering price of HEAD's stock in relation to the company's past earnings per share. In order accurately to reflect HEAD's earnings relative to the proposed offering, Mr. Long realized that the company's past per share earnings would have to be adjusted downward on the basis of the larger number of common stock shares that would be outstanding subsequent to the offering. An additional consideration concerned the company's dividend policy; Mr. Head desired to continue the policy of reinvesting all earnings in order to strengthen the company's working capital position in anticipation of increased sales and production levels. Mr. Long did not feel that such a policy would have an adverse effect upon the marketability of HEAD's stock, however, since the reinvestment of all earnings had become an accepted policy of many companies which were expanding rapidly and whose stock was actively traded.

To aid him in his pricing decision, Mr. Long had compiled comparative financial and descriptive data on selected companies in the recreational and amusement fields (Exhibits 6, 7, and 8). None of these companies concentrated solely on the manufacture and sale of skis since, to Mr. Long's knowledge, all such companies were either privately owned or were subsidiaries of larger, publicly owned corporations. Mr. Long had also compiled published statements regarding the future prospects for the amusement industry (Exhibit 9).

A corollary consideration in Mr. Long's pricing recommendation concerned the present conditions in the capital stock markets. The number of relatively small companies issuing stock publicly for the first time had shown a marked increase since the fall of 1959. According to many underwriting firms and security dealers, this had produced an oversupply of stocks in the new issues market, promoting lower prices for the stocks of many companies in relation to their past earnings records. On the other hand, Mr. Head anticipated that HEAD's new issue would generate considerably more investor appeal than the moderate interest expressed in some current new issues. He thought that many owners of Head skis would be potential buyers of HEAD's stock; this, coupled with the relatively small supply of stock anticipated in the proposed offering, would, he hoped, stimulate an active buying interest in the issue.

If Robert Garrett & Sons was accepted as HEAD's underwriter, it was Mr. Long's intention to distribute the stock to security dealers for resale to the public in those areas of the country where interest in skiing was most pronounced; specifically, he would allocate approximately half of the stock to dealers in California and Colorado, and the remainder to dealers along the East Coast. The offering would be scheduled for early April, 1960, and would be traded in the over-the-counter market. Under the terms of the proposed underwriting agreement, the selling stockholders would be restricted from selling additional stock for a period of one year from the date of the issue.

During that period, then, the trading activity in HEAD's stock would be confined to the number of shares offered through the underwriting.

Mr. Long's most important objective in his recommendation to Mr. Head was the determination of that price for HEAD's stock that would result in the highest proceeds and lowest dilution in earnings per share to the company and the selling shareholders, consistent with a price that would stimulate active and continued investor appeal. He would consider the issue successful if the stock rose to a premium of one or two points above the offering price in the trading market after the offering. If HEAD continued to grow at its present rate, the company might wish to return to the equity markets in the future; a successful offering at this time would certainly make it easier for HEAD to consider future public offerings of common stock.

Exhibit 1

HEAD SKI COMPANY, INC.

NET WORTH AND CAPITAL STOCK OUTSTANDING

April 30, 1955–January 2, 1960

	4/30/55	4/30/56	4/30/57	4/26/58	4/25/59	6/10/59	1/2/60
Net Worth:							
Common stock	$ 1,500	$ 4,000	$ 4,000	$ 4,000	$ 4,000	$158,400	$167,400
Preferred stock—5% cumulative	149,400	154,400	154,400	154,400	154,400		
Surplus	63,051	154,075	135,077	207,841	302,731	n.a.	366,340
Total	$213,951	$312,475	$293,477	$366,241	$461,131	n.a.	$533,740
Preferred stock dividends earned but not declared	$ 15,375	$ 23,062	$ 30,812	$ 38,562	$ 46,312		
Capital stock outstanding (number of shares):							
No-par value common	1,500	1,550	1,550	1,550	1,550		
No-par value new common						74,400*	
$1.50 par value common							111,600†
No-par value preferred	1,500	1,550	1,550	1,550	1,550		

* 74,400 no par shares new common stock outstanding following issuance of (1) 13 shares for each share of preferred stock and accumulated dividend arrearages thereon and (2) 35 shares for each share of old common stock.

† 111,600 shares of $1.50 par value common stock outstanding following issuance of 1½ shares of $1.50 par value common for each one share of no par value common.

Exhibit 2

HEAD SKI COMPANY, INC.

BALANCE SHEET* AS AT JANUARY 2, 1960

(Unaudited)

ASSETS

Current Assets:

Cash in bank and on hand	$ 64,107	
Trade acceptances	17,054	
Accounts receivable (net)	543,315	
Inventories (see Note A)†	316,251	
Prepaid expenses and other	$ 33,341	
Total Current Assets		$ 974,068

Fixed Assets:

Machinery and equipment	$211,477		
Less: Depreciation to date	100,847	$110,630	
Other	$ 40,472		
Less: Depreciation and amortization to date	16,195	24,277	
Building	$261,476		
Less: Depreciation to date	10,644	250,832	
Total Fixed Assets			385,739

Other Assets:

Cash surrender value—life insurance (see Note B)†	$ 36,918	
Miscellaneous	26,306	63,223
Total Assets		$1,423,031

LIABILITIES AND NET WORTH

Current Liabilities:

Vouchers payable	$206,839	
Notes payable	300,000	
Mortgage payable—current portion (see Note C)†	8,820	
Customers' advance payments	14,153	
Estimated federal and state income taxes payable	63,388	
Other	94,911	
Total Current Liabilities		$ 688,111

Long-Term Debt:

Mortgage payable—noncurrent portion (see Note C)†		201,180
Total Liabilities		$ 889,291

Commitments and Contingent Liabilities (see Note D)†

Net Worth:

Common stock, $1.50 par value, authorized, 200,000 shares; issued and outstanding, 111,600 shares	$167,400	
Retained earnings	366,340	
Total Net Worth		533,740
Total Liabilities and Net Worth		$1,423,031

* Figures are rounded and therefore may not add to totals.

† The notes to financial statements (see Exhibit 5) are an integral part hereof.

Exhibit 3

HEAD SKI COMPANY, INC.

DESCRIPTION OF COMMON STOCK, AS OF FEBRUARY, 1960

Prior to June 10, 1959, the authorized capital stock of the company consisted of 1,550 shares without par value of preferred stock and 1,550 shares without par value of common stock, all of which shares were issued and outstanding. By amendments of the charter and stock splits since that date, these shares have all been reclassified into the now outstanding 111,-600 shares of the par value of $1.50 per share of common stock of the company; and the authorized capital stock has been increased to the present 200,000 shares of common stock, all of one class.

All shareholders will participate equally, share for share, in any dividends which may be paid or on liquidation. On all matters of voting, each shareholder is entitled to one vote for each share of stock standing in his name. Cumulative voting for directors is not provided for by the charter or by the bylaws, and the shares have noncumulative voting rights; that is, the holders of more than 50% of the shares voting for the election of directors can elect 100% of the directors if they choose to do so; and in such event, the holders of the remaining less than 50% of the shares voting for the election of directors will not be able to elect any person or persons to the board of directors. The holders of the common stock have under the charter of the company no pre-emptive rights.

Exhibit 4

HEAD SKI COMPANY, INC.

STATEMENTS OF INCOME FOR THE PERIODS INDICATED BELOW

(Unaudited)

	Fiscal Year Ended April 30, 1957	52 Weeks Ended April 26, 1958	52 Weeks Ended April 25, 1959	36 Weeks Ended January 2, 1960
Sales	$1,076,652	$1,315,063	$1,613,872	$1,514,181
Less: Cost of Sales	800,190	919,762	1,122,578	1,085,095
Gross profit	$ 276,462	$ 395,301	$ 491,294	$ 429,086
Less: Expenses:				
Selling expenses	$ 76,848	$ 101,187	$ 109,305	$ 97,800
Administrative expenses	77,809	92,751	107,405	91,614
Corporate expenses	26,951	39,987	77,459	113,870
Total Expenses	$ 181,608	$ 233,926	$ 294,168	$ 303,284
Net Profit before Income Taxes	$ 94,854	$ 161,375	$ 197,126	$ 125,802
Federal and state income taxes	49,988	88,611	102,236	63,388
Net Profit after Income Taxes (See Note E)*	$ 44,866	$ 72,764	$ 94,890	$ 62,414
Earnings per Share (based upon 111,-600 shares outstanding on January 2, 1960, giving retroactive effect to recapitalization)	$0.40	$0.65	$0.85	$0.56

* The notes to financial statements (see Exhibit 5) are an integral part hereof.

Exhibit 5

HEAD SKI COMPANY, INC.

NOTES TO FINANCIAL STATEMENTS

Note A—Inventories

Inventories are valued at lower of cost or market and are detailed below:

Finished goods	$ 75,985
Goods in process	98,259
Raw materials	125,127
Manufacturing supplies	16,880
Total	$316,251

Note B—Cash Surrender Value of Life Insurance

The company is the owner and beneficiary of life insurance contracts in the face amount of $500,000 on the life of its president, Howard Head. The cash surrender value of these policies was $36,918 on January 2, 1960.

Insurance owned by the corporation on the life of its president, with maturity value of $50,000 and cash surrender value of $3,463 at January 2, 1960, has been pledged as additional security for the mortgage loan payable to Loyola Federal Savings and Loan Association.

Insurance owned by the corporation on the life of its president, with maturity values of $400,000 and aggregate cash surrender value of $28,581 at January 2, 1960, is held by a trustee pursuant to the terms of a stock redemption contract between the company and its president. The company is permitted by this contract to exercise various rights with respect to such policies, including the right to borrow and the right to change beneficiaries. The company is obligated to purchase only as much of the president's stock as the insurance proceeds can buy. Shares which are subject to the agreement are in the custody of the trustee. The president has limited rights to withdraw some of his shares from the trustee, thereby removing these shares from the effects of the contract.

Note C—Mortgage Payable

The company plant at Timonium, Maryland, and a life insurance contract owned by the company are pledged to secure a 6% mortgage loan payable in monthly instalments to Loyola Federal Savings and Loan Association. The last monthly payment will be due on December 1, 1974.

Note D—Long-Term Leases, Commitments, Contingent Liabilities

The company, prior to moving into its present facilities, occupied premises at 1507 Roland Heights Avenue in Baltimore under a lease which will expire on March 31, 1964. The rental under such lease is $7,520 per annum. The company has subleased said premises for the remaining term of the lease at an annual rental of $7,800.

Land upon which the company has constructed its plant is leased for twenty years beginning on September 1, 1959, at an annual rental of $7,200, subject to reduction until certain utilities and grading have been supplied by the lessor, and subject to an increase of $1,152 per acre in the annual

Exhibit 5—Continued

rental to the extent that a portion of the leased tract, consisting of 1.562 acres and reserved for storm drainage, is made available for company use. The lease gives the company options to renew for three successive 20-year terms followed by a final term of 19 years. In addition, the company has the option to purchase the land at any time during the last 15 years of the initial 20-year term of the lease at a price of $25,000 per acre of land not reserved for Baltimore County storm drainage less the sum of $12,500. If the present reservation for storm drainage purposes is not changed, upon exercise of the purchase option the company would acquire 6.25 acres, not subject to storm drainage use, for a price of $143,750.

Skis sold by the company bear a guaranty for one year from the retailer's sales date. The financial statements make no provision for the contingent liabilities created by such guaranties, since the extent of such liability is indeterminate and, in the opinion of the company's officials, based upon past experience, is not considered material.

Note E—Statements of Income and Retained Earnings

Examination indicates a correction is needed to the company's opening inventory for the thirty-six week fiscal period ended January 2, 1960, and here reported. Inventories as of April 25, 1959, were undervalued by $38,850. As a consequence, net profit after income taxes for the fiscal period April 26, 1959, to January 2, 1960, includes $11,888 which was earned prior to April 26, 1959, and which is computed as follows:

Increase in current-period income because of inventory undervaluation	$38,850
Less: Increase in current-period profit sharing and incentive bonus expenses as result of above increase	12,781
Increase in net profits before income taxes	$26,069
Less: Income taxes on above income	14,182
Increase in Net Profits after Taxes	$11,888

During the fiscal period April 26, 1959, to January 2, 1960, depreciation charges amounted to $47,117, and the following extraordinary expenses were incurred and charged off:

Expenses of moving plant from Baltimore to Timonium (included in corporate expenses)	$20,896
Contribution to Winter Olympic Ski Team (included in administrative expenses)	2,500
Total	$23,396

Testing and research expenses are included in corporate expenses. For the 52 weeks ended April 25, 1959, these expenses amounted to $28,417. Because of increased experimentation, research, and product development, testing and research expenses aggregated $36,147 for the 36 weeks ended January 2, 1960.

Because of increased borrowings, including interest paid on construction loans, interest expense for the 36 weeks ended January 2, 1960, was $19,471, as compared with $11,068 for the 52 weeks ended April 25, 1959. Interest expense is included in corporate expenses.

HEAD SKI COMPANY, INC.

COMPARATIVE STOCK PRICING AND FINANCIAL DATA ON SELECTED COMPANIES

February 26, 1960

	Head Ski Company, Inc.	MCA, Inc.	Shakespeare Company	Higbie Mfg. Company	A.G. Spalding & Bros., Inc.	Milton Bradley Co.	Murray Ohio Mfg. Co.	U.S. Playing Card Co.	Brunswick-Balke-Collender Co.	Outboard Marine Corp.
Fiscal Year End	4/25	12/31	7/31	7/31	7/31	12/31	12/31	12/31	12/31	9/30
Latest Complete Year	4/25/59	12/31/59	7/31/59	7/31/59	7/31/59	12/31/59	12/31/59	12/31/59	12/31/59	9/30/59
Sales (000)	$ 1,614	$ 56,929	$ 14,954	$ 7,748	$ 14,954	$ 12,336	$ 33,178	$ 21,547	$ 275,100	$ 171,569
Net income (000)	95	5,186	1,378	593	1,378	746	1,243	2,204	26,859	13,785
Net income/sales	5.9%	9.1%	9.2%	7.7%	9.2%	6.1%	3.8%	10.2%	9.7%	8.0%
Net income/net worth	20.5%	17.8%	10.6%	11.2%	8.2%	18.6%	10.0%	15.6%	26.6%	16.8%
Earnings per Share:										
1959	$0.85	$1.28	$2.85	$1.64	$1.35	$6.87	$4.23	$1.43	$3.42	$1.76
1958	0.65	1.18	2.73	0.74	1.21	3.02	2.74	1.40	2.13	1.16
1957	0.40	0.12	2.59	0.98	0.79	2.38	2.12	1.22	1.38	1.67
1956	0.82	0.74	2.00	0.96	1.32	2.60	2.28	1.18	0.77	1.69
1955	0.22	0.61	2.38	1.10	1.05	2.06	3.42	1.10	0.32	1.23
1959 versus 5-year average	143%	130%	114%	151%	118%	202%	142%	113%	213%	117%
Market Price[p]	....	25	28½[b]	15¾	23⅜	57[b]	31½	32⅜	58⅝	34¼
Price Earnings:										
1959	....	19.5	10.0	9.6	17.5	8.3	7.5	22.6	17.2	19.5
5-year average, 1955–59	....	25.4	11.4	14.4	20.6	16.8	10.6	25.6	36.5	22.6
Current Cash Dividend Rate	....	$ 0.00	$ 1.80	$ 0.60	$ 0.00	$ 0.95	$ 2.00	$ 1.25	0.53	0.80
Current Cash Yield	....	0.00%	6.3%	3.8%	0.00%	1.7%	6.3%	3.9%	0.9%	2.3%
Market Price/Net Tangible Assets per Share (Common)[n]	....	366%	128%[e]	168%[e]	118%[e]	167%	074%	353%	460%	330%
Common Shares:										
Total outstanding	111,600	3,996,000	483,000	363,000	855,000	106,000	294,000	1,540,000	7,823,000	7,854,000
Recent offering		400,000								
Date of offering		10/8/59								
Offering price		$17.50								
Traded	NYSE	NYSE	O.C	ASE	NYSE	O.C	ASE	NYSE	NYSE	NYSE

Symbols:
p = Closing quotations February 26, 1960.
b = Bid prices.
n = Based on capitalization 12/31/59.
e = Estimated.

Exhibit 7

HEAD SKI COMPANY, INC.

COMPARATIVE FINANCIAL DATA ON SELECTED COMPANIES

(Dollar figures in thousands)

Balance Sheet Analysis	Head Ski Company, Inc. 1/2/60	MCA, Inc. 12/31/59	Shakespeare Co. 7/31/59	Outboard Marine Corp. 9/30/59
ASSETS				
Cash	$ 64	$ 2,753	$ 2,579	$ 15,518
Marketable securities		2,407	2,384	5,424
Accounts receivable (net)	539	4,592	1,642	14,049
Inventories	316	18,786	3,280	37,468
Other current assets	55	354	128	.....
Total Current Assets	$ 974	$28,892	$10,013	$ 72,459
Land, buildings, etc.	$ 514	$17,537	$ 5,160	$ 62,804
Depreciation	128	3,122	2,278	22,394
Net property	$ 386	$14,415	$ 2,882	$ 40,410
Unamortized assets		25,093	.....	.....
Other assets	63	2,123	106	6,432
Total Assets	$1,423	$70,523	$13,001	$119,301
LIABILITIES AND CAPITAL				
Notes payable	$ 300	$ 3,000	$	$ 3,500
Accounts payable	207	6,915	428	6,672
Federal income taxes	63	4,020	1,203	998
Accruals and other	118	4,241	669	5,899
Total Current Liabilities	$ 688	$18,176	$ 2,300	$ 17,069
Contracts or notes payable, other long-term debt	$ 201	$23,232	$	$ 20,779
Preferred stock		1,799	.....	.....
Common stock	167	7,476	2,417	2,356
Retained earnings and surplus	367	19,840	8,284	79,097
Total Liabilities and Capital	$1,423	$70,523	$13,001	$119,301

Exhibit 7—Continued

Head Ski Company, Inc.

Sales	Sales	Increase over Previous Year
1959	$1,614	23%
1958	1,315	22%
1957	1,077	28%
1956	839	294%
1955	213	....

Net Earnings	Net Earnings	Increase over Previous Year
1959	$ 95	30%
1958	73	62%
1957	45	(51%)
1956	91	264%
1955	25	....

MCA, Inc.

Sales	Sales	Increase over Previous Year
1959	$56,929	20%
1958	47,473	22%
1957	38,878	24%
1956	31,392	31%
1955	23,895	....

Net Earnings	Net Earnings	Increase over Previous Year
1959	$ 5,106	20%
1958	4,328	5%
1957	4,121	49%
1956	2,758	21%
1955	2,286	....

Shakespeare Co.

Sales	Sales	Increase over Previous Year
1959	$14,954	7%
1958	13,962	(1%)
1957	14,099	13%
1956	12,456	3%
1955	12,112	....

Net Earnings	Net Earnings	Increase over Previous Year
1959	$ 1,378	4%
1958	1,320	5%
1957	1,253	29%
1956	969	(16%)
1955	1,154	....

Outboard Marine Corp.

Sales	Sales	Increase over Previous Year
1959	$171,569	8%
1958	158,713	6%
1957	150,476	23%
1956	122,045	42%
1955	85,856	....

Net Earnings	Net Earnings	Increase over Previous Year
1959	$ 13,785	52%
1958	9,095	(30%)
1957	13,071	8%
1956	12,098	54%
1955	7,864	....

Exhibit 8

HEAD SKI COMPANY, INC.

DESCRIPTIONS OF COMPANIES LISTED IN EXHIBITS 6 AND 7

Music Corporation of America, Inc. (MCA), produced television film series and distributed these films throughout the United States and to foreign countries. The company also acted as agents for artists in the entertainment business. On October 8, 1959, MCA's common stock became publicly owned through an issue of 400,000 shares at $17.50 a share.

The *Shakespeare Company* manufactured and sold steel tubing and fishing reels. Over 50% of the company's operations were devoted to the manufacture of small-diameter welded steel tubing, of which 80% was sold to the automobile industry. Fishing reels represented between 35% and 40% of the company's business.

A. G. Spalding & Bros., Inc., was a well-known manufacturer of a varied line of sporting goods.

Milton Bradley Company manufactured school materials, display booths, and a varied line of additional amusements, toys, and novelties.

The *Murray Ohio Manufacturing Company* manufactured a complete line of juvenile automobiles, bicycles, wagons, scooters, etc. In 1957, over 45% of the company's sales were to Sears Roebuck & Co.

U.S. Playing Card Company manufactured and sold all types of playing cards.

Brunswick-Balke-Collender Company was the largest manufacturer of bowling equipment in the United States. The company also manufactured and sold school furniture, sports equipment, nonpharmaceutical laboratory supplies, and various defense products.

Outboard Marine Corporation was the largest domestic producer of outboard motors. The company also manufactured power lawn mowers, chain saws, and similar types of equipment.

Exhibit 9

HEAD SKI COMPANY, INC.

SELECTED COMMENTS ON THE AMUSEMENT INDUSTRY*

All indications point to the greatest boom in the history of the amusement industry over the next decade and longer. . . .

Factors are:

. . . . current projections for a 41% rise in the number of persons between 15 and 29 years old in the 1960–1970 period. . . .

. . . . the substantial increase in consumer income anticipated in coming years. . . .

. . . . the growing amount of leisure time enjoyed by the average working man.

Current indications suggest the largest relative gains in sales and earnings will be experienced by those segments of the entertainment industry in which individuals are involved as participants rather than as spectators. . . .

. . . . Total spending on sporting goods in 1959 is expected to rise roughly 8% to a new peak of $1.97 billion. . . .

---

* Standard and Poor's Corporation. *Industry Surveys: Amusements*, May 21, 1959.

Case 28

American Machine & Foundry Company

In December, 1958, Mr. David S. Meiklejohn, vice president and treasurer of American Machine & Foundry Company (AMF), was reviewing the company's financial condition and its cash and earnings forecasts for the year 1959. He was preparing a recommendation to be submitted at the meeting of the AMF board of directors on January 6, 1959, regarding the company's two convertible debenture issues, one in the amount of $4,388,000 outstanding at 4¼%, the other in the amount of $12,286,000 outstanding at 5%. The question to come before the board was whether the company should plan to force conversion of the debentures in early 1959 by calling either or both of them for redemption. As of December, 1958, conversion of the 4¼'s outstanding would result in 140,400 additional common shares, and conversion of the 5's would add 321,200 shares.

Company Background

AMF was a large, diversified company engaged in manufacturing, selling, and leasing special automatic and semiautomatic machinery and equipment. It was composed of over 20 wholly owned domestic and international subsidiaries, with manufacturing plants and sales offices located throughout the United States and in many foreign countries. Its products were varied, including cigarette-making and -packing machines for the tobacco industry; stitching machines for the apparel and shoe industries; ovens, wrapping machines, and slicing machines for the baking industry; pinspotters, alleys, and pins for the bowling industry; bicycles and power shop equipment for the consumer; reactors, control systems, and remote handling equipment for the atomic energy field; radar, electronic, and missile control equipment for the defense industry; motors, engines, and special equipment for general industries. Consolidated gross sales and rentals of

843

the company and its subsidiaries had grown from $27,517,000 in the year 1950 to a high of $261,754,000 in 1957. Management expected 1958 gross sales and rentals to total approxinately $230,000,000.

A growing recreation field in recent years had enabled AMF to take good advantage of its bowling line, particularly the automatic pinspotter. Although the 1958 recession had decreased the company's over-all earnings and profits, leases of bowling equipment were running nearly two thirds greater in 1958 than in 1957. As AMF had continued to improve its position of leadership in this field, the need for funds to finance investment in leased bowling equipment had been a problem of increasing proportions. In fact, investment in bowling machines and equipment leased to customers had grown from $1,424,-476 in 1950 to approximately $112,000,000 in 1958, the latter figure being an increase over 1957 of $21,000,000. In an effort to free cash to help support the tremendous growth in sales and in investment in bowling equipment leased to customers, the company for a number of years had followed the practice of leasing rather than buying most of its own manufacturing plant and equipment.

Exhibits 1–4 present selected data on AMF's financial condition and operations.

Convertible Debentures Issued, 1956

In December, 1955, Mr. Meiklejohn received from the accounting department a cash forecast for 1956, showing that the company would need at least $10,000,000 by year end to meet the cash requirements for the year's operations. This amount was over and above funds which would be provided by borrowing[1] against new investment in bowling equipment to be leased to customers. The possibility of raising $10,000,000 through short-term borrowing was not considered as an alternative because the funds would be needed on a long-term basis. The company followed a policy of using short-term borrowing capacity only for seasonal requirements and "bridging" financing, and therefore tried to be out of debt on a short-term basis at the end of each year.

In the spring of 1956, Mr. Meiklejohn consulted with an investment banking firm for recommendations on the matter. After discussions with several institutional lenders and others, the investment banking firm came to the conclusion that AMF could not raise $10,-000,000 through a straight debt issue on satisfactory terms. AMF's relatively disappointing earnings during 1955 and its debt position

---

[1] See p. 847 for description of borrowing method.

were given as the primary reasons for this conclusion. AMF was also advised that a common stock issue to raise the funds would be inadvisable at that time, because a common stock offering had been made in 1955 and another issue coming so soon thereafter would probably have a depressing effect on market price.

It was recommended that AMF raise the funds through an issue of subordinated convertible debentures. Mr. Meiklejohn favored this method for several reasons: It presented an opportunity to raise funds through a device that substantially amounted to selling common stock at a premium above market price; AMF's long-term debt holders would view such an issue as equivalent to equity; if AMF's sales and rentals should take an unexpected slump, the debentures could still be sold by the company on a bond-yield basis; if the unexpected slump should happen to continue, AMF would be in a position to retire the debentures with cash released by resulting decreases in receivables, inventories, and investment in leased equipment. Convertible debentures seemed, therefore, to provide AMF with the greatest flexibility in light of the company's circumstances.

On June 26, 1956, a special stockholders' meeting was held, at which the stockholders authorized the issuance of subordinated convertible debentures by an affirmative vote of 85%. The following day, June 27, a $10,897,000 offering of 25-year debentures was made to stockholders, with subscription rights expiring on July 11. The interest rate was set at $4\frac{1}{4}\%$; and the conversion price, protected against future dilution, was set at $32.50 for 10 years, based on a closing price of $30 for AMF common on that day. (In December, 1958, the adjusted conversion price on this issue was $31.25.) Of the total offering, 95.67% was subscribed by company stockholders, and a tabulation of market prices during the period showed little effect on the price of AMF common stock.

Soon after the sale of the $4\frac{1}{4}\%$ convertible debentures, it became obvious to Mr. Meiklejohn that AMF's cash needs would exceed forecasts. Revised forecasts for the remainder of 1956 and for the year 1957 indicated a need of at least $10,000,000 of additional long-term money by December 31, 1957. This sum was in addition to another $20,000,000, which Mr. Meiklejohn thought could be raised during the period by borrowing against expected new investment in leased equipment.

Again, the investment banking firm was consulted for recommendations. A straight debt issue was ruled out on substantially the same grounds as before. Since AMF was planning to issue common stock in

1957 for the purpose of acquiring two companies, it was thought that the sale of an additional block of stock at this time might have a depressing effect on the market price.

After discussing the problem with the investment bankers, Mr. Meiklejohn decided that AMF should sell another issue of subordinated convertible debentures. The investment banking firm at first recommended that the 4¼% outstanding debentures, which were then selling at $125 to $129, should be called and conversion forced prior to sale of the new issue. In November, 1956, however, shortly after this recommendation, it became evident that a tremendous amount of new money would be raised by U.S. corporations in early 1957 to finance general business expansion. The investment banking firm became concerned about the delay involved in first calling the outstanding issue to force conversion and then making an offer to stockholders of a second debenture issue. In view of this, Mr. Meiklejohn decided that it would be best to sell the new issue without calling the first.

On January 24, 1957, without the earlier conducted formality of a special stockholders' meeting, a $12,725,800 offering of 20-year subordinated convertible debentures was made to AMF stockholders, with subscription rights expiring on February 7. The interest rate was set at 5% and the conversion price, protected against future dilution, at $38.25 for 20 years (based on a closing market price for AMF common on January 22 of $35.50).[2] Of the total offering, AMF stockholders subscribed to 96.3%. The closing market prices of AMF common during the period from announcement date, December 31, 1956, to expiration date, February 7, 1957, fell from 37¼ to 33½.

To Call Debentures and Force Conversion in 1959— Factors Considered

Management of AMF was confidently expecting that 1959 would be a record year in terms of sales, rentals, and profits. The company's rental business, however, was believed by several members of management to have reached a point where, instead of creating a demand for cash, it would provide a positive cash flow for expansion of the company's other business and for debt reduction. Partly in this light, the directors had recently voted to increase quarterly cash dividends on AMF common stock from 40 cents to 50 cents a share. Exhibit 5 presents the company's forecast of cash requirements and sources for the year 1959.

---

[2] Excerpts from the conversion provisions of this issue as contained in the indenture, which were almost identical with those of the 4¼% issue, are given in Appendix A.

As Mr. Meiklejohn reviewed the forecasts, however, he recalled that in recent years, investment in leased bowling equipment had continually exceeded management's expectations. In late 1957, for example, it had been forecast that 7,000 new automatic pinspotters would be leased during 1958. It was now apparent that new pinspotters leased in 1958 would total at least 10,000. While the cash reduction, as now forecast, would not particularly strain AMF's cash position, he thought it would be undesirable to risk reducing it any further. In this light, Mr. Meiklejohn was somewhat reluctant to place a high degree of confidence in the 1959 forecast of investment in pinspotters included in the forecast of company-wide cash requirements and sources (Exhibit 5).

Mr. Meiklejohn also recalled that in late 1956 the company had obtained an increase in its line of credit for financing pinspotter leases, but only after overcoming a noticeable reluctance on the part of some of the financing institutions. As of December 31, 1957, the full line of credit (a 15-year loan of $60,000,000) had been taken down by the company except for an unused $6,000,000 special cushion which had been provided for in the agreement to finance unanticipated pinspotter leases at 100% of equipment cost. Of the loan, $20,000,000 had been placed with a group of banks and included maturities for the first five years, payable at the rate of $5,000,000 a year for four years beginning in 1959; $40,000,000 had been placed with two insurance companies and included maturities for the remaining 10 years of the 15-year period. The $60,000,000 loan was based principally on the credit of AMF Pinspotters, Inc., a wholly owned subsidiary which had practically no other liabilities; it was guaranteed, however, by AMF, the parent company. The principal basis for credit to the subsidiary was the minimum rental of $800 a year guaranteed in the pinspotter leases (10-year leases), which involved an investment by AMF of approximately $2,000 for each pinspotter covered. The loan agreement required that the minimum rental ($800) times the unexpired terms of all pinspotters on lease must not be less than at least three times the outstanding amount of the loan. This requirement was covered by a significant margin of safety, but Mr. Meiklejohn questioned whether the banks and insurance companies would yet be willing to consider another increase in AMF's line of credit.

It seemed to Mr. Meiklejohn that if past experience of underestimating the next year's sales and investments in leased equipment should repeat itself, then some external financing late in 1959 would be difficult to avoid. In December, 1958, the market price of AMF common stock was at a level that would almost assure 100% conversion of both debenture issues if called for redemption. Mr. Meiklejohn knew that forcing conversion would greatly increase the company's financing flexibility. He knew that a delay in such action was always subject to the risk of the market. If general business or political conditions were to develop which depressed the market, the opportunity for forcing conversion might be lost for some time. On the other hand, AMF common stock would have to fall substantially from its price level to prevent forcing conversion of the debentures, probably over 21% for the convertible 5's and 35% for the convertible 4¼'s. Exhibit 6 presents recent market performance of AMF common stock and convertible debentures. Exhibit 7 presents a comparison of AMF common stock with *Moody's 125 Industrial Stocks.*

A provision in the company's agreement with certain long-term lenders required that an underwriting be secured for call of convertible debentures unless market price of AMF common stock on the call date was at least 150% of the conversion price. This was to protect the asset security position of debt holders in the company by providing assurance that AMF would not be required to pay out cash for redemption of any debentures not converted by the holders. An underwritten call arrangement would involve an agreement with an investment banking firm, wherein debentures turned back for cash redemption would be taken up by the underwriter, converted to common stock, and held for investment or for sale to the public. In any event, those holders redeeming for cash instead of converting would create no cash drain on the company if the call was underwritten. As long as the market price of AMF common stock remained above 46⅞, the necessity and expense of an underwritten call on the 4¼% debentures could be avoided. A price of 57⅜ or above was necessary, however, to avoid an underwriting of the 5% debentures. Mr. Meiklejohn had obtained an estimate of $100,000 as the underwriting fee on the call of the 5's at this time. This expense probably could have been avoided in recent weeks, when the common reached its all-time high of 59¾.

Mr. Meiklejohn thought that a gradual voluntary conversion of the 4.25% debentures would continue, owing to the cash dividend yield on the common stock. Holders of these debentures were in a position to receive a 6.4% yield on their investment by converting, as compared with 4.25% if they did not convert. He also thought that voluntary conversion of the 5% debentures would not be significant until the common dividend was again increased. Cash dividend yield on investment after conversion of a 5% debenture would be only 5.23%.

Exhibit 1

AMERICAN MACHINE & FOUNDRY COMPANY

Preliminary Consolidated Statement of Financial Condition for Company and Subsidiaries, as of December 31, 1958

(Dollar figures in thousands)

ASSETS

Current Assets:

Cash...		$ 21,000
Receivables...		56,000
Inventories (at cost or market, whichever is lower)..........		41,000
Other...		2,500
Total current assets...................................		$120,500
Property, plant, and equipment, net (at cost)*.................		23,000
Bowling machines and equipment leased to customers..........	$112,000	
Less: Reserve for depreciation............................	30,700	
		81,300
Patents, licenses, developments, investments, and other, net.....		6,700
		$231,500

LIABILITIES, CAPITAL STOCK, AND SURPLUS

Current Liabilities:

Current maturities on long-term debt.......................		$ 6,900
Accounts payable and accrued liabilities....................		20,300
Federal, state and other taxes (after deducting U.S. government securities, at cost—$4 million).......................		7,800
Total current liabilities...............................		$ 35,000
Long-term debt, less maturities included in current liabilities....		93,600
Deferred federal income taxes..............................		6,850
Minority interest in subsidiary.............................		150
Preferred stock...$	8,150	
Common stock and surplus (Issued and outstanding 3,347,000 shares, $7 par)......................................	88,250	
	$ 96,400	
Less: Treasury stock, preferred and common (at cost)........	500	
		95,900
		$231,500

* Aggregate annual rental payments for property, plant, and facilities on long-term leases at December 31, 1958, including rentals on properties sold and leased back, approximated $1,985,000.

Exhibit 2

AMERICAN MACHINE & FOUNDRY COMPANY

Selected Data on Consolidated Sales, Income, Dividends, Financial Position, Burden Coverage, and Common Stock for Company and Subsidiaries

(Dollar figures in thousands)

			Year		(Preliminary)
	1954	1955	1956	1957	1958
Sales	$117,143	$130,936	$175,225	$227,504	$184,140
Rental income from leased equipment	9,364	14,065	22,833	34,250	46,735
Total Sales and Rentals	$126,507	$145,001	$198,058	$261,754	$230,875
Earnings before interest, lease obligations, and taxes	$ 9,215	$ 11,516	$ 20,646	$ 28,775	$ 28,300
Interest expense	$ 1,347	$ 1,727	$ 2,670	$ 4,639	$ 5,298
Annual rental payments for property and facilities under long-term lease	n.a.	n.a.	1,266	1,968	1,985
Preferred dividends*	757	763	741	721	682
Retirement of preferred stock*	479	340	557	482	750
Current maturities paid on long-term debt*	4,130	7,810	10,300	16,800	3,660
Total Burden	$ 6,713	$ 10,640	$ 15,534	$ 24,610	$ 12,375
Burden coverage, exclusive of common dividends (times)	1.4	1.1	1.4	1.2	2.3
Net income	$ 4,023	$ 4,774	$ 8,976	$ 11,782	$ 11,000
Cash dividends paid:					
Preferred stock	363	366	355	346	327
Common stock	2,149	2,479	2,863	4,192	5,600
Shares of common stock outstanding at December 31†	2,238,372	2,660,204	2,847,923	3,258,739	3,347,000
Earnings per share at December 31 (after preferred dividend)	$ 1.64	$ 1.66	$ 3.03	$ 3.51	$ 3.19
Total assets, less reserves	105,662	132,625	182,385	225,619	231,500
Long-term debt, less current maturities	30,150	38,46~	67,480	102,868	93,600

* Including tax related (52%).
† Listed on the New York Stock Exchange.

Exhibit 3

AMERICAN MACHINE & FOUNDRY COMPANY

CONSOLIDATED STATEMENTS OF SOURCE AND DISPOSITION OF FUNDS FOR
COMPANY AND SUBSIDIARIES

(Dollar figures in thousands)

			Year		
					(*Preliminary*)
	1954	*1955*	*1956*	*1957*	*1958*
Source of Funds:					
Net earnings....................	$ 4,023	$ 4,774	$ 8,976	$ 11,782	$11,000
Depreciation and other noncash charges....................	4,611	6,080	8,351	11,857	15,700
Federal income taxes deferred........	.....	.....	555	3,408	1,850
Sale of 5% cumulative preferred stock.	556	.....	.....	......	.....
Sale of common stock..............	104	6,322	172	91	540
Long-term borrowing..............	21,415	8,318	38,242	92,926	.....
Decrease in working capital other than cash..........................	.....	.....	.....	......	7,270
Held by subsidiaries when acquired...	522	245	320	595	.....
Total........................	$31,231	$25,739	$56,616	$120,659	$36,360
Disposition of Funds:					
Investment in leased machines.......	$10,584	$10,869	$22,669	$ 25,260	$21,700
Property plant and equipment.......	3,437	3,988	5,820	4,808	2,600
Retirement of preferred stock........	230	163	267	231	360
Long-term debt paid or transferred to current liabilities..............	*	*	8,783	54,544	6,900
Dividends paid....................	2,512	2,845	3,218	4,538	5,930
Increase in working capital other than cash........................	12,020	6,778	6,276	22,358	.....
Other items, net..................	498	1,088	2,266	3,930	870
Total........................	$29,281	$25,731	$49,299	$115,669	$38,360
Increase (decrease) in cash.........	$ 1,950	$ 8	$ 7,317	$ 4,990	$(2,000)

* Netted against long-term borrowing in years 1954 and 1955.

Exhibit 4

AMERICAN MACHINE & FOUNDRY COMPANY
CONSOLIDATED SCHEDULE OF LONG-TERM DEBT, INTEREST RATES,
AND FUTURE MATURITIES FOR COMPANY AND SUBSIDIARIES
(Dollar figures in thousands)

	Total 12/31/58 (Preliminary)	Interest Rate	Maturities in Year Indicated				
			1959	1960	1961	1962	1963
Notes payable to insurance companies.................	$ 1,050	3¾%	$ 150	$ 150	$ 150	$ 150	$ 150
	1,000	4¾	100	100	100	100	100
	5,000	4¾	....	425	425	425	425
	40,000*	5¾	....	....	....	....	2,000
Note payable to banks..........	20,000*	5	5,000	5,000	5,000	5,000	....
Sinking fund debentures........	14,000	4	500	500	1,500	1,500	1,500
	1,750	3	1,000	750	....	....	....
First-mortgage note............	1,040	4¾	105	105	105	105	105
Convertible subordinated debentures...................	12,286	5	....	....	....	....	....
	4,388	4¼	....	....	....	....	....
Totals....................	$100,514		$6,855	$7,030	$7,280	$7,280	$4,280
Estimated annual rental payments for property and facilities under long-term lease.....			$2,200	$2,400	$2,500	$2,700	$3,000

* Loaned against bowling equipment as described on page 847.

Exhibit 5

AMERICAN MACHINE & FOUNDRY COMPANY
FORECAST OF CONSOLIDATED CASH REQUIREMENTS AND SOURCES FOR
COMPANY AND SUBSIDIARIES, YEAR 1959
(Dollar figures in millions)

Requirements:

Investment in leased machines...	$22.0
Additions to property, plant, and equipment...............................	4.5
Other investments...	3.0
Redemption of preferred stock...	0.3
Cash dividends on preferred stock..	0.3
Cash dividends on common stock...	6.8
Increase in receivables and inventories....................................	3.0
Current maturities on long-term debt.....................................	6.9
	$46.8

Sources:

Net earnings*...	$16.0
Depreciation and other noncash charges.................................	16.0
Increase in tax liabilities (including increase in deferred federal income taxes, $1.8 million)..	7.5
U.S. government securities (offset against tax liabilities on 1958 balance sheet)...	4.0
	$43.5
Decrease in cash..	$ 3.3

* Deductions included for annual rental payments on property and facilities under long-term lease were $2.2 million.

Exhibit 6

AMERICAN MACHINE & FOUNDRY COMPANY
RECENT MARKET PERFORMANCE OF AMF COMMON STOCK
AND CONVERTIBLE DEBENTURES

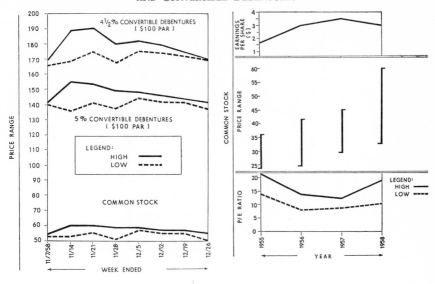

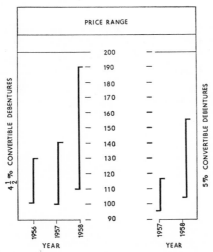

* SOURCE: Market prices from *Barron's* and *Commercial and Financial Chronicle.*

Exhibit 7

AMERICAN MACHINE & FOUNDRY COMPANY
SELECTED COMPARISONS OF AMF COMMON STOCK DATA
WITH "MOODY'S 125 INDUSTRIAL STOCKS"

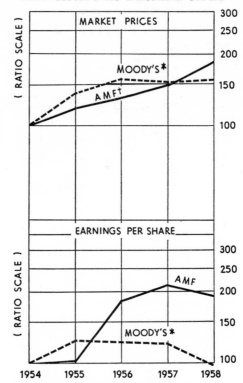

* Averages from *Moody's 125 Industrial Stocks.*
† Average of annual high and low market prices.

Appendix A

American Machine & Foundry Company

GENERAL PROVISIONS FOR CONVERSION OF THE 5 PER CENT DEBENTURE ISSUE, TAKEN FROM THE INDENTURE

· ·

ARTICLE FOUR

CONVERSION OF DEBENTURES

SECTION 4.01. *Conversion Privilege.* Subject to and upon compliance with the provisions of this Article Four, at the option of the holder, any Debenture, or any portion of the principal amount thereof which is $100 or a multiple thereof, may, at any time on or before February 1, 1977, or in case such Debenture or some portion thereof shall be called for redemption prior to such date, then with respect to such portion thereof as is so called, until and including, but (if no default is made in making due provision for the payment of the redemption price) not after, the date fixed for such redemption, be converted at 100% of so much of the principal amount of such Debenture as is so converted, into Common Stock at the conversion price in effect at the date of conversion.

SECTION 4.02. *Manner of Exercise of Conversion Privilege.* In order to exercise the conversion privilege, the holder of any Debenture or Debentures to be converted shall surrender such Debenture or Debentures, together with all unmatured coupons thereto appertaining, if any, to the Company at any time during usual business hours at its office or agency in the Borough of Manhattan, City and State of New York, and shall give written notice to the Company at such office or agency that the holder elects to convert such Debenture or Debentures, or a specified portion thereof. Such notice shall also state the name or names (with address) in which the certificate or certificates for shares of Common Stock which shall be issuable on such conversion shall be issued. . . . Such conversion shall be deemed to have been effected immediately prior to the close of business on the date (hereinafter called the date of conversion) on which such notice shall have been received by the Company and such Debenture or Debentures shall have been surrendered as aforesaid, . . . but such conversion shall be at

855

the conversion price in effect at the close of business on the date of such surrender. No adjustment shall be made for interest accrued on any Debenture that shall be converted or for dividends on any Common Stock that shall be issued upon the conversion of such Debenture as provided in this Article Four.

. . . .

SECTION 4.03. *Fractions of Shares.* The Company shall not be required to issue fractions of shares of Common Stock upon conversions of Debentures. If more than one Debenture shall be surrendered for conversion at one time by the same holder, the number of full shares which shall be issuable upon conversion thereof shall be computed on the basis of the aggregate principal amount of the Debentures (or specified portions thereof) so surrendered. If any fraction of a share of Common Stock would, except for the provisions of this Section 4.03, be issuable on the conversion of any Debenture or Debentures (or specified portions thereof), the Company shall, at its option, either (*a*) purchase such fraction for an amount in cash equal to the current value of such fraction (i) computed, if the Common Stock shall be listed or admitted to unlisted trading privileges on the New York Stock Exchange, on the basis of the last reported sale price of the Common Stock on such Exchange on the last business day prior to the date of conversion upon which such a sale shall have been effected, or (ii) computed, if the Common Stock shall not be so listed or admitted to unlisted trading privileges, on the basis of the average mean of the bid and asked prices for the Common Stock in the over-the-counter market in New York, New York, on the last business day prior to the date of conversion as reported by the National Quotation Bureau, Inc., or (*b*) issue scrip of the Company in lieu thereof. . . .

SECTION 4.04. *Conversion Price.* The basic conversion prices at which Common Stock shall be issuable upon conversion of Debentures shall be the following principal amounts of Debentures for each share of Common Stock: $38.25 if converted on or before February 1, 1967, and $43.25 if converted thereafter and on or before February 1, 1977.

The conversion price shall be the applicable basic conversion price or, after adjustment as provided in this Article Four, the conversion price as so adjusted.

SECTION 4.05. *Adjustment of Conversion Price.* The conversion price shall be subject to adjustment from time to time as follows:

(*a*) Except as hereinafter provided, in case the Company shall at any time after the date of this Indenture issue or sell any shares of Common Stock (including shares held in the Company's treasury) for a consideration per share less than the conversion price in effect immediately prior to the issuance or sale of such shares, or without consideration, then, and thereafter successively upon each such issuance or sale, the conversion price in effect immediately prior to each such issuance or sale shall forthwith be reduced to a price determined by dividing

(i) an amount equal to (*A*) the total number of shares of Common Stock outstanding immediately prior to such issuance or sale multiplied by the conversion price in effect immediately prior to such issuance or sale, plus (*B*) the consideration, if any, received by the Company upon such issuance or sale, by

(ii) the total number of shares of Common Stock outstanding immediately after such issuance or sale.

(*b*) In case the Company shall at any time after the date of this Indenture, issue options or rights to subscribe for shares of Common Stock (including shares held in the Company's treasury), or issue any securities (other than the Debentures, and scrip certificates issued pursuant to Section 4.03) convertible into or exchangeable for shares of Common Stock, for a consideration per share less than the conversion price in effect immediately prior to the issuance of such options or rights or convertible or exchangeable securities, or without consideration, the conversion price in effect immediately prior to the issuance of such options or rights or securities shall be reduced to a price determined by making a computation in accordance with the provisions of subsection (*a*) of this Section 4.05. . . .

(*c*) In case the Company shall at any time subdivide or combine the outstanding shares of Common Stock, the conversion price shall forthwith be proportionately decreased in the case of subdivision or increased in the case of combination.

(*d*) On the date when the new basic conversion price becomes effective (as provided in Section 4.04), the conversion price shall be the last preceding conversion price increased to an amount which shall bear the same proportion to such new basic conversion price as the last preceding conversion price bore to the preceding basic conversion price.

Case 29

Upstate Canning Company, Inc.

DURING THE period following his graduation from a business school in 1950, Mr. Nelson Shields had attempted to prepare himself for the opportunity of becoming the manager and sole or part owner of a company with real growth possibilities. Because he lacked financial resources, he had sought employment which offered substantial immediate income as well as managerial experience which would be useful in later years. This search led him successively through positions in three distinctly different businesses, in each of which experience was largely concentrated in the sales and sales management areas. By 1956, he had accumulated personal savings of $15,000 which, added to some family money placed at his disposal, gave him an investment fund of $35,000.

At this point, Mr. Shields had begun an active search for opportunities to purchase an existing business. In the course of the year, he looked into about 25 possibilities which came to his attention. Some of these were quickly rejected; others involved the expenditure of considerable time and some money before a negative decision was reached. While looking for business possibilities, Shields also sought to develop contacts with business and professional men who might be induced to invest equity capital in an attractive opportunity, should one be found requiring more capital than he possessed. By the end of 1956, Mr. Shields was still investigating business leads, but with no real prospect in sight. Meanwhile, the pressure to settle on a business was increasing. Shields had given up employment in October in order to devote full time to his search, and he realized that he could not afford many months of unemployment without eating into the sum set aside for investment.

In February of 1957 a business broker called Shields to advise him that a small cannery had just come up for sale. The property consisted of two plants, equipped for the canning of fruits and vegetables, which were located close to the source of supply in rural towns in New York State. The business, known as the Upstate Canning Company, Inc., was owned and managed by Mr. A. C. Fordham. Mr. Fordham's health was uncertain and, at 55, he had decided to sell out because he had no relatives to take his place in the business. The broker urged Shields to investigate this opportunity because it looked as though it might fit his circumstances.

Mr. Shields immediately set out to learn what he could about the fruit and vegetable canning industry in general and this business in particular. The broker arranged a meeting with Mr. Fordham; and from this and subsequent meetings and telephone conversations, Mr. Shields assembled a picture of the business.

In general, Mr. Fordham was very co-operative in providing the information requested from him. He was reluctant, however, to disclose the financial details of operations for the three years prior to 1956. During 1952, Fordham had brought in a general manager on a three-year employment contract as a means of easing himself out of the day-to-day responsibilities of the business. The new man had not worked out well, and sales and profits had suffered as a result. Upon the termination of this contract, Fordham had again assumed full management responsibilities, and results in 1956 improved substantially over those of 1953, 1954, and 1955. Fordham argued that these years were not representative of the earnings potential of the business and that 1956 should be taken as the most accurate measure of its possibilities. From what Shields had been able to find out about the business from other sources, he was inclined to accept Fordham's explanation and to base his estimates on the figures for 1956.

The physical plant of the business appeared to be in very good condition. The two buildings had been kept in excellent repair, and the canning equipment was modern. The combined plant and equipment had recently been appraised for insurance purposes, and their value had been placed at $200,000. Shields was assured that no major repairs would be necessary over the next few years.

Mr. Fordham had been accustomed to operating the plants only during the limited harvest season for the fruits and vegetables which he canned. The season lasted for four months, from July through October, with August and September normally accounting for two thirds of the company's total production. At times, Fordham had considered stretching out the production period with other canning operations, but he had never taken any action on the idea. During the 1956 season, Upstate had produced canned fruits and vegetables with a total value of $850,000 (valued at Upstate's selling price). This production represented only about 50% of combined productive capacity of the plants during the production season. Excess capacity was attributed to the substantial expansion of facilities which had been undertaken to meet wartime demands.

The vegetables and fruits canned by Upstate were bought on a contract basis from farmers in the surrounding area; farmers were paid cash on delivery on the basis of prevailing market prices at the time of delivery. The quantities canned by Upstate varied to some extent with the crop conditions from year to year; normally, output could be increased considerably, however, by noncontract purchases, if good marketing opportunities existed. The production process was almost entirely mechanical, and the towns and surrounding areas offered an ample supply of seasonal labor sufficiently skilled to perform the various operations in the plant. Labor was paid on a weekly basis.

The products of the Upstate Canning Company were marketed primarily under the Upstate brand through jobbers. It was the normal practice to sell the entire season's pack before the next canning season began, so that little inventory would be carried over from one year to the next. Sales tended to be concentrated during and immediately following the production period. Fordham indicated that about 50% of the pack would normally be sold by the end of the canning season (October) and 70% by the end of December. The balance of sales was customarily spread rather evenly over the remaining months through June.

Mr. Shields was particularly attracted by the marketing opportunities of the business. It was his impression that Fordham had not been aggressive in sales promotion—that much better use could be made of the company's productive capacity. Shields believed that he could greatly increase the scale of operations by undertaking an active but relatively inexpensive sales program. He had in mind direct sales to supermarket chains of both Upstate and private brands to be obtained largely through his own efforts with no significant increase in present selling costs.

Relying on these expectations, Shields prepared a five-year sales program (see Exhibit 1) which he planned to use as the basis of his estimates of profits and working capital requirements. He was informed by Fordham that collections on accounts receivable caused little trouble in this business; bad debt losses were rare, and accounts were normally collected within 30 days. Shields expected that the planned expansion would not affect this collection period and might even improve it because he would be increasing direct sales to large accounts.

In examining the cost aspects of the business, Shields soon became aware of the high proportion of variable costs. The principal items were the fruits and vegetables and other ingredients, cans, and direct labor. As previously indicated, fruits and vegetables were bought on a cash basis, labor was paid weekly at fixed hourly rates, and cans and "other ingredients" were purchased on normal terms of 2/10, net 30 days. The details of revenues and costs for 1956 are shown in Exhibits 2 and 3.

As negotiations proceeded, it became evident that Fordham was anxious to sell the business as soon as possible. The new crop season was coming on; and Fordham felt that if he were to operate the business for another year, it would soon be necessary to sign contracts with farmers for the year's production. After three weeks, during which Shields was gathering and studying information and talking to bankers, can company officials, government agencies, and others, Fordham came forward with a specific proposal for the sale of the business (see Exhibit 4).

The plan anticipated that Shields would organize a new company and purchase certain Upstate assets, namely, its plant and equipment, a small amount of finished goods inventory, and the right to use the Upstate brand names. Current assets (other than the inventory mentioned above) and liabilities of the old company would not pass to the new company. It was apparent from the plan that Fordham had guessed that Shields had very limited resources and, accordingly, had provided for an instalment purchase of Upstate assets through the gradual redemption of $300,000 of income bonds to be issued to Fordham. By this time, Shields had become convinced that this business was sufficiently promising to justify a full and detailed study of Fordham's proposal.

Before accepting Fordham's proposal or making a counterproposal, it was necessary for Shields to determine how the new company was to be financed. His best lead for additional equity capital was a professional man who had indicated that he was prepared to invest as much as $100,000 if the right opportunity came along. This man was 50 years of age, and his investment goal appeared to be that of capital appreciation over the years rather than immediate income.

Shields was determined that the plan for the new company would include a means by which he could become the owner of 51 per cent of the voting stock as soon as possible. More specifically, he hoped to obtain control within five years, and hence was intent on arranging a compensation plan for himself as manager which would enable him to accomplish this objective. Shields's plan, as tentatively formulated, provided for a basic salary of $15,000 plus 5% of profits before taxes; these figures took account of his estimate that roughly 60% of his annual income would be absorbed by living expenses and tax payments. His plan also included an option to buy enough additional shares—either new shares to be issued by the company or outstanding shares held by his associate(s)—to raise Shields's holdings to 51 per cent of all outstanding voting stock. It was clear, however, that the exact details of the final plan would have to be worked out with the other shareholder or shareholders before arrangements could be completed with Fordham.

As part of his program to assure an adequate supply of capital, Mr. Shields obtained an introduction, through a mutual friend, to one of the officers of a medium-sized bank in a nearby city. This officer indicated that it was the bank's normal policy to avoid substantial loans to new enterprises, but that exceptions were occasionally made where there was adequate security. Canning operations were important to the surrounding area, and he suggested that the bank might consider a secured loan to the new company if it looked promising on closer examination. From further conversation, Shields concluded that the best possibility would be a loan of up to 75 per cent of the cost of finished goods inventory under a field warehousing arrangement. The cost of this kind of financing, including field warehousing expenses, which would not otherwise have been incurred, would be about 6 per cent per annum. In addition to the bank loan, Shields also believed that it might be possible to stretch the payment period on cans to 60 days without creating serious credit problems.

In considering his preliminary calculations, Shields planned to make a detailed study of the year 1957–58 and to use this as a basis for approximating the necessary figures for the fiscal years 1958–59 through 1961–62. He had in mind a fiscal year beginning July 1.

Shields was aware that the next move was up to him. As he saw it, there were three obvious courses of action: (1) accept Fordham's proposal as presented; (2) reject the proposal and look for another business; (3) propose a compromise plan which would have a reasonable prospect of meeting the objectives of all interested parties.

Exhibit 1

UPSTATE CANNING COMPANY, INC.

PLANNED SALES VOLUME, 1957–1962

1957–1958	$ 850,000
1958–1959	1,050,000
1959–1960	1,250,000
1960–1961	1,450,000
1961–1962	1,650,000

Exhibit 2

UPSTATE CANNING COMPANY, INC.

INCOME STATEMENT FOR YEAR ENDED DEC. 31, 1956

(Dollar figures in thousands)

		Amount	*Per Cent of Sales*
Sales (net after returns and allowances)		$850	100%
Less: Cost of goods sold			
Beginning inventory, Jan. 1, 1956	$257		
Add: Cost of goods manufactured	630		
	$887		
Less: Ending inventory, December 31, 1956	254	633	74
Gross profit on sales		$217	
Less: Selling and administrative expense			
Selling and delivery	$ 64		8
Administrative and general (including salary to			
Fordham of $20,000)	56	120	7
Profit before taxes		$ 97	
Less: Federal income tax*		45	5
Net profit after taxes		$ 52	6

* Federal income tax is computed on the basis of 30% of the first $25,000 of taxable income plus 52% of income in excess of $25,000. For companies of this size the tax is payable in the succeeding fiscal year as follows: 50% on the 15th day of the 3d month following the end of the tax year and 50% on the 15th day of the 6th month following.

Exhibit 3

UPSTATE CANNING COMPANY, INC.

STATEMENT OF COST OF GOODS MANUFACTURED FOR
YEAR ENDED DEC. 31, 1956

(Dollar figures in thousands)

	Amount	Per Cent of Total Cost of Goods Manufactured
Direct costs		
Vegetables and fruit	$232	
Labor	138	
Cans	112	
Other ingredients	36	$518	82%
Variable overhead		
Fuel oil	$ 17	
Electricity and water	7	
Factory supplies	5	
Payroll taxes	7	
Truck and auto expenses	2	
Gas and oil	5	43	7
Fixed overhead		
Repairs and maintenance	$ 18	
Insurance	12	
Property taxes	10	
Depreciation—plant and equipment	24	
Machinery rental	5	$ 69	11
Total cost of goods manufactured		$630	100%

Exhibit 4

UPSTATE CANNING COMPANY, INC.

INITIAL PROPOSAL BY MR. FORDHAM FOR THE PURCHASE OF CERTAIN ASSETS OF THE UPSTATE CANNING COMPANY, INC., BY MR. SHIELDS AND ASSOCIATE(S)

1. New corporation to be formed with capitalization of $400,000 and with a capital structure as follows:

   a) $100,000 of common stock, $1.00 par, one vote per share, to be issued to Shields and associate(s) for $100,000 cash. Cash to be retained in new corporation.

   b) $300,000 of income bonds due on June 1, 1967; 3% interest per annum, payable semiannually (June 1 and December 1) if and when earned, cumulative, to be issued to Fordham in exchange for all plant and equipment of Upstate Canning Company, $50,000 of salable finished goods inventory, and the right to use the brand names of the Upstate Canning Company. (Prior to the exchange, the Upstate Canning Company will be liquidated and the assets distributed to Fordham as sole owner.)

2. Repayment provisions of income bonds:

   a) Company to repurchase $50,000 of income bonds on or before June 1, 1958.

   b) In succeeding years, company to repurchase income bonds equivalent in par value to 50% of the net profit after taxes, provided that the amount in any year will be no less than $15,000. The $15,000 will be due on June 1, and any balance within thirty days after the close of the fiscal year.

   c) Company to have the option of purchasing any amount of income bonds in excess of the minimum requirements according to a schedule of discounted prices as follows: in the first year at 80% of par, in the second year at 82½% of par, in the third year at 85% of par, and so on.

3. No fixed assets to be sold or encumbered in any way without the consent of the income bondholders.

4. Control of the company to be divided equally between the income bondholders and the common shareholders until the income bonds have been completely retired. Each group will elect two directors to a four-man board.

5. Fordham to act as chairman of the board and receive compensation for whatever time he spends on operating matters, beyond board meetings, on a basis to be determined in further negotiations.

6. Shields to act as president and general manager.

7. New company to be incorporated and assets of Upstate to be acquired on or about June 1, 1957. In the meantime, it is to be understood that Fordham and Shields will work together in negotiating contracts with farmers and arranging for an orderly transfer of ownership.

Case 30

Lestoil Products, Inc.

IN EARLY June, 1960, Mr. John Bolten, Sr. and Mr. Daniel E. Hogan, Jr., members of the executive committee of Lestoil Products, Inc., were studying the details of a proposed offering of the company's capital stock, which was to be traded over the counter. In light of the company's past record, its potential future earnings, and the terms of the issue, they were confident that the proposed stock would be sold with little difficulty. In this final analysis of the offering, they concentrated particularly on the price of the stock to the public. They believed that the offering price would certainly be attractive. They thought, however, that the offering was perhaps underpriced, and questioned whether the company should offer fewer units at a higher price to raise the necessary funds.

Company Background

Lestoil Products, Inc., was organized in the spring of 1960 for the purpose of purchasing Adell Chemical Company, Inc.; its wholly owned advertising affiliate, Jackson Associates, Inc.; and its wholly owned real estate subsidiary, J.L.B. Realty Trust. Adell Chemical Company had been organized in 1933 by Mr. Jacob L. Barowsky to manufacture and sell a synthetic liquid detergent. Until 1954, sales had been made primarily to commercial laundries and the paper and textile industries. In that year the Adell Company brought its detergent to the attention of the household trade through spot television advertising. The company later added several other items, including a concentrated, premeasured dry bleach sealed in individual, water-soluble packets. The two principal products, the detergent and the bleach, were widely advertised and known under the trade names of "Lestoil" and "Lestare." The company's offices and manufacturing facilities were located in Holyoke, Massachusetts. Financial data for Lestoil Products' predecessor are presented in Exhibits 1 and 2.

Acquisition of Adell Chemical Company, Inc.

In early 1960, Mr. Barowsky, the president and founder of Adell Chemical Company, decided to find a buyer for the company. He turned down several offers. One company, for instance, offered $8,000,000 in its own stock and $4,000,000 in cash, but Mr. Barowsky wanted a cash sale. Another company offered $7,000,000 in cash, but Mr. Barowsky thought that this amount was not enough. Mr. Samuel S. Dennis III, a member of the law firm of Hale and Dorr of Boston, Massachusetts, who had been counsel to the Adell Company, had been attempting to aid Mr. Barowsky in finding a buyer.

Mr. Dennis was also associated with a family group in Andover, Massachusetts, headed by Mr. Bolten, Sr., and Mr. Hogan, respectively chairman of the board and president of the Standard International Corporation. This corporation was a closely held investment company with substantial interests in a number of corporations. During the time that Mr. Dennis was trying to locate a buyer for Adell Chemical Company, he, Mr. Bolten, and Mr. Hogan concluded that perhaps a group associated with Standard International would find it worth while to buy the company. Recognizing a possible conflict of interest, Mr. Dennis immediately notified Mr. Barowsky that he should obtain new legal counsel to represent him in this transaction.

As the result of further negotiations a contract, dated March 25, 1960, was entered into between Adell Chemical Company and its stockholders as sellers and Standard International Corporation and Mr. Hogan, acting for himself and as agent for Mr. John Bolten, Sr., Mr. John Bolten, Jr., and Mr. Dennis, as purchasers. Lestoil Products, Inc., was formed subsequently by the purchasing group to become the acquiring corporation.

Lestoil Products agreed to pay the sellers a cash price of $8,000,000 and also agreed to assume a conditional liability to pay an additional sum in the maximum amount of $4,000,000. Payments on the conditional obligation were required to be made annually but only to the extent of one half of annual net profits in excess of $1,500,000 after income taxes. The obligation would expire on October 31, 1969, whether or not the maximum amount had been paid in full.

The purchase and sale agreement called for a deposit of $150,000 as option money and gave the purchasing group ninety days to complete the transaction. This sum was to be forfeited as damages in the

event that the transaction was not completed within this period. The
Standard International Corporation advanced the option money. In
addition, employment contracts were made with three of the former
officers for five years, beginning on June 1, 1960, at the following
salaries:

	First Year	Annually, Last Four Years
Jacob L. Barowsky	$100,000	$ 50,000
Isaac L. Eskenasy	30,000	30,000
Aaron L. Kingsberg	20,000	20,000
	$150,000	$100,000

These officers had received compensation at a higher rate in recent
years.

Mr. Hogan had always kept a business diary. The entries in the
spring of 1960 included a chronological account of the important
dates and events in connection with the acquisition of Adell Chemical
Company. A summary of these entries from February 1 to March 25
is given below:

1960

Monday, February 1—In Palm Beach with Sam Dennis. He called the president of a chemical company in New York and told him about the availability
of Adell Chemical and suggested that his company consider the possibility of
adding it as one of their divisions.

Friday, March 4—While in New York on another matter with Mr. Dennis,
we decided to visit the president of the chemical company personally and
tell him the latest news about Adell Chemical and give him the reasons why
his company should buy it, etc. En route to Boston the next day, the thought
occurred to us that maybe we could put together a group or a transaction
that would be attractive to all concerned, and where Standard International
and its stockholders could end up with a fairly good-sized piece of the Adell
equity.

Tuesday, March 8—Visit to Boston and preliminary discussions with
Mr. William L. Brown, vice president of the First National Bank of Boston,
regarding interim financing.

Wednesday, March 9—Visit to Holyoke and preliminary discussion with
Mr. and Mrs. Barowsky.

Thursday, March 10—Conferences in Boston regarding the amount and
terms of the loan which the bank was willing to give us to finance the
purchase.

[At this early stage of negotiations the bank indicated a willingness to
provide $7–$8,000,000 in "turn-around money" at an interest rate of 5½%.
The stocks of Lestoil Products and of Standard International were to be
pledged as security.]

Friday, March 11—Conferences in Boston with law firm of Hale and Dorr
to go over the preliminary drafts of the proposed employment contract for
the owners of Adell Chemical.

Saturday, March 12—Skiing at Mittersill and met Mr. [X] of a law firm in New York with contacts which might be helpful in a public underwriting.

Monday, March 14—Conferences at Holyoke with Mr. and Mrs. Barowsky.

Tuesday, March 15—Conference at the First National Bank of Boston with the senior loan officer.

Wednesday, March 16—Conference at Andover with Gale Deam and Charles McCarthy, who would be the vice presidents for manufacturing and sales in the new Lestoil organization. Aaron Kingsberg of Adell phoned to emphasize the fact that we would have to show them definitely where the $8,000,000 is coming from fairly soon.

Thursday, March 17—With McCarthy, Deam, and Sol Sackell, who will be in charge of advertising activities, to Holyoke for more negotiations regarding the purchase and sale contract.

Friday, March 18—In Andover and Boston, going over the various projections involved in paying off the interim bank loan.

Sunday, March 20—Conversations with S. Dennis about various financing alternatives.

Monday, March 21—In New Hampshire, conversations with Mr. [M] regarding the possibility of his firm's joining in an underwriting group re: Lestoil Products, Inc.

Tuesday, March 22—In Jackson, New Hampshire, more conversations with Mr. [M].

Wednesday, March 23—In New York City, initial conferences with institutional lenders regarding the possibility of their putting up $3–$4,000,000 of subordinated funds.

Thursday, March 24—In Andover, conversations with Mr. Bolten, Sr. and Mr. Bolten, Jr., regarding progress of the Lestoil situation.

Friday, March 25—Signing of purchase and sale agreement of Adell Chemical.

Financing the Acquisition

The formal closing of the purchase and sale transaction took place on May 31, 1960, when Lestoil Products paid $8,000,000 in cash to the sellers. It had raised the necessary funds to finance the acquisition of Adell Chemical Company in the following manner:

Sale of Lestoil common stock at 60 cents a share:

Purchasers	Shares	Amount
Standard International Corporation	249,406	
John Bolten, Sr.	396,599	
John Bolten, Jr.	396,598	
Daniel E. Hogan, Jr.	396,599	
Samuel S. Dennis, III	396,598	
Total	1,835,800	$1,101,480
Loan to Lestoil Products from The First National Bank of Boston on a demand promissory note		6,900,000
		$8,001,480

The bank loan was a temporary one, which had been granted to serve only as "turn-around money" while Lestoil Products raised permanent capital to finance the acquisition. The purchasers had spent the past two months working out the details of the permanent financing.

As one part of the financing, on May 27, 1960, the company received letters of commitment from representatives of institutional investors (several pension funds) stating their intention to purchase $3,200,000 principal amount of the company's 6¼% notes due in 1970, together with detachable and transferable ten-year warrants, protected against dilution, for the purchase of a total of 339,200 shares of common stock at $7.50 a share.[1] The agreement provided that the obligation of the institutional lenders was conditional on the sale by Lestoil Products to the public of certain of its equity securities as outlined in management's proposal for a public offering to raise approximately $4,000,000. Any excess over the $6,900,000 needed to repay the bank loan was to be used for general corporate purposes.

Important provisions of the loan agreement relating to the 6¼% notes to be purchased by the institutional lenders were as follows: Annual instalments on principal were payable in the amount of $300,000. The notes were redeemable for the first two years at a premium of 10%; the premium would be 4% for the third year, and then would diminish annually at the rate of 1% a year until 1966, after which date the notes would be redeemable at par. The company could not create liens or mortgages other than for the purpose of financing a maximum of 70% of plant and equipment purchases. It was required to maintain a minimum net working capital balance of $1,200,000 during the period July 1, 1961–June 30, 1962, and $1,500,000 after June 30, 1962. It was prohibited from making distributions on account of the common stock until such time and also thereafter if, as a result, consolidated net working capital would be less than $2,500,000. The notes were subordinated to bank loans up to a maximum of $3,000,000, which under certain circumstances could be increased to a maximum of $5,000,000.

The Public Offering of Equity Securities

The major part of the funds needed were to be raised by a public offering of equity securities. Mr. Hogan and a representative of one

---

[1] When the financing was completed, 339,200 shares would be approximately 14% of the common stock before conversion of the Class A shares, and approximately 11% after conversion.

of the two underwriting firms involved had conceived a plan that they believed would aid in assuring the success of the offering. The securities designed for the public sale were to be split into Class A shares and common shares and sold in units consisting of one common share and one Class A share. Certificates representing units were to be issued to purchasers. On January 2, 1961, the shares of Class A and common stock composing a unit would become separately transferable, and certificates representing units would become exchangeable for separate certificates for shares of Class A and common stock.

A complex of factors actually determined the size and price of the offering. The offerors naturally wanted the offering to be successful and hoped, therefore, that no questions would be raised regarding its attractiveness. At the same time, they wanted to hold dilution of their equity within reasonable limits. They knew that Mr. Barowsky had talked earlier with several investment banking houses regarding the possibility of selling the stock of Adell Chemical Company publicly. These discussions had indicated some interest on the part of investment bankers in underwriting such an issue at a price/earnings ratio of 15/1. Thus, from the start, the Standard International group had based its thinking on a price/earnings ratio in this range.

In preliminary talks with representatives of underwriting firms, an offering of only one class of common stock had been proposed. After a review of the situation the underwriters replied that, in their opinion, the company's earnings were not sufficiently stable to justify a 15/1 price/earnings ratio on a straight common issue. The package of two classes of stock was then conceived and decided upon, one class bearing a fixed and cumulative preferred dividend obligation, to add the appeal of an assured return to the offering for the investing public. As an additional capital gains incentive, the Class A stock would be made convertible into common stock at any time prior to redemption and within a limited time after any call for redemption.

On the basis of earnings after taxes in the year ended October 31, 1959, adjusted to allow for 6¼% interest payments on the notes to be purchased by institutional lenders, it was estimated that earnings after interest and taxes in future years were likely to be at least $1,-000,000. The offerors and underwriters agreed that a fixed dividend commitment on Class A stock should be covered a minimum of four times if it and the common stock were to be looked on with favor by investors. A computation revealed that it would be possible to maintain this coverage and still offer as much as a 6% return on the total funds to be raised through the offering ($4,000,000).

With this information at hand, specific details of the offering were "backed into." The conversion ratio of the Class A stock was set at two shares of common stock for each share of Class A, and a price of $14.40 and 60 cents, respectively ($15 a unit), was placed on the Class A and common shares on a total offering of 275,000 units—primarily on the following basis: It was determined that a fair offering price for the common shares would be the same as the Standard International group had paid for their shares, namely, 60 cents. The price and conversion ratio of the Class A stock were then determined at the amount per share that would give a price/earnings ratio of approximately 15/1 on the whole package, allowing for probable future dilution from the warrants issued to institutional investors. This automatically gave an acceptable result in terms of equity dilution on the basis of a $4,000,000 offering. The preferred dividend was then determined at 90 cents, to give a 6% plus return on the Class A shares. Other factors involved in setting the conversion privilege at two shares of common for each share of Class A were (1) to give additional desirability to the offering and (2) to be substantially consistent with the $7.50 warrant price to institutional investors.

	Shares of Common Stock	Percentage
Owned by promoting group	1,835,800	61.2
Reserved for exercise of warrants	339,200	11.3
Sold to public (275,000 units):		
Common stock	275,000	9.2
Reserved for conversion of Class A shares	550,000	18.3
Total	3,000,000	100.0

Earnings for year ended October 31, 1959 (adjusted)	$1,000,000
Total shares of common stock to be outstanding	3,000,000
Earnings per share	$ 0.333
Offering price per unit	$ 15.00
Effective cost to public per share of common stock	$ 5.00
Effective price/earnings ratio (after dilution)	15/1

Both the Standard International group and the underwriters were confident that this combination would make an attractive package for sale to the public.[2]

The "red-herring" prospectus[3] for the public offering was completed early in June, 1960. Other provisions of the two classes of

---

[2] Exhibit 3 presents selected data on certain other companies, and Exhibit 4 gives data from *Moody's Industrial Stock Averages.*

[3] Eric L. Kohler, *A Dictionary for Accountants* (2d ed.; Englewood Cliffs, N.J.: Prentice-Hall, Inc., 1957), p. 410, defines *red-herring prospectus* as follows: "An announcement and description of an anticipated issue of securities, given restricted circulation during the "waiting" period of 20 days or other specified period between the filing of a registration statement with the U.S. Securities and Exchange Commission and the effective date of the statement. It generally takes the form of the final prospectus except that

stock were described as follows: A provision was included for adjustment of the conversion ratio to prevent dilution of the rights of Class A shareholders. The Class A stock had a liquidation and redemption value of $15 a share. No dividends could be paid on the common stock while any shares of Class A stock were outstanding, and the prospectus stated that no dividends on the common stock should be expected in the near future. Management intended to retain all earnings until a substantial amount of working capital had been accumulated. The common shares and the Class A shares were entitled to one vote each and would vote together as a single class except where the separate consent of Class A shares was required.

Conferences with underwriters indicated an underwriting commission of 8%. Net proceeds to the company would therefore amount to $3,795,000. The effects of the proposed financing on the company's balance sheet and earnings statements are shown in the pro forma financial statements presented as Exhibits 5 and 6.

Mr. Hogan's business diary noted the development of the plans for the permanent financing:

Saturday, March 26—Conference in New York City with underwriters' representatives re: first studies as to the various methods that could be used in the Lestoil underwriting. We first came up with the possibility of the Class A and common stocks package at this conference.

Sunday, March 27—More conferences, New York City—conversations with Sam Dennis regarding the present proposal for the packaged security.

Monday, March 28—Additional conferences in New York City with representatives of the two underwriting firms.

Tuesday, March 29—We are now in effect running Lestoil. Held conferences with McCarthy, Deam, and others regarding immediate steps that should be taken to strengthen the business.

Wednesday, March 30—Conferences with the Barowskys at Holyoke on what is needed in Lestoil.

Friday, April 1—Finalized the arrangements with underwriters.

Monday, April 4—Conferences in New York with institutional lenders to discuss the intermediate financing plans and subordinated notes.

Tuesday, April 5—At Holyoke planning Lestoil strategy.

Wednesday, April 6—Left Holyoke with Mr. Barowsky, to packaging show in Atlantic City.

Thursday, April 7—Conference in New York City with a chemical company regarding possibility of bringing out a liquid starch made from their synthetic resins.

the offering price, commissions to dealers, and other data dependent on price are omitted; also emblazoned across each page is an inscription printed in red, stating that the document is not an offer to sell or the solicitation of an offer to buy and that neither kind of offer may be made until the registration statement has become effective."

Tuesday, April 12—Picked up representatives of the pension funds in Morristown, New Jersey, and flew them to Lestoil at Holyoke for the day. [One of the corporations controlled by Standard International owned an airplane as its only asset. Mr. Hogan held a pilot's license and often flew the plane on such trips.]

Thursday, April 14—Conferences in Boston regarding the closing of the Lestoil deal and the details of the underwriting.

Friday, April 15—In Andover and Boston, discussing details of financing with Messrs. Bolten, Senior and Junior. Then a luncheon conference with firm of Hale and Dorr to begin giving them the background work for the registration statement.

Monday, April 18—On the phone most of the day with representatives of pension funds trying to work out the details of their financing versus the underwriting. Pension funds thought the underwriters' deal was too rich, and the underwriters felt that the pension funds were asking for too much. [The institutional lenders thought that the underwriters were making the package more attractive than necessary to raise $4,000,000. The underwriters thought that the institutional lenders were getting too many warrants for purchase of stock at $7.50 a share.]

Tuesday, April 19—Writing up the brochure for consideration by the pension funds committees to help push the financing of the subordinated notes.

Thursday, April 21—Conferences in Boston with the underwriter. Then meeting with president of [XYZ Company]. He was interested in buying Lestoil. We had many feelers from various companies wanting to know if we would like to turn over our deal to them. [Mr. Hogan did not investigate any of these offers in any depth.]

Friday, April 22—Conferences wih underwriter in Boston.

Saturday and Sunday, April 23 and 24—Revising the brochure for the underwriters and the pension fund.

April 25–May 31—A lot of activity on the promotions at Lestoil, details of the underwriting, preparing the details for the SEC, etc.

Tuesday, May 31—We had the closing at The First National Bank of Boston.

Future Prospects

Lestoil Products maintained a research department to study production methods, quality controls, and development of new products by applying to practical uses current discoveries and developments in chemical science. The management intended to place the emphasis almost entirely on development and improvement of discoveries made by others in the field, rather than emphasizing basic research. The policy of the company would be to add new items for family and household use to its product line if and when suitable products were developed and proved. Management's objective was to develop and market companion products to Lestoil and Lestare, and thus offer a "family" of Lestoil products to the consumer.

In 1959, some of the major soap and detergent companies had introduced new brands of heavy-duty liquid detergents, accompanied by extensive television advertising and other unusually intensive methods of sales promotion. Partly as a result of this competition, sales of Lestoil had declined since September, 1959. Industry sales were also seasonally lower during the winter months. The new owners believed, however, that no permanent or continuing adverse trends in sales volume were necessarily indicated. In fact, they thought that a seasonal increase in industry sales, improvements in sales management, rapidly increasing sales of Lestare, and plans to advertise and market company products in the Western and Southwestern parts of the United States in the immediate future would push sales volumes to new highs. They felt that company profits before taxes during the calendar year 1960 could reasonably be expected to reach a level of $3,000,000, and that the before-tax profits for 1961 were likely to show an increase over the 1960 level. In their opinion, existing plant facilities would be adequate for some time. The company's net cash inflow during the next few years would therefore be substantial.

At this time the Standard International group foresaw no need for additional common stock issues in the future. In fact, they had stated that company policy would be to avoid any such dilution if at all possible. Acquisitions by or additions to Lestoil Products would be made with cash and new debt, with sale of equity only as a last resort.

Exhibit 1

LESTOIL PRODUCTS, INC.

CONSOLIDATED STATEMENT OF FINANCIAL CONDITION OF
ADELL CHEMICAL COMPANY, INC., AND SUBSIDIARIES
ON MARCH 31, 1960

(Dollar figures in thousands)

ASSETS

Current assets:

Cash and U.S. Treasury bills	$1,614	
Accounts receivable	1,605	
Inventories (at lower of cost or market)	1,304	
Other	65	
Total Current Assets		$4,588
Fixed assets (net)		3,415
Other assets		184
Total Assets		$8,187

LIABILITIES AND CAPITAL

Current liabilities:

Notes payable (banks)	$1,140	
Other	2,465	
Total Current Liabilities		$3,605
Noncurrent liabilities*		1
Capital stock and retained earnings		4,581
Total Liabilities and Capital		$8,187

* Commitments for noncancelable media advertising for a three-month period amounted to approximately $1,500,000.

Exhibit 2

LESTOIL PRODUCTS, INC.

CONSOLIDATED STATEMENTS OF INCOME AND EXPENSE OF ADELL CHEMICAL COMPANY, INC., AND SUBSIDIARIES, 1955–60

(Dollar figures in thousands)

	Year Ended October 31					Five Months Ended March 31	
	1955	1956	1957	1958	1959	1959	1960
Net sales	$474	$1,641	$7,220	$19,945	$22,467	$9,158	$8,719
Cost of sales*	218	625	2,553	7,319	8,731	3,399	3,959
Gross profit	$256	$1,016	$4,667	$12,626	$13,736	$5,759	$4,760
Advertising expense	$125	$ 497	$2,033	$ 6,008	$ 9,562	$3,648	$3,027
Selling, general, and administrative expenses	100	191	650	1,666	1,974	859	825
	$225	$ 688	$2,683	$ 7,674	$11,536	$4,507	$3,852
Net operating income	$ 31	$ 328	$1,984	$ 4,952	$ 2,200	$1,252	$ 908
Other income (expense):							
Interest income	$.....	$.....	$ 6	$ 9	$ 7	$ 6	$ 5
Miscellaneous	(2)	5	14	80	113	41	26
Interest expense	.....	(1)	(3)	(14)	(26)	(7)	(24)
	$(2)	$ 4	$ 17	$ 75	$ 94	$ 40	$ 7
Net income before taxes	$ 29	$ 332	$2,001	$ 5,027	$ 2,294	$1,292	$ 915
Provision for federal and state income taxes	10	178	1,091	2,763	1,226	695	499
Net Income	$ 19	$ 154	$ 910	$ 2,264	$ 1,068	$ 597	$ 416

* Depreciation charges included:
Year ended October 31:
1955 .... n.a.
1956 .... n.a.
1957 .... $ 49
1958 192
1959 318
Five months ended March 31:
1959 .... n.a.
1960 .... $168

Exhibit 3

LESTOIL PRODUCTS, INC.

SELECTED DATA ON CERTAIN COMPANIES IN THE SAME AND RELATED FIELDS OF BUSINESS

	Where Traded	Price/Earnings Ratios (1)*	(2)†	Cash Dividend Yield on Common Stock, 1959‡	Sales Year Ended	Amount (Millions)	Date	Capitalization Long-Term Debt	Preferred Stock	Common Stock and Surplus
Lestoil Products Inc. (pro forma)	O.C.	15§		6.0%#	10/31/59	$22.5	3/31/60	39.5%	45.0%	15.5%
Purex Corporation, Ltd.	O.C.	20	18	2.4%	6/30/59	$71.4	6/30/59	39.1%	.....	60.9%
Procter & Gamble Company	NYSE	20	24	2.7%	6/30/59	$1,368.5	6/30/59	14.7%	0.3%	85.0%
Stepan Chemical Company	O.C.	21	18	0.0%	12/31/59	$19.4	12/31/59	36.2%	.....	63.8%
Wyandotte Chemical Corporation	O.C.	20	28	1.9%	12/31/59	$93.9	12/31/59	10.1%	14.8%	75.1%
Witco Chemical Company, Inc.	O.C.	17	11	2.5%	12/31/59	$51.2	12/31/59	.....	.....	100.0%

Purex Corporation, Ltd. Manufactures and sells bleaches, disinfectants, synthetic detergents, ammonia, and other soaps, cleaners, and toiletries. Products are sold under a variety of trade names. Company was established in year 1927.

Procter & Gamble Company. Constitutes the largest factor in the domestic soap industry. Manufactures and sells soap, toothpaste, synthetic detergents, household cleansers, glycerine, cooking fats, peanut butter, cake mixes, and a variety of other products. Its products are marketed under numerous trade names. Company was established in year 1905.

Stepan Chemical Company. Manufactures organic chemicals which are sold primarily to processors and industrial users. Products include liquid detergents, chemicals for cosmetics, emulsifiers, insecticides, flavoring compounds, liquid fertilizers, and others. Company was established in year 1932.

Wyandotte Chemical Corporation. Produces cleansing products, sanitizing products, soda ash, caustic soda, chlorine, glycols, coke, cement, and other products. Sales are made primarily to industrial users. The existing company was incorporated in year 1942.

Witco Chemical Company, Inc. Produces chemicals, synthetic detergents, metallic stearates, emulsifiers, plasticizers, asphalts, and other products. Sales are made largely to industrial users. Company was formed in year 1920.

* Bid prices (or closing prices) on December 31, 1959, divided by earnings for year ended December 31, 1959.
† Bid prices (or closing prices) on May 31, 1960, divided by earnings for quarter ended March 31, 1960, on an annual basis.
‡ Annual cash dividend rate, divided by average of high and low market prices for the year.
§ Effective price/earnings ratio (after dilution) based on effective offering price per share of common stock ($5.00) divided by earnings for year ended October 31, 1959.
# Yield on offering price of unit.
SOURCE OF BASIC DATA: *Moody's Industrials.*

Exhibit 4

LESTOIL PRODUCTS, INC.

SELECTED DATA FROM "MOODY'S INDUSTRIAL STOCK AVERAGES"

MOODY'S INDUSTRIAL STOCK AVERAGES—
PRICE/EARNINGS RATIOS*

1955	12
1956	14
1957	14
1958	18
1959	19

* Moody's annual composite weighted average prices, divided by composite weighted average earnings for corresponding years (125 common stocks).

MOODY'S PREFERRED STOCK YIELD AVERAGES

	10 Medium-Grade Industrials	10 Speculative-Grade Industrials
1959	4.99%	5.58%
1960:		
January	5.23	5.78
February	5.22	5.72
March	5.21	5.79
April	5.25	5.80

Exhibit 5

LESTOIL PRODUCTS, INC.

PRO FORMA BALANCE SHEET GIVING EFFECT TO THE PROPOSED FINANCING
AS IF THE ACQUISITION TRANSACTION HAD BEEN COMPLETED
ON MARCH 31, 1960

(Dollar figures in thousands)

ASSETS

Current assets:

Cash and U.S. Treasury bills	$1,889	
Accounts receivable	1,605	
Inventories (at lower of cost or market)*	1,374	
Other*	58	
Total Current Assets		$ 4,926
Fixed assets (net)*		4,077
Other assets†		2,760
Total Assets		$11,763

LIABILITIES AND CAPITAL

Current liabilities:

Notes payable (bank)	$1,140	
Other‡	2,525	
Total Current Liabilities		$ 3,665
Noncurrent liabilities:		
6¼% notes		3,200
Other§		1
Capital stock:		
Class A (convertible, no par value; 275,000 shares)	$3,644	
Common stock (50¢ par value; 2,110,800 shares)	1,055	
		4,699
Capital paid in in excess of par value of common stock		198
Total Liabilities and Capital		$11,763

* Reflects adjustments made on the basis of values as determined by the new management and supported by independent appraisal.

† Reflects excess of cost of total assets over the amount allocated to tangible assets. Payments on the $4,000,000 conditional liability were to be allocated to intangible assets also.

‡ Reflects adjustment for estimated organization and financing charges in connection with acquisition transaction.

§ Commitments for noncancelable media advertising for a three-month period amounted to approximately $1,500,000.

Exhibit 6

LESTOIL PRODUCTS, INC.

PRO FORMA EARNINGS AS IF THE ACQUISITION TRANSACTION HAD BEEN EFFECTIVE
DURING THE PERIODS COVERED

(Dollar figures in thousands)

	Years Ended October 31		Five Months Ended March 31, 1960
	1958	1959	
Net income after taxes (as reported)	$2,264	$1,068	$ 416
Pro forma adjustments:			
Interest on 6¼% notes	$(200)	$(200)	$ (83)
Amortization of estimated organization and financing expenses	(12)	(12)	(5)
Changes in depreciation charges resulting from re-valuation of assets and change in method*	24	54	58
Estimated reduction in income taxes resulting from additional expenses	104	87	16
	$(84)	$(71)	$ (14)
Pro forma net income after taxes	$2,180	$ 997	$ 402
Dividends on 275,000 Class A shares	$ 248	$ 248	$ 103
Pro forma net income on common stock	$1,932	$ 749	$ 299
Pro forma net income per share—based on 2,110,800 common shares	$ 0.92	$ 0.35	$0.14

* Lestoil Products, Inc., would not be permitted to use accelerated methods used by the predecessor company.

Case 31

Kansas City Stock Yards Company of Maine

IN DECEMBER, 1951, the directors of the Kansas City Stock Yards Company of Maine had before them for decision a proposal that the company undertake a voluntary recapitalization under which holders of the noncallable 5% cumulative preferred stock of the company would be offered 40-year income debenture notes in exchange for their preferred stock.

The history of the Kansas City Stock Yards Company began in 1871, when the first independent stockyards company to serve all shippers of livestock to the Kansas City market was organized. From the outset the Kansas City Stock Yards Company engaged in no buying and selling activities itself; instead, it operated a "livestock hotel" for cattle, hogs, and sheep coming to the Kansas City public market for sale to and slaughter by local meat-packing companies or for sale and reshipment to farmers for further fattening. The stockyard company derived its revenues from service charges for receiving, yarding, watering, feeding, weighing, and shipping livestock and from building rentals.

As receipts of livestock to the Kansas City market increased, extensive stockyard facilities were installed. By 1951, the Kansas City Stock Yards Company had a gross investment of more than $16,000,-000 in 238 acres of land along the Kaw (Kansas) River, in livestock handling pens, buildings, and equipment, in hay and feed barns, and in a nine-floor office building housing the facilities of the Kansas City Livestock Exchange and other service activities. The stockyards company also owned rail facilities, connecting with twelve major railroads serving Kansas City, and extensive truck unloading docks.

The company had financed its expansion of physical facilities over the years without heavy use of debt. Operations had generally been profitable, and the company had been able to maintain dividend payments on its substantial issue of 5% preferred stock almost without interruption since the stock was issued in 1913. Common stock dividends included a 100% stock dividend in 1921. From 1924 to 1933, annual dividends of $8 per share were paid on the common stock. Dividends were reduced in 1934; and from 1942 through 1947, no common dividends had been paid. Although $1.00 was paid on each share of common stock in 1948 and $1.50 in 1949 and again in 1950, preferred dividend requirements of almost $237,000 absorbed a large part of the net earnings of the company in 1950.

Despite the long record of past profits, management in 1951 was concerned about several apparent long-run threats to the future profitability of the company.

First, several changes in livestock marketing methods in the last two decades had led to a relative decline in the number of livestock marketed at the large public markets (Chicago, Omaha, Kansas City, South St. Paul, St. Louis, Denver, etc.). One of the most important of these changes resulted from a marked increase in the direct purchase from the farmers of livestock, especially hogs, by the packers, who had constructed small packing plants in smaller cities in the producing areas. The farmers were able to truck their hogs from the farm directly to the decentralized packing plants for sale at a posted price and thus by-pass the large central markets. These and other developments had contributed to a decline in total animal receipts by Kansas City Stock Yards Company, illustrated by the drop from 6,460,000 animals in 1929 to 3,475,000 in 1950. In addition to the long-term decline in physical volume of operations, the company had experienced rises in operating expenses common to industry in general during recent years. Further, in 1951 the company faced the prospect of post-Korea increases in the rates of federal income taxation. The preferred dividend requirement of $236,950 had to be paid out of earnings after taxes. In order to cover the preferred dividends at the anticipated 1952 tax rate of 52%, earnings before income taxes of almost $494,000 were required. In the face of these developments, the management and board of directors had given continued consideration to possible measures by which the current modest return to common stockholders could be protected and perhaps enhanced.

The long-term problems of the company were aggravated in July, 1951, when its properties were completely inundated by a devastating flood. On the morning of Friday, July 13, with little warning, the Kaw River swept over its levees and spread over a wide area of indus-

trial Kansas City. The floodwaters covered all the company's proper-
ties, reaching a depth of 26 inches in the second floor of the Livestock
Exchange Building and more than 30 feet in some parts of the yard.
Damage by the rushing waters and by mud was severe.

Fortunately, at the time of the flood the company was in a strong
financial position (see balance sheet included as Exhibit 1), and the
directors, at a special session on July 19, determined to push rehabilitation measures vigorously. By dint of strenuous and expensive efforts, the yard was opened for part-scale operation within three weeks
after the flood, but it was apparent by September that complete rehabilitation would require more than a year. Even though it was decided
not to repair some facilities which were apparently in excess of current needs, the cost of planned repairs promised to near $1,000,000.
Of this sum, over $650,000 was expended in 1951.

At the meeting just after the flood the board decided to postpone
declaration of the quarterly preferred dividend, normally payable on
August 1, until the cost of rehabilitation could be assessed more accurately. By September, it appeared that the financial position of the
company would permit the early resumption of regular preferred
dividends; and the August dividend was voted for payment in October, although operations for the year were expected to result in a
large loss due to the extraordinary expenses of flood repair and to
loss of revenues resulting from the flood.

No action was taken on the preferred dividend due November 1, but it was planned to bring the stock up to date on dividends
before the exchange offer would be made.

No dividends were paid on the common after the distribution of
$1.00 per share in February.

The widely publicized flood damage had caused the market price
of the preferred stock to drop to a low of 82½ in August; but by November, quotations had risen to around 90.

As suggested above, there had been considerable discussion in top
management and board meetings in recent years of the possibilities of
reducing the demands upon profits of the noncallable 5% preferred
stock. After the flood, the board of directors authorized detailed investigation of the possibilities of reducing the burden of the preferred
stock by creation of a new issue of income notes and offer of these
notes to the preferred stockholders in exchange for the existing preferred stock. Consequently, management and legal counsel had
worked out plans for the new security issue and the terms of the exchange. In presenting the plan to the board, the management first re-

viewed the salient features of the existing preferred stock. They were as follows:

1. The 5% dividend on the $100 par shares was fully cumulative; that is, no dividends could be paid on the common stock until all back preferred dividends had been paid.

2. The preferred stock was *not* callable, and there was no provision for retirement through a sinking fund.

3. Preferred stockholders had no voting rights so long as dividend payments were current. In the event of default on two consecutive quarterly dividend payments, each share of preferred stock was entitled to one vote, along with each of the 50,000 shares of outstanding common stock, which otherwise held exclusive voting rights. The voting rights of the preferred stock terminated upon the clearing of arrearages.

4. In the event of liquidation and distribution of assets remaining after payment of creditors, the preferred stock was entitled to payment in the amount of the $100 par value per share plus any dividends in arrears. Common stockholders were entitled only to what remained after such payments.

5. Consent of holders of two thirds of the preferred stock was required before a mortgage or other lien could be placed on properties of the company.

Tentative provisions of the proposed 5% income notes were as follows:

1. The notes would be dated November 1, 1951, and would become due and payable on November 1, 1991.

2. The notes would be fully registered, and checks for quarterly interest payments would be mailed to the owners directly from the company.

3. Interest would be payable in $1\frac{1}{4}$% quarter-annual instalments on the first day of February, May, August, and November. However, the directors were required to make interest payments only to the extent that "net income"[1] for the current fiscal year proved sufficient for the payment of such interest. In the event net income was not sufficient to cover the interest payments, the unpaid interest was payable from the first subsequent "net income" of the company. In effect, interest payments then were "fully

---

[1] "Net income" would be defined to mean "the net income of the company, after deducting all proper operating expenses and all proper charges, including proper charges for depreciation, depletion, obsolescence, and all other proper purposes, amortization (if elected by the company), interest on all current liabilities, and all ad valorem taxes upon its properties and all occupation taxes and license fees, but before and without deducting federal, state, and other income, excess profits, war, and other similar taxes on income, and not including, but excluding, any profits or losses on the sale or other disposition, not in the ordinary course of business, of investments or fixed or capital assets, or on the acquisition or retirement or sale or other disposition of stock or securities of the company, and also excluding any taxes on such profits and any tax deductions or credits on account of any such losses, all as determined in accordance with sound accounting practice."

cumulative." Any accumulated interest unpaid at the maturity of the notes became unconditionally payable along with the principal amount.

4. Beginning in 1957, a sinking fund would be established under which 1% of the original amount of the notes would be required to be called with the premiums stated below, or purchased in the open market for redemption each year.

5. In addition to the required retirement of notes through the sinking fund, the notes could be called by the company in whole or in part at any time. If called for redemption, the following prices would be paid, along with any accumulated interest:

Nov., 1951—Nov. 1, 1955 110
Nov. 2, 1955—Nov. 1, 1956 108
Nov. 2, 1956—Nov. 1, 1957 106
Nov. 2, 1957—Nov. 1, 1958 104
Nov. 2, 1958—Nov. 1, 1959 102
Nov. 2, 1959 and thereafter 100

6. No dividends could be paid or stock purchased or retired as long as any interest or sinking fund payments were in arrears.

7. There would be no limit to the amount of securities, secured or unsecured, which might be issued at a later time, but this issue of bonds would be limited to the par value of the preferred actually exchanged.

8. The proceeds of any one sale of fixed assets for more than $100,000 must be reinvested in fixed assets or used to retire the income notes.

9. In the event of default, the trustee of the issue could declare all principal and accumulated interest due and payable.

The company's legal counsel and special counsel employed for the purpose had expressed opinions on several important legal issues raised by the proposals. The counsel had agreed that: (1) It would not be necessary to secure approval of either preferred or common stockholders in order to authorize the issue of income notes and their exchange for preferred stock. Of course, individual preferred stockholders could elect not to exchange their preferred stock for the new 5% income notes and would in such case continue to hold the preferred stock. (2) A preferred stockholder could exchange his preferred stock for the new note without realizing a taxable gain in so doing. (3) Interest paid by the company on the new income notes would be deductible as a business expense before calculation of the net income of the company for purposes of income taxation. (4) It was believed and intended by the counsel and management that the new noteholders would be general creditors of the company. However, there was some feeling that "there may be a legal possibility that the company's obligation to pay the principal and any accumulated unpaid interest on the notes might be held subordinate to the rights of other creditors in existence at the time payment is to be made."

Ownership of the 47,390 shares of preferred stock currently outstanding was widely distributed among 1,252 stockholders in 36 states. There were few large holders, and many stockholders held only one or two shares. Much of the stock was held in New England and in the Missouri-Kansas area. Most stockholders had held the stock for many years. The common stock was held by 513 owners in many states. A relatively small percentage of the preferred stock was owned by common stockholders.

Neither the common nor the preferred stock was listed on an organized security exchange. Several over-the-counter dealers were interested in the securities and maintained markets in them. Market price quotations are given in Exhibit 3 for the years 1938–50 and the available months of 1951.

If the decision to offer the exchange was made, management planned to seek the help of interested security dealers on a cost reimbursement basis in soliciting exchanges by stockholders.

Under Securities and Exchange Commission rules, it would be necessary to set a terminal date, perhaps four months after the offer, by which time the exchange would have to be accomplished. As indicated earlier, preferred stockholders who elected not to exchange their stocks would continue with the same rights as before. However, their claims would now be junior to the claims of the income noteholders.

Although the total costs of carrying out the proposed recapitalization could not be estimated with accuracy, management thought that direct costs might approximate some $25,000.

In earlier discussions of the proposal a director with wide financial experience had pointed out that income bonds as a class had long held a somewhat dubious reputation in investment circles. This was due, he felt, primarily to the fact that most currently outstanding income bonds had been created during reorganizations and issued in involuntary exchange to former bondholders. Created out of situations that were often fundamentally weak, the record of income bonds in general had not been one to inspire great investor confidence.[2]

---

[2] In their book, *Security Analysis* (2d ed.; New York: McGraw-Hill Book Co., Inc., 1940), B. Graham and D. L. Dodd assert, ". . . we know of only one income obligation which has maintained an investment standing continuously over any length of time, *viz.*, Atchison, Topeka and Santa Fe Railway Company Adjustment 4s, due 1955" (p. 209).

In recent years a few strong concerns had issued income bonds in exchange for outstanding preferred stock, but none of these companies was located in the Kansas City area.

Since the noncallable feature and the contingent voting rights attached to the preferred stock would not carry forward to the income bonds, the management expected that some of the directors would question the probable willingness of preferred stockholders to accept the exchange offer.

Exhibit 1

KANSAS CITY STOCK YARDS COMPANY OF MAINE

BALANCE SHEETS

(Dollar figures in thousands)

ASSETS

	Dec. 31 1950	Nov. 30 1951
Current assets:		
Cash.........................	$ 648	$ 99
U.S. Government bonds..........	380	410
Accounts receivable............	66	111
Inventories....................	71	24
Total current assets......	$ 1,165	$ 644
Other assets:		
Fixed assets...................	$10,639	$10,653
Reserve for depreciation........	88	97
Total other assets........	$11,892	$11,394

LIABILITIES

	Dec. 31 1950	Nov. 30 1951
Current liabilities:		
Accounts payable..............	$ 30	$ 32
Accrued expenses (payroll and local taxes).....	22	147
Accrued income taxes...........	261	50
Total current liabilities....	$ 313	$ 229
Reserves.......................	90	88
5% preferred stock.............	4,739	4,739
Common stock..................	5,000	5,000
Earned surplus.................	1,750	1,338
Total liabilities...........	$11,892	$11,394

Exhibit 2

KANSAS CITY STOCK YARDS COMPANY OF MAINE
SELECTED DATA
(Dollar figures in thousands)

Year	Gross Income	Net Income before Income Taxes	Net Income after Income Taxes
1940	$1,366	$389	$296
1941	1,414	438	301
1942	1,808	802	473
1943	2,095	864	511
1944	2,085	748	405
1945	1,938	564	321
1946	1,970	615	372
1947	2,148	737	435
1948	2,063	737	428
1949	2,211	824	514
1950	1,944	600	339
1951 (11 months)	1,620	184d	184d

d Loss.

Exhibit 3

KANSAS CITY STOCK YARDS COMPANY OF MAINE
MARKET PRICES OF SECURITIES

Year	Preferred Stock High	Preferred Stock Low	Common Stock High	Common Stock Low
1938	$ 93	$ 80	$62	$47
1939	90	81	50½	43
1940	90	62	48	19
1941	70¼	60	21	7
1942	68	61¾	13	6½
1943	85	67½	16	11
1944	99	84	22¼	15
1945	103½	99	29	22½
1946	103½	98	26	15
1947	105	100	23	18
1948	102	99	25	15
1949	101½	99½	23	15
1950	103	101	27	23
1951 (11 months)	102½	82½	26½	16¼

Case 32

Sheraton Corporation of America

IN THE late spring of 1959, Mr. Ernest Henderson III, treasurer of the Sheraton Corporation of America, was reviewing the company's policy and its decision rule regarding purchase of its own shares of common stock on the New York Stock Exchange. Within a limit of available and uncommitted funds, the company for a number of years had followed a policy of buying its own stock on the market whenever the selling price was below an estimated net asset value per share as determined by management. At the time, it appeared that uncommitted funds were not available, and Mr. Henderson thought that the necessary pause afforded an appropriate opportunity for examining the desirability of the general policy and of the company's specific decision rule.

Company Background and Nature of Operations

The Sheraton Corporation of America, a real estate holding and management company headquartered in Boston, Massachusetts, was formed in 1946 through a merger of two companies, the Sheraton Corporation and the reorganized United States Realty and Improvement Company.

In 1959 the company, through its subsidiaries, operated approximately fifty hotels in the United States and Canada as well as other real estate property, principally office buildings. It also held a 12% ownership interest in the Diner's Club, Inc., an all-purpose credit card company, and operated Thompson Industries, Inc., an 80% owned subsidiary which supplied stainless steel stampings and other parts to major automobile manufacturers. In recent years, hotel operations had accounted for approximately 80% of the company's gross operating income.

891

The company exercised considerable control over operations of subsidiaries, and had established uniform operating procedures throughout its chain of hotels to achieve cost reduction and efficiency. Average occupancy and room rates of Sheraton Hotels compared favorably with industry figures. Its hotels were nationally advertised, and business was efficiently channeled from one hotel in the chain to another through an internal electronic computer system (Reservatron) installed in fiscal 1959. This device recorded almost instantaneously the availability of 26,500 guest rooms in the chain for thirty-four days in advance.

In the past, Sheraton had acquired many properties at reasonable prices, and had increased their value through capital expenditures for improvement and through the techniques of better management. Management believed that its policy of making large annual expenditures on maintenance and renovation was largely responsible for the growth in the company's real property values. Owing to Sheraton's practice of writing off substantially all maintenance and renovation expenditures for accounting and tax purposes, these values did not show up in the conventional balance sheet figures; officers' estimates of real asset values, however, were noted on the balance sheet.

The large expenditures for improvement had resulted in very nominal, if any, "real depreciation" on company properties. A large tax shield was provided, however, through the use of accelerated depreciation methods for tax purposes, resulting in a substantial cash flow each year. Commenting on the company's tax and accounting practices for depreciation and earnings, Mr. Henderson had said, "It's important to recognize that the normal concept of depreciation does not apply in this business, because we do not expect to replace a hotel. Our basic operating philosophy, on the other hand, is that of minimizing income taxes rather than capitalizing earnings."

These factors had enabled the company to obtain considerable debt financing for its operations. Company policy maintained long-term debt at approximately 50% of market value of its properties, less current liabilities. With respect to the use of debt, Mr. Henderson had said:

We accept the "layer" philosophy here. We will even pay up to 10% and 12% for secondary debt funds if necessary, because leverage makes the last dollar invested the most profitable. The average person thinks of money as a medium of exchange; we think of it as a commodity that can be bought and sold much like an automobile. The true measure for the use of debt, of course, is the value of a dollar today versus the value of a dollar tomorrow.

Exhibits 1 and 2 present a consolidated balance sheet and an income statement of the company.

Convinced of the inadequacy of conventional methods of reporting, management had for a number of years attempted to evaluate the company's performance for its stockholders in the annual report. The following excerpts were taken from the company's annual report for the fiscal year ended April 30, 1959:

ECONOMIC GAINS

Sheraton earnings, adjusted for changes in the estimated market value of its assets, have been referred to in previous reports as "economic gains" or "gainings." This yardstick is of interest to the management for it measures—within the limits of accuracy of market value estimates—the actual progress of the company. Indicated "economic gains" per share for the year were $3.82 compared with $1.51 a year ago. . . .

The improvement reflects in part the rise in the value of many Sheraton properties following the "lifting" of the recent recession, and in part the effectiveness of many millions invested in improvements which often add more than their cost to the value of improved properties.

INTERPRETATION OF REPORTED EARNINGS

The conventional method of presenting so-called "reported earnings" is perhaps inadequate in two respects.

Since some latitude exists under Treasury rulings with respect to deductible depreciation reserves, there is a corresponding leeway in the amount of reportable earnings. Sheraton believes that with propriety its depreciation reserves could be reduced by several million dollars,—in part by eliminating accelerated depreciation, and in part by taking into account improvements which add more than their cost to the value of these properties, thereby reducing the need for as much depreciation. If reductions in depreciation reserves had been made, reported earnings might conceivably have been twice as large. Unfortunately such procedure would require added income taxes.

A second factor affecting "reported earnings" adversely, although actual losses are rarely involved, arises from the fact that many of Sheraton's subsidiaries are in the red ink, even though in most instances the Cash Flow they "generate" is satisfactory. Nearly three millions of "losses" were recorded during the past year by these "loss" companies. These losses were subtracted from the earnings of so-called profitable subsidiaries when determining "reported earnings."

The loss companies, many in the process of rehabilitation, might be termed "Development Corporations." They are valued by Sheraton at over $100,000,000, out of a total estimated valuation of some $280,000,000 for all Sheraton real estate, computed on the basis of the "cash throw off" of these properties, adjusted for any unusual or nonrecurring expenses. Even though a market exists for these "loss" companies of approximately

$100,000,000, if Sheraton disposed of these even by giving them away, the result would be to *increase* by nearly three million dollars the reported pre-tax earnings. This, however, would mean larger income tax payments and therefore reduced "cash flow."

We believe it would be unwise to sell these so-called "loss companies," even at their full market value,—for these present perhaps the most promising opportunity for further appreciation.

Inconsistencies which appear to exist in conventional accounting practice, presumably due to the custom of applying to real estate companies accounting procedures applicable to industries of a quite different nature, explains why Sheraton prefers the yardstick we call economic gains, to the more usual measure known as "reported earnings."

UNFAVORABLE FACTORS

A number of unfavorable factors, for the first time in many years, resulted in a slight decrease in cash flow.

The adverse factors were:

(*a*) Especially heavy competition from new hotels, to some extent Canadian Government subsidized, in Montreal and Toronto.

(*b*) A costly strike in Pittsburgh.

(*c*) The 1958 recession.

(*d*) Heavy promotional expenses in connection with the new Sheraton-Dallas Hotel.

(*e*) Losses of the Ritz-Carlton in Atlantic City, and the Terrace Motel in Austin, Texas. (Sold February and July 1959 respectively.)

(*f*) Heavy initial costs of introducing Sheraton's "Reservatron" electronic reservation system.

Most of the difficulties encountered in the past fiscal year will, it is hoped, be of a nonrecurring nature.

Exhibits 3–5 show financial and operating data for fiscal years 1955–59, as presented in the 1959 annual report.

Stock Purchase Policy and the Decision Rule

Owing to management's belief that the market had continually undervalued Sheraton common stock through conventional methods of capitalizing reported earnings, available and uncommitted funds were used by the company to purchase its common stock as long as the market price remained below estimated net asset value per share. Uncommitted funds were defined as funds available after allowance for sinking funds, new investment reserves, and "betterment" projects. The one other limitation to the policy was that management thought it inappropriate to use company funds in this manner if short-term debt was outstanding.

Estimated net asset value per share was computed semiannually by management in accordance with yardsticks often used by real estate buyers. Under this method, total fair market value of all the company's assets was first arrived at by capitalizing earnings of the individual properties, before deducting interest, depreciation, and income taxes, and after adjustment for unusual repairs. These earnings were capitalized at varying rates, generally 10% to 12%, depending upon the type, age, and location of the property, competition, debt financing, and other factors. All minority interests at their capitalized equity values and all known liabilities were then deducted to arrive at estimated net asset value of the company. This amount, divided by the common shares outstanding, plus shares reserved for exercise of warrants and conversion privileges, yielded an estimated net asset value per share.

The actual decision to buy (or not to buy) the company's common stock was made and implemented in the following manner: Each year a statistical department studied the cost and profitability of Sheraton's investment opportunities. The method used to screen opportunities was "average annual return, after investment amortization, divided by average investment." Projects failing to show a 20% return after taxes were discarded automatically from further consideration. All investment projects with a 20% return or better were then submitted to top management for consideration. If the funds that were expected to be generated from various sources during the year appeared adequate, the latter projects typically were accepted and included in the investment program. In any event, "betterments" on existing properties and investments for expansion purposes received priority treatment. If funds remained uncommitted on this basis, the balance was made available for purchase of Sheraton common stock as long as market price was below estimated net asset value per share.

From this point a specific decision to buy shares of Sheraton stock was made primarily on an *ad hoc* basis, depending on developments during the year regarding available funds and investment opportunities. With respect to timing of investment expenditures and stock purchases, Mr. Henderson had said, "We make a real effort to keep our money working for the stockholders most of the time, one way or another."

Orders to repurchase Sheraton stock were placed with various brokers at about one eighth to one quarter of a point below market. On this practice, Mr. Henderson had commented, "Then we just wait. Our bid tends to establish a floor under the market price without driving it up. Occasionally, of course, we revise our bid price to adjust for developments in the market."

During the fiscal year ended April 30, 1959, the company purchased on the market 51,471 shares of its common stock, at a cost of $969,380. Total reported earnings per share for the year were $1.1444. If the shares had not been purchased, earnings per share would have been $1.1320. During the past 10 years, $3,940,882 had been expended by the company for 310,335 shares of its common stock. Earnings per share for the fiscal year ended April 30, 1959, would have been $1.0733 if these shares had not been purchased and the funds had not been otherwise productively employed. Exhibit 6 presents a 10-year record of stock repurchases by the company. Exhibit 7 shows weekly market prices, volume of recorded sales, and purchases by the company of its common stock for the fiscal year ended April 30, 1959. Exhibit 8 compares cash dividend yield and market performance of Sheraton common stock with two other hotel corporation common stocks.

Mr. Henderson believed that the primary justification for Sheraton's stock repurchase policy was the resulting financial benefit to shareholders who did not sell their stock. He also believed that large differences between net asset value and market price of the stock might attract "raiders." In fact, during the previous year an offer from a New York syndicate had been received to purchase all of the company's assets at a price in excess of net asset value as estimated by management. By narrowing the spread between market price and net asset value through a stock repurchase policy, Mr. Henderson thought that attempts by outsiders to gain a position of strength or control on the board would be discouraged. The existing board of directors controlled 30% of the company's outstanding stock.

Since both the policy of purchasing its own stock when undervalued[1] and management's views regarding real values and earnings were clearly stated in the company's annual reports, Mr. Henderson questioned whether there existed any real ethical problems in such a policy.

When questioned about the policy of a company purchasing its own stock, an investment banker had made the following observations:

---

[1] The policy was stated in a recent year's annual report as follows: "If shares continue to be available at a substantial discount from asset value, additional shares may be repurchased from time to time when funds are conveniently available for such use, with a view to reacquiring at least in part the shares distributed as stock dividends. The repurchase of shares in the open market is an effective means of increasing the indicated net asset value of the outstanding shares because of the discount from such value at which stock can be purchased."

The net result of a company reacquiring its own shares is usually a relative increase in the earning power of the shares remaining. For this reason, it can be said that such a policy definitely benefits those stockholders who do not sell. This result would not necessarily be true, of course, if the funds used were needed to maintain the company's financial strength and flexibility, or if really attractive investment opportunities were being by-passed in favor of stock repurchases.

Certain questions can be raised regarding fair treatment of those stockholders who elect to sell their shares. This is especially true when stockholders have not been told that the company is buying its own stock; it is also true if management has not kept the stockholders adequately informed regarding circumstances and developments related to or affecting the value of the stock in question.

A few members of the investment banking profession continue to view a stock repurchase program with considerable suspicion; they tend to think of it as being indicative of something sinister taking place. By and large, however, I would say that the financial community looks on such programs with favor and as an expression of confidence by management of the particular company's future.

Exhibit 1

SHERATON CORPORATION OF AMERICA

CONSOLIDATED BALANCE SHEET OF COMPANY AND SUBSIDIARIES
AT APRIL 30, 1959

(Dollar figures in thousands)

ASSETS

Current assets:

Cash and marketable securities		$ 17,680
Accounts and notes receivable (net)		13,897
Other		10,092
Total current assets		$ 41,669
Investments		11,447
Property, plant, and equipment, net		187,395
Other		4,992
		$245,503*

LIABILITIES, CAPITAL SHARES, AND SURPLUS

Current liabilities		$ 28,641
Long-term indebtedness:		
Bonds and mortgages payable	$ 131,517	
Capital income sinking fund debentures	16,291	
Other	11,807	
		159,615
Minority interests		3,528
Capital shares:		
Common (par $0.50):		
Authorized	6,000,000	
Issued	5,055,451	
Less: In Treasury	380,017†	
Outstanding	4,675,434	2,338
Surplus		51,381
		$245,503
Book value		$ 53,719
Book value per common share		$ 11.50

* Officers' estimated value of total assets at April 30, 1959, was $346,910.
† Includes shares repurchased by company.

Exhibit 2

SHERATON CORPORATION OF AMERICA

CONSOLIDATED INCOME STATEMENT FOR COMPANY AND SUBSIDIARIES
FOR YEAR ENDED APRIL 30, 1959

(Dollar figures in thousands)

Gross operating income		$170,788
Operating costs and expenses		142,207
Operating income		$ 28,581
Other income		685
		$ 29,266
Depreciation	$14,144	
Interest and debt expense	7,292	
		21,436
Ordinary income		$ 7,830
Income taxes		3,914
Net income before profit from capital transactions		$ 3,916
Net profit from capital transactions		2,001
Net income and profits before minority interests		$ 5,917
Minority interests		566
Net income and profits for the year		$ 5,351
Net income and profits per common share		$ 1.14

Exhibit 3

SHERATON CORPORATION OF AMERICA

SHERATON'S GROWTH (CONSOLIDATED)

(Dollar figures in thousands)

Year Ended April 30	Total Assets at Estimated Values*	Total Assets at Book Values	Gross Income	Net Operating Income before Depreciation	Depreciation	Net Operating Income†	Net Profits on Capital Transactions†	Total Net Income and Net Profits†
1959	$346,910	$245,503	$171,474	$17,494	$14,144	$3,350	$2,001	$5,351
1958	304,007	217,325	159,014	17,896	14,164	3,732	1,101	4,833
1957	304,645	219,866	153,792	16,668	11,920	4,748	654	5,402
1956	243,697	172,468	121,672	12,534	8,098	4,436	2,215	6,651
1955	193,033	134,543	89,376	9,504	5,390	4,114	4,760	8,874
1954	132,520	89,568	72,771	7,924	4,507	3,417	1,878	5,295
1953	129,475	91,313	68,142	6,772	3,857	2,915	1,007	3,922
1952	113,524	82,459	62,773	6,062	3,490	2,986‡	1,196	4,182
1951	101,861	74,982	56,071	6,156	3,253	3,719‡	1,191	4,910
1950	87,874	73,029	39,739	4,594	2,626	2,107‡	1,457	3,564

* Estimated by company officers.
† After minority interests.
‡ Other credits included: $414 in 1952, $816 in 1951, $139 in 1950.

Exhibit 4

SHERATON CORPORATION OF AMERICA

SHERATON'S GROWTH PER COMMON SHARE* (CONSOLIDATED)

Year Ended April 30	Estimated Net Asset Value†	Book Net Asset Value†	Cash Flow‡	Depreciation	Net Operating Income§	Net Profits on Capital Transactions§	Total Net Income and Net Profits§
1959	$30.02	$11.49	$3.73	$3.02	$0.71	$0.43	$1.14
1958	26.80	11.04	3.80	3.01	0.79	0.24	1.03
1957	25.88	10.61	3.54	2.53	1.01	0.14	1.15
1956	22.72	10.06	2.66	1.72	0.94	0.47	1.41
1955	19.42	9.45	2.01	1.14	0.87	1.01	1.88
1954	16.50	7.94	1.65	0.94	0.71	0.39	1.10
1953	14.36	7.00	1.39	0.79	0.60	0.20	0.80
1952	12.23	6.33	1.21	0.70	0.59#	0.24	0.83
1951	10.97	5.76	1.25	0.66	0.76#	0.24	1.00
1950	7.74	4.79	0.91	0.53	0.41#	0.30	0.71

* All figures are adjusted to the basis of 4,675,434 shares outstanding at April 30, 1959.
† After liabilities and minority interests.
‡ Net operating income plus depreciation.
§ After minority interests.
# Other credits included: $0.08 in 1952, $0.17 in 1951, $0.03 in 1950.
NOTE: Estimated net asset values were estimated by company officers and allowed for exercise of warrants and first conversion privilege of 4¾% debentures outstanding.

Exhibit 5

SHERATON CORPORATION OF AMERICA

SHERATON'S "ECONOMIC PERFORMANCE" PER COMMON SHARE*

Year Ended April 30	Market Price†	Estimated Net Asset Value‡	Increase In Estimated Net Asset Value During Year	Cash Dividends Paid	"Economic Performance"§	Price/Performance Ratio#
1959	$18.50	$30.02	$3.22	$0.60	$3.82	4.8
1958	11.15	26.80	0.92	0.59	1.51	7.4
1957	12.13	25.88	3.16	0.50	3.66	3.3
1956	10.80	22.72	3.30	0.42	3.72	2.9
1955	12.14	19.42	2.92	0.28	3.20	3.8
1954	5.61	16.50	2.14	0.22	2.36	2.4
1953	4.57	14.36	2.13	0.19	2.32	2.0
1952	3.82	12.23	1.26	0.19	1.45	2.6
1951	3.16	10.97	3.23	0.19	3.42	0.9
1950	2.47	7.74	2.62	0.12	2.74	0.9

* All figures are adjusted to the basis of 4,675,434 shares outstanding at April 30, 1959.
† Closing price at year end, adjusted to basis of shares outstanding at April 30, 1959.
‡ See Exhibit 4 for basis of computation.
§ Increase in estimated net asset value, plus cash dividends paid.
# Shows ratio of market price to "economic performance."

Exhibit 6

SHERATON CORPORATION OF AMERICA

SHERATON'S TEN-YEAR STOCK REPURCHASE RECORD

Year Ended April 30	Number of Shares Purchased	Average Cost per Share (Unadjusted)	Approximate Cost per Share (Adjusted)*	Approximate Price/Earnings Ratio†	Approximate Price/Cash Flow Ratio‡	Total Amount Expended	Number of Shares Outstanding (End of Period)
1959	51,471	$18.83	$18.83	16.5	5.0	$969,830	4,675,434
1958	1,118	11.09	10.90	10.5	3.0	12,395	4,610,209
1957§	7,976	14.12	13.70	12.0	4.0	112,632	4,524,079
1956	64,376	14.49	11.50	8.0	4.5	933,037	3,706,252
1955	61,700	13.25	9.20	5.0	4.5	817,754	3,259,430
1954§	62,400	7.50	5.20	4.5	3.0	467,732	3,259,430
1953	24,610	14.34	4.80	6.0	3.5	352,872	1,580,554
1952	7,614	10.58	3.50	4.0	3.0	80,341	1,531,405
1951	12,570	8.44	2.70	2.5	2.0	105,866	1,503,874
1950	16,500	5.36	1.70	2.5	2.0	88,423	1,514,437

* Adjusted to a basis of 4,675,434 shares outstanding.
† Cost per share to net income and profits.
‡ Cost per share to net operating income plus depreciation.
§ Sold treasury stock: 1957—1,000 shares for $15,367; 1954—5,000 shares for 65,000.

NOTE: Stock dividends paid as follows:

1959	2%
1958	2
1957	2 and 20%
1956	10
1955	5
1954	5 (plus 2-for-1 split)
1953	5

Exhibit 7

SHERATON CORPORATION OF AMERICA

MARKET PRICES, VOLUME OF RECORDED SALES, AND PURCHASES BY THE COMPANY
OF ITS COMMON STOCK FOR THE WEEKS INDICATED

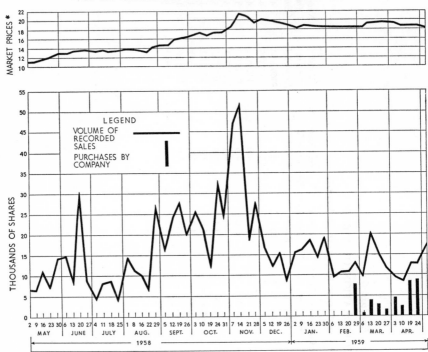

* Average weekly high and low market prices.

SOURCE: *Barron's, Commercial and Financial Chronicle,* and records of the company.

Exhibit 8

SHERATON CORPORATION OF AMERICA

COMPARISON OF MARKET PERFORMANCE AND CASH DIVIDEND YIELD OF SHERATON
COMMON STOCK WITH TWO OTHER HOTEL CORPORATION COMMON STOCKS

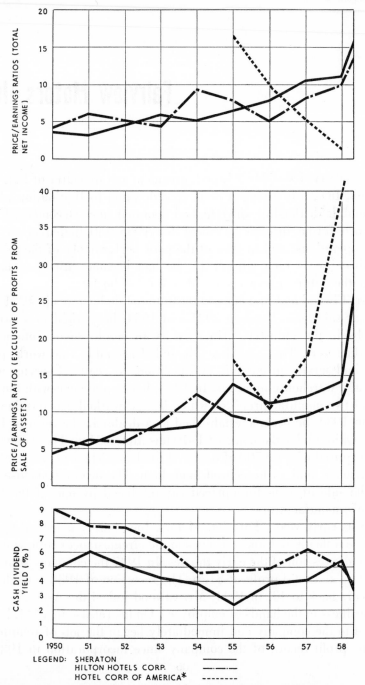

LEGEND: SHERATON
HILTON HOTELS CORP.
HOTEL CORP. OF AMERICA*

* For the Hotel Corporation of America, 1950 through 1954 were loss years.

Case 33

Fairview Motors, Inc.

IN FEBRUARY, 1955, Mr. Elwood, president and treasurer of Fairview Motors, Inc., was giving serious consideration to liquidation of his automobile dealership which he had operated since December, 1934. The pro forma income statement for 1955 anticipated a net loss from operations; and in view of the poor performance of the preceding three years (see Exhibit 1), he had become quite pessimistic about the future prospects for this line of business.

Mr. Elwood had first entered the automobile business in 1921 as a new-car salesman. Between 1921 and 1934, he worked in a variety of jobs in the industry, primarily as an employee of automobile manufacturers. This experience included assembly line work, parts sales and service promotion, and positions as regional service manager and warehouse manager. In 1933, his employment with the second of two manufacturers for which he had worked was terminated; and in 1934, he became established as a dealer in the town of Fairview, Ohio, under the name of Fairview Motors, Inc. The dealership was acquired with $2,700 of personal funds, assistance from relatives and friends, and an unsecured bank loan. The dealer franchise was for the sale of a medium-priced car produced by one of the "Big Three" manufacturers.

In its early years, Fairview Motors, Inc., barely managed to survive the difficult and uncertain economic circumstances following the severe depression of the early thirties. In 1937 the company sold 127 new cars at a total profit of $126. The recession of 1938 cut sales of new cars back to 40. In 1941, Mr. Elwood joined the Army, leaving the business in the hands of employees. On his release in 1944, he returned to the company and immediately began the job of rebuilding it. The profit record of the company since incorporation in 1938 is shown in Exhibit 2 and indicates the extent to which profits recovered through 1950. The results of this recovery period are reflected in company balance sheets, which are shown in Exhibit 3 for the years 1951 to 1954, inclusive. Throughout the life of the business, Mr. Elwood had remained sole owner. In recent years, he was assisted in its management by his son.

Because of what he considered to be highly unsatisfactory prospects for 1955, Mr. Elwood decided to discuss the matter with the automobile manufacturer's regional financial representative, Mr. Fairfax. After reviewing Mr. Elwood's financial statements and forecast, Mr. Fairfax suggested that there were three aspects of his business which Mr. Elwood should examine closely before coming to any final conclusions. These were: (1) pricing and bargaining with the customer, (2) cost control, and (3) the maximum investment necessary to operate the business. Mr. Fairfax stated that the manufacturer expected a well-managed dealership to return at least 15% on the owner's investment (after taxes and bonuses).

On the subject of pricing, Mr. Fairfax suggested that Mr. Elwood consider the practice of "packing." This was a practice in general use in the automobile business at the time whereby the list price of a new car quoted the customer was increased by what was known as a "pack" of, say, $200 to give the dealer more of a margin within which to bargain. With the shrewd bargainer, the dealer could make what appeared to be substantial concessions either in trade-in price or in the form of a cash discount in order to close the sale. The customer who failed to bargain effectively would pay the inflated price, thus increasing the over-all margin of profit on new-car sales. Mr. Elwood had very strong views on the use of the pack, feeling that it favored some customers at the expense of others on an unfair basis, and he had steadfastly refused to resort to it up to this point. These views were known to Mr. Fairfax from previous discussions with Mr. Elwood.

Mr. Fairfax also suggested that in some respects, Mr. Elwood's costs of operating the dealership were unnecessarily high. In particular, he took exception to the item: salaries—officers. It was his contention that the salary of the owner and manager of a dealership of this size (an average of 150 new cars sold per year) should not exceed $9,000. In addition, he objected to expenditures on leasehold improvements. Automobile manufacturers encouraged dealers to rent rather than own their own buildings and, in line with this, discouraged leasehold improvements as being just another way of investing in real estate. Countering this, Mr. Elwood insisted that he had not made any such expenditures that were not absolutely necessary to a well-run automobile business. Other items, such as travel and entertainment, were also questioned by Mr. Fairfax. On balance, he contended that Mr. Elwood could help his profit performance substantially by a more careful control of costs.

Subsequently, Mr. Elwood undertook to analyze his costs for 1954 to see how the profit would have appeared according to the line of reasoning taken by Fairfax. In doing so, he reduced certain costs by the following amounts:

Salaries and wages:	
Officers' salaries..............................	$11,200
Officers' bonuses.............................	5,800
Training school..............................	400
Other semifixed expenses:	
Company car................................	400
Advertising.................................	1,200
Travel and entertainment.....................	1,100
Memberships...............................	300
Fixed expenses:	
Maintenance—buildings........................	1,200
Maintenance—equipment.....................	1,300
Total reduction..............................	$22,900

The third aspect of the business questioned by Mr. Fairfax was the owner's investment. It was a basic policy of the manufacturer to discourage the dealer from investing any more than absolutely necessary. Fairfax drew up a balance sheet which, in his view, reflected the investment required to carry on a 200-car dealership (see Exhibit 4). In view of the fact that Mr. Elwood's agency was at a current level of 150 new cars a year, this balance sheet clearly suggested that his investment was excessive. The suggested balance sheet did not provide for any investment in new-car inventory, on the assumption that all new cars would be financed in full through a bank or other leading agent. The investment in used-car inventory was taken at a maximum 30 days' inventory of 25 cars. Mr. Fairfax pointed out that if this excess investment were withdrawn, the rate of return on the remaining investment would be proportionately improved.

Mr. Elwood came away from the interview with Mr. Fairfax feeling that the latter was not recognizing the "facts of life" of the automobile agency business. He felt that Fairfax had in mind a stripped-down, "shoestring" kind of dealership, whereas his objective had been to develop a well-equipped, well-run dealership which would justify a permanent and respected place in the business community.

In particular, he rejected the idea that $9,000 was an adequate salary for the manager of an $800,000-a-year business. He also questioned 15% as an adequate rate of return, particularly in view of the minimum investment suggested by Fairfax. Experience had taught him that there were considerable risks inherent in the business of selling automobiles.

In order to gain additional perspective on his problem, Mr. Elwood proceeded to gather information on other dealerships. In doing so, he interviewed other dealers and also sought the help of the National Automobile Dealers Association (N.A.D.A.). In particular, he wanted to know whether he was justified in his beliefs that he was above average in over-all efficiency of operations and that his investment was not excessive.

His primary source of information in this regard was the N.A.D.A. From this organization, he obtained national averages on costs as a percentage of sales for dealers in his make of car and in his size group. These figures were for 1954, and he proceeded to make similar calculations from the 1954 income statement of Fairview Motors, Inc. (see Exhibit 5). These comparisons were interpreted by Mr. Elwood as further evidence that he was above average in terms of operating efficiency. In previous years, he had shown up very favorably in dealer comparisons drawn up by the manufacturer and on more than one occasion had been "exhibited" as a sample of what could be done in the business.

In reviewing the industry cost figures supplied by N.A.D.A., Mr. Elwood noted a downward trend in profit margins beginning in 1950:

	Gross Profit	Operating Profit As a Per Cent of Sales	Total Expenses
1950	18.6%	6.3%	12.3%
1951	18.2	4.9	13.3
1952	17.2	3.6	13.6
1953	15.2	2.2	13.0
1954	14.8	0.6	14.2

Information on the average investment by automobile dealers was more difficult to find. The N.A.D.A. had only commenced collecting such information in 1954. The figures available for 1954 were on an industry-wide basis and showed an average per dealer net worth of $108,933 (average sales: 101 new cars). On this basis the ratio of operating profit to net worth was 5.83% (before federal income taxes).

Mr. Elwood was also giving some thought to the probable outcome of a decision to liquidate. He was certain that if he did so, he could work for another dealer as manager at a minimum salary of $15,000. On the other hand, he was quite uncertain as to what he could get for the business, in view of the special circumstances of the agency relationship. To clarify his thinking on this point, Mr. Elwood and his service superintendent took an inventory of all machinery, equipment, office furniture, and fixtures. They priced each item at replacement cost, taking into consideration the percentage of useful life remaining in each piece of equipment. This gave a figure that Mr. Elwood thought was a fair selling price for these assets. He also inventoried his spare parts, accessories, and supplies, which at cost would be valued at about $10,000. The manufacturer would buy back practically all of this at cost price if Mr. Elwood closed out the business without someone taking over as a dealer.

The total value of the physical assets of the business to be offered for sale was estimated as follows:

Machinery, equipment, office furniture, and fixtures	$47,000
Spare parts, accessories, and supplies	10,000
Company cars	4,000
	$61,000

If the business was to be sold as a going concern, Mr. Elwood felt he was justified in asking a price in excess of $61,000 in order to reimburse him for the expense of the development of the business which he had incurred over a twenty-year period. He was willing to spread the payment for the assets over a five-year period. He thought there would be several people interested in buying in on this basis. On the other hand, he was uncertain as to whether the manufacturer would be willing to franchise a new dealer on these terms. Previous experience of other dealers indicated that the manufacturer took an active interest in the price at which the dealership was to be sold and that it appeared to consider depreciated book value as the proper basis, with no allowance for goodwill.

Exhibit 1

FAIRVIEW MOTORS, INC.

INCOME STATEMENTS FOR YEARS ENDING DECEMBER 31, 1951–1955

	Actual				Pro Forma
	1951	1952	1953	1954	1955
Net sales	$486,800	$579,100	$698,400	$803,800	$753,600
Less cost of sales	381,600	474,800	563,400	665,300	624,700
Gross profit on sales	$105,200	$104,300	$135,000	$138,500	$128,900
Less:					
Variable expenses[1]	$ 11,700	$ 16,600	$ 21,400	$ 28,300	$ 31,900
Semifixed salaries and wages[2]	54,900	54,100	67,600	68,900	60,500
Other semifixed expenses[3]	12,200	15,400	20,100	20,500	15,700
Fixed expenses[4]	16,000	17,000	24,000	26,700	22,200
Total expenses	$ 94,800	$103,100	$133,100	$144,200	$130,300
Net profit (loss) from operations	$ 10,400	$ 1,200	$ 1,900	$ (5,700)	$ (1,400)
Add other income[5]	4,500	4,400	9,700	10,400	9,000
	$ 14,900	$ 5,600	$ 11,600	$ 4,700	$ 7,600
Less other expenses	400	500	1,400	1,000	....
Net profit before taxes	$ 14,500	$ 5,100	$ 10,200	$ 3,700	$ 7,600
Federal taxes	4,200	1,500	3,000	1,000	
Net profit after taxes	$ 10,300	$ 3,600	$ 7,200	$ 2,700	
[1] Includes salesmen's salaries and commissions	$ 6,000	$ 8,000	$ 10,000	$ 13,000	$ 12,500
[2] Includes officers' salaries	28,000	28,700	28,700	23,200	25,200
and bonus	....			5,800	

Note: Of the sum paid as officers' salaries and bonus, a part was paid to individual members of the Elwood family who served in management in some capacity. In recent years the amount paid to these individuals other than Mr. Elwood was approximately $10,000.

[3] Major item—advertising	4,300	4,800	5,400	6,600	4,800
[4] Includes rent, amortization of improvements, depreciation, etc.					
[5] Includes revenue received in connection with the financing of customer installment contracts	500	400	4,900	5,900	

Exhibit 2

FAIRVIEW MOTORS, INC.

NET PROFIT AFTER TAXES, 1938–1950

For Year	Net Profit (Loss) after Taxes	Salaries and Bonuses Paid to Owner and Officers
1938	$(1,400)	$ 2,700
1939	(4,000)	3,200
1940	500	5,600
1941	500	9,600
1942*	....	....
1943*	....	....
1944*	....	....
1945	1,200	7,500
1946	10,800	12,600
1947	13,600	21,000
1948	8,100	32,100
1949	14,500	25,700
1950	16,700	25,700

* Not given—period when Mr. Elwood was absent from the business.

Exhibit 3

FAIRVIEW MOTORS, INC.

BALANCE SHEETS, 1951–1954

ASSETS	1951	1952	1953	1954
Current				
Cash..	$ 6,800	$16,200	$ 21,800	$ 16,800
Contracts in transit...........................	1,500	1,400	2,300	2,700
Customers' accounts less reserve...............	9,400	10,700	13,200	11,500
Inventories: New cars.........................	2,100	2,100	10,500	13,300
Used cars.........................	14,400	14,400	7,500	7,100
Other...........................	12,400	13,500	12,600	19,500
Securities at cost.............................	14,100	10,100	10,100	8,300
Miscellaneous................................	900	1,900	2,300	2,800
Total current assets........................	$61,600	$70,300	$ 80,300	$ 82,000
Fixed (net of depreciation)				
Machinery and equipment.....................	$ 6,800	$ 6,500	$ 7,000	$ 6,300
Furniture and fixtures........................	2,300	2,600	3,600	3,900
Service cars..................................	100	1,900	1,400	4,300
Leaseholds and improvements.................	5,400	4,700	18,800	16,200
Total fixed assets..........................	$14,600	$15,700	$ 30,800	$ 30,700
Other				
Repossession reserve..........................	$ 2,300	$ 3,500	$ 4,800	$ 5,500
Miscellaneous................................	700			
Total other assets....................	$ 3,000	$ 3,500	$ 4,800	$ 5,500
Total assets......................	$79,200	$89,500	$115,900	$118,200
LIABILITIES AND NET WORTH				
Current liabilities				
Accounts payable............................	$ 800	$ 1,800	$ 7,600	$ 7,700
Accounts receivable—credit balance............	1,800	2,100	8,200	200
Service contract deposits......................	400	500	600	1,700
Accrued payroll and bonuses..................	1,100	800	7,600	600
Accrued taxes other than federal..............	4,500	3,900	4,100	2,500
Accrued federal income tax....................	4,700	1,500	3,000	....
New cars financed...........................	....	....	....	13,200
Due officers.................................	....	3,700	3,500	....
Total current liabilities....................	$13,300	$14,300	$ 34,600	$ 25,900
Current asset reserves.........................	$ 300	$ 800	$ 200	$ 9,400
Net worth				
Capital stock—common......................	$19,200	$26,600	$ 26,600	$ 26,600
Earned surplus...............................	46,400	47,800	54,500	56,300
Total net worth..........................	$65,600	$74,400	$ 81,100	$ 82,900
Total liabilities and net worth........	$79,200	$89,500	$115,900	$118,200

Exhibit 4

FAIRVIEW MOTORS, INC.

PROPOSED BALANCE SHEET, 200 CAR DEALERSHIP

ASSETS

Current assets
Cash	$ 15,000
Accounts receivable	12,000
Inventories: New cars	....
Used cars	25,000
Other	23,000
Securities	....
Due from finance companies	10,000
Other	5,500
Total current assets	$ 90,500
Fixed assets	25,000
	$115,500

LIABILITIES AND NET WORTH

Current liabilities	$ 15,500
Net worth	100,000
	$115,500

Exhibit 5

FAIRVIEW MOTORS, INC.

COSTS AND REVENUES AS PER CENT OF TOTAL SALES, 1954

	Fairview Motors, Inc.	The Industry Average	
		150–399 New Cars	1–149 New Cars
	% of Sales	% of Sales	% of Sales
Salaries, commissions and other compensation to salesmen	1.60	2.53	1.83
Salaries and wages			
Owners or officers	2.90	1.49	1.68
Supervision	1.25	1.45	1.10
Other	3.26	2.46	2.30
Total salaries and wages	7.41	5.40	5.68
Rent plus expenses in lieu of rent	1.15	1.25	1.21
Advertising, local	.82	1.11	.84
Total expenses	16.90	15.16	14.39
(Variable expense)	3.54	4.05	3.30
Total gross profit	17.30	16.09	14.77
Operating profit	.39	.93	.38
Operating profit before owners' and officers' salaries	3.29	2.42	2.06
Per cent return on invested capital*		5.1	2.1
Percentage of dealers who reported an operating loss		26.2	34.6

* Before income taxes.

Source: National Automobile Dealers Association, based on nation-wide information from dealers in the same make of car and in comparable size groups.

Case 34

The Penumbra Light and Power Company

IN MARCH, 1954, the treasurer of the Penumbra Light and Power Company was considering two proposals, each of which would require a substantial investment of funds. It was the treasurer's responsibility to analyze the financial implications of all such proposals and make recommendations to the company's board of directors. In view of the sums involved in the two proposals now before him and the current financial condition of the company, the treasurer had concluded that only one of the two could be implemented at this time.

One of the proposals, which had originated in his own department, was to refund a $5 million issue of callable bonds issued by the company in May, 1948, and due in 1973. The treasurer kept in close touch with the bond market, and it was apparent to him that a new $5 million issue of 25-year bonds could be sold in the near future at a significantly lower interest rate. The existing bonds would then be called for redemption, and the proceeds of the new issue would be used to pay off the holders of the existing $5 million issue. The other proposal, which had originated in the engineering department, was to invest $250,000 in rebuilding and re-equipping a steam generating unit which was expected to bring significant operating savings.

The bond issue which the proposed refunding issue would replace bore a 3⅞% coupon rate and was callable for redemption at any time on 30 days' notice. If called during 1954, the company was required by the terms of the bond indenture to pay the bondholders $105 for each $100 face value of bond. In view of the 30-day notice of call provision and of possible short delays in issuing the new bonds, the treasurer considered it conservative to assume that there would be a two-month period over which the company would be paying interest both on the old bonds and on the new. Two months' interest on the outstanding bonds amounted to $32,291. The legal and other costs associated with the refunding (other than compensation to the underwriters of the new issue) were expected to amount to approximately $75,000.

Barring an unexpected reversal in the securities market, the treasurer was satisfied that a new $5 million issue of bonds similar to the existing issue could be sold within the next couple of months with a coupon rate of 3% at a small premium. The premium would be just enough to provide the compensation required by the underwriter, and Penumbra Light and Power was expected to net the par value of the bonds. Neither of the issues contained sinking fund provisions.

The second alternative was the proposal to make certain alterations in an auxiliary power plant which provided additional electric power in peak periods when available hydroelectric sources were overloaded. This plant, which provided power through steam generation, although old, was still quite adequate to meet the needs of the company.

The engineering department of the company had estimated that by investing $250,000, annual cash savings of $50,000 could be realized in the operation of the plant. The proposed investment consisted in part of $200,000 for buying and installing new equipment, and the remaining $50,000 was for construction costs in building alterations. The expected savings were to be realized primarily through reduced costs of fuel but also in part through reduced labor costs resulting from a more automatic operation. There would be no significant increase in generating capacity. Estimates were based on company data on the operation of the plant during the period 1950–53.

The equipment which was to be replaced had a value on the company's books at the beginning of 1954 of $50,000. It was realized that this equipment would have no resale value except as scrap and therefore would realize no more than $10,000 if sold. The engineering department indicated that if the investment of $250,000 were made at this time, the entire plant would then operate efficiently and without major additional investment for a period of 20 years.

In considering investment opportunities, the management of Penumbra generally applied the standard of a minimum expected rate of return of 10% after taxes of 52%. This standard had been arrived at by taking an average of the cost of obtaining debt and equity capital weighted according to the normal proportion of each source in the company's capital structure. A prospective investment which did not promise at least a 10% return would be rejected unless there were strong nonprofit considerations to the contrary. The treasurer intended that if either of the two proposals was recommended to and approved by the board, it would be financed out of funds already in the business.

Case 35

Liquigas, Inc.

IN THE FALL of 1952, Mr. Bayard, treasurer of the Liquigas corporation, was studying a list of projects which had been proposed for capital investment in 1953. At the next meeting of the company's directors, to be held late in October, Mr. Bayard would be asked to make recommendations as to which projects should be adopted and how they should be financed.

The Liquigas corporation, located in Hillandale, New Jersey, was a large producer of diversified industrial and commercial chemicals and allied products. Organized in 1926 to manufacture certain chemical compounds used in the oil-refining industry, the company's sales volume expanded rapidly until 1931. During the depression years, operations were so successfully cut back that despite the poor position of the industry, the company showed a small profit in every year from 1931 to 1935. Interest payments were met on bank loans and on a mortgage bond issue; and cash dividends, though on a greatly reduced basis, were paid to shareholders each year.

In the latter thirties the company continued to expand its product line; and during World War II, it reached a position of prominence in the industry. The resurgence of demand for chemicals in the postwar period pushed the industry's and the company's sales to record levels.

In 1952 the company remained a leading producer of chemical compounds for the petroleum-refining industry and, in addition, had diversified its product line through the manufacture of polyethylene and polyvinyl plastics, soil conditioners, anhydrous ammonia for agricultural use, and a range of commercial and household chemicals. The company's directors had recently approved participation in a government-industry project leading to the improvement of synthetic rubber manufacture, and was considering the advisability of taking part in certain aspects of nuclear-chemical development at the request of a government agency.

Sales volume for the entire year 1952 was estimated, on the basis of the current rate of sales, to be approximately $27,500,000; a net profit of $2,800,000 after taxes was predicted.

The company's management had adopted a system of capital budgeting which involved the submission, by each individual department, of capital construction projects desired for the coming year; these programs contained, beside an estimate of the funds required, an estimate of the annual rate of return on the initial amount of the investment, after allowance for costs, including depreciation and amortization sufficient to maintain the earning power of the project by replacements, but before consideration of taxes. Estimates of the rate of return were made very carefully and, in recent years, had been proved reliable. The most promising proposals for calendar 1953 which had been submitted to Mr. Bayard are summarized as follows:

Nature of Proposal	Amount	Per Cent Return before Income Taxes
Mechanization of accounting and inventory control system	$ 118,000	25%
Acquisition of additional chemical storage tanks	1,750,000	20
Purchase of railroad tank cars and loading equipment	240,000	20
Purchase of leased space and facilities—Arkansas	800,000	15
Additions for plastics division, including machinery	1,100,000	14
Replacement of power facilities—New Jersey plant	620,000	12
Construction of new materials handling system	460,000	10–15
Construction of facilities for loading and transfer of explosives to barges— New Jersey	900,000	10
Purchase of New Jersey affiliate to handle export sales and relations	400,000	8
Modernization of New Jersey office building—relocation of functional departments	150,000	4
Purchase of adjacent office building offered for sale	1,000,000	4
	$7,533,000	

The company's expansion policies were based on a desire to satisfy only those demands which seemed to be of a permanent nature, and to avoid speculative prospects, however attractive they might appear.

On the basis of this policy, Mr. Bayard did not feel that any of the above proposals would compromise the long-range interests of the company; each one would be a desirable addition to the company's assets. Sales prospects for 1953 and 1954 were very promising; sales of plastics products had far exceeded expectations, and export sales had continued above the expected rate. The management had informed the company's stockholders, in a midyear letter, that they could look forward to a continued increase in sales volume and corresponding expansion of facilities for at least the next two years.

Mr. Bayard knew that the proposed projects would have to be financed largely through new funds obtained outside the company. The level of earnings remaining after dividends was insufficient to supply all desirable projects, so Mr. Bayard planned to count on no more than $1,750,000 as being available through internally generated sources for the 1953 projects as listed.

Mr. Bayard knew that new financing could be accomplished in several ways. The probable terms attending the sale of additional securities had been discussed with underwriters and bankers from time to time during recent months. Reviewing the possibilities of obtaining funds from outside sources, Mr. Bayard contemplated the following alternatives:

1. Bonds. Mr. Bayard knew, from conversations with underwriters, that it would be possible to sell mortgage bonds on the present market. Such a sale could be made to the public or could be privately placed with institutional investors. Bonds would be of 20- to 30-year maturity and would carry a sinking fund provision. The cost to the company would be, after usual expenses, approximately 3% annually.

Unsecured debentures, with a shorter maturity, were also possible, and would cost the company between 3 and 3½% annually.

2. Preferred Stock. Underwriters had told Mr. Bayard that it would be possible to sell a large issue of preferred stock on the present market at an attractive price. Such an issue would be cumulative and convertible, and would carry with it a sinking fund or retirement provision. The cost to the company would be, after expenses but before consideration of income taxes, between 5½% and 6%. The company's outstanding 4½% preferred stock was currently selling at about 100.

3. Common Stock. The company's postwar growth had been financed largely through the sale of common stock. An issue sold in 1948 had been very successful; and underwriters thought that a large issue, covering the present requirements, could be sold without difficulty at a return to the company, after all costs, of $41 per share. The stock currently outstanding yielded 5.6% on the present market price of 44½ and the cash dividend rate of $2.50; shares were listed on a national exchange and were actively traded. Since 1946 the price/earnings ratio of the common stock had varied from 9.5 to 13.1; the ratio was currently 12.7.

The company had, in 1951, paid federal income taxes of 52% and expected to pay, in 1952, this same rate, as well as excess profits taxes of 8%. Mr. Bayard decided to use an over-all figure of 60% in computing the future impact of taxes on earnings. He also decided to use the above costs of financing, for the various alternatives, in determining the costs of obtaining outside capital.

In considering the profitability of financing a given new project with a determinable rate of return through the use of new money, Mr. Bayard had always in the past used a weighted average cost of capital—that is, the cost of the various types of equity and debt capital weighted by the proportion of each type in the company's current capital structure. The present cost of capital computed by this method was 7.7%, arrived at as follows:

Type of Capital	Earnings Required to Cover Cost, before Taxes	Stated Amounts ($ Millions)	Weights	Weighted Average Calculation
Fixed debt.....................	3%	8.0	32	96
Preferred stock*...............	$\frac{5\%\ddagger}{.4} = 13$	2.4	10	130
Common stock†...............	$\frac{5.6\%\ddagger}{.4} = 14$	9.6	39	546
Surplus......................	No cost	4.8	19	0
		24.8	100	772 = 7.7

* 24,000 shares, $100 par.
† 411,428 shares, no par, book value $35 per share on December 31, 1951.
‡ Current yield = $\frac{\text{Dividend}}{\text{Price}}$.

The Surplus account was carried at no cost, since it was available and would not have to be raised outside the company.

Mr. Bayard had recently attended a businessmen's round-table discussion, at which the cost of financing in relation to rates of return had been the chief topic. At this meeting an economist had advanced several interesting arguments in favor of using the "marginal cost" of capital as the criterion for determining to what extent additional funds should be invested in productive capacity. On this basis, any project which would return, after allowances for depreciation and after consideration of taxes, more than the cost of the least expensive method of financing, again after tax considerations, was a legitimate and desirable investment.

In Mr. Bayard's opinion, employment of the "marginal rate" computation would make all the projects appear desirable, since it was possible to finance the total requirements in part with mortgage bonds costing only 3% and in part with reinvested earnings costing nothing.

Case 36

New England Telephone & Telegraph Company

LATE IN March, 1958, the management of New England Telephone & Telegraph Company (N.E.T.&T.) was considering the advisability of moving forward with plans for an imminent refunding of its outstanding $35 million issue of 4¾% debentures, due in 1986. The 4¾'s, rated Aa by Moody's Rating Service, had been sold at competitive bidding in January, 1957. The winning investment banking syndicate had bought the bonds from the company at a price of 101.-519.[1] The coupon rate of 4.75% ($47.50 for each $1,000 bond) represented an effective interest cost to the company of 4.65%, since the company actually received $1,015.19 for each $1,000 bond. The investment banking syndicate had resold the bonds to the public at 102.388, at which price the bonds yielded 4.60% to the investors.

As can be seen from the chart reproduced as Exhibit 1, the interest rates on long-term corporate bonds, as measured by bond yields on market prices of outstanding issues, had trended upward from late in 1954 until November, 1957. During this period, corporations marketing sizable issues of new bonds found it necessary to offer investors substantially higher yields than those established by market transactions on outstanding issues. For example, in October, 1957, outstanding corporate bonds of Aa rating were reported by Moody's to have sold on an average yield of 4.28%. In contrast, new corporate issues of the same quality rating in October, 1957, sold at an average yield of 4.91%.

Beginning in November, 1957, the Federal Reserve System took measures which were widely interpreted in financial circles as a reversal of its earlier policy of active restraint of the money supply.

---

[1] Bonds are typically issued in $1,000 denominations. The price "101.519" means 101.519% of face value, or $1,015.19 for a $1,000 bond.

Following these measures, interest rates fell sharply, and the general decline that began in November continued into early 1958. During the last week of February, 1958, Cleveland Electric Illuminating Company sold a $30 million issue of 3⅞% bonds, due in 1993 and rated Aaa, at $1,020 per $1,000 bond, to yield 3.77%. The same week, Southern New England Telephone and Telegraph Company sold a $30 million issue of 4⅛% bonds, due in 1991 and rated Aa, at $1,022.79 per $1,000 bond, to yield 4%. The downturn in interest rates suggested to the management of N.E.T.&T. the possibility of calling the 4¾'s due in 1986 with funds obtained through a new issue, as it appeared that a new isssue might be sold at a lower effective interest cost to the company, producing worth-while savings.

N.E.T.&T. was one of 20 operating telephone subsidiaries of the American Telephone & Telegraph Company, which, together with the parent company, comprised the Bell System. A.T.&T. owned about 70% of the outstanding common stock of N.E.T.&T. Like other operating companies of the Bell System, N.E.T.&T. had undergone a continued expansion of its facilities since 1945. The expansion had been financed by sale of common stock through pre-emptive rights to A.T.&T. and other stockholders, and by the sale through competitive bidding of a number of long-term debt issues. In addition, N.E.T.&T., like other operating companies of the Bell System, had borrowed on a short-term basis from A.T.&T. from time to time. Exhibit 2 shows the capital structure of N.E.T.&T. as of December 31, 1957.

The 4¾'s due in 1986 could be called on 30 days' notice. However, the terms of the issue required payment of a substantial premium if called prior to maturity. The precise premiums for early call are indicated by the following schedule of redemption prices.

If Called on or Prior to December 31	Redemption Price
1957	106.888
1958–1959	106.388
1960	105.888
1961	105.388
1962	105.12
1963	104.85
1964–1980	Preceding price reduced by about .27 annually
Thereafter	100

In addition, it was the general policy of the company not to call for redemption of an outstanding issue until the refunding issue had been successfully marketed. As a result, the company would find it necessary to pay interest on both the old and new issues for a period of 30 days. However, the burden of the double interest payments could be reduced somewhat by the investment of the funds received from the new issue in U.S. Treasury bills during the 30-day period until the holders of the called issue registered their debentures with the company for redemption.

As a part of the analysis of the possible savings through refunding, the controller of N.E.T.&T. had his staff prepare a comparison of interest paid on the outstanding 4¾'s due in 1986 with a range of possible interest rates at which the proposed new issue might be sold. This comparison is shown in Exhibit 3. The controller also undertook to estimate the costs that the company would incur in connection with the recall of the outstanding bonds and the issue of new securities. Estimates of these costs were as follows:

Company's internal administrative costs of calling the 4¾% debenture	$ 25,000
Company's costs of preparing and issuing the new debentures	114,000
Net cost of interest on 4¾% issue less short-term interest during 30-day call period	29,000
Call premium on 4¾% issue at 106.388	2,236,000
Total estimated before-tax cost of refunding	$2,404,000
Estimated after-tax cost (using 52% rate)	$1,154,000

Whereas the 4¾'s due in 1986 carried a 29-year maturity, management desired to give any new issue a 35-year maturity, pushing it out from 1986 to 1993. Public financing for the entire Bell System required considerable co-ordination to avoid market competition for funds in the future among the various operating companies and the parent company, and it was felt that a 35-year maturity would better suit the Company's and the System's needs. The pattern of Bell System maturities is given in Exhibit 4. Similarly, to avoid conflict with offerings by other Bell System companies, or other corporate offerings, management chose April 14 to receive and open bids from the various underwriting syndicates, since no other offerings were scheduled on that date.

During March, the controller watched the performance of the bond market with considerable interest. The downward trend of interest rates appeared to have come to an end during the first week in March (see Exhibit 5). However, on March 11, an issue of Indianapolis Power & Light 4⅛% first-mortgage bonds, due in 1988, rated Aa, was successfully sold to the public at 102.172, for a yield to investors of 4.00%.

On March 20, the Company filed the Registration Statement for the new $35 million debenture issue with the Securities and Exchange Commission. On Friday, April 4, the management of N.E.-T.&T. had to decide whether or not to advertise the issue for bidding on the following Monday, April 7. The bids were to be received and opened a week later, on Monday, April 14, in New York. If necessary, the Company could decide against marketing the issue any time up until the time of opening the bids. However, management decided to make a firm decision as early as possible.

As indicated earlier, the post-World War II expansion of the Bell System had required large amounts of outside financing by the A.T.&T. and its operating subsidiaries. N.E.T.&T. alone had increased its outlay on new construction expenditures from $40 million in 1952 to $110 million in both 1956 and 1957. In 1957, the assets of the Bell System had been increased by $1.5 billion, and it had been necessary to raise $1.2 billion through the sale of new securities. There appeared little likelihood that the need for additional capital would abate substantially in the foreseeable future. Although it was difficult to measure in quantitative terms, System financial experts believed that the refunding of existing obligations made the marketing of new issues of securities somewhat more difficult. Consequently, the N.E.T.&T. management wished to proceed with the refunding of the 4¾'s due in 1986 only if significant savings could be achieved.

Complicating the decision to go forward with a refunding issue in early April was the possibility that a deepening of the current recession might be accompanied by a further decline in interest rates. If a continuing decline were to take place, postponement of the refunding might lead to even greater savings in the long run.

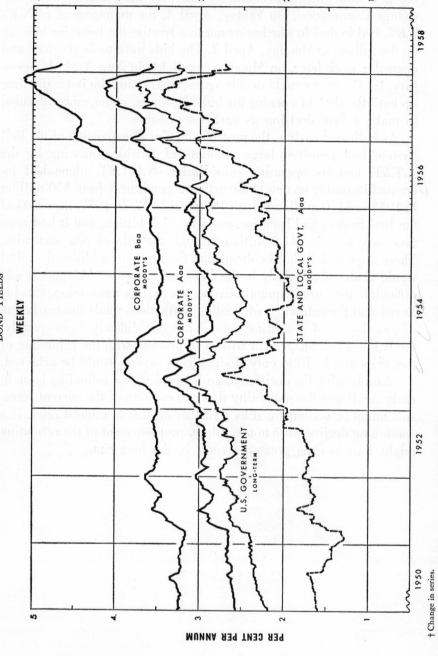
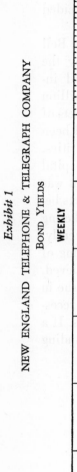

Exhibit 1

NEW ENGLAND TELEPHONE & TELEGRAPH COMPANY

BOND YIELDS

WEEKLY

† Change in series.

SOURCE: Board of Governors of the Federal Reserve System. Latest figures plotted: February 14.

Exhibit 2

NEW ENGLAND TELEPHONE & TELEGRAPH COMPANY
CAPITAL STRUCTURE AS OF DECEMBER 31, 1957

First mortgage bonds

Series B—$4\frac{1}{2}$%, due 1961	$ 40,000,000
Series D—$2\frac{3}{4}$%, due 1975	20,000,000

Debentures

25 Year—3%, due 1974	35,000,000
25 Year—$3\frac{1}{4}$%, due 1977	20,000,000
35 Year—3%, due 1982	40,000,000
29 Year—$4\frac{3}{4}$%, due 1986	35,000,000
34 Year—$3\frac{1}{8}$%, due 1988	30,000,000
36 Year—$3\frac{1}{4}$%, due 1991	30,000,000
Total	$250,000,000
Advances from American Telephone & Telegraph Co.	78,000,000
Stockholders equity (includes both public and A.T.&T. holdings)	392,406,318

Exhibit 3

NEW ENGLAND TELEPHONE & TELEGRAPH COMPANY
ANNUAL INTEREST SAVINGS RESULTING FROM REFUNDING $35,000,000
ISSUE OF $4\frac{3}{4}$% DEBENTURES

Proposed Issue		*Outstanding Issue—*	*Reduction in*
Rate	*Annual Interest*	*Annual Interest at 4.75%*	*Interest*
4.50%	$1,575,000	$1,663,000	$ 88,000
4.40	1,540,000	1,663,000	123,000
4.3	1,505,000	1,663,000	158,000
4.25	1,488,000	1,663,000	175,000
4.2	1,470,000	1,663,000	193,000
4.1	1,435,000	1,663,000	228,000
4.0	1,400,000	1,663,000	263,000
3.9	1,365,000	1,663,000	298,000
3.8	1,330,000	1,663,000	333,000
3.75	1,313,000	1,663,000	350,000
3.7	1,295,000	1,663,000	368,000
3.6	1,260,000	1,663,000	403,000
3.5	1,225,000	1,663,000	438,000

Exhibit 4

NEW ENGLAND TELEPHONE & TELEGRAPH COMPANY
BELL SYSTEM DEBT MATURITIES

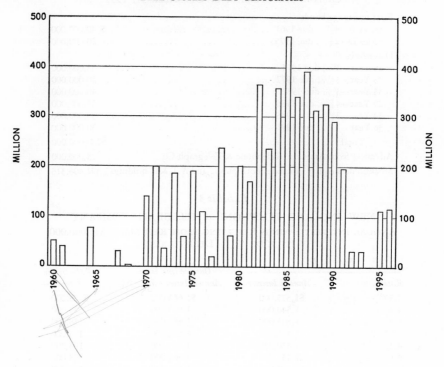

Exhibit 5

NEW ENGLAND TELEPHONE & TELEGRAPH COMPANY

NEW BOND ISSUES AND PROPOSED OFFERINGS, FEBRUARY 25 TO APRIL 15, 1958

Date	Company and Type of Issue	Moody's Aaa	Amount in Millions	Public Offering Price	Yield	Cost to Company
2/26	Cleveland El. Ill., First 3⅞s	1993	$ 30.0	$102.000	3.77%	3.80%
3/3	Baltimore Gas & El., First 4s,	1993	30.0	101.134	3.94	3.98
3/25	New Jersey Bell Tel., Debs.	1993	30.0	Postponed Indefinitely (1)		
4/9	Duquesne Light, First	1988	15.0			
4/15	Commonwealth Edison, First	1988	50.0			

		Moody's Aa				
2/25	Penn. El., First 4s,	1988	29.0	100.874	3.95	3.99
2/26	Cent. Ill. P. & L., First 4⅛s, G,	1988	15.0	102.172	4.00	4.04
2/27	So. New Eng. Tel., Debs. 4⅛s	1991	30.0	102.279	4.00	4.04
3/4	Ohio Edison, First 4¼s,	1988	40.0	101.706	4.15	4.20
3/5	Union Electric, First 4⅜s,	1988	35.0	102.623	4.22	4.27
3/11	Indianapolis P. & L., First 4⅛s,	1988	8.0	102.172	4.00	4.04
3/18	Carolina P. & L., First 4⅛s	1988	20.0	102.172	4.00	4.04
3/24	Florida Power & Light, First	1988	20.0	101.295	4.05	4.09
3/31	Wisconsin Electric Power, First 4⅛s	1988	30.0	102.526	3.98	4.03
4/1	Idaho Power, First	1988	10.0			
4/1	Idaho Power, Debs.	1983	10.0			
4/9	American Can, Debs.	1988	80.0			
4/11	Aluminum Co. of America, Debs.	1983	125.0			
4/14	N.E.T.&T., Debs.	1993	35.0			(2)

		Moody's A				
2/27	United Gas, First & Col. 4¼s,	1978	30.0	101.349	4.15	4.21
2/28	Calif. Elec. P., First 4½s,	1988	12.0	101.656	4.40	4.46
3/3	Iowa Pub. Ser., First 4¼s,	1988	10.0	100.000	4.25	4.31
3/5	Iowa-Ill. Gas & El. Conv. Debs. 3¼s,	1968	9.0	100.500	3.19	3.30
3/6	Columbia Gas Sys., Debs 4⅜s, J,	1983	30.0	99.623	4.40	4.45
3/10	Merrimack-Essex, First, C,	1988	20.0	Postponed Indefinitely (3)		
3/20	Georgia Power, First 4⅛s,	1988	24.0	100.947	4.07	4.12
3/26	Gen. Tel. Co. of Cal., First 4⅛s, L,	1988	20.0	100.429	4.10	4.15

		Moody's Baa				
3/12	Mississippi R. Fuel, Debs. 4¾s,	1978	30.0	100.500	4.71	4.79
3/18	Tenn. Gas Trans., Debs.	1978	30.0	Postponed Indefinitely		
3/19	Texas East Trans., First 4⅞s,	1978	25.0	99.500	4.92	5.00
4/10	Douglas Aircraft, Debs.	1978	60.0			

(1) Refunding $30M, 4⅞% debentures due 1993.
(2) Refunding $35M, 4¾% debentures due 1986.
(3) Refunding $20M, 5⅝% first, Series B, due 1987.
Issued: March 31, 1958.
Chief Statistician.

TABLE A

Present Value of $1

Periods until Payment	1%	2%	4%	6%	8%	10%	12%	14%	15%	16%	18%	20%	22%	24%	25%	26%	28%	30%	35%	40%	45%	50%
1	0.990	0.980	0.962	0.943	0.926	0.909	0.893	0.877	0.870	0.862	0.847	0.833	0.820	0.806	0.800	0.794	0.781	0.769	0.741	0.714	0.690	0.667
2	0.980	0.961	0.925	0.890	0.857	0.826	0.797	0.769	0.756	0.743	0.718	0.694	0.672	0.650	0.640	0.630	0.610	0.592	0.549	0.510	0.476	0.444
3	0.971	0.942	0.889	0.840	0.794	0.751	0.712	0.675	0.658	0.641	0.609	0.579	0.551	0.524	0.512	0.500	0.477	0.455	0.406	0.364	0.328	0.296
4	0.961	0.924	0.855	0.792	0.735	0.683	0.636	0.592	0.572	0.552	0.516	0.482	0.451	0.423	0.410	0.397	0.373	0.350	0.301	0.260	0.226	0.198
5	0.951	0.906	0.822	0.747	0.681	0.621	0.567	0.519	0.497	0.476	0.437	0.402	0.370	0.341	0.328	0.315	0.291	0.269	0.223	0.186	0.156	0.132
6	0.942	0.888	0.790	0.705	0.630	0.564	0.507	0.456	0.432	0.410	0.370	0.335	0.303	0.275	0.262	0.250	0.227	0.207	0.165	0.133	0.108	0.088
7	0.933	0.871	0.760	0.665	0.583	0.513	0.452	0.400	0.376	0.354	0.314	0.279	0.249	0.222	0.210	0.198	0.178	0.159	0.122	0.095	0.074	0.059
8	0.923	0.853	0.731	0.627	0.540	0.467	0.404	0.351	0.327	0.305	0.266	0.233	0.204	0.179	0.168	0.157	0.139	0.123	0.091	0.068	0.051	0.039
9	0.914	0.837	0.703	0.592	0.500	0.424	0.361	0.308	0.284	0.263	0.225	0.194	0.167	0.144	0.134	0.125	0.108	0.094	0.067	0.048	0.035	0.026
10	0.905	0.820	0.676	0.558	0.463	0.386	0.322	0.270	0.247	0.227	0.191	0.162	0.137	0.116	0.107	0.099	0.085	0.073	0.050	0.035	0.024	0.017
11	0.896	0.804	0.650	0.527	0.429	0.350	0.287	0.237	0.215	0.195	0.162	0.135	0.112	0.094	0.086	0.079	0.066	0.056	0.037	0.025	0.017	0.012
12	0.887	0.788	0.625	0.497	0.397	0.319	0.257	0.208	0.187	0.168	0.137	0.112	0.092	0.076	0.069	0.062	0.052	0.043	0.027	0.018	0.012	0.008
13	0.879	0.773	0.601	0.469	0.368	0.290	0.229	0.182	0.163	0.145	0.116	0.093	0.075	0.061	0.055	0.050	0.040	0.033	0.020	0.013	0.008	0.005
14	0.870	0.758	0.577	0.442	0.340	0.263	0.205	0.160	0.141	0.125	0.099	0.078	0.062	0.049	0.044	0.039	0.032	0.025	0.015	0.009	0.006	0.003
15	0.861	0.743	0.555	0.417	0.315	0.239	0.183	0.140	0.123	0.108	0.084	0.065	0.051	0.040	0.035	0.031	0.025	0.020	0.011	0.006	0.004	0.002
16	0.853	0.728	0.534	0.394	0.292	0.218	0.163	0.123	0.107	0.093	0.071	0.054	0.042	0.032	0.028	0.025	0.019	0.015	0.008	0.005	0.003	0.002
17	0.844	0.714	0.513	0.371	0.270	0.198	0.146	0.108	0.093	0.080	0.060	0.045	0.034	0.026	0.023	0.020	0.015	0.012	0.006	0.003	0.002	0.001
18	0.836	0.700	0.494	0.350	0.250	0.180	0.130	0.095	0.081	0.069	0.051	0.038	0.028	0.021	0.018	0.016	0.012	0.009	0.005	0.002	0.001	0.001
19	0.828	0.686	0.475	0.331	0.232	0.164	0.116	0.083	0.070	0.060	0.043	0.031	0.023	0.017	0.014	0.012	0.009	0.007	0.003	0.002	0.001	0.001
20	0.820	0.673	0.456	0.312	0.215	0.149	0.104	0.073	0.061	0.051	0.037	0.026	0.019	0.014	0.012	0.010	0.007	0.005	0.002	0.001	0.001	0.001
21	0.811	0.660	0.439	0.294	0.199	0.135	0.093	0.064	0.053	0.044	0.031	0.022	0.015	0.011	0.009	0.008	0.006	0.004	0.002	0.001		
22	0.803	0.647	0.422	0.278	0.184	0.123	0.083	0.056	0.046	0.038	0.026	0.018	0.013	0.009	0.007	0.006	0.004	0.003	0.001	0.001		
23	0.795	0.634	0.406	0.262	0.170	0.112	0.074	0.049	0.040	0.033	0.022	0.015	0.010	0.007	0.006	0.005	0.003	0.002	0.001			
24	0.788	0.622	0.390	0.247	0.158	0.102	0.066	0.043	0.035	0.028	0.019	0.013	0.008	0.006	0.005	0.004	0.003	0.002	0.001			
25	0.780	0.610	0.375	0.233	0.146	0.092	0.059	0.038	0.030	0.024	0.016	0.010	0.007	0.005	0.004	0.003	0.002	0.001	0.001			
26	0.772	0.598	0.361	0.220	0.135	0.084	0.053	0.033	0.026	0.021	0.014	0.009	0.006	0.004	0.003	0.002	0.002	0.001				
27	0.764	0.586	0.347	0.207	0.125	0.076	0.047	0.029	0.023	0.018	0.011	0.007	0.005	0.003	0.002	0.002	0.001	0.001				
28	0.757	0.574	0.333	0.196	0.116	0.069	0.042	0.026	0.020	0.016	0.010	0.006	0.004	0.002	0.002	0.002	0.001	0.001				
29	0.749	0.563	0.321	0.185	0.107	0.063	0.037	0.022	0.017	0.014	0.008	0.005	0.003	0.002	0.002	0.001	0.001	0.001				
30	0.742	0.552	0.308	0.174	0.099	0.057	0.033	0.020	0.015	0.012	0.007	0.004	0.003	0.002	0.001	0.001	0.001	0.001				
40	0.672	0.453	0.208	0.097	0.046	0.022	0.011	0.005	0.004	0.003	0.001	0.001										
50	0.608	0.372	0.141	0.054	0.021	0.009	0.003	0.001	0.001	0.001												

Source: Robert N. Anthony, *Management Accounting: Text and Cases* (rev. ed.; Homewood, Ill.: Richard D. Irwin, Inc., 1960), p. 656.

Authors' Note: These values are obtained by compounding at the end of each period. Other tables use different schemes of compounding, without changing the magnitudes greatly.

TABLE B

Present Value of $1 Received Annually

Periods to Be Paid	1%	2%	4%	6%	8%	10%	12%	14%	15%	16%	18%	20%	22%	24%	25%	26%	28%	30%	35%	40%	45%	50%
1	0.990	0.980	0.962	0.943	0.926	0.909	0.893	0.877	0.870	0.862	0.847	0.833	0.820	0.806	0.800	0.794	0.781	0.769	0.741	0.714	0.690	0.667
2	1.970	1.942	1.886	1.833	1.783	1.736	1.690	1.647	1.626	1.605	1.566	1.528	1.492	1.457	1.440	1.424	1.392	1.361	1.289	1.224	1.165	1.111
3	2.941	2.884	2.775	2.673	2.577	2.487	2.402	2.322	2.283	2.246	2.174	2.106	2.042	1.981	1.952	1.923	1.868	1.816	1.696	1.589	1.493	1.407
4	3.902	3.808	3.630	3.465	3.312	3.170	3.037	2.914	2.855	2.798	2.690	2.589	2.494	2.404	2.362	2.320	2.241	2.166	1.849	1.849	1.720	1.605
5	4.853	4.713	4.452	4.212	3.993	3.791	3.605	3.433	3.352	3.274	3.127	2.991	2.864	2.745	2.689	2.635	2.532	2.436	2.220	2.035	1.876	1.737
6	5.795	5.601	5.242	4.917	4.623	4.355	4.111	3.889	3.784	3.685	3.498	3.326	3.167	3.020	2.951	2.885	2.759	2.643	2.385	2.168	1.983	1.824
7	6.728	6.472	6.002	5.582	5.206	4.868	4.564	4.288	4.160	4.039	3.812	3.605	3.416	3.242	3.161	3.083	2.937	2.802	2.508	2.263	2.057	1.883
8	7.652	7.325	6.733	6.210	5.747	5.335	4.968	4.639	4.487	4.344	4.078	3.837	3.619	3.421	3.329	3.241	3.076	2.925	2.598	2.331	2.108	1.922
9	8.566	8.162	7.435	6.802	6.247	5.759	5.328	4.946	4.772	4.607	4.303	4.031	3.786	3.566	3.463	3.366	3.184	3.019	2.665	2.379	2.144	1.948
10	9.471	8.983	8.111	7.360	6.710	6.145	5.650	5.216	5.019	4.833	4.494	4.192	3.923	3.682	3.571	3.465	3.269	3.092	2.715	2.414	2.168	1.965
11	10.368	9.787	8.760	7.887	7.139	6.495	5.937	5.453	5.234	5.029	4.656	4.327	4.035	3.776	3.656	3.544	3.335	3.147	2.752	2.438	2.185	1.977
12	11.255	10.575	9.385	8.384	7.536	6.814	6.194	5.660	5.421	5.197	4.793	4.439	4.127	3.851	3.725	3.606	3.387	3.190	2.779	2.456	2.196	1.985
13	12.134	11.343	9.986	8.853	7.904	7.103	6.424	5.842	5.583	5.342	4.910	4.533	4.203	3.912	3.780	3.656	3.427	3.223	2.799	2.468	2.204	1.990
14	13.004	12.106	10.563	9.295	8.244	7.367	6.628	6.002	5.724	5.468	5.008	4.611	4.265	3.962	3.824	3.695	3.459	3.249	2.814	2.477	2.210	1.993
15	13.865	12.849	11.118	9.712	8.559	7.606	6.811	6.142	5.847	5.575	5.092	4.675	4.315	4.001	3.859	3.726	3.483	3.268	2.825	2.484	2.214	1.995
16	14.718	13.578	11.652	10.106	8.851	7.824	6.974	6.265	5.954	5.669	5.162	4.730	4.357	4.033	3.887	3.751	3.503	3.283	2.834	2.489	2.216	1.997
17	15.562	14.292	12.166	10.477	9.122	8.022	7.120	6.373	6.047	5.749	5.222	4.775	4.391	4.059	3.910	3.771	3.518	3.295	2.840	2.492	2.218	1.998
18	16.398	14.992	12.659	10.828	9.372	8.201	7.250	6.467	6.128	5.818	5.273	4.812	4.419	4.080	3.928	3.786	3.529	3.304	2.844	2.494	2.219	1.999
19	17.226	15.678	13.134	11.158	9.604	8.365	7.366	6.550	6.198	5.877	5.316	4.844	4.442	4.097	3.942	3.799	3.539	3.311	2.848	2.496	2.220	1.999
20	18.046	16.351	13.590	11.470	9.818	8.514	7.469	6.623	6.259	5.929	5.353	4.870	4.460	4.110	3.954	3.808	3.546	3.316	2.850	2.497	2.221	1.999
21	18.857	17.011	14.029	11.764	10.017	8.649	7.562	6.687	6.312	5.973	5.384	4.891	4.476	4.121	3.963	3.816	3.551	3.320	2.852	2.498	2.221	2.000
22	19.660	17.658	14.451	12.042	10.201	8.772	7.645	6.743	6.359	6.011	5.410	4.909	4.488	4.130	3.970	3.822	3.556	3.323	2.853	2.498	2.222	2.000
23	20.456	18.292	14.857	12.303	10.371	8.883	7.718	6.792	6.399	6.044	5.432	4.925	4.499	4.137	3.976	3.827	3.559	3.325	2.854	2.499	2.222	2.000
24	21.243	18.914	15.247	12.550	10.529	8.985	7.784	6.835	6.434	6.073	5.451	4.937	4.507	4.143	3.981	3.831	3.562	3.327	2.855	2.499	2.222	2.000
25	22.023	19.523	15.622	12.783	10.675	9.077	7.843	6.873	6.464	6.097	5.467	4.948	4.514	4.147	3.985	3.834	3.564	3.329	2.856	2.499	2.222	2.000
26	22.795	20.121	15.983	13.003	10.810	9.161	7.896	6.906	6.491	6.118	5.480	4.956	4.520	4.151	3.988	3.837	3.566	3.330	2.856	2.500	2.222	2.000
27	23.560	20.707	16.330	13.211	10.935	9.237	7.943	6.935	6.514	6.136	5.492	4.964	4.524	4.154	3.990	3.839	3.567	3.331	2.856	2.500	2.222	2.000
28	24.316	21.281	16.663	13.406	11.051	9.307	7.984	6.961	6.534	6.152	5.502	4.970	4.528	4.157	3.992	3.840	3.568	3.331	2.857	2.500	2.222	2.000
29	25.066	21.844	16.984	13.591	11.158	9.370	8.022	6.983	6.551	6.166	5.510	4.975	4.531	4.159	3.994	3.841	3.569	3.332	2.857	2.500	2.222	2.000
30	25.808	22.396	17.292	13.765	11.258	9.427	8.055	7.003	6.566	6.177	5.517	4.979	4.534	4.160	3.995	3.842	3.569	3.332	2.857	2.500	2.222	2.000
40	32.835	27.355	19.793	15.046	11.925	9.779	8.244	7.105	6.642	6.234	5.548	4.997	4.544	4.166	3.999	3.846	3.571	3.333	2.857	2.500	2.222	2.000
50	39.196	31.424	21.482	15.762	12.234	9.915	8.304	7.133	6.661	6.246	5.554	4.999	4.545	4.167	4.000	3.846	3.571	3.333	2.857	2.500	2.222	2.000

SOURCE: Robert N. Anthony, *Management Accounting: Text and Cases* (rev. ed.; Homewood, Ill.: Richard D. Irwin, Inc., 1960), p. 657.

AUTHORS' NOTE: These values are obtained by compounding at the end of each period. Other tables use different schemes of compounding, without changing the magnitudes greatly.

Tax Table

FEDERAL TAX RATES ON CORPORATE INCOME, AND PAYMENT DATES

(To be used in connection with cases in this book)

Note: This is not a complete statement of applicable rates, and it should not be used as a reference for general purposes.

Income Years	Rate	Income Years	Rate	Income Years	Rate
1940*	24.0%	1947	38.0%	1954	52.0%
1941*	31.0	1948	38.0	1955	52.0
1942*	40.0	1949	38.0	1956	52.0
1943*	40.0	1950*	47.0	1957	52.0
1944*	40.0	1951*	52.0	1958	52.0
1945*	40.0	1952*	52.0	1959	52.0
1946	38.0	1953*	52.0	1960	52.0

* Excess profits tax also applied for at least part of year.

It should be noted that the 52 per cent rate breaks down into normal tax and surtax. The normal tax is equal to 30 per cent of taxable income. The surtax is equal to 22 per cent of the amount by which the taxable income exceeds $25,000. For a company with a low level of income this breakdown becomes important.

Recent revenue acts have made provisions to move corporate income tax payments closer to "pay as you go." Beginning in 1950, payments were gradually accelerated until in 1954 they were brought entirely into the first half of the year following the tax liability. The Revenue Act of 1954 set up a still more accelerated schedule for tax liabilities in excess of $100,000: payment of part of the estimated tax liability for the current year was moved into the current year. The schedule below lists the due dates for companies on a calendar year basis.

Year	Percentage Paid in Income Year*		Percentage Paid in Following Year†			
	September 15	December 15	March 15	June 15	September 15	December 15
1949	—	—	25%	25%	25%	25%
1950	—	—	30	30	20	20
1951	—	—	35	35	15	15
1952	—	—	40	40	10	10
1953	—	—	45	45	5	5
1954	—	—	50	50	—	—
1955	5%	5%	45	45	—	—
1956	10	10	40	40	—	—
1957	15	15	35	35	—	—
1958	20	20	30	30	—	—
1959	25	25	25	25	—	—
1960	25	25	25	25	—	—

* These are percentages of the estimated tax liability on income of the current year.
† These are percentages of the tax liability on income of the previous year.

Indexes

Indexes

Index

Index of Cases

This book has been set on the Linotype in 12 and 10 point Bodoni Book, leaded 1 point. Part and chapter numbers are in 18 point Bonodi #175 Italics; part and chapter titles are in 24 point Alternate Gothic. The size of the text page is 27 by 46½ picas.